Innovations in Optimization and Machine Learning

Toufik Mzili
Chouaib Doukkali University, Morocco

Adarsh Kumar Arya
Harcourt Butler Technical University, India

IGI Global
Scientific Publishing
Publishing Tomorrow's Research Today

Vice President of Editorial	Melissa Wagner
Managing Editor of Acquisitions	Mikaela Felty
Managing Editor of Book Development	Jocelynn Hessler
Production Manager	Mike Brehm
Cover Design	Phillip Shickler

Published in the United States of America by
    IGI Global Scientific Publishing
    701 East Chocolate Avenue
    Hershey, PA, 17033, USA
    Tel: 717-533-8845
    Fax: 717-533-8661
    Website: https://www.igi-global.com E-mail: cust@igi-global.com

Library of Congress Cataloging-in-Publication Data

Names: Mzili, Toufik, 1995- editor. | Arya, Adarsh, 1979- editor.
Title: Innovations in optimization and machine learning / edited by Toufik
    Mzili, Adarsh Arya.
Description: Hershey PA : Engineering Science Reference, [2025] | Includes
    bibliographical references and index. | Summary: "This book aspires to
    be a valuable resource for researchers, practitioners, students, and
    enthusiasts seeking to deepen their understanding of optimization,
    machine learning, and AI, and contribute to the continual advancement of
    these fields"-- Provided by publisher.
Identifiers: LCCN 2024038691 (print) | LCCN 2024038692 (ebook) | ISBN
    9798369352311 (h/c) | ISBN 9798369352328 (s/c) | ISBN 9798369352335
    (ebook)
Subjects: LCSH: Decision making--Technological innovations. |
    Multidisciplinary design optimization--Data procesing. | Artifical
    intelligence--Industrial applications. | Machine learning--Industrial
    applications.
Classification: LCC T57.95 .I5493 2024 (print) | LCC T57.95 (ebook) | DDC
    006.3/1--dc23/eng/20241108
LC record available at https://lccn.loc.gov/2024038691
LC ebook record available at https://lccn.loc.gov/2024038692

British Cataloguing in Publication Data
A Cataloguing in Publication record for this book is available from the British Library.

Table of Contents

Detailed Table of Contents

Chapter 1
A Web Content Identification and Classification System Using Natural
Language Processing and Machine Learning Techniques 1

    C. Balakumar, Karpagam Academy of Higher Education, India
    N. Divya, Karpagam Academy of Higher Education, India
    J. Gokulapriya, Rathinam College of Arts and Science, India
    M. Kokilamani, Kamalam College of Arts and Science, India

The majority of systems used to filter web pages rely on naive bayes, k-nearest neighbour, and SVM algorithms. These methods are not perfect in extracting valuable information from unstructured online content. These systems lack the cognitive ability to discern between erotic and other common information on websites by intelligently filtering web pages. In order to convert the freely available unstructured text information on the search engine into structured data, the suggested effort would be used to classify the web content using the artificial neural network (ANN) technique. This work provides a semantic knowledge system based on machine learning (ML) with the help of ant colony optimization (ACO) technique that addresses these issues by identifying and blocking access to filtering web content in an organised manner. In order to provide accuracy and speed, the suggested method uses a blacklist of restricted websites to classify URLs into wanted and unwanted categories

    Ahmed Raza, School of Systems and Technology, University of
        Management and Technology, Lahore, Pakistan
    Usama Ahmed, School of Systems and Technology, University of
        Management and Technology, Lahore, Pakistan
    Kainat Saleem, COMSATS University Islamabad, Lahore, Pakistan
    Muhammad Sarwar, School of Systems and Technology, University of
        Management and Technology, Lahore, Pakistan
    Momina Shaheen, School of Arts Humanities and Social Sciences,
        University of Roehampton, London, UK
    Muhammad Sohail Farooq, Comsat Institute of Information Technology,
        Lahore, Pakistan

The process of sequence labeling (POS) by assigning syntactic tags to words in the given context is an important role in various NLP applications. The core motive of this work is to tackle the morpho-syntactic category of words in Urdu language. This language has lots of computational challenges because of its dual nature. The work comprises different tasks as initially the authors tracked the best combination of feature sets in terms of CRF to entitle the previous results on two stable and well-known datasets Bushra Jawaid dataset and CLE dataset. Due to syntactic ambiguity, a state-of-the-art voting method has been introduced which is being implemented to overcome the contradictory results of the different machine learning classifiers. The results show significant improvement in the baseline results as the F1-score on a primary dataset is 94.8% and 95.7% on the succeeding dataset. Long short-term memory (LSTM) is used for one of the most diverse and inflectional tasks like part of speech tagging for the Urdu language by achieving an F1-score of 86.7% and 96.1% respectively for both datasets.

    S. Sasikumar, Karpagam Academy of Higher Education, India
    G. Ravishankar, Karpagam Academy of Higher Education, India
    P. Poongothai, Kristu Jayanti College, India
    Suresh Palarimath, University of Technology and Applied Sciences,
        Salalah, Oman

The gathering of tweets from before and after the companies' involvement in the metaverse allowed for the investigation of how potential users perceived their involvement. The numerous applications of metaverse technology are attracting the attention of experts and researchers. It serves as an immersive virtual environment that encourages user social interaction. However, we don't know how customers feel about this technology, particularly how positive they view it. To evaluate the chosen dataset from the Kaggle website, the hybrid particle swarm optimization with support vector machine (HPSOSVM) approach was also employed. The suggested HPSOSVM outperforms the other classifiers, according to the results. Features may be extracted using the HPSOSVM with an accuracy of 90.12%. The outcomes demonstrate that ensemble classifiers outperform individual classifiers in terms of accuracy. Being relatively new phenomena, there are many opportunities to reorient the Metaverse on humanist values instead of specialized interests.

Chapter 4

This study explores the complex field of edge computing, emphasising optimisation techniques that are vital for enhancing data management, resource allocation, energy usage, and offloading efficiency. This chapter investigates new approaches to improve edge computing system quality, providing a thorough analysis that incorporates knowledge from several fields. By resolving important issues and opening the door for more long-lasting and efficient quality control methods, the findings improve edge computing applications. Through a comprehensive examination of various optimization methodologies, this study aims to enhance the efficiency and quality management of edge computing systems, providing valuable insights for researchers, practitioners, and industry stakeholders in the rapidly evolving domain of edge computing.

Chapter 5

In this work, the authors investigate the resolution of the permutation flow shop scheduling problem by minimizing total tardiness. First, they explore different approaches, and they utilize nature-inspired metaheuristics. The proposed solution approach incorporates three metaheuristics: genetic algorithm (GA), migratory bird optimization (MBO), and artificial bee colony (ABC) algorithm. These metaheuristics are combined with local search procedures to explore neighboring solutions. Additionally, two constructive algorithms, Nawaz-Enscore-Ham (NEH) and artificial neural networks (ANN), are introduced for generating optimal sequences initially. The effectiveness of the proposed approach and algorithms is evaluated through comprehensive tests on various instance sizes. The simulations demonstrate that the population-based ABC with the NEH outperforms other algorithms in terms of efficiency. This comparative analysis reveals that the ABC_NEH metaheuristic achieves better results than other algorithms, resulting in a good success rate.

Chapter 6

Feature selection is crucial in data analytics, as it helps identify the most relevant features for modeling. This improves efficiency and interpretability by reducing data dimensionality. Conventional methods optimize a single criterion, such as accuracy or information gain. However, these methods may not fully capture the complexity of real-world problems with multiple competing objectives. Recently, multi-objective optimization techniques have been applied to traditional algorithms, offering a framework for optimizing feature subsets that balance several objectives, such as precision and robustness. However, determining the most efficient algorithm for a specific dataset is challenging. This chapter aims to provide practitioners with a detailed examination of various multi-objective feature selection approaches, including their strengths, weaknesses, and a case study. By understanding the benefits of considering multiple objectives, professionals can apply these advanced methods to research projects, decision-making, and real-world data analytics problems.

Chapter 7

Time series forecasting is crucial for various real-world applications, such as energy consumption, traffic flow estimation, and financial market analysis. This chapter explores the application of deep learning models, specifically transformer-based models for long-term time series forecasting. Despite the success of transformers in sequence modeling, their permutation-invariant nature can lead to the loss of temporal information, posing challenges for accurate forecasting. Especially, the embedding of the position-wise vector or the time-stamp vector is the key to the success of the long time series forecasting. Another noted headache of the standard transformer-based model is the squared computation complexity. This chapter studies the development of the research field of the long timer series forecasting, challenging pain point, popular data sets, and state-of-the-art benchmarks. The discussion covers the implications, limitations, and future research directions, offering insights for applying these advanced techniques to real-world forecasting problems.

Chapter 8

Bimol Chandra Das, Trine University, USA
Munir Ahmad, Survey of Pakistan, Pakistan
Maida Maqsood, Government College Women University, Sialkot,
*   Pakistan*

Cloud platforms can enhance spatial data management with specialized services like databases, geocoding, and geospatial analytics. Databases such as Amazon Redshift with PostGIS, Microsoft Azure's Cosmos DB, and Google Cloud Spanner offer efficient storage, retrieval, and spatial data analysis. Geocoding services convert addresses into geographic coordinates, including Google's Geocoding API, OpenStreetMap Nominatim, and Mapbox's Geocoding API. Geospatial analytics tools from Amazon, Microsoft Azure, and Google Earth Engine provide actionable insights from spatial data. Optimization techniques like spatial indexing, partitioning, caching, and parallel processing (MapReduce and Apache Spark) enhance data access and processing. Security measures include access control, data encryption, and anonymization to protect sensitive information. Disaster recovery and backup strategies can ensure data resilience and business continuity. Utilizing these cloud services can transform spatial data management, unlocking its potential for analysis, visualization, and decision-making.

Chapter 9

S. Jasmine, P.S.R. Engineering College, India
P. Marichamy, P.S.R. Engineering College, India
K. Ramalakshmi, P.S.R. Engineering College, India
Aqil Ahmed J., P.S.R. Engineering College, India

This work focuses on human gait detection, a branch of biometrics that examines people's specific walking patterns. Walking pattern, or gait, has drawn interest because of its potential in several applications, such as surveillance and medical monitoring, where non-intrusive identification is critical. The CASIA-B dataset, which included samples with varying gait patterns, clothing changes, and luggage presence, was used for this study. High accuracy rates were attained by the suggested MobileNet with BiLSTM model: 94.52% accuracy with bags and 96.89% accuracy without them. These findings highlight the model's practical applicability and further the development of gait analysis techniques.

    Ayoub Ouchlif, Hassan II Agronomic and Veterinary Institute, Morocco
    Oumaima Kabba, Hassan II Agronomic and Veterinary Institute,
      Morocco
    Majda Guendour, Hassan II Agronomic and Veterinary Institute,
      Morocco
    Hicham Hajji, Hassan II Agronomic and Veterinary Institute, Morocco
    Kenza Aitelkadi, Hassan II Agronomic and Veterinary Institute,
      Morocco

In this study, the authors aim to explore the potential of machine learning (ML) in real estate valuation, particularly in Morocco where challenges include intelligent and sustainable valuation methods and transitioning to smart urban planning aligned with the eleventh sustainable development goal. To tackle these, they analyzed, processed, and tested seven ML architectures using real estate ads from Casablanca and Rabat collected over three months (April to June 2022). Support vector regression (SVR) led with 92.6% accuracy, followed by neural networks at 90%, then random forest, gradient boosting, XGBoost, and ridge and lasso regressions. SVR, a validated model, produced predictions depicted in an interactive thematic map showing their distribution across the two cities, underscoring the influence of digital real estate on conventional valuation methods.

    R. Chennappan, Karpagam Academy of Higher Education, India
    A. Vinitha, Karpagam Academy of Higher Education, India
    S. Vinitha, Sankara College of Science and Commerce, India
    R. Gunasundari, Karpagam Academy of Higher Education, India

Comprehending location-specific attitudes regarding crisis scenarios is crucial for political leaders and those making strategic decisions. To this aim, the authors introduce a novel fully automated technique for extracting the public feelings on global crisis situations, through the social media posts using artificial intelligence (AI) method based on sentimental analysis. They created the suggested system using sentiment analysis based on AI and NLP, regression, optimization-based algorithm, and using artificial neural network (ANN) for classifying technique to get thorough understanding and perceptions on social media feeds connected to disasters in different languages. The rate of average sensitivity is 93.56%, and the obtained specificity is 94.52% measured with the execution time duration of

5.68 ms. Overall, the fully automated disaster monitoring solution using AI-based sentimental analysis demonstrated the 94.25% accuracy.

Chapter 12

Youssra El Idrissi El-Bouzaidi, Team-ISISA, Faculty of Science,
    Abdelmalek Essaadi University, Tetouan, Morocco
Fatima Zohra Hibbi, ISIC Research Team of ESTM, Moulay Ismail
    University, Meknes, Morocco
Otman Abdoun, Team-ISISA, Faculty of Science, Abdelmalek Essaadi
    University, Tetouan, Morocco

This chapter examines skin cancer, particularly melanoma, which has a high mortality rate, making early diagnosis essential. It explores how convolutional neural networks (CNNs) can improve melanoma detection, providing a detailed technical analysis of hyperparameters and their impact on model performance. Strategies for tuning hyperparameters, including random search and Bayesian optimization, are demonstrated. Using the HAM10000 dataset, the chapter assesses the impact of different hyperparameter settings on accuracy, sensitivity, and specificity. Issues like class imbalance are addressed with data augmentation and resampling. The optimization methods improve DenseNet121 and MobileNetV2 accuracies to 85.65% and 84.08%, respectively.

Chapter 13

Mehrajudin Aslam Aslam Najar, Communication University of China,
    China

This chapter explores how artificial intelligence (AI) augments human capabilities across sectors like healthcare, education, and business, emphasizing ethical considerations. It addresses challenges such as bias in algorithms and workforce displacement while discussing future trends like natural language interfaces and brain-computer interfaces. It advocates for ethical governance, proactive reskilling, and inclusive AI development to ensure equitable societal benefits and sustainable progress.

    T. Venkat Narayana Rao, Sreenidhi Institute of Science and Technology,
       India
    M. Stephen, Sreenidhi Institute of Science and Technology, India
    E. Manoj, Sreenidhi Institute of Science and Technology, India
    Bhavana Sangers, Sreenidhi Institute of Science and Technology, India

When developing and implementing machine learning algorithms, bias and fairness are essential factors to consider. Systematic mistakes or inconsistencies in the data or the algorithmic decision-making process are the root cause of bias in machine learning algorithms. In algorithmic systems, ensuring fairness is crucial to preventing harm and advancing equity and justice. In order to assess the fairness of machine learning algorithms, several measures and criteria have been put forth, such as differential impact, equal opportunity, and demographic parity. This study reviews how these algorithms work and their applications in real-world scenarios such as healthcare, hiring and recruitment, financial services, and recommender systems. In conclusion, in order to guarantee fair results and minimize potential harm, machine learning algorithms must address prejudice and promote fairness. Through the chapter the authors hope the readers will be able to review the fairness on existing algorithms and become responsible AI practitioners by addressing bias and fairness.

    Evariste Gatabazi, The Open University of Tanzania, Tanzania
    Maad M. Mijwil, Al-Iraqia University, Iraq
    Mostafa Abotaleb, South Ural State University, Russia
    Saganga Kapaya, The Open University of Tanzania, Tanzania

This study reviewed a total of 3171 published articles, mainly from 1992-2024. The review was performed using scientifically cited and indexed databases, namely Dimensions, Web Science, Elsevier Scopus, and Google Scholar. This study demonstrates how AI technologies, such as computer vision and system learning, may revolutionize industrial efficiency, productivity, and satisfactory control. Superior algorithms, neural networks, and big data analytics are integrated to optimize manufacturing strategies and enable intelligent decision-making, which is where the innovation lies. Also, it was found that building workforce capacity through collaborations and customized training programs can help close the skills gap, while improving cybersecurity and implementing efficient data management frameworks can help with privacy issues. However, despite the growing body of literature on AI packages, studies specializing in AI embracing on the organizational level stay restrained.

Preface

Welcome to *Innovations in Optimization and Machine Learning*. This book is a testament to the evolving and interdisciplinary nature of optimization, machine learning, and artificial intelligence (AI), fields that continue to redefine the boundaries of what technology can achieve. As editors, we, Toufik Mzili from Chouaib Doukkali University, Morocco, and Adarsh Arya from Harcourt Butler Technical University, India, are thrilled to present this collection of cutting-edge research, which captures the essence of these dynamic domains.

The confluence of optimization techniques and machine learning methodologies is driving innovations across industries. Optimization enhances efficiency in various domains, from healthcare and finance to supply chain networks, while machine learning empowers systems to autonomously learn, adapt, and make intelligent decisions based on data. AI, as the broader umbrella, encompasses both of these, extending human capabilities through advanced problem-solving and decision-making systems.

This book brings together contributions from experts who are at the forefront of these fields, aiming to provide comprehensive insights that traverse theoretical foundations and practical implementations. By exploring topics such as evolutionary algorithms, deep learning architectures, swarm intelligence, and convex optimization, this volume offers both breadth and depth. It extends into applied areas, highlighting the role of optimization in domains like healthcare, robotics, and hydrogen supply chains, and tackling crucial ethical considerations such as bias and fairness in machine learning.

Each chapter is meticulously crafted to offer readers not only an understanding of the latest advances but also a glimpse into the future of optimization, machine learning, and AI. Whether you are a researcher seeking to expand your knowledge, a practitioner looking for practical applications, or a student exploring these fields for the first time, we believe this book will serve as an invaluable resource.

As editors of this reference book, we are pleased to present an insightful and diverse collection of research contributions that address key advancements, challenges, and applications in machine learning, artificial intelligence, and related fields.

Each chapter delves deeply into specific topics, showcasing innovative solutions and cutting-edge methodologies. Below is an overview of the chapters included in this book:

CHAPTER OVERVIEW

Chapter 1: This chapter tackles the challenge of automatically detecting adult content to block access to inappropriate websites. Traditional filtering systems often fall short due to their reliance on algorithms like Naive Bayes, K-Nearest Neighbour, and SVM, which struggle to extract meaningful information from unstructured data. This work introduces an Artificial Neural Network (ANN)-based semantic knowledge system enhanced with Ant Colony Optimization (ACO) techniques. By employing a blacklist of restricted websites, the proposed method classifies URLs into desired and undesired categories with improved accuracy and speed, addressing a critical issue in web content filtering.

Chapter 2: The complexities of sequence labeling for Urdu language pose significant computational challenges. This chapter explores syntactic tagging of words using Conditional Random Fields (CRF) and introduces a state-of-the-art voting method to mitigate syntactic ambiguities. By testing on the Bushra Jawaid and CLE datasets, the authors achieve notable F1-scores, validating their approach. Furthermore, the integration of Long Short-Term Memory (LSTM) models offers advancements in Part-of-Speech tagging for Urdu, achieving high levels of accuracy and establishing benchmarks for morpho-syntactic analysis.

Chapter 3: Examining public perceptions of the metaverse, this chapter analyzes tweets collected before and after companies' engagement with this virtual technology. Employing the Hybrid Particle Swarm Optimization with Support Vector Machine (HPSOSVM) approach, the authors demonstrate its superior accuracy in extracting features from the dataset. With results highlighting the potential of ensemble classifiers, the chapter discusses the humanistic reorientation of the metaverse to align with broader societal values.

Chapter 4: Edge computing systems face numerous challenges, including data management, resource allocation, and energy efficiency. This chapter provides a comprehensive analysis of optimization techniques that address these challenges. Drawing on interdisciplinary knowledge, the authors explore methodologies to enhance the quality and efficiency of edge computing systems, paving the way for more sustainable and effective applications in this rapidly evolving field.

Chapter 5: This chapter addresses the permutation flow shop scheduling problem, focusing on minimizing total tardiness. Utilizing nature-inspired metaheuristics such as genetic algorithms, migratory bird optimization, and artificial bee colony algorithms, the authors combine these techniques with local search procedures for optimal sequence generation. The comparative analysis highlights the effectiveness of the population-based ABC_NEH metaheuristic, which consistently outperforms other algorithms in efficiency and success rates.

Chapter 6: Feature selection plays a pivotal role in data analytics by identifying relevant features and reducing data dimensionality. This chapter explores multi-objective optimization techniques that balance accuracy, precision, and robustness. By providing a detailed examination of various approaches, including case studies, the authors equip practitioners with advanced methods for tackling complex real-world data analytics challenges.

Chapter 7: Focusing on time series forecasting, this chapter investigates the application of Transformer-based models for long-term predictions. The authors address challenges such as loss of temporal information and computational complexity, emphasizing the role of position-wise vectors in achieving accurate forecasts. By exploring state-of-the-art benchmarks and datasets, the chapter offers valuable insights for leveraging advanced deep learning techniques in practical applications.

Chapter 8: Cloud platforms revolutionize spatial data management with specialized services such as geocoding and geospatial analytics. This chapter examines tools like Amazon Redshift, Microsoft Azure Cosmos DB, and Google Cloud Spanner, highlighting optimization techniques and security measures. By leveraging these services, the authors demonstrate how spatial data can be transformed for enhanced analysis, visualization, and decision-making.

Chapter 9: Human gait detection emerges as a critical area in biometrics, offering non-intrusive identification methods for applications like surveillance and medical monitoring. Using the CASIA-B dataset, this chapter evaluates a MobileNet with BiLSTM model, achieving remarkable accuracy rates even under varying conditions. The findings underscore the practical applicability and advancements in gait analysis technologies.

Chapter 10: Real estate valuation in Morocco presents unique challenges, including intelligent and sustainable approaches aligned with smart urban planning. This chapter explores machine learning architectures such as Support Vector Regression (SVR), which achieves impressive accuracy. By integrating predictions into an interactive thematic map, the authors highlight the transformative potential of digital tools in modernizing real estate valuation methods.

Chapter 11: This chapter introduces a fully automated AI-based sentiment analysis system to monitor public attitudes toward global crises through social media. By leveraging advanced techniques such as Artificial Neural Networks and optimization algorithms, the system achieves high accuracy and specificity. The findings emphasize the importance of understanding public sentiments to inform strategic decision-making and crisis management.

Chapter 12: Early detection of melanoma, a highly lethal form of skin cancer, is the focus of this chapter. Through Convolutional Neural Networks (CNNs) and the HAM10000 dataset, the authors optimize hyperparameters to enhance model performance. Addressing challenges like class imbalance, the study demonstrates significant improvements in accuracy, sensitivity, and specificity, showcasing the potential of AI in medical diagnostics.

Chapter 13: Artificial intelligence is transforming sectors such as healthcare, education, and business by augmenting human capabilities. This chapter discusses ethical challenges, including bias and workforce displacement, while advocating for inclusive AI development. Future trends like natural language and brain-computer interfaces are explored, underscoring the need for ethical governance and proactive reskilling.

Chapter 14: Bias and fairness are critical considerations in machine learning algorithm development. This chapter reviews measures such as differential impact and demographic parity, analyzing their application in sectors like healthcare, hiring, and financial services. By addressing prejudice and promoting fairness, the authors aim to foster responsible AI practices and equitable outcomes.

Chapter 15: Based on an extensive review of over 3,000 articles published from 1992 to 2024, this chapter synthesizes key developments and research trends in the field, providing a comprehensive perspective on advancements and future directions in machine learning and AI.

It is our hope that this compilation will inspire further innovation, encourage cross-disciplinary collaboration, and contribute to the ongoing advancement of these exciting fields.

We invite you to delve into the world of *Innovations in Optimization and Machine Learning* and explore the transformative potential these technologies hold for the future.

Toufik Mzili

Chouaib Doukkali University, Morocco

Adarsh Kumar Arya

Harcourt Butler Technical University, India

Chapter 1
A Web Content Identification and Classification System Using Natural Language Processing and Machine Learning Techniques

C. Balakumar
Karpagam Academy of Higher Education, India

N. Divya
Karpagam Academy of Higher Education, India

J. Gokulapriya
Rathinam College of Arts and Science, India

M. Kokilamani
Kamalam College of Arts and Science, India

ABSTRACT

The majority of systems used to filter web pages rely on naive bayes, k-nearest neighbour, and SVM algorithms. These methods are not perfect in extracting valuable information from unstructured online content. These systems lack the cognitive ability to discern between erotic and other common information on websites by intelligently filtering web pages. In order to convert the freely available unstructured text information on the search engine into structured data, the suggested effort would be used

DOI: 10.4018/979-8-3693-5231-1.ch001

to classify the web content using the artificial neural network (ANN) technique. This work provides a semantic knowledge system based on machine learning (ML) with the help of ant colony optimization (ACO) technique that addresses these issues by identifying and blocking access to filtering web content in an organised manner. In order to provide accuracy and speed, the suggested method uses a blacklist of restricted websites to classify URLs into wanted and unwanted categories

1. INTRODUCTION

A component of an information retrieval application that presents necessary beneficial information is the classification of web page content. The goal of this procedure is to swiftly classify web items from the extensive world wide web that provide pertinent information. The issue of machine learning is becoming increasingly important as millions of websites continue to grow. Due to the epidemic condition, learning methodologies have drastically changed worldwide in the last two to three years, analysed by Lalitha, T. B., & Sreeja, P. S. (2023). Because there is so much content on the Internet, automatic fake news detection is a useful natural language processing (NLP) problem that can help all online content producers cut down on the time and effort that it takes for humans to identify and stop the dissemination of false information. In this work, we outline the challenges posed by detecting fake news as well as associated activities. We thoroughly examine and contrast the task descriptions, datasets, and NLP solutions created for this assignment by Oshikawa, R., et al (2018). The general web content classification is shown in the figure 1.

Figure 1. Web content classification

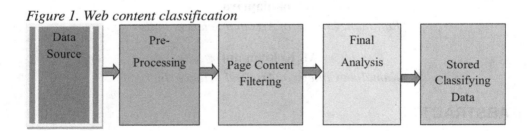

Adult (pornographic) content is currently available on the Internet in large quantities and is growing quickly. It is clear that the adult content filtering technologies in place are unable to effectively categorise webpage context in order to block inappropriate information. For teenagers the abundance may have a negative impact on one's physical and emotional well-being of pornographic websites that are freely accessible to all users on the Internet. It also causes issues for parents who want to prevent their kids from visiting these websites, analysed by Kotenko, I., et al (2017). Furthermore, a significant quantity of combined information about sexual and medical topics diseases, mental health, physical fitness, birth controls, treatment during pregnancy, etc. It can be found on several web pages. To quickly access the content of these web pages, search engines recommend using keyword-based queries. Through a comparison of the query keywords and online content terms, the data is retrieved. But the adult content screening mechanisms that are now in place are not very good at telling if a webpage is about medicine or pornography, detailed by Rowland, D. L., & Uribe, D. (2020) et al (2020).

Narayanan, B. K. (2018) said that, currently, technologies for dynamic filtering, picture filtering, and Universal Resource Locator (URL) filtering are used to detect adult content. Using URL blacklists instead of assessing a webpage's content increases the likelihood of making a mistaken conclusion when using URL filtering techniques. Image filtering systems have a low performance capability and may identify photos related to medicine as adult images. Using a variety of algorithms, a dynamic filtering system examines the content of a webpage.

Nevertheless, these technologies find it difficult to extract significant terms to categorise webpage content. In addition to being a research subject in and of itself, determining the kind of website whose internal keywords are not accessible is also required for additional analyses. Present systems employ common characteristics to block access to content that they consider immoral. Additionally, the existing mechanisms only distinguish broad categories of adult content, like sedition and obscenity. Meaningful keywords, however, are hidden, subject to sudden change, and may not resemble standard features. The majority of current systems extract and categorise undesirable content using naïve Bayes, the bag-of-words model, or a classical ontology. Varshney, G., et al (2016) discussed, these algorithms are unable to identify and eliminate irrelevant stuff from useful content. Furthermore, websites have been categorised into a whitelist and a blacklist using the Platform for Internet Content Selection (PICS), which also employs a common vocabulary and data label format. However, due to its semantic restrictions, the PICS-based technique is not suitable for efficiently identifying websites related to medicine.

Enabling computers to understand written or spoken language is the aim of natural language processing. Numerous fields are combined in NLP, including as statistics, machine learning, deep learning, and computation linguistics. In order to teach computers to comprehend and analyse natural language, NLP algorithms are intricate mathematical formulas. Machine learning (ML) for text analytics and natural language processing (NLP) employs "narrow" artificial intelligence (AI) and machine learning algorithms to read text documents. Text-based data is analysed, processed, and interpreted by NLP algorithms, whereas generalised machine learning algorithms concentrate more on other kinds of data, such image or numeric data, said by Ali, F., et al (2017).

To deal with this problem, two basic approaches are employed. The first tactic is to classify the URL in order to offer speed and accuracy. The second tactic involves categorising data labels, which serve as resource descriptions. Furthermore, a classical NLP serves as the foundation for the majority of information extraction and retrieval. A traditional NLP-based system is inadequate and has a limited capacity to retrieve meaningful data obtained via the internet. In order to extract relevant data from the combined online content, adult content filtering algorithms are thought to benefit greatly from the use of machine learning techniques. Varshney, G., et al (2016).

This research presents a machine learning based webpage content detection system and ACO approach to optimize these issues. NLP filters out pertinent text, and the proposed ANN classification method provides semantic information to identify unsuitable content.. In order to avoid poor picture scanning performance, we examine the context of webpages without image filtering in this paper. The main components of the suggested system's workflow are the pre-processing of web content, the representation of NLP-based information and an optimization, and also the classification of the ANN type of webpage.

> The suggested method compares URLs with an NLP URL list and an online URL blacklist in order to add them to either a whitelist or a blacklist during the erotic content-filtering phase. This phase's main benefits are speed and accuracy. Once informal data has been extracted from the internet content, the online contents are intelligently analysed to identify the relevant webpages. The webpage's accessibility will be gradually blocked if the volume of unofficial data above a predetermined threshold value.
> It properly detects the websites and lessens confusion caused by mistaking general information for web content.
> To extract significant keywords from webpages and remove unnecessary phrases, an unsupervised linear algorithm is utilised.
> Every visited URL, as well as supporting, normal, and abnormal words, is all included in the machine learning. For the purpose of specific data optimization and intelligent classification. To identify and prevent explicit online content, the suggested ANN with ACO semantic knowledge is used.

This chapter is organised, the current research is compiled in Section II. In contrast, Section III provides a brief explanation of the overall situation and internal workings of the suggested ANN of machine learning system. The results and experimental work are detailed in Section IV. Section V serves as the final section of this work.

2. LITERATURE SURVEY

The proliferation of adult websites on the Internet has increased the difficulty of web filtering. The majority of technologies designed to filter content from pornographic websites are ineffective in keeping teenagers from accessing them. To address this, extensive technological development is needed to routinely block access to inappropriate URLs and take out and carefully filter web data. Keeping track of the URLs of inappropriate websites is one way to filter webpages. The primary benefit is speed. However, because many URLs do not display the actual information, a URL-based filtering mechanism is not always perfect. To filter webpages, methods such as Filtering and censoring websites depending on their content is necessary. effectively in order to address this constraint. Filtering can be done using a lot of the information included in hyperlinks and HTML tags on websites. Similar to this, methods for screening and blocking images and videos are also employed to prevent access to inappropriate websites. Various neural network methods are used in these techniques to identify and block offensive images on webpages, Ariyadasa, S., et al (2022).

Aljabri, M., et al (2022) introduce a technique based on machine learning algorithms was introduced to categorise webpage URLs. Every URL is compared against the ODP blacklist during execution in order to filter webpages. The algorithm classifies URLs into categories with or without pornographic elements using two methods: token and n-gram. There are restrictions, though. There are situations when a URL phrase misrepresents the content of the webpage. Immoral information is concealed within the webpages content. It is impossible for a URL-based filtering system to block objectionable websites.

Awal, M. A., et al (2018), told that, by dividing the URL into tokens, a naïve Bayes algorithm was applied for supervised learning and weblog classification. Several issues with the spam blog (splog) system were resolved by this system. The majority of URL phrases, such as http://adult-videompegs.blogspot.com, are composed of concatenated words and punctuation segmentations that the splog system is unable to filter. Sahoo, D., et al (2017) discuss that, a technique to classify weblogs as spam or good was developed in order to solve the problem of URL phrases. The technology compares the URL with a URL repository. The weblog category is changed and the URL is added if it is not already included in the repository.

In order to address the challenging problem of parental control so that kids can use the internet safely and securely, Kenan Enes Aydın, and Sefer Baday, (2020) have developed a model to categorise website contents. Natural language processing, text categorization, and machine learning methods like support vector machines are used to simulate the dynamic classification of webpages. Using SVM, the classification success rate achieved good results. A. Cavalieri et al., (2022) have released a clever technique that will help political science researchers by classifying some political documents including parliamentary questions automatically. These questions are gathered at the Italian Republic's Chamber of Deputies the technology employs text classification through machine learning and deep learning during the weekly Question Times. techniques to make this process easier. Goyal, A., et al. (2018) presented a method for named entity recognition (NER)-based web content filtering. The use of fundamental methods like keyword matching and URL blocking by this system limits its capacity to screen pornographic information. In order to illustrate the web content filtering process, a model lexical NER system uses training pages from the internet. The NER system uses a support vector machine (SVM) to extract and tokenize words in order to assign a weight vector. It enhanced the way webpage text was categorised. With reference to visiting unsuitable websites at home, at school, and in organisations, significant difficulties were highlighted. Preventing employees and youngsters from accessing these pages is getting harder and harder.

Recent times have seen the implementation of content-based filtering to achieve webpage filtering. The training set's noisy data is eliminated using SVM with K-nearest Neighbour. This algorithm used a training set of 1,400 webpages and attained an accuracy of 86%. Websites were categorised using a naïve Bayes method. The central limit theorem is then used to determine the weight of the features that the system has extracted from HTML tags. A Gaussian model is used to classify the web content, while a naïve Bayes theorem computes the probabilities of distinct data sets and events. These functions determine frequencies and weight by utilising the HTML document's plain language, told by Kumar, S., et al (2016). Host blacklisting and thresholding are accomplished using a dynamic threshold and speculative aggregation technique. This system uses local data, such as usage trends, network usage visibility, and worldwide usage, to describe the blacklisting policy. There is a predetermined threshold, and if spam volume surpasses that, Blacklisting the email server will happen. The dynamic threshold method is utilised to determine the server that has to be blocked by dividing the percentage of emails that contain a spam trap,focussed by Lykousas, N. (2022). Logical and organisational boundaries are identified, and autonomous systems exchange routing information via the Border Gateway Protocol (BGPThe proposal for a set of indices for an external universal recommender was made via a higher level recommender insert approach. It compares keywords with the organization's internal dataset, which has a few particular terms in it. It is possible for this recommender system to keep an eye on software development activity. It looks for the index title, uniqueness of the URL, and material relevancy within the webpage content. It resolves privacy concerns across organisational boundaries, explores by Sahingoz, O. K., et al (2019).

Roldán, J. C., et al (2020) introduced a method for classifying web content was introduced in order to add unsuitable websites to a blacklist. This method executes an incremental update and categorization procedure. Then, by giving each page a value, these items are divided into three groups. This method builds a feature set, extracts keywords from the content data, identifies the encoding language, and eliminates HTML elements. These webpages are given a category level and given a specified value. Nichita Utiu, and Vlad-Sebastian Ionescu, (2018) have suggested a structure for keeping the template and other ornamental components off the text and keeping the text on the page separate from the rest of it. The method obtains the primary contents of the webpages using machine learning classification algorithms using well-known datasets such as the Cleaneval and Dragnet datasets, and it achieves 0.95 as f1 score in performance evaluation without requiring extensive pre-processing steps. T. Karthikeya et al., (2019) A model that is designed to classify documents extracted with a higher accuracy rate has been constructed by better feature subsets can be chosen by applying machine learning algorithms and efficient web scraping techniques for recursive feature removal.

An intelligent system for web filtering, called XFighter, was introduced to filter web content. A filtering agent for the internet and an offline classification agent and an access control database make up XFighter's three primary parts. The offline classification agent finds webpages that are inappropriate. Details about URLs are contained in the access control database. The internet filtering agent blocks websites and keeps track of web usage, given by Invernizzi, L., et al (2016). To filter unwanted URLs, a descriptive model based on Naïve Bayesian categorization was presented by Rodríguez, J. E., & Pimiento, J. P. O. (2017). This model is based on term variation, textual modelling (HTML elements, metadata), and structured modelling (images, linkages). High accuracy was achieved via Bayesian categorization for both non-pornographic and pornographic content. Typically, the most widely utilised characteristic for identifying and preventing pornographic photos is skin detection. Two types of filters are used in adult picture categorization methods: hazardous symbol and adult image filters. The adult image filter classifies adult images using a neural network and detects skin using a statistical model. The experimental findings exhibited encouraging performance with both filters. The following sections described the proposed system design architectural functioning.

3. SYSTEM DESIGN

The suggested study discusses the experiment on machine learning techniques of Artificial Neural Networks (ANN) for web content identification and classification of unstructured web content or pages, with Ant Colony Optimisation (ACO) performing the optimisation process. In the discipline of computer science, the model created for this study is based on freely accessible Natural Language Processing (NLP) method.

3.1 Natural Language Processing (NLP)

Specifically, the field of artificial intelligence in computer science known as natural language processing, or NLP, seeks to make it possible for machines to understand spoken and written language similarly to how humans do. Two key approaches in NLP are syntax and semantic analysis. Making grammatical sense out of a sentence's word order is known as syntax. As stated by Kang, Y., et al. (2020), grammatical norms state that NLP uses syntax to ascertain the meaning of a language.

3.2 Ant Colony Optimization (ACO)

A metaheuristic called Ant Colony Optimisation (ACO) was developed after observing how some ant species leave and follow pheromone trails. Making use of tailored (false) pheromone data Based on the ant's search history and any potentially accessible heuristic data provided by Dorigo, M., & Stützle, T. (2019), artificial ants in ACO are stochastic techniques for generating solutions that propose potential fixes for the issue instance in question. To locate the area in the input text data that is affected, the ACO method is employed. Where different iterations of the ACO algorithm are present and it clearly explained in below figure 2. In each iterations, a number of ants construct comprehensive answers based on heuristic input and the knowledge collected by prior populations of ants. A component of a solution leaves a pheromone trail that is a representation of these collected experiences. This initial stage involves setting up all settings and pheromone variables. A group of ants builds a solution to the problem at hand after initiating it by using pheromone values and extra information. In this optional stage, the ants refine the created solution. At this step, pheromone variables are modified depending on observations from search behaviour in ants.

Figure 2. ACO algorithm pseudocode

<u>Ant Colony Optimization:</u>

Initialise the pheromone experiments and relevant parameters;

Do not terminate, but instead

Create an ant colony;

Determine the fitness ratings for each ant;

Using selection techniques, determine the optimal option;

Pheromone trial updates;

Stop while

Process over

Now that we are aware of how the ants acted in the example above, we can construct an algorithm. For simplicity's sake, one food source, one ant colony, and two potential travel routes have been examined. The complete scenario may be simulated using weighted graphs: the paths are the edges, the ant colony and food source are the vertices (or nodes), and the weights associated with the pathways are the pheromone levels.

Take into account the graph as $G = (V, E)$, where V, E are the graph's vertices and edges, respectively. Assuming that we take it into mind, the vertices are (V_s - Source vertex, an ant colony, and V_d - Destination vertex, a food source). The lengths of the two edges, E_1 and E_2, are L_1 and L_2, respectively. Now, it may be hypothesised that, depending on their strength, Vertices E_1 and E_2 have related pheromone values of R_1 and R_2, respectively. As a result, the probability that each ant will first select a path (between E_1 and E_2) is as follows:

$$Pi = \frac{Ri}{R1 + R2}; i = 1, 2$$

Apparently, if R1>R2 and vice versa, there is a larger possibility of choosing E1. As you return along that path, say along, the pheromone value for that route now changes, Ei.

1. Considering the length of the path

$$Ri \leftarrow Ri + \frac{K}{Li}$$

In the aforementioned update, "K" and "i=1, 2" serve as model parameters.

2. Dependent on the pheromone's rate of evaporation

$$Ri \leftarrow (1 - v)*Ri$$

"V," a parameter with a range of [0, 1], controls the evaporation of pheromones. Similarly, "i" is equal to 1 plus 2 plus 3.

The optimized values are fed to the classification based Artificial Neural Network techniques.

3.3 Artificial Neural Network (ANN)

These components, which are grouped in various layers, make up a system's entire artificial neural network (ANN). Depending on how complex the system is, a layer may include a few hundred or millions of units. Input, output, and other layers are routinely combined with hidden layers in artificial neural networks. The outside information that the neural network needs to assess or learn is sent to the input layer. This input is then changed into useable data for the output layer after travelling through one or more hidden layers. Kubat, M., & Kubat, M. (2021). The output layer responds to input data by creating an output in the form of an artificial neural network, is the last but not least. Figure 3 below shows how ANNs function.

Figure 3. ANN performances

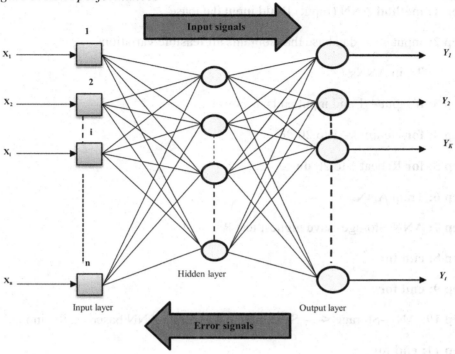

According to its name, the input layer in the above image takes in inputs in a variety of formats specified by the programme. The hidden layer lies between the input and output layers. It does every computation necessary to find buried patterns and features. The hidden layer transforms the input into a variety of outputs before it reaches this layer. The artificial neural network adds a bias to the weighted sum of the inputs when it receives input. An illustration of this technique uses a transfer function which is known as output layer.

$$\sum_{i=1}^{n} Wi * Xi + b$$

The below figure 4 shows the Pseudo-code for ANN in this system. The weighted sum is fed through an activation function to obtain the result, which is then displayed. The firing behaviour of a node depends on its activation functions. Only people who have been fired have access to the output layer. Depending on the kind of task we are completing, we can use any number of activation functions.

Figure 4. Pseudocode for ANN

Step 1: method ANN (Input) Build input database

Step 2: Input <---- database that contains all feasible variations

Train ANNs

Step 3: if input = 1 and input ends, perform

Step 4: for Neurons= 1 to 20 **do**

Step 5: for Repeat 1 to 20 **do**

Step 6: Train ANN

Step 7: ANN-Storage- save highest test R^2

Step 8: end for

Step 9: end for

Step 10: ANN-Storage <---- Save the most accurate ANN based on the inputs.

Step 11: end for

Step 12: return ANN-Storage

Step 13: end procedure

3.4 Mathematical Model for ANN

There are three fundamental elements that are crucial for developing a functional model of the biological neuron. The neuron's connections are first modelled as weights. The weight's value indicates the degree of coupling between an input and a neuron. Positive weight values represent excitatory connections, whereas negative weight values represent inhibitory ones. The next two elements simulate how a neuron cell actually functions. Each input is modified by its corresponding weight before being added together. A linear combination is the phrase employed to describe this action. The activation function of a neuron, finally, regulates the strength of its output. An output range between 0 and 1, or between -1 and 1, is typically regarded as acceptable.

$$V_k = \sum_{j=1}^{p} w_{kj} x_j$$

Figure 5. Mathematical flow of ANN

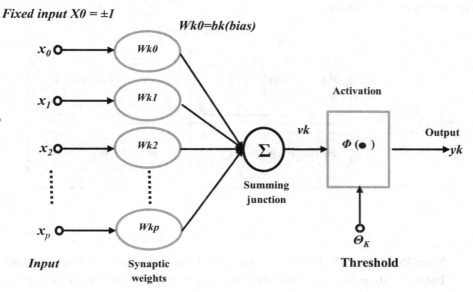

Fixed input X0 = ±1

This model demonstrates that the neuron's interval activity is the above figure 5 shows the mathematical model for ANN. The following section elaborate the data-set, confusion matrix and proposed system result comparison with existing system performance are described.

4. RESULT AND DISCUSSION

In this session, a newly designed Ant Colony Optimisation Algorithm (ACO) and Artificial Neural Network (ANN) combination is compared with the old one in terms of precision, accuracy, recall, and time duration characteristics. ANNACO methods for webpage categorization and web content identification use Naïve Bayes, SVM, and K means algorithms, which are drawn from the literature. It also explains the results of the suggested system (ACOANN). The recently presented study evaluates a classifier mean's efficacy using MATLAB 2013A. Utilising performance evaluation indicators, it may assess the effectiveness of the machine learning models that have been trained. By doing this, it will be able to a dataset that it has never seen before to see how well the machine learning model will perform. The performance effectiveness of a categorization approach is displayed and summarised using a confusion matrix. The confusion matrix is shown in figure 6 below.

Figure 6. Confusion matrix

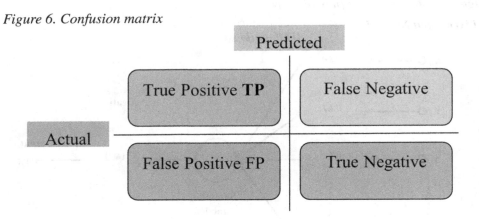

True Positive (TP): Effective detection of the bounding box on the ground.
False Positive (FP): Incorrectly detecting an object that is present or incorrectly detecting one that is not.
False Negative (FN): A bounding box for ground truth that is hidden.
True Negative (TN): Because there are numerous bounding boxes in every image that shouldn't be recognised, a true negative (TN) outcome is irrelevant while discussing object detection.

4.1 Precision

The degree of precision indicates how closely the various measurements match one another. Finding the average deviation, which computes the average of the measurement discrepancies, allows you to assess precision.

$$\text{Precision} = \frac{TP}{(TP + FP)}$$

4.2 Accuracy

By deviating from 100% in the error rate, the accuracy formula represents accuracy. Before we can assess accuracy, we must first assess error rate. Next, we divide the observed value by the actual value to get a percentage that represents the mistake rate.

Accuracy =

Table 1. Result of precision and accuracy

Classification Method	Precision (%)	Accuracy (%)
Naive Bayes	84.49	85.64
SVM	82.56	87.26
K-Means	87.21	89.54
ACOANN	92.68	94.23

The classification result of existing and proposed system is listed in the table 1. In this table, the overall precision and accuracy of both existing (Naïve Bayes, SVM, K means) and proposed (ACOANN) system is mentioned. The existing models achieve precision of 84.49, 82.56%, 87.21% vice versa and the proposed model achieves the best precision value of 92.68% comparing than the other models. Its output result graph is plotted in figure 7. And also it delivers the high accuracy of 94.23% whereas the Naïve Bayes, SVM, K means delivers the accuracy of 85.64%, 87.26%, 89.54% respectively, and also the result is shown by graph in figure 8.

Figure 7. Precision graph

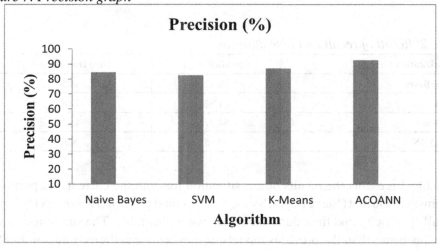

Figure 8. Accuracy graph

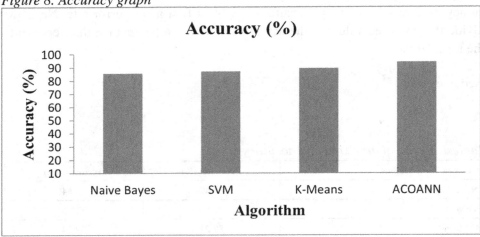

4.3 Specificity

Calculating specificity (SP) involves dividing the entire number of accurate negative predictions by the total number of negatives. The specificity is calculated using the formula shown below.

Specificity = 4.4 Time Duration

Choosing the best machine learning model to solve a problem can be time-consuming if done carelessly.

Table 2. Result of recall and time duration

Classification Method	Specificity (%)	Time Duration (ms)
Naive Bayes	86.42	14.56
SVM	81.82	12.82
K-Means	84.37	13.28
ACOANN	93.85	8.37

Table 2 presents the results of classification for both the current and proposed systems. The current (Naïve Bayes, SVM, K means) and planned (ACOANN) system's overall specificity and time duration are shown in this table. The suggested model performs better than the previous models, achieving a specificity value of 93.85%

when compared to the current model's results of 86.42, 81.82%, and 84.37%, and also its output result graph is shown in figure 9. It also takes up the least amount of time of 8.37ms, in contrast to the execution time of 14.56ms, 12.82ms, and 13.28ms provided by Naïve Bayes, SVM, and K means, also its output graph is plotted in figure 10.

Figure 9. Specificity graph

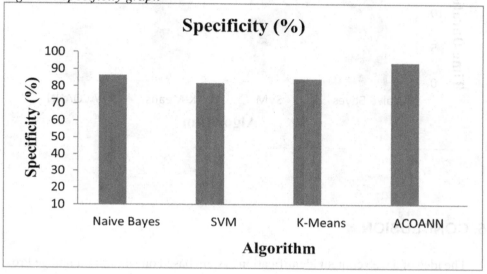

Figure 10. Time duration graph

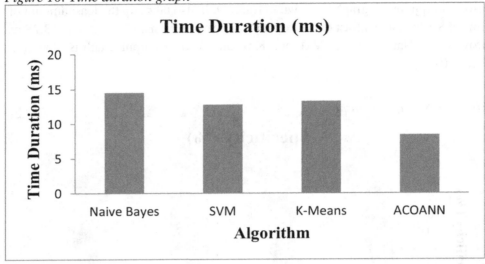

5. CONCLUSION

The idea of a web content identification system based on Natural Language Processing (NLP) is presented in this research in order to automate the classification of needy websites from other websites. Various difficulties related to sensitivity are taken into account, such as classifying the URL, utilising unsupervised linear algorithms to eliminate unnecessary words, extracting and optimizing relevant keywords, and utilising intelligent online content analysis to identify adult content. Using attributes taken from extracted web content, the suggested mechanism provides a useful web content recognition system that can distinguish the appropriate webpages. In fact, the suggested method obtains NLP variables and effectively helpful for optimization by using ACO from web content to the webpage classification using ANN method. And also ACOANN improves the overall performances with the same time it takes the minimum computation time duration. With the use of this methodology, adult material websites can be found and blocked by methodically retrieving and analysing all online content. To intelligently study a network, it can also be used at home, in workplaces, educational institutions, and other public settings. Moreover, this system can solve the categorization issue with medical and other webpages because it can identify adult or medical features from confusing webpage material, extract medical features from those features, and compute a value that serves as a signal for the system of decisions. In subsequent research, Machine Learning (ML) techniques will be employed to enhance the adult content detection algorithm even more.

REFERENCES

Ali, F., Khan, P., Riaz, K., Kwak, D., Abuhmed, T., Park, D., & Kwak, K. S. (2017). A fuzzy ontology and SVM–based Web content classification system. *IEEE Access : Practical Innovations, Open Solutions*, 5, 25781–25797. DOI: 10.1109/ACCESS.2017.2768564

Aljabri, M., Altamimi, H. S., Albelali, S. A., Maimunah, A. H., Alhuraib, H. T., Alotaibi, N. K., & Salah, K. (2022). Detecting malicious URLs using machine learning techniques: Review and research directions. *IEEE Access : Practical Innovations, Open Solutions*, 10, 121395–121417. DOI: 10.1109/ACCESS.2022.3222307

Ariyadasa, S., Fernando, S., & Fernando, S. (2022). Combining long-term recurrent convolutional and graph convolutional networks to detect phishing sites using URL and HTML. *IEEE Access : Practical Innovations, Open Solutions*, 10, 82355–82375. DOI: 10.1109/ACCESS.2022.3196018

Awal, M. A., Rahman, M. S., & Rabbi, J. (2018, October). Detecting abusive comments in discussion threads using Naïve Bayes. In *2018 International Conference on Innovations in Science, Engineering and Technology (ICISET)* (pp. 163-167). IEEE. DOI: 10.1109/ICISET.2018.8745565

Aydın, K. E., & Baday, S. (2020). Machine Learning for Web Content Classification. 2020 Innovations in Intelligent Systems and Applications Conference (ASYU), 1-7. DOI: 10.1109/ASYU50717.2020.9259833

Cavalieri, A. (2022). An Intelligent System for the Categorization of Question Time Official Documents of the Italian Chamber of Deputies. *Journal of Information Technology & Politics*.

Dorigo, M., & Stützle, T. (2019). *Ant colony optimization: overview and recent advances*. Springer International Publishing.

Goyal, A., Gupta, V., & Kumar, M. (2018). Recent named entity recognition and classification techniques: A systematic review. *Computer Science Review*, 29, 21–43. DOI: 10.1016/j.cosrev.2018.06.001

Invernizzi, L., Thomas, K., Kapravelos, A., Comanescu, O., Picod, J. M., & Burgztein, E. (2016, May). Cloak of visibility: Detecting when machines browse a different web. In *2016 IEEE Symposium on Security and Privacy (SP)* (pp. 743-758). IEEE. DOI: 10.1109/SP.2016.50

Kang, Y., Cai, Z., Tan, C. W., Huang, Q., & Liu, H. (2020). Natural language processing (NLP) in management research: A literature review. *Journal of Management Analytics*, 7(2), 139–172. DOI: 10.1080/23270012.2020.1756939

Karthikeya, T. (2019). Personalized Content Extraction and Text Classification Using Effective Web Scraping Techniques. *International Journal of Web Portals*, 11(2), 41–52. DOI: 10.4018/IJWP.2019070103

Kotenko, I., Chechulin, A., & Komashinsky, D. (2017). Categorisation of web pages for protection against inappropriate content in the internet. *International Journal of Internet Protocol Technology*, 10(1), 61–71. DOI: 10.1504/IJIPT.2017.083038

Kubat, M., & Kubat, M. (2021). Artificial neural networks. An Introduction to Machine Learning, 117-143.

Kumar, S., Gao, X., Welch, I., & Mansoori, M. (2016, March). A machine learning based web spam filtering approach. In 2016 IEEE 30th International Conference on Advanced Information Networking and Applications (AINA) (pp. 973-980). IEEE. DOI: 10.1109/AINA.2016.177

Lalitha, T. B., & Sreeja, P. S. (2023). Potential Web Content Identification and Classification System using NLP and Machine Learning Techniques. *International Journal of Engineering Trends and Technology*, 71(4), 403–415. DOI: 10.14445/22315381/IJETT-V71I4P235

Lykousas, N. (2022). Analysis and detection of deviant and malicious behaviors in social media and beyond (Doctoral dissertation, University of Piraeus (Greece)).

Narayanan, B. K., M, R. B., J, S. M., & M, N. (2018). Adult content filtering: Restricting minor audience from accessing inappropriate internet content. *Education and Information Technologies*, 23(6), 2719–2735. DOI: 10.1007/s10639-018-9738-y

Oshikawa, R., Qian, J., & Wang, W. Y. (2018). A survey on natural language processing for fake news detection. arXiv preprint arXiv:1811.00770.

Rodríguez, J. E., & Pimiento, J. P. O. (2017). Bayesian methods for classification inappropriate web pages. Visión electrónica, 11(2), 179-189.

Roldán, J. C., Jiménez, P., & Corchuelo, R. (2020). On extracting data from tables that are encoded using HTML. *Knowledge-Based Systems*, 190, 105157. DOI: 10.1016/j.knosys.2019.105157

Rowland, D. L., & Uribe, D. (2020). Pornography use: what do cross-cultural patterns tell us?. Cultural differences and the practice of sexual medicine: A guide for sexual health practitioners, 317-334.

Sahingoz, O. K., Buber, E., Demir, O., & Diri, B. (2019). Machine learning based phishing detection from URLs. *Expert Systems with Applications*, 117, 345–357. DOI: 10.1016/j.eswa.2018.09.029

Sahoo, D., Liu, C., & Hoi, S. C. (2017). Malicious URL detection using machine learning: A survey. arXiv preprint arXiv:1701.07179.

Utiu, N., & Ionescu, V.-S. (2018). Learning Web Content Extraction with DOM Features. IEEE 14th International Conference on Intelligent Computer Communication and Processing (ICCP), 5-11. DOI: 10.1109/ICCP.2018.8516632

Varshney, G., Misra, M., & Atrey, P. K. (2016). A survey and classification of web phishing detection schemes. *Security and Communication Networks*, 9(18), 6266–6284. DOI: 10.1002/sec.1674

Chapter 2
Employing Natural Language Processing Techniques for the Development of a Voting–Based POS Tagger in the Urdu Language

Ahmed Raza
https://orcid.org/0009-0000-3095-2158
School of Systems and Technology, University of Management and Technology, Lahore, Pakistan

Muhammad Sarwar
School of Systems and Technology, University of Management and Technology, Lahore, Pakistan

Usama Ahmed
School of Systems and Technology, University of Management and Technology, Lahore, Pakistan

Momina Shaheen
https://orcid.org/0000-0001-9424-9787
School of Arts Humanities and Social Sciences, University of Roehampton, London, UK

Kainat Saleem
COMSATS University Islamabad, Lahore, Pakistan

Muhammad Sohail Farooq
Comsat Institute of Information Technology, Lahore, Pakistan

ABSTRACT

The process of sequence labeling (POS) by assigning syntactic tags to words in the given context is an important role in various NLP applications. The core motive of this work is to tackle the morpho-syntactic category of words in Urdu language. This language has lots of computational challenges because of its dual nature. The

DOI: 10.4018/979-8-3693-5231-1.ch002

work comprises different tasks as initially the authors tracked the best combination of feature sets in terms of CRF to entitle the previous results on two stable and well-known datasets Bushra Jawaid dataset and CLE dataset. Due to syntactic ambiguity, a state-of-the-art voting method has been introduced which is being implemented to overcome the contradictory results of the different machine learning classifiers. The results show significant improvement in the baseline results as the F1-score on a primary dataset is 94.8% and 95.7% on the succeeding dataset. Long short-term memory (LSTM) is used for one of the most diverse and inflectional tasks like part of speech tagging for the Urdu language by achieving an F1-score of 86.7% and 96.1% respectively for both datasets.

INTRODUCTION

Part of Speech (POS) Tagging plays a core part in numerous languages like Urdu, Hindi, Arabic, and Persian, etc. It also helps in understanding the script of a particular language for assigning syntactic tags. Tags involve in Part of Speech are composed of various tag sets (Penn Treebank, Sajjad's tag set, and CRULP tag set). Tagging highly relies on these tag sets to improve the efficiency of different tags and the combination of these tags. POS tagging is a preliminary step in many NLP tasks which gives detailed information of the given text. Tagging also plays an important role in various applications like Information Extraction (IE), Name Entity Recognition (NER), Machine Translation (MT), Word Sense Disambiguation (WSD) and many other NLP applications. The major part of POS is to boost the accuracy and robustness in different NLP domains and benefited to extract the accurate & related data from the training corpus. Generally, syntactic categories of the words help to identify the corpora. Broadly the work has been done regarding POS tagging in many European languages like English, French and South Asian languages, etc. Meanwhile, in the Urdu language, less work has been done because it has fewer resources according to linguistic knowledge. Part of speech tagging task in this language is conceived as a crucial & complex challenge due to the dual behavior of Urdu POS-tags or morpho-syntactic ambiguity in various situations. Majorly POS Taggers performed tagging using two key steps initially they need a Gold-standard-tagged dataset for training secondly those algorithms that helps to assign tags to words in a particular context. Initially, Liner-chain CRF1 worked as a learning-algorithm for part of speech tagging. It includes the language-independent and language-dependent features that are intense, firm and equitable for Urdu. Latterly point out numerous challenges that could make part of speech tagging difficult for Urdu (Khan et al., 2019). In Natural-language-processing (NLP) POS tagging is basic tasks to conclude the effectiveness and efficiency among text and tags. By applying various taggers and models such as Conditional Random Field (CRF) proves exceptional execution in association with numerous types of linguistic ambiguities. It also plays a vital role in capturing various sorts of linguistic knowledge. We have also worked on neural network variation i-e Bi-LSTM for sequence tagging task which helps in accessing the both past and future input for a certain data. This helps to back and forth propagation for tagging data. The main focus of this paper is to assist the POS tagging using different models in the Urdu language. POS tagging is an emergent field for Asian languages because the models developed by researchers for POS tagging for English and other languages are unable to address the problems in Asian languages like Urdu and Hindi etc.

The main contributions of this work are as follows:

1. Explored POS tagging in Urdu Language using various tag sets.
2. Developing a comparison & evaluation of different statistical models to overcome the issue of ambiguity of various tags and performed neural network analysis for tagging.
3. Proposing an ensemble method for different taggers & statistical models.

Previously support vector machine (SVM) also shows remarkable results in the field of Part of Speech (POS) tagging but CRF has outdone the SVM. Our results show that CRF outperforms the previous results and we also made voting criteria that show betterment in the results.

LITERATURE REVIEW

Nowadays the number of techniques has been introduced for Part of Speech tagging for words in a particular sentence. These techniques have been divided into two categories first one is Rule-based technique which works as assigning tags based on rules. Whereas later one is a stochastic-based approach in which probability models help to assign tags (Tian and Lo, 2015). The sparsity problem is the major issue in the NLP task due to morphological richness which incorporates the out-of-vocabulary problem. It might be the congestion state in POS tagging due to which POS tagging becomes crucial & challenging task for agglutinative languages as compared to other languages that have poor morphology (Bölücü and Can, 2019). POS tagging for the Urdu language is similar to Hindi but the difference is in vocabulary and its writing style. Data preprocessing is highly important which did by removing stop words, diacritics initially from the data then make a standard format of it and use hybrid techniques for achieving accuracy (Ali Daud et .al 2017). The importance of POS tagging in linguistics is the basic step of text processing in many NLP applications like NER, Machine Translation (MT) POS tagging, etc. It describes the features of the Urdu language in the context of POS tagging. These are the morphological features of Urdu language like Number, Gender & case. Whereas the Urdu language "case" hasp three subcategories like vocative, nominative, and oblique (Asif et al., 2015). Numerous problems are involved in POS tagging failure in which one is unknown words. They might be referred to as spelling errors in learner English that are being tackled by using Bidirectional LSTM (Nagata et al., 2018). UDPipe 1.0 is the pre-trained pipeline for performing NLP tasks like POS tagging, Dependency Parsing, Lemmatization, Sentence segmentation & Tokenization. That is issued as a baseline model for CoNLL 2017 UD shared-tasking using raw text for training data. Meanwhile, a modified version of UDPipe 1.2 which is used for CoNLL 2017 as a contestant system being introduced. Whereas hyperparameters are used for the sake of improving accuracy (Straka and Straková, 2018).

The effect of the evolution of Treebank with annotated tags of POS is highly efficient for Urdu language processing. It is the scarce resource language and requires countless resources to overcome the challenge of computational resources (Abbas, 2014). The accuracy of POS tagging is refined by using CRF with a fine-grained label set (Silfverberg et al., 2014). A special model is introduced for semantic and syntactic information by using deep learning in which their representation and morphemic semantics with their compositional features have been tackled. It also helps in representing the word better by combining both the Recurrent Neural Network (RNN) & Neural Language Model (NLM). It shows improved results for semantic and syntactic information in clustering related words (Luong et al., 2013). Space insertion and space omission are major challenges in Word segmentation for the Urdu language. They are being covered using CRF based model (Wahab Khan et al., 15). Part of speech tagging can be classified in open class type and close class type. Whereas for the stochastic based tagger SVM, CRF, and HMM-based approaches used for classification which helps to assign adequate tags to the words (Vaishali Gupta et al., 2016). Standard datasets including the Center for Language Engineering (CLE) and Bushra Jawaid (BJ) has been used for implementing previously mentioned algorithms as well as Deep Recurrent Neural Network (DRNN) which involves LSTM-RNN with CRF and forward LSTM-RNN for word features. It shows that CRF performs better on the CLE dataset while DRNN outperforms other algorithms on the BJ dataset (Khan et al., 2019). Long-Short Term Method (LSTM) based on feature-extraction that is used for handling Out of Vocabulary problems in POS tagging by utilizing sequence labeling for the learning system on the character level. This task is performed on four typologically different languages which don't require annotation because it deals with known and unknown words (Zhandos Yessenbayev et al., 2016). The neural network helps in representing both character and word level by using Bidirectional-LSTM and CRF. Convolutional-

Neural-Network (CNN) for encoding character-level information of words into the character-level representation is being used on two datasets one is CoNLL 2003 and Penn Treebank for POS tagging (Xuezhe Ma et al., 2018).

POS TAGGING IN URDU LANGUAGE

Urdu is less resource language due to rich morphology: therefore, POS-tagging is a more crucial task in this language. In the Urdu language, it is difficult to identify nouns from pronouns while there is a proper distinction between noun & pronoun. The occurrence of the dropping of words is frequent in the Urdu language as compared to other languages. In Urdu, POS-tagging is a difficult process due to the dual behavior of tags. To conquer this issue context-based POS-tagging for the Urdu language is performed by using different taggers & machine learning algorithms.

Challenges in Urdu POS Tagging

The majority of the work has been carried out regarding POS-tagging in resource-rich languages but Urdu still needs a lot of work to do. Issues involved in Urdu POS-tagging are in the infancy stage due to resources that are required for handling the Urdu language.

Contextual Features

It is a significant problem to pinpoint the exact word according to the sense of the core sentence. An example of clear identification of this type of feature is given in table 1.

Table 1. Contextual feature

Aajkal sone ka bhao kaya hai ? What is the price of Gold nowadays?

In this sentence, we don't know about the word "Sone" either it is used for sleeping or Gold. When it is used for sleeping it is a Verb & for Gold, it is used as a Noun. The ambiguity of these two forms of one word is resolved by seeing [daam] (price) word in a sentence. So it is difficult to identify these types of words with the exact meaning of that word in the sentence.

Categorical Features

It is a crucial feature for unseen words in data where an artificial bias is used with the help of a Specific tag set. Instead of using explicit bias for these types of words in the built model. As for the understanding example is given in figure 1.

Figure 1. Categorical example

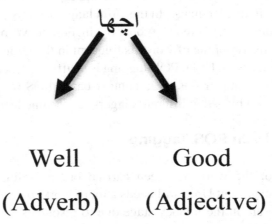

Some of the noun in the Urdu language used as an adjective. When we removed the noun from the sentence the adjective plays as a noun in that particular sentence given in table 2.

Table 2. Noun as adjective sentence

Do mulazmat ko logun berozgar Employ unemployed people
Do mulazmat ko berozgar Employ the unemployed

Similarly, when an adjective modifies an adverb in Urdu text it behaves like an adverb in a sentence as given in the table 3.

Table 3. Adverb as adjective sentence

hay insan azeem bada wo He is a great man	
hay insan bada wo He is a big man	

DATASET

We have used two benchmark datasets that are Bushra Jawaid dataset and the CLE dataset. The first is publicly available whereas the second one has the restricted access.

Bushra Jawaid Dataset

The Bushra Jawaid dataset consists of data that is gathered from web resources like BBC, Awaz-e-Dost and Digital Urdu Library while a major part of the data is gathered from Urdu planet in contrast to other resources. Approximately the total number of sentences in this corpus is 5.4 million but due to limited hardware resources we have worked on 200k sentences.

CLE Dataset

We have worked on another dataset that was evaluated on the dataset of Urdu Digest which is POS tagged and published by "The Center for Language Engineering" (CLE) for the sake of Urdu language computational processing. The data consist of different domains like politics, health, education, world affairs etc. The restriction of this dataset is we need a license to use it. Statistics of both datasets are given in the table 4.

Table 4. Dataset description

Datasets	Bushra Jawaid	CLE
No. of Sentences	2,00,000	4981
No. of Tokens	3,539,944	8,95,344
No. of Unique Tokens	1,25,965	10,871
No of Tags	42	35

29

Tag sets are the integral part of POS tagging having two type of classes one is morpho-syntactic and other is syntactical class. Different tag sets have various numbers of categories of tags. The Hardie tag set consists of 350 tags having two types of categories in it. Our main focus is on Sajjad Tag set which is based on Urdu Grammar and the tag sets that are previously made and it belongs to syntactic category of tag sets. Another tag set is CRULP which stands for "Center for Research in Urdu Language Processing" which have 46 Part of Speech tags in it. The second majorly focused tag set is CLE which have 35 POS tags having 12 integral categories in it. These tag sets are keenly observed and selected according to our dataset.

MATERIALS AND METHODS

This section is describing the work flow which shows that starting from the corpus selection we have done our tagging after preprocessing initially then training data and further steps discussed in detail as shown in "Figure 2" then model implementation and finally evaluating results.

Figure 2. Proposed system architecture

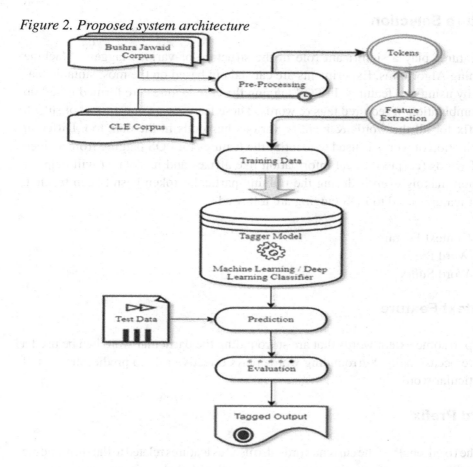

Preprocessing

The preprocessing has an important step which leads to implementing different algorithms of machine learning. The data is preprocessed by removing noise like bullets, arrows, commas, etc. We know that brackets haven't played any role in Urdu that's why it is also discarded from the data. The tokenization of data is done by using NLTK (Natural language Tool Kit). After tokenization of data, by using Urdu sentence boundary like full stop we split paragraphs into sentences. The major challenge in data preprocessing in the Urdu language is "|" delimiter sign which is used to separate the tags from words because the compiler is not familiar to this operator & it is stuck when reading Urdu file in which this operator is used so it should be discarded.

Feature Selection

Features play a significant role in the structure of various taggers, Machine Learning Algorithms. Experiments are carried out based on the most suitable features by using get_features. In POS tagging the core features are formed based on the combination of required tags & words. These features are constituted of suffix, a prefix for all the words & identify various numerals in the data too. Different combination of words is used to identify the features for POS tagging from a given set of words (corpus). Local information like affixes and its context will help for decision making even if during the training particular token hasn't been tackled. Set of features used to POS tagging are followed as:

- Context Feature
- Word Prefix
- Word Suffix

Context Feature

Up to some extent words that are surrounding the particular word can be used a feature occasionally. Surrounding words plays effective role to predict the tags of a particular word.

Word Prefix

The fixed length of the current words also used as features related to the surrounding words. The prefix information helps to identify the POS class for a particular token in a given context. On the basis of this model can easily predict the tag for the token.

Word Suffix

Word suffixes efficiently worked to extract information therefore it is used as a feature in some era. These features are split up in two types, initial one is using the fixed length of current & its surrounding words formed a feature secondly more advanced feature used to modify binary values. Different features in the set format are given in the table 5. We have given an example of a sentence that is extracted from a training file shown in table 6 which clearly describing the tagging criteria for a particular word according to the tagset for part of speech tagging.

Table 5. Feature description

Feature	Feature Description	Set of Feature
Fe1: Wr	Lexemic Word	[0,0]
Fe2: Pr	Previous Word	[-1,0]
Fe3: Nx	Next Word	[0,1]
Fe4: Wr+Pfx1	Lexemic Word + Prefix -1	[0,0], [-1,0]
Fe5: Wr+Pfx1+Pfx2	Lexemic Word + Prefix-1 + Prefix-2	[0,0], [-1,0],[-2,0]
Fe6: Wr+Sfx1	Lexemic Word + Suffix-1	[0,0], [0,1]
Fe7: Wr+Sfx1+Sfx2	Lexemic Word + Suffix-1 + Suffix-2	[0,0], [0,1], [0,2]

Table 6. Word Tagging for a sentence in a training file

Lexemic Word	Suffix-1	Suffix-2	Prefix	Previous Word	Previous Word Tag	Actual Tag	Next Word
				-	SM	PN	
					PN	I	
					I	NN	
					NN	NN	
					NN	VB	-
-	-	-	-		VB	SM	

MODELS

Different machine learning models are being used for Part of Speech tagging in Urdu.

CRF

Conditional Random Field (CRF) is an approach belongs to the conditional-probabilistic model. This includes the most frequent sequential segmentation and different functions related to labeling that has up-to-the-mark results. The expression for CRF is given in equation 1.

$$P\left(\acute{Y} \mid X\right) = \frac{1}{ZX} * \exp\left(\sum_{t}\sum_{k}\lambda_k \cdot f_k\left(\acute{Y}_{t-1}, \acute{Y}_t, X\right)\right) \tag{1}$$

In this equation $f_k(y_{t-1}, y_t, x)$ is the feature function & λ_k is used to assigning weights to the different features during training. In the second equation $Z(x)$ represents the normalization factor that is given in equation 2:

$$Z\left(X\right) = \sum_{\acute{Y} \in Y} exp\left(\sum_t \sum_k \lambda_k \cdot f_k\left(\acute{Y}_{t-1}, \acute{Y}_t, X\right)\right) \tag{2}$$

Random Forest

Random forest is used to solve the problems related to classification and regression which helps in decision-making by forming trees for them. It works for categorical and numerical features whereas for our classification problem it gives us the probability according to specific classes.

Tree Tagger

It's an open-source and multilingual technique to annotate part of speech and lemma information to any text. The Parameter file is necessary to use this tagger which is created according to our data. The core part of Tree Tagger is to estimate with the binary decision tree of transitional probabilities.

TnT

Trigrams'n Tags tagging (TnT) is a statistical tagger that requires input data in form of one token per line in which the first column has words and the second has tags most of the time this tagger works on probability distribution. We can calculate the probabilities according to the sequence of words using equation 3.

$$argmax_{t1\ldots tT}\left[\prod_{i=1}^{T} P\left(t_i \mid t_{i-1}, t_{i-2}\right) P\left(w_i \mid t_i\right)\right] P\left(t_{T+1} \mid t_T\right) \tag{3}$$

$w_1 \ldots w_T$ is the sequences of words in length T & t_{i-1}, t_0 are the additional tags while $t_1 \ldots t_T$ are the tagset components. While t_{T+1} is used as a sequence markers. In TnT uni, bi & trigrams frequencies are calculated which helps to select the best model for tagging. The formulas that we use are given in equation 4,5 and 6.

For Unigram $P\left(t_3\right) = \dfrac{f(t_3)}{N} \quad (4)$

For Bigram $P\left(t_3 \mid t_2\right) = \dfrac{f(t_2, t3)}{f(t_2)} \quad (5)$

For Trigram $P(t_3|t_1,t_2) = \dfrac{f(t_1,t_2,t3)}{f(t_1,t_2)}$ $\left(6\right)$

It is quite speedy and optimized. For the generation of parameters, the elements used to train on tagged corpora. To get the efficient result in the context of precision log addition is used over multiplication in this tagger.

Decision Tree

Decision tree is basically rule based technique and has three types of nodes namely root, lead and decision nodes respectively. We have used it according to our data by splitting up the data on the nodes until all the attributes have assigned the same values which helps in getting results.

LSTM

LSTM stands for Long-Short Term Memory; it's the deep learning type technique. In LSTM an epoch called hyperparameter should be initialized before the training of the model which helps in periodic evaluation. The best part of it is that it is the classification of data, processing of data and finally predicting against the particular data. Our focus is on Bi-Directional LSTM which controls the input both from past to future and future to past which helps in understanding the results in the given context more precisely. In terms of tagging Bi-LSTTM handles the data for long range dependencies by tagging the particular word on forward and backward information. Equation for forward function of Bi-LSTM has given equation 7 and 8.

$$a_h^t = \sum_{l=1}^{L} x_l^t w_{lh} + \sum_{h'=1,t>0}^{H} b_{h'}^{t-1} w_{h'h} \tag{7}$$

$$b_h^t = \Theta_h\left(a_h^t\right) \tag{8}$$

In equations x^t is considered as an input and a_h^t network input for h unit to LSTM, whereas b_h^t haves the h and t activation functions. w_{lh} is the input weight and $w_{h'h}$ is the hidden unit weight. Θ_h represents the activation function for hidden layer. The backward function has been calculated by the given equation 9 and 10.

$$\frac{\delta O}{\delta w_{hk}} = \sum_{t=1}^{T} \frac{\delta O}{\delta a_h^t} b_h^t \tag{9}$$

$$\frac{\delta O}{\delta a_h^t} = \Theta_h\left(a_h^t\right)\left(\sum_{K=1}^{K} \frac{\delta O}{\delta a_h^t} w_{hk} + \sum_{h'=1,t>0}^{H} \frac{\delta O}{\delta a_{h'}^{t+1}} w_{hh'}\right) \tag{10}$$

Voting

It is a method that helps us to incorporate more than one classifiers to improve the baseline results. The fundamental reason to do voting among all classifiers is a particular token that is tagged wrongly by any classifier & correctly tagged by another one. We have used Weighted Voting to combine the output of all these classifiers to get effective results so that the correct tag classifier take into consideration. To overcome this issue we assign weights to each classifier. We have used the formula to assigning weights to the classifiers given in equation 11.

$$Output = \left(Max \left(Set \left(\sum_{i=1}^{5} Tag[id(i)] + + \right) \right) \right) \tag{11}$$

Weighting criteria based on the performance of individual classifier. The higher the performance, higher the weights of the model in voting method (Asif Eqbal et. al 2018). Voting technique gives a promising improvement for various classifiers efficiency as well as noticeable increments in predicted scores.

EXPERIMENTAL RESULTS

We have enumerated our results on the Bushra Jawaid corpus and CLE corpus using supervised machine learning algorithms. We have extracted features that are based on the Urdu language that helps in assigning tags to the words according to the context. In addition, to improve the accuracy of Urdu POS tagging these kinds of features provide necessary information regarding the specific word in a specific sentence in the Urdu language. We have observed that different POS tags of one word are significant in classification for a specific word in part of speech tagging. After executing statistical model we make a voting method by assigning weights to models then calculate the results. We have evaluated our results using different evaluation measures including F1-score, Recall and Precision. The table 7 represents the detailed result that we calculate on the Bushra Jawaid Dataset. The detailed results for the second dataset is given in table 8.

Table 7. Results on BJ dataset

Models	Recall			Precision			F1-Score		
	Micro	Macro	Weighted	Micro	Macro	Weighted	Micro	Macro	Weighted
Conditional Random Field	94.9	88.3	94.8	94.9	89.4	94.8	94.9	88.7	94.8
Tree Tagger	93.3	91.6	93.3	93.3	90.2	93.2	93.3	90.2	93.2
Decision Tree Classifier	91.2	86.6	91.6	91.2	86.8	91.6	91.2	86.7	91.6
TnT Tagger	91.3	86.3	91.3	91.3	86.6	92.9	91.3	86.2	92.1
Random Forest	92.2	86.6	92.2	92.2	86.8	92.1	92.2	86.7	92.1
Voting	94.6	90.6	94.6	94.6	91.1	94.6	94.6	90.7	94.6

Table 8. Results on CLE dataset

Models	Recall			Precision			F1-Score		
	Micro	Macro	Weighted	Micro	Macro	Weighted	Micro	Macro	Weighted
Conditional Random Field	95.5	82.6	95.5	95.5	91.2	95.5	95.5	85.0	95.4
Tree Tagger	90.6	89.6	90.6	90.6	79.5	91.0	90.6	83.0	90.2
Decision Tree Classifier	90.5	81.6	90.5	90.5	82.5	90.5	90.5	81.1	90.5
TnT Tagger	90.7	82.4	90.7	90.7	90.4	96.3	90.7	85.0	93.3
Random Forest	92.2	80.3	92.2	92.2	85.3	92.2	92.2	81.1	92.1
Voting	95.8	83.3	95.8	95.8	91.5	95.9	95.8	85.5	95.7

In table 9 CRF shows better results than the voting method the reason behind is that CRF tagger is much better than the other classifiers. The combination of different classifiers doesn't have a major impact on voting that's why we try different CRF features combinations such as (weight regularization, different feature set, number of training iterations, etc.) which will ultimately help to find out best suitable combination.

Table 9. CRF Variations on BJ and CLE datasets

Combination of best suitable Features	F-Measure in Terms of % on BJ	F-Measure in Terms of % on CLE
Wr,Nx	75.0	80.3
Wr,Nx,Pfx1	71.2	73.7
Wr,pr,pfx1	75.3	77.3
Wr,Nx,Pr,Pfx1	69.3	80.9
Wr,Nx,Pr,Sfx1	84.9	84.4
Wr,Nx,Pr,Pfx1,Sfx1	78.6	81.7
Wr,Nx,Pr,Sfx1,Sfx2	84.3	88.4
Wr,Nx,Pr,Pfx1,Pfx2	77.5	83.8
Wr,Nx,Pr,Sfx2,Pfx1	80.7	84.2
Voting	85.0	88.3

Table 10. Comparative analysis

Study	Corpus	Techniques	F1-score %	
			BJ Dataset	CLE Dataset
(Khan et al., 2018)	CLE, Bushra Jawaid	CRF	93.56	86.99
(Khan et al., 2019)	CLE, Bushra Jawaid	Lstm-Rnn	88.7 (Acc.)	75.64 (Acc.)
Proposed Work	CLE, Bushra Jawaid	CRF, Voting	94.8	95.7
		Bi-Lstm	86.7	96.1

Table 10 represents the comparative analysis of our work with the baseline results. They have used a feature set which included (Previous word, Current word, Next word, Next-1, Next-2, Next+1, Next+2, POS tags of previous word, Suffix of current word, length of current word). We have used more distinct features from the baseline features set. These features are (lexemic word, previous word, next word, Prefix-1, Prefix-2, Suffix-1, and Suffix-2). Our results show promising improvement for both the datasets. Table 11 presents the deep learning techniques results on both discussed earlier datasets.

Table 11. LSTM result

Model	Recall	Precision	F1-Score
LSTM on BJ	95.8	96.5	96.1
LSTM on CLE	85.6	87.8	86.7

DISCUSSION

In the Urdu language, a major issue is that a substantial amount of Urdu words have different meanings according to their (different) context. Just for an example, the word (, sona) has two different tags due to the same words in different context either it is a noun (NN) or a verb (VB) (gold, sleep). This desperate and dual behavior of the tags makes the POS tagging more challenging.

For sequence classification (tagging) of text, different machine learning algorithms are used like CRF, Tree Tagger, Random Forest, TnT Tagger & Decision tree. CRF outperformed overall classifiers. The core reason behind its exceptional performance is that it is a discriminative probabilistic classifier. It's working based on conditional probabilities and try to model these probabilities distribution i.e P (bla). Due to these distributions, CRF has a considerable good set of label distributions. We have analyzed Urdu language-dependent features and critically scrutinize the impact of different combinations of features on our datasets in the case of CRF. The major motivation behind our improved results in terms of CRF is choosing the best fitting combination of the feature set that helps to outperform the existing baseline results. We have a noticeable increment in the experimental results that is 94.8% F1-score which is 1.24% higher than the previous results in terms of CRF using Bushra Jawaid and 95.4% F1-score which is 8.41% using CLE corpus (Khan et al., 2019). We have implemented a neural network on our data sets which shows more promising results than the previous results. We primarily apply Bi-LSTM which observes remarkable improvement in the results. It involves backward and forwards information for a current word which plays an important part in POS tagging and helps in digging out the tag of the next word on the basic information of that previous tag. In Urdu language, subcategories of conjunction composed of coordination conjunction and subordinating conjunction. Because CC (Coordination Conjunction) is used to connect two or more sentences, words & clauses while SC (Subordinating Conjunction) like " " word in the Urdu language is used at the start of the sentence as a clause, this word is also used in our test data & there is a confusion of SC tag with NN (Noun). Most of the tags are chosen by different classifiers according to their probabilities. PN (Proper noun) tag is mostly confused with the NN tag that puts a deep effect on the sense of the whole context. Table 12 clearly explains some of the words having ambiguous tags assigned by different classifier.

Table 12. Ambiguous tags

Words	Actual Tags	Tag Assigned by CRF	Tag Assigned by TnT	Tag Assigned by Random Forest	Tag Assigned by Tree Tagger	Voting
	NN	NN	NN	ADJ	ADJ	NN
	VB	VB	PN	NN	PN	VB
	PN	PN	MUL	VB	VB	PN
	PN	PN	VB	TA	AA	PN
	NN	NN	UNK	NN	NN	PN
	INT	ADJ	NN	INT	PN	INT
	VB	VB	VB	AA	AA	VB
	SC	SC	SC	SC	NN	SC
	PN	NN	NN	PN	NN	NN
	NN	ADJ	ADJ	NN	NN	ADJ
	G	G	G	NN	NN	G
	ADV	NN	ADV	NN	NN	ADV

To overcome these confusions of dual behavior of the tags we develop a voting technique. In which, we take prediction on test data by all classifiers & vote that prediction which has the highest confidence. Sometimes the tags are equally voted by classifiers in this case the best individual tag is chosen based on the best-weighted classifier. To increase efficiency and resolve this ambiguity we have used weighted voting. In this type of voting, we assign weights to each classifier and based on weights, we have predicted the correct tag of each token by taking the sum of similar tags assigned by classifiers and take the highest weighted tag for this particular token. In this way, we overcome the issue of ambiguous tags assigned by different classifiers. By using the voting technique we see that it enhances the efficiency of different classifiers and also increases the score. This method shows that some of the tags perform well when voting is applied like for Bushra Jawaid PN (Proper noun), NN (Noun), and VB (Verb) while for CLE SC (Subordinate Conjunction), ADV (Adverb), and G (Genitive). The remaining tags are described as ADJ (Adjective), MUL (Multiplicative), TA (Ten Auxiliaries), INT (Interjection), AA (Aspectual Auxiliaries), and UNK stand for Unknown tag.

CONCLUSION

POS tagging gives grammatical categories of words. The integral part played by Part of speech tagging is to understand the meaning of the particular words in a given text and extract the association among these words. Countless applications of POS tagging show that POS taggers have tags ambiguity. It is conquered by presenting a tagging model for Urdu language focusing to enrich the POS tagging in Urdu. Two convenient means that are proposed for Urdu language processing. A substantial monolingual corpus in the form of ordinary text as well as automatically tagged and an unprecedented tagger that is being trained on the monolingual data (Jawaid et al., 2014). We explore major issues in sequence labeling like dual behavior of the various tags in the Urdu language. We also introduced voting criteria for diverse kinds of taggers & statistical models to get efficient & better results in POS tagging. Several machine learning algorithms for POS tagging in the Urdu language have been used in this work namely Conditional Random Field, Decision tree, Random forest, TnT, and Tree tagger. Datasets named Bushra Jawaid and CLE have been used in our work for the sake of experiments. The most suitable features which are formed by a combination of required words & tags show that Condition Random Fields (CRF) outperformed all classifiers in terms of precision, recall, and f1-score. Unique voting criteria have also been developed to address the problem of confusing tags for one particular token by combining (integrate) diverse types of taggers for part of speech tagging that increase the efficiency of different taggers. The voting technique gives the state of the art result upon all taggers. To avoid various predictions on test data for a particular token weighted voting has been applied. By applying weighted voting the issue of multiple predictions is resolved & achieves F1-score on the Bushra Jawaid dataset is 94.6% and on CLE F1-score is calculated as 95.7%. We have applied a neural network that is LSTM which achieved F1-score 96.1 & 86.7 respectively for both the datasets.

REFERENCES

Abbas, Q. (2014, August). Semi-semantic part of speech annotation and evaluation. In *Proceedings of LAW VIII-The 8th Linguistic Annotation Workshop* (pp. 75-81). DOI: 10.3115/v1/W14-4911

Ahmed, U., Issa, G. F., Khan, M. A., Aftab, S., Khan, M. F., Said, R. A. T., Ghazal, T. M., & Ahmad, M. (2022). Prediction of Diabetes Empowered With Fused Machine Learning. *IEEE Access : Practical Innovations, Open Solutions*, 10, 8529–8538. DOI: 10.1109/ACCESS.2022.3142097

Alharbi, R., Magdy, W., Darwish, K., Abdelali, A., & Mubarak, H. (2018). Part-of-Speech Tagging for Arabic Gulf Dialect Using Bi-LSTM. *Proceedings of the Eleventh International Conference on Language Resources and Evaluation(LREC 2018)*, 3925–3932.

Asif, T., Ali, A., & Malik, K. (2015). Developing a POS Tagged Resource Of Urdu. Developing a POS tagged Resource in Urdu. Punjab University College of Information Technology, University of the Punjab.

Bölücü, N., & Can, B. (2019). Unsupervised joint PoS tagging and stemming for agglutinative languages. *ACM Transactions on Asian and Low-Resource Language Information Processing*, 18(3), 1–21. DOI: 10.1145/3292398

Bryant, C., & Briscoe, T. (2017). *Automatic Annotation and Evaluation of Error Types for Grammatical Error Correction*. Association for Computational Linguistics. DOI: 10.18653/v1/P17-1074

Darwish, K., & Abdelali, A. (2017). Arabic POS Tagging : Don't Abandon Feature Engineering Just Yet. *Proceedings of the Third Arabic Natural Language Processing Workshop*, 130–137. DOI: 10.18653/v1/W17-1316

Daud, A., Khan, W., & Che, D. (2017). Urdu language processing : A survey. *Artificial Intelligence Review*, 47(3), 279–311. DOI: 10.1007/s10462-016-9482-x

Dell'Orletta, F. (2009). Ensemble system sfor Part-of-Speech tagging. *Proceedings of EVALITA*, 1-8.

Ekbal, A., & Bandyopadhyay, S. (2008). Part of Speech Tagging in Bengali Using Support Vector Machine. *International Conference on Information Technology*. IEEE. DOI: 10.1109/ICIT.2008.12

Ekbal, A., Hasanuzzaman, M., & Bandyopadhyay, S. (2009). Voted approach for part of speech tagging in bengali. Proceedings of the 23rd Pacific Asia Conference on Language, Information and Computation, 1, 120-129.

Go, M. P. V. (2017). Using Stanford Part-of-Speech Tagger for the Morphologically-rich Filipino Language. *Proceedings of the 31st Pacific Asia Conference on Language, Information and Computation*, 81–88.

Gupta, V., Joshi, N., & Mathur, I. (2016). POS tagger for Urdu using Stochastic approaches. *Proceedings of the Second International Conference on Information and Communication Technology for Competitive Strategies*, 56. DOI: 10.1145/2905055.2905114

Huang, Z., Xu, W., & Kai, Y. (2015). Bidirectional LSTM-CRF Models for Sequence Tagging. arXiv preprint arXiv: 1508.01991.

J. A. P & Forcada. (2001). Part-of-Speech Tagging with Recurrent Neural Networks. *International Joint Conference on Neural Networks*, IEEE.

Jahangiri, N., Kahani, M., Ahamdi, R., & Sazvar, M. (2015, January). A study on part of speech tagging. *Review - Americas Society*.

Janicki, A. (2004). *Application of Neural Networks for POS Tagging and Intonation Control in Speech Synthesis for Polish. Soft Computing and intelligent systems*. SCIS.

Jatav, R. (2017). Improving Part-of-Speech Tagging for NLP Pipelines.

Jawaid, B., & Bojar, O. (2012, December). Tagger voting for Urdu. In *Proceedings of the 3rd Workshop on South and Southeast Asian Natural Language Processing* (pp. 135-144).

Jawaid, B., Kamran, A., & Bojar, O. (2014, May). A Tagged Corpus and a Tagger for Urdu. In *LREC* (Vol. 2, pp. 2938-2943).

Khan, Khan, Khan, Khan, Khan, & Ullah. (2018). Urdu Word Segmentation using Machine Learning Approaches. Inernational Journal of Advanced Computer Science and applications, 9(6), 193–200.

Khan, W., Daud, A., Khan, K., Nasir, J. A., Basheri, M., & Alotaibi, F. S. (2019). Part of Speech Tagging in Urdu : Comparison of Machine and Deep Learning Approaches. *IEEE Access : Practical Innovations, Open Solutions*, 7, 38918–38936. DOI: 10.1109/ACCESS.2019.2897327

Khan, W., Daud, A., Nasir, J. A., & Amjad, T. (2016). A survey on the state-of-the-art machine learning models in the context of NLP. *Kuwait Journal of Science*, 43(4), 95–113.

Khan, W., Daud, A., Nasir, J. A., Amjad, T., Arafat, S., Aljohani, N., & Alotaibi, F. S. (2019). Urdu part of speech tagging using conditional random fields. *Language Resources and Evaluation*, 53(3), 331–362. DOI: 10.1007/s10579-018-9439-6

Khanam, M. H., Madhumurthy, K. V., & Khudhus, A. (2013). Part-Of-Speech Tagging for Urdu in Scarce Resource : Mix Maximum Entropy Modelling System. *International Journal of Advanced Research in Computer and Communication Engineering*, 2(9), 3421–3425.

Kumawat, D., & Jain, V. (2015). POS Tagging Approaches: A Comparison. *International Journal of Computer Applications*, 118(6), 32–38. DOI: 10.5120/20752-3148

Luong, M. T., Socher, R., & Manning, C. D. (2013, August). Better word representations with recursive neural networks for morphology.

Ma, J., Zhang, Y., & Zhu, J. (2014). Tagging The Web: Building A Robust Web Tagger with Neural Network. *Proceedings 52nd Annual Meeting Association Computing Linguistics*, 1, 144–154. DOI: 10.3115/v1/P14-1014

Ma & Hovy. (2016). End-to-end Sequence Labeling via Bi-directional LSTM-CNNs-CRF. *Proceedings of the 54th Annual Meeting of Proceedings of the 54th Annual Meeting of the Association for Computational Linguistics*, 1, 1064–1074.

Nagata, R., Mizumoto, T., Kikuchi, Y., Kawasaki, Y., & Funakoshi, K. (2018, November). A POS tagging model adapted to learner English. In *Proceedings of the 2018 EMNLP Workshop W-NUT: The 4th Workshop on Noisy User-generated Text* (pp. 39-48). DOI: 10.18653/v1/W18-6106

Naseem, A., Anwar, M., Ahmed, S., Satti, Q. A., Hashmi, F. R., & Malik, T. (2017). Tagging Urdu Sentences from English POS Taggers. *International Journal of Advanced Computer Science and Applications*, 8(10), 231–238. DOI: 10.14569/IJACSA.2017.081030

Raghu, M., Balusu, B., Merghani, T., & Eisenstein, J. (2018). Stylistic Variation in Social Media Part-of-Speech Tagging. *Proceedings of the Second Workshop on Stylistic Variation*, 11-19.

Saha, S., & Ekbal, A. (2013). Combining multiple classifiers usin vote based classifier ensemble technique for named entity recognition. Data & Knowledge Engineering, 15-39.

Sajjad, H., & Schmid, H. (2009). Tagging Urdu Text with Parts of Speech: A Tagger Comparison. Proccedings 12th Conferrence Euopian, 692–700.

Shao, Y., Hardmeier, C., & Nivre, J. (2017). Character-based Joint Segmentation and POS Tagging for Chinese using Bidirectional RNN-CRF. The 8th International Joint Conference on Natural Language Processing, 173-183.

Silfverberg, M., Ruokolainen, T., Linden, K., & Kurimo, M. (2014, June). Part-of-speech tagging using conditional random fields: Exploiting sub-label dependencies for improved accuracy. In *Proceedings of the 52nd Annual Meeting of the Association for Computational Linguistics(*Volume 2*: Short Papers)* (pp. 259-264). DOI: 10.3115/v1/P14-2043

Silva, A. P., Silva, A., & Rodrigues, I. (2013). A New Approach to the POS Tagging Problem Using Evolutionary Computation. *Proceedings of the International Conference Recent Advances in Natural language Processing RANLP*, 619–625.

Straka, M., & Straková, J. (2017, August). Tokenizing, pos tagging, lemmatizing and parsing ud 2.0 with udpipe. In *Proceedings of the CoNLL 2017 shared task: Multilingual parsing from raw text to universal dependencies* (pp. 88-99). DOI: 10.18653/v1/K17-3009

Stratos, K., Collins, M., & Hsu, D. (2016). Unsupervised Part-Of-Speech Tagging with Anchor Hidden Markov Models. *Transactions of the Association for Computational Linguistics*, 4, 245–257. DOI: 10.1162/tacl_a_00096

Tian, Y., & Lo, D. (2015, March). A comparative study on the effectiveness of part-of-speech tagging techniques on bug reports. In *2015 IEEE 22nd International Conference on Software Analysis, Evolution, and Reengineering (SANER)* (pp. 570-574). IEEE. DOI: 10.1109/SANER.2015.7081879

Toutanova, K., Klein, D., Manning, C. D., & Singer, Y. (2003). Feature-Rich Part-of-Speech Tagging with a Cyclic Dependency Network. *Association for Computational Linguistic*, (June), 173–180. DOI: 10.3115/1073445.1073478

Wang, P., Qian, Y., Soong, F. K., He, L., & Hai, Z. (2015). Part-of-Speech Tagging with Bidirectional Long Short-Term Memory Recurrent Neural Network. arXiv preprint arXiv: 1510.0616.

Yao, K., Peng, B., Zweig, G., Yu, D., Li, X., & Gao, F. (2014). Recurrent Conditional Random Field for Language Understanding. *2014 IEEE International Conference on Acoustics, Speech and Signal Processing (ICASSP)*, 4077–4081. DOI: 10.1109/ICASSP.2014.6854368

Yessenbayev, Z. (2016). Character-based Feature Extraction with LSTM Networks for POS-tagging Task. 2016 IEEE 10th International. Conference on. Application of. Information and. Communication Technologies., 1–5.

Chapter 3
Sentiment Analysis of Guardian Metaverse Articles With Leximancer Tool Using HSVMPSo Technique

S. Sasikumar
Karpagam Academy of Higher Education, India

G. Ravishankar
Karpagam Academy of Higher Education, India

P. Poongothai
Kristu Jayanti College, India

Suresh Palarimath
https://orcid.org/0000-0002-3099-3926
University of Technology and Applied Sciences, Salalah, Oman

ABSTRACT

The gathering of tweets from before and after the companies' involvement in the metaverse allowed for the investigation of how potential users perceived their involvement. The numerous applications of metaverse technology are attracting the attention of experts and researchers. It serves as an immersive virtual environment that encourages user social interaction. However, we don't know how customers feel about this technology, particularly how positive they view it. To evaluate the chosen dataset from the Kaggle website, the hybrid particle swarm optimization with

DOI: 10.4018/979-8-3693-5231-1.ch003

support vector machine (HPSOSVM) approach was also employed. The suggested HPSOSVM outperforms the other classifiers, according to the results. Features may be extracted using the HPSOSVM with an accuracy of 90.12%. The outcomes demonstrate that ensemble classifiers outperform individual classifiers in terms of accuracy. Being relatively new phenomena, there are many opportunities to reorient the Metaverse on humanist values instead of specialized interests.

I. INTRODUCTION

People can now express their opinions online thanks to the World Wide Web's array of text-based channels, such as social media and online reviews. The ability to use these opinions to ascertain people's opinions about a specific product or location is highly advantageous for many enterprises. Businesses can improve their products based on client input, restaurants can adjust their menus in response to online food reviews, and political campaigns can be evaluated by analyzing social media posts. As a result, sentiment analysis has expanded in importance with the expansion of the Internet said Birjali, Marouane (2021).

Sentiment analysis collects and assesses people's opinions about specific topics from text sources. Another term for sentiment analysis that is occasionally used in literature is opinion mining. However, it's important to distinguish between "sentiments" and "opinions". In other words, views describe one's convictions about a particular subject, while feelings reflect how someone feels about something. Nonetheless, opinion statements are frequently helpful in evoking feelings, and the two concepts are intimately associated. The goal is to identify the sentiment polarity within a body of text. "Polarity" and "sentiment" are not the same things, even though they are often used synonymously by Kausar, Samina, et al (2019). The finest example of a consumer review is shown in figure 1, which has three goals with varying degrees of sentiment polarity.

Figure 1. Represent varied sentiment polarities

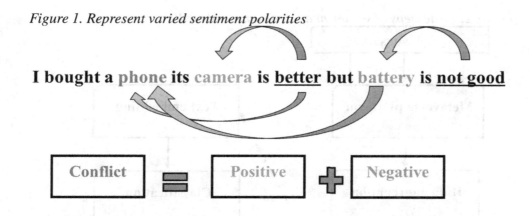

Whether they actual or virtual, we are always dependent on technology in one form or another. This includes both more complex gadgets like smart washing machines and simpler tasks like using a toaster. Thanks to technology, we are maximizing our social lives, and this tendency is likely to continue. The human need to find new ways to interact socially, communicate, and optimize routines is the root reason of all of this. All the same, we need to examine this idea using the Metaverse of Mind paradigm, keep in mind the significance of interpersonal interactions and representations in and among peopleWang, Fei-Yue(2022).Virtual reality makes it possible to create our own virtual realities by using a computer as a simulation. It also turns the Metaverse into a communication tool. In the event as virtual reality is regarded as a type of dream, and the Metaverse is in charge of compiling every dream that might ever exist and constructing a world that we and they can live in.

Extended, Virtual, Augmented and Mixed Reality

Components of XR include MR, AR, and VR. A completely fake environment created digitally is called virtual reality (VR). Users of virtual reality (VR) feel as though they are immersed in a new environment, acting as they would in real life Servotte, Jean-Christophe, et al (2020). Taking a novel approach to physical settings rather than immediately improving them. It combines spatially the real and virtual worlds. Furthermore, augmented reality can be utilized in virtual reality headsets that support the fundamental stages of sentiment analysis on social media are shown in figure 2.

Figure 2. Basic steps of sentiment analysis on social media.

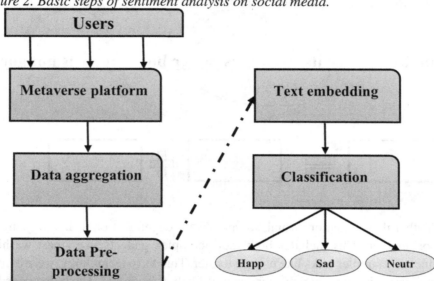

The machine learning take into account popular narratives, language interpretations, and new technological advancements. "MR" is a more complicated word. Mixed reality (MR) is sometimes compared to an enhanced version of augmented reality (AR) due to its ability to facilitate real-time interaction between the projected digital data and the physical world. For example, an author Yin, Ruiyang, et al (2021) programmed non-player character in a manipulative role-playing game would be aware of its physical surroundings and would conceal itself behind a desk or a couch. Consequently, MR's combination of VR and AR remains the two main technologies.

Multimodal Metaverse Interactions

It is possible for stereoscopic displays to provide depth awareness, it is possible to simulate real-world sight using slightly yet independent displays for each eye. When contrasting 2D and XR systems, the latter offer superior sound quality. Soundscapes that greatly enhance immersion can be produced with 3D, spatial, or binaural audio dispersion cues their routes, making sound cues an excellent tool attracting users promoting navigation. Because of this ability, they actively participate in every educational experience by Pfanzagl-Cardone, Edwin (2023). A more natural interface will be achieved for the user experience through thorough hand tracking development. Furthermore, research is being conducted on wearable technologies, including suits and gloves with touch sensitivity. Ongoing sensory research efforts center on the digitization and simulation of smells.

Sentiment analysis (SA) is one of the active fields of text mining study at the moment. It recognizes, extracts, quantifies, and addresses subjectivity and emotional states in literature using a methodical and quantitative approach. Artificial intelligence (AI) has many applications, including automated historical corpus analysis, product review analysis to forecast sales and gather real customer feedback, and social media text analysis (such as tweets) to analyze public opinion on a range of socio-political topics. The world's population stores a lot of data every day since data storage costs are decreasing and information technology is evolving swiftly. Using Artificial Intelligence (AI) techniques to build and develop computational platforms is one of the primary goals of Natural Language Processing (NLP). These systems automate the process of identifying patterns and information from both structured and unstructured text sources that were previously undiscovered.

A document's sentiment can be classified as either positive or negative based on its overall assessment, which is done at the Sentiment Identification (pre-processing) layer. Layer for classifying sentiments in which feelings are categorized based on the particular characteristics of entities that need to be identified at the outset of this process. Nowadays, most approaches to supervised artificial intelligence (SA) rely on supervised learning, which is based on manually labeled samples such as product reviews from commercial websites like Google, Amazon, and other social networks, where users explicitly state their overall attitude by using stars, numbers, and other symbols. Text-based applications can be enhanced by combining machine learning and transfer learning models.

Leximancer Tool

In addition to searching, adding, removing, and merging terms, lexicamers can also retrieve relational and semantic data. Additionally, by comparing key concepts to other words and applying ML to build and classify a dictionary for each set of data, it may recognize significant ideas. These configurations show how this software has supported the data analysis for similar research.

Support Vector Machine (SVM)

SVM determines set support vectors that are components of the labeled training data samples. The linear SVM is a binary classifier that classifies multi-dimensional data by maximizing the margin between hyper-planes created from some of the closest training data points from each class by Gos, Magdalena, et al (2020). SVMs are also useful for categorizing data that is. The SVM classifier aims to enhance its classification of non-linear data by attempting to transfer the data to a higher dimension using kernel functions.

Particle Swarm Optimization (PSO)

For optimization problems, swarm optimisation (PSO) is a well-liked population-based metaheuristic technique. Combining their communal and individual experiences, a flock of birds makes their way toward its feeding source. They constantly adjust their positions based on the best positions of the swarm as well as their own, striving to produce the greatest possible arrangement. This program simulates swarm intelligence based on natural selection through iterations. The method starts with a swarm a collection of possible solutions. Each iteration updates each individual in the population's position and velocityFreitas, Diogo (2020). Eberhart and Kennedy determined that pbest and gbest are two essential values.

This essay is divided into the following five sections: Session 2 describes the shortcomings of the existing system, which analyzes sentiment in the Guardian Metaverse using kaggle datasets and a range of machine learning techniques. The proposed sentiment analysis system, which combines the concepts of Hybrid Particle Swarm Optimization and Support Vector Machine (HPSOSVM), demonstrated the third session. The outcomes of the proposed system are shown in Session 4. A review conclusion of the suggested technique for the Sentimental Analysis for Guardian Metaverse concludes Session 5.

II. LITERATURE REVIEW

This section covers machine learning and sentiment analysis techniques. Before utilizing this evaluation to identify knowledge gaps and clarify specific research objectives, relevant literature is outlined.

Sentiment Analysis

As one type of categorization method, sentiment analysis Sentiment analysis makes use of a variety of NLP approaches. A good illustration of this method is VADER from NLTK package. VADER can distinguish between polarities that is positive or negative as well as perceptual strength and intensity explain by Wankhade, Mayur (2022). It is the basis for numerous previous research studies. Sentiment classification was applied right away via LTG in current study using a Python-coded VADER. For every piece of content, VADER automatically calculated the compound score. The book was read and assessed using the calculated score as a guide. Using it, the metaverse articles were categorized in this study. Based on the text's content, three automatic classifications were created: "Event Classifier," "Role Industry Classifier," and "Business Classifier". The content was interpreted and displayed after the guardian.com metaverse were determined based on the scores.

Research Birjali, Marouane, (2021) elucidate how sentiment analysis uses mind extraction, feeling, or emotion-based summarization. Opinion mining, often known as sentiment analysis, is the application of NLP, to track the sentiments emotions general regarding a certain subject kind of product or service. The Sentiment Analysis Categories are described in Figure 3.

Figure 3. Categories of sentiment analysis

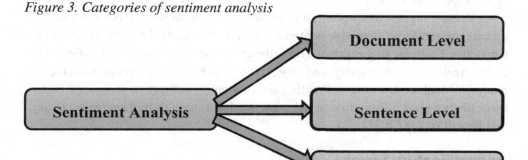

Opinion mining, or sentiment analysis, is the technique of determining, recognizing, or classifying a user's sentiment or opinion regarding any services, such as films, troubles with products, events, or any attribute that is neutral, positive, or negative. The analysis's key sources are social media websites, including reviews, forum conversations, blogs, microblogs, Twitter, and so forth. Due of its slanted data, which enables consumers to read reviews for any service that might be beneficial in their day-to-day lives, this study subject is becoming increasingly popular. Digital formats are used to store the vast quantity of biased data. Sentiment analysis, which links data mining operations to specific topics or opinions, produces results.

Document Level

Opinion mining, also known as sentiment analysis, starts at this extremely basic level and is document-based. In this stage, we determine the polarity by taking the entire document into consideration. We can categorize whether the opinions and feelings that are available to us give us a favorable or negative attitude via this level, or with this level's assistance. This is why document needs to focus on just one subject explained by Yadav, Ashima, and Dinesh Kumar Vishwakarma (**2020**). Sentiment or feelings serve as this document's primary source to be given careful thought. For example, if a text file just contains one product evaluation, the algorithm will now decide if the review conveys a positive or negative opinion about the product overall.

Sentence Level

Sentence-level sentiment analysis is a sort of sentiment analysis in which the polarity of each sentence is determined via processing and examination, yielding a positive, negative, or neutral outcome judgment on sentence. Views, opinions, and perspectives about the sentence comprise subjective sentences. When a sentence doesn't suggest aviewpoint; it is unbiased. A neutral remark is more likely to be categorized as an objective sentence that presents factual information than as subjective language that expresses the subject's personal opinions and beliefs. The categorization of subjectivity and objectivity is the main advantage of sentence analysis. Machine learning is usually used to identify subjective sentences. Sentiment analysis has a limitation at the sentence level, though by Nandwani, Pansy, and RupaliVerma (2021).

Aspect/Feature Level

The author Yue, Lin, et al (2019) explain about aspect level is often referred to as the feature level or entity level. The analysis at the sentence level as well as document allow us to determine people's preferences. Ultimately, this aspect level results in the most comprehensive type of sentiment analysis since it presents the output as an opinion. Either the two results or the target value are viewed as POSITIVE or NEGATIVE. Understanding the importance of this level is made easier by target opinion, which expresses feelings about entities and their characteristics. At this stage, comments, complaints, so on completed.

Metaverse

Since then, Garcia, Manuel B., et al (2023) deal of progress has been made in understanding and describing it. Technology enabling augmented and virtual reality has created a shared, three-dimensional virtual environment known as the "Metaverse," which sits between reality and ourselves. We can define it as a composite word that combines the meanings of "meta" and "universe," providing a definition of the digital world that is useful for both daily life and business. Through avatars, users can establish social, professional, and cultural connections with one another in that emulates real borders by Krietemeyer, Bess (2019).This multiuser environment, sometimes referred to as a "post-reality universe," combines digital and physical virtuality to create networked worlds and multisensory interactions. Virtual reality, augmented reality, social networking, online gaming, and other aspects that facilitate digital involvement are also believed to be a part of the Metaverse.

In addition Lee, Chang Won (2022) having a significant impact on the healthcare system, education, entertainment, business, and information and services, term "metaverse" in the book large shared includes all VR, AR. In the contemporary term "metaverse" describes a hybrid reality in which individuals and virtual reality to manage their social and professional lives. This virtual environment is the first of its kind to aim for comprehensiveness, utilizing a range of technologies to create a private sector. Through this platform, people can participate in social networking and experiences. The metaverse's ability to do anything is what gives it such significance by Koohang, Alex, et al (2023).

Gui, Rong, et al (2020) provides a clear-cut, logical explanation for our chaotic, disorganized world. Similar to how atoms and quarks make up a physical chair, digital processes create virtual objects. As such, categorization of "traditional" or "non-traditional" elements of the metaverse is ambiguous. This world will explore the connection between AI technology and human experience, as well as the prospects for humankind, by drawing. Only tech merchants that produce incredibly diverse artwork, terminology "cryptoverse" truly said to represent the metaverse as spiritually weak. On this platform, our genuine identities will be powered by AI and avatars. It affects not only people, but also digital people.

Virtual World versus Virtual Reality

Barhorst, Jennifer Brannon, et al (2021) declared, "Everything in life is a test." The adage "the more experiments you make, the better" holds true. We have definitely accepted them if we take into account how technologies have changed our life and produced these parallel realms. Understanding have brought to us in the future is therefore crucial, regardless of whether they are a component of the Metaverse or a concept unto themselves. Some writers suggest that virtual worlds could be compared to persistent and dynamic computer games that promote it also possible to make and sell friends and buy real estate. They offer a viewpoint on social spaces, virtual environments, or formative settings. These online social spaces have dual use as educational and recreational resources by Oranç, Cansu, and Aylin C. Küntay (2019). Virtual reality has previously been used to describe computer-generated simulations that include three-dimensional objects or obviously authentic, direct, or tactile human interactions. It is also emphasized that these virtual settings are non-pausible.

The Chalmers, David J (2022) explain in his studies largely focused on techniques that demonstrate physical digital realms described tactics were suggested using user input and metaverse user interaction analysis. Sentiment analysis is an analytical technique that is employed to determine the opinions of users regarding a topic. According to Cambria, sentiment analysis is a prerequisite for the development of artificial intelligence. Since sentiment analysis also makes use of visual materials in addition to text. Due to the importance of public sentiments and opinions to daily life, it is vital to analyze user opinions in order to understand public opinion and make judgments on a subject. Twitter provides the majority of the data used in sentiment analysis.

Lee, Han Jin, and Hyun HeeGu (2022) examined and evaluated metaverse-relevant Twitter data. Examining tweets related to the metaverse makes this study distinct. Based on their investigation, they found that the bulk of the tweets they collected were related to positive feelings. Turkish people suggested various terms that may be used in place of "metaverse," even though only that phrase was included in the tweets they obtained. To do a sentiment analysis on the tweets, we selected those that included the substitute words. From Stephenson's perspective, socially interactive world computers most of the techniques discussed above focused on the future course of interactions between the virtual and physical worlds. It is also crucial to investigate the connection between people's emotions and the metaverse. Alam, Ashraf, and AtasiMohanty (2022) are having more passionate online chats as a result of technical advancements and artificial intelligence.The standard SA researcher works with an emoji or text. Most South African social media research has concentrated. The most popular emoticons have the highest rating, the least popular are the lowest, and the remaining ones are in the middle. Emojis can, however, be added at the end and in groups to tweets.

Entiment Analysis Based on Sentimentlexicon

Basiri, Mohammad Ehsan, et al. (2021) proposed the Semantic Orientation Calculator, a new lexicon-based sentiment analysis technique that uses sentiment normalization and an evidence-based combination function, to extract sentiment from text utilizing dictionaries of words annotated with polarity and strength. To assess sentiment analysis of online user comments, sentiment terms are not the only tools used. Emojis, modifiers, and domain-specific phrases are also integrated. Microb-log by combining corpus and lexicons to create adaptive sentiment vocabulary that will increase Weibo's sentiment classification accuracy. This is done by employing extended sentiment lexicons of increased degree adverb lexicon, network word lexicon, and negative word lexicon.

Emoticon Sentiment Aggregation Approach

The author Ghosh, Anupam, and Sudipta Roy (2023) effectiveness of any prediction model is contingent upon the caliber of data collecting. Emojis related to those tweets are also considered, but only tweets that contain the term "metaverse" are analyzed. An examination of actual tweets is essential and priceless in this case since it illuminates Twitter's sentiment. To forecast sentiment for a given unknown text, the machine learning makes use of a number of patterns it has learnt from the dataset. Classifying Human Emotions using twitter on the Metaverse.

The standard method used for Twitter sentiment analysis is text categorization. Different results may be obtained depending on the pre-processing technique used to classify texts. Certain investigations may make use of techniques like retrieval, categorization, and document filtering.In author Ezugwu, Absalom E., et al (2022) recent proposals for a number of term weighted techniques have been made for various research domains. An approach to phrase weighting was suggested for sentiment analysis on Twitter. Bag of Words (BoW) and character level (N-gram) models were used in this study's feature extraction process. English and Turkish-language tweets made up the dataset. Utilized was a Latent Dirichlet Allocation (LDA)-based subject model for sentiment categorization. They claim this is the most effective strategy based on the results of their experiments. In specific research projects, sentiment analysis on Twitter was used to determine customer opinions. As such, companies and institutions get the opportunity to hear feedback regarding how they are performing in the market.AĞRALI, Özgür, and Ömer AYDIN (2021) carried out research that made extensive use of tweet analysis and prototyping. Based on their investigation, 84.1% of the tweets were classified as "null," 6.5% as "negative," and 9.4% as "positive." The results clearly show that the study has to be rectified because it contains serious faults.

The author George, AS Hovan, et al(2021) through the utilization of VR, 3D internet, and AR, the metaverse builds new worlds by fusing. That changes with VR/AR. It offers an interface for seeing a hybrid, half and partially real environment through eventually outperform VR in terms of effectiveness, completely replacing digital stuff on top of the actual world is virtual reality.Using virtual reality headsets outside, users, or digital avatars, interact with one another within this reality. Interestingly, Chalmers projected that virtual and actual worlds would be identical in a century. Its decentralized structure allows it to generate wealth and assets on its own. People can get income from this that is unique to their own world by sharing them. The metaverse democratizes its own social structure through the creation of user thanks to the sale of digitally created assets by Huang, Huakun, et al (2022). It aims to change the status quo while acknowledging these realities at the same time by fusing the digital and physical domains. Despite the accomplishment of these important goals, a comprehensive field of metaverse research is still small, uncommon, and relatively new. By identifying themes that arise and, subsequently, conceptions related to the metaverse and their possible impact reality as we know it the concept of the metaverse.

III. SYSTEM DESIGN

An explanation of the suggested research architecture and methodology is given in this section. Using Google's Kaggle dataset (Positive Negative, Neutral), a hybrid machine learning approach is utilized to train the system with data from metaverse posts covering a wide range of activities, including different doing so. To improve the outcomes, a collection of activities that enable farmers to forecast an individual's guardian with improved sensitivity, specificity, accuracy, and precision must be developed in order to practically integrate and apply the offered ways. Scientists also use machine learning approaches that are more potent and less expensive, taking into account their own financial limits and preferences. Figure 4 shows a flow chart for the recommended methodology.

Figure 4. Flow chart of the proposed method to be applied

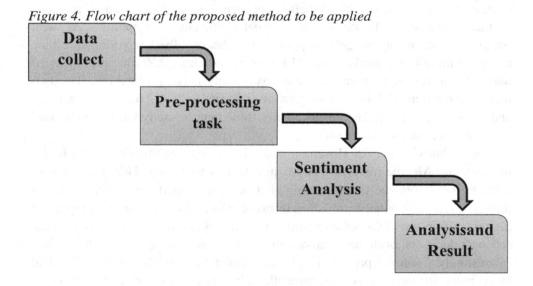

Dataset

Since pre-made data on the study's subject could not be found, these data were gathered utilizing specialist web mining and web scraping methods. There are numerous methods for obtaining data from the metaverse. Although not all of these methods utilize MetaAPI, some do. Twitter API, Orange frameworks, and Tweedy are the sources of Metaverse API data scraping. Most of these methods are available for free and are Python libraries. The best method out of all which lets you retrieve a limitless amount of data within specific time frames.

Pre-Processing Text

Not every tweet's content is suitable for analysis. To improve the outcome, these sections must be removed and the tweets must be tokenized. The collected social media data contains a lot of noise and meaningless words. Pre-processing and data purification done well are crucial. Certain elements are removed during the noise-removal process: symbols, stop words, digits, hyperlinks, and punctuation.

Hybrid Particle Swarm Optimization with Support Vector Machine

In order to better understand how population size affects PSO algorithms, we define the fundamental PSO variation with inertia weight (PSO-iw) in this section. The source, to which the reader is directed, provides definitions and parameterization for the remaining seven PSO versions taken into consideration in this work.

Particle Swarm Optimization

The initial translations xi_0 inside bounds to the challenge the user has to set the population size (p_s) beforehand. $P_{Besti,g}$ is the result of evaluating and storing values of the particle starting points for the objective function. The generation counter, represented by g in this instance, starts at 0the following equation:

$$v^d_{i,g+1} = w_g \cdot v^d_{i,g} + c_1 rand1^d_{i,g}(0,1) \cdot \left(pBest^d_{i,g} - x^d_{i,g}\right) + C_2 rand2^d_{i,g}(0,1) \cdot \left(gBest^d_g - x^d_{i,g}\right)$$

$$x^d_{i,g+1} = x^d_{i,g} + v^d_{i,g+1}$$

The user-specified acceleration coefficients c1 and c2 are the inertia weight, and all other particles in the swarm are represented by d = 1,...,D (where D is the problem dimensionality). For every i^{th} particle and d^{th} dimension, two random numbers, rand1$_{di,g}$(0,1) and rand2$_{di,g}$ (0,1), are generated independently using the [0,1] interval.In addition to the matching each particle in the run is associated with three vectors: the particle's $x_{i,g}$, v$_i$g, and the best position ($P_{Besti,g}$) it has visited since the search was started. The procedure keeps on until the predefined maximum number of function calls are completed.

PSO Algorithmic Structure

From one iteration to the next, particle swarms modify their relative positions, which allows the PSO algorithm to efficiently conduct the search. To find the best feasible solution, each particle in the swarm moves toward its prior Pbest and gbest. Assume, f is objective function to minimized or optimized, t is the number of the current iteration, and i is the particle index. The Pseudo-Code of the Particle Swarm Optimization given in figure 5.

A swarm a group of people in the PSO algorithm, whereas an individual represents a possible solution. The PSO algorithm is a widely used population-based evolutionary computing method. In an N-dimensional optimization problem, the ith particle's velocity is represented by a vector, vi = (vi1, vi2,...,viN). Similarly, xi = $(x_{i1}, x_{i2}, ...,x_{iN})$ represents the position vector of the ith particle. The equations for updating the position and velocity of particle I are given below:

$$v_i(k+1)= w \times v_i(k)+c_1 \times r_1 \times (p_i(k)-x_i(k))+c_2 \times r_2 \times (p_g(k)-x_i(k))x_i(k+1)$$

$$= x_i(k)+v_i(k+1)$$

Table 1. Pseudo-Code of the Particle Swarm Optimization

```
Initialization
Define the swarm size S and the number of dimensions D
for each particle i [1..S]
Randomly generate X_i and V_i, and evaluate the fitness of X_i denoting it as f(X_i)
SetPbest_i = X_i and f(Pbest_i) = f(X_i)
end for
Set Gbest = Pbest_1 and f(Gbest) = f(Pbest_1)
for each particle i [1..S]
   iff(Pbest_i) < f(Gbest)then
      f(Gbest) = f(Pbest_i)
   end if
end for
while t < maximum number of iterations
for each particle i [1..S]
Evaluate its velocity v_id (t + 1) using Equation (1)
Update the position x_id (t + 1) of the particle using Equation (2)
iff (x_i (t + 1)) < f (Pbest_i)then
Pbest_i = x_i (t + 1)
   f(Pbest_i) = f(x_i(t + 1)
end if
iff(Pbest_i) < f(Gbest)then
   Gbest = Pbest_i
   f(Gbest) = f(Pbest_i)
end if
end for
t = t + 1
end while
returnGbest
```

Members of interval [0, 1] are the two unique random integers, r1 and r2. The range of m, the domain of the optimization problem, is where the particle's position can only be. The following represents the updated equation for the inertia weight w at the kth iteration:

$$w=(w_1-(w_1-w_2)\times k) /maxiter$$

While w1 and w2 show the maximum and minimum inertia weights, respectively; maxiter is the number of iterations that can be made.

Parameters Adjustment

It's commonly acknowledged that while a smaller w facilitates exploitation, greater w facilitates exploration. During the optimization process, the most used update rule of w drops linearly from 0.9 to 0.4, despite the fact that it is still utilized in a lot of PSOs today. Built upon an iterative procedure employing (HPSO-TVAC) with time-varying acceleration coefficients. With PSO search being complex and nonlinear, several nonlinear-varying methods have been proposed to adjust the parameters and provide particles different search behaviors. The previously stated strategies improve PSO's performance to variable degrees, however because the iteration-based strategies misuse information from different evolutionary phases, they might be susceptible to incorrect tuning parameters.To build various academics suggested various adjustments as a more appropriate modification for the modifications based on historical data from the entire population. For instance, in PSO, tweaking w, c1, and c2 is independent of iteration counts. An evolutionary state estimator, whose evaluation is reliant on particle fitness and distribution, is selected as a substitute criterion for changing the parameters. The second term, called the cognitive component, simulates a particle's "personal" experience and drives it toward the best location (pbest) it has found up to the current function assessment. The third term, dubbed the collective component, mimics the effect of particles working together to reach the global optimum by directing a particle toward the best position ever found among all of the swarm's members (gbest). We provide a novel concept, random self-cognition that drives a particle toward an arbitrarily selected ideal position that other particles have found (pbesti−1 rand). In fact, this allows other particles to randomly exchange their knowledge.Here's another new term: the fifth term adds the Prtvelrand random velocity parameter, which broadens the swarm's range and enhances its capacity to move through challenging and constrained search regions.

Support Vector Machine (SVM)

Since the greatest interval is desired, the computation of the sample space interval is important. The split of the hyperplane is described by the following linear equation in the sample space:

$$W^T x + b = 0$$

The normal vector W in this instance determines the hyperplane's direction, while the displacement b establishes its distance from the origin. Let's say the training samples satisfy the following formula and the hyperplane is able to classify them appropriately:

$$W^t x_i + b >= 1, y = 1$$

$$W^t + b <= 1, y = -1$$

The sample positive, as indicated by the fact that it is a negative sample. The values of 1 or −1 given here are actually just for the sake of calculation; you can use any constant in their place. Especially in apps that use text categorization. SVMs can potentially solve the locally extreme dilemma that plagues machine learning algorithms by solving a convex quadratic optimization problem and producing a globally optimal solution. SVM belongs to the category of nonparametric super-vised techniques and is insensitive to the distribution of the underlying data. This is one of SVMs' advantages over other statistical techniques like machine learning, where data distribution must be understood beforehand. The figure 6 explain SVM classification Pseudo-Code.

Table 2. SVM classification Pseudo-Code

Request: X and y loaded with test labelled data $\alpha \leftarrow 0$ to $\alpha\leftarrow$ **partially test SVM**
$C\leftarrow$some value
Repeat
  For all $\{x_i, y_i\}\{x_j, y_j\}$**do**
    Optimize α_i and α_j
End for
Until no changes in αor other resource constraint criteria met
Ensure: retain only the support vector $(\alpha_i > 0)$

Finding a single boundary between two groups is the task of a linear binary classifier, or SVM for short. It is possible to separate the multidimensional data the input space linearly, according to the linear SVM. In particular, SVMs use the training data to find the optimal hyper line in the most basic scenario for partition-ing the dataset into a predetermined number of predefined classes. SVMs employ the training sample as a support vector to maximize the separation or margin based on how near it is to the ideal decision boundary in the feature space. Placing the decision border depends on the most challenging classification of these samples. Mathematically and geometrically, the maximal margin, or ideal hyperplane, can be defined. It proposes a threshold for decision-making that lowers the number of false positives during the training phase. Many hyperplanes with no sample in between are chosen, and it indicates that the ideal hyperplane is identified when the margin of separation is highest. The "learning process" is the method of creating a classifier by iteration that has an ideal decision boundary. Where,

- K(xi, xj) is the kernel function that determines how similar two samples, xi and xj, are to one another. The samples are implicitly mapped into a feature space of greater dimensions, SVM may effectively address nonlinear classifi-cation issues.
- The term $\sum\alpha i$ represents the sum of all Lagrange multipliers.

Soft-Margin

SVM can be expanded using the hinge loss function in scenarios when the data cannot be divided linearly. $\max(0, 1-y_i(w^Tx_i - b))$.

Note that y_i is the ith target (i.e., in this case, 1 or -1), and $w^Tx_i - b$ is the ith output. After the dual problem is resolved and the ideal Lagrange multipliers are identified, the SVM decision boundary can be expressed in terms of these multipliers and the support vectors. The decision boundary is provided as needed, and training samples with i> 0 act as the support vectors.

IV. RESULT AND DISCUSSION

This session presents the findings from the proposed system, Hybrid Particle Swarm Optimization with Support Vector Machine (HPSOSVM). The recently constructed categorization approach is validated and introduced through sentiment analysis of metaverse data, with datasets supplied from the Kaggle website. The training raw dataset contains a large number of metavers data features. The proposed system uses HPSOSVM and Leximancer v5.0 for sentimental analysis with metaverse data. A 13th generation Intel i3 CPU with 16GB RAM and 512GB ROM powers the machine. We compare the accuracy and sensitivity measures of the newly constructed PSO with SVM, the RF, the DT, and CNN.

Confusion Matrix

It is frequently employed in evaluating effectiveness categorization models, which strive to assign a categorical label to each instance of input. The quantity of TP, TN, FP, and FN generated by the model with the test data set is displayed in Figure 7 below.

Figure 5. Confusion matrix

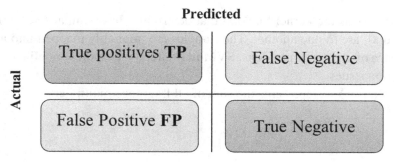

Predicted

	True positives TP	False Negative
Actual		
	False Positive FP	True Negative

Accuracy

The model's correctness is a critical performance parameter that determines if our assumptions about the positive and negative classes are accurate.

$$\text{Accuracy} = \frac{TP + TN}{TP + TN + FN + FP}$$

Table 3. result values for Accuracy with proposed and existing system

Algorithm	Accuracy
RF	83.22
DT	87.06
CNN	84.31
HPSOSVM	90.12

The accuracy of the current system, as evaluated by 84.31, is 5.81 times less accurate than the accuracy of the proposed system, as determined by HPSOSVM at 90.12, as shown in Figure 8Table 1.

Figure 6. Accuracy graph of the proposed and current systems as a result

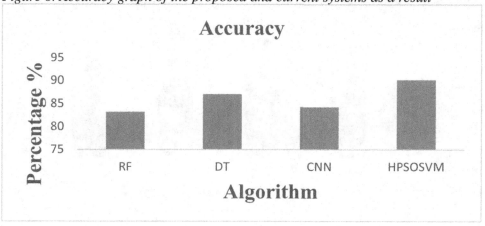

Sensitivity

The sensitivity (SN) can be calculated simply calculating the ratio of all the positives to all the correct positive forecasts.

$$\text{Sensitivity} = \frac{TP}{TP + FN}$$

Table 4. result values for sensitivity with present and existing system

Algorithm	Sensitivity
RF	86.06
DT	76.92
CNN	87.56
HPSOSVM	92.33

Table 2's findings show, as seen in Figure 9, that the suggested system's HPSOSVM-determined sensitivity is 92.33, 4.77 times greater than the 87.56 sensitivity of the current system.

Figure 7. Sensitivity graph of the proposed and current systems as a result

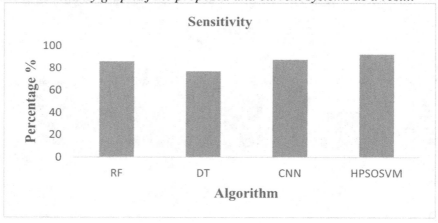

Precision

Counting the number of classes that are actually positive that we expected to be positive will help you understand the following equation better. A model's precision reveals how effectively it can forecast the future.

$$\text{Precision} = \frac{TP}{TP + FP}$$

Table 5. Result values for precision with proposed and existing system

Algorithm	Precision
RF	81.29
DT	83.1
CNN	85.96
HPSOSVM	93.55

Table 3's findings indicate that the recommended system has a precision rating of 93.55 based on HPSOSVM analysis. Figure 10's 85.96 evaluation indicates that this is 7.59 times more accurate than the system in use today.

Figure 8. Precision graph of the proposed and current systems as a result

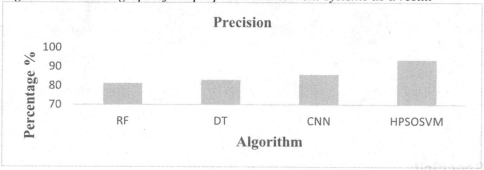

F1 Score

Recall and precision ratings are used to illustrate a classification model's overall performance. The accuracy statistic tracks how many times a model has accurately predicted throughout the entire dataset.

$$F1 - score = 2 * \frac{percision * recall}{precision + recall}$$

Table 6. result values for F1-score with proposed system

Algorithm	F1-score
RF	78.33
DT	80.96
CNN	83.16
HPSOSVM	88.75

The table 4 contains an information of a result obtained from the proposed and existing system similarly the figure 11 contains a graph which shows proposed system HPSOSVM obtain 88.75% in F1-Score which is 5.59 times greater than present system of CNN that gives 83.16%.

Figure 9. F1-score graph of the proposed and current systems as a result

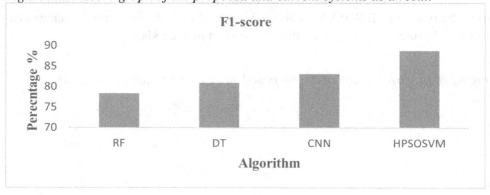

Specificity

The percentage of real numbers that may be expected to match each actual number precisely is known as the specificity indicator. TNR is an additional term that could be utilized.

$$Specificity = \frac{TN}{TN + FP}$$

Table 7. result values for specificity with existing system

Algorithm	Specificity
RF	81.36
DT	83.2
CNN	84.69
HPSOSVM	90.96

As illustrated in Figure 12, Table 5's findings show that the recommended system's specificity, as measured by HPSOSVM, is 90.96, 6.27 times higher than the current system's, as measured by 84.69.

Figure 10. Specificity graph of the proposed and present systems as a result

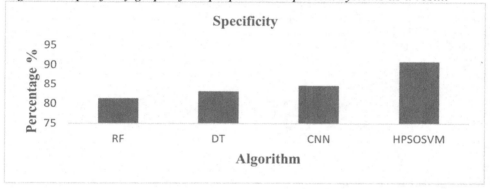

The graph below tables 1, 2, 3, 4, and 5 above shows how much better the suggested system performs than the current one. The aforementioned Figures 8, 9, 10, 11 and 12 show the specificity results. As a result, the recommended solution performs better when the HPSOSVM technique is used for metaverse data processing for Guardian. This illustrates recommended strategies fared better in data processing analysis study than the control group.

V. CONCLUSION

This guardian has proven benefits for both data science and sentiment analysis. This study compares the accuracy of many popular classification techniques. There has been relatively little study on sentiment analysis for metaversives. Software and a Hybrid Particle Swarm Optimization with Support Vector Machine (HPSOSVM) processing were employed in the technique to improve the outcomes. This simplified the information for the metaverse, giving them an advantage in trying to enhance the aspects that don't seem to be as excellent or as popular with the metaverse. The findings demonstrate that the current CNN, DT, and RF system is not a good fit for the chosen dataset.The research asserts, however, that the HPSOSVM findings provide compelling proof that the suggested system's PSO and SVM outperform machine learning classifiers. Unfortunately, this analysis is currently inadequate because it is fresh and has not been tested on a wide number of other classification models. Users must choose one of the choices; Rapid Miner's main drawback is that it only allows users to analyze up to 100,000 emotion data for free each day. Thus, in order to build upon our current research and analysis in the future, we aim to collect a substantial amount of data and enhance the data mining methodology employed in this analytical approach.

REFERENCES

Ağrali, Ö., & Aydin, Ö. (2021). Tweet Classification and Sentiment Analysis on Metaverse Related Messages. *Journal of Metaverse*, 1(1), 25–30.

Alam, A., & Mohanty, A. (2022). Metaverse and Posthuman animated avatars for teaching-learning process: interperception in virtual universe for educational transformation. In *International Conference on Innovations in Intelligent Computing and Communications* (pp. 47-61). Springer.

Barhorst, J. B., McLean, G., Shah, E., & Mack, R. (2021). Blending the real world and the virtual world: Exploring the role of flow in augmented reality experiences. *Journal of Business Research*, 122, 423–436.

Basiri, M. E., Nemati, S., Abdar, M., Cambria, E., & Acharya, U. R. (2021). ABCDM: An attention-based bidirectional CNN-RNN deep model for sentiment analysis. *Future Generation Computer Systems*, 115, 279–294.

Birjali, M., Kasri, M., & Beni-Hssane, A. (2021). A comprehensive survey on sentiment analysis: Approaches, challenges and trends. *Knowledge-Based Systems*, 226, 107134.

Chalmers, D. J. (2022). *Reality+: Virtual worlds and the problems of philosophy.* Penguin UK.

Ezugwu, A. E., Ikotun, A. M., Oyelade, O. O., Abualigah, L., Agushaka, J. O., Eke, C. I., & Akinyelu, A. A. (2022). A comprehensive survey of clustering algorithms: State-of-the-art machine learning applications, taxonomy, challenges, and future research prospects. *Engineering Applications of Artificial Intelligence*, 110, 104743.

Freitas, D., Lopes, L. G., & Morgado-Dias, F. (2020). Particle swarm optimisation: A historical review up to the current developments. *Entropy (Basel, Switzerland)*, 22(3), 362. PMID: 33286136

Garcia, M. B., Adao, R. T., Pempina, E. B., Quejado, C. K., & Maranan, C. R. B. (2023, August). MILES Virtual World: A Three-Dimensional Avatar-Driven Metaverse-Inspired Digital School Environment for FEU Group of Schools. In *Proceedings of the 7th International Conference on Education and Multimedia Technology* (pp. 23-29).

George, A. H., Fernando, M., George, A. S., Baskar, T., & Pandey, D. (2021). Metaverse: The next stage of human culture and the internet. *International Journal of Advanced Research Trends in Engineering and Technology*, 8(12), 1–10.

Ghosh, A., & Roy, S. (2023, February). An Emoticon-Based Sentiment Aggregation on Metaverse Related Tweets. In *The 3rd International Conference on Artificial Intelligence and Computer Vision (AICV2023), March 5–7, 2023* (Vol. 164, p. 358). Springer Nature.

Gos, M., Krzyszczak, J., Baranowski, P., Murat, M., & Malinowska, I. (2020). Combined TBATS and SVM model of minimum and maximum air temperatures applied to wheat yield prediction at different locations in Europe. *Agricultural and Forest Meteorology*, 281, 107827.

Gui, R., Wang, Y., Yao, Y., & Cheng, G. (2020). Enhanced logical vibrational resonance in a two-well potential system. *Chaos, Solitons, and Fractals*, 138, 109952.

Huang, H., Zeng, X., Zhao, L., Qiu, C., Wu, H., & Fan, L. (2022). Fusion of building information modeling and blockchain for metaverse: A survey. *IEEE Open Journal of the Computer Society*, 3, 195–207.

Kausar, S., Huahu, X. U., Ahmad, W., & Shabir, M. Y. (2019). A sentiment polarity categorization technique for online product reviews. *IEEE Access : Practical Innovations, Open Solutions*, 8, 3594–3605.

Koohang, A., Nord, J. H., Ooi, K. B., Tan, G. W. H., Al-Emran, M., Aw, E. C. X., & Wong, L. W. (2023). Shaping the metaverse into reality: A holistic multidisciplinary understanding of opportunities, challenges, and avenues for future investigation. *Journal of Computer Information Systems*, 63(3), 735–765.

Krietemeyer, B., Bartosh, A., & Covington, L. (2019). A shared realities workflow for interactive design using virtual reality and three-dimensional depth sensing. *International Journal of Architectural Computing*, 17(2), 220–235.

Lee, C. W. (2022). Application of metaverse service to healthcare industry: A strategic perspective. *International Journal of Environmental Research and Public Health*, 19(20), 13038. PMID: 36293609

Lee, H. J., & Gu, H. H. (2022). Empirical Research on the Metaverse User Experience of Digital Natives. *Sustainability*, 14(22), 14747.

Nandwani, P., & Verma, R. (2021). A review on sentiment analysis and emotion detection from text. *Social Network Analysis and Mining*, 11(1), 81. PMID: 34484462

Oranç, C., & Küntay, A. C. (2019). Learning from the real and the virtual worlds: Educational use of augmented reality in early childhood. *International Journal of Child-Computer Interaction*, 21, 104–111.

Pfanzagl-Cardone, E. (2023). '3D'-or 'Immersive'Audio—The Basics and a Primer on Spatial Hearing. In *The Art and Science of 3D Audio Recording* (pp. 51–91). Springer International Publishing.

Servotte, J. C., Goosse, M., Campbell, S. H., Dardenne, N., Pilote, B., Simoneau, I. L., & Ghuysen, A. (2020). Virtual reality experience: Immersion, sense of presence, and cybersickness. *Clinical Simulation in Nursing*, 38, 35–43.

Wang, F. Y. (2022). The metaverse of mind: Perspectives on DeSci for DeEco and DeSoc. *IEEE/CAA Journal of AutomaticaSinica, 9*(12), 2043-2046.

Wankhade, M., Rao, A. C. S., & Kulkarni, C. (2022). A survey on sentiment analysis methods, applications, and challenges. *Artificial Intelligence Review*, 55(7), 5731–5780.

Yadav, A., & Vishwakarma, D. K. (2020). Sentiment analysis using deep learning architectures: A review. *Artificial Intelligence Review*, 53(6), 4335–4385.

Yin, R., Wang, D., Zhao, S., Lou, Z., & Shen, G. (2021). Wearable sensors-enabled human–machine interaction systems: From design to application. *Advanced Functional Materials*, 31(11), 2008936.

Yue, L., Chen, W., Li, X., Zuo, W., & Yin, M. (2019). A survey of sentiment analysis in social media. *Knowledge and Information Systems*, 60, 617–663.

Chapter 4
An Analysis of Optimization Methodologies on Edge Computing

R. Ramya

https://orcid.org/0000-0002-8071-9343

Sathyabama Institute of Science and Technology, India

ABSTRACT

This study explores the complex field of edge computing, emphasising optimisation techniques that are vital for enhancing data management, resource allocation, energy usage, and offloading efficiency. This chapter investigates new approaches to improve edge computing system quality, providing a thorough analysis that incorporates knowledge from several fields. By resolving important issues and opening the door for more long-lasting and efficient quality control methods, the findings improve edge computing applications. Through a comprehensive examination of various optimization methodologies, this study aims to enhance the efficiency and quality management of edge computing systems, providing valuable insights for researchers, practitioners, and industry stakeholders in the rapidly evolving domain of edge computing.

1. INTRODUCTION

Edge devices, with their limited resources, demand clever optimization techniques. (Adu, 2023) Task allocation and model downsizing are two strategies that address constraints in order to meet objectives such as reduced energy usage, quicker

DOI: 10.4018/979-8-3693-5231-1.ch004

reaction times, and enhanced overall performance. The capabilities of the devices themselves and the priorities of the application will determine which technique is best. We can fully realise the potential of edge computing for effective and profitable deployments by optimising it.

1.1. Introduction to Optimization

A key idea in several academic disciplines, including computer science, business, engineering, and mathematics, is optimisation. Fundamentally, optimisation is the process of maximising something's usefulness or effectiveness. With the main objective of maximising benefits, lowering costs, or reaching optimal performance, it entails methodically choosing the best option from a range of workable alternatives.

Generally speaking, optimisation can be used to solve a wide range of issues, each with its own special set of limitations and goals. (Ramya, 2023) Whether it is optimising algorithms for efficient computation, maximising profit in a business model, or minimising energy consumption in engineering systems, the basis of optimisation is identifying the most advantageous collection of parameters or variables that lead to the desired outcome.

Mathematically speaking, tasks involving maximisation or minimization are frequently used to formulate optimisation issues, with the quantity to be optimised being represented by the objective function. These issues become much more difficult due to constraints, which are limitations or restrictions on the variables. To negotiate the complex terrain of these problems, a variety of optimisation approaches are used, including metaheuristic algorithms, nonlinear optimisation, and linear programming.

In order to solve problems in the real world, optimisation is essential. It advances operations research, technology, and decision-making techniques. The concepts of optimisation offer a potent foundation for improving systems, processes, and solutions, regardless of the field—finance, artificial intelligence, or supply chain management. This introduction only touches on the surface of optimization's immense and multidisciplinary nature, highlighting its importance in promoting effectiveness, efficiency, and creativity in a wide range of fields.

1.2. Introduction to Edge Computing

The concept of edge computing has surfaced as a revolutionary response to the ever-increasing demands for distributed, high-performance, low-latency computing capabilities in the ever changing world of modern computing. In contrast to conventional centralised cloud computing models, edge computing brings computational resources closer to the data source, frequently at the network's edge—hence the term "edge."

Edge computing operates on local devices or edge servers as opposed to traditional cloud computing, which processes and stores data in remote data centres. The goals of this decentralised method are to improve real-time processing, lower latency, and lessen the load on network capacity. In situations when quick decision-making, responsiveness, and bandwidth efficiency are critical, edge computing is especially important.

The popularity of edge computing has been driven by the spread of smart sensors, Internet of Things (IoT) devices, and the exponential expansion of data generated at the edge. Applications can now take advantage of the processing capacity of devices located closer to the site of data production thanks to this paradigm change. Smart cities, self-driving cars, industrial automation, and healthcare monitoring are a few examples.

Edge computing's architecture consists of a hierarchy of nodes, with data processing taking place at different levels, starting from edge devices and moving up to intermediate edge servers and, if necessary, centralised cloud data centres. A flexible and scalable deployment is made possible by this hierarchical structure, which enables businesses to customise their edge computing infrastructure to meet their unique needs and use cases.

Edge computing presents both intriguing prospects and challenges as it develops further. Although it has benefits like lower latency, better privacy, and increased bandwidth efficiency, it also adds complexity to resource optimisation, security, and distributed system management. This introduction lays the groundwork for an exploration of the complex world of edge computing, where technological advancements meet the demands of an increasingly data-driven and connected society.

1.3. Importance of Edge Computing Technology

Edge computing is essential, and here are some of its biggest advantages:

The Significance of Edge Computing: The Key is Speed (Low Latency): Edge computing drastically cuts down on how long it takes for devices and apps to react to events by processing data closer to the source. This is essential for uses such as: Self-driving cars: In quickly changing settings, they must make quick decisions. Real-time interactions are essential for a smooth user experience in augmented and virtual reality. Industrial automation: Near-zero delays are necessary for precision control. Bandwidth conservation: By processing at the edge, core networks are not as taxed. (Safavat, 2020)

Savings: There is no longer a requirement for costly cloud data transmission for each item of information.

Preventing bottlenecks is essential for managing the vast amounts of data that the Internet of Things generates.

Reliability and Resilience: In the event that there is a brief loss of cloud connectivity, Edge devices can still function and make choices. For mission-critical applications such as: this is crucial.

Healthcare: Regardless of network connectivity, real-time patient monitoring and remote operations are required.

Disaster response: Localised edge nodes can still coordinate efforts in the event that the communication infrastructure fails.

Data security and privacy: It's usually best to store sensitive data at the edge for analysis. This gives users more precise control over data access while reducing the chance of exposure during transmission.

Scalability: As networks expand and the number of connected devices rises, edge computing can readily keep up. Distributing computing power enables companies to change swiftly.

Novelties and Innovation: With its edge computing, centralised models make impractical new possibilities possible.

Location-aware personalisation: Businesses can present tailored content to customers according to their precise location.

Intelligent traffic control, environmental monitoring, and energy grid optimisation are examples of smart cities.

The Final Word Edge computing is a necessary addition to the cloud, not its replacement. Through the process of decentralising computing power, a more intelligent, responsive, and efficient technological landscape is created, revolutionising the ways in which we analyze, respond to, and use data.

2. THE COMBINATION OF OPTIMIZATION AND EDGE COMPUTING-AN OVERVIEW

The confluence of edge computing and optimisation approaches has become a crucial study field in the dynamic landscape of computing, with the potential to significantly alter the efficacy and efficiency of decentralised computational systems. The complex interactions between optimisation strategies and edge computing are explored in this paper, with particular attention to offloading, resource allocation, energy usage, and data optimisation. As more and more sectors depend on edge computing for processing and decision-making in real-time, improving quality control becomes critical. (Bajic, 2023)

Sophisticated optimisation algorithms are required to achieve optimal resource utilisation while meeting strict quality criteria due to the integration of varied devices at the edge of the network. Offloading, or the deliberate division of processing work between edge servers and local devices, is essential for reducing latency and optimising performance. In order to ensure that activities are completed as quickly and reliably as possible in decentralised contexts, resource allocation algorithms work simultaneously to manage computational resources efficiently.

Considering the resource-constrained nature of edge devices, energy consumption plays a crucial role in the design and functioning of edge computing systems. Examining approaches that seek to achieve a fine balance between preserving optimal performance and reducing energy consumption is important for sustainability and extended device life.

Moreover, quality management increasingly depends on the optimisation and control of data at the edge. Effective data optimisation techniques are necessary to maintain data security, integrity, and optimal use of storage capacity as the amount of data created and processed at the edge continues to soar.

The study provided here aims to navigate this difficult terrain by elucidating the intricacies and interrelationships of optimisation approaches within the edge computing setting. Through an examination of the subtleties surrounding offloading, resource distribution, energy usage, and data optimisation, this research aims to provide insightful information to scholars, practitioners, and industry stakeholders in equal measure, promoting improvements in quality control in the context of the changing edge computing paradigm.

- Optimisation and edge computing together provide a number of noteworthy benefits. Below is a summary of the main advantages:

Benefits

Ultra-low latency decision making: Near-instantaneous data analysis and decision-making are possible thanks to optimisation techniques at the edge. This lessens the latency involved in transferring data to the cloud for processing, facilitating vital applications that need replies almost instantly (e.g., industrial process control, autonomous vehicles).

Effective Resource Management: Optimisation strategies guarantee the efficient use of edge device computing, network, and energy resources.

Task distribution: Performance is maximised and bottlenecks are avoided by strategically distributing workloads among several edge nodes.

Dynamic resource scaling is the process of matching application requirements, preserving energy, and adjusting compute power or network bandwidth as needed.

Decreased Bandwidth Expenses and Network Congestion: Only necessary data is transmitted to the cloud after pre-processing and filtering at the edge. This reduces expenses, maximizes network utilisation, and lessens the burden on key networks.

Enhanced Security and Privacy: Localising sensitive data contributes to increased privacy. To lessen the exposure of data during transmission, optimisation can assist in deciding which data should remain at the edge. Moreover, intrusion and anomaly detection can be improved via edge-based security optimisations.

Resilience and Autonomy: Edge computing nodes possess the ability to function even in the event of a cloud connection loss. By maximising performance while utilising the resources at hand, optimisation increases uptime in places with sporadic access.

illustrative instances

Manufacturing: maximising throughput on production lines, anticipating possible problems, and reducing energy consumption via real-time sensor data.

Intelligent energy grid management, dynamic parking management systems, and real-time traffic camera feeds are examples of smart city traffic flow optimisation.

Personalised Retail Experiences: By leveraging local data, businesses may optimise shop layouts and focus promotions and recommendations while maintaining privacy.

Predictive maintenance reduces unexpected downtime in sectors like energy and logistics by using optimisation algorithms to forecast equipment faults based on data from edge sensors.

Important Points

Though it is still in its infancy, the convergence of edge computing and optimisation has great promise for productivity, novel application creation, and addressing the difficulties associated with data-driven operations at the edge of the network.

3. OPTIMIZATION FOR EDGE COMPUTING OFFLOADING

Optimising edge computing offloading is essential for improving decentralised computational systems' overall functionality, performance, and efficiency. Offloading is the deliberate division and assignment of computational work between local devices and edge servers with the goal of reducing latency, optimising resource use, and raising overall quality of service. (Ramya, 2022) This explains how optimisation for edge computing offloading offers essential assistance:

Reduction of Latency:

Real-time Processing: Vital operations can be carried out in closer proximity to the data source by shifting computational responsibilities to edge servers. By minimising the round-trip time for data to reach centralised cloud servers and return, this lowers latency and guarantees that applications respond in real time.

Utilisation of Resources:

Optimal Allocation: Based on variables including device capabilities, network conditions, and job needs, optimisation techniques assist in determining the most effective way to divide up tasks between edge devices and servers. By doing this, it is made sure that computational resources are used as efficiently as possible, avoiding overloading or underuse.

Energy Effectiveness:

Task Offloading Strategies: When making decisions during offloading, optimisation approaches take energy consumption into account. Energy-intensive calculations can be carried out on more potent edge servers by intelligently allocating jobs, which saves energy on resource-constrained edge devices and increases their operational lives.

Management of Bandwidth:

Data Offloading: Effective offloading techniques aid in the efficient management of network capacity. The overall demand on the network is decreased, minimising congestion and guaranteeing a smoother flow of information between edge devices and servers by offloading only necessary data or computation results.

Enhancement of Quality of Service (QoS):

Task Prioritisation: When deciding which jobs to offload, optimisation approaches take into account the importance and priority of each task. By ensuring that high-priority tasks—like those pertaining to quality management—get special attention, this raises the standard of service as a whole. (Ramya, 2024)

Both adaptability and scalability:

Dynamic Decision-Making: Offloading, adjusting to shifting network conditions, device capacities, and workload demands are all made possible by optimisation approaches. The capacity to scale guarantees that the edge computing system can effectively manage changing demands and workloads over time.

Economy of scale:

Resource Cost Considerations: Whether at the edge or in the cloud, optimisation takes into account the expenses related to using various resources. Through cost-effective decision-making, organisations can attain efficient computing without incurring needless expenses.

Table 1. List of optimization algorithms for different edge computing aspects.

Edge computing Aspect	Optimization Algorithm Types
Task Offloading	- Genetic Algorithms
	- Particle Swarm Optimization (PSO)
	- Ant Colony Optimization
	- Reinforcement Learning
	- Markov Decision Processes (MDP)
Resource Allocation	- Linear Programming
	- Integer Programming
	- Dynamic Programming
	- Game Theory
	- Machine Learning (e.g., Neural Networks)
Energy Consumption	- Dynamic Voltage and Frequency Scaling (DVFS)
	- Sleep Scheduling Algorithms
	- Energy-Aware Scheduling Algorithms
	- Genetic Algorithms for Energy Optimization
	- Reinforcement Learning for Energy Efficiency
Data Optimization	- Data Compression Algorithms
	- Deduplication Techniques
	- Differential Privacy Techniques
	- Machine Learning for Data Compression
	- Data Encryption and Secure Transmission

continued on following page

Table 1. Continued

Edge computing Aspect	Optimization Algorithm Types
Quality of Service (QoS)	- QoS-Aware Task Scheduling
	- Load Balancing Algorithms
	- Service Level Agreements (SLA) Management
	- Feedback Control Systems
	- Multi-objective Optimization

The table1 represents the List of optimization algorithms for different edge computing aspects.

To sum up, optimizing for edge computing offloading is essential to building a computational environment that is economical, resource-efficient, and responsive. The success and profitability of edge computing systems across a range of sectors are greatly enhanced by these optimisation tactics, which address critical factors including latency, resource utilisation, energy efficiency, and quality of service.

4. OPTIMIZATION METHODOLOGY FOR ENERGY EFFICIENCY

The fundamental goal of energy optimisation approach is to identify the most effective way to do tasks while consuming the least amount of energy. (Adu, 2023) This touches on a number of important areas:

Algorithm Design: The cornerstone is based on effective algorithms. This entails choosing algorithms with minimal computational complexity and steering clear of pointless procedures.

Hardware optimisation is the process of selecting low-power, energy-consuming hardware parts including memory, storage, and processors.

Load balancing: Energy-intensive surges on individual systems are avoided by distributing workloads evenly among computer resources.

Power management is the application of strategies to dynamically modify power usage in response to workload. This could entail reducing CPU frequency or placing devices into sleep mode while not in use.

Data management and transfer: reducing the amount of energy used during movement by optimising data processing, storage, and transportation.

Predictive modelling: This technique forecasts usage patterns using AI and machine learning, enabling systems to make proactive changes to power states and resource distribution.

Edge Computing Optimisation Data processing and storage are moved closer to the "edge" of the network, where data is generated, thanks to edge computing. Energy efficiency becomes even more important for edge devices since they frequently have constrained power supplies and processing capabilities. This is how it's relevant:

Modest Offloading Not all data processing must take place at the edge. By lowering the amount of energy used at the edge, optimisation algorithms assist identify which data must be processed immediately and which may be transferred to a central data centre or the cloud for further analysis.

Power-Concerned Planning Energy-sensitive tasks should be prioritised and intelligently distributed over time and among edge devices to prevent overloading any one device.

Network Enhancement Minimising the energy draw associated with communication can be achieved by optimising data transmission over the network, for example, by compressing data before transmitting.

Edge Device Sleep Modes intelligently shutting off edge components or devices when not in use without compromising the edge network's ability to respond to queries.

As an example Smart Buildings: To optimise energy use, energy-intensive jobs (such as HVAC) can be scheduled to run during off-peak hours. Lighting and temperature can also be adjusted based on occupancy in real time.

Manufacturing: Optimisation aids in the analysis of factory energy usage patterns, the streamlined execution of manufacturing procedures, and the identification of possible energy savings through equipment maintenance or improvements.

Self-Driving Cars (Edge Applications): Real-time object detection and navigation decisions must be made by edge devices in these vehicles. Optimising is essential to reduce the amount of processing power needed and increase battery life.

Table 2. Lists the optimization algorithms used for energy consumption

Category	Algorithm	Description
Nature-Inspired	Genetic Algorithm (GA)	Mimics the process of natural selection to find optimal solutions, but can be computationally expensive.
	Particle Swarm Optimization (PSO)	Simulates the behavior of birds in a flock searching for food, good for continuous optimization problems.
	Artificial Bee Colony (ABC)	Inspired by foraging behavior of bees, efficient for finding near-optimal solutions.
	Ant Colony Optimization (ACO)	Based on how ants find paths, suitable for routing and scheduling problems.

continued on following page

Table 2. Continued

Category	Algorithm	Description
Machine Learning & AI	Deep Reinforcement Learning (DRL)	Trains an agent to learn optimal behavior through trial and error, powerful but requires significant data and processing power.
	Support Vector Machines (SVM)	Can be used for classification tasks related to energy usage patterns, helping to predict and optimize future consumption.
	Artificial Neural Networks (ANN)	Can learn complex relationships between variables influencing energy consumption, allowing for predictive modeling and control.
Other Techniques	Linear Programming (LP)	Solves mathematical problems involving linear inequalities, useful for optimizing resource allocation with specific constraints.
	Dynamic Programming (DP)	Breaks down complex problems into smaller sub-problems, efficient for optimizing sequential decision-making processes.
	Heuristics	Rule-based algorithms that provide approximate solutions, often used when exact solutions are difficult or impractical.

Table 2 shows the Development of Energy Consumption Optimisation Algorithms: Algorithms Inspired by Nature

The Genetic Algorithm (GA) replicates natural selection in order to function. It starts with a population of solutions (individuals) and combines and selects them repeatedly according to an objective function called "fitness" (which has to do with energy consumption). This mechanism guides the population towards the best answers by imitating the survival of the fittest. However, for complicated issues, GA can be computationally costly.

> Optimisation of Particle Swarms (PSO): The collective behaviour of fish or birds in a school or flock serves as the inspiration for this algorithm. Every "particle" in the search space is a solution, and it moves based on its own past position as well as the optimal position that the swarm has discovered. PSO works well for ongoing optimisation issues such as determining the device power levels that use the least amount of energy.
> Artificial Bee Colony (ABC): This algorithm attempts to replicate how bees forage. It makes use of three different kinds of "bees": scout bees, who investigate new areas when available resources are exhausted, employed bees, who look for food sources (solutions), and observer bees, who make decisions based on the information provided by employed bees. This method effectively locates solutions for energy optimisation issues that are close to ideal.
> Ant Colony Optimisation (ACO): Using "artificial ants" that leave behind virtual pheromones as they scan the area, ACO is modelled after how ants locate the shortest path to food. Stronger pheromone trails draw the attention

of other ants, who eventually follow these trails to more promising solutions (paths that use less energy).

AI & Machine Learning

Through trial and error, an AI agent is trained to learn optimal behaviour in an environment (e.g., managing energy usage in a building) through the use of Deep Reinforcement Learning (DRL), a potent technique. Although it necessitates a large amount of data and processing capacity, in complex settings it can be very effective.

SVMs, or support vector machines: SVMs can be applied to energy optimisation jobs even though they don't directly do optimisation. Their proficiency in classification can be advantageous in discerning trends within energy consumption information. SVMs can assist in anticipating and optimising future consumption by categorising usage patterns.

Artificial Neural Networks (ANN): Networks designed with the brain's architecture in mind. They are able to pick up on intricate connections between various factors affecting energy usage. ANNs enable proactive optimisation techniques by enabling predictive modelling and control after training.

Additional Methods

Resource restrictions and other problems involving linear inequalities are resolved through the use of linear programming, or LP. It is helpful for allocating resources as efficiently as possible while taking particular constraints into account, including energy budgets for various system components.

Dynamic Programming (DP): DP divides a large problem into smaller, more manageable subproblems rather than attempting to solve it all at once. This method works well for optimising energy-related sequential decision-making processes, when decisions made at one stage influence choices made at a later stage.

Heuristics are rule-based algorithms that give approximations of solutions; they are frequently employed when it is difficult or impracticable to obtain exact solutions. Heuristics are helpful in time-constrained real-world applications because they can yield workable answers rapidly, even though they cannot always identify the perfect solution.

5. CHALLENGES OF IMPLEMENTING OPTIMIZATION METHODOLOGIES IN EDGE COMPUTING OFF LOADING AND ENERGY CONSUMPTIONS

5.1 The Difficulties in Applying Optimisation Techniques to Edge Computing Offloading, as Well as Suggestions for Possible Fixes

Principal Difficulties

Heterogeneous and Dynamic Environment: Edge computing is characterised by a constantly changing network and a range of devices with different capacities. For effective offloading, optimisation techniques must adjust in real-time to these modifications.

Restricted Resources: In comparison to cloud servers, edge nodes usually have lower processing and storage capacities. In order to operate within these limitations, optimisation algorithms need to be efficient and lightweight.

Maintaining equilibrium Trade-offs: The goals of offloading are to increase performance overall, latency, and energy consumption. The goal of optimisation is to strike the ideal balance between these variables, which are frequently at odds with one another.

Security and Privacy: There may be security and privacy issues when sending sensitive data to edge nodes. Strong security mechanisms must be incorporated into optimisation frameworks.

Interoperability: Interoperability problems arise from the variety of devices and protocols at the edge. For offloading to occur seamlessly, optimisation techniques need to work with a variety of technological platforms.

Possible Remedies and Strategies Machine Learning Techniques: ML can be very useful in forecasting network circumstances, offloading decisions that are flexible, and device profiling. Particularly promising in the dynamic edge environment is reinforcement learning.

Lightweight Algorithms: It is crucial to provide optimisation algorithms that are specific to the resource limitations of edge nodes. Techniques that combine heuristic and metaheuristic methods can often provide an accurate and speedy solution.

Collaborative Offloading: Several edge nodes working together to offload can increase processing power. Such cooperative efforts can be coordinated with the use of game theory or distributed optimisation techniques.

Security-focused Design: The optimisation process itself must incorporate security. While data is being offloaded and computed, methods like differential privacy and homomorphic encryption can protect its confidentiality.
Standardisation: Optimising systems and devices for edge computing will be made simpler and less complex by promoting interoperability standards.

As an illustration, think about processing videos in real time in an edge setting. The decision of whether to process frames locally on a device, transfer them to a nearby edge node, or send them to the cloud must be made continually by an optimisation algorithm.

5.2. The Difficulties in Putting Optimisation Techniques Into Practice, Particularly to Reduce Energy Usage in Edge Computing

Principal Difficulties

Complex Energy Profiles: Depending on the hardware, software, and workloads, edge devices and nodes have different patterns of energy consumption. For optimisation algorithms to make wise choices, these profiles must be adequately modelled.
Multi-objective Optimisation: Cutting energy use frequently runs counter to other objectives, such as enhancing performance (throughput, latency). Energy minimization requires optimisation to identify a sweet spot rather than a single solution.
Dynamic Workloads: Depending on user requests or sensor data, edge nodes may complete extremely erratic workloads. For optimisation to continue saving energy, it must be flexible and quick to adjust to changes in workload.
Computational and communication energy trade-off: While assigning a task to an edge node may reduce compute energy consumption locally, data transfer may result in an increase in communication energy. Optimisation must take this trade-off into account in its entirety.
Restricted Control over Edge Infrastructure: In third-party maintained edge nodes, energy-saving techniques could necessitate system-level or hardware-level alterations (such dynamic voltage/frequency scaling).
Possible Remedies and Strategies Workload Prediction and Profiling: Proactive offloading choices and resource allocation are made possible by employing methods such as machine learning to forecast future workloads and energy consumption patterns.

The goal of energy-aware scheduling is to reduce total energy consumption by creating scheduling algorithms that take into account energy consumption on both local and edge nodes.

Hierarchical Optimisation: Using several layers may be helpful. methods of optimisation that function at the levels of individual devices, edge nodes, and the larger edge-cloud system.

Collaboration and Workload Sharing: To increase energy efficiency throughout the network, jobs can be moved or spread thanks to coordination between edge nodes.

Optimising with consideration for hardware features like as low-power modes and tailoring optimisation techniques to their unique capabilities is known as hardware-aware optimisation.

An example of an optimisation algorithm in a smart home scenario might be: Examine past energy trends from sensors and devices.

Estimate the likelihood of energy-intensive tasks occurring.

Either carry out these operations locally when energy costs are lower or preemptively offload them to an edge node during off-peak energy consumption hours.

6. FUTURE RESEARCH DIRECTIONS OF OPTIMIZATION METHODOLOGIES IN EDGE COMPUTING TECHNOLOGY

upcoming paths for edge computing optimisation research, including a few major areas of interest:

Important Topics and Patterns Multi-Objective Optimisation (MOO): In edge networks, balancing competing goals such as latency, energy consumption, resource usage, and security is a major difficulty. MOO is going to be important. Methods that include optimisation techniques (e.g., reinforcement learning, evolutionary algorithms) will become more important for more intelligent decision-making.

AI-Driven Optimisation: Intelligent edge computing systems will be powered by the integration of deep learning and machine learning. Anticipate attention to be focused on:

AI models for forecasting and prediction can be used to anticipate resource requirements, network usage trends, and possible bottlenecks, enabling proactive optimisation.

Self-learning optimisation loops: To increase efficiency, systems will adjust their optimisation tactics on their own, taking into account changes in the environment and real-time data.

Federated Learning and Optimisation: Handling the edge computing-related privacy and data sensitivity issues. Without centralising data, federated learning enables cooperative model training on dispersed data. To identify the best answers in these decentralised situations, optimisation techniques will be created.

Optimisation Throughout the Continuum: Cloud resources are a part of a wider ecosystem that includes edge computing. The goal of the research is to ensure task distribution that optimises the advantages of each tier by focusing on seamless optimisation across the edge, fog, and cloud levels.

Security-Focused Optimisation: Edge situations present special security risks and limits. Algorithms for optimisation must take security metrics into account by default, determining the optimum balance between attack defence and performance.

Human-Centric Optimisation: The user experience is directly impacted by edge computing. In addition to conventional technological characteristics, future study should take into account optimising QoS (Quality of Service) indicators including responsiveness and user happiness.

Particular Research Paths Adapting in real time to changes in edge device capabilities, network conditions, and application requirements through dynamic task offloading and resource allocation Energy-efficient algorithm design is the process of creating optimisation methods with the primary goal of reducing edge device power consumption.

Context-aware optimisation: Adapting optimisation tactics for certain conditions by utilising sensor data and user behaviour patterns.

Optimisation for heterogeneous edge environments: A wide range of devices with different functionalities are present in edge networks. Flexible optimisation frameworks that accommodate this variation will be the main focus of research.

Optimisation in the face of uncertainty: Edge computing handles erratic variables. Sturdy optimisation techniques that function effectively even with noisy or imperfect data will be beneficial.

7. CONCLUSION

An investigation of the complex field of optimisation approaches in the context of edge computing, it is clear that the combination of state-of-the-art methods and decentralised computing architectures has enormous potential to influence the direction of information technology. The four main pillars of our thorough investigation were offloading, resource allocation, energy usage, and data optimisation. These pillars are all essential to improving the effectiveness, performance, and quality control of edge computing systems. The analysis of offloading techniques brought to light how important it is to divide up computing work between local devices and edge servers in order to cut down on latency and facilitate real-time processing. Different optimisation methods, from reinforcement learning to evolutionary algorithms, were found to be important facilitators of making judgements that are specific to each offloading case. The key component of efficient edge computing, resource allocation, demonstrated the significance of ideal task distribution for balanced computational resource use. Algorithms like game theory and linear programming have become effective tools for scalability, dynamic resource management, and responding to the changing needs of decentralised systems.

Our analysis addressed the constant worry about energy usage and emphasised the need of using energy-efficient algorithms and techniques. Energy-saving techniques, including as dynamic voltage and frequency scaling and sophisticated scheduling algorithms, prolong the operating life of resource-constrained edge devices while simultaneously promoting sustainability. A range of strategies were made available by the management and optimisation of data at the edge, an essential component of quality management. These strategies included encryption, secure transmission, deduplication, and compression. Together, these techniques help to protect privacy, security, and data integrity while guaranteeing effective storage capacity use.

Upon considering the complex terrain covered in this analysis, it is evident that the convergence of edge computing and optimisation techniques has the potential to completely transform a wide range of businesses. This study adds to the expanding body of knowledge influencing the direction of decentralised computing by offering practical insights. Edge computing systems drive improved performance, responsiveness, and overall quality control through the dynamic interaction of offloading, resource allocation, energy consumption, and data optimisation. This represents a major turning point in the development of contemporary computing paradigms.

REFERENCES

Adu. (2023). Optimal Computation Resource Allocation in Energy-Efficient Edge IoT Systems With Deep Reinforcement Learning. *IEEE Transactions on Green Communications and Networking.* .DOI: 10.1109/TGCN.2023.3286914

Afrin, M., Jin, J., Rahman, A., Tian, Y., & Kulkarni, A. (2019). Multi-objective resource allocation for edge cloud based robotic workflow in smart factory. *Future Generation Computer Systems*, 97, 119–130.

Alam, M. G. R., Hassan, M. M., Uddin, M. Z., Almogren, A., & Fortino, G. (2019). Autonomic computation offloading in mobile edge for iot applications. *Future Generation Computer Systems*, 90, 149–157.

Alelaiwi, A. (2019). An efficient method of computation offloading in an edge cloud platform. *Journal of Parallel and Distributed Computing*, 127, 58–64.

Alkhalaileh, M., Calheiros, R. N., Nguyen, Q. V., & Javadi, B. (2020). Data-intensive application scheduling on mobile edge cloud computing. *Journal of Network and Computer Applications*, 167, 102735.

Bajic, , Nikola, Slobodan, Miladin, Milos, & Aleksandar. (2023). Edge Computing Data Optimization for Smart Quality Management: Industry 5.0 Perspective. *Sustainability*, 15(7), 6032. DOI: 10.3390/su15076032

Baktir, A. C., Ozgovde, A., & Ersoy, C. (2017). How can edge computing benefit from software defined networking: A survey, use cases, and future directions. *IEEE Communications Surveys and Tutorials*, 19, 2359–2391.

Bertsekas, D. P. (2019). *Reinforcement Learning and Optimal Control.* Athena Scientific Belmont.

Chen, J., Chen, S., Luo, S., Wang, Q., Cao, B., & Li, X. (2020). An intelligent task offloading algorithm (itoa) for uav edge computing network. *Digital Communications and Networks*, 6, 433–443.

Chen, X., Zhang, H., Wu, C., Mao, S., Ji, Y., & Bennis, M. (2019). Optimized computation offloading performance in virtual edge computing systems via deep reinforcement learning. *IEEE Internet of Things Journal*, 6, 4005–4018.

Cui, L., Xu, C., Yang, S., Huang, J. Z., Li, J., Wang, X., Ming, Z., & Lu, N. (2019). Joint optimization of energy consumption and latency in mobile edge computing for internet of things. *IEEE Internet of Things Journal*, 6, 4791–4803.

Cui, Y., Zhang, D., Zhang, T., Chen, L., Piao, M., & Zhu, H. (2020). Novel method of mobile edge computation offloading based on evolutionary game strategy for iot devices. *AEÜ. International Journal of Electronics and Communications*, 118, 153134.

Cutress, I. (2022). Intel's manufacturing roadmap from 2019 to 2029: back porting, 7nm, 5nm, 3nm, 2nm, and 1.4 nm. https://www.anandtech.com/show/15217/intels .manufacturing-roadmap-from-2019-to-2029

Danilak, R. (2022). Why energy is a big and rapidly growing problem for data centers. https://www.forbes.com/sites/forbestechcouncil/2017/12/15/why-energy -is-a-big-and-rapidly-growing-problem-for-data-centers

Feng, L., Li, W., Lin, Y., Zhu, L., Guo, S., & Zhen, Z. (2020). Joint computation offloading and URLLC resource allocation for collaborative MEC assisted cellular- v2x networks. *IEEE Access: Practical Innovations, Open Solutions*, 8, 24914–24926.

Ghobaei-Arani, M., Souri, A., Safara, F., & Norouzi, M. (2020). An efficient task scheduling approach using moth-flame optimization algorithm for cyber-physical system applications in fog computing. *Transactions on Emerging Telecommunications Technologies*, 31, 2.

Gsma. (2022). Definitive data and analysis for the mobile data industry. https:// www.gsmaintelligence.com/data/

Guo, S., Liu, J., Yang, Y., Xiao, B., & Li, Z. (2019). Energy-efficient dynamic computation offloading and cooperative task scheduling in mobile cloud computing. *IEEE Transactions on Mobile Computing*, 18, 319–333.

Hu, J., Li, K., Liu, C., & Li, K. (2020). Game-based task offloading of multiple mobile devices with qos in mobile edge computing systems of limited computation capacity. *ACM Transactions on Embedded Computing Systems*, 19(29), 1–29.

Hu, M., Xie, Z., Wu, D., Zhou, Y., Chen, X., & Xiao, L. (2020). Heterogeneous edge offloading with incomplete information: A minority game approach. *IEEE Transactions on Parallel and Distributed Systems*, 31, 2139–2154.

Huang, L., Feng, X., Zhang, C., Qian, L., & Wu, Y. (2019). Deep reinforcement learning-based joint task offloading and bandwidth allocation for multi-user mobile edge computing. *Digital Communications and Networks*, 5, 10–17.

Huawei. (2022). Touching an intelligent world. https://www.huawei.com/minisite/ giv/Files/whitepaper_en_2019.pdf

Jiang, C., Cheng, X., Gao, H., Zhou, X., & Wan, J. (2019). Toward computation offloading in edge computing: A survey. *IEEE Access : Practical Innovations, Open Solutions*, 7, 131543–131558.

Khan, W. Z., Ahmed, E., Hakak, S., Yaqoob, I., & Ahmed, A. (2019). Edge computing: A survey. *Future Generation Computer Systems*, 97, 219–235.

La, Q. D., Ngo, M. V., Dinh, T. Q., Quek, T. Q., & Shin, H. (2019). Enabling intelligence in fog computing to achieve energy and latency reduction. *Digital Communications and Networks*, 5, 3–9.

Li, C., Bai, J., Chen, Y., & Luo, Y. (2020). Resource and replica management strategy for optimizing financial cost and user experience in edge cloud computing system. *Inf. Sci.*, 516, 33–55.

Li, C., Jianhang, T., & Luo, Y. (2019). Dynamic multi-user computation offloading for wireless powered mobile edge computing. *Journal of Network and Computer Applications*, 131, 1–15.

Li, C., Jianhang, T., Tang, H., & Luo, Y. (2019). Collaborative cache allocation and task scheduling for data-intensive applications in edge computing environment. *Future Generation Computer Systems*, 95, 249–264.

Li, J., Gao, H., Lv, T., & Lu, Y. (2018). *Deep reinforcement learning based computation offloading and resource allocation for MEC. 2018 IEEE Wireless Communications and Networking Conference, WCNC 2018.* IEEE.

Li, Y., Ma, H., Wang, L., Mao, S., & Wang, G. (2020). Optimized content caching and user association for edge computing in densely deployed heterogeneous networks. *IEEE Transactions on Mobile Computing*. Advance online publication. DOI: 10.1109/TMC.2020.3033563

Li, Y., Xia, S., Zheng, M., Cao, B., & Liu, Q. (2019). Lyapunov optimization based trade-off policy for mobile cloud offloading in heterogeneous wireless networks. *IEEE Transactions on Cloud Computing*, 10, 491–505.

Lin, L., Liao, X., Jin, H., & Li, P. (2019). Computation offloading toward edge computing. *Proceedings of the IEEE*, 107, 1584–1607.

Liu, M., Yu, F. R., Teng, Y., Leung, V. C. M., & Song, M. (2019). Distributed resource allocation in blockchain-based video streaming systems with mobile edge computing. *IEEE Transactions on Wireless Communications*, 18(1), 695–708.

Liu, P., Xu, G., Yang, K., Wang, K., & Meng, X. (2019). Jointly optimized energy-minimal resource allocation in cache-enhanced mobile edge computing systems. *IEEE Access : Practical Innovations, Open Solutions*, 7, 3336–3347.

Liwang, M., Wang, J., Gao, Z., Du, X., & Guizani, M. (2019). Game theory based opportunistic computation offloading in cloud-enabled iov. *IEEE Access : Practical Innovations, Open Solutions*, 7, 32551–32561.

Mach, P., & Becvar, Z. (2017). Mobile edge computing: A survey on architecture and computation offloading. *IEEE Communications Surveys and Tutorials*, 19, 1628–1656.

Mahmud, M. S., Huang, J. Z., Salloum, S., Emara, T. Z., & Sadatdiynov, K. (2020). A survey of data partitioning and sampling methods to support big data analysis. *Big Data Mining and Analytics*, 3(2), 85–101.

McClellan, M., Cervello-Pastor, C., & Sallent, S. (2020). Deep learning at the mobile edge: Opportunities for 5g networks. *Applied Sciences (Basel, Switzerland)*, 10, 4735.

Nguyen, Q. H., & Dressler, F. (2020). A smartphone perspective on computation offloading—A survey. *Computer Communications*, 159, 133–154.

Paymard, P., Rezvani, S., & Mokari, N. (2019). Joint task scheduling and uplink/downlink radio resource allocation in PD-NOMA based mobile edge computing networks. *Physical Communication*, 32, 160–171.

Ramya, R. (2024). *Analysis and Applications Finding of Wireless Sensors and IoT Devices With Artificial Intelligence/Machine Learning. AIoT and Smart Sensing Technologies for Smart Devices*. IGI Global. DOI: 10.4018/979-8-3693-0786-1.ch005

Ramya, R., Padmapriya, R., & Anand, M. (2024). *Applications of Machine Learning in UAV-Based Detecting and Tracking Objects: Analysis and Overview. Applications of Machine Learning in UAV Networks*. IGI Global. DOI: 10.4018/979-8-3693-0578-2.ch003

Ramya, R., & Ramamoorthy, S. (2022). Development of a framework for adaptive productivity management for edge computing based IoT applications. *AIP Conference Proceedings*, 2519, 030068.

Ramya, R., & Ramamoorthy, S. (2022). Analysis of machine learning algorithms for efficient cloud and edge computing in the IoT, Challenges and Risks Involved in Deploying 6G and NextGen Networks, 72–90.

Ramya, R., & Ramamoorthy, S. (2022)... *Survey on Edge Intelligence in IoT-Based Computing Platform, Lecture Notes in Networks and Systems, Springer*, 356, 549–556. DOI: 10.1007/978-981-16-7952-0_52

Ramya, R., & Ramamoorthy, S. (2023). Lightweight Unified Collaborated Relinquish Edge Intelligent Gateway Architecture with Joint Optimization. *IEEE Access : Practical Innovations, Open Solutions*, 11, 90396–90409. DOI: 10.1109/ACCESS.2023.3307808

Ramya, R., & Ramamoorthy, S. (2024). QoS in multimedia application for IoT devices through edge intelligence. *Multimedia Tools and Applications, Springer*, 83, 9227–9250. DOI: 10.1007/s11042-023-15941-6

Ramya, R., & Ramamoorthy, S. (2024). Hybrid Fog-Edge-IoT Architecture for Real-time Data Monitoring. *International Journal of Intelligent Engineering and Systems*, 17(1), 2024. DOI: 10.22266/ijies2024.0229.22

Sadatdiynov, , Cui, Zhang, Huang, Salloum, & Mahmud. (2022). A review of optimization methods for computation offloading in edge computing networks. *Digital Communications and Networks*, 9. Advance online publication. DOI: 10.1016/j.dcan.2022.03.003

Safavat, S., Sapavath, N. N., & Rawat, D. B. (2020). Recent advances in mobile edge computing and content caching. *Digital Communications and Networks*, 6, 189–194.

Salmani, M., & Davidson, T. N. (2020). Uplink resource allocation for multiple access computational offloading. *Signal Processing*, 168, 107322.

Shakarami, A., Ghobaei-Arani, M., & Shahidinejad, A. (2020). A survey on the computation offloading approaches in mobile edge computing: A machine learning-based perspective. *Computer Networks*, 182, 107496.

Shakarami, A., Shahidinejad, A., & Ghobaei-Arani, M. (2020). A review on the computation offloading approaches in mobile edge computing: A game-theoretic perspective. *Software, Practice & Experience*, 50, 1719–1759.

Shao, Y., Li, C., Fu, Z., Jia, L., & Luo, Y. (2019). Cost-effective replication management and scheduling in edge computing. *Journal of Network and Computer Applications*, 129, 46–61.

Storck, C. R., & Duarte-Figueiredo, F. (2020). A survey of 5g technology evolution, standards, and infrastructure associated with vehicle-to-everything communications by internet of vehicles. *IEEE Access : Practical Innovations, Open Solutions*, 8, 117593–117614.

Tan, Z., Yu, F. R., Li, X., Ji, H., & Leung, V. C. M. (2018). Virtual resource allocation for heterogeneous services in full duplex-enabled scns with mobile edge computing and caching. *IEEE Transactions on Vehicular Technology*, 67, 1794–1808.

Tong, Z., Deng, X., Basodi, F. Ye. S., Xiao, X., & Pan, Y. (2020). Adaptive computation offloading and resource allocation strategy in a mobile edge computing environment. *Inf. Sci.*, 537, 116–131.

Wang, X., Ning, Z., & Guo, S. (2021). Multi-agent imitation learning for pervasive edge computing: A decentralized computation offloading algorithm. *IEEE Transactions on Parallel and Distributed Systems*, 32, 411–425.

Xia, S., Yao, Z., Li, Y., & Mao, S. (2021). Online distributed offloading and computing resource management with energy harvesting for heterogeneous mec-enabled iot. *IEEE Transactions on Wireless Communications*, 20, 6743–6757.

Xu, X., Fu, S., Yuan, Y., Luo, Y., Qi, L., Lin, W., & Dou, W. (2019). Multi objective computation offloading for workflow management in cloudlet-based mobile cloud using NSGA-II. *Computational Intelligence*, 35, 476–495.

Xu, X., Li, Y., Huang, T., Xue, Y., Peng, K., Qi, L., & Dou, W. (2019). An energy-aware computation offloading method for smart edge computing in wireless metropolitan area networks. *Journal of Network and Computer Applications*, 133, 75–85.

Xu, X., Liu, X., Yin, X., Wang, S., Qi, Q., & Qi, L. (2020). Privacy-aware offloading for training tasks of generative adversarial network in edge computing. *Inf. Sci.*, 532, 1–15.

Yang, L., Zhong, C., Yang, Q., Zou, W., & Fathalla, A. (2020). Task offloading for directed acyclic graph applications based on edge computing in industrial internet. *Inf. Sci.*, 540, 51–68.

Yang, X., Chen, Z., Li, K., Sun, Y., Liu, N., Xie, W., & Zhao, Y. (2018). Communication-constrained mobile edge computing systems for wireless virtual reality: Scheduling and tradeoff. *IEEE Access : Practical Innovations, Open Solutions*, 6, 16665–16677.

Yang, Y., Ma, Y., Xiang, W., Gu, X., & Zhao, H. (2018). Joint optimization of energy consumption and packet scheduling for mobile edge computing in cyber-physical networks. *IEEE Access : Practical Innovations, Open Solutions*, 6, 15576–15586.

You, Q., & Tang, B. (2021). Efficient task offloading using particle swarm optimization algorithm in edge computing for industrial internet of things. *J Cloud Comp*, 10, 41. DOI: 10.1186/s13677-021-00256-4

Zhang, C., & Zheng, Z. (2019). Task migration for mobile edge computing using deep reinforcement learning. *Future Generation Computer Systems*, 96, 111–118.

Zhang, J., Xia, W., Yan, F., & Shen, L. (2018). Joint computation offloading and resource allocation optimization in heterogeneous networks with mobile edge computing. *IEEE Access : Practical Innovations, Open Solutions*, 6, 19324–19337.

Zhang, L., Cao, B., Li, Y., Peng, M., & Feng, G. (2021). A multi-stage stochastic programming based offloading policy for fog enabled iot-ehealth. *IEEE Journal on Selected Areas in Communications*, 39(2), 411–425.

Zhang, Q., Lin, M., Yang, L. T., Chen, Z., & Li, P. (2019). Energy-efficient scheduling for real-time systems based on deep q-learning model. *T-SUSC*, 4, 132–141.

Zhao, M., Wang, W., Wang, Y., & Zhang, Z. (2019). Load scheduling for distributed edge computing: A communication-computation tradeoff. *Peer-to-Peer Networking and Applications*, 12, 1418–1432.

Zheng, T., Wan, J., Zhang, J., Jiang, C., & Jia, G. (2020). A survey of computation offloading in edge computing. 2020 International Conference on Computer, Information and Telecommunication Systems (CITS), 1–6.

Zhou, J., Zhang, X., & Wang, W. (2019). Joint resource allocation and user association for heterogeneous services in multi-access edge computing networks. *IEEE Access : Practical Innovations, Open Solutions*, 7, 12272–12282.

Zhu, Z., Peng, J., Gu, X., Li, H., Liu, K., Zhou, Z., & Liu, W. (2018). Fair resource allocation for system throughput maximization in mobile edge computing. *IEEE Access : Practical Innovations, Open Solutions*, 6, 5332–5340.

Chapter 5
Optimal Population–Based Metaheuristics With NEH and ANN Algorithms for Minimizing Total Tardiness in Flow Shop Scheduling Problem

Hajar Sadki

Laboratory of Mathematics, Computer Science and Applications, FST Mohammedia, University Hassan II of Casablanca, Mohammedia, Morocco

Karam Allali
 https://orcid.org/0000-0002-9463-4295

Laboratory of Mathematics, Computer Science and Applications, FST Mohammedia, University Hassan II of Casablanca, Mohammedia, Morocco

ABSTRACT

In this work, the authors investigate the resolution of the permutation flow shop scheduling problem by minimizing total tardiness. First, they explore different approaches, and they utilize nature-inspired metaheuristics. The proposed solution approach incorporates three metaheuristics: genetic algorithm (GA), migratory bird optimization (MBO), and artificial bee colony (ABC) algorithm. These metaheuristics are combined with local search procedures to explore neighboring solutions. Additionally, two constructive algorithms, Nawaz-Enscore-Ham (NEH) and artificial

DOI: 10.4018/979-8-3693-5231-1.ch005

neural networks (ANN), are introduced for generating optimal sequences initially. The effectiveness of the proposed approach and algorithms is evaluated through comprehensive tests on various instance sizes. The simulations demonstrate that the population-based ABC with the NEH outperforms other algorithms in terms of efficiency. This comparative analysis reveals that the ABC_NEH metaheuristic achieves better results than other algorithms, resulting in a good success rate.

1. INTRODUCTION

The permutation flow shop scheduling problem (PFSSP) has been a fascinating research area for over forty years. Production scheduling is a crucial aspect of manufacturing system planning and operations, with flow shop scheduling being one of the different scheduling systems available Framinan et al. (2004); Yenisey and Yagmahan (2014). Flow shop scheduling involves sequencing n jobs that must be processed on m machines to optimize performance measures such as minimum makespan, minimum tardiness, etc. However, difficulties arise when dealing with large sets of jobs and machines in real-life applications, making the PFSSP more complex. Traditional methods have been used to solve the problem, but they are often found to be insufficient.

In this study, we investigate the PFSSP problem with a focus on minimizing total tardiness (TT). Over the years, various solution approaches have been proposed for tackling the PFSSP problem Zobolas et al. (2009); Lian et al. (2008), utilizing both approximate and exact methods. Specifically, the exact methods include mathematical formulation and the branch and bound technique. Mixed Integer Linear Programming (MILP) has been established to optimize the flow shop scheduling problem in manufacturing Gmys et al. (2020); Sadki et al. (2021); Aqil and Allali (2021). Likewise, the approach methods are based on heuristics and metaheuristics, with the latter constituting the majority of efforts to resolve the PFSSP problem. With the advancement of computer technology, we turned to metaheuristic algorithms due to their computational power. Iterative approaches in metaheuristics algorithms have proven effective in solving various optimization scheduling problems. Industrial problems often involve large batch sizes, making exact methods impractical for real-world applications. The PFSSP flow shop problem has been the subject of much research on industrial optimization problems. In Onwubolu and Mutingi (1999), Genetic Algorithm (GA) used in solving hybrid optimization and scheduling for minimizing tardiness PFSSP. Tang et al. (2005), a neural network algorithm for solving the hybrid PFSSP in a dynamic environment. In Li et al.(2022) The Artificial Bee Colony (ABC) algorithm is employed to decrease the makespan, while in Sioud and Gagne (2018) the migratory bird optimization (MBO) method is utilized to minimize the maximum completion time. In Cui and Gu (2015), an improved version of the artificial bee colony algorithm is suggested to minimize the makespan of an HFS-SDST problem. Also, in Ta et al. (2018), the authors used metaheuristics and methods based on MILP formulation in PFSSP. Additionally, authors in Rahman et al. (2021) have addressed the PFSSP-SDST setup time constraint in the analysis of the problem. In Rouhani et al. (2010), the authors aimed to develop an artificial intelligence capable of performing scheduling tasks through the process of neural network training. Also, in Radha Ramanan et al. (2011) the authors proposed two approaches in which the artificial neural network algorithms (ANN) generate priorities of a scheduling action, which is subsequently optimized by a heuristic or genetic algorithm. Motivated by these contributions, we have conducted further investigation using nature-inspired metaheuristics to tackle the PFSSP problem with greater efficiency. We employ two constructive algorithms based on the NEH Nawaz et al. (1983) procedure and the ANN Kumar and Giri (2019) algorithm to enhance the effectiveness of the inspired nature metaheuristics.

Our contribution consists of three nature-inspired metaheuristic algorithms. The proposed solution approach comprises three population-based metaheuristics inspired by nature: the genetic algorithm, migratory bird optimization, and the artificial bee colony algorithm. These metaheuristics are complemented by various approaches incorporating local search procedures to explore neighboring solutions Dong et al. (2009). Additionally, two constructive algorithms, namely the Nawaz-Enscore and Ham algorithm and the artificial neural network algorithms, are introduced to generate optimal sequences in the initial phase. The work presents three population-based metaheuristics, namely GA_ANN, MBO_NEH, and ABC_NEH, which aim to address the optimization problem in the context of manufacturing. Our objective is to employ the ABC, GA, and MBO algorithms along with various local search techniques to achieve the best possible solution. These methods make it possible to best explore the neighborhood of the current solution by a simple disruption of the sequence. Indeed, our improvement consists of generating sequences by insertion, permutation, or a large neighborhood system. Our improvement therefore consists of better choosing the variable settings of each algorithm to obtain the best possible result. Such an approach allows having no redundancy on the solutions already treated during the evolution of the local search. We give in detail our exploration approach for each metaheuristic. Motivated by the industrial interest in optimizing the TT criterion, we introduced a range of diverse constructive approaches for solving the manufacturing PFSSP problem. To effectively address the optimization scheduling problem, our contribution is based on three population-based metaheuristics. We improved by utilizing approximate local search methods in the global form of population-based metaheuristics. Moreover, in the initial phase, two powerful NEH and ANN algorithms with constructive solutions are used to generate the population. This implementation model allows us to save enough computation time to reach the right solution from the initial phase. Other enhancements concern the strengthening of the current solution's neighborhood generation mechanism. The strengths of our approach are summarized for solving this kind of problem in the following indications:

- The new model and implementation scheme of the genetic algorithm with a population-based approach have been unveiled based ANN algorithm. This novel approach is aptly named population-based genetic algorithm based artificial neural network algorithm (GA _ANN). To enhance the exploration of the neighborhood system, the algorithm incorporates the crossover and mutation technique inspired by the genetic algorithm.
- The iterative local search structure, known as The neighborhood structure, represents a significant advancement in the field. This structure incorporates various local neighborhood search techniques making it highly effective.
- The three metaheuristics are utilized to solve the PFSSP scheduling optimization problem.

Our motivation is to tackle the PFSSP problem by employing innovative approaches based on population algorithms. The primary objective is to develop a platform that offers a variety of solution methods. This platform will act as a valuable decision-support tool for industries engaged in this area. It will enable decision-makers to select the most appropriate method based on the problem size and available technological resources. In the end, our contribution introduces a novel approach to solving workshop scheduling problems. In the subsequent section, we provide a comprehensive explanation of the various methodologies employed to address the optimization scheduling problem in the manufacturing environment.

This work is organized as follows: Section 2 provides a comprehensive literature review. Section 3 presents the PFSSP model. Section 4 gives the proposed neural network approach and the methods for solving the problem. Section 5 provides the numerical outcomes and a comparative evaluation of the methods developed. Finally, Section 6 highlights the advantages of our research and suggests avenues for future exploration.

2. LITERATURE REVIEW

In this work, our specific focus is on the PFSSP scheduling problem, which aims to minimize TT criterion. We adopt the standard notation $Fm|PFSSP, prum, d_{(j)}|$ $\sum_{j=1}^{n} T_{\sigma_j}$ given by Graham et al. (1979) for denoting the problem, where the three fields represent the machine flow shop problem, the problem constraints, and the minimization criterion, respectively. The PFSSP scheduling problems consider various constraints. In this literature review, several important elements are discussed, including the earliest arrival date $r_{(j)}$, predictive maintenance, and the due date constraint $d_{(j)}$. In addition to production-related criteria like C_{max} and TFT, which is characterized by $\sum_{j=1}^{n} Ct_{m,\sigma_j}$, there are also criteria associated with customer satisfaction. To provide an overview of related research in the field, we present Table 1 summarizing the various studies conducted on the PFSSP problem.

Table 1. A summary of previous work on PFSSP scheduling problems

	Type of problem	Method	Comments
Gelders and Sambandam (1978)	Total tardiness	Four heuristic methods for obtaining a good solution	The computational results indicate that all four heuristic methods performed well
Onwubolu and Mutingi (1999)	Total tardiness	Campbell, Dudeck and Smith (CDS) and GA	The proposed GA outperforms traditional heuristics
Allahverdi and Aydilek (2015)	Total tardiness	An insertion algorithm (PIA), GA, two proposed of simulated annealing algorithm (PSA)	The PSA algorithm combined with the proposed insertion algorithm (PIA) significantly outperforms other methods
Vallada et al. (2008)	Total tardiness	SA, Tabu search methods (TS), differential evolution method reported in Onwubolu and Davendra(2006)	Simulated annealing and job insertion/interchange heuristics are the top-performing methods
Vallada and Ruiz (2010)	Total tardiness	Genetic algorithm	Random initialization, two-point crossover and swap mutation
Karacan et al. (2023)	Total tardiness and the total earliness	TS, particle swarm optimization (PSO), local search (LS)	The Simulated Annealing Multithread (SAMT) significantly outperforms classical SA, PSO, and TS Algorithms
Yu and Seif (2016)	Total tardiness	MILP and a lower bound based on GA (LBGA)	The proposed LBGA effectively addresses the NP-hard permutation flow shop scheduling problem
Ta et al. (2018)	Total tardiness	A mixed integer linear programming, GA	The proposed metaheuristics Algorithm consistently outperforms the GA in most cases
Pan et al. (2002)	Total tardiness	Branch-and-bound algorithm	The proposed branch-and-bound algorithm significantly outperforms

continued on following page

Table 1. Continued

	Type of problem	Method	Comments
Fernandez-Viagas et al. (2018)	Total tardiness	The beam search-based heuristics, iterated greedy, LS	The beam search heuristics achieved better results than NEH_{edd}, and the iterated greedy algorithm with adjacent swaps outperformed other method
Nejjarou et al. (2023)	Total tardiness	Artificial bee colony algorithm, the genetic algorithm and the migratory bird optimization algorithm	The migratory bird optimization is highly effective
Sadki et al. (2024)	Makespan and total flow time	The GA, the iterative greedy algorithm, the ILS	The iterative greedy method provided the best results
Yang and Xu (2021)	Total tardiness	The double deep Q network (DDQN)	The DDQN-based scheduling outperforms several well-known dispatching rules

2. THE DESCRIPTION OF THE FLOW SHOP SCHEDULING PROBLEM

The permutation flow shop scheduling problem optimization problem involves configuring a group of production equipment to operate in a sequential and efficient production line. In this context, the resources typically refer to a collection of machines, denoted as $M = \{M_1, M_2, \ldots, M_m\}$, positioned throughout the manufacturing process. Within this workshop, a set of jobs, denoted by $J = \{J_1, J_2, \ldots, J_n\}$, is processed together in a production batch that starts with M1 and ends with Mm. Each job has a defined processing time, $p_{i,j} > 0$, which determines its duration. Additionally, a flow shop represents a manufacturing system where a collection of n jobs follows the same path through a sequence of m machines. It's important to note that the traditional flow shop configuration has been adapted in various ways to meet the requirements of real-world manufacturing systems. The primary model is the standard flow shop, which is based on the following assumptions:

- Only one job can be assigned to a machine at any given time, and each job can be executed by only one machine at a time.
- At time zero, all tasks are readily accessible.
- All machines are consistently and permanently accessible.

- The preparation times for operations are not reliant on their sequence and are included in the processing times.

The subsequent notation will be utilized, to formulate the routing model:

- j Refers to a group of n jobs j = 1 . . . n.
- i Refers to a group of m machines i = 1 . . . m.
- $p_{i,k}$ Denotes the duration required to complete job J_k on machine M_i.
- $\sigma = \{\sigma_1, . . ., \sigma_n\}$ Represents the order of n jobs.
- CT_{i,σ_j} Refers to the time taken to finish job σ_j on machine m_i the completion time.
- T_{σ_j} The tardiness of each job
- d_j Indicates the due date for job j.

Since the goal is to minimize the total tardiness of each job, the subsequent formulas are implemented to compute TT:

$$CT_{1,\sigma_1} = p_{1,\sigma_1} \tag{1}$$

The completion time of the job σ_j on the initial machine is:

$$CT_{1,\sigma_j} = CT_{1,\sigma_{j-1}} + p_{1,\sigma_j} \tag{2}$$

The time to complete the first job on the remaining machines is:

$$CT_{i,\sigma_j} = CT_{i-1,\sigma_{j-1}} + p_{1,\sigma_1}, i = 2, ..., m \tag{3}$$

The completion time for job σ_j on the remaining machines is determined by:

$$CT_{i,\sigma_j} = max\left\{CT_{i,\sigma_{j-1}}, CT_{i-1,\sigma_j}\right\} + p_{1,\sigma_j}, i = 2, ..., m, j = 2, ..., n \tag{4}$$

The main objective of this study is to minimize the total tardiness of all jobs. To achieve this, we determine the tardiness of each job using the formula:

$$T_{\sigma_j} = max\left(CT_{\sigma_j,m} - d_{\sigma_j}, 0\right) \text{ for } j = 1, ..., n$$

And the total tardiness will be indicated by:

$$TT = \sum_{j=1}^{n} T_{o_j}, j = 1,\ldots,n \qquad (5)$$

2.1. Example

To demonstrate the effectiveness of the proposed model, we give an example illustration of five jobs and three machines creating our workshop. Table 2 presents the processing times and the due date for executing jobs on the machines. Our goal is to schedule the sequence $\sigma = [J4, J2, J3, J1, J5]$, where the $\tau = (1+\text{Rand}())$. In Figure 1 the total tardiness of each job is denoted as TT = 30-time units.

Table 2. The processing time of five jobs on three machines

Job (j)	Machine (i)			Due Date
	M_1	M_2	M_3	$d_{(j)} = \lfloor \tau \times \sum_{i=1}^{m} p_{i,j} \rfloor$
J_1	2	2	1	5
J_2	2	6	5	18
J_3	6	5	1	16
J_4	1	4	1	8
J_5	3	3	4	10

Figure 1. Gantt chart for five jobs and three machines.

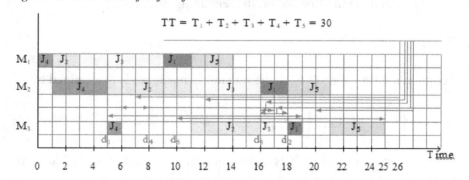

3. RESOLUTION APPROACHES

The flow shop scheduling problems are resolved through the implementation of optimization methods. We propose three metaheuristics to solve the scheduling problem of PFSSP. The first approach is a genetic algorithm based on an artificial neural network approach. The second approach is the artificial bee colony algorithm. Lastly, we employ the migratory bird optimization algorithm, both of which are based on the Nawaz-Enscore and Ham algorithms.

3.1. Genetic Algorithm

The genetic algorithm draws inspiration from the workings of biological organisms, as it is a metaheuristic approach to the progression of genetic code through successive generations. Its effectiveness in resolving optimization problems within the manufacturing industry has been remarkable. Various implementations of this metaheuristic have proven to be effective in addressing PFSSP problems and their extensions. In Onwubolu and Mutingi (1999), an improvement of the genetic algorithm is proposed for minimizing tardiness in flow shop scheduling. To solve this problem, we propose a new version of the GA algorithm. We introduce a new iteration of the population-based Artificial Neural Network (ANN) algorithm, which is utilized during the generation phase of the initial population in the population-based genetic algorithm. In Radha Ramanan et al. (2011), researchers utilized a GA-based ANN approach (GA_ANN) to address the permutation flow shop scheduling problem. The steps of the GA procedure are presented in Algorithm 1.

To illustrate the three phases of the GA algorithm. Starting from an initial population, in the selection phase, two parents: $Parent_1 = [4, 7, 4, 1, 6, 3, 8, 2]$ and $Parent_2 = [4, 3, 8, 5, 1, 2, 7, 6]$ are selected according to a previously defined procedure. In the crossover phase: the genetic code of $child_1 = [5, 7, 4, 3, 1, 6, 8, 2]$ is divided into three sub-sequences so that the first and last sub-sequences $[5, 7], [8, 2]$ are the same as those of $Parent_1$. This sub-sequencing within the bound is found using the parameter $\rho = n/4 = 2$. The second sub-sequence is taken from $Parent_2$ with the condition that the genetics that already exist in $Child_1$ will not be duplicated. The same process is made for $child_2$. For the mutation neighborhood phase: we apply the insert procedure on the second sub-sequence of $Child_1$ to generate the set neighborhood structure. Figure 2, we illustrate the phases of GA.

Figure 2. Example of crossover and mutation operation.

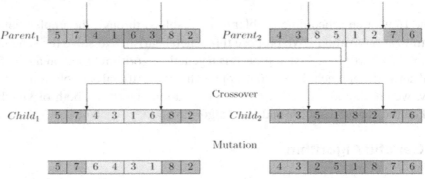

Algorithm 1: The GA algorithm

Input:
　　Create initial population **H** constructed by artificial neural network approach.
　　Determine the TT of every element in **H**, and then construct the optimal sequence σ^{op}.
　while Condition not satisfied **do**:
　　Select two $Parent_{1,2}$ from the population **H**
　　Generate two $Child_{1,2}$ using the crossing procedure
　　Apply the mutation procedure to $Child_{1,2}$
　　Evaluate the set of generated individuals
　　Update population **H** and the σ^{op}
　end
Output σ^{op}

In our improvement of the GA algorithm, we propose to use the artificial neural network (ANN) technique in the initial phase. Algorithm 2 shows the different steps of the ANN procedure. We have chosen to adopt this technique because of its simplicity and ease of implementation. This procedure is very interesting because it allows us to create new high-quality neighborhood structures in scheduling optimization problems. By integrating this procedure into the GA algorithm, we observed accelerated convergence of the GA metaheuristic. The integration of the ANN procedure into the GA algorithm represents a valuable improvement, as it enables the creation of a hybrid algorithm (GA _ANN).

Creating Data for Giving to the Artificial Neural Network

This work describes an approach that utilizes Artificial Neural Network (ANN) Tang et al. (2005); Radha Ramanan et al. (2011); Kumar and Giri (2020) to generate the initial schedule for the flow shop problem. The proposed ANN requires an input layer whose size depends on the number of machines, making it necessary to use distinct and trained networks for each machine in flow shop problems. The input patterns should be constrained to values ranging between zero and one, requiring normalization of the input data. To represent each job and its relationship to other scheduled jobs, a vector is employed, where the vector's size is three times that of the number of machines, denoted as 3m. The neural network proposed in this work features an input layer containing 3m nodes. When a job j is presented to the network, the values of the input layer's nodes are calculated using the following equations:

$$Node_q = \begin{cases} \frac{P_{i,q}}{100}, & q = 1,\ldots,m \\ \frac{\frac{1}{n}\sum_{i=1}^{n}P_{i,q-m}}{100}, & q = m+1,\ldots,2m \\ \sqrt{\frac{Y_{(q-2m)}-n\bar{p}_{(q-2m)}^2}{(n-1)\times 10^4}}, & q = 2m+1,\ldots,3m \end{cases} \tag{6}$$

where

$$\bar{P}_{(k)} = \frac{1}{n}\sum_{i=1}^{n}P_{i,k}, \text{ where } k = q - m \tag{7}$$

and

$$Y_{(r)} = \sum_{i=1}^{n}p_{i,k}^2, \text{ where } r = q - 2m \tag{8}$$

Equation (6) incorporates a divisor of 100 to ensure that the normalization encompasses the entire spectrum of processing times. The initial m nodes contain the processing times for a job on each of the m machines, while the intermediate m nodes represent the mean processing times for each machine, and the final m nodes store the standard deviation of the processing times for each machine. In this case, the network is trained on the correlations and relationships among the jobs within a designated batch. To establish these correlations, the standard deviation and averages of the jobs performed on each machine are utilized. By using average and standard deviation, the identification of identical jobs across distinct batches is ensured, facilitating the training of the ANN. Regardless of the value of m, the output layer of the network consists of only one node, which takes on values ranging from 0.1 to 0.9. In this particular model, a single hidden neuron layer is allocated for each job, and an output neuron layer with one neuron also exists. In the current model designed for problems involving n jobs and m machines, the network architecture entails 3m input neurons, one hidden neuron, and an output neuron. The architecture representation of this neural model's working mechanism for the flow shop problem is illustrated in Figure 3.

Figure 3. Input/Output values of neurons for J, and ten machine.

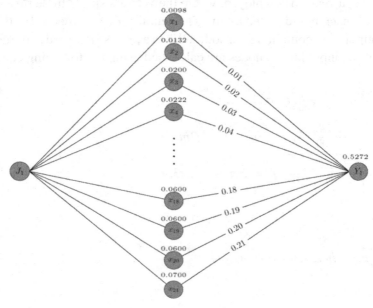

Algorithm 2: The artificial neural network algorithm

Input: Generate the P using the processing time $p_{i,j}$
   Step 1: Apply the same procedure as in Eqs (6) – (8) to determine the input values for a job j when it is presented to the network
   Step 2: The weight values on the connections between the hidden neuron and the others should be calculated as follows:
       - Order the input values in ascending order
       - Rank their priorities in order from 1 to 3m, then divide each one by 100
   Step 3: Apply the activation function to the net input $y_{\_in}$:
   $y_{\_in} = \sum_{i=1}^{n} x_i w_i$
   Step 4: Using the following function, determine the output values y_k
$y_k = F(y_{\_in}), \quad k = 1,\dots,n$
     $F(x) = \dfrac{1}{1 + \exp(-x)}$
   Where:
   Step 5: Arranged the output values of L_k in increasing order to obtain the sequence of jobs
Output: σ^*, $TT(\sigma^*)$

To illustrate how the neural network is utilized to generate a sequence from a group of jobs, we examine the instance of a 6-jobs, 7-machine problem taken from the datasets. The processing times of these jobs on each machine are presented in Table 3. Utilizing Equations (6) − (8), each of the six jobs is initially transformed into a 21-element vector (i.e., a vector with 21 rows) of input nodes. The outcomes of this phase are presented in Table 4. The neural sequence can be obtained by sorting the six jobs in ascending order of their neural outputs, as illustrated in the following $\sigma^*_{ANN} = [J_4, J_3, J_1, J_6, J_2, J_5]$.

Table 3. The processing time of six jobs on seven machines

Job	:	J_1	J_2	J_3	J_4	J_5	J_6
M_1	:	5	6	4	6	4	6
M_2	:	6	9	9	4	9	5
M_3	:	6	7	1	1	4	3
M_4	:	2	1	3	6	1	7
M_5	:	3	6	3	3	3	5
M_6	:	5	3	2	4	8	5
M_7	:	6	4	7	4	8	2
$d_{(j)}$	:	46	42	36	30	51	44

Table 4. Input/Output values of neurons for six jobs and ten machine

Input elements	Jobs					
	J_1	J_2	J_3	J_4	J_5	J_6
1	0.0500	0.0600	0.0400	0.0600	0.0400	0.0600
2	0.0600	0.0900	0.0900	0.0400	0.0900	0.0500
3	0.0600	0.0700	0.0100	0.0100	0.0400	0.0300
4	0.0200	0.0100	0.0300	0.0600	0.0100	0.0700
5	0.0300	0.0600	0.0300	0.0300	0.0300	0.0500
6	0.0500	0.0300	0.0200	0.0400	0.0800	0.0500
7	0.0600	0.0400	0.0700	0.0400	0.0800	0.0200
8	0.0516	0.0516	0.0516	0.0516	0.0516	0.0516
9	0.0700	0.070	0.0700	0.0700	0.0700	0.0700
10	0.0366	0.0366	0.0366	0.0366	0.0366	0.0366
11	0.0333	0.0333	0.0333	0.0333	0.0333	0.0333

continued on following page

Table 4. Continued

Input elements	Jobs					
	J_1	J_2	J_3	J_4	J_5	J_6
12	0.0383	0.0383	0.0383	0.0383	0.0383	0.0383
13	0.0450	0.0450	0.0450	0.0450	0.0450	0.0450
14	0.0516	0.0516	0.0516	0.0516	0.0516	0.0516
15	0.0098	0.0098	0.0098	0.0098	0.0098	0.0098
16	0.0228	0.0228	0.0228	0.0228	0.0228	0.0228
17	0.0250	0.0250	0.0250	0.0250	0.0250	0.0250
18	0.0258	0.0258	0.0258	0.0258	0.0258	0.0258
19	0.0132	0.0132	0.0132	0.0132	0.0132	0.0132
20	0.0207	0.0207	0.0207	0.0207	0.0207	0.0207
21	0.0222	0.0222	0.0222	0.0222	0.0222	0.0222
Output	0.5272	0.5292	0.5269	0.5256	0.5299	0.5272

3.2. The NEH Algorithm

The NEH heuristic, outlined in Algorithm 3, is a widely recognized and effective constructive solution approach introduced in Nawaz et al. (1983). It is highly regarded as one of the most influential heuristics in the scheduling field. Numerous adaptations and comprehensive explanations of this method can be found in Jin et al. (2007). To improve the performance of the algorithms, we opted to incorporate the NEH technique during the initial stage of every population-based metaheuristic.

Algorithm 3: The algorithm of NEH

Input: For a processing time $p_{1,\sigma j}, \cdots, p_{m,\sigma j}$
    Calculate total the processing time for each job by: $T(\sigma_j) = \sum_{i=1}^{m} p_{i,\sigma_j}$
    Construct the sequence $\sigma = (\sigma_1,\ldots, \sigma_n)$ by sorting the jobs in descending order of $T(\sigma_j)$.
    Determine the optimum sequence for the first two jobs by taking σ_1 and σ_2.
    for j = 3 to n **do**
        Add σ_j to every point of the current sequence being created, choose the sequence with the minimum TT in the previous machine, and update the σ_{NEH} of the best sequence.
    end for
Output: σ_{NEH}

3.3. Artificial Bee Colony Algorithm

The ABC Karaboga and Basturk (2007) method was introduced as a population-based optimization algorithm. The population comprises three distinct groups of bees, namely: the workers, the spectators, and the scouts. In Allali et al. (2022), the ABC approach was presented to address the distributed flexible flow shop optimization problem, focusing on minimizing the makespan and maximum tardiness. In our study, we introduce an enhanced version of the ABC algorithm which reinforced incorporates diversification into the neighbor exploration system. Our suggestion involves utilizing a space neighborhood system exploration strategy that incorporates a three-neighborhood structure NS, specifically denoted as V_1, V_2, and V_3. Algorithm 4 presents the procedural steps for the implementation of the ABC algorithm. To demonstrate the neighborhood system (refer to Figure 4), the current sequence is $\sigma = [5, 7, 9, 6, 1, 2, 4, 8, 3]$, and we randomly generate two positions p=2 and q= 7. In the first neighborhood V_1, the work in position p is swapped with the work in position q. In the second neighborhood V_2, we give the new sequence by inserting and shifting right. Finally, the third neighborhood V_3 of the neighboring sequence is generated by an insertion and shift to the left.

Algorithm 4: The ABC algorithm

Input: Create a population initial $H = [\sigma^1, \sigma^2, \ldots \sigma^k]$ using NEH algorithm
    Evaluate TT each sequence σ^k where k = 1 . . . K in H
    $\sigma^{ABC} = \min_{1 \leq k \leq m} \{TT_{min}(\sigma^k), \sigma^k \in H\}$
    while Condition not satisfied **do**
    for k = 1 to K do
      Construct the new sequence utilizing the V_1 neighborhood "employed phase"
      Create the new sequence utilizing the V_2 neighborhood "onlooker phase"
      Built the new sequence utilizing the V_3 neighborhood "scout phase"
      Updated H and give the best sequence σ^{ABC}
Output: σ^{ABC}

3.4. Migratory Bird Optimization Algorithm

The MBO technique is a highly effective metaheuristic that can be used to solve optimization problems in the industry. This iterative method is founded on simulating the behavior of migratory birds. Recently, Duman et al. (2012) introduced the MBO method, which has demonstrated exceptional performance. Several optimization problems Cao et al. (2020); Ulker and Tongur (2017). The principal idea is to split the population H into two sub-populations on the right H_R and the left H_L. The steps to implement the algorithm are presented in Algorithm 5. We use the V_1 neighborhood on sub-population H_R and apply the V_2 neighborhood to subpopulation H_L. We have enhanced this metaheuristic by applying a total permutation of a portion of the sequence to the current optimal solution. This technique enables an extensive search in the local space, referred to as the NS total neighborhood (refer to Figure 4).

Figure 4. The neighborhood structure for ABC and MBO algorithms.

$$p = 2 \qquad q = 7$$

$$\sigma = [5\ 7\ 9\ 6\ 1\ 2\ 4\ 8\ 3]$$
$$V_1 = [5\ 4\ 9\ 6\ 1\ 2\ 7\ 8\ 3]$$
$$V_2 = [5\ 7\ 4\ 9\ 6\ 1\ 2\ 8\ 3]$$
$$V_3 = [5\ 9\ 6\ 1\ 2\ 7\ 4\ 8\ 3]$$

$$\text{NS} \begin{cases} 5\ 4\ 2\ 6\ 1\ 9\ 7\ 8\ 3 \\ 5\ 4\ 9\ 2\ 1\ 6\ 7\ 8\ 3 \\ \chi \begin{cases} 5\ 4\ 9\ 6\ 2\ 1\ 7\ 8\ 3 \\ 5\ 4\ 1\ 6\ 9\ 2\ 7\ 8\ 3 \\ 5\ 4\ 9\ 1\ 6\ 2\ 7\ 8\ 3 \\ 5\ 4\ 6\ 9\ 1\ 2\ 7\ 8\ 3 \end{cases} \end{cases}$$

Algorithm 5: The MBO Algorithm

Input:
Step 1: Create the starting population **H** and divide it into two sub-population H_R, H_L using NEH algorithm, θ: number of turns
$H = H_R \cup H_L : \sigma^* \leftarrow best(\sigma, \sigma \in H), H = [\sigma^1, \sigma^2, \ldots, \sigma^{|H|}]$
Step 2
while Condition not satisfied **do**
  for k = 1 to θ **do**
    $\bar{\sigma}$ is the optimal sequence in χ given by NS applied to σ^*
    if $TT(\bar{\sigma}) \leqslant TT(\sigma^*)$ **then**
      $\sigma* \leftarrow \bar{\sigma}$
    end
    for r = 1 to $|H_R|$ **do**
      $\sigma' \leftarrow V_1(\sigma^r)$
      if $TT(\sigma') \leqslant TT(\sigma^r)$ **then**
        $\sigma^r \leftarrow \sigma'$
        if $TT(\sigma^r) \leqslant TT(\sigma^*)$ **then**
          $\sigma^* \leftarrow \sigma^r$
        end
      end
    end
    for l = 1 to $|H_L|$ **do**
      $\sigma' \leftarrow V_2(\sigma^l)$
      if $TT(\sigma') \leqslant TT(\sigma^l)$ **then**
        $\sigma^l \leftarrow \sigma'$
        if $TT(\sigma^l) \leqslant TT(\sigma^*)$ **then**
          $\sigma^* \leftarrow \sigma^l$
        end
      end
    end
  end
end
Output: σ*

4. THE COMPUTATIONAL RESULT

In this section, we present the results of our experimental research conducted to evaluate various algorithms for addressing the PFSSP, with a focus on minimizing the maximum tardiness. The problem can be characterized by two variables: the number of jobs and the number of machines. To evaluate the performance of the developed algorithms, we generate instances of varying sizes. We have chosen a set of intermediate-sized examples, where the problem instances consist of varying numbers of machines $m \in \{5, 10\}$ and numbers of jobs $n \in \{10, 20. . . 190\}$, where the processing times $p_{i,j} \in [1, 49]$. The instances with a specific size of n jobs and m machines are defined as combinations of m × n. The stopping criterion for the three metaheuristics is determined by the following expression: $\tau_{limit} = \alpha \times n \times m$ seconds CPU time. The outcomes are presented for different values of $\alpha \in [0.03, 0.06, 0.09]$. This adjustment primarily focuses on two aspects: the population size (Pop_size) for each algorithm and the neighborhood structure, along with the number of turns θ for the MBO algorithm. Additionally, it is important to note that the parameter ρ, which represents the number of jobs inherited, plays a vital role in the GA algorithm. *Table 5* provides a summary of the selected parameter in our comparative study among the algorithms.

Table 5. The parameters for the algorithms.

Instance	GA_ANN Size_Pop	ρ	ABC_NEH Size_Pop	MBO_NEH Size_Pop	Θ
Small size (n < 60, m∈ {5, 10})	5	$\lfloor n/5 \rfloor$	20	11	15
Medium size (n∈[60, 90], m∈ {5, 10})	15	$\lfloor n/4 \rfloor$	30	21	30
Large size (n > 90), m∈ {5, 10}	25	$\lfloor n/3 \rfloor$	40	31	45

Table 6 presents the simulation results for different instances with three values of $\alpha = 0.03$, $\alpha = 0.06$ and $\alpha = 0.09$, considering a computation time limit that constrains the search according to the instance size $\tau_{limit} = \alpha \times n \times m$. It presents the objective function values obtained by different metaheuristics for problem resolution. Based on this simulation, for $\alpha = 0.03$, $\tau_{limit} = 0.03 \times n \times m$ and 38 instances across three approaches, we have 114 simulated test problems. The simulation demonstrates the dominance of the ABC_NEH algorithm, which achieves a remarkable success rate of 19.29% across the set of 22 instances, outperforming other algorithms. Similarly, for $\alpha = 0.06$, $\tau_{limit} = 0.06 \times n \times m$ and 38 instances across three algorithms, we have 114 simulated test problems. This comparative analysis shows that the ABC_NEH algorithm achieved 26 better results compared to other algorithms, with a success rate of 22.80%. Also, for $\alpha = 0.09$, $\tau_{limit} = 0.09 \times n \times m$, and 38 instances across three approaches, we have 114 simulated test problems. The ABC_NEH algorithm achieves a success rate of 20.17% across a set of 23 instances, outperforming other algorithms.

Overall, the ABC_NEH algorithm exhibits strong performance, achieving a success rate of 20.76% across 342 tests for $\alpha = 0.03$, $\alpha = 0.06$, and $\alpha = 0.09$ for instance size with n ranging from 10 to 190 and m for 5 and 10. It outperformed the other two metaheuristics, with the minimum value recorded being 3.21% obtained by MBO_NEH. From this last result, we can confirm that the algorithm ABC_NEH is an effective method for solving the PFSSP scheduling problem.

The second analysis examines how the objective function value varies when the weighting coefficient α changes for different metaheuristics. The figure below illustrates the progression of the objective function value about the weighting coefficient α to be optimized. In the plot Figure 5 The evolution of the objective function value as a function of processing time CPU time for the instance size 20×10 is represented in (a) and the instance size 30×10 is presented in (b) by choosing the value of α = 0.03. This instance can serve as a reference to represent the performance across different instances.

We conduct five replications of tests and we only keep the best result obtained. From the plot, we can observe that the artificial bee colony algorithm, based on the NEH algorithm, achieves the best result compared to the other two metaheuristics. In case(a), the algorithm achieves a final value of 4400 units of time, while in case (b), it achieves 3550 units of time. It is worth noting that the ABC NEH algorithm reaches its stable limit quickly, as seen in plot (a) at $\tau_{\text{limit}} = 0.03 \times 20 \times 10$ CPU seconds and in plot (b) at $\tau_{\text{limit}} = 0.03 \times 30 \times 10$ CPU seconds.

It is worth noting that increasing the population size tends to yield better results, indicating the importance of this parameter. Similarly, the values of ρ and the step length in the neighborhood structure need to be increased by the size of the simulated instance for the ABC_NEH algorithm to achieve successful outcomes. In this study, our attention is solely directed towards the population size and the neighborhood system.

Table 6. The total tardiness value of various problems.

n×m	$\alpha = 0.03$			$\alpha = 0.06$			$\alpha = 0.09$		
	ABC_NEH	GA_ANN	MBO_NEH	ABC_NEH	GA_ANN	MBO_NEH	ABC_NEH	GA_ANN	MBO_NEH
10×5	322	322	323	281	285	293	276	282	276
10×10	717	717	717	658	658	658	441	444	441
20×5	3733	3818	3862	3804	3847	3935	3687	2824	3687

continued on following page

116

Table 6. Continued

n×m	α = 0.03			α = 0.06			α = 0.09		
	ABC_NEH	GA_ANN	MBO_NEH	ABC_NEH	GA_ANN	MBO_NEH	ABC_NEH	GA_ANN	MBO_NEH
20×10	4378	4505	4586	4458	4540	4448	1481	1517	1503
30×5	8250	8459	8414	8205	8406	8324	8204	8496	8335
30×10	3247	3357	3301	3671	3717	3731	3517	3633	3569
40×5	16014	16282	16298	16008	16264	16189	15849	16208	16142
40×10	6336	6443	6413	6759	6866	6850	6357	6493	6464
50×5	24675	25066	24924	24473	24954	24686	24472	24703	24577
50×10	10470	10591	10691	10410	10515	10533	10549	10733	10732
60×5	38864	39673	39257	39152	39274	39635	38978	38645	38966
60×10	15279	15349	15561	15227	15457	15357	15211	15376	15296
70×5	19918	19836	20015	19185	19336	19215	19075	19186	19148
70×10	56902	56837	58121	57254	57281	58308	55202	56177	55838
80×5	26473	26481	26583	24242	24249	24356	25365	25434	25342
80×10	77319	76668	77954	77061	76842	77539	76356	77623	76916
90×5	88829	88509	88760	88212	87800	88999	88003	88524	88090
90×10	97916	97207	98781	96482	958251	95588	96979	96468	97383
100×5	110236	109801	110992	108981	109453	109394	108561	109397	108822
100×10	117832	115615	117170	116836	116918	118074	115617	114244	115606
110×5	135818	135440	135859	134453	134576	135127	134389	134694	134496
110×10	145841	145398	147870	145245	144946	147277	144640	146583	144988
120×5	156379	157411	158246	157178	155749	158150	155339	155244	155393
120×10	167110	162829	167752	168220	170775	169286	164746	167930	167806
130×5	69427	68486	69605	69739	70139	69730	68944	68818	69064
130×10	73470	73694	74153	72696	72537	73472	71175	70984	71495
140×5	75424	74810	75966	78961	78887	79021	79602	79497	79023
140×10	85537	85838	86193	88587	88818	88836	83990	84274	84397
150×5	93192	92585	93477	91868	91273	91894	91284	91430	91445
150 ×10	96901	97755	98159	98738	99035	99272	95604	95263	96296
160×5	106860	109008	107354	104871	105057	104977	104737	106216	105061
160×10	114923	115124	116268	112505	112640	112889	113758	112712	114597
170×5	119884	120199	119545	117430	116811	117529	119092	118819	119483
170×10	127400	128763	127632	123396	125087	124472	127152	126796	128221
180×5	136081	134551	136616	131481	130521	131150	129087	129874	129130

continued on following page

Table 6. Continued

n×m	α = 0.03			α = 0.06			α = 0.09		
	ABC_NEH	GA_ANN	MBO_NEH	ABC_NEH	GA_ANN	MBO_NEH	ABC_NEH	GA_ANN	MBO_NEH
180×10	143304	144952	144599	142300	143361	143903	139979	139968	140388
190×5	149447	148702	151831	150053	151148	149445	143290	143009	143929
190×10	159424	160566	160332	156898	157527	157828	159918	160613	161096

Figure 5. Variation of the objective function value as a functions of CPU time.

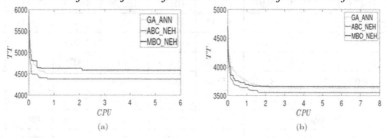

5. CONCLUSION

This work proposes three population-based metaheuristics algorithm to optimize manufacturing flow shop scheduling problems. The objective of minimizing total tardiness. The population-based metaheuristics are GA_ANN, MBO_NEH, and ABC _NEH using the NEH (Nawaz, Enscore, and Ham) and ANN (Artificial Neural Network). A set of neighborhood system exploration procedures has been employed to enhance the diversifying the neighbor solution space. The efficiency of our method is tested through a comparative simulation study, which includes a series of tests on instances of varying sizes based on the number of machines and jobs. Through extensive simulations on various instances, it is evident that the ABC_NEH algorithm, which combines the population-based artificial bee colony approach with the NEH heuristic, consistently outperforms other algorithms. This clear dominance highlights the effectiveness of the ABC_NEH algorithm in solving the permutation flow shop scheduling problem. Indeed, the ABC_NEH metaheuristic demonstrates a success rate of 20.76% and achieves a minimum value recorded is 3.21%.

As a perspective of this work, one can use both approximate and exact methods while also integrating additional constraints such as blocking and machine unavailability. Moreover, examining various optimization criteria, including energy efficiency and production costs, and assessing machine performance in the scheduling process. Additionally, developing and implementing new local search algorithms to improve the quest for optimal or near-optimal solutions to the problems under investigation can be interesting for future researches.

REFERENCES

Allahverdi, A., & Aydilek, H. (2015). The two stage assembly flowshop scheduling problem to minimize total tardiness. *Journal of Intelligent Manufacturing*, 26, 225–237.

Allali, K., Aqil, S., & Belabid, J. (2022). Distributed no-wait flow shop problem with sequence dependent setup time: Optimization of makespan and maximum tardiness. *Simulation Modelling Practice and Theory*, 116, 102455.

Aqil, S., & Allali, K. (2021). On a bi-criteria flow shop scheduling problem under constraints of blocking and sequence dependent setup time. *Annals of Operations Research*, 296(1), 615–637.

Cao, J., Guan, Z., Yue, L., Ullah, S., & Sherwani, R. A. K. (2020). A bottleneck degreebased migrating birds optimization algorithm for the pcb production scheduling. *IEEE Access : Practical Innovations, Open Solutions*, 8, 209579–209593.

Cui, Z., & Gu, X. (2015). An improved discrete artificial bee colony algorithm to minimize the makespan on hybrid flow shop problems. *Neurocomputing*, 148, 248–259.

Dong, X., Huang, H., & Chen, P. (2009). An iterated local search algorithm for the permutation flowshop problem with total flowtime criterion. *Computers & Operations Research*, 36(5), 1664–1669.

Duman, E., Uysal, M., & Alkaya, A. F. (2012). Migrating birds optimization: A new metaheuristic approach and its performance on quadratic assignment problem. *Information Sciences*, 217, 65–77.

Fernandez-Viagas, V., Valente, J. M., & Framinan, J. M. (2018). Iterated-greedy-based algorithms with beam search initialization for the permutation flowshop to minimise total tardiness. *Expert Systems with Applications*, 94, 58–69.

Framinan, J. M., Gupta, J. N., & Leisten, R. (2004). A review and classification of heuristics for permutation flow-shop scheduling with makespan objective. *The Journal of the Operational Research Society*, 55(12), 1243–1255.

Gelders, L. F., & Sambandam, N. (1978). Four simple heuristics for scheduling a flow-shop. *International Journal of Production Research*, 16(3), 221–231.

Gmys, J., Mezmaz, M., Melab, N., & Tuyttens, D. (2020). A computationally efficient branchand-bound algorithm for the permutation flow-shop scheduling problem. *European Journal of Operational Research*, 284(3), 814–833.

Graham, R. L., Lawler, E. L., Lenstra, J. K., & Kan, A. R. (1979). Optimization and approximation in deterministic sequencing and scheduling: a survey. In *Annals of discrete mathematics* (Vol. 5, pp. 287–326). Elsevier.

Jin, F., Song, S., & Wu, C. (2007). An improved version of the neh algorithm and its application to large-scale flow-shop scheduling problems. *IIE Transactions*, 39(2), 229–234.

Karaboga, D., & Basturk, B. (2007). A powerful and efficient algorithm for numerical function optimization: Artificial bee colony (abc) algorithm. *Journal of Global Optimization*, 39, 459–471.

Karacan, I., Senvar, O., & Bulkan, S. (2023). A novel parallel simulated annealing methodology to solve the no-wait flow shop scheduling problem with earliness and tardiness objectives. *Processes (Basel, Switzerland)*, 11(2), 454.

Kumar, H. & Giri, S. (2019). A flow shop scheduling algorithm based on artificial neural network.

Kumar, H., & Giri, S. (2020). Optimisation of makespan of a flow shop problem using multi layer neural network. *International Journal of Computing Science and Mathematics*, 11(2), 107–122.

Li, H., Gao, K., Duan, P.-Y., Li, J.-Q., & Zhang, L. (2022). An improved artificial bee colony algorithm with q-learning for solving permutation flow- shop scheduling problems. *IEEE Transactions on Systems, Man, and Cybernetics. Systems*, 53(5), 2684–2693.

Lian, Z., Gu, X., & Jiao, B. (2008). A novel particle swarm optimization algorithm for permutation flow-shop scheduling to minimize makespan. Chaos, Solitons &amp. *Fractals*, 35(5), 851–861.

Nawaz, M., Enscore, E.Jr, & Ham, I. (1983). A heuristic algorithm for the m-machine, n-job flow-shop sequencing problem. *Omega*, 11(1), 91–95.

Nejjarou, O., Aqil, S., & Lahby, M. (2023). Inspired nature meta-heuristics minimizing total tardiness for manufacturing flow shop scheduling under setup time constraint. In *International Conference on Digital Technologies and Applications*. Springer.

Onwubolu, G. & Davendra, D. (2006). Scheduling flow shops using differential evolution algorithm. European Journal of Operational Research, 171(2):674–692.

Onwubolu, G. C., & Mutingi, M. (1999). Genetic algorithm for minimizing tardiness in flow-shop scheduling. Production Planning &amp. *Control*, 10(5), 462–471.

Pan, J. C.-H., Chen, J.-S., & Chao, C.-M. (2002). Minimizing tardiness in a two-machine flow shop. *Computers & Operations Research*, 29(7), 869–885.

Radha Ramanan, T., Sridharan, R., Shashikant, S. K., & Haq, A. N. (2011). An artificial neural network based heuristic for flow shop scheduling problems. *Journal of Intelligent Manufacturing*, 22, 279–288.

Rahman, H., Janardhanan, M., Chuen, L., & Ponnambalam, S. (2021). Flowshop scheduling with sequence dependent setup times and batch delivery in supply chain. Computers &amp. *Industrial Engineering (American Institute of Industrial Engineers)*, 158, 107378.

Rouhani, S., Fathian, M., Jafari, M., & Akhavan, P. (2010). Solving the problem of flow shop scheduling by neural network approach. *Networked Digital Technologies: Second International Conference, NDT 2010, Prague, Czech Republic, July 7-9, 2010Proceedings*, 2(Part II), 172–183.

Sadki, H., Aqil, S., Belabid, J., & Allali, K. (2024). Multi-objective optimization flow shop scheduling problem solving the makespan and total flow time with sequence independent setup time. *Journal of Advanced Manufacturing Systems*, 23(01), 163–184.

Sadki, H., Belabid, J., Aqil, S., & Allali, K. (2021). On permutation flow shop scheduling problem with sequence-independent setup time and total flow time. In *International Conference on Advanced Technologies for Humanity*. Springer International Publishing.

Sioud, A., & Gagne, C. (2018). Enhanced migrating birds optimization algorithm for the permutation flow shop problem with sequence dependent setup times. *European Journal of Operational Research*, 264(1), 66–73.

Ta, Q., Billaut, J.-C., & Bouquard, J.-L. (2018). Matheuristic algorithms for minimizing total tardiness in the m-machine flow-shop scheduling problem. *Journal of Intelligent Manufacturing*, 29, 617–628.

Tang, L., Liu, W., & Liu, J. (2005). A neural network model and algorithm for the hybrid flow shop scheduling problem in a dynamic environment. *Journal of Intelligent Manufacturing*, 16, 361–370.

Ulker, E., & Tongur, V. (2017). Migrating birds optimization (mbo) algorithm to solve knapsack problem. *Procedia Computer Science*, 111, 71–76.

Vallada, E., & Ruiz, R. (2010). Genetic algorithms with path relinking for the minimum tardiness permutation flowshop problem. *Omega*, 38(1-2), 57–67.

Vallada, E., Ruiz, R., & Minella, G. (2008). Minimising total tardiness in the m-machine flowshop problem: A review and evaluation of heuristics and metaheuristics. *Computers & Operations Research*, 35(4), 1350–1373.

Yang, S., & Xu, Z. (2021). Intelligent scheduling for permutation flow shop with dynamic job arrival via deep reinforcement learning. In 2021 IEEE 5th Advanced Information Technology, Electronic and Automation Control Conference (IAEAC). IEEE.

Yenisey, M. M., & Yagmahan, B. (2014). Multi-objective permutation flow shop scheduling problem: Literature review, classification and current trends. *Omega*, 45, 119–135.

Yu, A. J., & Seif, J. (2016). Minimizing tardiness and maintenance costs in flow shop scheduling by a lower-bound-based ga. *Computers & Industrial Engineering*, 97, 26–40.

Zobolas, G., Tarantilis, C. D., & Ioannou, G. (2009). Minimizing makespan in permutation flow shop scheduling problems using a hybrid metaheuristic algorithm. Computers &amp. *Operations Research*, 36(4), 1249–1267.

Chapter 6
Multi–Objective Optimization of Traditional Feature Selection Methods

Hetavi Dilip Mehta

Dwarkadas J. Sanghvi College of Engineering, India

Ramchandra Mangrulkar

https://orcid.org/0000-0002-9020-0713

Dwarkadas J. Sanghvi College of Engineering, India

ABSTRACT

Feature selection is crucial in data analytics, as it helps identify the most relevant features for modeling. This improves efficiency and interpretability by reducing data dimensionality. Conventional methods optimize a single criterion, such as accuracy or information gain. However, these methods may not fully capture the complexity of real-world problems with multiple competing objectives. Recently, multi-objective optimization techniques have been applied to traditional algorithms, offering a framework for optimizing feature subsets that balance several objectives, such as precision and robustness. However, determining the most efficient algorithm for a specific dataset is challenging. This chapter aims to provide practitioners with a detailed examination of various multi-objective feature selection approaches, including their strengths, weaknesses, and a case study. By understanding the benefits of considering multiple objectives, professionals can apply these advanced methods to research projects, decision-making, and real-world data analytics problems.

DOI: 10.4018/979-8-3693-5231-1.ch006

INTRODUCTION

Vilfredo Pareto proposed multi-objective optimization as a mathematical field which can be applied in the realm of decision-making. It focuses on solving problems that require concurrent optimization of two or more objective functions. Generally, these problems concern optimizing objectives that exhibit conflicting nature, whereby improvement to one objective implies the expense of another. Such problems do not provide a single best solution for all objectives, rather a set of optimal solutions are obtained which represent the most efficient trade-offs possible among the conflicting objectives that are considered. This type of optimization problem can be used by professionals in various fields, such as mathematics, engineering, economics, aviation, automotive, and many others.

Elements of Multi-Objective Optimization Problem

The components of a multi-objective optimization (MOO) problem serve to collectively define the problem and direct the exploration for Pareto-optimal solutions. These components are comprised of the following:

Decision Variables. They refer to the parameters that are manipulated by a multi-objective optimization algorithm in order to seek optimal solutions. Decision variables often have a physical interpretation in the context of the problem. For example, in a manufacturing optimization problem, decision variables could represent production quantities, energy utilization, or material allocation. More variables may result in a larger search space, which may increase the computational complexity associated with the optimization process. A careful selection of decision-making factors is crucial as they have a direct impact on the final outcome of the problem. Thorough deliberation and precise definition of decision variables are essential for formulating an accurate and effective multi-objective optimization problem.

Objective Functions. In the context of multi-objective optimization (MOO), multiple objective functions are defined, each representing a different criterion or aspect of the given problem. The optimization process is guided by the quantification of objectives in a mathematical manner, taking into account the choice variables and problem context. This quantification facilitates the search for solutions that achieve the best possible balance among them. Objectives can be assigned weights to accurately represent their relative influence on the problem in question. Each objective function pertains to a direction of optimization, which is either minimization or maximization. For example, in the context of a manufacturing optimization problem, an objective function would aim to maximize production quantities while another would be focused on minimizing energy utilization. In multi-objective optimization, the primary challenge is to find a set of optimal solutions that consider the trade-offs between conflicting objectives, while ensuring that no single solution dominates the others.

Constraints. Constraints are mathematical expressions that involve decision variables and are used to describe the constraints, boundaries, and conditions that solutions must adhere to. Constraints are used to define the feasible region within the decision space. This region represents an array of valid solutions that satisfy the requirements of the problem. Any solution that fails to meet one or more constraints is deemed infeasible and is hence eliminated from further consideration. Constraints often have a physical interpretation. In the context of the manufacturing optimization problem, constraints can be defined involving many factors such as the availability of materials, production capacity, and equipment efficiency. Constraints are of utmost importance in multi-objective optimization (MOO) since they are crucial in ensuring the practicality and feasibility of solutions. These constraints interact with the objective functions to establish the feasible region, where solutions must strike a balance among many conflicting objectives.

Feasible Region. The feasible region defines the space within which the decision variables must lie to be regarded as feasible solutions. Infeasible solutions, which are beyond the feasible region, are excluded from consideration throughout the optimization process. The feasible area is defined as the set of points that satisfy all constraints, including both equality and inequality constraints. The feasible region can introduce trade-offs between constraints and objectives. By relaxing a single constraint, it is possible to get enhancements in specific objectives; nevertheless, this action may have adverse effects on other objectives. The concept of feasibility refers to the set of limitations that solutions must comply to in order to be deemed viable. Feasibility plays a crucial role in directing the optimization process towards identifying Pareto-optimal solutions that satisfy the constraints associated with the problem.

Formulating a Multi-Objective Optimization Problem

Formulating a multi-objective optimization (MOO) problem entail defining the key components (decision variables, objective functions, and constraints) in a way that captures the trade-offs among multiple conflicting objectives (Gunantara, 2018).

1. Identify the decision variables: This includes assigning symbols to represent each decision variable and determining its type (continuous, discrete, mixed).
2. Define objective functions: Identify the objectives that need to be optimized, even though they are conflicting. Formulate a mathematical expression for each objective function and specify the direction of optimization i.e., minimization or maximization.

3. Specify constraints: Formulate mathematical expressions – equality or inequality – for each constraint, based on the decision variables.
4. Combine objectives and constraints: Combining the objective functions and constraints is a requisite step while formulating a multi-objective optimization problem. The general form is:

Minimize/Maximize $F = \{f_1(x), f_2(x), ..., f_n(x)\}$ (Gunantara, 2018)
Subject to:
$$g_1(x) \leq 0; g_2(x) \leq 0; ... ; g_m(x) \leq 0$$
$$h_1(x) = 0; h_2(x) = 0; ... ; h_p(x) = 0$$
where x is the vector of decision variables, F is the set of all objective functions $f_k(x)$, $g_i(x)$ denote the inequality constraints, while $h_j(x)$ correspond to the equality constraints.

1. Assign weights: If some objectives are more important than others, assign weights to the objective functions to reflect their relative priorities.
2. Define feasible region: This establishes the boundaries within which the optimization will occur.

Now, the formulated problem can be solved for set of optimal solutions, which can be achieved with the help of any multi-objective optimization algorithm.

Pareto Optimality. The theory of Pareto optimality was initially introduced by Vilfredo Pareto within the field of economics. However, the concept exhibits widespread relevance across a variety of different fields, encompassing engineering, economics, finance, healthcare, and various other domains, owing to its foundational role in the sphere of multi-objective optimization. The framework offers a systematic approach for managing complex decision problems that involve competing objectives. This enables decision-makers to analyze and comprehend the compromises involved, facilitating informed decision-making based on their preferences.

Pareto optimality (or Pareto efficiency) refers to a condition in which resource allocation is most effective, so that enhancing one criterion does not result in a deterioration of other criteria. (M. C. Kennedy et al., 2007). Pareto optimality aptly captures the inherent trade-offs that arise from addressing many objectives simultaneously. A solution qualifies as Pareto-optimal when it is not possible to enhance any single objective without adversely impacting another objective. This suggests that a Pareto-optimal solution exhibits the quality of not being superior to any other solution in the given set, rendering it a distinct and valuable point of compromise. The set of Pareto-optimal solutions constitutes a non-dominated front within the objective space. Solutions present on this front represent potential trade-offs between competing objectives. Convexity of the Pareto front signifies that no solution within the front is superlative among all solutions across the entire objective space. The decision-maker possesses the power to select the best alternative from the Pareto front considering the demands and priorities of the problem at hand.

Various techniques, such as Multi-Objective Differential Evolution (MODE), Multi-Objective Particle Swarm Optimization (MOPSO), and Non-dominated Sorting Genetic Algorithms (NSGA), have been specifically developed to identify Pareto-optimal solutions for problems that require multi-objective optimization. As optimization algorithms evolve, they aim to enrich the quality and expand the coverage of the Pareto front. The aforementioned algorithms explore the decision space to determine solutions that are not dominated by others and gradually build the Pareto front.

RELATED WORKS

Single-Objective Feature Selection

The recent years have witnessed a substantial rise in the focus on feature selection as a vital step in pre-processing data used for machine learning and data analysis. This section provides an exhaustive review of the existing literary works associated with single-objective feature selection. It seeks to explain the evolution of techniques in this field and their impact in enhancing both the performance and interpretability of models.

Filter Methods

Filter methods represent an initial approach to feature selection, wherein the evaluation of features is conducted independently of the learning process. The concept of utilizing correlation and statistical tests for feature ranking was first established in the seminal dissertations of (Kohavi & John, n.d.). Furthermore, (Guyon & De, 2003) conducted a comprehensive assessment on different filter algorithms, highlighting their computational efficiency and model-agnostic characteristics. Filter methods are commonly used as a fundamental approach to assess the significance of features. However, it is necessary to note that these methods may not thoroughly capture the interactions between features.

Wrapper Methods

The concept of wrapper techniques was first presented by (Kohavi & John, n.d.). These methods involve treating feature selection as an optimization problem as well as incorporating the performance of the chosen machine learning algorithm as the fitness function for selecting features. (Kohavi & John, n.d.) underscored the significance of considering the correlation between feature selection and the learning strategy opted. However, it also highlighted some of the limitations, such as computational cost and the risk of overfitting to a particular learning algorithm. Following this, (Brownlee, 2011) introduced Clever Algorithm, a parallel particle swarm optimization toolkit, which enabled the application of wrapper methods on various datasets. Wrapper methods provide an excellent technique for evaluating the impact of feature subsets on model performance.

Recent Advancements and Challenges

Most recent research studies have proposed extended feature selection techniques wherein domain-specific knowledge has been integrated, ensemble methods have been explored, and high-dimensional datasets have been addressed. In their study, (Saeys et al., 2007) conducted a thorough examination of feature selection methods in the sector of bioinformatics. The significance of these techniques in enhancing the performance and interpretability of models when dealing with intricate biological data is very well highlighted in the paper. Nevertheless, there still persist issues that need to be addressed in this domain. These challenges include the curse of dimensionality, which refers to the difficulty of analyzing and interpreting data in high-dimensional spaces, as well as the necessity of efficiently managing noisy or redundant attributes to provide accurate and reliable results. The studies discussed above have made substantial contributions to the field of feature selection, with a primary emphasis on optimizing a single objective.

Multi-Objective Optimization Methods

This section offers a comprehensive overview of laudable developments and contemporary advancements that have influenced multi-objective optimization. The article emphasizes notable contributions within the discipline and presents research publications that have had a substantial impact on its progress.

Multi-Objective Genetic Algorithms

Genetic Algorithms (GA) are computational algorithms that draw inspiration from the principles of natural selection. These algorithms aim to solve complex problems by iteratively evolving viable solutions through time, with the ultimate objective of identifying the optimal solution. (Goldberg & Holland, 1988) offers a thorough overview of genetic algorithms, elucidating the fundamental concepts of natural selection and evolution, and their use in the context of optimization problems. The proposed utilization of crossover and mutation operators in genetic algorithms enables quick traversal of the search space and ensures preservation of diversity within the population.

The NSGA-II algorithm, which was proposed by (Deb et al., 2002) in a seminal publication, represents a significant contribution to the domain of multi-objective optimization. It addresses the challenges of optimizing problems with multiple conflicting objectives. It also introduces an innovative non-dominated sorting algorithm that effectively classifies solutions into distinct Pareto fronts, preserving the best solutions while maintaining diversity. The NSGA-II algorithm provides a reliable and scalable methodology for addressing complex multi-objective problems. (Hamdani et al., 2007) provides a comprehensive exploration of multi-objective feature selection using NSGA-II, highlighting its advantages over traditional single-objective methods, and demonstrating its efficacy through empirical validation. The proposed framework offers a principled approach to address the inherent trade-offs in feature selection, paving the way for improved model interpretability, generalization, and scalability in various machine learning applications.

(L. E. A. Santana & Canuto, 2012) proposes a bi-objective genetic algorithm that simultaneously optimizes two criteria: maximizing classification accuracy and minimizing the number of selected features. Further advancing the study of the MOGA technique, (Spolaôr et al., 2017) employs Pareto dominance principles within genetic algorithms to identify a set of non-dominated solutions, each representing a different trade-off between objectives. This approach ensures that no single solution is considered best across all objectives, allowing for a diverse set of potential feature subsets to be evaluated. (Spolaôr et al., 2011) discusses the significant advantages over traditional methods by simultaneously optimizing multiple criteria, leading to more efficient and accurate models. It highlights the potential of MOGAs in feature selection, providing a robust method for handling multiple criteria and offering valuable insights into the benefits of multi-objective optimization in machine learning tasks.

Multi-Objective Particle Swarm Optimization

(J. Kennedy & Eberhart, 1995) proposed particle swarm optimization as a technique that is especially applicative for feature selection tasks, owing to its competency to effectively traverse extensive search spaces. (Coello et al., 2004) laid the foundation for Multi-Objective Particle Swarm Optimization (MOPSO), emphasizing the handling of multiple conflicting objectives in particle swarm optimization. (Zhang & Li, 2007) extended the concept of MOPSO by employing a decomposition approach to break down multi-objective problems into various single-objective sub-problems. The proposed method leverages decomposition-based hyper-heuristics to optimize multiple conflicting objectives simultaneously. (L. A. Santana & Canuto, 2013) underscores the potential of using metaheuristic algorithms like PSO for feature selection that can enhance the performance of ensemble systems by selecting an optimal subset of features, thereby contributing to the broader field of multi-objective optimization in feature selection methods.

(Parsopoulos & Vrahatis, 1 C.E.) discusses hybridization of PSO with other metaheuristics and emphasizes the algorithm's robustness and efficiency in finding diverse solutions along the Pareto front, making it particularly suitable for complex feature selection tasks. (Zhu & Han, 2021) demonstrates that the hybrid approach of combining PSO with space decomposition techniques significantly outperforms traditional PSO methods in terms of finding diverse Pareto-optimal solutions, making it a promising technique for complex multi-objective optimization problems in feature selection. (Vashishtha et al., 2020) proposes modifications to the particle update rules of the standard PSO algorithm, providing a robust method for handling the trade-offs between different objectives in feature selection tasks.

Multi-Objective Optimization in Feature Selection

(Zhang & Li, 2007) centers around the topic of multi-objective feature selection (MOFS) using decomposition-based hyper-heuristics. Instead of a single objective (e.g., accuracy), it considers multiple objectives, such as accuracy, dimensionality reduction, and robustness. The authors apply the principles of balancing trade-offs between conflicting objectives to feature selection, highlighting the potential benefits of employing multi-objective optimization techniques to obtain feature subsets that are both resilient and interpretable. (Deb et al., 2021) discusses the hybrid approach of integrating surrogate modelling with multi-objective optimization. The deployment of surrogate models for efficient approximation of the Pareto front is introduced, hence enhancing the computational feasibility of MOFS.

(Siedlecki & Sklansky, 2011) provides a comprehensive overview of various automatic feature selection methods like filter method, wrapper methos, and embedded methods, highlighting their importance in improving machine learning model accuracy, reducing overfitting, and enhancing interpretability. It emphasizes the need for continued research and innovation particularly regarding the integration of feature selection with advanced machine learning techniques, such as deep learning, and the development of more robust and scalable algorithms.

The insights provided by (Al-Tashi et al., 2020) are highlight how MOFS can enhance traditional feature selection methods, with a particular focus on evolutionary algorithms such as Genetic Algorithms (GAs) and Particle Swarm Optimization (PSO). By emphasizing the advancements and ongoing challenges, it sets the stage for exploring hybrid MOFS strategies in greater detail. The integration of MOFS with traditional methods such as wrapper, filter, and embedded techniques can significantly improve their performance, making feature selection more robust and efficient.

Challenges and Emerging Trends

(Al-Tashi et al., 2020) presents an extensive review of the potential challenges associated with the multi-objective feature selection problem. Additionally, it offers a critical analysis of the many strategies employed to address this problem. (L. Li et al., n.d.) focuses on the issue of scalability in MOFS. The authors propose an algorithm that is specifically designed to handle scalability concerns, using dominance and roughness-based selection strategies. (Yuan et al., 2014) underscores the substantial impact of noise in data on the performance of feature selection algorithms. (Zhou et al., 2023) studies multi-objective optimization techniques to select pertinent features within deep learning models, addressing the challenge of feature selection in complex deep neural networks.

The subsequent sections emphasize the importance of multi-objective feature selection, followed by the analyses of the strengths and limitations of four MOFS approaches along with a real-world case study for each. This chapter aims to underscore the importance of MOFS and to provide a comprehensive review of several multi-objective feature selection algorithms, challenges of MOFS methods, comparison between MOFS and SOFS.

IMPORTANCE MULTI-OBJECTIVE OPTIMIZATION FOR FEATURE SELECTION

Limitations of Single-Objective Feature Selection

Single-objective feature selection (SOFS) methodologies enable the identification of relevant features from large datasets, enhancing the interpretability and efficiency of models. Nevertheless, these methodologies possess inherent constraints that could potentially hinder their applicability in specific situations.

The SOFS approach may fail to consider those subsets that have the potential to enhance several aspects of a model simultaneously. Consequently, useful solutions that optimize multiple objectives may be inadvertently omitted. The choice of the single objective is often context-dependent and subjective, making SOFS inflexible and dependent on problem context. Additionally, these methodologies evaluate the relevance of each feature independently, disregarding the potential interdependencies across features, which are frequently observed in real-world datasets. SOFS algorithms typically employ heuristic search methods to find the best feature subset. Nevertheless, if the initial selection fails to yield substantial enhancements in the selected objective, these algorithms may become bound to local optima.

Another significant drawback of employing algorithms that optimize a single objective, often pertaining to model performance metrics, is the risk of overfitting (Kohavi & Sommerfield, 1995) . The selected features may exhibit a high degree of specificity to the training set by capturing noise and idiosyncrasies rather than the underlying patterns. Overfitting occurs when a model is excessively sensitive to variations in the training data or outliers, resulting in a disproportionate influence on the model's predictions. This could lead to the production of unreliable and unstable results, undermining the model's practicality.

The scalability of SOFS algorithms may be compromised when confronted with high-dimensional datasets that encompass numerous features (Bolón-Canedo et al., 2018). The pursuit for the most optimal feature subset can become computationally intensive as the number of features increases. Such methods that require evaluation of each subset might result in exponential time complexity. They also demand substantial computer resources, encompassing both memory capacity and processing capabilities. Moreover, it is essential to note that the feature subset selected by SOFS for a particular model may not exhibit strong adaptability when implemented in other machine learning techniques. Consequently, the selected features may lack compatibility, limiting their broader applicability.

Advantages of Multi-Objective Feature Selection

In a medical diagnosis application, focusing exclusively on optimal classification accuracy might lead to the selection of a feature subset that is difficult for medical practitioners to interpret. A better solution might involve a compromise between accuracy and interpretability. As we know, optimizing a single objective may lead to suboptimal feature subsets in multi-criteria scenarios due to its inability to effectively handle trade-offs between different objectives.

In contrast, multi-objective optimization aims to find results that balance multiple, and often competing, objectives simultaneously. An objective function is formulated to optimize a system by integrating various objectives into a unified composite objective function. A variety of techniques have been suggested for addressing composite objective functions. Each optimization algorithm requires thorough exploration of the search space to identify a set of suitable solutions. This set of solutions allows practitioners to select a solution from the set that aligns with their specific priorities or preferences, effectively balancing objectives according to the problem context.

Multi-objective feature selection (MOFS) can identify feature subsets that are robust to noisy data (Dong et al., 2020). The feature selection process aims to identify and prioritize those features that have a noteworthy influence on the desired objectives, while simultaneously reducing the impact of irrelevant or noisy features. Robust models built with MOFS are less sensitive to outliers or small fluctuations in the data. They offer stable predictions, making them accurate and reliable machine learning models. In addition, the inclusion of feature selection techniques in machine learning models helps mitigate the danger of overfitting by excluding noisy characteristics that may contribute to the development of overfitted models.

As opposed to single-objective feature selection, MOFS techniques often explicitly consider feature dependencies. While assessing feature subsets, they consider feature interactions and redundancy. Consequently, MOFS tends to select feature subsets that accurately capture the complex relationships within the data more accurately, thereby resulting in feature subsets that are more informative and effective. Feature interactions are frequently observed in applications of natural language processing (NLP) as feature interactions are common because words or phrases may have different meanings when combined. MOFS can enhance the performance of sentiment analysis (I. S. Ahmad et al., 2019) or language translation models (Jumelet & Zuidema, 2023) by facilitating the selection of feature subsets that effectively capture these intricate relationships.

Evidently, MOFS is adaptable to evolving objectives. As objectives undergo adaptations, MOFS can provide novel Pareto-optimal feature subsets that are in accordance with the updated criteria. Moreover, MOFS method employs a ranking system to determine the significance of features in the optimization of several objectives. This approach provides valuable insights into the relevance of individual characteristics within the chosen subsets.

Algorithms and Approaches for Multi-Objective Feature Selection

Multi-Objective Wrapper Methods

Wrapper methods capture complex interactions between features because they evaluate the impact of each feature in the context of the subset. Multi-objective wrapper methods primarily aim to determine the feature subset that simultaneously optimize numerous objectives that reflect different aspects of model performance (accuracy, precision, recall, etc.). A specific supervised machine learning model or algorithm is employed to evaluate the quality of feature subsets (Nouri-Moghaddam et al., 2021). The process of feature selection involves evaluating different subsets of features by training and testing the chosen model on each subset. Wrapper methods can capture complex feature interactions, as they assess the impact of every feature on model performance in combination with other features. They start with an initial feature subset (empty or the full feature set) and then iteratively add or remove features based on the model's performance. This process continues until certain stopping criteria are met. To avoid overfitting and ensure robustness, wrapper methods employ cross-validation approaches, which involves splitting the data into multiple subsets (e.g., training and validation sets) to evaluate the model's ability to generalize. A Pareto-front is generated, encompassing solutions that represent trade-offs between conflicting objectives. Decision-makers have the liberty to choose a solution from the Pareto front that aligns with their specific priorities or preferences.

Evaluating the performance of multi-objective wrapper methods for feature selection involves a comprehensive approach that includes assessing multiple performance metrics, ensuring robustness through cross-validation, analyzing the Pareto front, performing statistical tests, and using visualizations. This thorough evaluation ensures that the selected feature subsets are not only optimal in terms of the specified objectives but also robust, generalizable, and efficient.

Strengths

Multi-objective wrapper methods are particularly valuable when there are trade-offs between different aspects of model performance, such as accuracy, interpretability, and computational efficiency. These strategies aid in the identification of feature subsets that strike the right balance according to the problem context. Global search strategy, which is adopted by multi-objective wrapper methods, helps identify feature subsets that might be missed by other feature selection methods (Njoku et al., 2023). Practitioners can define and prioritize objectives based on the specific requirements of their application. This adaptability allows for tailoring feature selection to meet specified objectives and constraints. The methods employed yield a Pareto front that offers a transparent representation of the trade-offs between objectives. Allowing practitioners to opt a solution from the Pareto-front that aligns with their priorities empowers them to make informed decisions based on the inherent trade-offs in the problem.

Multi-objective wrapper methods are model agnostic allowing practitioners to select the best appropriate model for their particular problem while still benefiting from the advantages of multi-objective feature selection (Njoku et al., 2023). Feature subsets selected by multi-objective wrapper methods are often robust to changes in data distribution or shifts in problem requirements. Since they consider multiple aspects of performance, they tend to produce solutions that are less sensitive to variations in data. In situations where the relationships between features are intricate and nonlinear, these methods can identify feature subsets that account for these interactions, leading to improved model performance.

Limitations

The effectiveness of multi-objective wrapper methods heavily depends on how well the objectives are defined to represent the problem's goals. Along with this, correctly determining their relative weights can be challenging. Poorly chosen objectives can lead to suboptimal results. Apart from this, the selection of a solution from the Pareto front is often subjective and depends on the practitioner's preferences and priorities. This subjectivity can introduce bias into the feature selection process.

Multi-objective wrapper methods, while theoretically powerful, may have limited real-world applications due to their computational demands and complexity. Generating a Pareto front and depicting probable non-dominated (Pareto-optimal) solutions, can be computationally intensive. This complexity grows significantly with the scope of the feature space, number of objectives, and complexity of the machine learning model. Consequently, multi-objective wrapper methods may not be feasible for large datasets or complex models (Njoku et al., 2023). The advanced optimization techniques employed by multi-objective wrapper methods demand considerable computational resources, including memory and processing power.

The multi-objective optimization process in feature selection may be more challenging when dealing with categorical data. Most multi-objective wrapper methods are designed for continuous feature spaces. Adapting them to handle categorical or mixed-type data can be non-trivial and may require additional pre-processing steps. One-hot encoding is a common approach to handle categorical data, wherein each category is converted into a binary feature (0 or 1). However, this can substantially expand the dimensionality of the dataset. The non-linear relationships and non-convex spaces that can arise from one-hot encoding make it harder to explore the objective space effectively.

Case Study: Multi-Objective Wrapper Methods for Credit Scoring in Banking

Background. Credit scoring is a critical task in the banking industry, as it involves making loan decisions that must effectively consider a range of objectives (Simumba et al., 2021). Banks aim to minimize credit risk while maximizing profitability and ensuring regulatory compliance. Traditional credit scoring models often rely on a single objective, such as minimizing default rates, which can lead to overly conservative lending practices. There exists a risk of algorithmic bias in traditional feature selection methods, which can be overcome by employing multi-objective approaches with one of the objectives being detection and elimination of biases. Hence, the bank decides to utilize multi-objective wrapper algorithm for feature selection as a means to optimize its credit scoring model (Simumba et al., 2022).

Data and Features. The bank collects historical data on loan applicants, including their financial information, credit history, employment status, and demographic data. Features include both numerical variables (e.g., income, credit score) and categorical variables (e.g., employment type, education level).

Multi-Objective Feature Selection.

1. Objective Definition: The bank formulates its objectives as follows:
   - Objective 1 (Default Risk Minimization): Minimize the number of false negatives (applicants wrongly classified as low risk but default) to accurately identify high-risk applicants.
   - Objective 2 (Profit Maximization): Maximize the net profit, which is the difference between interest income and expected default losses.
   - Objective 3 (Fair Lending Practices): Ensure that the model does not discriminate against any protected attribute while maintaining objectives 1 and 2.
2. Feature Subset Evaluation: Multi-objective wrapper methods involve systematic assessment of various feature subsets by training and testing a machine learning model (e.g., a gradient boosting classifier) on each subset. Each subset is evaluated based on the pre-defined objectives.
3. Pareto Front Search: A multi-objective optimization algorithm (e.g., NSGA-II (Hamdani et al., 2007b)) is employed to search for the Pareto front, which represents feature subsets that balance the three objectives. It identifies solutions

that provide trade-offs between objectives, such as including demographic features to ensure fairness yet preserving default risk and profitability.

4. Solution Selection: The bank selects a solution from the Pareto front that aligns with its particular priorities. For instance, it may choose a feature subset that balances fairness with default risk and profitability, ensuring that loan decisions are both equitable and financially sound.

Challenges (Onay & Öztürk, 2018).

1. Data Privacy: Ensuring impartiality of the model while adhering to privacy regulations, such as GDPR, requires careful handling of sensitive information.
2. Model Interpretability: Highly accurate models, especially those using complex algorithms, often suffer from a lack of interpretability.
3. Biasness: Optimizing for maximum predictive performance might lead to the selection of features that are correlated with sensitive attributes (e.g., race, gender), potentially introducing or perpetuating bias.
4. Model Validation: Rigorous model validation and continuous monitoring are needed to assess the model's performance against the defined objectives in real-world scenarios.

Multi-Objective Genetic Algorithm-Based Approaches

Multi-Objective Genetic Algorithm (MOGA) (Saroj & Jyoti, 2014) strategies leverage genetic algorithm, a search and optimization heuristic inspired by natural selection, to address multiple conflicting objectives in feature selection. Like other multiple-objective optimization methods, MOGA starts by establishing multiple objectives that capture different aspects of model performance and feature subset quality. These objectives often include model complexity, classification accuracy, robustness, and interpretability. An initial population of feature subsets needs to be generated either randomly or through heuristic methods. The quality of each feature subset is calculated based on the defined objectives by training and testing machine learning models. The process of selecting feature subsets to create a new generation of solutions is accomplished through the utilization of mechanisms that draw inspiration from natural selection. These mechanisms favor solutions that perform well across multiple objectives. Genetic operators (crossover and mutation) are applied to produce the next generation of solutions from the selected feature subsets. These operations introduce diversity into the population and enable exploration of the search space. A set of non-dominated solutions are generated along the Pareto front and are retained across generations. The algorithm continues to evolve the population for a predefined number of generations or until termination criteria are met. Typical termination criteria include a limit on the number of generations, convergence of the Pareto front, or a user-defined stopping point.

One of the most widely used MOGA technique is Non-dominated Sorting Generic Algorithm II (NSGA-II), which is particularly effective for feature selection because it can handle complex, non-linear relationships between features and the target variable. NSGA-II maintains a population of candidate solutions (feature subsets) that evolve over successive generations. These solutions are ranked based on dominance. A solution dominates another if it is no worse in all objectives and better in at least one.

Strengths

Multi-objective genetic algorithms are model agnostic, meaning they can be applied in conjunction with a wide spectrum of machine learning algorithms. This adaptability allows practitioners to opt for the most suitable model for their specific problem while still benefiting from their advantages. Also, they are highly flexible and adaptable to different feature selection scenarios. Practitioners can define and prioritize objectives based on the specific requirements of their application. This adaptability allows for customization of feature selection to meet diverse goals and constraints (Imani et al., 2023).

Genetic algorithm-based feature selection typically results in feature subsets that exhibit resilience to variations in data distribution. This approach employs global search strategies inspired by natural evolution, such as crossover and mutation. This enables them to explore the feature space more effectively and discover feature subsets that might be missed by other feature selection methods, particularly in high-dimensional spaces. The utilization of genetic operators in these approaches facilitates the exploration of feature subsets that encompass a broad range of potential solutions, hence ensuring diversity in the set of solutions generated, as indicated by the Pareto front (Hamdani et al., 2007b) . By offering a set of Pareto-optimal solutions, MOGA enhances decision support in complex feature selection tasks. Practitioners can explore the trade-offs and select the most suitable solution for their individual requirements, leading to better-informed decision-making.

Moreover, the transparency of the trade-offs between different objectives offered by the Pareto-front aids the practitioners to make informed decisions by selecting the most suitable solution for their specific application.

Limitations

MOGA faces the curse of dimensionality. Exploring a vast search space becomes increasingly challenging and may necessitate an impractically high number of generations and assessments, rendering the optimization process infeasible. The iterative progression of evolving a population over multiple generations, evaluating solutions for multiple objectives, and maintaining a Pareto front proves to be very time-consuming, thus increasing the computational complexity.

The efficacy of this strategy in properly exploring the objective space may be variable. The algorithm's convergence behavior and the quality of the Pareto front can vary depending on factors like population size, mutation rates, and crossover operators. Finding an optimal configuration for these parameters can be a non-trivial task. Furthermore, the parameters (e.g., population size, mutation rate, selection mechanism) of genetic algorithms require parameter fine-tuning for optimal performance. Determining the right parameter settings can be time-consuming and may require expert knowledge.

The effectiveness of MOGA depends on the precise design of genetic operators (crossover and mutation) (Khan & Baig, 2015). Poorly chosen operators can lead to premature convergence, suboptimal solutions, or computational inefficiency. Additionally, this approach may struggle with scalability when dealing with many objectives. The Pareto front may become overcrowded with solutions, making it challenging in discerning distinct trade-offs and choosing the most suitable option.

Case Study: Multi-Objective Genetic Algorithm for Feature Selection in Medical Diagnosis

Background. Medical diagnosis is a critical domain where the selection of relevant features for predictive models is crucial. Inaccurate or overly complex models can lead to misdiagnosis, increased healthcare costs, and patient discomfort. Moreover, a single-objective feature selection method could lead to overfitting. By considering multiple objectives (accuracy, generalizability, interpretability), the resulting models are less likely to overfit and more likely to perform well on new, unseen patient data. Therefore, a healthcare institution decides to leverage multi-objective genetic algorithm - based (MOGAs) feature selection for development of a diagnostic model for a specific disease (Hajimani et al., 2015). The proposed diagnostic model will adopt a patient-centric approach, prioritizing the safety and well-being of individuals.

Data and Features. The institution gathers a comprehensive dataset that includes patient demographics, medical history, and results from various medical tests. This dataset contains mainly numerical and categorical features.

Multi-Objective Feature Selection.

1. Objective Definition: The institution formulates objectives as follows:
   - Objective 1 (Diagnostic Accuracy): Maximize the classification accuracy of the diagnostic model.
   - Objective 2 (Model Simplicity): Minimize the number of selected features to create a model that is simple, interpretable, and requires fewer resources.
   - Objective 3 (Patient Safety): Prioritize features that do not require invasive or expensive tests to minimize healthcare cost and patient discomfort.
2. Population Initialization: An initial population of feature subsets is generated using random sampling or a heuristic method. Each feature subset represents a potential solution.
3. Fitness Evaluation: The quality of each feature subset is determined based on the defined objectives. A machine learning model (e.g., a support vector machine (Hajimani et al., 2015) or decision tree) is trained and tested using the selected feature subset, and performance is assessed across multiple objectives.
4. Selection: Feature subsets are selected to form a new generation of solutions, favoring those that perform well across multiple objectives while balancing diagnostic accuracy, simplicity, and patient safety.
5. Crossover and Mutation: The genetic operators are applied to produce offspring solutions. These operations introduce diversity into the population and enable exploration of the feature space.
6. Pareto-Front Maintenance: A set of Pareto-optimal solutions are mapped on the Pareto-front. Each solution on the Pareto front represents compromises between different objectives. The institution selects a solution from the Pareto front that aligns with their specific priorities.

Challenges (Abdullah et al., 2021).

1. Data Quality: Ensuring data quality and reliability is crucial, as inaccurate, or biased data can lead to suboptimal feature selection and model performance.
2. Ethical Considerations: The institution must carefully consider ethical implications, especially when dealing with patient data, to ensure privacy and compliance with regulations like HIPAA.
3. Validation: Rigorous validation and testing are necessary to assess the generalization of the diagnostic model to new patient cases and different healthcare settings.

4. Data Privacy: The feature selection process requires access to sensitive medical data. Ensuring that this data is kept confidential and secure is critical.

Multi-Objective Particle Swarm Optimization

Particle swarm optimization (PSO) is a very effective algorithm for addressing continuous optimization problems, drawing inspiration from the collective behavior observed in bird flocking or fish schooling. In PSO, each potential solution to an optimization problem is depicted as a particle in a multidimensional search space. All particles have a velocity that determines their traversal inside the search space. This algorithm employs an iterative approach to continuously update the positions and velocities of all particles, enabling them to explore the search space and ulti-mately discover solutions that are either optimal or near-optima. The velocity of each particle is updated based on its best-known position (personal best) and the best-known position among all particles in the swarm (global best). A fitness func-tion assesses the quality of each particle's solution in the search space. It quantifies how well the solution satisfies the optimization objectives.

Similarly, each particle in the MOPSO swarm represents a feature subset (Nguy-en et al., n.d.). The presence or absence of features in the subset is encoded in the particle's position while the velocity vector denotes the speed and direction of the particle's movement in the search space. Particles keep a track of their personal as well as global best-known positions and utilize this information to guide their movement through the search space. Multiple objective functions are defined to evaluate the fitness of each particle based on its performance across all defined ob-jectives. Given its iterative nature, this methodology involves updating the velocities and positions of each particle with the aim of exploration (moving towards global best-known position) and exploitation (following personal best-known position). Exploration aims to find diverse solutions across the entire search space which prevents the algorithm from getting trapped in local optima and ensures that it has a chance to discover potentially better solutions. On the contrary, exploitation focuses on refining and improving the solutions that are already known. It aims to converge toward the best-known solutions and enhance them further.

Maintaining diversity within the population of particles in a MOPSO swarm is essential to prevent premature convergence and facilitate effective exploration of the entire Pareto front effectively. Crowding distance is a common diversity maintenance metric used in MOPSO (Raquel & Naval, 2005). It quantifies how densely particles are distributed in the objective space. Crowding distance is used to prioritize particles for selection and removal. Some MOPSO algorithms employ the utilization of multiple sub-swarms that operate independently and periodically exchange information to introduce diversity. This multi-swarm approach allows for diverse exploration and can help avoid premature convergence.

Strengths

The strength of PSO lies in its competence to efficiently explore the search space by combining both local search (personal best) and global search (global best) strategies. It's a population-based optimization technique that does not require gradient information, making it suitable for solving problems where gradients are unknown or discontinuous.

The MOPSO algorithm indirectly addresses the issue of feature dependencies by promoting the selection of relevant feature subsets that balance objectives and eliminate redundancy. The optimization procedure of MOPSO does not make any assumptions about linearity. Instead, it allows for the discovery of nonlinear relationships between attributes and the target variable. The reason for this is that the optimization process is designed to identify subsets of features that optimize multiple objectives, and these objectives can capture nonlinear feature importance. This is valuable for capturing complex patterns that might be missed by linear feature selection methods.

MOPSO algorithm incorporates methods of preserving diversity within the population of solutions. This prevents premature convergence to a single solution and ensures that a wide range of trade-off solutions is available. One of these mechanisms is elitism (Amoozegar & Minaei-Bidgoli, 2018) which involves preserving the best solutions (non-dominated particles) from the current population to the next generation without modification. These elite solutions are considered as benchmarks of high quality and contribute to maintaining diversity. Elitism guarantees that the best solutions are retained during optimization. MOPSO's diversity and exploration capabilities make it robust to noisy or uncertain data. It can discover solutions that are less sensitive to noise and outliers, leading to more reliable results.

MOPSO can be parallelized for more efficient exploration of the search space (J.-Z. Li et al., 2015). The population of particles can be divided into subsets, with each subset being subjected to individual processing by a separate computing unit. Each subset evolves independently, with its own set of particles, and periodically, these subsets exchange information to share promising solutions. The parallelization of MOPSO is feasible across multiple computing nodes in a distributed computing environment (Arun et al., 2011), such as a cluster or cloud infrastructure. This enables the algorithm to harness significant computational power, making it suitable for large-scale optimization problems.

MOPSO is capable of finding global optimal or near-optimal solutions, provided sufficient exploration is allowed. This makes it suitable for finding the best solutions in complex and high-dimensional spaces. Near-optimal solutions often represent practical and implementable solutions that are closer to real-world feasibility. This makes them valuable for applications in various spheres including engineering, design, and operations.

Limitations

MOPSO requires the tuning of many parameters, including the inertia weight, acceleration coefficients, and population size. The presence of very sensitive parameters can result in variable performance throughout multiple iterations of the algorithm, making it challenging to obtain consistently high-quality solutions. MOPSO algorithm for feature selection typically encompasses several hyperparameters, such as the number of particles, the maximum iteration count, and coefficients associated with the particle motion equation. Tuning these parameters for optimal performance can be challenging and may require substantial trial and error.

Another issue lies in achieving a balance between exploration (searching for new solutions) and exploitation (refining promising solutions). MOPSO may struggle achieving an optimal trade-off, and possibly leading to premature convergence or slow exploration. Evidently, feature selection problems often have non-convex search spaces with multiple local optima. Balancing exploration and exploitation in such spaces requires careful consideration of how to escape local optima while converging to global optima.

MOPSO is inherently designed for continuous optimization problems and may not adequately handle discrete or categorical features. Categorical attributes are not amenable to the continuous movement mechanisms used in MOPSO. This incompatibility can lead to difficulties in representing and updating discrete features. Adapting MOPSO to accommodate discrete features can be complex and may require additional discretization techniques. Additionally, the conversion of features into binary variables might result in the loss of significant information regarding their true influence on the objective functions. This can provide a greater difficulty for the algorithm to distinguish between subtle differences in feature importance.

Case Study: Multi-Objective Particle Swarm Optimization (MOPSO) for Feature Selection in Weather Predictions

Background. Weather prediction is a complex and critical task that relies on various meteorological data sources and models to forecast weather conditions accurately. Feature selection is of utmost importance in enhancing the precision and effectiveness of weather prediction models. This is achieved by finding the meteorological variables that are most pertinent and informative. The aim of this case study is to improve the precision of weather forecasts by accurately choosing the most pertinent meteorological characteristics while simultaneously minimizing the quantity of features employed (Lv & Wang, 2022; Sarangi et al., 2023). MOP-SO considers computational costs, resource usage, and model interpretability as part of the optimization process. It seeks to minimize the number of features while maintaining high predictive power. It increases transparency and trust in weather forecasts, aiding better decision-making.

Dataset and Features. The case study utilizes a historical weather dataset containing various meteorological variables such as temperature, humidity, wind speed, atmospheric pressure, and precipitation, collected over several years. These attributes have continuous numeric values.

Multi-Objective Feature Selection.

1. Objective Definition: The objectives can be formulated as follows:
   - Objective 1 (Accuracy): Maximize prediction accuracy (e.g., minimizing mean squared error).
   - Objective 2 (Dimensionality): Minimize the number of selected features to improve model simplicity and reduce computational costs.
   - Objective 3 (Interpretability): Maximize model interpretability by selecting meteorological features that align with known weather patterns and meteorological principles.
2. Initialization: A population of potential feature subsets is generated. Every subset is a binary vector that indicates selection (1) or non-selection (0) of meteorological features. Velocity vectors are also initialized for each subset, which determine the direction and magnitude of movement in the feature space.
3. Evaluation: The quality of each feature subset is evaluated using a forecasting model. This model is trained and tested on historical weather data.
4. Pareto Dominance: Pareto dominance is used to compare solutions. One solution is considered better than another if it performs better or equivalent in all objectives and strictly better in at least one. Over multiple iterations (generations), the algorithm aims to converge toward a set of non-dominated solutions along the Pareto front.
5. Updating Velocity and Positions: The updates of velocity and position are guided by the trade-offs between objectives. The primary aim of this algorithm is to balance improving forecast accuracy while reducing the number of selected features and ensuring interpretability.

6. Termination: The algorithm runs for a predefined number of generations or until convergence criteria are met. After termination, the array of non-dominated solutions along the Pareto front is analyzed to select the most suitable feature subset(s) based on the problem's specific objectives and priorities.

7. Interpretability Analysis: To ensure that the selected features are interpretable, they are subjected to further analysis to evaluate their alignment with known meteorological principles and their contribution to weather patterns. Features that do not provide meaningful insights or are not relevant to weather prediction can be filtered out.

Challenges (F. Ahmad et al., 2023).

1. Dynamic Data: Weather data is inherently dynamic, with temporal dependencies and varying patterns over time. MOPSO may need adaptations to account for time-dependent feature selection, which is essential for accurate weather forecasting.

2. Real-Time Application: In operational weather forecasting, decisions need to be made in real time. MOPSO-based feature selection should be efficient enough to work within the time constraints of real-time forecasting systems.

3. Limited Domain Knowledge: Effective feature selection often requires domain knowledge. Integrating meteorological expertise into the optimization process can be challenging, especially when domain experts are not familiar with optimization techniques.

4. Environmental Impact: High computational demands for complex models can lead to greater energy consumption and a larger carbon footprint. Thus, a trade-off between these parameters must be maintained.

Other Hybrid Approaches

The following sections provide a concise overview of various other Multi-Objective Feature Selection (MOFS) techniques. This discussion aims to highlight the advancements in the field of MOFS achieved by integrating multiple traditional methods with multi-objective optimization frameworks.

Multi-Objective Feature Selection with Metaheuristics

Metaheuristics are a class of algorithms that are characterized by their iterative nature and reliance on heuristics. These algorithms are designed to effectively navigate through extensive solution spaces to identify high-quality solutions for complex optimization problems (Amarnath & Appavu alias Balamurugan, 2016).

When employed in context to multi-objective feature selection (MOFS), they aim to discover feature subsets that balance multiple objectives effectively. Several commonly used metaheuristics for MOFS include Simulated Annealing, Ant Colony Optimization (ACO), and Differential Evolution, among others (Agrawal et al., 2021). The selection of algorithm is reliant upon the requirements of the problem at hand as well as the availability of computational resources.

A fitness function is defined to quantify the performance of a feature subset in relation to various objectives. The fitness function combines the values of these objectives into a single scalar value, often using weighted sums or Pareto dominance. This function guides the metaheuristic algorithm its exploration of the solution space. The metaheuristic algorithm iteratively explores the solution space by creating new candidate solutions through operations such as perturbations. Upon the termination of the metaheuristic algorithm, a set of feature subsets that are Pareto-optimal will be obtained. These subsets offer different trade-offs between objectives.

Metaheuristic algorithms are well-suited for handling high-dimensional feature spaces, where traditional methods may struggle due to computational complexity. Moreover, these methods are generally data-driven (Gopalakrishnan & Vadivel, 2023) and do not require prior domain knowledge or manual feature engineering. They can discover relevant features automatically. In addition, many metaheuristic algorithms can be parallelized, allowing for efficient exploration of the solution space across multi-core processors or distributed computing environments.

However, metaheuristic algorithms, particularly those that involve many iterations, can be computationally intensive and time-consuming for complex problems. Furthermore, properly configuring metaheuristic algorithms and tuning their corresponding hyperparameters can be challenging and may require extensive experimentation. While metaheuristics aim to find good solutions, they do not guarantee finding the global optima. The quality of solutions can be sensitive to algorithmic configurations and initial conditions.

Multi-Objective Feature Selection with Deep Learning

In the hybrid approach of multi-objective feature selection with deep learning (Zhou et al., 2023), integration with deep neural networks (DNNs) is vital to simultaneously optimize multiple objectives. This approach is advantageous especially when dealing with high-dimensional and complex data. Deep learning architecture commonly include Convolutional Neural Networks (CNNs) for image data, Recurrent Neural Networks (RNNs) for sequential data, and various layers of feedforward neural networks (including fully connected and deep learning models like deep autoencoders) for structured data. Selection of architecture depends on the nature of data available, and the problem being addressed.

A feature selection layer is integrated into the deep learning model (Zou et al., 2015). This layer is responsible for selecting a subset of input features that will be used for training the subsequent layers. Feature selection layer can be added as an initial layer in the neural network. Subsequently, during training, the model learns to extract relevant features from the input data to optimize the defined objectives. Optimization of the model's hyperparameters is necessary to identify the optimal configuration that aligns with the desired objectives. Upon training the deep learning model and optimizing its hyperparameters, it is possible to obtain many configurations that constitute the Pareto front. This front illustrates the trade-offs between different objectives.

The primary advantage of this methodology is in its incorporation of multi-objective optimization alongside deep learning models, which facilitate autonomous acquisition of pertinent features from unprocessed data, eliminating the need for manual feature engineering and domain expertise. Deep neural networks can capture complex and hierarchical patterns in data, making them effective for feature selection in high-dimensional and unstructured data. Deep learning models can model nonlinear relationships between features and targets, allowing them to discover intricate feature interactions.

However, deep learning typically requires large volumes of labelled data for training, which may be tough to elicit, especially in domains with limited data. Training deep learning models can severely augment time-complexity, especially for complex architectures and large datasets. Deep learning often relies on specialized hardware (e.g., GPUs or TPUs) for efficient training, which can be costly and may not be available to all users. Deep learning models are often deemed as black-box models, which can restrict their utility in certain domains.

Multi-Objective Feature Selection with Ensemble Methods

Multi-objective feature selection with embedded methods entails the utilization of machine learning algorithms, typically integrated as part of the model-building process, to concurrently optimize various objectives associated to feature selection (Nouri-Moghaddam et al., 2021) . It allows for automated and data-driven feature selection, making it particularly useful when dealing with high-dimensional data and complex feature spaces. Frequently employed machine learning techniques include decision tree-based algorithms (e.g., Random Forests, Gradient Boosting), regularized linear models (e.g., Lasso regression), and support vector machines (SVMs) (Bolón-Canedo & Alonso-Betanzos, 2019). The choice of algorithm depends on the type of data and the task at hand. The embedded algorithm or its objective function is modified to incorporate multiple objectives. Typically, the process requires modification of the loss function or regularization terms to incorporate the objectives associated with feature selection.

One of the notable advantages of ensemble methods is their ability to combine the decisions of multiple models, reducing the impact of individual model errors and enhancing robustness. Moreover, they can provide estimates of feature importance based on their contributions to model performance, thereby aiding feature selection. Feature importance scores are computed to facilitate the interpretation of the relevance of features in the model's predictions.

The drawback to these methods is that they require diverse and representative data to perform well. Ensembles may exhibit reduced effectiveness in situations when datasets are uneven or biased. Achieving a balance between diversity and accuracy among base models in the ensemble can be challenging. Overly similar models may not contribute significantly to feature selection. Ensemble methods are prone to overfitting, particularly if the ensemble is too complex or if individual models are not properly regularized.

Comparison of Multi-Objective Feature Selection with Single-Objective Approaches

Table 1. Multi-Objective Feature Selection vs Single-Objective Feature Selection

Parameter	Multi-Objective Feature Selection	Single-Objective Feature Selection
Objective	It considers trade-offs between multiple objectives such as accuracy, simplicity, and interpretability.	It focuses on optimizing one objective function, often accuracy or precision; it does not consider other criteria concurrently.
Solution(s)	A set of Pareto-optimal solutions is produced; final selection is made in accordance with the problem's requirements.	Feature subset selected may be more biased toward that objective, potentially neglecting other important factors.
Exploration of the Solution Space	It explores a broader solution space by considering a diverse set of non-dominated solutions along the Pareto front.	Single-objective approaches explore a narrower solution space, typically focused on optimizing a single criterion.
Robustness	Non-dominant solutions generated may offer better generalization to unseen data.	It is more susceptible to overfitting and sensitive to noisy data as only one criterion is optimized.

continued on following page

Table 1. Continued

Parameter	Multi-Objective Feature Selection	Single-Objective Feature Selection
Computational Intensity	Exploring the entire Pareto front requires evaluating many feature subsets. Dealing with high-dimensional data or complex objective functions requires high computational power.	It is more computationally efficient and hence more appropriate for large datasets.
Application	It is well-suited for complex decision-making scenarios where multiple criteria need to be considered, as discussed above.	It more suitable for scenarios where a single criterion is of paramount importance, and other factors are less critical.

Challenges and Limitations of Multi-Objective Feature Selection

Defining appropriate and meaningful objective functions for MOFS (Multi-Objective Feature Selection) can be challenging. Combing multiple objectives, especially when they are conflicting, requires careful consideration. The selection of objectives and the determination of their respective weights can possess a certain degree of subjectivity (Al-Tashi et al., 2020). The selection of distinct subsets of attributes may vary depending on how objectives are defined and weighted. This subjectivity can introduce bias into the feature selection process. MOFS often requires domain expertise to design meaningful objective functions for real-world problems and interpret the results effectively. Complex, and often conflicting, objectives may require advanced mathematical modelling or domain-specific knowledge. Without domain knowledge, it may be challenging to make informed decisions.

When dealing with imbalanced datasets, MOFS may inadvertently assign higher priority to features belonging to the majority class, hence impacting the performance of models trained on the selected subsets (Al-Tashi et al., 2020). In such case, considering metrics like accuracy can be misleading because a model that is biased towards predicting the majority class can still achieve high accuracy, even if it performs inadequately on the minority class.

In high-dimensional datasets, the search space for feature subsets becomes exponentially large, making it computationally expensive and potentially impractical to explore exhaustively. Datasets characterized by a large crowding distance exhibit sparsity, which can give rise to challenges such as overfitting. This occurs when models encounter difficulties in identifying significant patterns within sparsely populated areas of the feature space. Additionally, MOFS may struggle with large datasets or those with many features due to computational and resource constraints. Storing high-dimensional datasets and intermediate results during MOFS can consume substantial memory, especially when dealing with large-scale data. Memory limitations can hinder the execution of MOFS algorithms on standard computing platforms. Scaling up MOFS for big data applications can be difficult.

MOFS algorithms can sometimes get stuck in local optima or fail to explore the entire Pareto front effectively. This can restrict the potential improvements in objectives for feature selection. Improving the exploration-exploitation balance is a popular research topic. Limited exploration often results in a lack of diversity among the solutions along the Pareto front. This implies that the selected features exhibit significant similarities to one another, presenting identical trade-offs between objectives, rather than providing a diverse set of options for decision-makers.

CONCLUSION

This chapter has explored complex domains of data science, optimization, and machine learning intersect to address the issue of identifying the most informative characteristics from intricate datasets. Throughout this chapter, a wide array of topics has been covered, ranging from the fundamental concepts of multi-objective optimization to the practical implementation of MOFS in various fields. Extensive discussions have been conducted regarding advantages and limitations associated with algorithms that are most employed.

Future Scope

Given the continuous expansion of data, it is imperative to ensure the scalability of multi-objective optimization methods in the context of feature selection Researchers are continuously developing innovative approaches to enhance scalability and experimenting various combinations of multi-objective feature selection strategies to establish hybrid methodologies. These studies aim to contribute to increasing the robustness of the selected features. For all the aforementioned methodologies, domain knowledge and demand human intervention are requisite. Techniques to automate feature selection without any human intervention could also be explored.

REFERENCES

Abdullah, T. A. A., Zahid, M. S. M., & Ali, W. (2021). A Review of Interpretable ML in Healthcare: Taxonomy, Applications, Challenges, and Future Directions. *Symmetry*, 13(12), 2439. DOI: 10.3390/sym13122439

Agrawal, P., Abutarboush, H. F., Ganesh, T., & Mohamed, A. W. (2021). Meta-heuristic algorithms on feature selection: A survey of one decade of research (2009-2019). *IEEE Access : Practical Innovations, Open Solutions*, 9, 26766–26791. DOI: 10.1109/ACCESS.2021.3056407

Ahmad, F., Tarik, M., Ahmad, M., & Ansari, M. Z. (2023). Weather Forecasting Using Deep Learning Algorithms. *2023 International Conference on Recent Advances in Electrical, Electronics & Digital Healthcare Technologies (REEDCON)*, 498–502. https://doi.org/DOI: 10.1109/REEDCON57544.2023.10150439

Ahmad, I. S., Bakar, A. A., & Yaakub, M. R. (2019). A review of feature selection in sentiment analysis using information gain and domain specific ontology. *International Journal of Advanced Computer Research*, 9(44), 283–292. DOI: 10.19101/IJACR.PID90

Al-Tashi, Q., Abdulkadir, S. J., Rais, H. M., Mirjalili, S., & Alhussian, H. (2020). Approaches to Multi-Objective Feature Selection: A Systematic Literature Review. *IEEE Access : Practical Innovations, Open Solutions*, 8, 125076–125096. DOI: 10.1109/ACCESS.2020.3007291

Amarnath, B., & Appavu alias Balamurugan, S. (2016). Metaheuristic Approach for Efficient Feature Selection: A Data Classification Perspective. *Indian Journal of Science and Technology*, 9(4). Advance online publication. DOI: 10.17485/ijst/2016/v9i4/87039

Amoozegar, M., & Minaei-Bidgoli, B. (2018). Optimizing multi-objective PSO based feature selection method using a feature elitism mechanism. *Expert Systems with Applications*, 113, 499–514. DOI: 10.1016/j.eswa.2018.07.013

Arun, J. P., Mishra, M., & Subramaniam, S. V. (2011). Parallel implementation of MOPSO on GPU using OpenCL and CUDA. *2011 18th International Conference on High Performance Computing*, 1–10. DOI: 10.1109/HiPC.2011.6152719

Bolón-Canedo, V., & Alonso-Betanzos, A. (2019). Ensembles for feature selection: A review and future trends. *Information Fusion*, 52, 1–12. DOI: 10.1016/j.inffus.2018.11.008

Bolón-Canedo, V., Rego-Fernández, D., Peteiro-Barral, D., Alonso-Betanzos, A., Guijarro-Berdiñas, B., & Sánchez-Maroño, N. (2018). On the scalability of feature selection methods on high-dimensional data. *Knowledge and Information Systems*, 56(2), 395–442. DOI: 10.1007/s10115-017-1140-3

Brownlee, J. (2011). *Clever Algorithms: Nature-Inspired Programming Recipes* (1st ed.). Lulu.com.

Coello, C. A. C., Pulido, G. T., & Lechuga, M. S. (2004). Handling multiple objectives with particle swarm optimization. *IEEE Transactions on Evolutionary Computation*, 8(3), 256–279. DOI: 10.1109/TEVC.2004.826067

Deb, K., Pratap, A., Agarwal, S., & Meyarivan, T. (2002). A fast and elitist multi-objective genetic algorithm: NSGA-II. *IEEE Transactions on Evolutionary Computation*, 6(2), 182–197. DOI: 10.1109/4235.996017

Deb, K., Roy, P. C., & Hussein, R. (2021). Surrogate Modeling Approaches for Multiobjective Optimization: Methods, Taxonomy, and Results. *Mathematical & Computational Applications*, 26(1). Advance online publication. DOI: 10.3390/mca26010005

Dong, H., Sun, J., Sun, X., & Ding, R. (2020). A many-objective feature selection for multi-label classification. *Knowledge-Based Systems*, 208, 106456. DOI: 10.1016/j.knosys.2020.106456

Goldberg, D. E., & Holland, J. H. (1988). Genetic Algorithms and Machine Learning. *Machine Learning*, 3(2), 95–99. DOI: 10.1023/A:1022602019183

Gopalakrishnan, A., & Vadivel, V. (2023). Multi-objective metaheuristic optimization algorithms for wrapper-based feature selection: A literature survey. *Bulletin of Electrical Engineering and Informatics*, 12(5), 3061–3066. DOI: 10.11591/eei.v12i5.4757

Gunantara, N. (2018). A review of multi-objective optimization: Methods and its applications. *Cogent Engineering*, 5(1), 1–16. DOI: 10.1080/23311916.2018.1502242

Guyon, I., & De, A. M. (2003). An Introduction to Variable and Feature Selection André Elisseeff. In *Journal of Machine Learning Research* (Vol. 3).

Hajimani, E., Ruano, M. G., & Ruano, A. E. (2015). MOGA design for neural networks based system for automatic diagnosis of Cerebral Vascular Accidents. *2015 IEEE 9th International Symposium on Intelligent Signal Processing (WISP) Proceedings*, 1–6. DOI: 10.1109/WISP.2015.7139170

Hamdani, T. M., Won, J. M., Alimi, A. M., & Karray, F. (2007a). Multi-objective Feature Selection with NSGA II. *Lecture Notes in Computer Science (Including Subseries Lecture Notes in Artificial Intelligence and Lecture Notes in Bioinformatics), 4431 LNCS*(PART 1), 240–247. DOI: 10.1007/978-3-540-71618-1_27

Hamdani, T. M., Won, J.-M., Alimi, A. M., & Karray, F. (2007b). Multi-objective Feature Selection with NSGA II. *International Conference on Adaptive and Natural Computing Algorithms.* https://api.semanticscholar.org/CorpusID:26841901

Imani, V., Sevilla-Salcedo, C., Fortino, V., & Tohka, J. (2023). *Multi-Objective Genetic Algorithm for Multi-View Feature Selection.* http://arxiv.org/abs/2305.18352

Jumelet, J., & Zuidema, W. (2023). *Feature Interactions Reveal Linguistic Structure in Language Models.* http://arxiv.org/abs/2306.12181

Kennedy, J., & Eberhart, R. (1995). Particle swarm optimization. *Proceedings of ICNN'95 - International Conference on Neural Networks, 4*, 1942–194. DOI: 10.1109/ICNN.1995.488968

Kennedy, M. C., Ford, E. D., Singleton, P., Finney, M., & Agee, J. K. (2007). Informed multi-objective decision-making in environmental management using Pareto optimality. *Journal of Applied Ecology, 45*(1), 181–192. DOI: 10.1111/j.1365-2664.2007.01367.x

Khan, A., & Baig, A. R. (2015). Multi-Objective Feature Subset Selection using Non-dominated Sorting Genetic Algorithm. *Journal of Applied Research and Technology, 13*(1), 145–159. DOI: 10.1016/S1665-6423(15)30013-4

Kohavi, R., & John, G. H. (n.d.). *Wrappers for feature subset selection.* http://robotics.stanford.edu/

Kohavi, R., & Sommerfield, D. (1995). Feature Subset Selection Using the Wrapper Method: Overfitting and Dynamic Search Space Topology. *Knowledge Discovery and Data Mining.* https://api.semanticscholar.org/CorpusID:5147685

Li, J.-Z., Chen, W.-N., Zhang, J., & Zhan, Z.-H. (2015). A Parallel Implementation of Multiobjective Particle Swarm Optimization Algorithm Based on Decomposition. *2015 IEEE Symposium Series on Computational Intelligence*, 1310–1317. DOI: 10.1109/SSCI.2015.187

Li, L., Liu, H., Ma, Z., Mo, Y., Duan, Z., Zhou, J., & Zhao, J. (n.d.). *Multi-label Feature Selection via Information Gain.*

Lv, S. X., & Wang, L. (2022). Deep learning combined wind speed forecasting with hybrid time series decomposition and multi-objective parameter optimization. *Applied Energy*, 311. Advance online publication. DOI: 10.1016/j.apenergy.2022.118674

Nguyen, H. B., Xue, B., & Zhang, M. (n.d.). *Similarity based Multi-objective Particle Swarm Optimisation for Feature Selection in Classification.*

Njoku, U. F., Abelló, A., Bilalli, B., & Bontempi, G. (2023). *Wrapper Methods for Multi-Objective Feature Selection.* DOI: 10.48786/edbt.2023.58

Nouri-Moghaddam, B., Ghazanfari, M., & Fathian, M. (2021). A novel multi-objective forest optimization algorithm for wrapper feature selection. *Expert Systems with Applications*, 175. Advance online publication. DOI: 10.1016/j.eswa.2021.114737

Onay, C., & Öztürk, E. (2018). A review of credit scoring research in the age of Big Data. *Journal of Financial Regulation and Compliance*, 26(3), 382–405. DOI: 10.1108/JFRC-06-2017-0054

Parsopoulos, K. E., & Vrahatis, M. N. (1 C.E.). Multi-Objective Particles Swarm Optimization Approaches. DOI: 10.4018/978-1-59904-498-9.CH002

Raquel, C. R., & Naval, P. C. (2005). An effective use of crowding distance in multi-objective particle swarm optimization. *Proceedings of the 7th Annual Conference on Genetic and Evolutionary Computation*, 257–264. DOI: 10.1145/1068009.1068047

Saeys, Y., Inza, I., & Larrañaga, P. (2007). A review of feature selection techniques in bioinformatics. In *Bioinformatics* (Vol. 23, Issue 19, pp. 2507–2517). Oxford University Press. DOI: 10.1093/bioinformatics/btm344

Santana, L. A., & Canuto, A. M. P. (2013). Particle swarm intelligence as feature selector in ensemble systems. *Proceedings - 2013 Brazilian Conference on Intelligent Systems, BRACIS 2013*, 89–94. DOI: 10.1109/BRACIS.2013.23

Santana, L. E. A., & Canuto, A. M. P. (2012). Bi-objective Genetic Algorithm for Feature Selection in Ensemble Systems. *Lecture Notes in Computer Science (Including Subseries Lecture Notes in Artificial Intelligence and Lecture Notes in Bioinformatics), 7552 LNCS*(PART 1), 701–709. DOI: 10.1007/978-3-642-33269-2_88

Sarangi, S., Dash, P. K., & Bisoi, R. (2023). Probabilistic prediction of wind speed using an integrated deep belief network optimized by a hybrid multi-objective particle swarm algorithm. *Engineering Applications of Artificial Intelligence*, 126. Advance online publication. DOI: 10.1016/j.engappai.2023.107034

Saroj & Jyoti. (2014). Multi-objective genetic algorithm approach to feature subset optimization. *2014 IEEE International Advance Computing Conference (IACC)*, 544–548. DOI: 10.1109/IAdCC.2014.6779383

Siedlecki, W., & Sklansky, J. (2011). On automatic feature selection. DOI: 10.1142/S0218001488000145

Simumba, N., Okami, S., Kodaka, A., & Kohtake, N. (2021). Comparison of Profit-Based Multi-Objective Approaches for Feature Selection in Credit Scoring. *Algorithms*, 14(9), 260. DOI: 10.3390/a14090260

Simumba, N., Okami, S., Kodaka, A., & Kohtake, N. (2022). Multiple objective metaheuristics for feature selection based on stakeholder requirements in credit scoring. *Decision Support Systems*, 155. Advance online publication. DOI: 10.1016/j.dss.2021.113714

Spolaôr, N., Lorena, A. C., & Diana Lee, H. (2017). Feature Selection via Pareto Multi-objective Genetic Algorithms. *Applied Artificial Intelligence*, 31(9–10), 764–791. DOI: 10.1080/08839514.2018.1444334

Spolaôr, N., Lorena, A. C., & Lee, H. D. (2011). Multi-objective Genetic Algorithm Evaluation in Feature Selection. *Lecture Notes in Computer Science (Including Subseries Lecture Notes in Artificial Intelligence and Lecture Notes in Bioinformatics)*, 6576 LNCS, 462–476. DOI: 10.1007/978-3-642-19893-9_32

Vashishtha, J., Puri, V. H., & Mukesh. (2020). Feature Selection Using PSO: A Multi Objective Approach. *Communications in Computer and Information Science, 1241 CCIS*, 106–119. DOI: 10.1007/978-981-15-6318-8_10

Yuan, W., Guan, D., Shen, L., & Pan, H. (2014). An empirical study of filter-based feature selection algorithms using noisy training data. *2014 4th IEEE International Conference on Information Science and Technology*, 209–212. DOI: 10.1109/ICIST.2014.6920367

Zhang, Q., & Li, H. (2007). MOEA/D: A Multiobjective Evolutionary Algorithm Based on Decomposition. *IEEE Transactions on Evolutionary Computation*, 11(6), 712–731. DOI: 10.1109/TEVC.2007.892759

Zhou, Z., Wong, J., Yu, K., Li, G., & Chen, S. (2023). *Feature Selection on Deep Learning Models: An Interactive Visualization Approach*. https://api.semanticscholar.org/CorpusID:260140100

Zhu, M., & Han, F. (2021). Multi-objective Particle Swarm Optimization based on Space Decomposition for Feature Selection. *Proceedings - 2021 17th International Conference on Computational Intelligence and Security, CIS 2021*, 387–391. https://doi.org/DOI: 10.1109/CIS54983.2021.00087

Zou, Q., Ni, L., Zhang, T., & Wang, Q. (2015). Deep Learning Based Feature Selection for Remote Sensing Scene Classification. *IEEE Geoscience and Remote Sensing Letters*, 12(11), 2321–2325. DOI: 10.1109/LGRS.2015.2475299

KEY TERMS AND DEFINITIONS

Feature Selection: The process of identifying and selecting the most relevant subset of features from a dataset to enrich model performance, reduce dimensionality, and enhance interpretability.

Filter Methods: Feature selection strategies that assess the intrinsic characteristics of features without incorporating any learning algorithm, typically relying on statistical measures or information-theoretic criteria.

Genetic Algorithm: An optimization algorithm inspired by the process of natural selection, involving the evolution of solutions across multiple generations through operations such as selection, crossover, and mutation. The aim is to find near-optimal solutions to optimization problems.

Objectives: Quantifiable goals or metrics used to evaluate the performance of a system or solution in optimization problems, guiding the search for solutions that optimize multiple conflicting objectives.

Pareto Optimality: A state where there is no other feasible solution that can improve one objective without negatively impacting another, thus emphasizing the trade-offs between competing objectives in multi-objective optimization.

Particle Swarm Optimization: An optimization technique inspired by the social behavior of birds flocking or fish schooling, where particles in a search space iteratively update their positions depending on their individual best position and the overall best position determined by the swarm.

Trade-Offs: The process of evaluating and deciding which objectives are more critical to optimize, while accepting compromises in other objectives to achieve optimal performance. It involves weighing the importance of the competing objectives and making informed decisions based on priorities and constraints.

Wrapper Methods: Feature selection approaches that evaluate the performance of a subset of features using a specific learning algorithm. This process treats the selection of features as a search problem within the space of potential feature subsets.

Chapter 7
A Comprehensive Study on Transformer–Based Time Series Forecasting

Di Wang

https://orcid.org/0000-0002-7992-7743

Foxconn, USA

ABSTRACT

Time series forecasting is crucial for various real-world applications, such as energy consumption, traffic flow estimation, and financial market analysis. This chapter explores the application of deep learning models, specifically transformer-based models for long-term time series forecasting. Despite the success of transformers in sequence modeling, their permutation-invariant nature can lead to the loss of temporal information, posing challenges for accurate forecasting. Especially, the embedding of the position-wise vector or the time-stamp vector is the key to the success of the long time series forecasting. Another noted headache of the standard transformer-based model is the squared computation complexity. This chapter studies the development of the research field of the long timer series forecasting, challenging pain point, popular data sets, and state-of-the-art benchmarks. The discussion covers the implications, limitations, and future research directions, offering insights for applying these advanced techniques to real-world forecasting problems.

INTRODUCTION

Time series forecasting is a fundamental task with a wide range of applications in various fields such as energy management(D. Wang et al., 2022; D. Wang, 2023b; D. Wang et al., 2018), traffic flow prediction(D. Wang et al., 2023; D. Wang, 2023c;

DOI: 10.4018/979-8-3693-5231-1.ch007

Yun et al., 2023), and financial market analysis(D. Wang, 2024a, 2024b). Accurate time series forecasting is essential for informed decision-making, effective resource management, and strategic planning. Despite its importance, long-term time series forecasting (LTSF) remains a challenging problem due to the complex temporal dependencies, non-stationary nature, and high dimensionality of real-world time series data.

The difficulties and challenges in time series forecasting include the following items:

1. Poor data quality, insufficient data points, or gaps in data can significantly hinder the accuracy of forecasts.
2. Effectively identifying and separating trends, seasonal effects, and irregular components from the time series can be complex, especially in data with multiple seasonal cycles or non-linear trends.
3. Choosing the right model to fit the data can be challenging, as different models may perform better or worse depending on the characteristics of the time series.
4. Time series data often involve non-stationary processes where statistical properties change over time, requiring models to adapt to these changes.
5. The length of the forecasting horizon greatly affects accuracy; longer horizons typically lead to less accurate predictions.
6. Accounting for external influences that are not reflected in the past data but could affect future outcomes.
7. Some advanced forecasting models, particularly in deep learning, demand significant computational resources and expertise to implement effectively.
8. Quantifying the uncertainty and establishing confidence intervals for forecasts, especially in dynamic environments, is crucial but challenging.

In recent years, deep learning models have emerged as powerful tools for time series forecasting (D. Wang, 2022; D. Wang & Hu, 2021, 2023). These models, particularly Recurrent Neural Networks (RNNs) and Convolutional Neural Networks (CNNs) (Kirisci & Cagcag Yolcu, 2022; Z. Zeng et al., 2018) have demonstrated the ability to capture complex patterns and dependencies in sequential data. However, they also come with their own set of limitations. RNNs, including Long Short-Term Memory (LSTM) and Gated Recurrent Unit (GRU) networks, are designed to handle sequential data by maintaining a memory of previous inputs (Livieris et al., 2020; Madan & Mangipudi, 2018; Tokgöz & Ünal, 2018). They have shown success in capturing short-term dependencies but struggle with long-term dependencies due to issues like vanishing gradients. CNNs, adapted for time series forecasting by applying convolutions along the time axis, can capture local patterns and are computationally efficient but may not effectively model long-range dependencies(D. Wang, 2023a, 2023d).

Transformer models, initially proposed for natural language processing (NLP) tasks, have been adapted for time series forecasting due to their ability to capture long-range dependencies using the self-attention mechanism. The Transformer architecture has revolutionized sequence modeling in various domains including finance (Lezmi & Xu, 2023; Xu et al., 2023; C. Zhang et al., 2024), transportation (Hu & Xiong, 2023; Koohfar et al., 2023; Yue & Ma, 2023), energy (L'Heureux et al., 2022; C. Wang et al., 2022; Zhu et al., 2023) and others. The parallelization schema of Transformer models can lead to faster training times and more effective handling of long sequences (Tuli et al., 2022).

Besides, the power of multi-head self-attention mechanism makes it possible to learn correlations between data points or data segments. Notable Transformer-based models for time series forecasting include Linear (A. Zeng et al., 2023), Informer (Zhou et al., n.d.), Autoformer (Wu et al., 2021), Reformer (Kitaev et al., 2020), and LogTrans (S. Li et al., 2019). These models have demonstrated superior performance compared to traditional statistical methods and other machine learning techniques, significantly advancing the state-of-the-art in time series forecasting. Figure 1 presents the architecture differences among different models including CNN model, RNN model and attention model.

Figure 1. Architecture comparison between different models

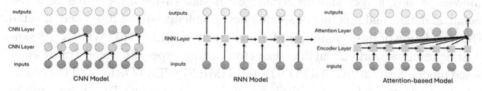

Forecasting long-term time series data is highly challenging due to three main reasons (Wen et al., 2022). First, directly identifying temporal dependencies is unreliable because they are often obscured by complex, entangled temporal patterns. Second, canonical Transformers with self-attention mechanisms struggle with long-term forecasting due to the quadratic complexity of sequence length. Although some Transformer-based models have improved self-attention to a sparse version, these models still rely on point-wise representation aggregation. This approach, while enhancing performance, sacrifices information utilization due to sparse connections, creating a bottleneck in long-term forecasting. Thirdly, the permutation-invariant nature of the self-attention mechanism, which is the cornerstone of Transformer models, poses a significant challenge in time series forecasting. Self-attention treats all elements in a sequence as equally important without considering their original order, leading to the loss of temporal information. This characteristic is particularly problematic for time series forecasting, where the order of data points is crucial to understanding the underlying patterns and trends. Unlike natural language processing tasks, where the overall meaning can often be preserved despite some reordering of words, time series data relies heavily on the precise sequence of data points to capture temporal dependencies accurately. Any disruption in the order can obscure the inherent patterns, making it difficult to model the temporal changes accurately. This loss of temporal information can result in less accurate forecasts and reduced performance of the model.

The multi-head self-attention mechanism of Transformers is powerful in extracting semantic correlations in long sequences, such as words in texts or image patches. However, self-attention is permutation-invariant and tends to lose temporal information, even when positional encoding techniques are employed. This loss of temporal information is less problematic in semantic-rich applications like NLP, where the overall meaning is preserved despite word reordering. However, in time series data, which lacks inherent semantics, accurately modeling temporal changes among continuous data points is essential.

Except deep learning approaches, there are rich studies existed for time series forecasting, which will be discussed in the Section 'RELATED WORK'. The goal of this chapter is to provide a comprehensive overview of the application of Transformer-based models for long-term time series forecasting. Background knowledge, advantages and disadvantages of state-of-the-art, popular data sets, technical details and pipeline of solving new problems will be discussed in detail. The foundation of this chapter is as follows: Section 'RELATED WORK' presents existing research works about time series forecasting, especially about Transformer-based model. Section 'FOUNDATION OF TIME SERIES FORECASTING,' presents the mathematical basics of the time series forecasting and Transformer model. Section 'TRANSFORMER-BASED TIME SERIES FORECASTING APPROACH' defines the architectures of different transformer-based models, their advantages and disadvantages. Section 'RESULTS' shows performances of nine baselines on six datasets. Section 'DISCUSSION' analyzes the details of experiment results and features of each approach. Section 'LIMITATIONS' discusses the limitations of the mentioned works. Section 'CONCLUSION' summarizes this chapter and talks about future works.

RELATED WORK

Time series forecasting has long been a crucial task across various domains, relying heavily on traditional statistical methods as its foundation. Among these, the AutoRegressive Integrated Moving Average (ARIMA) model (Shumway et al., 2017) stands out as one of the most commonly used techniques. ARIMA addresses the challenge of forecasting by converting non-stationary time series data into stationary series through differencing, autoregression, and moving average components. This idea motivates the following neural network architecture designs. Although effective in certain contexts, ARIMA often struggles with capturing non-linear patterns and long-term dependencies, limiting its effectiveness in complex real-world datasets (Kalpakis et al., 2001; G. P. Zhang, 2003). Another prominent method, the Exponential Smoothing State Space Model (ETS), focuses on emphasizing trend and seasonality components to improve forecasting accuracy (Dong et al., 2013; Kitagawa & Gersch, 1984). While ETS models are flexible and adept at handling various seasonal patterns, they also fall short in scenarios involving highly non-linear and multivariate time series data due to their linear assumptions.

The advent of machine learning enhances the accuracy and robustness of time series forecasting. One such method is Gradient Boosting Regression Trees, which builds an ensemble of weak prediction models, typically decision trees, to improve performance. GBRT is capable of capturing complex patterns in time series data but can be computationally intensive and requires meticulous hyperparameter tuning (L. Li et al., 2020). Support Vector Machines (Sapankevych & Sankar, 2009) and Gaussian Processes (Roberts et al., 2013) have also been employed in time series forecasting, particularly excelling with smaller datasets due to their strong theoretical foundations. However, their performance tends to degrade with increasing data dimensionality and volume, making them less suitable for large-scale applications.

Transformer-based models attract great attention in the area of time series forecasting. As mentioned before, one main challenge is the quadratic computational complexity of sequence length. Increasing cheerful works have been proposed. For instance, LogTrans (S. Li et al., 2019) offers several advantages, including enhanced locality awareness through convolutional self-attention, which improves the model's ability to capture local context and patterns, leading to higher forecasting accuracy. Additionally, the introduction of LogSparse Transformer significantly reduces memory complexity to $O(L(\log L)^2)$, enabling efficient modeling of long time series with fine granularity under constrained memory budgets. Informer (Zhou et al., n.d.) enhances time-series forecasting by introducing a ProbSparse self-attention mechanism and self-attention distilling, significantly reducing time complexity and memory usage. This allows for efficient handling of long sequences. Additionally, its generative style decoder improves inference speed by predicting long sequences in one forward operation. These advancements lead to superior performance on large-scale datasets. However, the algorithm's increased implementation complexity and dependency on large datasets for optimal performance are notable limitations. The Reformer algorithm (Kitaev et al., 2020) enhances the efficiency of Transformers in time-series forecasting by significantly reducing memory usage through reversible residual layers and introducing locality-sensitive hashing attention, which lowers the complexity from $O(L^2)$ to $O(L \log L)$. These advancements allow the Reformer to handle long sequences more efficiently and with less memory, making it suitable for large-scale applications. However, the increased implementation complexity and dependency on large datasets for optimal performance remain notable limitations. The Autoformer (Wu et al., 2021) algorithm improves long-term time-series forecasting by introducing a progressive decomposition architecture and an Auto-Correlation mechanism. The decomposition architecture effectively separates long-term trends and seasonal components, enhancing the model's ability to handle complex temporal patterns. The Auto-Correlation mechanism, based on series periodicity, replaces traditional self-attention, reducing computational complexity to $O(L \log L)$. These innovations result in superior forecasting accuracy and efficiency on extensive real-world datasets. However, the increased complexity of implementation and the reliance on large datasets for optimal performance remain challenges.

Another challenge is the permutation-invariant nature of the self-attention mechanism. To solve this problem, absolute-position encoding schema (Lee & Toutanova, 2018) and relative-position encoding schema (Huang et al., 2020) are proposed. Moreover, a time Absolute Position Encoding (tAPE) and an efficient Relative Position Encoding schemas are proposed in (Foumani et al., 2024), which emphasize the combination of the absolute and relative position encoding considering computation efficiency.

However, Linear (A. Zeng et al., 2023) questions the effectiveness of Transformer-based models for long-term time-series forecasting (LTSF) and introduces a simple one-layer linear model, LTSF-Linear, which outperforms existing sophisticated Transformer-based models on multiple benchmarks. The key advantage of LTSF-Linear is its simplicity and efficiency, providing better prediction accuracy and reducing complexity compared to Transformer models. However, the study highlights that Transformers tend to lose temporal information due to their permutation-invariant self-attention mechanism and are prone to overfitting on noisy data, leading to suboptimal performance in LTSF tasks. The results suggest that while Transformers have advanced the field, simpler models like LTSF-Linear may offer more reliable performance for certain time-series forecasting tasks.

FOUNDATION

Time series forecasting models are designed to predict future values of a target variable $y_{i,t}$ for a specific entity i at time t. Each entity corresponds to a logical grouping of temporal data, such as sensor readings from various weather stations in climate studies or vital statistics from different patients in healthcare. These entities are observed simultaneously. Typically, one-step-ahead forecasting models predict the next value in the sequence based on the most recent data points Eq. (1).

$$\hat{y}_{i,t+1} = f\left(y_{i,t-k:t}, x_{i,t-k:t}, s_i\right) \tag{1}$$

where $\hat{y}_{i,t+1}$ denotes the forecasting value, $y_{i,t-k:t}, x_{i,t-k:t}$ are observation values, k is the look-back window, and s_i is the static metadata.

Iterated multi-step (IMS) forecasting involves training a model to make single-step predictions, which are then applied iteratively to generate multi-step forecasts. This method benefits from the autoregressive estimation procedure, resulting in smaller prediction variances. However, it is prone to accumulating errors over multiple steps. IMS forecasting is most effective when the single-step forecaster is highly accurate, and the forecasting horizon (T) is relatively short. On the other hand, direct multi-step (DMS) forecasting directly optimizes the multi-step forecasting objective, aiming to improve accuracy over longer horizons. DMS is preferable when it is challenging to achieve an unbiased single-step model or when the forecasting horizon is large, as it reduces the compounding of errors seen in IMS methods.

The Transformer model, originally proposed by Vaswani et al., (Vaswani et al., 2017) has revolutionized the field of sequence modeling and has been particularly influential in natural language processing. Its architecture relies on self-attention mechanisms, which allow the model to weigh the importance of different parts of the input sequence, providing flexibility. The core component of the Transformer model is the self-attention mechanism, which computes a weighted sum of input values, allowing the model to focus on different parts of the sequence. The self-attention operation is defined as Eq. (2).

$$Attention(Q.K.V) = softmax\left(\frac{QK^T}{\sqrt{d_k}}\right)V \tag{2}$$

where Q denotes the query vector, K the key vector, and V the value vector. They are calculated from the input sequence through linear transformations. d_k is the dimensionality of the keys. In the context of time series forecasting, the Transformer model has been adapted to handle the unique challenges of temporal data. For instance, the incorporation of positional encodings helps the model retain information about the order of the sequence, which is vital for time series data. The positional encoding for each position *pos* and dimension *i* can be computed as:

$$PE_{(pos,2i)} = sin\left(\frac{pos}{10000^{2i/d_{model}}}\right) \tag{3}$$

$$PE_{(pos,2i+1)} = cos\left(\frac{pos}{10000^{2i/d_{model}}}\right) \tag{4}$$

Proposed Algorithm

Figure 2. The pipeline of transformer-based solution to time series forecasting problems

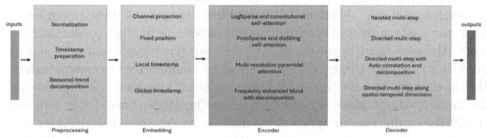

As shown in Figure 2, in Transformer models, the self-attention layer does not inherently encode the positional information of time series data, which is crucial for maintaining the sequence's temporal structure. To address this, several strategies are employed to inject positional context into the model. These include fixed positional encodings, channel projection embeddings, and learnable temporal embeddings. Additionally, temporal convolutions or learnable timestamps can be integrated to further enhance the temporal context. These strategies help the model understand both local positional information (the order of data points) and global temporal context (like hierarchical timestamps such as weeks, months, and years, as well as special events or holidays).

The self-attention mechanism in Transformers identifies dependencies between different parts of the input sequence. However, the traditional self-attention approach has a computational complexity of O (L²), where LL is the sequence length. To improve efficiency, various techniques have been proposed. LogTrans introduces a Logsparse mask to reduce complexity to O (L log L), while Pyraformer uses a pyramidal attention mechanism to capture multi-scale temporal dependencies with O (L) complexity. Informer employs a ProbSparse self-attention mechanism and self-attention distillation, achieving O (L log L) complexity. FEDformer utilizes Fourier and wavelet-enhanced blocks to reduce the complexity to O (L). Autoformer replaces traditional self-attention with a series-wise auto-correlation mechanism to maintain efficiency while capturing temporal dependencies.

The original Transformer decoder generates sequences in an autoregressive manner, which can be slow and prone to error accumulation over long sequences. To address this, Informer and other Transformer variants employ direct multi-step forecasting strategies. Informer uses a generative-style decoder to produce predictions in one forward pass, significantly speeding up inference. Pyraformer combines spatial and temporal information in a fully connected layer for decoding, while Autoformer integrates trend-cyclical components and seasonal auto-correlation mechanisms for final predictions. FEDformer utilizes a decomposition-based approach with frequency attention blocks to enhance the accuracy and efficiency of the decoding process.

Among these strategies, Autoformer is important, where series decomposition block, auto-correlation mechanism and time delay aggregation pave the way for success. In this section, these techniques details will be discussed.

Figure 3. The architecture of Autoformer (Wu et al., 2021)

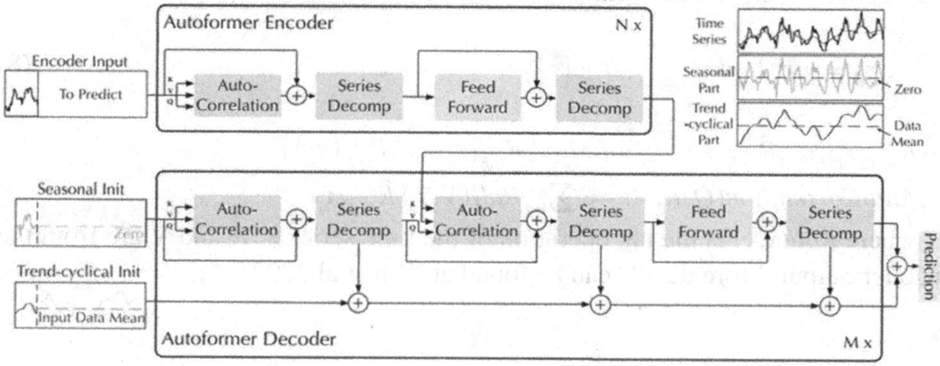

Series decomposition block splits a time series into its trend-cyclical and seasonal components, representing the series' long-term behavior and seasonal variations, respectively. Directly decomposing future series poses a challenge due to the unpredictability of future data. To overcome this, Autoformer incorporates a series decomposition block within the Autoformer framework as shown in Figure 3, which progressively isolates the long-term stationary trends from predicted intermediate hidden states. In summary, there are several blocks in the Encoder and Decoder parts, each of which is composed of the correlation part, series decomposition part, and feed forward part. In detail, a moving average technique is taken to smooth out periodic fluctuations and accentuate long-term trends as shown below:

$$x_t = AvgPool(Padding(x)) \tag{5}$$

$$x_s = x - x_t \tag{6}$$

where x_t is the trend-cyclical component while x_s is the seasonal one.

Auto-correlation mechanism calculates the correlation between different series segments instead of data points. Interestingly, the series segments are selected by time delay rollout strategies. The correlation between time series x_t and another lagged time series $x_{t-\tau}$ is presented in Eq. (7).

$$R_{xx}(\tau) = \lim_{L \to \infty} \frac{1}{L} \sum_{t=1}^{L} x\, x_{t-\tau} \tag{7}$$

where τ is the lagged time period. But the next challenging question will be the selection of the best τ or the combination of candidates of τ values. In the time delay aggregation block, k lagged time series are selected as follows:

$$\tau_1, \ldots, \tau_k = argTopk_{\tau \in \{1,\ldots,L\}}\left(R_{Q,K}(\tau)\right) \tag{8}$$

$$\widehat{R}_{Q,K}(\tau_1), \ldots, \widehat{R}_{Q,K}(\tau_k) = SoftMax\left(R_{Q,K}(\tau_1), \ldots, R_{Q,K}(\tau_k)\right)$$
$$AutoCorrelation(Q, K, V) = \sum_{i=1}^{k} Roll(V, \tau_i)\, \widehat{R}_{Q,K}(\tau_i)$$

where $Roll(x, \tau)$ is the lag operation of the time series x. K and V are from the encoder output. More details can be found at (Wu et al., 2021).

Figure 4. Performance comparison between different attention mechanisms (Wu et al., 2021)

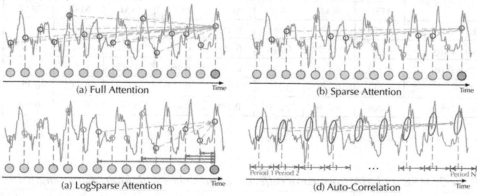

(a) Full Attention

(b) Sparse Attention

(a) LogSparse Attention

(d) Auto-Correlation

As shown in Figure 4, different attention mechanisms focus on correlations among different parts. Full attention studies all-time series points with full-connection models. Sparse attention selects partial points instead of using all points according to calculated similarity values. LogSparse attention selects points based on the exponentially time intervals. Auto correlation attention studies the correlation between different time series segments with complicated selection strategies.

RESULTS

The performances of five different Transformer-model based time series forecasting approaches are evaluated on five real-world datasets (Lai et al., 2018; Zhou et al., n.d.). The Electricity Transformer Temperature (ETT) dataset includes data from two electricity transformers, recording load and oil temperature every 15 minutes between July 2016 and July 2018. This dataset aims to support research on long sequence time-series forecasting. In addition to the ETT dataset, the Electricity1 dataset documents hourly electricity consumption for 321 customers from 2012 to 2014. The Exchange dataset covers daily exchange rates for eight countries from 1990 to 2016, providing a rich source for financial forecasting models. The Traffic2 dataset comprises hourly road occupancy rates collected by sensors on freeways in the San Francisco Bay Area, courtesy of the California Department of Transportation. The Weather3 dataset, recorded every 10 minutes throughout 2020, includes 21 meteorological indicators such as air temperature and humidity. For different target tasks, training settings like hyperparameters vary. Details can be found at (Kitaev et al., 2020; S. Li et al., 2019; Wu et al., 2021; Zhou et al., n.d.).

Table 1. MSE and MAE results of different approaches with forecasting length 96

Models Metric	Autoformer		Informer		LogTrans		Reformer	
	MSE	MAE	MSE	MAE	MSE	MAE	MSE	MAE
ETT	0.255	0.339	0.365	0.453	0.768	0.642	0.658	0.619
Electricity	0.201	0.317	0.274	0.368	0.258	0.357	0.312	0.402
Exchange	0.197	0.323	0.847	0.752	0.968	0.812	1.065	0.829
Traffic	0.613	0.388	0.719	0.391	0.684	0.384	0.732	0.423
Weather	0.266	0.336	0.300	0.384	0.458	0.490	0.689	0.596

Table 2. MSE and MAE results of different approaches with forecasting length 192

Models Metric	Autoformer		Informer		LogTrans		Reformer	
	MSE	MAE	MSE	MAE	MSE	MAE	MSE	MAE
ETT	0.281	0.340	0.533	0.563	0.989	0.757	1.078	0.827
Electricity	0.222	0.334	0.296	0.386	0.266	0.368	0.348	0.433
Exchange	0.300	0.369	1.204	0.895	1.040	0.851	1.188	0.906
Traffic	0.616	0.382	0.696	0.379	0.685	0.390	0.733	0.420
Weather	0.307	0.367	0.598	0.544	0.658	0.589	0.752	0.638

Table 3. MSE and MAE results of different approaches with forecasting length 336

Models Metric	Autoformer		Informer		LogTrans		Reformer	
	MSE	MAE	MSE	MAE	MSE	MAE	MSE	MAE
ETT	0.339	0.372	1.363	0.887	1.334	0.872	1.549	0.972
Electricity	0.231	0.338	0.300	0.394	0.280	0.380	0.350	0.433
Exchange	0.509	0.524	1.672	1.036	1.659	1.081	1.357	0.976
Traffic	0.622	0.337	0.777	0.420	0.733	0.408	0.742	0.420
Weather	0.359	0.395	0.578	0.523	0.797	0.652	0.639	0.596

Table 4. MSE and MAE results of different approaches with forecasting length 720

Models Metric	Autoformer		Informer		LogTrans		Reformer	
	MSE	MAE	MSE	MAE	MSE	MAE	MSE	MAE
ETT	0.422	0.419	3.379	1.388	3.048	1.328	2.631	1.242
Electricity	0.254	0.361	0.373	0.439	0.283	0.376	0.340	0.420
Exchange	1.337	0.941	2.478	1.310	1.941	1.127	1.510	1.016
Traffic	0.660	0.408	0.864	0.472	0.717	0.396	0.755	0.423
Weather	0.419	0.428	1.059	0.741	0.869	0.675	1.130	0.792

DISCUSSION

Table 1 compares the Mean Absolute Error and Mean Squared Error performance of different models across five datasets with the prediction length of 96. In the ETT dataset, Autoformer exhibits the best performance, with the lowest MSE (0.255) and MAE (0.339), indicating its superior accuracy. Informer, LogTrans, and Reformer show higher error rates, with LogTrans performing the worst (MSE: 0.768, MAE: 0.642). For the Electricity dataset, Autoformer again leads with the lowest MSE (0.201) and MAE (0.317), followed by LogTrans (MSE: 0.258, MAE: 0.357). Informer and Reformer have higher errors, with Reformer having the highest MAE (0.402). In the Exchange dataset, Autoformer achieves the best results, with the lowest MSE (0.197) and MAE (0.323). The other models perform significantly worse, particularly Reformer, which has the highest MSE (1.065) and MAE (0.829). Overall, Autoformer consistently provides the most accurate predictions across all datasets, demonstrating its effectiveness in long-term forecasting tasks.

Then the prediction length is increased from 96 to 192. As shown in Table 2, in the ETT dataset, Autoformer stands out with the lowest MSE (0.281) and MAE (0.340), indicating its superior predictive accuracy. In contrast, Reformer has the highest error rates (MSE: 1.078, MAE: 0.827), followed by Informer and LogTrans. For the Electricity dataset, Autoformer again proves to be the best performer, achieving an MSE of 0.222 and MAE of 0.334. LogTrans follows with slightly higher errors (MSE: 0.266, MAE: 0.368), while Informer and Reformer show greater inaccuracies, with Reformer having the highest MAE (0.433). In the Exchange dataset, Autoformer delivers the most accurate predictions with an MSE of 0.300 and MAE of 0.369. Other models perform considerably worse, particularly Informer (MSE: 1.204, MAE: 0.895) and Reformer (MSE: 1.188, MAE: 0.906). When it comes to the Traffic dataset, Autoformer achieves the lowest MAE (0.382), although its MSE (0.616) is slightly higher than that of LogTrans (MSE: 0.685, MAE: 0.390).

Reformer again exhibits the highest error rates (MSE: 0.733, MAE: 0.420). Lastly, in the Weather dataset, Autoformer leads with the lowest MSE (0.307) and MAE (0.367), outperforming Informer, LogTrans, and Reformer, with Reformer showing the poorest performance (MSE: 0.752, MAE: 0.638).

To further test the performances of these approaches, the prediction length is increased to 336. As shown in Table 3, in the ETT dataset, Autoformer outperforms all other models with an MSE of 0.339 and an MAE of 0.372. In contrast, Reformer has the highest error rates, with an MSE of 1.549 and an MAE of 0.972. This means Autoformer's MSE is approximately 78% lower than Reformer's, and its MAE is about 62% lower. For the Electricity dataset, Autoformer again shows the best performance with an MSE of 0.231 and an MAE of 0.338. Compared to Reformer, which has an MSE of 0.350 and an MAE of 0.433, Autoformer's MSE is around 34% lower, and its MAE is about 22% lower. In the Exchange dataset, Autoformer achieves the lowest MSE of 0.509 and MAE of 0.524. Informer and LogTrans perform significantly worse, with Informer having an MSE of 1.672 and an MAE of 1.036. This indicates that Autoformer's MSE is approximately 70% lower, and its MAE is 49% lower compared to Informer. Regarding the Traffic dataset, Auto-former shows the best MAE of 0.337 and a competitive MSE of 0.622. Informer, LogTrans, and Reformer have higher errors, with Reformer having the highest MSE (0.742) and MAE (0.420). Autoformer's MSE is about 16% lower than Reformer's, and its MAE is around 20% lower. In the Weather dataset, Autoformer leads with the lowest MSE of 0.359 and MAE of 0.395. Reformer has an MSE of 0.639 and an MAE of 0.596, indicating Autoformer's MSE is approximately 44% lower and its MAE is 34% lower than Reformer's.

Finally, the prediction length is extended to 720 for an extremely challenging case, as presented in Table 4. In the ETT dataset, Autoformer outperforms the other models with an MSE of 0.422 and an MAE of 0.419. Compared to Informer, which has the highest MSE of 3.379 and an MAE of 1.388, Autoformer's MSE is approximately 87.5% lower, and its MAE is around 69.8% lower. Similarly, Autoformer shows a 86.1% lower MSE and a 68.4% lower MAE compared to LogTrans (MSE: 3.048, MAE: 1.328). When compared to Reformer, Autoformer's MSE is 84.0% lower, and its MAE is 66.3% lower (Reformer MSE: 2.631, MAE: 1.242). For the Electricity dataset, Autoformer demonstrates the best performance with an MSE of 0.254 and an MAE of 0.361. Compared to Informer (MSE: 0.373, MAE: 0.439), Autoformer's MSE is about 31.9% lower, and its MAE is 17.7% lower. Autoformer also shows a 10.2% lower MSE and a 4.0% lower MAE compared to LogTrans (MSE: 0.283, MAE: 0.376). Compared to Reformer (MSE: 0.340, MAE: 0.420), Autoformer's MSE is 25.3% lower and its MAE is 14.0% lower. In the Exchange dataset, Autoformer achieves the best results with an MSE of 1.337 and an MAE of 0.941. Informer, which has the highest errors (MSE: 2.478, MAE: 1.310), shows an MSE that is 46.0% higher and an MAE that is 28.2% higher compared to Autoformer. LogTrans (MSE: 1.941, MAE: 1.127) has an MSE 31.1% higher and an MAE 16.5% higher than Autoformer. Reformer (MSE: 1.510, MAE: 1.016) shows an MSE 11.5% higher and an MAE 7.4% higher compared to Autoformer. For the Traffic dataset, Autoformer leads with an MSE of 0.660 and an MAE of 0.408. Informer (MSE: 0.864, MAE: 0.472) has an MSE that is 23.6% higher and an MAE that is 15.7% higher than Autoformer. LogTrans (MSE: 0.717, MAE: 0.396) shows an MSE that is 7.9% higher and an MAE 3.0% lower than Autoformer. Reformer (MSE: 0.755, MAE: 0.423) has an MSE that is 12.6% higher and an MAE 3.7% higher than Autoformer. In the Weather dataset, Autoformer also leads with an MSE of 0.419 and an MAE of 0.428. Compared to Informer (MSE: 1.059, MAE: 0.741), Autoformer's MSE is 60.4% lower and its MAE is 42.2% lower. LogTrans (MSE: 0.869, MAE: 0.675) has an MSE 51.8% higher and an MAE 36.6% higher than Autoformer. Reformer (MSE: 1.130, MAE: 0.792) shows an MSE 62.9% higher and an MAE 45.9% higher compared to Autoformer.

LIMITATIONS

Despite the significant advancements brought by Transformer-based models in time series forecasting, several limitations persist, challenging their broad applicability and effectiveness. One primary issue is the high computational complexity inherent in the self-attention mechanism, which has quadratic complexity with respect to the sequence length. This makes it computationally expensive and memory-intensive to handle long time series data, even with advancements such as LogTrans and Reformer attempting to reduce this complexity. Additionally, the permutation-invariant nature of Transformers can lead to the loss of crucial temporal information. Although positional encoding techniques are employed to mitigate this, they may not fully preserve the sequential order's importance, which is vital for capturing temporal dependencies accurately. This issue is particularly problematic because the precise sequence of data points is essential for understanding underlying patterns and trends in time series data.

Another significant challenge is the quality and quantity of data required for effective forecasting. Transformer models demand large volumes of high-quality data, and any gaps, inconsistencies, or noise can significantly impair their performance. Furthermore, real-world time series data often exhibit non-stationary behaviors, with statistical properties that change over time. This non-stationarity poses additional challenges for Transformers, which may struggle to adapt without dynamic mechanisms for handling trend and seasonality shifts. Additionally, the interpretability of these models remains limited, posing problems for applications where understanding the decision-making process is crucial. The high resource intensity for training and deployment, along with the risk of overfitting due to their high capacity, further complicates their practical use. These challenges necessitate ongoing research into more efficient architectures, enhanced interpretability, and robust handling of real-world data characteristics to fully harness the potential of Transformer-based models in time series forecasting.

CONCLUSION

In conclusion, Transformer-based models have significantly advanced the field of time series forecasting, offering improved performance over traditional methods and other machine learning techniques. These models, leveraging the self-attention mechanism, excel in capturing long-range dependencies, which is crucial for accurate long-term forecasting. Autoformer, Informer, LogTrans, and other Transformer variants have demonstrated their capabilities across various datasets, showcasing their potential to handle complex temporal patterns in real-world applications like energy consumption, traffic flow estimation, and financial market analysis.

However, despite their successes, Transformer-based models are not without limitations. The high computational complexity, particularly the quadratic complexity of the self-attention mechanism, poses challenges for scaling these models to very long sequences. Additionally, the permutation-invariant nature of Transformers can lead to the loss of crucial temporal information, which is essential for understanding time series data. The need for large volumes of high-quality data, along with the models' sensitivity to data quality and non-stationarity, further complicates their practical deployment. These limitations underscore the importance of continued research and development to address these challenges.

Future research directions should focus on developing more computationally efficient Transformer architectures that can handle long sequences without compromising performance. Improving the models' ability to retain temporal information and adapt to non-stationary data is also critical. Enhancing the interpretability of Transformer-based models will be crucial for their application in domains where understanding the decision-making process is vital. Additionally, exploring hybrid models that combine the strengths of traditional methods with deep learning approaches could provide more robust solutions for time series forecasting. By addressing these areas, future studies can unlock the full potential of Transformer-based models, paving the way for more accurate and reliable long-term forecasting in various real-world applications.

REFERENCES

Dong, Z., Yang, D., Reindl, T., & Walsh, W. M. (2013). Short-term solar irradiance forecasting using exponential smoothing state space model. *Energy*, 55, 1104–1113. DOI: 10.1016/j.energy.2013.04.027

Foumani, N. M., Tan, C. W., Webb, G. I., & Salehi, M. (2024). Improving position encoding of transformers for multivariate time series classification. *Data Mining and Knowledge Discovery*, 38(1), 22–48. DOI: 10.1007/s10618-023-00948-2

Hu, S., & Xiong, C. (2023). High-dimensional population inflow time series forecasting via an interpretable hierarchical transformer. *Transportation Research Part C, Emerging Technologies*, 146, 103962. DOI: 10.1016/j.trc.2022.103962

Huang, Z., Liang, D., Xu, P., & Xiang, B. (2020). Improve transformer models with better relative position embeddings. DOI: 10.18653/v1/2020.findings-emnlp.298

Kalpakis, K., Gada, D., & Puttagunta, V. (2001). Distance measures for effective clustering of ARIMA time-series. *Proceedings 2001 IEEE International Conference on Data Mining*, 273–280. DOI: 10.1109/ICDM.2001.989529

Kirisci, M., & Cagcag Yolcu, O. (2022). A new CNN-based model for financial time series: TAIEX and FTSE stocks forecasting. *Neural Processing Letters*, 54(4), 3357–3374. DOI: 10.1007/s11063-022-10767-z

Kitaev, N., Kaiser, Ł., & Levskaya, A. (2020). Reformer: The efficient transformer. *ArXiv Preprint ArXiv:2001.04451*.

Kitagawa, G., & Gersch, W. (1984). A smoothness priors–state space modeling of time series with trend and seasonality. *Journal of the American Statistical Association*, 79(386), 378–389.

Koohfar, S., Woldemariam, W., & Kumar, A. (2023). Prediction of electric vehicles charging demand: A transformer-based deep learning approach. *Sustainability (Basel)*, 15(3), 2105. DOI: 10.3390/su15032105

L'Heureux, A., Grolinger, K., & Capretz, M. A. M. (2022). Transformer-based model for electrical load forecasting. *Energies*, 15(14), 4993. DOI: 10.3390/en15144993

Lai, G., Chang, W.-C., Yang, Y., & Liu, H. (2018). Modeling long-and short-term temporal patterns with deep neural networks. *The 41st International ACM SIGIR Conference on Research & Development in Information Retrieval*, 95–104.

Lee, J., & Toutanova, K. (2018). Pre-training of deep bidirectional transformers for language understanding. *ArXiv Preprint ArXiv:1810.04805, 3(8)*.

Lezmi, E., & Xu, J. (2023). Time series forecasting with transformer models and application to asset management. *Available atSSRN* 4375798. DOI: 10.2139/ssrn.4375798

Li, L., Dai, S., Cao, Z., Hong, J., Jiang, S., & Yang, K. (2020). Using improved gradient-boosted decision tree algorithm based on Kalman filter (GBDT-KF) in time series prediction. *The Journal of Supercomputing*, 76(9), 6887–6900. DOI: 10.1007/s11227-019-03130-y

Li, S., Jin, X., Xuan, Y., Zhou, X., Chen, W., Wang, Y.-X., & Yan, X. (2019). Enhancing the locality and breaking the memory bottleneck of transformer on time series forecasting. *Advances in Neural Information Processing Systems*, 32.

Livieris, I. E., Pintelas, E., & Pintelas, P. (2020). A CNN–LSTM model for gold price time-series forecasting. *Neural Computing & Applications*, 32(23), 17351–17360. DOI: 10.1007/s00521-020-04867-x

Madan, R., & Mangipudi, P. S. (2018). Predicting computer network traffic: a time series forecasting approach using DWT, ARIMA and RNN. *2018 Eleventh International Conference on Contemporary Computing (IC3)*, 1–5. DOI: 10.1109/IC3.2018.8530608

Roberts, S., Osborne, M., Ebden, M., Reece, S., Gibson, N., & Aigrain, S. (2013). Gaussian processes for time-series modelling. *Philosophical Transactions of the Royal Society A: Mathematical, Physical and Engineering Sciences, 371*(1984), 20110550.

Sapankevych, N. I., & Sankar, R. (2009). Time series prediction using support vector machines: A survey. *IEEE Computational Intelligence Magazine*, 4(2), 24–38. DOI: 10.1109/MCI.2009.932254

Shumway, R. H., Stoffer, D. S., Shumway, R. H., & Stoffer, D. S. (2017). ARIMA models. *Time Series Analysis and Its Applications: With R Examples*, 75–163.

Tokgöz, A., & Ünal, G. (2018). A RNN based time series approach for forecasting turkish electricity load. *2018 26th Signal Processing and Communications Applications Conference (SIU)*, 1–4.

Tuli, S., Casale, G., & Jennings, N. R. (2022). Tranad: Deep transformer networks for anomaly detection in multivariate time series data. *ArXiv Preprint ArXiv:2201.07284*.

Vaswani, A., Shazeer, N., Parmar, N., Uszkoreit, J., Jones, L., Gomez, A. N., Kaiser, Ł., & Polosukhin, I. (2017). Attention is all you need. *Advances in Neural Information Processing Systems*, 30.

Wang, C., Wang, Y., Ding, Z., Zheng, T., Hu, J., & Zhang, K. (2022). A transformer-based method of multienergy load forecasting in integrated energy system. *IEEE Transactions on Smart Grid*, 13(4), 2703–2714. DOI: 10.1109/TSG.2022.3166600

Wang, D. (2022). Meta Reinforcement Learning with Hebbian Learning. *2022 IEEE 13th Annual Ubiquitous Computing, Electronics & Mobile Communication Conference (UEMCON)*, 52–58.

Wang, D. (2023a). Explainable deep reinforcement learning for knowledge graph reasoning. In *Recent Developments in Machine and Human Intelligence* (pp. 168–183). IGI Global. DOI: 10.4018/978-1-6684-9189-8.ch012

Wang, D. (2023b). Reinforcement Learning for Combinatorial Optimization. In *Encyclopedia of Data Science and Machine Learning* (pp. 2857–2871). IGI Global.

Wang, D. (2023c). Obstacle-aware Simultaneous Task and Energy Planning with Ordering Constraints. *2023 11th International Conference on Information and Communication Technology (ICoICT)*, 289–294.

Wang, D. (2023d). Out-of-Distribution Detection with Confidence Deep Reinforcement Learning. *2023 International Conference on Communications, Computing, Cybersecurity, and Informatics (CCCI)*, 1–7. DOI: 10.1109/CCCI58712.2023.10290768

Wang, D. (2024a). Robust Adversarial Deep Reinforcement Learning. In *Deep Learning, Reinforcement Learning, and the Rise of Intelligent Systems* (pp. 106–125). IGI Global. DOI: 10.4018/979-8-3693-1738-9.ch005

Wang, D. (2024b). Multi-agent Reinforcement Learning for Safe Driving in On-ramp Merging of Autonomous Vehicles. *2024 14th International Conference on Cloud Computing, Data Science & Engineering (Confluence)*, 644–651.

Wang, D., & Hu, M. (2021). Deep Deterministic Policy Gradient With Compatible Critic Network. *IEEE Transactions on Neural Networks and Learning Systems*. PMID: 34653007

Wang, D., & Hu, M. (2023). Contrastive learning methods for deep reinforcement learning. *IEEE Access : Practical Innovations, Open Solutions*, 11, 97107–97117. DOI: 10.1109/ACCESS.2023.3312383

Wang, D., Hu, M., & Gao, Y. (2018). Multi-criteria mission planning for a solar-powered multi-robot system. *International Design Engineering Technical Conferences and Computers and Information in Engineering Conference, 51753*, V02AT03A026.

Wang, D., Hu, M., & Weir, J. D. (2022). Simultaneous Task and Energy Planning using Deep Reinforcement Learning. *Information Sciences*, 607, 931–946. DOI: 10.1016/j.ins.2022.06.015

Wang, D., Zhao, J., Han, M., & Li, L. (2023). 4d Printing-Enabled Circular Economy: Disassembly Sequence Planning Using Reinforcement Learning. DOI: 10.2139/ssrn.4429186

Wen, Q., Zhou, T., Zhang, C., Chen, W., Ma, Z., Yan, J., & Sun, L. (2022). Transformers in time series: A survey. *ArXiv Preprint ArXiv:2202.07125*.

Wu, H., Xu, J., Wang, J., & Long, M. (2021). Autoformer: Decomposition transformers with auto-correlation for long-term series forecasting. *Advances in Neural Information Processing Systems*, 34, 22419–22430.

Xu, C., Li, J., Feng, B., & Lu, B. (2023). A financial time-series prediction model based on multiplex attention and linear transformer structure. *Applied Sciences (Basel, Switzerland)*, 13(8), 5175. DOI: 10.3390/app13085175

Yue, M., & Ma, S. (2023). LSTM-based transformer for transfer passenger flow forecasting between transportation integrated hubs in urban agglomeration. *Applied Sciences (Basel, Switzerland)*, 13(1), 637. DOI: 10.3390/app13010637

Yun, L., Wang, D., & Li, L. (2023). Explainable multi-agent deep reinforcement learning for real-time demand response towards sustainable manufacturing. *Applied Energy*, 347, 121324. DOI: 10.1016/j.apenergy.2023.121324

Zeng, A., Chen, M., Zhang, L., & Xu, Q. (2023). Are transformers effective for time series forecasting? *Proceedings of the AAAI Conference on Artificial Intelligence*, 37(9), 11121–11128. DOI: 10.1609/aaai.v37i9.26317

Zeng, Z., Xiao, H., Zhang, X., Koprinska, I., Wu, D., Wang, Z., Kirisci, M., & Cagcag Yolcu, O. (2018). Self CNN-based time series stream forecasting. *2018 International Joint Conference on Neural Networks (IJCNN), 54*(4), 1–8.

Zhang, C., Sjarif, N. N. A., & Ibrahim, R. (2024). Deep learning models for price forecasting of financial time series: A review of recent advancements: 2020–2022. *Wiley Interdisciplinary Reviews. Data Mining and Knowledge Discovery*, 14(1), e1519. DOI: 10.1002/widm.1519

Zhang, G. P. (2003). Time series forecasting using a hybrid ARIMA and neural network model. *Neurocomputing*, 50, 159–175. DOI: 10.1016/S0925-2312(01)00702-0

Zhou, H., Zhang, S., Peng, J., Zhang, S., Li, J., Xiong, H., & Informer, W. Z. (n.d.). Beyond efficient transformer for long sequence time-series forecasting. Https:// Doi. Org/10.1609/Aaai

Zhu, J., Zhao, Z., Zheng, X., An, Z., Guo, Q., Li, Z., Sun, J., & Guo, Y. (2023). Time-series power forecasting for wind and solar energy based on the SL-transformer. *Energies*, 16(22), 7610. DOI: 10.3390/en16227610

ADDITIONAL READING

Lim, B., & Zohren, S. (2021). Time-series forecasting with deep learning: A survey. *Philosophical Transactions. Series A, Mathematical, Physical, and Engineering Sciences*, 379(2194), 20200209. DOI: 10.1098/rsta.2020.0209 PMID: 33583273

Masini, R. P., Medeiros, M. C., & Mendes, E. F. (2023). Machine learning advances for time series forecasting. *Journal of Economic Surveys*, 37(1), 76–111. DOI: 10.1111/joes.12429

Torres, J. F., Hadjout, D., Sebaa, A., Martínez-Álvarez, F., & Troncoso, A. (2021). Deep learning for time series forecasting: A survey. *Big Data*, 9(1), 3–21. DOI: 10.1089/big.2020.0159 PMID: 33275484

Zerveas, G., Jayaraman, S., Patel, D., Bhamidipaty, A., & Eickhoff, C. (2021, August). A transformer-based framework for multivariate time series representation learning. In Proceedings of the 27th ACM SIGKDD conference on knowledge discovery & data mining (pp. 2114-2124). DOI: 10.1145/3447548.3467401

KEY TERMS AND DEFINITIONS

Deep Learning: Deep learning is a subset of machine learning that involves neural networks with multiple layers, or "deep" architectures, which enable the learning of complex patterns in large amounts of data.

Long Time Series Forecasting: Long time series forecasting is an extension of standard time series forecasting that specifically aims to predict outcomes far into the future, distinguishing it from shorter-term forecasts that may focus on immediate or near-term predictions. This method typically requires handling more complex patterns and long-range dependencies, which can increase the challenge of making accurate predictions.

Machine Learning: Machine learning is a branch of artificial intelligence that focuses on the development of algorithms and statistical models that enable computers to perform tasks without explicit instructions, relying instead on patterns and inference derived from data. It encompasses a range of techniques that allow systems to learn from and make predictions or decisions based on data.

Neural Network: A neural network is a computational model inspired by the structure of the brain, consisting of layers of interconnected nodes or "neurons" that process data through a network.

Time Series Forecasting: Time series forecasting is the process of analyzing time-ordered data points to predict future values. It utilizes statistical and machine learning methods to identify and extrapolate patterns observed in past data.

Chapter 8
Strategies for Spatial Data Management in Cloud Environments

Bimol Chandra Das
https://orcid.org/0009-0007-8388-8883
Trine University, USA

Munir Ahmad
https://orcid.org/0000-0003-4836-6151
Survey of Pakistan, Pakistan

Maida Maqsood
Government College Women University, Sialkot, Pakistan

ABSTRACT

Cloud platforms can enhance spatial data management with specialized services like databases, geocoding, and geospatial analytics. Databases such as Amazon Redshift with PostGIS, Microsoft Azure's Cosmos DB, and Google Cloud Spanner offer efficient storage, retrieval, and spatial data analysis. Geocoding services convert addresses into geographic coordinates, including Google's Geocoding API, OpenStreetMap Nominatim, and Mapbox's Geocoding API. Geospatial analytics tools from Amazon, Microsoft Azure, and Google Earth Engine provide actionable insights from spatial data. Optimization techniques like spatial indexing, partitioning, caching, and parallel processing (MapReduce and Apache Spark) enhance data access and processing. Security measures include access control, data encryption, and anonymization to protect sensitive information. Disaster recovery and backup strategies can ensure data resilience and business continuity. Utilizing these cloud services can transform spatial data management, unlocking its potential for analysis,

DOI: 10.4018/979-8-3693-5231-1.ch008

visualization, and decision-making.

INTRODUCTION

Geolocation data, or information about the location and attributes of objects located on the Earth's surface, is the basis for many disciplines (Apollo et al., 2023; Li et al., 2020). Spatial data is essential in urban planning which entails planning and management of infrastructures to reflect the sustainable development of cities (Gede Suacana et al., 2024; Huang et al., 2024). This data can be employed in environmental science to study and assess the condition of ecosystems, climate variations, and conservation of natural resources (de Lourdes Berrios Cintrón et al., 2024; Stankovics et al., 2024). Spatial data is also important in logistics, for instance, it enables effective planning of routes, supply chains, and delivery methods (Korpinen et al., 2023; P. Zhao et al., 2020; X. Zhao & Miao, 2023). Because of its complicated form, spatial data is normally incorporated into several layers of information including topographical maps, satellite images, and GPS coordinates. These formats need high skills in their storage format to facilitate easy storage and retrieval of large volumes of data. Some of the data manipulation techniques include georeferencing which links a dataset with geographical coordinates, and spatial interpolation which estimates values between two points.

However, processing spatial data requires specific methods and techniques such as Geographic Information Systems and remote sensing (Sangeetha et al., 2024; Sunkur & Mauremootoo, 2024; Yusuf & Jauro, 2024). Due to its capability of storing, processing, and portraying spatial data, GIS makes it easier to identify trends or patterns that are hard to notice. Aerial photography, which is the use of satellite or aircraft data to capture information on the environment, is a valuable information source used in studying changes in the environment, and the growth of towns and cities among other factors. Cloud computing has brought about global opportunities as well as challenges that affect management of spatial data. Cloud solutions offer great flexibility due to the ability to scale capacity very easily including the storage and computing capabilities (Alhaidari et al., 2023; Dhifaoui et al., 2024; Doo et al., 2024). This is particularly useful in managing large and highly volatile spatial data sets that can undergo frequent changes in their size and /or structure. Moreover, cost-savings can be seen in the utilization of the cloud computing model due to the lack of large and costly investments in hardware and equipment.

This provides the organizations with the opportunity to subsidize only the resources they consume and this cuts down the expenses greatly. One of the most important pillars with which cloud computing is confidently presenting itself is on-demand access. Users can get spatial data and processing tools from any internet connection and share their work and ideas from any place globally, making the work progressive. This is particularly helpful for international groups to have a flow of their working process, especially for projects that include the exchange of real-time data. However, the use of cloud computing in management of spatial data also comes with challenges. Location-based applications do not perform well when traditional data management practices are used on cloud platforms, it is mainly due to the dissimilarities in architecture as well as operation. For example, in cloud computing, there is need to come up with different ways of putting, retrieving, and protecting data. Therefore, there is a need for effective and efficient data governance policies when implementing spatial data in the cloud as well as an understanding of the cloud security relevancies.

It also poses challenges that concern data transfer and bandwidth in cloud infrastructure, in a process of optimizing spatial data (Ahmad et al., 2023; Ahmad & Ali, 2023). Opting for a large spatial dataset can prove to be expensive and time taking since the data is required to migrate to the cloud and back. These problems relate to both device configuration and the underlying methods of transferring data, for which the application of suitable compression algorithms can be a viable solution. Also, spatial data processing in the cloud is frequently needed to utilize preprogrammed software and platforms capable of taking advantage of parallel computing in the shortest time possible for data analysis.

This chapter aims at focusing on the proper management of spatial data in the cloud platform. Through these strategies, the users can be enabled to grasp knowledge and resources to harness cloud computing for spatial data analysis and applications fully. The subsequent subtopics provide insights into the functional approaches to the optimization and management of geographical data on the cloud. We then highlight the selection factors to store spatial data, describe cloud services for spatial-context data, and describe methods for improving spatial data access and processing. Additionally, we will touch upon security considerations and best practices for ensuring the integrity and privacy of spatial data in the cloud.

DATA STORAGE FORMATS FOR CLOUD-BASED SPATIAL DATA

Choosing the optimal data storage format for your cloud-based spatial data is crucial for efficient management, analysis, and scalability. This section explores various popular formats, their advantages and limitations, and introduce cloud-native options offered by different cloud providers.

Popular Spatial Data Formats

Geodatabases

Geodatabases are comprehensive file formats designed to store spatial features such as points, lines, and polygons, along with associated attributes and metadata. These databases provide a robust framework for managing and analyzing spatial data, offering advanced functionality for data integrity, topology, and spatial relationships. Popular examples include the File Geodatabase (FGDB) and Personal Geodatabase. The FGDB is known for its scalability and support for large datasets, while the Personal Geodatabase is more suitable for smaller projects and individual users. Despite their rich functionality, geodatabases can be complex to use and often require specialized software, such as Esri's ArcGIS, for creation, editing, and analysis (Allen & Gerike, 2021; Bajjali, 2018; Nikolov & Atanasova, 2024; Pászto et al., 2021).

Shapefiles

Shapefiles are a widely used vector format composed of multiple files, typically including .shp (geometry), .shx (shape index), and .dbf (attribute data). This format is known for its simplicity and interoperability with various GIS software packages, making it a standard choice for many GIS professionals. Shapefiles are particularly well-suited for smaller datasets due to their straightforward structure. However, they can become cumbersome when dealing with large or complex datasets, as they lack support for advanced data types and relationships. Additionally, shapefiles have a size limitation of 2 GB per file, which can be restrictive for extensive datasets (Batcheller et al., 2007; Hu et al., 2015; Zhu et al., 2019).

GeoJSON

GeoJSON is a text-based format that offers a lightweight and human-readable way to represent vector geospatial data. It uses JavaScript Object Notation (JSON) to encode geographic features, making it easily parsable by various programming languages and web services. GeoJSON is ideal for data exchange and integration with web applications, enabling seamless interaction with mapping libraries such as Leaflet and OpenLayers. This format is particularly advantageous for web-based visualizations and applications due to its simplicity and compatibility with web technologies. However, GeoJSON can be less efficient than binary formats for storing and querying large datasets, as its text-based nature can lead to increased file sizes and slower processing times (Butler et al., 2016; Horbiński & Lorek, 2022).

KML (Keyhole Markup Language)

KML is a text-based format primarily used for creating map overlays and visualizations. Developed by Google, it is widely used for sharing geospatial information with tools like Google Earth and Google Maps. KML files support the representation of vector data, such as points, lines, and polygons, and can include additional elements like images, 3D models, and descriptive text. This makes KML suitable for creating rich, interactive maps and visualizations. However, KML offers limited functionality for complex spatial analysis and is not as efficient as other formats for handling large datasets or performing advanced geospatial operations. Despite these limitations, its ease of use and integration with popular mapping tools make KML a popular choice for many applications (De Paor & Whitmeyer, 2011; Li & Lu, 2018).

Each of these spatial data formats has its strengths and weaknesses. Geodatabases offer comprehensive functionality but require specialized software. Shapefiles are simple and widely compatible but can be cumbersome for large datasets. GeoJSON is ideal for web applications due to its lightweight and human-readable nature but may be less efficient for large data. KML excels in creating visualizations but is limited in analytical capabilities. Table 1 shows the comparison of the popular spatial data formats.

Table 1. Comparison of Popular Spatial Data Formats

Features	Geodatabase	Shapefile	GeoJSON	KML
Format Type	Vector	Vector	Text-based	Text-based
Ideal for	Complex datasets with rich attributes	Smaller datasets, interoperability	Data exchange, web applications	Map overlays, visualizations
Advantages	Rich functionality supports metadata	Simple, widely used, multiple software compatibility	Lightweight, human-readable	Easy sharing, works with Google Earth
Limitations	The complex structure requires specialized software	Can be cumbersome for large datasets	Less efficient for querying large datasets	Limited functionality for complex analysis

Cloud-Native Storage Options

Cloud providers offer specialized storage solutions designed to handle large datasets, including spatial data. These services are optimized for scalability, cost-effectiveness, and ease of access, making them ideal for managing complex spatial information.

Amazon S3 (Simple Storage Service)

Amazon S3 is a highly scalable and cost-effective object storage service provided by Amazon Web Services (AWS). It supports a wide range of data formats, including those commonly used for spatial data such as GeoTIFF and GeoJSON. S3 allows for efficient data access and retrieval through its robust API, which can be easily integrated with various cloud-based processing tools. This makes it suitable for applications requiring frequent data retrieval and manipulation. S3's flexible storage classes also allow users to optimize costs based on data access patterns, with options like Standard, Intelligent-Tiering, and Glacier for long-term archival storage (Dubey et al., 2023; Kingsley, 2024a).

Azure Blob Storage

Azure Blob Storage, offered by Microsoft Azure, provides a scalable and cost-effective solution for storing unstructured data, including spatial datasets. Similar to Amazon S3, Azure Blob Storage is designed for high availability and durability, ensuring that spatial data remains accessible and secure. It integrates seamlessly with other Azure services, such as Azure Synapse Analytics and Azure Machine Learning, enabling comprehensive spatial data processing and analysis. Azure Blob Storage supports multiple storage tiers, including Hot, Cool, and Archive, allowing users to manage costs by selecting the appropriate tier based on their data usage needs (Brendan Brow, 2021; Kingsley, 2024b).

Google Cloud Storage

Google Cloud Storage is another robust object storage solution that offers platform-agnostic support for various data formats, including spatial data. It provides seamless integration with other Google Cloud services, such as BigQuery for data analysis and Google Earth Engine for geospatial visualization and analysis. Google Cloud Storage is designed for high performance and reliability, featuring multiple storage classes like Standard, Nearline, Coldline, and Archive, which cater to different access and cost requirements. The service's API and SDKs enable easy integration with custom applications and workflows, making it a versatile choice for managing spatial data in the cloud (Bisong, 2019; Cloud, 2023).

Benefits and Considerations

Each of these cloud-native storage options offers unique advantages for handling spatial data. All three services—Amazon S3, Azure Blob Storage, and Google Cloud Storage—provide virtually unlimited storage capacity, allowing users to scale up as their data grows. Moreover, by offering multiple storage tiers, these services enable users to optimize costs based on data access frequency and retention requirements. Furthermore, seamless integration with their respective cloud ecosystems allows users to leverage a wide range of tools for data processing, analysis, and visualization. Additionally, robust APIs and SDKs facilitate easy data access and manipulation, supporting diverse applications and workflows.

However, there are also considerations to keep in mind. For example, transferring large datasets to and from the cloud can incur significant costs, so it's essential to factor in data egress charges. Similarly, ensuring data security and compliance with regulations is crucial. Each provider offers robust security features, but users must configure them correctly to protect sensitive spatial data. Further, while cloud storage is generally reliable, the performance can vary based on the chosen storage class and the specific use case. It's important to select the appropriate storage tier to meet performance requirements.

Cloud-native storage options from leading providers like AWS, Microsoft Azure, and Google Cloud offer powerful solutions for managing spatial data. By understanding the strengths and considerations of each service, users can make informed decisions to optimize their spatial data storage and processing needs. Table 2 shows the cloud-native storage options for spatial data.

Table 2. Cloud-Native Storage Options for Spatial Data

Cloud Provider	Service Name	Description
Amazon Web Services (AWS)	Amazon S3 (Simple Storage Service)	Scalable, cost-effective object storage for various data formats, including GeoTIFF and GeoJSON
Microsoft Azure	Azure Blob Storage	Similar to S3, offers scalable storage for unstructured data including spatial datasets
Google Cloud Platform	Google Cloud Storage	Platform-agnostic object storage for various data formats, including spatial data

Choosing the Right Format

Selecting the optimal data storage format is critical and depends on several specific factors.

Data Size and Complexity

Geodatabases are well-suited for managing smaller datasets with complex spatial relationships and extensive metadata. They provide robust functionality for maintaining data integrity, managing topology, and supporting sophisticated spatial analysis. In contrast, Cloud-Native Options (e.g., Amazon S3, Azure Blob Storage, Google Cloud Storage) are ideal for handling large and scalable datasets. These options offer virtually unlimited storage capacity, making them suitable for datasets that grow over time or require high availability. They also support various spatial data formats and provide cost-effective solutions for extensive data storage needs.

Interoperability

GeoJSON format is excellent for data exchange due to its lightweight, text-based structure, which makes it easily readable by both humans and machines. It integrates well with web applications and is supported by many programming languages and web services. GeoJSON is ideal for scenarios where interoperability and ease of data sharing are paramount. Whereas, Native Formats (e.g., FGDB for Esri's ArcGIS) are suitable when workflow relies heavily on specific software tools, using native formats ensures seamless integration and optimal performance. For instance, File Geodatabases are tailored for use with Esri's ArcGIS platform, offering advanced features and efficient data management within that ecosystem.

Processing Needs

Cloud storage solutions like Amazon S3, Azure Blob Storage, and Google Cloud Storage are designed to integrate seamlessly with their respective cloud ecosystems. This integration facilitates efficient data processing and analysis using cloud-based tools. For example, Amazon S3 can work with AWS Lambda for serverless computing, Azure Blob Storage can integrate with Azure Synapse Analytics for big data processing, and Google Cloud Storage can be used with BigQuery for large-scale data analysis. These options provide the flexibility to leverage powerful cloud computing resources, enabling scalable and efficient processing workflows.

By understanding the advantages and limitations of various data storage formats, one can choose the most suitable option for managing your cloud-based spatial data effectively.

LEVERAGING CLOUD SERVICES FOR SPATIAL DATA MANAGEMENT

Cloud platforms offer a robust ecosystem of specialized services designed to streamline and optimize spatial data management. This section delves into some key services that can significantly enhance your workflow:

Spatial Databases

Managing geospatial data can be challenging for traditional relational databases due to their inherent limitations in handling complex spatial queries and data types. To address these challenges, cloud providers have introduced specialized spatial databases designed specifically for efficient storage, retrieval, and analysis of spatial features.

Amazon Redshift with PostGIS is a powerful combination that integrates Amazon Redshift, a high-performance cloud data warehouse, with PostGIS, a leading open-source spatial database extension. By leveraging PostGIS's robust spatial capabilities within Amazon Redshift, users can execute intricate spatial queries and perform detailed spatial analyses on vast datasets. This solution is particularly advantageous for applications requiring scalable and performant spatial data handling in a cloud environment (Aws, 2023; Mete & Yomralioglu, 2021).

Microsoft Azure's Cosmos DB, a globally distributed NoSQL database service, includes built-in support for geospatial data types and operations. Cosmos DB Geospatial enables developers to effortlessly store, manage, and query location-based data at scale. Its flexible schema and automatic indexing streamline the process of storing and retrieving spatial data, making it suitable for applications demanding real-time geospatial analytics and insights (Flowers, 2023; Kingsley, 2024b).

Google Cloud Spanner is a fully managed, globally distributed relational database service that offers robust support for geospatial data. Spanner's unique architecture combines the scalability of NoSQL databases with the transactional consistency of traditional relational databases. It supports geographically distributed data storage and efficient querying of spatial data, making it an ideal choice for applications requiring strong consistency and high availability across large geographic regions (Kingsley, 2023; Shashi, 2023).

These specialized spatial databases not only address the limitations of traditional relational databases in handling geospatial data but also provide scalable and efficient solutions for organizations looking to leverage spatial information for analytics, mapping, and location-based services in a cloud-native environment.

Geocoding Services

Geocoding, a crucial process in spatial data management, transforms textual addresses or locations into precise geographic coordinates (latitude and longitude). Cloud-based geocoding services have simplified this task, offering efficient ways to enhance spatial datasets with accurate location information.

Google's Geocoding API enables developers to convert addresses into geographic coordinates programmatically. It supports batch geocoding for processing large datasets efficiently and offers reverse geocoding capabilities to retrieve addresses from given coordinates. The API also provides advanced features like viewport biasing to prioritize results within a specific geographic area, making it suitable for diverse applications requiring reliable and detailed location data (Lemke et al., 2015; Saha et al., 2022).

Moreover, OpenStreetMap Nominatim is a robust open-source geocoding service that accesses a global database of geographic information. It provides free access to geocoding functionality, making it an economical choice for users working with open data or seeking a cost-effective geocoding solution. Nominatim supports both forward and reverse geocoding operations, allowing users to convert between textual addresses and geographic coordinates seamlessly (Kilic et al., 2023; Pérez & Aybar, 2024).

Similarly, Mapbox offers a versatile Geocoding API tailored for businesses needing comprehensive geocoding solutions. The API includes features such as address autocomplete to assist users in entering locations accurately, fuzzy matching for handling incomplete or misspelled addresses, and robust reverse geocoding capabilities. Mapbox's geocoding service is known for its reliability and scalability, making it suitable for applications ranging from mobile navigation to enterprise GIS solutions (Airlangga & Rachman, 2022; Rzeszewski, 2023).

These cloud-based geocoding services not only streamline the process of converting addresses into spatial coordinates but also provide additional functionalities that enhance spatial data management and application development. Whether for mapping applications, logistics optimization, or location-based services, leveraging these services enables businesses and developers to integrate precise location intelligence into their solutions effectively.

Geospatial Analytics Tools

Cloud platforms offer a diverse array of geospatial analytics tools designed to extract actionable insights from spatial datasets, enabling informed decision-making and enhancing business operations.

Amazon provides a comprehensive suite of geospatial analytics services tailored for various spatial analysis tasks. This includes route optimization to streamline logistics and transportation planning, heatmap generation for visualizing spatial data intensity and geofencing capabilities for defining virtual perimeters and triggering alerts based on geographic boundaries. Amazon Location Analytics empowers businesses to leverage spatial data effectively for improving operational efficiency and customer experience.

Similarly, Microsoft Azure Maps offers robust spatial analysis tools that facilitate detailed examination of spatial relationships within data. This includes functionalities for identifying nearest neighbors to optimize resource allocation or service delivery, performing network analysis on transportation routes to enhance route planning and efficiency, and conducting geospatial queries to extract relevant insights from location-based data. Azure Maps Spatial Analysis supports businesses in making data-driven decisions by providing actionable spatial intelligence (Andersson, 2023; Wolf et al., 2022).

Further, Google Earth Engine is a powerful cloud-based platform designed for accessing, processing, and analyzing vast geospatial datasets. It offers advanced tools for image analysis, such as spectral indices calculation and classification, enabling users to monitor environmental changes, land cover dynamics, and vegetation health over time. Earth Engine also supports time series analysis of satellite imagery, facilitating the study of temporal trends and patterns across different geographic regions. Additionally, it integrates machine learning capabilities for automated feature extraction and prediction tasks based on geospatial data, making it a valuable tool for research, conservation efforts, and disaster response planning (Amani et al., 2020; Kumar & Mutanga, 2018; Q. Zhao et al., 2021).

These geospatial analytics tools provided by Amazon, Microsoft Azure, and Google Cloud enable organizations to derive valuable insights from spatial data, ranging from optimizing resource allocation and improving operational workflows to advancing scientific research and environmental monitoring initiatives. By leveraging these cloud services, you can transform your spatial data management from a cumbersome task to a streamlined and efficient process that unlocks the true potential of your geospatial data for analysis, visualization, and informed decision-making.

OPTIMIZING DATA ACCESS AND PROCESSING

The vast storage capacity of the cloud, while advantageous, can also present challenges for efficient data access and processing, especially with large spatial datasets. This section outlines various strategies for optimizing data access and processing in the cloud environment, allowing you to unlock the full potential of your spatial data for analysis.

Optimizing Data Access in Spatial Databases

Similar to traditional databases, spatial databases employ indexing techniques to expedite data retrieval based on spatial relationships. Spatial indexes such as R-trees and B-trees organize spatial data in a hierarchical structure, facilitating quicker access to features within specific geographic areas. By indexing spatial data, databases can efficiently handle complex spatial queries and spatial joins, improving overall query performance and response times.

Moreover, partitioning involves dividing large datasets into smaller, more manageable segments based on spatial or thematic criteria. For instance, a national dataset can be partitioned by geographic regions (e.g., states, and provinces) or by thematic attributes (e.g., land use categories). This strategy enables selective querying of specific partitions rather than the entire dataset, thereby reducing computational overhead and improving query efficiency. Partitioning also enhances scalability by allowing parallel processing of data segments across distributed computing resources.

To minimize latency and optimize data access, caching frequently accessed spatial data is crucial. Cloud providers offer caching services that store data on high-performance storage closer to compute resources. By caching spatial data, organizations can reduce the frequency of data retrieval from the primary storage location, thereby accelerating data access times for applications and queries. Caching strategies can be tailored to prioritize frequently accessed spatial datasets or specific layers within spatial databases, enhancing overall system performance and responsiveness.

Implementing these optimization techniques—indexing for efficient spatial query processing, partitioning for targeted data retrieval, and caching for reduced latency can empower organizations to maximize the performance and scalability of their spatial databases in cloud environments. By strategically managing data access and storage, businesses can enhance operational efficiency, support real-time analytics, and deliver responsive geospatial applications to meet diverse business needs.

Parallel Processing for Large Datasets

Traditional single-threaded processing methods often struggle to efficiently handle the vast volumes of data involved in spatial analytics. Cloud platforms provide robust solutions for parallel processing, enabling organizations to distribute computational workloads across multiple virtual machines or containers.

MapReduce is a widely adopted programming paradigm designed for parallel processing of large datasets. In the context of spatial data, the "map" phase divides the dataset into smaller partitions and processes them independently across distributed nodes. The "reduce" phase then consolidates and aggregates the intermediate results to produce the final output. Cloud platforms offer managed MapReduce services that simplify the deployment and management of distributed computing tasks, making it easier to implement scalable spatial analytics workflows (Hedayati et al., 2023; Sun et al., 2023).

Apache Spark is also a powerful open-source framework renowned for its capabilities in distributed data processing. Spark excels in handling large-scale analytics tasks, including spatial data analysis. It supports in-memory processing, which significantly accelerates data processing speeds for iterative algorithms and complex computations. Spark's rich ecosystem includes libraries for machine learning (MLlib), graph processing (GraphX), and streaming data analysis (Spark Streaming), making it a versatile choice for performing advanced spatial analytics on distributed datasets (Manconi et al., 2023; Salloum et al., 2016).

Moreover, cloud providers offer specialized services tailored for distributed processing within their ecosystems. For example, Amazon Web Services (AWS) provides Elastic MapReduce (EMR), a managed Hadoop framework that supports MapReduce applications and other distributed computing paradigms. AWS Lambda enables serverless computing, allowing for event-driven parallel processing without managing infrastructure. Similarly, Microsoft Azure offers Azure Batch for executing parallel jobs at scale and Azure Functions for serverless compute tasks, both integrating seamlessly with Azure's suite of spatial data services.

These parallel processing approaches empower organizations to overcome the limitations of single-threaded processing, enabling faster and more efficient analysis of large spatial datasets. By leveraging cloud-based distributed computing frameworks and managed services, businesses can achieve enhanced scalability, performance, and agility in their spatial analytics workflows, ultimately deriving valuable insights and making data-driven decisions more effectively.

SECURITY CONSIDERATIONS FOR SPATIAL DATA IN THE CLOUD

The security of spatial data in the cloud environment is paramount. Spatial data can be sensitive, revealing locations of critical infrastructure, sensitive ecosystems, or even private residences. A typical security measures for cloud-based spatial data is depicted in Figure 1. This section highlights essential considerations for securing your spatial data in the cloud, ensuring its confidentiality, integrity, and availability.

Access Control Mechanisms

Effective access control mechanisms are essential for securing spatial data in cloud environments, ensuring that only authorized users and applications can access, modify, or manage sensitive information.

Cloud providers offer comprehensive Identity and Access Management (IAM) systems that enable organizations to manage user identities and define fine-grained access policies. IAM allows administrators to create roles with specific permissions tailored to different user groups or individuals. For spatial data, IAM can be used to restrict access based on factors such as data sensitivity or operational roles, ensuring that users have minimal privileges necessary to perform their tasks without compromising security.

Moreover, multi-factor authentication (MFA) enhances security by requiring users to provide multiple verification factors during the authentication process. Beyond the standard username and password, MFA may involve a one-time code sent to a registered device, biometric verification (e.g., fingerprint scan), or hardware security token. By adding a layer of authentication, MFA mitigates the risks associated with compromised credentials and unauthorized access attempts, particularly critical for accessing sensitive spatial data stored in the cloud.

Further, network security groups (NSGs) are cloud-based firewall rules that control inbound and outbound network traffic to virtual machines and other cloud resources. Organizations can define NSGs to restrict access based on IP addresses, port ranges, and protocols, thereby safeguarding spatial data from unauthorized network access. NSGs help enforce security policies by limiting communication to approved networks or specific endpoints, reducing the surface area for potential security threats, and ensuring compliance with data protection regulations.

By implementing these access control mechanisms—leveraging IAM for role-based access control, integrating MFA for enhanced authentication security, and utilizing NSGs to manage network traffic—organizations can strengthen the security posture of their spatial data in cloud environments. These measures not only protect against unauthorized access and data breaches but also uphold confidentiality, integrity, and availability of critical spatial data assets.

Data Encryption

Securing spatial data at rest is crucial for protecting sensitive information stored in cloud environments. Cloud providers offer robust encryption mechanisms to safeguard data stored in cloud storage services. Cloud providers typically offer Server-Side Encryption (SSE), where encryption and decryption are managed by the cloud service. SSE encrypts spatial data before it is written to disk and decrypts it when accessed by authorized users or applications. Encryption keys are managed and controlled by the cloud provider, ensuring data confidentiality without requiring additional management overhead from the user. Moreover, for enhanced control over encryption keys and added security, client-side encryption allows organizations to encrypt spatial data before uploading it to the cloud storage service. Encryption keys are managed by the user, providing complete ownership and control over data access and decryption. Client-side encryption ensures that data remains encrypted throughout its lifecycle in the cloud, offering an additional layer of protection against unauthorized access and data breaches.

Encrypting data during transit between on-premises environments and cloud storage services is essential to prevent interception and maintain data confidentiality. Secure protocols such as HTTPS (Hypertext Transfer Protocol Secure) encrypt data transmissions using Transport Layer Security (TLS) or Secure Sockets Layer (SSL) protocols. By encrypting data in transit, organizations ensure that spatial data remains protected from eavesdropping and unauthorized interception during transmission over public networks.

Data Anonymization

Data anonymization is crucial for protecting privacy when handling sensitive spatial data. It involves modifying data to remove or obfuscate identifying information while retaining its utility for analysis. Combine individual data points into larger groups to obscure specific details while retaining overall trends. For spatial data, this could involve aggregating individual location points into clusters or summarizing data at higher geographic levels (e.g., city or region). Similarly, replace precise data values with more generalized ones to reduce granularity. For example, instead of storing exact GPS coordinates of buildings, generalize the data to represent broader areas or zones. This approach protects individual privacy while still enabling analysis of spatial patterns and trends, such as creating heatmaps to visualize population density across neighborhoods.

Differential privacy is an advanced technique that adds calibrated noise to data queries or outputs, ensuring that statistical analyses do not reveal sensitive individual information. This method is particularly effective for protecting privacy in datasets used for research, policy analysis, and public health studies. In the context of spatial data, differential privacy can be applied to queries or aggregated results to prevent the identification of specific individuals or locations while still providing accurate statistical insights. This approach maintains the utility of spatial data for analysis without compromising individual privacy.

By implementing aggregation, generalization, and differential privacy techniques, organizations can effectively anonymize spatial data to comply with privacy regulations and protect sensitive information. These methods enable responsible data sharing for research, public policy, and commercial applications while minimizing the risks associated with re-identification and unauthorized disclosure of personal or sensitive spatial data.

Figure 1. Security measures for cloud-based spatial data

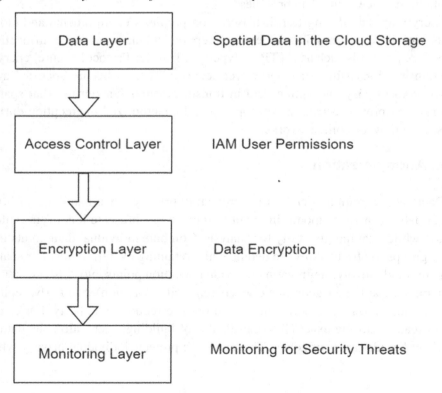

Disaster Recovery and Backups

To safeguard spatial data against unforeseen events and ensure business continuity, it's essential to establish robust disaster recovery (DR) and backup strategies.

Disaster Recovery Plans

Create a detailed disaster recovery plan that outlines procedures, responsibilities, and resources for recovering spatial data in various disaster scenarios. Identify critical spatial datasets, applications, and dependencies that require prioritized recovery efforts. Similarly, leverage cloud providers' data replication and recovery services to enhance resilience. Cloud platforms offer options such as geo-redundant storage, which replicates data across multiple geographic regions to mitigate risks from regional outages or disasters. Further, regularly test your disaster recovery procedures to validate their effectiveness and identify any gaps or issues. Conduct simulated disaster scenarios to ensure readiness and optimize recovery times.

Regular Backups

Establish a consistent backup schedule for spatial data, considering the frequency of updates and the criticality of the information. Automated backup solutions can streamline the process and ensure backups are performed at regular intervals. Similarly, store backups in a separate cloud storage location from your primary data or consider on-premises backups for added redundancy. Offsite backups protect against data loss due to site-specific disasters or localized failures. Further, implement versioning and retention policies for backups to maintain multiple historical copies of spatial data. This enables recovery from specific points in time, facilitating data rollback in case of accidental deletion, corruption, or ransomware attacks.

By implementing a comprehensive disaster recovery plan and regular backup strategy, organizations can mitigate the impact of disruptions on spatial data operations. Leveraging cloud infrastructure for data replication and storage diversification enhances resilience, ensuring that spatial data remains accessible and recoverable in adverse scenarios. These practices not only safeguard against data loss but also support compliance with regulatory requirements and stakeholder expectations for business continuity.

CONCLUSION

Cloud platforms offer a robust ecosystem of specialized services designed to streamline and optimize spatial data management. They include spatial databases, geocoding services, and geospatial analytics tools, all of which enhance workflow efficiency and data handling capabilities. Spatial databases like Amazon Redshift with PostGIS, Microsoft Azure's Cosmos DB, and Google Cloud Spanner are tailored for efficient storage, retrieval, and analysis of spatial features, addressing traditional databases' limitations. Geocoding services such as Google's Geocoding API, OpenStreetMap Nominatim, and Mapbox's Geocoding API facilitate the transformation of textual addresses into geographic coordinates, essential for spatial data management. Geospatial analytics tools from Amazon, Microsoft Azure, and Google Earth Engine enable the extraction of actionable insights from spatial datasets, aiding in decision-making and business operations. To optimize data access and processing, techniques like spatial indexing, data partitioning, caching, and parallel processing (using frameworks like MapReduce and Apache Spark) are employed. Security considerations for spatial data in the cloud encompass robust access control mechanisms, data encryption, and anonymization techniques to protect sensitive information and ensure privacy. Effective disaster recovery and backup strategies, including regular backups, geo-redundant storage, and comprehensive disaster recovery plans, are essential to safeguard against data loss and ensure business continuity. By leveraging these cloud services and strategies, organizations can transform spatial data management from a cumbersome task to a streamlined, efficient process that unlocks the full potential of geospatial data for analysis, visualization, and informed decision-making.

REFERENCES

Ahmad, M., & Ali, A. (2023). Mapping the future of sustainable development through cloud-based solutions: A case study of openstreetmap. In *Promoting Sustainable Management Through Technological Innovation* (pp. 153–176). IGI Global. DOI: 10.4018/978-1-6684-9979-5.ch011

Ahmad, M., Ali, A., & Khiyal, M. S. H. (2023). Fog Computing for Spatial Data Infrastructure: Challenges and Opportunities. In D. P. Acharjya & K. Ahmed P. (Eds.), *Multi-Disciplinary Applications of Fog Computing: Responsiveness in Real-Time* (pp. 152–178). IGI Global. DOI: 10.4018/978-1-6684-4466-5.ch008

Airlangga, P., & Rachman, A. A. (2022). Deployment of Location Mapping Results Based on Application Programming Interface. *NEWTON: Networking and Information Technology*, 1(3). Advance online publication. DOI: 10.32764/newton.v1i3.1922

Alhaidari, F., Rahman, A., & Zagrouba, R. (2023). Cloud of Things: Architecture, applications and challenges. *Journal of Ambient Intelligence and Humanized Computing*, 14(5). Advance online publication. DOI: 10.1007/s12652-020-02448-3

Allen, D. W., & Gerike, M. J. (2021). Focus on Geodatabases in ArcGIS Pro. *Photogrammetric Engineering and Remote Sensing*, 87(7). Advance online publication. DOI: 10.14358/pers.87.7.468

Amani, M., Ghorbanian, A., Ahmadi, S. A., Kakooei, M., Moghimi, A., Mirmazloumi, S. M., Moghaddam, S. H. A., Mahdavi, S., Ghahremanloo, M., Parsian, S., Wu, Q., & Brisco, B. (2020). Google Earth Engine Cloud Computing Platform for Remote Sensing Big Data Applications: A Comprehensive Review. *IEEE Journal of Selected Topics in Applied Earth Observations and Remote Sensing*, 13. Advance online publication. DOI: 10.1109/JSTARS.2020.3021052

Andersson, J. C. (2023). *Learning Microsoft Azure*. O'Reilly Media, Inc.

Apollo, M., Jakubiak, M., Nistor, S., Lewinska, P., Krawczyk, A., Borowski, L., Specht, M., Krzykowska-Piotrowska, K., Marchel, Ł., Peska-Siwik, A., Kardoš, M., & Maciuk, K. (2023). Geodata in science: A review of selected scientific fields. *Acta Scientiarum Polonorum. Formatio Circumiectus*, 22(2). Advance online publication. DOI: 10.15576/ASP.FC/2023.22.2.02

Aws. (2023). *Amazon Redshift Cloud Data Warehouse*. https://aws.amazon.com/redshift/

Bajjali, W. (2018). Geodatabase. In *ArcGIS for Environmental and Water Issues* (pp. 103–116). Springer International Publishing., DOI: 10.1007/978-3-319-61158-7_7

Batcheller, J. K., Gittings, B. M., & Dowers, S. (2007). The performance of vector oriented data storage strategies in ESRI's ArcGIS. *Transactions in GIS*, 11(1). Advance online publication. DOI: 10.1111/j.1467-9671.2007.01032.x

Bisong, E. (2019). Google Cloud Storage (GCS). In *Building Machine Learning and Deep Learning Models on Google Cloud Platform*. DOI: 10.1007/978-1-4842-4470-8_4

Brendan Brow. (2021). *Azure Blob Storage | Microsoft Azure*. Microsoft.

Butler, H., Daly, M., Doyle, A., Gillies, S., Schaub, T., & Schmidt, C. (2016). The GeoJSON format specification. In *IRFC 7946* (Vol. 67).

Cloud, G. (2023). *Cloud Storage | Google Cloud*. Google.

de Lourdes Berrios Cintrón, M., Broomandi, P., Cárdenas-Escudero, J., Cáceres, J. O., & Galán-Madruga, D. (2024). Elucidating Best Geospatial Estimation Method Applied to Environmental Sciences. *Bulletin of Environmental Contamination and Toxicology*, 112(1). Advance online publication. DOI: 10.1007/s00128-023-03835-0 PMID: 38063862

De Paor, D. G., & Whitmeyer, S. J. (2011). Geological and geophysical modeling on virtual globes using KML, COLLADA, and Javascript. *Computers & Geosciences*, 37(1). Advance online publication. DOI: 10.1016/j.cageo.2010.05.003

Dhifaoui, S., Houaidia, C., & Saidane, L. A. (2024). Computing paradigms for smart farming in the era of drones: A systematic review. *Annales Des Telecommunications. Annales des Télécommunications*, 79(1–2). Advance online publication. DOI: 10.1007/s12243-023-00997-0

Doo, F. X., Kulkarni, P., Siegel, E. L., Toland, M., Yi, P. H., Carlos, R. C., & Parekh, V. S. (2024). Economic and Environmental Costs of Cloud Technologies for Medical Imaging and Radiology Artificial Intelligence. *Journal of the American College of Radiology*, 21(2). Advance online publication. DOI: 10.1016/j.jacr.2023.11.011 PMID: 38072221

Dubey, P., Kumar Tiwari, A., & Raja, R. (2023). Amazon Web Services: the Definitive Guide for Beginners and Advanced Users. In *Amazon Web Services: the Definitive Guide for Beginners and Advanced Users*. DOI: 10.2174/97898151658211230101

Flowers, S. (2023). *Designing and Implementing Cloud-native Applications Using Microsoft Azure Cosmos DB*.

Gede Suacana, I. W., Sudana, I. W., Wiratmaja, I. N., & Rukmawati, D. (2024). Urban Land Consolidation Policy in the Context of Creating a Good Environment According to Spatial Planning in Indonesia. *Journal of Wood Science*, 3(2). Advance online publication. DOI: 10.58344/jws.v3i2.559

Hedayati, S., Maleki, N., Olsson, T., Ahlgren, F., Seyednezhad, M., & Berahmand, K. (2023). MapReduce scheduling algorithms in Hadoop: a systematic study. In *Journal of Cloud Computing* (Vol. 12, Issue 1). DOI: 10.1186/s13677-023-00520-9

Horbiński, T., & Lorek, D. (2022). The use of Leaflet and GeoJSON files for creating the interactive web map of the preindustrial state of the natural environment. In *Journal of Spatial Science* (Vol. 67, Issue 1). DOI: 10.1080/14498596.2020.1713237

Hu, D., Ma, S., Guo, F., Lu, G., & Liu, J. (2015). Describing data formats of geographical models. *Environmental Earth Sciences*, 74(10). Advance online publication. DOI: 10.1007/s12665-015-4737-4

Huang, X., Jiang, Y., & Mostafavi, A. (2024). The emergence of urban heat traps and human mobility in 20 US cities. *NPJ Urban Sustainability*, 4(1). Advance online publication. DOI: 10.1038/s42949-024-00142-3

Kilic, B., Hacar, M., & Gülgen, F. (2023). Effects of reverse geocoding on OpenStreetMap tag quality assessment. *Transactions in GIS*, 27(5). Advance online publication. DOI: 10.1111/tgis.13089

Kingsley, M. S. (2023). Cloud Platform. In *Cloud Technologies and Services: Theoretical Concepts and Practical Applications* (pp. 143–156). Springer.

Kingsley, M. S. (2024a). Amazon Web Services (AWS). In *Textbooks in Telecommunications Engineering: Vol. Part F1656*. DOI: 10.1007/978-3-031-33669-0_6

Kingsley, M. S. (2024b). Microsoft Azure. In *Cloud Technologies and Services : Theoretical Concepts and Practical Applications* (pp. 127–141). Springer International Publishing. DOI: 10.1007/978-3-031-33669-0_7

Korpinen, O. J., & Aalto, M. KC, R., Tokola, T., & Ranta, T. (2023). Utilisation of Spatial Data in Energy Biomass Supply Chain Research—A Review. In *Energies* (Vol. 16, Issue 2). DOI: 10.3390/en16020893

Kumar, L., & Mutanga, O. (2018). Google Earth Engine applications since inception: Usage, trends, and potential. *Remote Sensing*, 10(10). Advance online publication. DOI: 10.3390/rs10101509

Lemke, D., Mattauch, V., Heidinger, O., & Hense, H. W. (2015). Who Hits the Mark? A Comparative Study of the Free Geocoding Services of Google and OpenStreetMap. *Gesundheitswesen (Bundesverband der Ärzte des Öffentlichen Gesundheitsdienstes (Germany))*, 77(8–9). Advance online publication. DOI: 10.1055/s-0035-1549939 PMID: 26154258

Li, D., Guo, W., Chang, X., & Li, X. (2020). From earth observation to human observation: Geocomputation for social science. *Journal of Geographical Sciences*, 30(2). Advance online publication. DOI: 10.1007/s11442-020-1725-8

Li, D., & Lu, M. (2018). Integrating geometric models, site images and GIS based on Google Earth and Keyhole Markup Language. *Automation in Construction*, 89. Advance online publication. DOI: 10.1016/j.autcon.2018.02.002

Manconi, A., Gnocchi, M., Milanesi, L., Marullo, O., & Armano, G. (2023). Framing Apache Spark in life sciences. In *Heliyon* (Vol. 9, Issue 2). DOI: 10.1016/j.heliyon.2023.e13368

Mete, M. O., & Yomralioglu, T. (2021). Implementation of serverless cloud GIS platform for land valuation. *International Journal of Digital Earth*, 14(7). Advance online publication. DOI: 10.1080/17538947.2021.1889056

Nikolov, H., & Atanasova, M. (2024). Local Geodatabase as Tool for Monitoring the Landslide "Thracian Cliffs." *Advances in Science. Technology and Innovation*. Advance online publication. DOI: 10.1007/978-3-031-48715-6_27

Pászto, V., Pánek, J., & Burian, J. (2021). Geodatabase of publicly available information about czech municipalities' local administration. *Data*, 6(8). Advance online publication. DOI: 10.3390/data6080089

Pérez, V., & Aybar, C. (2024). Challenges in Geocoding: An Analysis of R Packages and Web Scraping Approaches. *ISPRS International Journal of Geo-Information*, 13(6), 170.

Rzeszewski, M. (2023). Mapbox. In *Evaluating Participatory Mapping Software*. DOI: 10.1007/978-3-031-19594-5_2

Saha, S., Basu, S., Majumder, K., & Chakravarty, D. (2022). Extension of Search Facilities Provided by 'CoWIN' Using Google's Geocoding API and APIs of 'CoWIN' and 'openweathermap.org.' *Communications in Computer and Information Science, 1534 CCIS*. DOI: 10.1007/978-3-030-96040-7_14

Salloum, S., Dautov, R., Chen, X., Peng, P. X., & Huang, J. Z. (2016). Big data analytics on Apache Spark. In *International Journal of Data Science and Analytics* (Vol. 1, pp. 3–4). Issues. DOI: 10.1007/s41060-016-0027-9

Sangeetha, C., Moond, V., Rajesh, G. M., Damor, J. S., Pandey, S. K., Kumar, P., & Singh, B. (2024). Remote Sensing and Geographic Information Systems for Precision Agriculture: A Review. *International Journal of Environment and Climate Change*, 14(2). Advance online publication. DOI: 10.9734/ijecc/2024/v14i23945

Shashi, A. (2023). Designing Applications for Google Cloud Platform. In *Designing Applications for Google Cloud Platform*. DOI: 10.1007/978-1-4842-9511-3

Stankovics, P., Schillaci, C., Pump, J., Birli, B., Ferraro, G., Munafò, M., Di Leginio, M., Hermann, T., Montanarella, L., & Tóth, G. (2024). A framework for co-designing decision-support systems for policy implementation: The LANDSUPPORT experience. *Land Degradation & Development*, 35(5). Advance online publication. DOI: 10.1002/ldr.5030

Sun, X., He, Y., Wu, D., & Huang, J. Z. (2023). Survey of Distributed Computing Frameworks for Supporting Big Data Analysis. *Big Data Mining and Analytics*, 6(2). Advance online publication. DOI: 10.26599/BDMA.2022.9020014

Sunkur, R., & Mauremootoo, J. (2024). Spatio-temporal Analysis of An Invasive Alien Species, Vachellia nilotica, on Rodrigues Island, Mauritius, Using Geographic Information Systems and Remote Sensing Techniques. *Indonesian Journal of Earth Sciences*, 4(1). Advance online publication. DOI: 10.52562/injoes.2024.835

Wolf, K., Dawson, R. J., Mills, J. P., Blythe, P., & Morley, J. (2022). Towards a digital twin for supporting multi-agency incident management in a smart city. *Scientific Reports*, 12(1). Advance online publication. DOI: 10.1038/s41598-022-20178-8 PMID: 36171329

Yusuf, M. B., & Jauro, U. A. (2024). *Impact of Land Use and Land Cover Change on Deforestation in the Central Taraba State: A Geographic Information System and Remote Sensing Analysis*. Environmental Protection Research. DOI: 10.37256/epr.4120243326

Zhao, P., Liu, X., Shi, W., Jia, T., Li, W., & Chen, M. (2020). An empirical study on the intra-urban goods movement patterns using logistics big data. *International Journal of Geographical Information Science*, 34(6). Advance online publication. DOI: 10.1080/13658816.2018.1520236

Zhao, Q., Yu, L., Li, X., Peng, D., Zhang, Y., & Gong, P. (2021). Progress and trends in the application of google earth and google earth engine. In *Remote Sensing* (Vol. 13, Issue 18). DOI: 10.3390/rs13183778

Zhao, X., & Miao, C. (2023). Research on the Spatial Pattern of the Logistics Industry Based on POI Data: A Case Study of Zhengzhou City. *Sustainability*, 15(21). Advance online publication. DOI: 10.3390/su152115574

Zhu, J., Wang, X., Wang, P., Wu, Z., & Kim, M. J. (2019). Integration of BIM and GIS: Geometry from IFC to shapefile using open-source technology. *Automation in Construction*, 102. Advance online publication. DOI: 10.1016/j.autcon.2019.02.014

Chapter 9
Efficient Human Gait Detection Hybrid Approach With MobileBiLSTM

S. Jasmine
P.S.R. Engineering College, India

P. Marichamy
P.S.R. Engineering College, India

K. Ramalakshmi
P.S.R. Engineering College, India

Aqil Ahmed J.
P.S.R. Engineering College, India

ABSTRACT

This work focuses on human gait detection, a branch of biometrics that examines people's specific walking patterns. Walking pattern, or gait, has drawn interest because of its potential in several applications, such as surveillance and medical monitoring, where non-intrusive identification is critical. The CASIA-B dataset, which included samples with varying gait patterns, clothing changes, and luggage presence, was used for this study. High accuracy rates were attained by the suggested MobileNet with BiLSTM model: 94.52% accuracy with bags and 96.89% accuracy without them. These findings highlight the model's practical applicability and further the development of gait analysis techniques.

DOI: 10.4018/979-8-3693-5231-1.ch009

I. INTRODUCTION

Biometrics encompasses the assessment and analysis of distinctive physical and behavioral traits to authenticate identity. Gait, defined as a person's unique walking pattern, is a crucial biometric trait for identification purposes. Unlike other biometric traits such as fingerprints or iris patterns, gait can be captured at a distance and without the subject's cooperation, making it particularly useful for surveillance applications. This ability to non-invasively identify individuals in various settings has spurred significant research interest and technological advancements in gait recognition.

Gait detection strategies can be divided into three primary techniques: machine vision method, floor sensor method, and wearable sensor method. In the machine vision approach, video capture and image processing using one or more cameras extract gait features from silhouette images obtained from the video. This approach is widely used due to its non-intrusive nature and the ability to capture gait patterns in natural settings. For instance, the use of the CASIA-B dataset, which contains various gait patterns under different conditions, has been pivotal in training and testing gait recognition models. This dataset includes sequences with different viewing angles, clothing variations, and the presence of carried objects, providing a comprehensive evaluation framework for gait recognition algorithms.

The floor sensor method involves gait feature extraction from images generated by floor sensors. These sensors capture pressure and motion data as individuals walk over them, allowing for the analysis of foot pressure patterns and stride lengths. Studies have shown that floor sensors can achieve high accuracy in controlled environments, such as smart homes or secure facilities, where the deployment of such sensors is feasible. For example, research conducted in smart home environments has demonstrated that floor sensor-based gait recognition can be effectively used for elder care, monitoring movements to detect falls or irregularities in walking patterns.

The wearable sensor method utilizes a range of techniques, such as gait kinematics, kinetics, and electromyography, to derive gait signatures. Wearable sensors, such as accelerometers and gyroscopes, are typically embedded in devices like smartphones or smartwatches. These sensors collect detailed motion data, which can then be analyzed to extract gait features. This method is particularly effective in clinical settings for monitoring patients with gait abnormalities or assessing the effectiveness of rehabilitation programs. Wearable technology has advanced significantly, enabling continuous gait monitoring and real-time feedback, which is beneficial for personalized healthcare and fitness tracking.

Gait recognition systems have significant applications in surveillance, particularly in security sectors such as railway stations and airports, where monitoring for shoplifters, criminals, and maintaining public safety is critical. These systems can identify individuals from a distance, without the need for physical contact or cooperation, making them ideal for use in crowded and dynamic environments. For example, gait recognition has been used to identify suspects in criminal investigations and to monitor the movements of individuals under surveillance. In recent years, advancements in video surveillance technology and the integration of artificial intelligence have further enhanced the capabilities of gait recognition systems, enabling more accurate and real-time identification. In addition to security applications, gait recognition is also employed in other contexts, such as identifying individuals in malls, during protests, and in various public spaces. For instance, during large public gatherings, gait recognition systems can help authorities monitor crowd dynamics and identify potential threats. In healthcare, gait analysis is used to assess and diagnose gait disorders, design personalized rehabilitation programs, and monitor patient progress. Moreover, in the field of sports, gait analysis is used to optimize athletic performance by identifying and correcting inefficient movement patterns.

A gait cycle acts as the core time unit in gait recognition, depicting a repeated sequence from a resting position to right-foot-forward (RFF), back to rest, then left-foot-forward (LFF), and returning to rest. This cycle encapsulates all body positions during walking and contains crucial information regarding dynamic and relative motion among body parts. The dynamics and periodicity of the gait cycle characterize the individual's motion, making it a vital element in gait recognition. Figure 1 illustrates the typical positions observed throughout a human gait cycle.

Figure 1. Typical positions observed throughout a human gait cycle

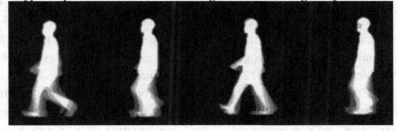

The gait cycle provides a comprehensive representation of an individual's walking pattern, including parameters such as stride length, step width, and joint angles. These parameters are essential for distinguishing between different individuals and for detecting any abnormalities in gait, which may indicate underlying health issues. Detailed analysis of the gait cycle can also provide insights into the biomechanics of walking, helping in the design of assistive devices and prosthetics.

Historically, gait recognition depended on manual methods, categorized into model-based and model-free approaches. Model-based methods employ a structural framework to extract gait features but often require substantial computational resources. These methods typically involve creating a detailed model of the human body, capturing the positions and movements of various joints and limbs. While accurate, model-based approaches are computationally intensive and may not be suitable for real-time applications. For example, model-based techniques like the use of kinematic models have been employed to study gait in clinical settings, providing valuable information about joint movements and muscle coordination. Conversely, model-free methods capture gait information directly from silhouettes, making them more computationally efficient. These methods analyze the overall shape and motion of the silhouette as it moves through different gait phases. However, they may miss some critical details, such as the precise movements of individual body parts, which can affect recognition accuracy. Despite their limitations, model-free approaches have been widely adopted in practical applications due to their simplicity and effectiveness.

The Gait Energy Image (GEI) method represents the energy distribution of a person's gait pattern, condensing temporal information into a single image. It captures the spatiotemporal characteristics of the gait for analysis and recognition, considering factors such as viewing perspective, object carriage, walking pace, and clothing obstructions. The robustness of GEI is particularly notable in scenarios where individuals wear multiple layers of clothing or carry bags, enhancing system resilience (Babaee et al. 2020). For instance, GEI has been successfully used to recognize individuals carrying backpacks or wearing long coats, which can significantly alter their silhouette.

Recent advances in deep learning, particularly Convolutional Neural Networks (CNNs), have significantly improved detection and grouping tasks. CNNs' ability to comprehend intricate and distinctive features from input images has led to their widespread adoption in gait recognition. Pre-trained CNNs like ResNet (He et al. 2016), AlexNet (Krizhevsky 2012), DenseNet (Huang et al. 2017), and VGG (Simonyan and Zisserman 2014) have been leveraged for their proficiency in extracting pertinent features from extensive datasets. These models are capable of learning complex patterns and representations from large amounts of data, which can then be used to distinguish between different individuals. For example, studies have demonstrated the effectiveness of using CNNs for gait recognition under varying conditions, such as changes in lighting, background, and viewing angles.

Techniques such as image augmentation (Saleh and Hamoud 2021) and models utilizing Gait Pal and Pal Entropy (GPPE) images combined with proposed distances (Ehaimir et al. 2017) have also been implemented to enhance recognition accuracy. Image augmentation involves artificially increasing the diversity of training data by applying random transformations, such as rotations, translations, and scaling, to the input images. This helps improve the robustness of the trained model to variations in viewing angles and lighting conditions. Additionally, the use of GANs (Generative Adversarial Networks) for synthetic data generation has emerged as a novel approach to augmenting training datasets, providing diverse and realistic gait patterns for model training. An improved version of the GEI-based gait recognition system utilizing neural networks, including the Unet architecture, has been implemented for better results. Unet is particularly advantageous in capturing intricate spatial features while preserving contextual information, making it well-suited for gait recognition tasks. By combining GEI with deep learning techniques, researchers have developed models that achieve high accuracy in challenging conditions, such as occlusions and variations in clothing. The incorporation of attention mechanisms in CNNs has further enhanced the performance of gait recognition models by allowing them to focus on the most informative regions of the gait sequence.

The field of gait recognition has witnessed several recent innovations aimed at improving accuracy, robustness, and applicability. One notable development is the integration of multimodal data, combining visual data with other types of sensor data to enhance recognition performance. For instance, fusing video data with data from inertial measurement units (IMUs) has shown promise in improving the robustness of gait recognition systems under varying conditions. Another significant innovation is the use of transfer learning, where models pre-trained on large, generic datasets are fine-tuned on gait-specific datasets. This approach leverages the knowledge acquired from large-scale datasets to improve the performance of gait recognition models, especially when limited gait-specific data is available.

Advancements in explainable AI (XAI) have also contributed to the field by making gait recognition models more interpretable and trustworthy. By understanding how these models make decisions, researchers can identify potential biases and improve the fairness and transparency of gait recognition systems. Furthermore, the development of lightweight and efficient deep learning models has made it feasible to deploy gait recognition systems on edge devices, such as smartphones and IoT devices. This enables real-time gait analysis and recognition in various applications, from mobile security to personalized healthcare.

The proposed work integrates MobileNet and BiLSTM, two state-of-the-art algorithms, to create an efficient hybrid approach for gait detection. MobileNet, renowned for its lightweight and efficient architecture, is ideally suited for deployment on mobile and edge devices, enabling real-time gait recognition. Meanwhile, BiLSTM excels at capturing temporal dependencies in sequential data, thereby enhancing the model's ability to accurately interpret and analyze gait patterns over time. By combining the strengths of both algorithms, this hybrid approach achieves superior performance in gait detection, offering a robust solution that is both highly effective and computationally efficient.

The subsequent sections of this paper are organized as follows: Section 2 illustrates existing works related to gait detection, providing a comprehensive review of the state-of-the-art techniques and their respective advantages and limitations. Section 3 outlines the materials and methods used in this study, detailing the dataset, pre-processing steps, and the proposed model architecture. Section 4 presents the results and discussions, highlighting the performance of the proposed model compared to existing methods and discussing the implications of the findings. Finally, Section 5 concludes the paper and suggests future developments, identifying potential areas for further research and improvement in gait recognition technology.

II. EXISTING WORKS

In the field of gait detection, Investigators have offered diverse approaches, broadly classified into two categories: manual approaches and automatic approaches. Manual approaches require extensive effort to extract predetermined features from gait data. This procedure typically involves identifying particular gait attributes such as cadence, length of the stride, and rhythm, and using these attributes to distinguish between individuals. However, manual methods suffer from reliance on extensive expertise to select pertinent features and may overlook the intricate nuances and complexities within gait patterns. In contrast, automatic methods autonomously encrypt complex features without human intervention. These techniques utilize neural networks to differentiate underlying patterns in gait data and subsequently identify individuals based on these differentiated patterns. Automatic approaches offer the benefit of capturing subtle and intricate features inherent in gait patterns, thereby enhancing recognition accuracy compared to manual approaches.

A. Manual Approach

Manual techniques for gait detection are typically classified into two primary categories: model-based and model-free approaches. The model-based approach utilizes a structured representation of a human figure, often depicted as stick figures with joint configurations, to extract motion data. On the other hand, the model-free approach directly analyzes motion data without relying on a predefined human prototype (Lee et al. 2014; Lee et al. 2014; Mogan et al. 2017; Mogan et al. 2017; Arshad et al. 2019; Lee et al. 2017 and Lee et al. 2013).

1) Model-Based Approach

A deterministic learning process was utilized to capture spatial-temporal and kinematic features. The spatial-temporal aspects included measurements like the dimensions of lower limbs and the combined silhouette area, while kinematic features encompassed the angles of four joints in the lower limbs (Deng et al. 2017). Additionally, a gait detection technique based on posture was introduced, employing a weighted K-nearest neighbor (KNN) model (Sah et al. 2020). This method involved 20 coordinates extracted from a Kinect skeletal model, then transforming them into Center of Body (CoB) coordinates, capturing the spatial positioning and dimensions of various body parts in each frame. Further, in a research the Shape features were obtained using Histograms of Oriented Gradients (HOG), with subsequent dimensionality reduction via Principal Component Analysis (PCA). Geometric features were computed alongside statistical measures, and the feature of the texture were acquired using a Volume Local Binary Pattern (VLBP) method (Sharif et al. 2020).

A method for gait detection was proposed utilizing relative triangle area and cosine dissimilarity which were optimized with the Adam optimization method (Bari et al. 2019). Su et al. (2005) employed discrete cosine analysis to examine hand and limb movements, applying multi-class support vector machines (SVMs) to distinguish between different gaits. Further, a pose-centered gait recognition system was proposed emphasizing the importance of movement around human joints as key features (Sokolova et al. 2018). Lishani et al. (2019) focused on gait identification by extracting features using multi-scale local binary patterns and Gabor filters. Also an automatic biometric system was designed to recognize individuals based on gait patterns extracted from video frame skeletons (Bhargavas et al. 2017). Babaee et al. (2018) introduced a gait recognition algorithm that identifies individuals even from partial gait cycles. Wang et al. (2017) devised a gait assessment system based on measures of gait variability and shapes of gait cycle trajectories, providing insights into gait characteristics. Chaitanya et al. (2020) explored continuous authentication of smartphone users by analyzing physiological or behavioral attributes, extending gait recognition to mobile device security. Few researchers employed angle calculation and convolutional neural networks for precise identification of the human gait (Elharrouss et al. 2020). Finally a system was designed to learn distinctive gait features from raw motion capture data, facilitating classification through template comparison in a centralized database (Balazia et al. 2018). These techniques contribute significantly to advancing gait recognition methodologies, each offering unique insights and applications in the field.

2) Model-Free Approach

Transient Binary Patterns (TBP) are texture classifiers of motion characteristics generated along the temporal axis. This approach was introduced in 2015. Numerous scales, including pixel-by-pixel, regional, and global, are estimated for these patterns. Histogram representations are produced at each scale to offer a thorough picture of motion characteristics (Lee et al. 2015). An approach was put out to extract gait characteristics devoid of the need for silhouettes. This method uses optical flow to directly capture complex sequences from gait videos. These sequences are used to compute features including Histograms of Oriented Gradients (HOG), Histograms of Optical Flow (HOF), as well as the horizontal and vertical components of optical flow. This method successfully renders persons' appearance traits as well as their motion dynamics (Khan, M.H.; Farid, M.S.; Grzegorzek, M 2019). In addition, a different research addressed issues with gait analysis such as disturbances, obstruction, and partial silhouettes. The method comprised convolving frames from gait sequences with pre-trained filters, producing feature maps for every frame. After that, the gradients of these feature maps were calculated, and techniques like majority voting and Euclidean distance were used to classify the subjects.

Liao et al. (2020) introduced the PoseGait model, which utilizes a human 3D pose estimated from images by convolutional neural networks (CNNs) for gait identification. This approach extracts gait features directly from image data, enabling robust recognition without the need for explicit modeling of human anatomy. Gao et al. (2021) focused on optimizing support vector machines (SVMs) for gait recognition using an artificial bee colony algorithm and a combination of multiple features. By leveraging nature-inspired optimization techniques, this method enhances the performance of SVM classifiers, leading to more accurate gait recognition systems. Sepas-Moghaddam et al. (2022) conducted a comprehensive survey on various technologies, methodologies, and approaches for gait recognition. Their work includes comparisons of datasets and neural network architectures, providing valuable insights into the existing techniques. Together, these model-free approaches contribute to the advancement of gait recognition technology by offering novel strategies for feature extraction and classification.

B. Automatic Methods

Deep learning networks have been increasingly popular in the past decade, especially when processing unstructured input such as text and pictures. These networks are made to automatically identify important information in data, which minimizes the need for human interaction. Convolutional Neural Networks (CNNs) are a prominent deep learning architecture used for image identification and categorization. A

CNN model consisting of convolutional layers in addition to max-pooling layers, with a fully connected layer, was suggested (Wu et al. 2018). Max-pooling layers are incorporated to assist reduce noise and distortions, while convolutional layers extract attributes that are essential for recognition. The logistic loss function is used to determine classification. In order to handle three input images concurrently, a multichannel CNN was devised. This model consists of a classifier layer, one fusion layer, five pooling layers, five convolution layers, and one fully connected layer. Using various convolutional kernels, features are retrieved from the three channels concurrently, and discrepancies between the channels are calculated in the fusion layer. The softmax function is used for classification (Wang et al. 2020). In a similar way research was done on using 3D CNNs to identify spatiotemporal gait characteristics. Four layers of convolution, two layers for pooling, two layers that are fully connected, a classifier layer, and a final convolution layer that applies batch normalization constitute the network (Gul et al. 2021). Few researchers explored employing triplet loss to produce unique features using angular Softmax loss to improve feature variety (Han et al. 2022). Using GaitSet as the core of the network, researchers added a batch normalization layer to improve the loss functions following the feature extraction layers (Chao et al. 2021). The field of gait recognition has been using transfer learning techniques more and more. The VGG-D model was used for classification, and Joint Bayesian was used to compute view variance (Li, C.; Min, X.; Sun, S.; Lin, W.; Tang, Z 2017).

Furthermore, gait feature extraction was performed using The VGG-19 model and AlexNet model, which combined the obtained features via parallel fusion. By evaluating the fused features' entropy and skewness, the ideal feature set was identified (Arshad et al. 2020). The optimal features were chosen using the Kurtosis and Principle Score approaches, with a pre-trained VGG-16 network being used for feature extraction. One versus All Multi Support Vector Machine (OAMSVM) was used for the classification (Mehmood et al. 2022). Ensemble approaches are becoming popular for improving the accuracy of gait identification. A method for transforming gait energy into a framework was created, and it uses a classifier ensemble for classification and temporal and spatial filtering for feature extraction (Ghaeminia, M.H.; Shokouhi, S.B 2019). Moreover, ensemble learning was applied, using other classifiers for result aggregation and a main classifier made up of five CNN models. Additionally, transformer integration into architectures of CNN for gait recognition has been investigated by researchers (Wang et al. 2021). To reduce the effects of external elements such as clothing and carrying circumstances, a CNN-based network including a discrimination net, joint intensity transformer, and joint intensity metric estimate net was developed

(Li et al. 2019). In a similar vein, to handle intra- and inter-subject variances, a paired spatial transformer network was created (Xu, C.; Makihara, Y.; Li, X.; Yagi, Y.; Lu, J 2020). Furthermore, a network was created to encode non-local and regionalized characteristics during the categorization step by utilizing self-attention processes (Wang et al. 2021). The feature extractor was pre-trained using the DINO algorithm that uses Vision Transformer architecture and input into a fully interconnected neural network for classification

(Pinci´c et al. 2022). In order to achieve improved performance with greater accuracies for Brodatz texture and brain MRI/CT images, respectively, this study (Kusakunniran 2014) introduces a Stochastic Multinomial Logarithmic (SML) based approach using deep convolutional neural networks for accurate medical image classification. This approach outperforms previously available techniques. Moreover, Gait-ViT was presented, which uses a Vision Transformer (ViT) model that has already been trained to understand gait features. For subject identification, the retrieved characteristics were fed into a multi-layer perceptron (MLP) (Mogan et al. 2022).

A method employing deep convolutional neural networks (CNNs) for gait recognition was introduced, utilizing similarity learning to extract discriminative features. This approach has been extensively tested on various network architectures and preprocessing techniques, ensuring robust performance across different conditions (Wu et al. 2016).

Qiu et al. (2021) introduced an ensemble empirical mode decomposition method tailored for analyzing and recognizing gait motions, particularly suitable for individuals using exoskeletons. This technique enhances the understanding of gait patterns and facilitates accurate recognition, even in complex scenarios. Si et al. (2020) developed a remote sensing system for security area monitoring, integrating face detection with gait signals to enhance classification accuracy. By combining multiple biometric modalities, their system provides a robust solution for person identification and surveillance. To increase the accuracy and versatility of gait tracking systems, a model incorporating LSTM (Long Short-Term Memory) together with an orthogonalization technique for exoskeleton following was proposed (Zhou et al. 2021). Furthermore, a gait identification system with great accuracy was presented by using several classification methods and the SOTON compact dataset together with multi-view normalization approaches (Ng et al. 2014). Luo et al. (2015) devised a gait system that incorporates Accumulated Frame Difference Energy Image (AFDEI) alongside Gait Energy Image (GEI) for classification, enhancing the representation of gait dynamics and improving recognition performance. Hanqing chao et al. (2019) developed the Gaitset algorithm, which performs Set Pooling for gait recognition based on the CASIA-B dataset, offering a novel approach to feature aggregation and classification. These automatic methods demonstrate the forefront of gait recognition technology, providing efficient and effective solutions for diverse application scenarios.

The existing body of work in gait detection has demonstrated significant progress through diverse methodologies, classified into manual and automatic approaches. Manual methods, including model-based and model-free techniques, have contributed foundational knowledge by leveraging structural representations and direct motion data analysis. However, they often require extensive expertise and may miss intricate details within gait patterns. In contrast, automatic methods have harnessed the power of deep learning, particularly Convolutional Neural Networks (CNNs) and Long Short-Term Memory (LSTM) networks, to autonomously extract complex features from gait data, achieving higher accuracy and robustness in various conditions.

Despite these advancements, there remains a critical need for more efficient and effective gait detection systems, particularly those that can operate in real-time on mobile and edge devices. The integration of MobileNet and BiLSTM in this research addresses this need by combining the lightweight and efficient architecture of MobileNet with the temporal dependency capturing capabilities of BiLSTM. This hybrid approach not only enhances recognition accuracy but also ensures computational efficiency, making it well-suited for deployment in practical, real-world scenarios. The present research work is poised to significantly advance the field by providing a robust, real-time solution for gait detection that leverages the strengths of both MobileNet and BiLSTM, addressing the limitations of previous methods and opening new avenues for application in surveillance, healthcare, and mobile security.

III. MATERIALS AND METHODS

This section outlines the methodologies employed for efficient human gait detection using a hybrid approach that combines MobileNet and BiLSTM. The study leverages the CASIA-B dataset, which provides a comprehensive set of gait patterns under varying conditions, including different viewing angles, clothing variations, and the presence of carried objects.The workflow begins with data collection and preprocessing. The CASIA-B dataset was selected for its diverse gait patterns. Initial steps involved cleaning the data to remove noise and standardizing the dataset through normalization. The gait sequences were then segmented into manageable units for further analysis. Silhouette images obtained from video frames were used to extract relevant gait features. MobileNet, a lightweight convolutional neural network (CNN), was employed for this task, efficiently capturing spatial features from the input images.

The hybrid model integrates MobileNet for spatial feature extraction and BiLSTM (Bidirectional Long Short-Term Memory) to capture temporal dependencies in the sequential data. This combination leverages the strengths of both architectures to enhance gait pattern analysis.The model was trained using augmented data from the CASIA-B dataset to ensure robustness. Performance metrics such as accuracy, precision, recall, and F1-score were used to evaluate the model, demonstrating its effectiveness in different scenarios. By integrating MobileNet and BiLSTM, the proposed approach achieves a robust and efficient solution for human gait detection, suitable for applications in surveillance and medical monitoring.

Figure 2. Workflow of the Proposed Mobile BiLSTM Gait Detection Model

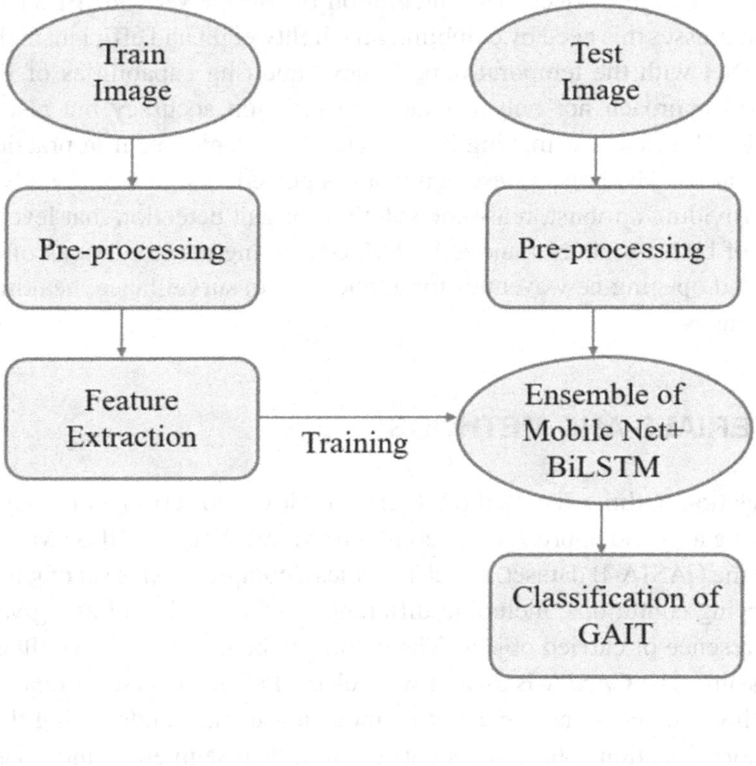

A. Dataset

Initially, the CASIA-B dataset comprises photographs featuring 124 male and female subjects from various angles relative to the camera, totaling 11 different views. Within this dataset, each subject contributes 6 instances of normal walking, along with 2 instances of walking while carrying baggage and 2 instances of walking with an additional layer of clothing. Notably, the dataset excludes instances of both unimpaired and pathological gaits. It additionally involves variances like individuals putting on jackets or other several layers of clothes and bearing backpacks or other items of luggage, which can dramatically alter their profile. The CNN uses the Gait Energy Image (GEI) as inputs for gait representation; this image is obtained by slicing apart an individual's silhouette and with an average of it over a series of silhouettes (Elharrouss et al. 2020). As a leading method for representing the human gait cycle in a single picture, GEI is notable for its ability to capture both spatial and temporal information. The durability and effectiveness of GEI as a gait recon-struction approach have been confirmed by experimental results (Han et al. 2005).

Equation 1 can be used to calculate the Gait Energy Image, with N denoting the overall amount of frames that are in a gait cycle. The series of pictures in the gait cycle is represented by the equation I(x, y, t), where t is the total number of frames in the cycle and (x, y) specifies the image coordinates. GEIs capture information about the silhouette and the changing walking environment. The gait sequences are extracted using background removal and normalization techniques prior to GEI calculation. A series of GEIs for a topic from different perspectives are shown in Figure 1. The training dataset included four examples of typical walking sequences from all viewpoints, as well as one example of each of carrying luggage and wear-ing additional layers of clothes while walking. The test data, on the other hand, had two examples of typical walking patterns and one example of each of walking with additional layers of costumes and walking when bearing baggage. After the division of the dataset into train and test, there were 7657 pictures for training and 4945 images for testing, spread among 124 classes.

$$G(x,y) = \frac{1}{N}\sum_{t=1}^{N}I(x,y,t) \tag{1}$$

B. MobileNet Architecture

MobileNet represents a leading-edge convolutional neural network structure extensively employed in vision-related tasks like detecting objects, categorizing im-ages, and segmentation Due to their lightweight characteristics suitable for efficient inference on resource-constrained platforms, the network was initially designed for mobile and embedded devices. However, MobileNet has been widely used. MobileNet is a good fit for the gait detection challenge for the following reasons: Gait detection is the process of identifying how people walk, which can be captured in the form of movies or sequences. Depthwise separable convolutions, the foundation of MobileNet's calculation, minimize computational effort while enabling effective feature extraction from the input frames. The traditional standard convolution process is divided into two layers: depth-wise convolution and point-wise convolution. This factorization reduces the number of parameters and computation expenses by orders of magnitude in contrast to standard convolutions. That is why MobileNet is suitable for real-time applications such as gait recognition. MobileNet can work with gait sequences of various resolutions given the network's capability of spatial hierarchies of features capturing and handling various input sizes. Moreover, even on devices with limited computational resources, gait detection systems can achieve real-time high-accuracy performance due to MobileNet's feature extraction efficiency.

Depthwise separable convolutions, a kind of factorized convolution that splits a regular convolution into a depthwise convolution and a pointwise convolution, are the foundation of the MobileNet model. In MobileNets, depthwise convolution is used to get a single filter for each input channel. The pointwise convolution employs a 1×1 convolution to combine the outputs of the depthwise convolution. In a single step, a conventional convolution filter and mixes inputs to produce a new set of outputs. This is split into two layers by the depthwise separable convolution: a filtering layer and a combining layer. The model size and computation time are greatly decreased by this factorization..

A DF × DF × M feature map F is fed into a conventional convolutional layer, producing a DF × DF × N feature map G. The spatial dimensions of the square input feature map are represented here by DF. M is the number of input channels, DG is the square output feature map's spatial dimensions, and N is the number of output channels. A convolution kernel K sized DK × DK × M × N defines the convolutional layer. DK stands for the spatial dimensions of the kernel, where M and N are the input and output channels, respectively. In ordinary convolution, the output feature map assumes a stride of one, and padding is estimated as:

$$G_{k,l,n} = \sum_{i,j,m} K_{i,j,m,n} \bullet F_{k+i-1,l+j-1,m} \tag{2}$$

The computational cost of standard convolutions is:

$$D_K \bullet D_K \bullet M \bullet N \bullet D_F \bullet D_F \tag{3}$$

The computational expense is directly related to the following: the size of the feature map (DF × DF), the number of input channels (M), the number of output channels (N), and the kernel size (Dk × Dk). In comparison to ordinary convolution, depthwise convolution is 8 to 9 times faster.

Figure 3. Typical convolution filters.

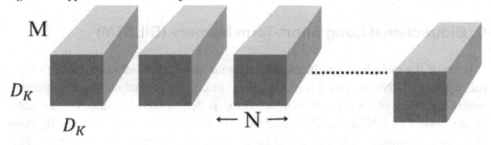

Figure 4. Depthwise convolutional filters involve convolving each input channel with its own set of filters.

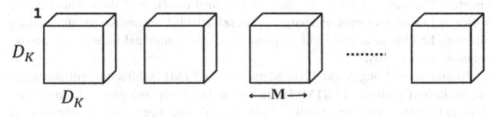

Figure 5. Depiction of pointwise convolution

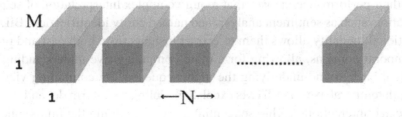

The depthwise convolution can be denoted as:

$$\widehat{G}_{k,l,m} = \sum_{i,j} \widehat{K}_{i,j,m} \cdot F_{k+i-1,l+j-1,m} \qquad (4)$$

where $\widehat{K}$ denotes the kernel size of the depth-wise convolutions, and $\widehat{G}$ denotes the output feature map. The depth-wise convolution has a computational cost of:

$$M \cdot D_F \cdot D_F \cdot D_K \cdot D_K \qquad (5)$$

C. Bidirectional Long Short-Term Memory (BiLSTM)

One of the main building blocks of artificial neural networks is Recurrent Neural Networks (RNNs), which are designed particularly to analyze input sequences where the order of each piece of information is determined by time. Unlike static neural networks, RNNs include linked loops that allow them to retain a recollection of previous inputs, which is essential for understanding temporal correlations. This trait enables RNNs to simulate dynamic sequences, which is useful in a variety of applications like language processing, and audio recognition..

The long Short-Term Memory (LSTM) model are a significant improvement in the RNN sector, designed to address the problem of disappearing gradients during training, which impedes the learning of long-term dependencies. LSTMs introduce customized memory units with gates that control the flow of data. These gates, which include input, forget, and output gates, selectively keep or discard information, allowing LSTMs to acquire and propagate relevant contextual information across sequences efficiently.

Bidirectional Long Short-Term Memory (BiLSTM) architecture enhances the capabilities of traditional LSTMs by including data from both past and future time steps in the input sequence. Unlike unidirectional equivalents, which only process input in one temporal direction, BiLSTMs use two independent LSTM layers—one for forward processing and one for backward processing—to enable thorough assimilation of contextual information. This bidirectional strategy gives BiLSTMs the capacity to extract subtle contextual knowledge from input data, which improves their performance in tasks that require complex interpretation of sequential information, such as sentiment analysis and named entity identification. BiLSTMs' bidirectional modality allows them to extract insights from both past and prospective temporal domains, allowing for a more comprehensive understanding of the contextual background underlying the input sequence. By combining viewpoints from both temporal axes, BiLSTMs excel at modeling long-term dependencies and complicated interactions within sequential data, overcoming the limits inherent in unidirectional RNN design. This increased contextual awareness makes BiLSTMs beneficial for a wide range of natural language processing applications that need subtle linguistic context capture.

Figure 6. The architecture of BiLSTM.

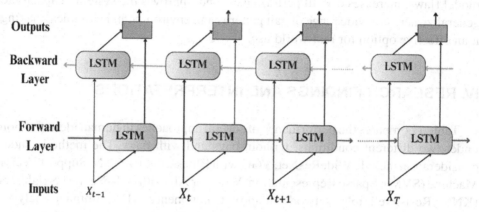

D. Integration of the MobileNet with BiLSTM

During the integration phase, predictions from many models are combined using an average ensemble approach. Class scores are generated by each model for every class in a test sample. These numbers, which go from 0 to 1, show how likely it is that the sample will fall into each class. The class having the highest probability among all ensemble members is chosen as the final prediction for a test sample. To minimize the hazards associated with overfitting, this is accomplished by averaging the class scores across all models. The goal is to decrease variance and improve the overall prediction's robustness. The class with the greatest likelihood corresponds to the ultimate outcome of the ensemble, represented by $h_{final}(W)$. It can be formulated as:

$$h_{final}(W) = \mathrm{argmax}_j \mu_j(W) \tag{6}$$

Using an average ensemble technique helps to reduce the variance of individual models, increasing the robustness of the estimator and lowering the vulnerability of overfitting. By combining forecasts from numerous models, the risk of erroneous predictions from any single model is reduced, resulting in better overall performance. This strategy uses the ensemble's collective wisdom to make more credible predictions, improving the model's generalizability. Combining the strengths of MobileNet with BiLSTM via an average ensemble provides various benefits for gait detection.

MobileNet efficiently extracts features from picture data, whereas BiLSTM captures temporal dependencies in sequential data. By combining their complementary qualities, the ensemble improves feature representation and temporal modeling, resulting in more robust and accurate gait recognition. This fusion strategy reduces individual model flaws, increases overall performance, and improves the system's capacity to generalize across a wide range of gait patterns and environmental variables, making it an effective option for real-world use.

IV. RESEARCH FINDINGS AND INTERPRETATIONS

Table 1 compares the performance of several approaches in human identification under two different conditions: without bags and with bags. The methods under consideration include WideResNet, VGG with Blocks, Gait + CNN, Support Vector Machine (SVM), Sparse Representation, Wrapper Algorithm, K-Nearest Neighbors (KNN), Resistive Triplet Network, Adaptive Component and Discriminant Analysis, Frequency-Domain Gait Entropy, Local Features Flow Regulation, SVM + Histogram of Oriented Gradients (HOG), and the proposed MobileBiLSTM.

WideResNet demonstrates perfect accuracy when individuals are not carrying bags, indicating its robustness in ideal conditions. However, its accuracy drops significantly to 89.4% when bags are introduced. This significant drop suggests that WideResNet is sensitive to changes in gait patterns caused by carrying objects. Similarly, VGG with Blocks performs well without bags at 94.5% accuracy but experiences a substantial drop to 65.1% with bags, indicating difficulties in adapting to variations in gait due to external factors. The significant drop in accuracy highlights the method's limitations in real-world applications where individuals might carry objects.

In contrast, the Gait + CNN approach maintains high accuracy even when bags are introduced, with only a slight reduction from 95.45% to 91.8%. This suggests that the method is quite robust and can effectively handle gait variations caused by carrying bags. The minor drop in accuracy indicates that Gait + CNN can be relied upon in practical scenarios where individuals might be carrying objects. On the other hand, the Support Vector Machine (SVM) method shows a drastic drop from 94.50% without bags to 60.90% with bags. This significant reduction highlights the method's sensitivity to changes in gait patterns, making it less reliable for real-world applications where individuals might carry objects.

Sparse Representation exhibits high accuracy without bags at 99% but sees a noticeable decline to 79% with bags. While the performance drop is not as severe as some other methods, it still indicates a moderate level of sensitivity to gait variations caused by external objects. This suggests that Sparse Representation might still be useful in scenarios where individuals are less likely to carry objects. The Wrapper Algorithm shows good performance in both scenarios, with a reduction from 93.60% without bags to 81.70% with bags. This modest decline suggests that the Wrapper Algorithm can still be effective in less controlled environments where individuals might carry objects.

K-Nearest Neighbors (KNN) performs reasonably well in both scenarios, with accuracy dropping from 85.36% without bags to 79.90% with bags. This indicates that KNN is relatively robust to changes in gait patterns, although its overall accuracy is lower than some other methods. The Resistive Triplet Network method shows a noticeable drop from 89% without bags to 72% with bags, indicating significant sensitivity to changes in gait patterns. This could limit its practical applications in real-world scenarios where individuals might carry objects.

The Adaptive Component and Discriminant Analysis method achieves perfect accuracy without bags but experiences a considerable drop to 78.30% with bags. This suggests a high sensitivity to gait pattern variations, which could affect its reliability in practical applications. Frequency-Domain Gait Entropy maintains high accuracy even with bags, with a modest reduction from 97.61% to 83.87%. This indicates that the method is relatively robust and can handle variations in gait caused by external objects effectively, making it suitable for real-world applications.

Local Features Flow Regulation performs well in both scenarios, with a relatively small drop in accuracy from 91.90% without bags to 80.30% with bags. This suggests it is quite robust to changes in gait patterns, indicating its suitability for practical applications where individuals might carry objects. The SVM combined with Histogram of Oriented Gradients (HOG) features results in a method that performs similarly well in both scenarios, with a very small drop in accuracy from 82.30% without bags to 79.80% with bags. This indicates good robustness to gait variations caused by external objects, making it a reliable choice for real-world scenarios.

The proposed MobileBiLSTM method shows high accuracy in both scenarios, with minimal reduction from 96.89% without bags to 94.52% with bags. This suggests that the method is highly robust to changes in gait patterns and can handle variations caused by carrying objects effectively. The slight decrease in accuracy indicates that MobileBiLSTM can be relied upon in practical applications where individuals might carry objects, making it a promising approach for real-world scenarios.

In summary, the methods vary significantly in their sensitivity to changes in gait patterns caused by carrying bags. While some methods, like WideResNet and VGG with Blocks, show substantial drops in accuracy, others like Gait + CNN and MobileBiLSTM maintain high accuracy even with bags. The proposed Mobile-BiLSTM method stands out for its robustness and high accuracy in both scenarios, making it a promising approach for practical applications where individuals may carry objects. This comparison highlights the importance of considering real-world conditions when evaluating gait recognition methods, as robustness to variations in gait patterns is crucial for their practical applicability.

The ability of a gait recognition method to handle variations caused by carrying objects is critical for its effectiveness in practical applications. Methods that show high sensitivity to such changes might perform well in controlled environments but fail in real-world scenarios. On the other hand, methods like MobileBiLSTM that maintain high accuracy despite these variations demonstrate their potential for practical use.

For instance, in surveillance and security applications, individuals often carry bags or other objects, making it essential for gait recognition systems to account for these variations. The robustness of MobileBiLSTM in such scenarios makes it a valuable tool for these applications. Additionally, in healthcare, where gait analysis can be used for monitoring and diagnosing conditions, the ability to accurately recognize gait patterns despite variations is crucial.

The significant drops in accuracy seen in methods like WideResNet and VGG with Blocks suggest that while they might be effective in controlled environments, their practical applicability is limited. Conversely, the minimal reduction in accuracy for methods like MobileBiLSTM and Gait + CNN indicates their suitability for real-world applications.

In conclusion, the proposed MobileBiLSTM method offers a highly robust and accurate approach to human gait recognition, capable of handling variations caused by carrying objects. Its performance in both scenarios highlights its potential for practical applications in various fields, making it a promising choice for real-world implementation. This comparison underscores the importance of evaluating gait recognition methods under conditions that reflect practical use, ensuring their effectiveness and reliability in real-world scenarios.

Table 1. Results for casia B dataset in different conditions

Methods	Without bags (%)	With bags (%)
WideResNet (Sokolova et al. 2018)	100	89.4
VGG with blocks (Chao et al. 2019)	94.5	65.1
Gait + CNN (Sheth et al. 2023)	95.45	91.8
Support vector machine (Kusakunnira 2014)	94.50	60.90
Sparse Representation (Rida et al. 2015)	99.00	79.00
Wrapper Algorithm (Rida et al. 2015)	93.60	81.70
KNN (Lishani et al. 2017)	85.36	79.90

continued on following page

Table 1. Continued

Methods	Without bags (%)	With bags (%)
Resistive Triplet Network (Tong et al. 2019)	89	72.00
Adaptive Component and Discriminant Analysis (Bashir et al. 2010)	100.0	78.30
Frequency-Domain Gait Entropy (Rokanujjaman et al. 2015)	97.61	83.87
Local Features Flow Regulation (Huang et al. 2020)	91.90	80.30
Support vector machine (SVM) + Histogram of oriented gradients (HOG) (Asif et al. 2022)	82.30	79.80
MobileBiLSTM [Proposed]	**96.89**	**94.52**

Figure 7 shows a classification of human gait using the proposed technique, which is swiftly integrated with a user-friendly GUI (Graphical User Interface). Figure 8 shows a comparison of existing approaches with the proposed approach, with and without bags.

Figure 7. Classification of the Gait using the proposed method.

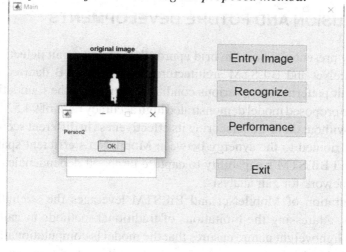

Figure 8. Example Accuracy comparison of human gait recognition methods with and without bags.

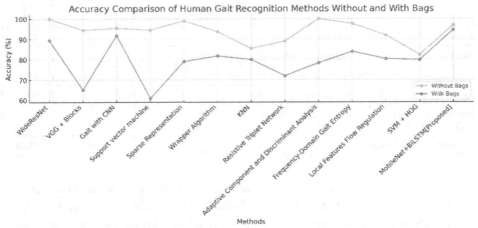

V. CONCLUSION AND FUTURE DEVELOPMENTS

The study presented a novel hybrid approach for human gait detection by combining MobileNet and BiLSTM architectures. The CASIA-B dataset, known for its diverse gait patterns under various conditions, served as the foundation for this research. The proposed model demonstrated high accuracy rates of 94.52% with bags and 96.89% without them, underscoring its effectiveness in different scenarios. This success is attributed to the synergy between MobileNet's efficient spatial feature extraction and BiLSTM's capability to capture temporal dependencies, providing a robust framework for gait analysis.

The integration of MobileNet and BiLSTM leverages the strengths of both architectures, addressing the limitations of traditional methods in gait detection. MobileNet's lightweight nature ensures that the model is computationally efficient, making it suitable for real-time applications on mobile and edge devices. BiLSTM, on the other hand, enhances the model's ability to understand the sequential nature of gait patterns, thereby improving its accuracy and robustness.

The results obtained in this study signify a substantial advancement in the field of gait analysis. The high accuracy rates achieved across different conditions highlight the model's potential for practical applications in areas such as security surveillance, medical diagnosis, and human-computer interaction. The ability to accurately detect gait patterns even in the presence of obstructions or variations in clothing suggests that the model is versatile and can be adapted to real-world scenarios where such variations are common.

While the proposed hybrid model has shown promising results, there are several avenues for future research and development that can further enhance its performance and applicability. One potential area is dataset expansion and diversity. Including additional datasets from different sources can help in generalizing the model further. Datasets with varying environmental conditions, different demographic characteristics, and diverse backgrounds can be used to train and validate the model. Employing advanced data augmentation techniques to simulate various real-world conditions such as occlusions, different lighting conditions, and more complex backgrounds can make the model more robust.

Another area for improvement is advanced feature extraction. Utilizing 3D gait data, if available, can provide additional spatial information that can be beneficial for more accurate gait analysis. Techniques such as 3D pose estimation can be integrated into the model to enhance feature extraction. Combining features from other domains such as audio, inertial sensors, or additional visual cues can provide a multi-modal approach to gait detection, potentially increasing accuracy and robustness.

Enhancing the model architecture is also crucial. Exploring advanced neural network architectures such as transformers, which have shown remarkable success in other domains, can be investigated for gait analysis. The attention mechanism in transformers can potentially capture more intricate details in gait sequences. Leveraging pre-trained models on large datasets and fine-tuning them on specific gait datasets can reduce training time and improve performance.

Real-time implementation and optimization are essential for practical applications. Optimizing the model for edge computing devices to ensure real-time processing capabilities includes reducing the model's computational complexity and memory footprint without compromising accuracy. Utilizing hardware accelerators such as GPUs and TPUs can further speed up the processing time, making the model suitable for deployment in real-time surveillance systems.

Integration with other biometric systems can provide a multi-layered security approach. Combining gait detection with other biometric systems such as facial recognition, fingerprint analysis, or iris scanning can significantly enhance the reliability and accuracy of identity verification systems. Integrating gait analysis with behavioral biometrics like keystroke dynamics, mouse movement patterns, and other user interaction data can offer a comprehensive understanding of an individual's identity.

Applications in healthcare are promising. The model can be adapted for medical applications such as diagnosing and monitoring gait-related disorders. By analyzing gait patterns, the system can assist in the early detection of neurological diseases like Parkinson's disease, multiple sclerosis, and other motor function impairments.

Implementing the model in rehabilitation centers to monitor patients' progress during physical therapy can help in tailoring rehabilitation programs to individual needs.

Ethical considerations and privacy are paramount. Ensuring the privacy and security of the collected gait data is essential. Developing secure data handling practices and anonymization techniques can help in protecting individuals' privacy. Addressing ethical concerns related to the deployment of gait detection systems, particularly in surveillance, ensures they are used responsibly and do not infringe on personal freedoms or privacy rights.

User adaptability and customization can enhance the model's usability. Developing personalized gait detection models that can adapt to individual users over time can be particularly useful in applications like user authentication, where the system can learn and adapt to subtle changes in an individual's gait. Incorporating user feedback mechanisms to continuously improve and refine the model can further enhance its performance.

Cross-domain applications can broaden the utility of gait detection. Integrating gait detection with human-computer interaction systems can enable more intuitive and natural interactions between humans and computers. For instance, gait recognition can be used to control smart home devices or personalize user experiences in virtual environments. Applying gait analysis in sports to improve athletes' performance by providing detailed insights into their running or walking patterns can help optimize training programs and prevent injuries.

Conducting longitudinal studies can provide valuable insights into how gait patterns change over time due to aging, lifestyle changes, or medical conditions. This can be beneficial for various applications, including healthcare and security.

In conclusion, while the hybrid MobileNet and BiLSTM model has demonstrated significant potential in human gait detection, ongoing development and enhancement of this technology hold even greater promise. By addressing the areas outlined above, future research can further improve the model's accuracy, robustness, and applicability, making it an invaluable tool in a wide range of fields from security to healthcare. The continued evolution of gait detection technology will undoubtedly lead to more sophisticated and efficient systems, contributing to advancements in both academic research and practical applications.

REFERENCES

Arshad, H., Khan, M. A., Sharif, M., Yasmin, M., & Javed, M. Y. (2019). Multi-level features fusion and selection for human gait recognition: An optimized framework of Bayesian model and binomial distribution. *International Journal of Machine Learning and Cybernetics*, 10(12), 3601–3618. DOI: 10.1007/s13042-019-00947-0

Arshad, H., Khan, M. A., Sharif, M. I., Yasmin, M., Tavares, J. M. R., Zhang, Y. D., & Satapathy, S. C. (2020). A multilevel paradigm for deep convolutional neural network features selection with an application to human gait recognition. *Expert Systems: International Journal of Knowledge Engineering and Neural Networks*, 39(7), e12541. DOI: 10.1111/exsy.12541

Asif, M., Tiwana, M.I., Khan, U.S., Ahmad, M.W., Qureshi, W.S., & Iqbal, J. (2022). Human gait recognition subject to different covariate factors in a multi-view environment. *Results in Engineering,15*, 100556.

Babaee, M., Li, L., & Rigoll, G. (2018). Gait recognition from incomplete gaitcycle. 2018 25th IEEE International Conference on Image Processing (ICIP), 768-772. DOI: 10.1109/ICIP.2018.8451785

Babaee, M., Zhu, Y., Köpüklü, O., Hörmann, S., & Rigoll, G. (2019). Gait energy image restoration using generative adversarial networks. *2019 IEEE Internationa Conference on Image Processing (ICIP)*, 2596-2600, DOI: 10.1109/ICIP.2019.8803236

Balazia, M., & Sojka, P. (2018). Gait recognition from motion capture data. *ACM Transactions on Multimedia Computing Communications and Applications*, 14(1s), 1–18. DOI: 10.1145/3152124

Bari, A. S. M., & Gavrilova, M. L. (2019). Artificial neural network based gait recognition using kinect sensor. *IEEE Access : Practical Innovations, Open Solutions*, 7, 162708–162722. DOI: 10.1109/ACCESS.2019.2952065

Bashir, K., Xiang, T., & Gong, S. (2010). Gait recognition without subject cooperation *Elsevier Journal of Pattern Recognition Letters,31*(13), 2052-2060.

Bhargavas, W. G., Harshavardhan, K., Mohan, G. C., Sharma, A. N., & Prathap, C. (2017). Human identification using gait recognition. In 2017 International Conference on Communication and Signal Processing (ICCSP), 1510-1513, DOI: 10.1109/ICCSP.2017.8286638

Chaitanya, G. K., & Raja Sekhar, K. (2020). A human gait recognition against information theft in smartphone using residual convolutional neural network. *International Journal of Advanced Computer Science and Applications*, 11(5). Advance online publication. DOI: 10.14569/IJACSA.2020.0110544

Chao, H., He, Y., Zhang, J., & Feng, J. (2019). Gaitset: Regarding gait as a set for cross-view gait recognition. *Proceedings of the AAAI Conference on Artificial Intelligence*, 33(1), 8126–8133. DOI: 10.1609/aaai.v33i01.33018126

Chao, H., Wang, K., He, Y., Zhang, J., & Feng, J. (2021). GaitSet: Cross-view gait recognition through utilizing gait as a deep set. *IEEE Transactions on Pattern Analysis and Machine Intelligence*, 44, 3467–3478. DOI: 10.1109/TPAMI.2021.3057879 PMID: 33560976

Deng, M., Wang, C., Cheng, F., & Zeng, W. (2017). Fusion of spatial-temporal and kinematic features for gait recognition with deterministic learning. *Pattern Recognition*, 67, 186–200. DOI: 10.1016/j.patcog.2017.02.014

Ehaimir, M. E., Jarraya, I., Ouarda, W., & Alimi, A. M. (2017). Human gait identity recognition system based on gait pal and pal entropy (GPPE) and distances features fusion. In 2017 Sudan Conference on Computer Science and Information Technology (SCCSIT) 1-5. DOI: 10.1109/SCCSIT.2017.8293061

Elharrouss, O., Almaadeed, N., Al-Maadeed, S., & Bouridane, A. (2020). Gait recognition for person re-identification. *The Journal of Supercomputing*, 1–20. DOI: 10.1007/s11227-020-03409-5

Gao, F., Tian, T., Yao, T., & Zhang, Q. (2021). Human gait recognition based on multiplefeature combination and parameter optimization algorithms. *Computational Intelligence and Neuroscience*, 2021(1), 6693206. Advance online publication. DOI: 10.1155/2021/6693206 PMID: 33727913

Ghaeminia, M. H., & Shokouhi, S. B. (2019). On the selection of spatiotemporal filtering with classifier ensemble method for effective gait recognition. *Signal, Image and Video Processing*, 13(1), 43–51. DOI: 10.1007/s11760-018-1326-5

Gul, S., Malik, M. I., Khan, G. M., & Shafait, F. (2021). Multi-view gait recognition system using spatio-temporal features and deep learning. *Expert Systems with Applications*, 179, 115057. DOI: 10.1016/j.eswa.2021.115057

Guo, H., Li, B., Zhang, Y., Zhang, Y., Li, W., Qiao, F., Rong, X., & Zhou, S. (2020). Gait recognition based on the feature extraction of gabor filter and linear discriminant analysis and improved local coupled extreme learning machine. *Mathematical Problems in Engineering*, 2020, 1–9. Advance online publication. DOI: 10.1155/2020/5393058

Han, F., Li, X., Zhao, J., & Shen, F. (2022). A unified perspective of classification-based loss and distance-based loss for cross-view gait recognition. *Pattern Recognition*, 125, 108519. DOI: 10.1016/j.patcog.2021.108519

Han, J., & Bhanu, B. (2005). Individual recognition using gait energy image. *IEEE Transactions on Pattern Analysis and Machine Intelligence,28*(2) 316-322. DOI: 10.1109/TPAMI.2006.38

He, K., Zhang, X., Ren, S., & Sun, J. (2016). Deep residual learning for image recognition. *Proceedings of the 2016 IEEE Conference on Computer Vision and Pattern Recognition (CVPR)*, 27-30.

Huang, G., Liu, Z., Van Der Maaten, L., & Weinberger, K. Q. (2017). Densely connected convolutional networks. *Proceedings of the 2017IEEE Conference on Computer Vision and Pattern Recognition (CVPR)*, 21-26.

Huang, G., Lu, Z., Pun, C., & Cheng, L. (2020). 'Flexible gait recognition based on flow regulation of local features between key frames. *IEEE Access : Practical Innovations, Open Solutions*, 8, 75381–75392. DOI: 10.1109/ACCESS.2020.2986554

Khan, M. H., Farid, M. S., & Grzegorzek, M. (2019). Spatiotemporal features of human motion for gait recognition. *Signal, Image and Video Processing*, 13(2), 369–377. DOI: 10.1007/s11760-018-1365-y

Krizhevsky, A., Sutskever, I., & Hinton, G. E. (2012). *Imagenet classification with deep convolutional neural networks*. Adv. Neural Inf.Process. Syst.

Kusakunniran, W., (2014). Attribute-based learning for gait recognition using spatio-temporal interest points. *Elsevier Journal of Image and Visio Computing*, 32(12), 1117-1126.

Lee, C. P., Tan, A., & Lim, K. (2017). Review on vision-based gait recognition: Representations, classification schemes and datasets. *American Journal of Applied Sciences*, 14(2), 252–266. DOI: 10.3844/ajassp.2017.252.266

Lee, C. P., Tan, A. W., & Tan, S. C. (2013). Gait recognition via optimally interpolated deformable contours. *Pattern Recognition Letters*, 34(6), 663–669. DOI: 10.1016/j.patrec.2013.01.013

Lee, C. P., Tan, A. W., & Tan, S. C. (2014). Gait probability image: An information-theoretic model of gait representation. *Journal of Visual Communication and Image Representation*, 25(6), 1489–1492. DOI: 10.1016/j.jvcir.2014.05.006

Lee, C. P., Tan, A. W., & Tan, S. C. (2014). Time-sliced averaged motion history image for gait recognition. *Journal of Visual Communication and Image Representation*, 25(5), 822–826. DOI: 10.1016/j.jvcir.2014.01.012

Lee, C. P., Tan, A. W., & Tan, S. C. (2015). Gait recognition with transient binary patterns. *Journal of Visual Communication and Image Representation*, 33, 69–77. DOI: 10.1016/j.jvcir.2015.09.006

Li, C., Min, X., Sun, S., Lin, W., & Tang, Z. (2017). DeepGait: A learning deep convolutional representation for view-invariant gait recognition using joint bayesian. *Applied Sciences (Basel, Switzerland)*, 7(3), 210. DOI: 10.3390/app7030210

Li, X., Makihara, Y., Xu, C., Yagi, Y., & Ren, M. (2019). Joint intensity transformer network for gait recognition robust against clothing and carrying status. *IEEE Transactions on Information Forensics and Security*, 14(12), 3102–3115. DOI: 10.1109/TIFS.2019.2912577

Liao. (2020). A model-based gait recognition method with body pose and human prior knowledge. *Pattern Recognition,98*, 107069. DOI: 10.1016/j.patcog.2019.107069

Lishani, A. O., Boubchir, L., Khalifa, E., & Bouridane, A. (2017). Human gait recognition based on Haralick feature journal of Signal. *Signal, Image and Video Processing*, 11(6), 1123–1130. DOI: 10.1007/s11760-017-1066-y

Lishani, A. O., Boubchir, L., Khalifa, E., & Bouridane, A. (2019). Human gait recognition using GEI-based local multi-scale feature descriptors. *Multimedia Tools and Applications*, 78(5), 5715–5730. DOI: 10.1007/s11042-018-5752-8

Luo, J., Zhang, J., Zi, C., Niu, Y., Tian, H., & Xiu, C. (2015). Gait recognition using GEI and AFDEI. *International Journal of Optics*, 2015, 1–5. Advance online publication. DOI: 10.1155/2015/763908

Mehmood, A., Tariq, U., Jeong, C., Nam, Y., Mostafa, R., & Elaeiny, A. (2022). Human Gait Recognition: A Deep Learning and Best Feature Selection Framework. *Computers, Materials & Continua*, 70, 343–360. DOI: 10.32604/cmc.2022.019250

Mogan, J. N., Lee, C. P., & Lim, K. M. (2020). Gait recognition using histograms of temporal gradients. *Journal of Physics: Conference Series*, 1502(1), 012051. DOI: 10.1088/1742-6596/1502/1/012051

Mogan, J. N., Lee, C. P., Lim, K. M., & Muthu, K. S. (2022). Gait-ViT: Gait Recognition with Vision Transformer. *Sensors (Basel)*, 22(19), 7362. DOI: 10.3390/s22197362 PMID: 36236462

Mogan, J. N., Lee, C. P., Lim, K. M., & Tan, A. W. (2017). Gait recognition using binarized statistical image features and histograms of oriented gradients. *Proceedings of the 2017 International Conference on Robotics, Automation and Sciences (ICORAS)*, 1-6. DOI: 10.1109/ICORAS.2017.8308067

Mogan, J. N., Lee, C. P., & Tan, A. W. (2017). Gait recognition using temporal gradient patterns. Proceedings of the 2017 5th International Conference on Information and Communication Technology (ICoIC7), 1-4. DOI: 10.1109/ICoICT.2017.8074680

Ng, H., Tan, W. H., Abdullah, J., & Tong, H. L. (2014). Development of vision based multi-view gait recognition system with MMUGait database. *TheScientificWorldJournal*, 2014, 1–13. Advance online publication. DOI: 10.1155/2014/376569 PMID: 25143972

Pinčić, D., Sušanj, D., & Lenac, K. (2022, September 21). Pinči c, D., Sušanj, D., & Lenac, K. Gait recognition with self-supervised learning of gait features based on vision transformers. *Sensors (Basel)*, 22(19), 7140. DOI: 10.3390/s22197140

Qiu, J., & Liu, H. (2021). Gait recognition for human-exoskeleton system in locomotion based on ensemble empirical mode decomposition. *Mathematical Problems in Engineering*, 2021, 1–13. Advance online publication. DOI: 10.1155/2021/5039285

Rida, I., Almaadeed, S. A., & Bouridane, A. (2015). Unsupervised feature selection method for improved human gait recognition. 23rd European Signal Processing Conference (EUSIPCO), 1128-1132.

Rida, I., Almaadeed, S.A., & Bouridane, A. (2015). Gait recognition based on modified phase-only correlation. Journal of Signal, Image and Video Processing, 463-470.

Rokanujjaman, M., Islam, M. S., Hossain, M. A., Islam, M. R., Makihara, Y., & Yagi, Y. (2015). Effective part-based gait identification using frequency-domain gait entropy features Multimed. *Tool. Appl.*, 74(9), 3099–3120.

Sah, S., & Panday, S. P. (2020). Model-Based Gait Recognition Using Weighted KNN. *Proceedings of the 8th IOE Graduate Conference*, 5-7.

Saleh, A. M., & Hamoud, T. (2021). Analysis and best parameters selection for person recognition based on gait model using CNN algorithm and image augmentation. *Journal of Big Data*, 8(1), 1–20. DOI: 10.1186/s40537-020-00387-6 PMID: 33425651

Sepas-Moghaddam, A., & Etemad, A. (2022). Deep gait recognition: A survey. *IEEE Transactions on Pattern Analysis and Machine Intelligence*. Advance online publication. DOI: 10.1109/TPAMI.2022.3151865 PMID: 35167443

Sharif, M., Attique, M., Tahir, M. Z., Yasmim, M., Saba, T., & Tanik, U. J. (2020). A machine learning method with threshold-based parallel feature fusion and feature selection for automated gait recognition. *Journal of Organizational and End User Computing*, 32(2), 67–92. DOI: 10.4018/JOEUC.2020040104

Sheth, A. A., Sharath, M., Reddy, A. S. C., & Sindhu, K. (2023). *Gait Recognition Using Convolutional Neural Network*. International Journal of Online and Biomedical Engineering. DOI: 10.3991/ijoe.v19i01.33823

Si, W., Zhang, J., Li, Y. D., Tan, W., Shao, Y. F., & Yang, G. L. (2020). Remote identity verification using gait analysis and face recognition. *Wireless Communications and Mobile Computing*, 2020, 1–10. Advance online publication. DOI: 10.1155/2020/8815461

Simonyan, K., & Zisserman, A. (2014). Very deep convolutional networks for large-scale image recognition. arXiv 2014, arXiv:1409.1556.

Sokolova & Konushin. (2018). Pose-based deep gait recognition. *IET Biometrics, 8*(2), 134-143. .DOI: 10.1049/iet-bmt.2018.5046

Su & Huang. (2005). Human gait recognition based on motion analysis. *2005 International Conference on Machine Learning and Cybernetics, 7*, 4464-4468.

Tong, S., Fu, Y., & Ling H. (2019). Cross-view gait recognition based on a restrictive triplet network. *Elsevier Journal of Pattern Recognition Letters, 125*, 212-219.

Wang, X., Ristic-Durrant, D., Spranger, M., & Gräser, A. (2017). Gait assessment system based on novel gait variability measures. 2017 International Conference on Rehabilitation Robotics (ICORR), 467-472. DOI: 10.1109/ICORR.2017.8009292

Wang, X., & Yan, W. Q. (2021). Non-local gait feature extraction and human identification. *Multimedia Tools and Applications*, 80(4), 6065–6078. DOI: 10.1007/s11042-020-09935-x

Wang, X., Zhang, J., & Yan, W. Q. (2020). Gait recognition using multichannel convolution neural networks. *Neural Computing & Applications*, 32(18), 14275–14285. DOI: 10.1007/s00521-019-04524-y

Wu, H., Weng, J., Chen, X., & Lu, W. (2018). Feedback weight convolutional neural network for gait recognition. *Journal of Visual Communication and Image Representation*, 55, 424–432. DOI: 10.1016/j.jvcir.2018.06.019

Xu, C., Makihara, Y., Li, X., Yagi, Y., & Lu, J. (2020). Cross-view gait recognition using pairwise spatial transformer networks. *IEEE Transactions on Circuits and Systems for Video Technology*, 31(1), 260–274. DOI: 10.1109/TCSVT.2020.2975671

Zhou, Q., Shan, J., Fang, B., Zhang, S., Sun, F., Ding, W., Wang, C., & Zhang, Q. (2021). Personal-specific gait recognition based on latent orthogonal feature space. *Cognitive Computation and Systems*, 3(1), 61–69. DOI: 10.1049/ccs2.12007

Chapter 10
Predicting Property Prices With Machine Learning:
A Case Study in the Moroccan Real Estate Market

Ayoub Ouchlif

https://orcid.org/0000-0002-2001-2178

Hassan II Agronomic and Veterinary Institute, Morocco

Oumaima Kabba

Hassan II Agronomic and Veterinary Institute, Morocco

Majda Guendour

Hassan II Agronomic and Veterinary Institute, Morocco

Hicham Hajji

Hassan II Agronomic and Veterinary Institute, Morocco

Kenza Aitelkadi

Hassan II Agronomic and Veterinary Institute, Morocco

ABSTRACT

In this study, the authors aim to explore the potential of machine learning (ML) in real estate valuation, particularly in Morocco where challenges include intelligent and sustainable valuation methods and transitioning to smart urban planning aligned with the eleventh sustainable development goal. To tackle these, they analyzed, processed, and tested seven ML architectures using real estate ads from Casablanca and Rabat collected over three months (April to June 2022). Support vector regression (SVR) led with 92.6% accuracy, followed by neural networks at 90%, then random

DOI: 10.4018/979-8-3693-5231-1.ch010

forest, gradient boosting, XGBoost, and ridge and lasso regressions. SVR, a validated model, produced predictions depicted in an interactive thematic map showing their distribution across the two cities, underscoring the influence of digital real estate on conventional valuation methods.

INTRODUCTION

Morocco integrated the SDGs very early in its economic and social development policies; significant progress achieved notably in improving the living conditions of the population, facilitating access to basic services as well as infrastructure development. In this context, we focus on the eleventh goal, entitled "Sustainable cities and communities", which aims to make cities inclusive, safe, resilient and sustainable. As such, real estate constitutes a key facilitating the transition from conventional urban planning to smart, sustainable planning in its broadest context.

The real estate market is experiencing significant dynamism and rapid, unrationalized evolution. Demand has increased considerably in recent years and reflects a high level of expectations in terms of value for money.

In this regard, the fairness of real estate taxation, which represents more than a simple source of revenue for the state and which depends closely on the real estate price, requires the rationalization of the latter. Otherwise, the country may face political instability and a decline in the population's standard of living. As a result, the state's executive, legislative, and judicial institutions (Bajeddi, 2017) will not reassure the population.

The relevant authorities, namely the National Agency for Land Registration, Cadastre, and Mapping (ANCFCC) and the General Directorate of Taxes (DGI), have published a common reference framework for real estate prices, which includes reference prices by zone and type of property. This framework intended for the calculation of conservation fees and taxes on income from real estate. However, it lacks precision since, within a given area, real estate properties differ from one another with their unique characteristics. Therefore, it would be necessary to define prices for each specific property rather than generalizing the task for given zones.

In the presence of the technological revolution in the current era, artificial intelligence (IA), particularly machine learning, brings significant interest to the real estate market by stimulating the prediction of its prices. With colossal data containing all types of property characteristics, machine learning (ML) can produce useful models that provide information on real estate prices and help accomplish the primary task of real estate appraisal: the estimation of the market value of properties.

With the shift towards digitalization of information that some administrations have undergone, it would be wise to move in this direction to facilitate the task. It would also be a powerful tool to aid decision-making regarding investments in the real estate sector.

Problematic and Objectives

Upon either examining the organizations and actors involved in the Moroccan real estate market, in the private or public sector, we have identified the following limitations:

■   The absence of a database dedicated to the property value map, which results in the divergence of references among the different administrations and real estate actors;

■   The market is informal and lacks transparency; real estate appraisal expertise faces the unavailability of information on comparable in the exploitation of estimation methods that require their existence;

■   Real estate appraisal in the public sector is limited to the estimation of market values through the comparative method;

■   Real estate expertise is based on heterogeneous and diverse information and does not yet seem to benefit from the digital revolution in Morocco;

■   The trend of prices not regularized, especially for the prices of real estate offers from property developers.

In light of the above context and the problems highlighted, the issue at hand, which this project aims to address, is "How to exploit machine learning to predict real estate prices?"

The main objective of this study is to predict real estate market prices using machine-learning algorithms. This will firstly produce beneficial information for real estate appraisers in private companies and administrations that use the comparative method. It will also initiate the unification of real estate actors' references in a thematic map representing the market values of properties.

To accomplish this project, the following specific objectives must be achieved:

■   Obtain a rich database with variables affecting the real estate price;
■   Exploit this data in the training of predictive models of machine learning;
■   Validate the models and select the most powerful one;
■   Deploy this model in an interactive cartographic representation that allows the visualization of the predictions made.

REAL ESTATE APPRAISAL AND ITS PRACTICE IN MOROCCO

Introduction and Generalities on Real Estate Appraisal

In order to best approach the exploitation of Machine Learning in the prediction of real estate prices in Morocco, it is essential to understand the preliminary notions on real estate appraisal and its practice in Morocco.

In this context, this section first explains generalities on real estate appraisal, namely the different missions requiring an expertise and the different concepts of value. Secondly, it specifies the set of factors that can affect the value of real estate properties and then it mentions the usual real estate appraisal methods that the expert uses in his estimation of the value. Finally, it focuses particularly on the framework of expertise in Morocco in order to highlight the importance of the exploitation of artificial intelligence in real estate appraisal.

Initially considered as the "exchange value" of movable properties for a long time, the concept of "value" has continued to evolve and expand to also cover real properties, thus giving birth to real estate appraisal.

Although the latter seems to be restricted to determining the value of a real property based on its characteristics and on the data of the real estate market, it still carries other aspects. Indeed, the practical guide of real estate appraisal (Polignac et al. 2019) explains the following missions, which can be the subject of a real estate appraisal:

The evaluation or expertise operation inevitably refers to a visit of the real property and to a well-conducted investigation in this sense, in order to estimate its value in the real estate market. In this regard, the international standards relating to evaluation according to the RICS clearly define the term "Evaluation" as follows: "Opinion relating to the value of an asset or a liability on a given date and according to specified value bases. Unless otherwise agreed in the terms of the contract, it is provided following a visit and, if necessary, more in-depth investigations and information research which depend on the nature of the asset and the purpose of the evaluation." (RICS, 2020). This evaluation is accompanied either by a detailed expertise report, a summary expertise report or a certificate of expertise in the case of repetitive expertise or investigation into many properties.

The Value of a Real Property and the Factors That Influence It

In the field of real estate appraisal, several aspects are to be considered in order to determine the value of a property. Real estate appraisal expertise is a crucial discipline that takes into account various factors to accurately evaluate the value of a property. Among these factors are:

Figure 1. Market value factors

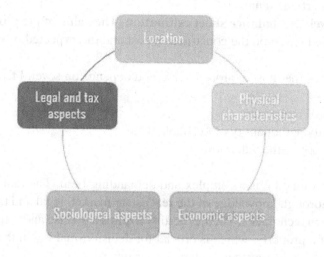

- **The location of the property**: its accessibility, environment, and nearby infrastructure are important factors to consider.
- **The physical characteristics of the property**, such as its living area, number of rooms, condition, materials used, and equipment present, influence its value.
- **Economic factors**: such as the local real estate market, general economic trends, and the potential for market evolution, should be analysed.
- **Sociological factors**: such as the population composition, rental demand, and housing needs in the area, should be taken into account.
- **Legal and tax factors**: such as applicable regulations, land taxes and property taxes, easements, and other charges on the property, should be examined.

The value of a property is influenced by the complex interaction of these different factors.

In the real estate valuation process, different methods can be used:

Direct comparison estimation: The property is compared to similar properties recently sold in the same sector.
- **Estimation by the cost of land and construction**: The value of the land and the construction cost of the buildings are estimated.
- **Income capitalization estimation**: The potential income generated by the property is taken into account.

- **Discounted cash flow estimation**: The future cash flows related to the property are analyzed.
- **Developer balance sheet estimation**: The value of the property is estimated based on the construction cost and the expected profit.

The choice of the most appropriate method depends on several factors:

- The type of real estate
- The quality and quantity of available data
- The purpose of the valuation

Real estate valuation is a complex and demanding field. The real estate expert must have a thorough knowledge of the real estate market, legal and tax aspects, as well as valuation techniques. Their expertise ensures a precise and reliable estimate of the value of a property, which is crucial for decision-making in the context of a real estate transaction, mortgage financing, or inheritance.

Framework of Real Estate Valuation in Morocco

The practice of real estate valuation in Morocco is based on global valuation standards such as RICS standards, the Guide to Real Estate Valuation in Europe, and the Charter for Real Estate Valuation applied in France. However, it lacks clear regulations governing all valuation activities at the national level. Specifically, real estate valuation and the definition of values are not regulated by legal provisions or implementing texts (Bajeddi, 2015). Three types of real estate valuation activities are distinguished in Morocco (EL IDRISSI, 2015):

- **Judicial expertise:**

This is regulated by Law 45.00 relating to judicial experts. According to Article 2 of this law, the judicial expert is appointed by a magistrate to investigate points of a purely technical nature.

- **Amicable or conventional expertise:**

This is partially regulated by Circular No. 19 relating to the classification of receivables and their coverage by provisions, applied by the Central Bank of the Kingdom "Bank Al-Maghrib" since 2002.

It is emphasized that the determination of the provisions of mortgages exceeding one million dirhams is only taken into account by the banking institutions after having been the subject of a rigorous appraisal by a qualified expert.

At this stage, the only law that grants the title of real estate expert is Law 30-93 relating to the practice of the profession of land surveyor in its first article.

■ **Administrative expertise:**

The public accounting decree mentions this type of expertise by appointing an administrative commission chaired by the local authority to evaluate the properties of the State or to be acquired by it.

Among the members of the commission are representatives of the following administrations: Private properties of the State, registration and stamps, urban planning or agriculture administration according to the vocation of the property, the ministerial department concerned...

All real estate valuation activities in Morocco use the previously mentioned valuation methods, with the exception of administrative expertise, which uses the direct comparison method in particular. Therefore, we already conclude the disparity between the functioning of the Moroccan types of expertise in terms of the estimation methods used. For this reason, we will focus in the following on the direct comparison method, since it is the basic estimation technique. It represents the common method used between the practitioners of amicable, judicial, and administrative expertise, and it is fully in line with the logic of our study. Real estate valuation in the private and public sectors is based on a set of multisource data, including data on paper supports. Consequently, the various organizations that practice valuation by direct comparison lack a rich and standardized digital database containing the different transactions carried out on the market and the real estate offers proposing the prices of the properties for sale. It should also contain all the information on the real estate properties from any establishment acting on the Moroccan real estate properties. Especially with the comparative method, which is in direct relation with the real estate market, it is essential to refer to reliable and available data. This means that real estate valuation, although it is a regulated practice with its own texts and attitudes of operation, it is also important that it deals with the important and heterogeneous data on which it is based. Therefore, it would be wise to couple the practice of real estate valuation in Morocco with a science of intelligent information processing of real estate information, which would thus facilitate the estimation of the market values of real estate properties.

SUMMARY

Real estate valuation, and more specifically real estate appraisal, is a practice that depends heavily on various value factors and the estimation methods used.

Therefore, the expert must be able to appreciate the value by studying in depth the information collected on the property to choose the best methods to use. In all cases, the estimation of the value of a property always comes down to finding reliable references from the real estate market.

In Morocco, the situation is even more complex. Real estate valuation, which does not have a clear and unique reference, generates disparities in terms of the practice of expertise in its different activities. On the other hand, the diversity of the information consulted during the valuation, of an economic, legal, tax, and physical nature, necessitates the implementation of a process for the intelligent treatment of massive data, particularly machine learning, to facilitate the prediction of the market values of the real estate market.

State of the Art on the Prediction of Real Estate Market Prices Using AI

Today, data is undergoing an important revolution, requiring careful and intelligent treatment for its exploitation in different fields. Data Science or Data Science is the science purely dedicated to this mission. Indeed, it consists of researching, cleaning, and processing raw data to extract meaning for analytical purposes. At this stage, it uses intelligent algorithms and iterative processing of a large amount of data by exploiting what is called Artificial Intelligence.

Wish means an experimental science designed to reconstitute, using artificial means (usually computers), reasoning and intelligent actions. It allows testing and refining the models expressed in programs on many examples, to discover and better understand the functioning of human intelligence (Laurière, 1987). Its practical objective is the design and realization of IT devices whose behavior seems intelligent to a human observer (Balacheff, 1994). That is to say, to create systems endowed with an intelligence capable of learning and reasoning like human beings (Zhao et al. 2021). Because of its many advantages, artificial intelligence has been successfully applied in multiple fields such as image classification, facial and voice recognition, the manufacture of autonomous vehicles, remote consulting, predictive analysis, etc.

Most of its applications often rely on machine learning, which is a branch of artificial intelligence. It describes the ability of systems to learn from specific problem-related training data to automate the process of building analytical models and solve related problems (Janiesch et al. 2021). It is used to teach machines to process data faster and more efficiently than a human being, to perform a specific task without being explicitly programmed, using algorithms and statistical models (Batta, 2020).

Machine Learning Algorithms in Real Estate Price Prediction

It is important to note that machine learning is not based on a single type of algorithm considered to be the best for solving a problem. The type of algorithm used depends on the type of problem to be solved, the type of model that is most suitable, the number and type of variables (Batta, 2020). For this reason, we distinguish three main Machine Learning techniques that are most commonly used. These are supervised learning, unsupervised learning, and reinforcement learning.

Table 1. Comparison between types of machine learning

Type of machine learning	Characteristics	Algorithms	
supervised learning	Well-defined objectives. Dedicated to classification and regression problems. Requires training.	**Classification**	**Regression**
		Naive Bayes ; Decision Trees ; Support Vector Machine ; Random Forest ; K-Nearest Neighbors.	Linear Regression ; Neural Network Regression ; Support Vector Regression ; Lasso Regression ; Ridge Regression.
unsupervised learning	▪ The result is not known. ▪ Dedicated to clustering and segmentation problems. ▪ Does not require training.	▪ K Means clustering ; ▪ Mean-shift clustering ; ▪ BDSCAN clustering ; ▪ Agglomerative Hierarchical clustering ; ▪ Gaussian Mixture.	
reinforcement learning	▪ The start and end states are defined. ▪ The agent discovers the path and makes its own decision.	▪ R Learning ; ▪ TD Learning ; ▪ Q Learning.	

Each type of machine learning is distinguished by the nature of the problems it solves and its own learning modalities. The table below provides a comparison between the different types of machine learning mentioned above (Batta, 2020; Janiesch et al., 2021; Sur, 2021):

In this study, we are focusing on the algorithms for predicting real estate prices on the Moroccan market. This topic is among the problems solved by supervised learning algorithms, and more specifically, those related to regression. Indeed, we are looking for a continuous numerical result, which requires prior training.

The structuring of the prediction problem in supervised learning in our case is based on four fundamental elements:

- A well-structured database with independent variables serving as input to the machine and the dependent variable to be predicted by it (price in our case);
- The machine learning model that will train on the data;
- The cost function represents the average of the errors between the real and predicted values, which shows how well the model has trained;
- The cost function minimization algorithm allows for finding the best parameters of the model by minimizing the prediction error each time.

In practice, three minimization algorithms are generally used: minimization by least squares, by gradient descent, or by stochastic gradient descent.

The least squares method consists of finding the minimum of the cost function and deriving the parameters of the model. Gradient descent, on the other hand, uses a learning rate to find the parameters of the model by first seeking the minimum of the cost function in a small neighborhood. The algorithm then moves on to search in the next interval as long as there is a value of the function inferior to the minimum found. It does this iteratively until it finds the absolute minimum and thus the best parameters (Tamenu, 2021). Stochastic gradient descent is a particular case of gradient descent where the algorithm performs the same process at each iteration of the model's learning. It is often used with neural networks (Imran et al., 2021).

Another notion of machine learning that is worth mentioning is cross-validation. Its principle is based on the distribution of the training over the entire database so as to have n-1 parts of training samples and a nth part for the validation of the model. It repeats these parts so that all the observations have the opportunity to be both training data and validation data, thus avoiding the model being biased because of the database. Cross-validation also provides the advantage of allowing the model to determine its best hyperparameters (John, 2014).

Despite the variety of qualities and performances of the algorithms mentioned above, they are not without disadvantages. These two characteristics are related to the ability of the algorithms to provide a reliable prediction on any kind of data, to execute in a reasonable amount of time, to handle missing data in the database, and to be relatively sensitive to outliers. The table below summarizes some advantages and disadvantages of the aforementioned algorithms (Gupta et al., 2020; Ho et al., 2021; Mullainathan and Spiess, 2017):

Table 2. Comparative study of the above algorithms

Type of Algorithms	Machine Learning Algorithms	Advantages	Disadvantages
Parametric Predictors	Linear Regression	■ Very simple method. ■ Useful for finding the nature of the relationship between two variables.	■ The linear function may not fit any database. ■ Trouble with a large number of variables.
	Polynomial Regression	■ Integration of all independent variables into a linear model.	■ Risk of over fitting or under fitting when choosing an unsuitable degree.
	Lasso Regression	■ Applies the shrinkage process. ■ Reduction of some coefficients to zero, allowing for variable selection and model simplification.	■ Possible elimination of the most important variables for prediction.
	Ridge Regression	■ Useful when variables are highly correlated. ■ ■ The coefficients of useless variables tend towards zero without reaching it.	■ Difficulty of interpretation, as it does not proceed with variable selection.
	Elastic Net	■ Combines the advantages of Ridge and Lasso regressions. ■ Model with better predictive power.	----------------
	Support Vector Regression	■ Effective in high dimensions. ■ Ability to adapt to non-linear limits. ■ The multiplicity of kernel functions can adapt to different types of problems. ■ The risk of over fitting is minimal.	■ Requires more time to execute compared to linear regression. ■ Does not perform well when the number of variables exceeds the number of training data.
Non-parametric predictors	Regression tree	■ Simple to understand. ■ Handles categorical and numerical data. ■ Uses several variables.	■ Sometimes trees become complex. ■ Decision trees can be unstable. ■ High probability of sampling error due to over-fitting of data.
Mixed predictors	Neural Networks	■ Memory space is distributed for processing. ■ Works well with massive amounts of data. ■ Works well with noisy data. ■ - Robust prediction mechanism	■ Consumes a lot of physical memory and CPU. ■ Requires parallel processing. ■ Difficult for everyone to understand.

continued on following page

Table 2. Continued

Type of Algorithms	Machine Learning Algorithms	Advantages	Disadvantages
Combined predictors (Ensemble learning)	Random Forest	■ More accurate than regression trees. ■ Reduces over-fitting of weak models. ■ Works well with missing values by replacing them with the variables that appear most often in a node.	■ Requires a longer execution time than SVR. ■ Complex algorithm. ■ Takes up a lot of memory. ■ Difficult to interpret.
	Gradient Boosting	■ Provides accurate prediction. ■ Flexible model fitting with hyper-parameter tuning options ■ Solves multi-colinearity problems when correlation between variables is high ■ Works well with missing data.	■ Requires a longer execution time than SVR. ■ Sensitive to outliers. ■ Difficult to interpret.
	AdaBoost	■ Trees can have different weights depending on their importance and performance. ■ Each tree compensates for the weaknesses of the one before it. ■ Emphasises poorly ranked examples.	■ It requires a high-quality dataset that contains no outliers or noisy values.

Discussion of ML-Based Approaches for Real Estate Price Prediction

In the indexed scientific databases, no bibliographic reference has been identified on the prediction of real estate prices in Morocco using machine learning. Our study is thus distinguished as the first of its kind in this specific context. However, various research has been conducted on this topic in other foreign countries. The exploitation of Machine Learning algorithms has proven their effectiveness in real estate evaluation, particularly those of ensemble learning. For example, in India, Borde et al. (2017) used linear regression and Random Forest (RF) on a database collected between 2005 and 2016, finding that RF offered better predictions. Wu and Wang (2018) in Virginia, USA, who trained RF and linear regression, drew similar conclusions.

In other studies, such as that of Ravikumar (2017), Random Forest (RF) was compared to other algorithms, including Gradient Boosting (GB), Neural Networks, and SVR, on data from the UCI Machine Learning repository, where RF showed better performance. Ho et al. (2021) in Hong Kong, who used SVR, RF, observed similar results and GB on a real estate database over an eighteen-year period, demonstrating the effectiveness of the RF and GB ensemble algorithms. In France, Tchuente and Nyawa (2022) also found that RF, GB, and AdaBoost had better performance in estimating real estate prices, using historical data provided by the French government. However, other studies have shown that parametric algorithms such as Ridge, Lasso, and ElasticNet regression can also offer accurate predictions, as observed by Abbasi (2020) in Iran and Fan et al. (2018) in Ames, Spain. The Support Vector Machine (SVM) in regression (SVR) has also proven effective in some studies, such as that conducted in Pakistan by Imran et al. (2021) and in Australia by Phan (2019), where it was combined with the PCA tool to analyze datasets with imprecise measures.

In conclusion, several models have demonstrated their ability to accurately predict real estate prices, but the effectiveness depends on each case study and the database used. Ensemble learning algorithms generally seem to perform well, followed by Neural Networks, SVM regression, and Lasso and Ridge regression. However, no category of algorithms can be considered superior to the other without taking into account the specific context of the study and the available data.

METHODOLOGY AND TOOLS FOR REAL ESTATE PRICE PREDICTION IN MOROCCO

Introduction and Presentation of the Study Area and the Tools Used

After highlighting the advantages of artificial intelligence in the field of real estate evaluation through Machine Learning, through the analysis and discussion of several articles dealing with part or our entire project at the international level, this part focuses on the practical aspect of this study. First, it presents the area concerned by our study, whose real estate offers were used to feed our dataset. Then, it emphasizes the tools used to achieve our goals. Finally, it discusses in detail the methodology adopted and the steps followed, from data collection to model training.

Study Area

The study area covers two major Moroccan cities: Rabat and Casablanca.

Rabat, the capital of Morocco, is located on the banks of the Bouregreg River on the Atlantic coast in the northwest of Morocco. It has an area of 118 km2 and corresponds to the prefecture of Rabat, which is composed of the urban commune of Rabat, divided into five districts: Hassan, Agdal-Ryad, el-Youssoufia, Yacoub el-Mansour, and Souissi, and the urban commune of Touarga, where the main royal palace of the country is located (@reseau-euromed, 2021). According to the 2014 General Census of Population and Housing, the population of Rabat was 578,519 inhabitants (Direction-régional-de Rabat-Sale-Kenitra, 2014).

Casablanca, the economic capital of Morocco, has an area of 384 km2. Its population was 3,359,818 inhabitants in 2014. It is a large prefecture located in the Casablanca-Settat region, which contains sixteen districts: Sidi Belyout, Anfa, Maârif, Al Fida, Mers Sultan, Aïn Sebaâ, Hay Mohammadi, Roches Noires, Aïn Chock, Hay Hassani, Ben M'sick, Sbata, Sidi Bernoussi, Sidi Moumen, Moulay Rachid, and Sidi Othmane (@Casablanca).

We chose to work with the real estate offers related to these two cities because of their national economic and social importance. Indeed, they are very dynamic and continue to expand because they are characterized by massive demographic growth that increases day after day. This is due to the favorable living conditions that the two cities offer at all levels, as well as to the variety of employment opportunities they present in the different sectors and for all social classes. This proves the strong demand for housing that they experience year after year.

Figure 2. Extent of the study area: city of Casablanca

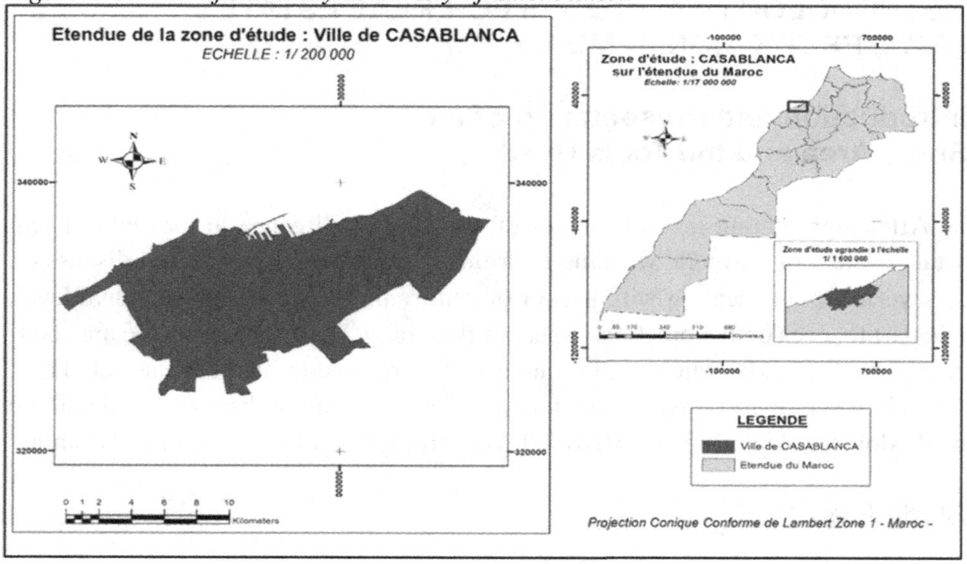

Figure 3. Extent of the study area: city of Rabat

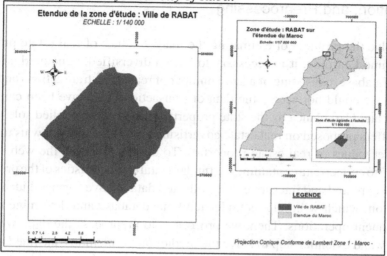

Legal Framework of Web Scraping

Before starting with web scraping, it is important and mandatory to question the legality of this practice and the laws that govern it.

In Morocco, there are no laws that explicitly deal with web scraping. However, we can refer to certain laws related to this subject to determine its legality, namely Law 02.00 on copyright and related rights. According to this law, particularly articles 3 and 15, we conclude that the automatic extraction of data from any website and their use for educational and non-profit purposes is authorized without prior authorization from the author, if the source and the name of the author are indicated. Law 5.20 on cybersecurity only penalizes acts that have disrupted websites or threatened their security. Therefore, web scraping in our case is legal since we will neither attack the security of the website nor disrupt its functioning. We will also use it as a work (computer program) exploited in our study while indicating its author.

The main idea to keep in mind is that as long as there is no use of others' work through illegal means for the purpose of gaining competitive interests, this practice remains legal.

In order to collect information from a website, it is wise to determine the source that will meet the criteria of the study. Several real estate portals have been consulted for this purpose. Unfortunately, the majority of Moroccan real estate websites, with the exception of a few sites such as Mubawab.ma, sarouty.ma, etc., lack spatial information which is of great importance in our project.

Methodology Adopted for Data Collection, Exploration, and Preprocessing

To solve the problem of estimating the market values of real estate properties via Machine Learning, it is necessary to have a diversified, structured, and well-cleaned database, consisting of a large number of real estate transactions and offers.

Since we could not access the data of transactions that have been carried out on Rabat and Casablanca by the state property department, we relied solely on the data of offers proposed on real estate advertising sites. This will allow us to predict the market values of real estate properties. To do this, we used the web scraping technique to collect data containing the fundamental characteristics of the properties. Then, we explored and interpreted the collected data to have a general idea of their distribution, which will help us understand our database and determine the type of subsequent operations. Then, we proceeded to preprocess the data, which is a necessary and essential step to solve the prediction problem in Machine Learning.

In this phase, we accomplished several tasks to prepare our database for subsequent operations:

- Treatment of missing values;
- Detection of outliers and their deletion;
- Encoding of qualitative variables;
- Selection of variables to train;
- Normalization of quantitative variables.
- Finally, after preparing our data, we moved on to training our models to choose the most performing and best suited to our database.

The following flowchart illustrates all the steps followed for the realization of this study:

Figure 4. steps followed for the realization of this study

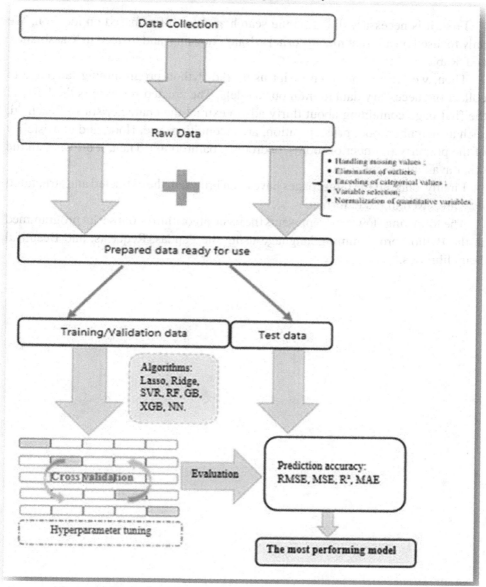

Steps for Data Collection

First, it is necessary to define the search area for offers based on location. We only focused on ads that met the criteria 'sale', 'housing' and located in 'Casablanca' and 'Rabat'.

Then, we created our own script using the Python programming language to collect the necessary data to train our models. The created script uses the URL of the first page containing about thirty ads to extract the characteristics of each ad, such as neighborhood, price, position, area, condition, age, floor, and consistency of the property (number of rooms, bedrooms, bathrooms). Then, it browses all the other available pages.

Finally, once all the target pages have been browsed, the extracted and structured data are saved in Excel format.

The following flowchart represents the basic algorithm of our script programmed in the Python programming language using the Pandas, Requests, and Beautiful Soup libraries:

Figure 5. Flowchart of the algorithm used for data collection

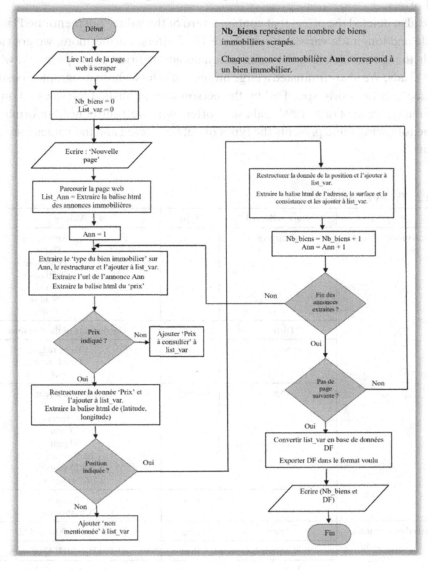

In this part of the report, we will analyze the scraped real estate offers to understand their consistency, nature, and the relationship between all the characteristics.

Initially, we had a noisy database of 1801 real estate offers in Rabat and 8318 in Casablanca, totaling 10119 offers. We proceeded with a manual cleaning to eliminate all incorrect observations, including those that will not be useful for training the models. We removed the lines containing very low prices that are suitable for rental offers.

We also deleted the offers that contain a zero or the value "not mentioned" in the latitude and longitude variables, which are 1337 offers. Furthermore, we got rid of the ads that do not disclose the information about the price of the property, which are 1943 ads. We also eliminated a large number of offers whose geographic position was incorrect or poorly specified by the person who published the sales ad on the site. Finally, we kept only 1994 real estate offers with well-introduced information.

The following table presents the types of data collected and the values they may contain:

Table 1. Types of data collected

	Data collected	Type	Values
Qualitative variables	**Property**	string	- Apartment - Duplex - Penthouse - Penthouse - Riad - Studio - Villa
	District	string	The districts of the two towns
	Status	string	To be renovated Good condition Newly built
	Age	string	Less than a year 1-5 years 5-10 years 10-20 years 20-30 years 30-50 years 50-70 years 70-100 years
	City	string	- Rabat - Casablanca
Quantitative variables	Price	Integer	[190000,99000000] MAD
	Latitude	Real	[33.50423, 34.0314] degrees
	Longitude	Real	[-7.72646, -6.80012] degrees
	Surface	Integer	[30,6489] m^2
	Number of pieces	Integer	[1,30]
	Number of rooms	Integer	[1,15]
	Number of bathrooms	Integer	[1,10]
	Floor	Integer	From the first floor to the 29th floor

In order to spatially the distribution of the real estate offers selected in Rabat and Casablanca, we have drawn up the following two maps:

Figure 6. distribution of the real estate offers selected in Rabat

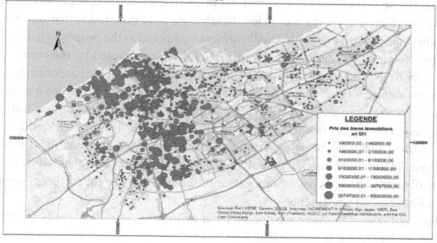

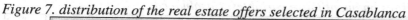

Figure 7. distribution of the real estate offers selected in Casablanca

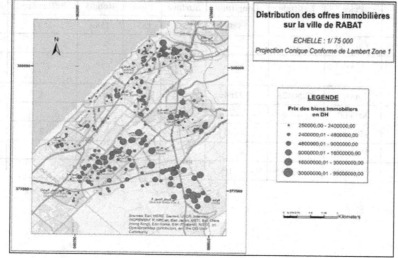

These two maps show that the collected data is almost distributed throughout the territory of the two cities, which gives us a general overview of the price range in each area. Thus, this distribution will help to overcome all the problems of under and overestimation of prices during the learning of the models. We have chosen to present the spatial component of the total price of the buildings because it is more significant than that of the unit price. Indeed, we have concluded that our dataset contains houses with relatively small surfaces compared to the proposed price. This can be explained by the inaccuracy of the information entered by the owner who may refer to the surface of one of the floors instead of taking into account the total living area of the house. Based on an analysis of the obtained maps, we notice that the prices of real estate properties differ from one district to another according to the urban planning of the area. The price is higher in the districts with villa zones than in those that contain only apartments. Moreover, we notice that the prices are dispersed in the same district, notably in the Medina district of Rabat, which is due to the diversity of the types of real estate properties that are found there, namely: riads, houses, and apartments.

To clarify our data, we have conducted a descriptive statistical study for all the qualitative and quantitative variables.

The two tables below present, by city, the statistics on the quantitative variables:

Table 3. Statistics on quantitative variables, Casablanca

	Price	Latitude	Longitude	Surface	Piece	Rooms	Bathrooms	Floor
Frequency	1589	1589	1589	1589	1587	1589	1587	1137
Average	2794760	----	----	190.47	----	----	----	----
Standard deviation	4474183	----	----	273.02	----	----	----	----
Min	190000	33.50423	-7.72646	3	1	1	1	1
Q1 = 25%	880000	----	----	80	3	2	1	2
Median	1500000	----	----	111	4	3	2	3
Q3 = 75%	2550000	----	----	166	5	3	2	4
Max	55000000	33.62602	-7.47169	35000	28	15	10	20

Table 4. Statistics on quantitative variables, Rabat

	Price	Latitude	Longitude	Surface	Piece	Rooms	Bathrooms	Floor
Frequency	405	405	405	405	403	403	402	240
Average	4079920	----	----	344.77	----	----	----	----
Standard deviation	6601456	----	----	686.86	----	----	----	----
Min	250000	33.93724	-6.90507	30	1	1	1	1
Q1 = 25%	1320000	----	----	90	3	2	1	2
Median	2180000	----	----	133	4	3	2	3
Q3 = 75%	4400000	----	----	218	6	4	3	4
Max	99000000	34.0314	-6.80012	6489	30	12	9	29

For the other categorical variables, we have represented their statistics in the following graphs:

Figure 8. Statistics on qualitative variables

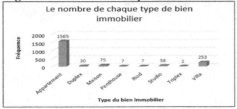

We notice that apartments are the most frequent type of property in the real estate market. Most of the properties are in good condition and are 10 to 20 years old. It is obvious that the price of real estate differs from one area to another. For example, two identical apartments located in two different neighborhoods will have completely different prices. To emphasize this difference in price, we have compared the unit price of apartments located in the most popular neighborhoods of the two cities Rabat and Casablanca in order to have an approximate idea of the price range of apartments in these cities. We have chosen to compare this type of property because it is the most available in the different neighborhoods compared to other types: villa, duplex, studio or other.

The results are presented in the two following graphs:

Figure 9. Unit price per district, Casablanca

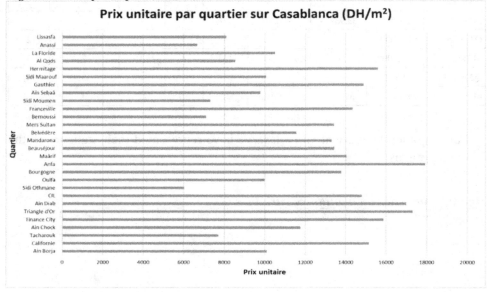

Figure 10. Unit price per district, Rabat

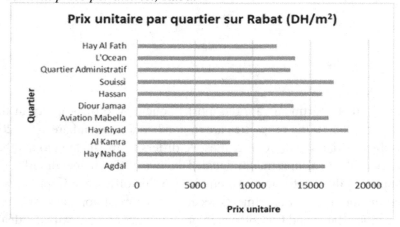

Based on the information collected in our database, we observe that Anfa is the most expensive neighborhood among the selected neighborhoods in Casablanca, where the price per square meter of living space reaches 18,000 Dhs. Whereas in Rabat, Hay Riad has the highest unit price of the order of 18,200 Dhs/m2.

The following steps detail the preprocessing steps that we have performed before training the machine learning models. First, we have treated the missing values using two different techniques for the qualitative and quantitative variables. Then, we have detected and eliminated the outliers using the interquartile range method. After that, we have encoded the qualitative variables using the simple encoding method with LabelEncoder. Then, we have selected the most correlated variables with the dependent variable "price" using the correlation matrix. Finally, we have normalized the quantitative variables using the RobustScaler transformation of python to obtain data on a common scale. These preprocessing steps are important to improve the quality of the database and the accuracy of the prediction results.

Therefore, the proposed methodology presents all the necessary elements to conduct a prediction project using machine learning algorithms, from data collection to obtaining the desired results. It is demanding in terms of the data preprocessing step, which is the most important step in the process followed because it is closely related to the accuracy of the obtained results.

In the following part, we will present, interpret, and discuss the results that we have obtained.

RESULTS AND DISCUSSION

This section is devoted to highlighting the results of the comparative study between the learning models on our database in order to estimate housing market prices with good performance.

First, we will briefly present the results of the training and validation of each algorithm, and then we will evaluate all the models on test data with a view to selecting the best among them. These results will then be displayed in an interactive map. Finally, a general discussion will be held to summarise the stages followed in carrying out our project and the results obtained.

Results of the Hyperparameters Selected For Learning

A rigorous selection of hyperparameters was carried out for each algorithm. This selection was based on graphical analyses and on the literature specialising in property valuation using machine learning. The qualitative and numerical values selected for each estimator are shown in the following table:

Table 5. Sample values of the hyperparameters selected for each model

Estimator	Selected hyperparameters	
	Parameter	Sample values
Lasso	Alpha	[1, 0.5, 0.0001]
Ridge	Alpha	[1, 0.1, 0.5, 0.0001]
SVR	kernel	[Rbf]
	C	[15, 12, 20]
	gamma	[0.001, 0.002, 0.003]
RF	n_estimators	[27, 29, 100, 200]
	max_depth	[30, 40, 50, 100]
	min_samples_leaf	[1, 2, 3]
	min_samples_split	[2, 3, 4]
	Bootstrap	[True]
GB	max_depth	[2, 3, 4, 5]
	n_estimators	[100, 150, 200, 250]
	learning_rate	[0.5, 0.1, 0.01, 0.05]
XGB	max_depth	[2, 3, 4, 5]
•	min_child_weight	[22, 25, 30, 35]
	n_estimators	[100, 150, 200, 250]
	learning_rate	[0.5, 0.1, 0.01, 0.05]
NN	Solver	[adam]
	hidden_layer_sizes	[(90,), (100,), (200,), (500,)]
	learning_rate_init	[0.002, 0.001, 2]

Results of Training and Model Validation

After configuring the hyperparameters in GridSearch, it evaluates all possible combinations using five iterations for each combination, corresponding to five cross-validation steps. GridSearch then averages the validation scores for each combination and selects the best hyperparameters using grid.best_params_ and the best estimation score using grid.best_score_. The results obtained, including the best hyperparameter combinations, their scores and the training time, are presented in the tables below for each model.

Table 6. Hyperparameter combinations with good validation scores for SVR, RF, GB, XGB and NN

Model	Optimum combination	Validation score (%)	Training time
SVR	{'C': 20, 'gamma': 0.001, 'kernel': 'rbf'}	88.76	15.32 s
RF	{'bootstrap': True, 'max_depth': 40, 'min_samples_leaf': 3, 'min_samples_split': 4, 'n_estimators': 29}	87.85	9 min et 27,16 s
GB	{'learning_rate': 0.1, 'max_depth': 2, 'n_estimators': 100}	87.21	4 min et 8,53 s
XGB	{'learning_rate': 0.05, 'max_depth': 2, 'n_estimators': 200}	87.73	10 min et 26,11s
NN	{'hidden_layer_sizes': (100,), 'learning_rate_init': 0.001, 'solver': 'adam'}	88.72	1 min et 231s

Note that the Ridge and Lasso regressions have a single parameter, which is why GridSearch has adopted a single value for each.

Table 7. Value of the hyperparameter selected for each of the Lasso and Ridge models

Model	Optimum value	Validation score (%)	Training time
Lasso	{'alpha': 0.0001}	83.51	0,46 s
Ridge	{'alpha': 0.0001}	83.52	5,20 s

he results show that the SVR and NN models have the highest validation scores (around 88.7%). The Random Forest and XGBoost models obtained slightly lower scores (around 87.5%). Ridge and Lasso regressions scored significantly lower than the other algorithms (around 83.5%).

In terms of training time, the Lasso and Ridge regressions stand out for their speed, followed by the SVR. The NN, GB, RF and XGBoost algorithms require a longer training time.

MODEL TEST RESULTS

Results of Model Testing Metrics

After selecting the best estimators, they were trained again on a test dataset representing 20% of the total database. Estimation accuracy metrics such as R2, MSE, RMSE and MAE were used to assess the effectiveness of the estimators in predicting property sales values.

The results showed that the higher the coefficient of determination R2 and the fact that the other metrics have values close to zero, the more accurate the model is in its predictions. The sklearn.metrics sub-library was used to calculate all the evaluation metrics for each model, and the results are presented in Table:

Table 8. Values of metrics , MAE, MSE, RMSE for each model

Model	Test score ^{2}(%)	MAE	MSE	RMSE
Lasso	79,11	0.44791	0.75141	0.86684
Ridge	79,12	0.44793	0.75089	0.86654
SVR	92,57	0.29665	0.26727	0.51698
RF	88.56	0.31317	0.41156	0.64153
GB	87,30	0.34273	0.45681	0.675884
XGB	87,28	0.34739	0.45741	0.67632
Neural Networks	90.02	0.34878	0.35890	0.59909

Results of Predicted Price Values

In order to get an idea of the predictions made for each estimator, we have drawn up the graphs below in python language, which illustrate the predicted selling prices as a function of the existing values in the test data.

The graph is also fitted with a linear function, which represents the values that the predictions should normally have in the ideal case, whose equation is ($y = x$) where x represents the prices in MAD in the test data. The results obtained are illustrated below:

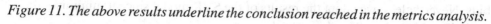

Figure 11. The above results underline the conclusion reached in the metrics analysis.

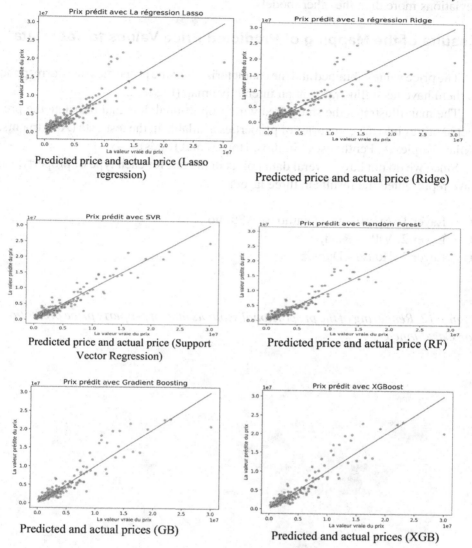

Predicted price and actual price (Lasso regression)

Predicted price and actual price (Ridge)

Predicted price and actual price (Support Vector Regression)

Predicted price and actual price (RF)

Predicted and actual prices (GB)

Predicted and actual prices (XGB)

The SVR model produces a scatterplot that best matches the line of true price values that exist on the test data.

For all models including SVR, we find that the predictions deviate from the linear representation at given prices, i.e. values from Dhs 300,000 to Dhs 400,000 and values above Dhs 10,0000,000. This can be explained by the lack of sufficient training data having the said prices and the same characteristics of the mispredicted bids. Nevertheless, we adopt the results of the SVR model since it minimises these deviations more than the other models.

Results of the Mapping of Predicted Price Values to Test Data

The price values obtained and the characteristics of the properties that correspond to them have been illustrated in an interactive map (Figure ...).

The map illustrates the study area with proportional dots that translate the predicted prices into the categories of properties available in the test data (Apartments, Villas, Duplexes, Penthouses, Studios, Houses and Riads).

Since we do not have several data points in the test for each type of property, we have represented the results in three layers:

- Layer 1: Apartment - Penthouse - Studio ;
- Layer 2: Villa - Riad;
- Layer 3: House - Duplex.

Figure 12. Rendering of the proportional symbols map of property price predictions for Casablanca

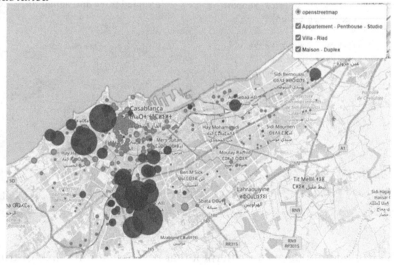

The result is as follows:

Figure 13.

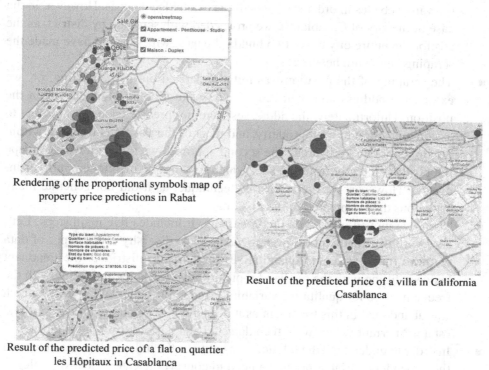

Rendering of the proportional symbols map of property price predictions in Rabat

Result of the predicted price of a villa in California Casablanca

Result of the predicted price of a flat on quartier les Hôpitaux in Casablanca

The cartographic illustration has allowed us to better represent the results of the SVR model's predictions. These results effectively reflect the distribution of real estate prices in the neighborhoods of the two cities of Rabat and Casablanca.

General Discussion

The sequence followed in this chapter, from data extraction using web scraping, to the necessary preprocessing steps carried out on the database, and finally to the selection of the most powerful model, has truly proven to us the importance of the logic adopted to achieve a good prediction of real estate sales values. The steps we followed are as follows:

■ We started by collecting data from Moroccan real estate ads in order to obtain the prices of the offers available in Rabat and Casablanca. This step took a lot of time, especially to evaluate the script that must target the customized 'html' tags on the website and restructure them in a way that is useful for the objective of our study. The developed script allows for automatic pagination of the relevant websites in order scraping all the available ad pages. However, in the case of the city of Casablanca, we proceeded with scraping by district, as the ads for the entire city cover two hundred pages, which would have made the scraping algorithm heavier.

- The scraping of the position was initially carried out by geocoding, i.e. we extract the address and then send a request to Google Maps to obtain the position. Unfortunately, the addresses were not precise enough to be able to assign a position to each property, and most of the positions were not within the limits of our study area. The second approach we followed was to scrape the position directly from the site, which may not be mentioned, null, or incorrect. However, we opted for this technique, as it did not generate many erroneous data compared to the first one.

- Then, we moved on to data preprocessing. It includes five main steps. Let's start with the treatment of missing values. The diversity of the types of data we have (qualitative and quantitative) forced us to distribute the treatment between filling with the median for quantitative variables and filling with the frequent value for qualitative variables, except for the variable "floor" which was abandoned in this treatment as it does not correspond to all types of real estate. Aberrant values were then detected and deleted from the database.

- In order to understand the relationship between the independent variables and the dependent variable price, we need to convert the categorical variables to be able to calculate their correlations with the price. To do this, we evaluated three types of encoding. First, the encoding proposed by the Pandas library with the get_dummies function allows encoding each qualitative variable with a binary matrix that represents the categories of values it contains. It returns a new database that contains the set of new binary columns created. This method helps to execute the training in little time with binary values recorded in memory. However, the correlation matrix it generated was very dense. We then tried to work with OneHotEncoder and OrdinalEncoder from the sklearn.preprocessing sub-library. These allow encoding separately the variables with an ordinal (hierarchical) character, such as the variable "age," and those that are nominal, such as "city." This type of encoding also generates binary matrices but which are not introduced into a database. The third method used was to encode each variable with simple numerical values using LabelEncoder. This allowed us to generate a correlation matrix that was lighter in comparison with the others. That is why we opted for this method. Then, we generated two correlation matrices, the first one corresponds to the relationship between all the variables and the price, while the second one highlights the relationship between the unit price and the position variables. The latter gave weak correlations, which can be explained by the non-regularization of the real estate offer on the two cities.

- We kept the contribution of the different variables in the training, except for the "floor" variable. Then, we proceeded to train the models after having normalized all the quantitative variables with RobustScaler. The training used cross-validation, and we generated only the validation scores of the models. A second training on test data was executed to select the appropriate prediction model for our study.

- We evaluated the performance of each model based on the calculated metrics and the generated prediction graphs. The models seem to have poorly predicted the prices of offers with very high prices. This is due to the minority of this type of sample in our database. Indeed, the majority of the observations we have have prices between 190,000 Dhs and 10,000,000 Dhs, and as a result, the models could not give good results for these data. However, we adopted the SVR model since it generated the best predicted prices in comparison with the other models.

- The results of the SVR predictor on the test data were then presented in the form of an interactive map that highlights the predicted prices in the form of proportional symbols. The map has three layers of information that correspond to the types of real estate. It facilitates the obtaining of information on each property in a pop-up by clicking on the proportional symbol, and the predicted price with SVR is also displayed there.

In summary, thanks to the machine learning models and the data we have, we have been able to touch on the contribution of artificial intelligence to the real estate field, according to the analysis of the results, but also to highlight the weak points to be improved in the proposed approach. The following section will present the constraints encountered and a general conclusion with a set of recommendations for improving this work.

Constraints Encountered

In the context of our study, which focuses on real estate evaluation through the prediction of real estate prices, machine learning requires a solid and rich database in terms of quantity and quality of information.

Unfortunately, Moroccan administrations and private sector companies involved in the real estate sector do not have a common and exhaustive real estate and geographic information system on which they can all rely for the realization of their tasks. The data on transactions are therefore not accessible.

As a result, we had to turn to the practice of web scraping of real estate ads on the web to be able to obtain the necessary data for our study. Although these data will allow us to predict the prices of real estate for sale before negotiation, they have enabled us to understand the offer of the Moroccan real estate market in part and to open up other avenues of reflection on the regularization of the real estate offer.

In truth, the scraped real estate ads also have their disadvantages. On the one hand, the prices were not always mentioned; some advertisers prefer to have direct contact with the buyer to disclose the price they are offering for their property. In addition, some information on the consistency, condition, and age of the property were not precisely indicated. On the other hand, the poor spatialization of the data on the website led to the deletion of more than half of the raw ads scraped.

Moreover, relying only on web scraping has also limited the diversity of the variables or factors of value of socio-economic, fiscal, and legal order that we could have used in the models. The offers were not structured according to the existing administrative districts, and this prevented us from enriching the database further with statistics from the High Commission for Planning, such as household income by district....

GENERAL CONCLUSION AND RECOMMENDATIONS

At the end of our final year project, a brief summary allows us to take stock of all the steps of the methodology followed. Indeed, the aim of this project is to predict the prices of the Moroccan real estate market in Casablanca and Rabat, more specifically the housing market.

To carry out this study, we first conducted a bibliographical research touching on the two aspects of our objective, firstly real estate expertise in Morocco and then machine learning applied to real estate, which highlights its contribution to real estate evaluation.

Afterward, we extracted the data from real estate offers on a real estate website and applied the necessary preprocessing. Then, we proceeded to train and test the models that we have chosen based on their advantages and the results of their use in various studies of real estate price prediction.

The results are very encouraging, where Support Vector Regression has the best precision. Neural Networks have also proven their prediction performance compared to ensemble learning models. Illustrated on an interactive map, the predictions obtained with SVR on the test data allow us to grasp the potential of machine learning, offering a promising alternative alternative in the search for the evaluation and estimation of real estate. The model brings amplitude to every real estate player:

administration, investor, real estate expert, citizen in search of housing to feed on the necessary information on real estate prices.

However, the design of an approach cannot be done without raising difficulties and axes of improvement. Following the results obtained from the case study and the various analyses carried out, we recommend the following for future work:

- Train the models on a database encompassing both real estate transactions and offers;
- Expand the database with information of legal, fiscal, economic, and socio-economic order;
- Consider other types of real estate, such as those dedicated to commerce or vacant land in urban and rural areas;
- The case study also highlights the importance of Neural Networks, we, therefore, recommend the use of these with more than one hidden layer, provided that the data is very rich to avoid overfitting;
- Realize an application that allows the implicit use of the model in the same concept as the interactive map realized.

REFERENCES

Abbasi, S. (2020). Advanced Regression Techniques Based Housing Price Prediction Model. *13th International Conference of Iranian Operations Research Society,* 1–10. DOI: 10.13140/RG.2.2.18572.87684

Ahn, J. J., Byun, H. W., Oh, K. J., & Kim, T. Y. (2012). Using ridge regression with genetic algorithm to enhance real estate appraisal forecasting. *Expert Systems with Applications*, 39(9), 8369–8379. DOI: 10.1016/j.eswa.2012.01.183

Al-Jawarneh, A. S., Ismail, M. T., Awajan, A. M., & Alsayed, A. R. M. (2020). Improving accuracy models using elastic net regression approach based on empirical mode decomposition. *Communications in Statistics. Simulation and Computation*, 0(0), 1–20. DOI: 10.1080/03610918.2020.1728319

Avanija, J., Sunitha, G., Reddy Madhavi, K., Korad, P., & Hitesh Sai Vittale, R. (2021). Prediction of House Price Using XGBoost Regression Algorithm. DOI: 10.17762/turcomat.v12i2.1870

Awad, M., & Khanna, R. (2015). *Efficient Learning Machines*. Editions Apress., DOI: 10.1007/978-1-4302-5990-9

Bajeddi A. (2015). Property Valuation and Ethics in Morocco.

Bajeddi, A. (2017). Land Valuation. In *Morocco*. Challenges And Prospects.

Balacheff, N. (1994). Didactique et intelligence artificielle. *Recherches En Didactique Des Mathematiques*, 14(June), 9–42. https://telearn.archives-ouvertes.fr/hal-00190648/

Batta, M. (2020). Machine Learning Algorithms - A Review. *International Journal of Science and Research*, 9(1), 381–386. DOI: 10.21275/ART20203995

Bishop, C. M. (2006). *Pattern recognition and machine learning (Information science and statistics)*. Springer-Verlag New York, Inc.

Borde, S., Rane, A., Shende, G., & Shetty, S. (2017). Real Estate Investment Advising Using MachineLearning. *International Research Journal of Engineering and Technology (IRJET)*, 4(3), 1821–1825. https://irjet.net/archives/V4/i3/IRJET-V4I3499.pdf

Bounajma, N. (2014). Cours d'expertise immobilière pour le compte de l'ONIGT / CRC, Casablanca.

Comité d'Application de la Charte de l'Expertise en Evaluation Immobilière (CACE-EI). (2017). Charte de l'Expertise en Evaluation Immobilière. 5e édition. Editions PALaroche.Paris, 89p.

Deberlanger, J. (2020). *Machine Learning Price Prediction on Green Building Prices*.

Direction-régional-de Rabat-Sale-Kenitra. (2014). *Projections de la population de la région de Rabat-Salé-Kénitra, 2014-2030*. 1–70. https://www.hcp.ma/region - rabat/attachment/1048729/

Dong, X., Yu, Z., Cao, W., Shi, Y., & Ma, Q. (2020). A survey on ensemble learning. In *Frontiers of Computer Science* (Vol. 14, Issue 2). DOI: 10.1007/s11704-019-8208-z

El Idrissi Abdelwahed. (2015). Réflexions sur la politique foncière au Maroc. Travaux de la commission Foncière du Cadastre et Cartographie de l'Ordre National des Ingénieurs Géomètres Topographes (Maroc), Marrakech.

Fan, C., Cui, Z., & Zhong, X. (2018). House prices prediction with machine learning algorithms. In *ACM International Conference Proceeding Series*. DOI: 10.1145/3195106.3195133

Fois, M., Fenu, G., & Bacchetta, G. (2019). Estimating land market values from real estate offers: A replicable method in support of biodiversity conservation strategies. In *Ambio* (Vol. 48, Issue 3). Springer Netherlands. DOI: 10.1007/s13280-018-1074-3

Fonti, V., & Belitser, E. (2017). Feature selection-using lasso. *VU Amsterdam Research Paper in Business Analytics, 30*, 1–25. https://www.researchgate.net/profile/David-Booth-7/post/Regression-of-pairwise-trait-similarity-on-similarity-in-personal-attributes/attachment/5b18368d4cde260d15e3a4e3/AS%3A634606906785793%401528 313485788/download/werkstuk-fonti_tcm235-836234.pdf

Freund, Y., & Schapire, R. E. (1995). A decision-theoretic generalization of on-line learning and an application to boosting. In *European Conference on Computational Learning Theory*. DOI: 10.1007/3-540-59119-2_166

Gupta, S., Kaur, M., Lakra, S., & Dixit, Y. (2020). A comparative theoretical and empirical analysis of machine learning algorithms. In *Webology* (Vol. 17, Issue 1). DOI: 10.14704/WEB/V17I1/WEB17011

Ho, W. K. O., Tang, B. S., & Wong, S. W. (2021). Predicting property prices with machine learning algorithms. *Journal of Property Research*, 38(1), 48–70. DOI: 10.1080/09599916.2020.1832558

Imran, Z. U., Waqar, M., & Zaman, A. (2021). Using Machine Learning Algorithms for Housing Price Prediction: The Case of Isalamabad Housing Data. *Soft Computing and Machine Intelligence Journal*, 1(1), 11–23.

Jamil, S., Mohd, T., Masrom, S., & Ab Rahim, N. (2020). Machine Learning Price Prediction on Green Building Prices.

Janiesch, C., Zschech, P., & Heinrich, K. (2021). Machine learning and deep learning. *Electronic Markets*, 31(3), 685–695. DOI: 10.1007/s12525-021-00475-2

Krotov, V., Johnson, L., & Silva, L. (2020). Tutorial: Legality and ethics of web scraping. *Communications of the Association for Information Systems*, 47(1), 539–563. DOI: 10.17705/1CAIS.04724

Krotov, V., & Silva, L. (2018). Legality and ethics of web scraping. *Americas Conference on Information Systems 2018: Digital Disruption, AMCIS 2018, May.*

Laurière, J. (1987). *Intelligence artificielle – Résolution de problèmes par l' homme et la machine Intelligence Artificielle Résolution de problème par l'Homme et la machine Jean- Louis Laurière.*

Madhuri, C. H. R., Anuradha, G., & Pujitha, M. V. (2019). House Price Prediction Using RegressionTechniques: A Comparative Study. DOI: 10.1109/ICSSS.2019.8882834

Maulud, D., & Abdulazeez, A. M. (2020). A Review on Linear Regression Comprehensive in Machine Learning. *Journal of Applied Science and Technology Trends*, 1(4), 140–147. DOI: 10.38094/jastt1457

Mitchell, J. B. O. (2014). Machine learning methods in chemoinformatics. *Wiley Interdisciplinary Reviews. Computational Molecular Science*, 4(5), 468–481. DOI: 10.1002/wcms.1183 PMID: 25285160

Mullainathan, S., & Spiess, J. (2017). Machine learning: An applied econometric approach. In *Journal of Economic Perspectives* (Vol. 31, Issue 2). DOI: 10.1257/jep.31.2.87

Ourouadi, T. (2021). *Cours d'Expertise Immobilière au profit des étudiants du département des Sciences Géomatiques et Ingénierie Topographique.* IAV.

Phan, T. D. (2019). Housing price prediction using machine-learning algorithms: The case of Melbourne city, Australia. In *Proceedings - International Conference on Machine Learning and Data Engineering, iCMLDE 2018.* IEEE. DOI: 10.1109/iCMLDE.2018.00017

Polignac, B., Monceau, J. P., Cussac, X., & Lesieur, P. (2019). *Expertise Immobilière, guide pratique, 7e édition.* Editions EYROLLES.

Priya, P. M, A. K., K, D. K., & Singha, N. (2021). Prediction of Property Price and Possibility Prediction Using Machine Learning. *Annals of the Romanian Society for Cell Biology, 25*(4), 3870–3882. http://annalsofrscb.ro3870

Ravikumar, A. S. (2017). Real Estate Price Prediction Using. *Machine Learning*.

Royal Institution of Chartered Surveyors (RICS). (2020). *RICS professional standards and guidance.*

Silver, D., Hubert, T., Schrittwieser, J., Antonoglou, I., Lai,M., Guez, A., Lanctot, M., Sifre, L., Kumaran, D., Graepel, T., Lillicrap, T., Simonyan, K., & Hassabis, D. (2018). A general reinforcement learning algorithm that masters chess, shogi, and go through self-play. Science, 362(6419), 1140 1144. .DOI: 10.1126/science.aar6404

Sur, F. (2021). *Introduction à l'apprentissage automatique Tronc commun scientifique FICM 2A École des Mines de Nancy.* https://members.loria.fr/FSur/

Tamenu, Y. (2021). Proptech: la Data Science appliquée à l'immobilier. Haute École de Gestion de Genève. Travail de Bachelor réalisé en vue de l'obtention du Bachelor HES.1- 77

Tchuente, D., & Nyawa, S. (2022). Real estate price estimation in French cities using geocoding and machine learning. In *Annals of Operations Research* (Vol. 308, Issues 1– 2). Springer US. DOI: 10.1007/s10479-021-03932-5

Worzala, E., Lenk, M., & Silva, A. (1995). An Exploration of Neural Networks and Its Application to Real Estate Valuation. In *Journal of Real Estate Research* (Vol. 10, Issue 2). DOI: 10.1080/10835547.1995.12090782

Wu, H., & Wang, C. (2018). A new machine learning approach to house price estimation. *New Trends in Mathematical Science*, 4(6), 165–171. DOI: 10.1016/j.tins.2018.02.002

Yan, Z., & Zong, L. (2020). Spatial Prediction of Housing Prices in Beijing Using Machine Learning Algorithms. In *ACM International Conference Proceeding Series.* DOI: 10.1145/3409501.3409543

Zhao, B. (2017). Web Scraping. DOI: 10.1007/978-3-319-32001-4_483-1

Zhao, S., Blaabjerg, F., & Wang, H. (2021). An overview of artificial intelligence applications for power electronics. *IEEE Transactions on Power Electronics*, 36(4), 4633–4658. DOI: 10.1109/TPEL.2020.3024914

Chapter 11
Automated Disaster Monitoring Through Social Media Posts Using Whale Optimization and ANN

R. Chennappan
Karpagam Academy of Higher Education, India

A. Vinitha
Karpagam Academy of Higher Education, India

S. Vinitha
Sankara College of Science and Commerce, India

R. Gunasundari
Karpagam Academy of Higher Education, India

ABSTRACT

Comprehending location-specific attitudes regarding crisis scenarios is crucial for political leaders and those making strategic decisions. To this aim, the authors introduce a novel fully automated technique for extracting the public feelings on global crisis situations, through the social media posts using artificial intelligence (AI) method based on sentimental analysis. They created the suggested system using sentiment analysis based on AI and NLP, regression, optimization-based algorithm, and using artificial neural network (ANN) for classifying technique to get thorough understanding and perceptions on social media feeds connected to disasters in

DOI: 10.4018/979-8-3693-5231-1.ch011

different languages. The rate of average sensitivity is 93.56%, and the obtained specificity is 94.52% measured with the execution time duration of 5.68 ms. Overall, the fully automated disaster monitoring solution using AI-based sentimental analysis demonstrated the 94.25% accuracy.

I. INTRODUCTION

People who are unprepared for the aftermath are put in danger when natural catastrophes occur since risks and vulnerabilities coexist in these situations. Natural and man-made disasters pose a persistent threat to human safety, which frequently result in significant destruction, agony for individuals, and detrimental effects on the economy. Yu, M., et al (2018). The unpredictable nature of natural disasters, the dearth of resources in the impacted areas, and the ever-changing environment are their defining characteristics, Martinelli, E., et al (2018).

Their surprising nature suggests that we will never be able to foresee with sufficient precision the catastrophic consequences that natural disasters will exact on persons and property, Sivanantham, K., & Kumar, R. M. (2023). Because it is challenging to provide sufficient resources ahead of Unpredictability causes the problem of finite resources to surface from time to time. Since it is challenging to predict people's movements and what kind of damage a natural disaster may produce, there are dynamic changes in the environment. Predicting such shifts with data from normal periods is challenging. There is a great deal of room for improvement when it comes to disaster management policy capabilities when they are introduced and the proper equipment and information technology are used. Furthermore, the changing trends have made enormous technology resources available for lowering the danger of disasters, Merz, B., et al (2020).

Every second, social networks produce large amounts of data, and the main hurdles are in filtering and analysing that enormous data to answer a particular query. Big data analytics is still in its infancy when it comes to its application in disaster response, despite its successful application in many other sectors. In times of crisis, appeals for emergency assistance are rarely made via social media. Since crisis situations tend to be more disorderly and chaotic, analysing the large amounts of data created during such times is ideal for managing the turbulent atmosphere. Making the appropriate choice during a crisis is crucial to meeting the needs of those impacted, Kim, J., & Hastak, M. (2018).

1.1 Disaster Management Cycle

F. K. Sufi and M. Alsulami, (2021) says, disaster data must be gathered, compiled, curated, analysed, and understood in an effort to decrease the harmful repercussions of natural catastrophes. The United Nations states that "Disaster risk knowledge based on the systematic collection of data and disaster risk assessments" is the first component of effective Early Warning Systems (EWS).

Palen, L., & Hughes, A. L. (2018), explained the distinctions in meaning between the terms "disaster," "emergency," and "crisis." They said that an emergency and a crisis are circumstances that, if ignored, might turn into a disaster. For the balance of this study report, we will refer to emergencies and disasters interchangeably based on the authors' explanation.

The catastrophe There are 4 main levels in the management cycle, which are generally "mitigation," "preparedness," "responses," and "recovery." Reducing the impact of a disaster is the aim of the mitigation phase, which includes risk assessments, public education, and the creation of warning codes and risk zones. Preparing a disaster response is the primary goal of the preparation phase. Erdelj, M., and Natalizio, E. et al (2016) said that, it comprises training, emergency drills, and readiness ambitions in addition to the development and use of the Early Warning System (EWS). The provision of the necessary disaster management services to preserve life, protect property, and preserve the environment in times of disaster is the focus of response actions. "Recovery" is the process of restoring normalcy to systems after an incident.

1.2 Social Media Resources for Disaster Actionable Information

How social media affects citizens' independence has been discussed in light of its abilities to gather and disseminate important information. M. Jurgens and I. Helsloot, (2018), give a review of social media platform use in emergency scenarios by examining research published between 2007 and 2014 regarding the use of diverse social media networks following a calamity. Twitter is the social media platform that has been studied the most, according to this review paper. Furthermore, four distinct categories of social media users have been found and classified in relation to crisis situations: (1) Resourceful and innovative users; (2) Reactive users who aid the affected population; (3) Responsive users who act as responders; and (4) Proactive users who operate as organisations.

Information more readily available online during a crisis. Procopio & Procopio was one of the pioneering works in the subject of disaster communication utilising Information and Communications Technology (ICT). According to a poll that looked at the use of the internet for crisis communication, people utilised it to communicate with others in order to reduce ambiguity and obtain assistance during a crisis. Examined were the features of Computer-Mediated Communication (CMC) in emergency situations and how it can be used by Schwarz, A., et al (2016).

Dos Santos Rocha, R., et al (2016), given the details that, The majority of the literature on disaster management in recent years has been on the possibilities for employing particular types of data for natural catastrophe management, said by Cinnamon, J., et al (2016). This context informs the review of major social media sources based AI sentimental analysis in this paper, together with the related successes in all phases of catastrophe management and state-of-the-art technical subjects pertaining to the use of this new ecosystem of sentimental analysis powered by artificial intelligence to monitor and identify natural hazards, lessen their effects, support relief efforts, and assist in the healing and rebuilding processes. According to the literature and what we know, this work is the first application of social media sentiment as an ANN-based deep learning input feature to extract the most precise location intelligence about catastrophes from social media.

K. Rudra, et al (2018) gives the details of due to the disadvantage of using geo-tagged tweets that contain location data researchers in retrieved potential location data using a local lookup table to take the location data out of the tweet's text. While employing compare the location of the tweet with its content database allows for the utilisation of nearly all tweet messages (compared to just 2% of geotagged tweets), it is limited to a specific area of interest.

One of the top disciplines for handling the humanitarian side of crises is Disaster Management (DM). Researchers are drawn to this topic because there is a growing need to discover better and more effective ways to manage disaster situations in order to lessen human suffering. a few reviews of papers published in conferences and journals on Artificial Neural Networks (ANN), a subset of Deep Learning (DL), and its applications in machine learning (DM) from 2010 to 2021. To determine the causes of ANN-based strategies' better performance in comparison to alternative approaches. Sort the existing material based on how it has been applied to various stages and kinds of disasters. "Mitigation and Preparedness" and "Response and Recovery" are the phases. The various types of disasters include wildfires, floods, earthquakes, and storms. It can extract some significant patterns from this analysis. The results confirm the following: The most innovative design for gathering data from social media in an emergency is Convolutional Neural Networks (CNN). (i) Back Propagation Neural Networks (BPNN) are commonly utilised to forecast and control floods. (ii) ANNs are frequently employed in flood management and prediction. The study's shortcomings and provide a number of possible next directions, by Guha, S., et al (2021).

More study has recently been conducted on the topic of using machine learning techniques to distinguish beneficial posts on social media that indicate disasters from posts that do not. Fan, C., et al (2020), their objective, in contrast to the previous review papers, is to assess academic publications on machine learning techniques for emergency coordination from four angles: quality assessment, communication, event detection, and disaster information extraction.

This paper consists of five parts. The section I discussed about the introduction of the work. The drawbacks and limitations of present systems are discussed in the section II. The section III explained about our new suggested system design. Section IV contains our newly constructed system's overall result and discussion. Section V covers this paper's conclusion.

II. LITERATURE REVIEW

In this literature survey section is discussing about the limitations and drawbacks of the current systems used in automated disaster monitoring using AI based sentiment analysis process. The discussion of the literature review includes noteworthy contributions from a wide range of academics in this topic. Japanese tweets were used to track the earthquake. Tokenized words were subjected to the support vector machine (SVM) method. A system that only functioned on floods and with a very small number of languages (English, Italian, Portuguese, and Turkish) was presented by researchers in S. B. Park et al (2020). A classifier was combined with an n-gram token and a word tokenizer. Using English tweets, the study showed situational awareness.

Researchers in W. Qi, R. Procter, et al (2019), evaluated consumer's happiness with wireless services by analysing English tweets using Sentiment Analysis, Naïve Bayes (NB), Support Vector Machines (SVM), and Recurrent Neural Networks (RNN).

Using SVM, a study in G. Vashisht and Y. N. Sinha, (2021), conducted sentiment analysis on the fiercely contested Citizenship Amendment Act (CAA) political discussion. Ten distinct regions of India were used for this study (Tamil Nadu, Andhra Pradesh, Kerala, Karnataka, Assam, Punjab, Uttar Pradesh, Maharashtra, West Bengal, and Delhi) to extract English tweets. Researchers did not employ sentiment analysis output as a forerunner to deep learning techniques like CNN, nor did they use NER to identify location from tweets. Consequently, these investigations had subpar location intelligence performance.

Ragini, J. R., et al (2018), suggest a technique for determining how people feel about the charitable assistance they got both during and after a crisis. Even when the government and other relief agencies make an effort to assist individuals after a crisis, people rarely receive the full advantages since there are insufficient tools to identify their precise requirements at the moment. This study categorises tweets sent out after a crisis and assists in developing a sentiment model based on the diverse requirements of the populace. Rescue workers can better comprehend the disaster scenario and take appropriate action with the aid of this model. This research makes three important contributions. The first step is to classify and examine the many requirements that individuals have both during and after a disaster. Subsequently, an analysis is conducted on multiple features, containing a sack of words, parts of speech based features, and numerous lexicon based features. Based on this analysis, the optimal algorithm is determined for each category. Finally, a technique for visualising the sentiment surrounding fundamental needs is suggested, which could aid emergency responders in providing better care.

2.1 Using Machine Learning Techniques for Emergency Responses through Social Media

Dwarakanath, L., et al (2021), constructed a model using machine learning to extract useful "information nuggets" from posts on social media. The authors define "information nuggets" as concise, self-contained facts about catastrophe response. A dataset of 207510 tweets from the Joplin (2011) tornado, which rocked Joplin, Missouri, USA, was used to validate the results. The most notable aspect of this work is how automatic the suggested approach is for information extraction. The messages were classified using a Naive Bayes machine learning classifier. AUC was used to gauge the performance of the classification. After tenfold cross-validation, with an accuracy of 0.80, recall of 0.78, and AUC of 0.81, the classifier successfully identified the informative tweets. As a supervised machine learning classifier, Support Vector Machine (SVM) has demonstrated robustness in text categorization due to its ability to handle multiple features at once.

Bouzidi, Z., et al (2020), examines the challenge of combining social networks, artificial intelligence, disaster management, neural learning, and intelligent disaster education. It is comprised of an automated learning environment that combines search results to get information and merges summaries from multiple sources. The Real-Time Alert Model is expanded upon in its construction. which is used for managing anthropogenic and natural disasters. This event serves as inspiration and context for our automated learning environment. In conclusion, highlight the key components of this strategy, offer a few citations for relevant literature, and go over some concerns regarding disaster relief, social media, and artificial intelligence.

2.2 Text-Based Deep Learning Classification Techniques

Toivonen, T., et al (2019) tackled the issue of social media post summary through model development to distinguish between those who are in need of assistance and those who are able to deliver it in an emergency. By observing the conversational conduct, posts from the deluge of social media are conversationally classified using this method. The authors created a detection method for location and helpful resource identification. Semantic web content, the domain model, and Natural Language Processing (NLP) approaches were combined to construct the model. The authors developed a model to categorise micro-blog posts during a crisis using a hybrid of crowdsourcing (human intelligence) and machine learning.

By looking at the conversational behaviour, Zheng, Z., et al (2022), examines and classifies coordinating data from the plethora of posts on social media. The authors devised a detection technique for location and relevant resource identification. Semantic web material, natural language processing (NLP) tools, and the domain model were combined to produce the model. This is a model to classify microblog messages in a crisis by combining crowdsourcing (human intelligence) with machine learning.

In a different study, Ruz, G. A., et al (2020), shown that deep neural networks perform better than conventional machine learning methods by creating models of convolutional and recurrent neural networks (RNN) and contrasting them with the Naïve Bayes approach for the purpose of selecting educational tweets from a variety of tweets that indicate disasters. The authors come to the conclusion that machine learning models that were trained on datasets without natural disasters do not perform well when used on datasets with natural disasters. On the other hand, a model developed by deep learning.

Liu, D., et al (2020), addresses the fuzziness issue in resilience evaluations by building on an enhanced flood catastrophe resilience assessment model using a random forest model. The model generates the resilience index of the research area by combining the assessment index set generated by the Driving forces-Pressure-State-Impact-Response (DPSIR) model. It accomplishes this by determining the crucial parameters in the conventional random forest regression (RFR) model using the whale optimisation algorithm (WOA). It is possible to resolve the disaster resilience problem of spatiotemporal dispersion with some advantages using this approach, which can also be used to analyse the important driving variables and the study region's variability in both space and time. Furthermore, there were regional differences in the degree of flood resistance, as demonstrated by the north eastern low level and the south westerly high level. Between 2006 and 2011, there was a greater degree of differentiation between farms; between 2012 and 2016, there was less of a difference. Additionally, the study discovered that demographic and economic variables had a bigger influence on the evaluation outcomes. The WOA-RFR model offers notable the improved stochastic forest regression model and the RFR model, with respect to fitting accuracy and generalisation performance by particle swarm optimisation (PSO-RFR). The WOA-RFR's stability and rationality coefficients have both attained a high level, at 0.976 and 0.964, respectively. The suggested WOA-RFR model can be used to evaluate resilience to regional disasters, offer trustworthy technical help, and create a scientific foundation for mitigating and preventing regional catastrophes in order to guarantee regional production safety and sustainable development.

Sufi, F. K., & Khalil, I. (2022), analysed the evaluation of the shortcomings of previous studies on Twitter-based disaster monitoring would take into account, in addition to the deep learning approach, the following factors: "Language coverage," "number of disasters monitored," "using sentiment analysis," "mobile app availability," "type of location service used" (e.g., Geotagged, NER, or Lookup), and "data availability for research reusability." They describe a brand-new, fully automated approach for extracting location-specific public attitudes about worldwide disaster situations, based on artificial intelligence (AI) and Natural Language Processing (NLP). Entity Recognition (NER), regression method, anomaly detection to acquire comprehensive information and insights on social media feeds relevant to disasters in 110 languages.

III. SYSTEM DESIGN

The following graphic describes the suggested design framework for automated disaster monitoring using social media posting that uses artificial intelligence (AI) based sentiment analysis and explained in detail. As seen in figure 1, the pre-possessing step receives live social media feeds such as tweets as input. Several features are extracted during the pre-processing phase. In later phases, the AI models are trained and tested using the features derived from the category classification, sentiment analysis processes. In the context of artificial intelligence and ANN-based anomaly detection are utilised. And this method used with optimization using whale Optimization algorithm (WOA) and classification done by Artificial Neural Network (ANN).

Figure 1. Framework of Automated Disaster Monitoring

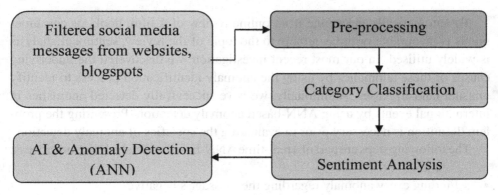

3.1 Category Classification

In order to classify text inputs into groups appropriate for a given business situation, category classification is used. Using prebuilt category classification models (such as Customer Feedback), a text input can be categorised falling into any of the subsequent groups: issues, complements, customer service, feedback, documentation, and so on.

3.2 Sentiment Analysis

Sentiment analysis is a relatively young field that aims to automatically identify the sentiment present in text by combining computer science and linguistics. Sentiment is defined as an assessment stated verbally, either good or negative. Sivanantham, K., et al (2023) said, Sentiment analysis is frequently used to automatically ascertain whether an online review of a movie, book, or consumer product is favourable or unfavourable to the subject of the review.

These days, political analysts, marketers, and businesses all use sentiment analysis as a standard tool in their social media analytic arsenal. Sentiment analysis research uses text's linguistic structure, the context of its words, and its positive and negative terms to glean information, detailed by Gandhi, A., et al (2023). Sentiment analysis was not used in any of the previous research to pre-process AI-based algorithms in order to extract feature properties from text inputs.

3.3 Anomaly Detection

To automatically determine if an online review of a film, book, or consumer goods is favourable or unfavourable to the topic of the review, sentiment analysis is widely utilised. In our most recent investigation, we discovered the underlying causes of these anomalies by using the anomaly identification process to identify unusual landslip cases. Additionally, we have successfully detected anomalies in international events by using ANN-based anomaly detection. Presenting the problem definition is necessary prior to evaluating the specifics of anomaly detection.

The following steps are part of a real-time ANN-based anomaly detection process:

- Finding every anomaly regarding the message's negative
- Determining every anomaly's potential underlying cause
- Using natural language processing, explain the anomaly and all of its underlying reasons in simple terms.

Table 1. Tweets for different categories

Category	Number of Tweet ID
Documentation	375
Feedback	180
Customer Service	15
Issues	2240
Compliment	650

The number of tweets occurring for the various categories is listed in table 1. It has the categories of documentation, feedback, complement, customer service and issues. We can easily access and taken action through this tweet data.

3.4 Whale Optimization Algorithm (WOA)

Whale Optimisation Algorithm (WOA) has certain advantages over conventional swarm intelligence algorithms, such as high search precision and great generalisation ability. It has a unique mechanism and simple parameters.

Figure 2. Flowchart for WOA

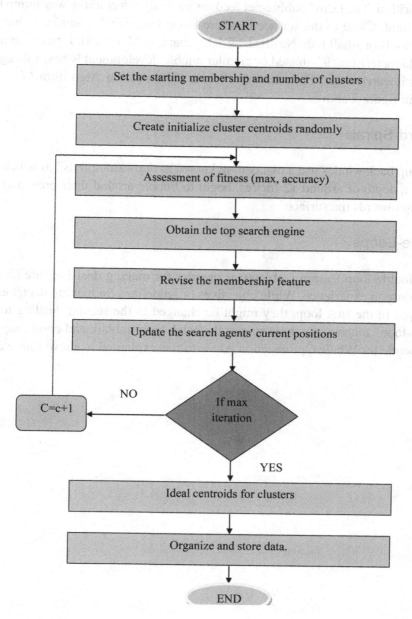

An optimisation algorithm is a methodical procedure that determines the objective function's maximum or minimal value. a meta-heuristic optimisation system that mimics the hunting strategies of humpback whales by taking inspiration from the natural world. The bubble-net searching technique serves as an inspiration for the algorithm. The term "bubble-net feeding method" refers to the way hump back whales hunt. Close to the surface is where hump back whales admire to hunt for Krill schools or small fish, Nasiri, J., & Khiyabani, F. M. (2018). It has been noted that a characteristic "9"-shaped or circular bubble development is how this ageing process is carried out. Flowchart for Whale Optimization Algorithm (WOA) is shown in figure 2 above.

Upward-Spirals

Hump back whales use a manoeuvre known as "upward-spirals" in which they dive to a depth of around 12 metres, begin to bubble around their prey, and then swim up towards the surface.

Double-Loops

In double-loop learning, objectives or rules for making decisions are changed in response to experience. While objectives or guidelines for making decisions are employed in the first loop, they might be changed in the second, leading to the" double-loop" maneuver's three stages: the catch loop, lobtail, and coral loop. The pseudocode for Whale Optimization Algorithm is explained in above figure 3.

Figure 3. Pseudocode for Whale Optimization Algorithm

Establish the whale population from scratch. $X_i(i = 1,2, ..., n)$

determine how fit each search agent is.

X^* = the best search agent

while(t < *maximum number of iterations*)

for every search engine

Update a, A, C, l, and p

***if*1**(p < 0.5)

***if*2**(/A/< 1)

***else if*2**(/A/≥ 1)

Select a random search agent(X_{rand})

***else if*2**

***else if*1**($p ≥ 0.5$)

***else if*1**

end for

Any search agents should be examined and modified if they traverse search space.

Assess the the suitability of every search agent.

Upate X^* if there is a better solution

$t = t + 1$

end while

return X^*

3.5 Artificial Neural Network (ANN)

Sivanantham, K., et al (2022), explains these components, which are grouped in various layers, make up a system's entire artificial neural network. Depending on how complex the system is, a layer may include a few hundred or millions of units. Input, output, and other layers are routinely combined with hidden layers in artificial neural networks. The outside information that the neural network needs to assess or learn is sent to the input layer. This input is then changed into useable data for the output layer after travelling through one or more hidden layers. Kubat, M., & Kubat, M. (2021). The output layer responds to input data by creating an output in the form of an artificial neural network, is the last but not least. Figure 4 below shows how ANNs function.

Figure 4. ANN performances

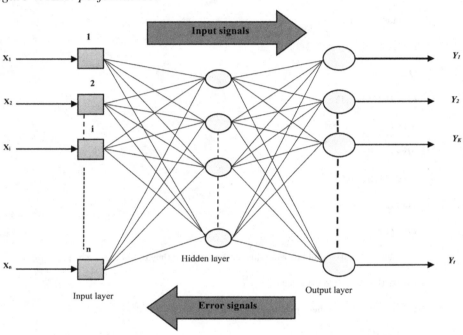

As may be inferred from the below image, the input layer takes in inputs in a variety of formats specified by the programming. The hidden layer divides the input and output layers apart.

It does all the calculations required to uncover hidden patterns and characteristics. The hidden layer converts the input into a range of outputs before it goes through this layer. An artificial neural network modifies the weighted total of the inputs by adding a bias when it receives data. An output layer, or transfer function, is used as an example of this technique.

The suggested design framework for automated social media posting disaster monitoring makes use of ANN-based anomaly detection and AI-based sentiment analysis. Additionally, this technique (WOAANN) uses an artificial neural network (ANN) for classification and optimisation utilising the whale optimisation algorithm (WOA).

IV. RESULT AND DISCUSSION

The functionality of the existing system was covered in this section which has accuracy, sensitivity, specificity, and resolution time ratings as performance parameters. When compared to the current system, the suggested system with the innovative approach to business intelligence and analytics using artificial neural network machine learning will be more effective. Additionally, the accuracy, sensitivity, specificity, and resolution time of this system is improved. Sentiment analysis based automated disaster monitoring and classification was performed. These results were finally stored in tabulation as well as the corresponding graphs were drawn.

4.1 Evaluation Metrics

A series of error calculations known as evaluation metrics are used to verify the model's accuracy. We frequently employ statistical techniques that calculate margins of error between actual values and predictions. Differently, we evaluated the relevant algorithms for each of our use cases. Figure 5 below depicts the performance evaluation confusion matrix.

Cross validation technique is used to evaluate the text similarity model. Calculating out-of-sample error is a common practise in machine learning known as cross-validation. For instance, a substantial training batch and a smaller testing sample were created from the data. After training the model on the first batch of data across a number of iterations, we use the test set to confirm that it can make predictions on data that it has never seen before. The number of data points that were anticipated wrongly based on the unknown data is then determined.

Figure 5. Confusion Matrix

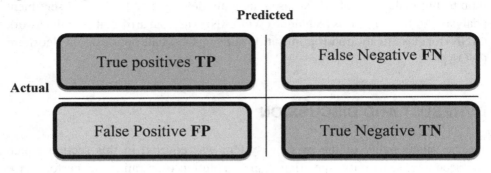

Predicted

	True positives **TP**	False Negative **FN**
Actual		
	False Positive **FP**	True Negative **TN**

Accuracy

The error rate's divergence from 100% is how the accuracy formula represents accuracy. Accuracy cannot be determined until the error rate is ascertained. Furthermore, by dividing the observed value by the actual value, the error rate can be expressed as a percentage.

$$\text{Accuracy} = \frac{TP + TN}{TP + TN + FN + FP}$$

Table 2. Accuracy Table

Algorithm	Accuracy (%)
Decision Tree	83.14
SVM	84.68
Random Forest	90.53
WOAANN	94.25

The table 2 shows the accuracy of proposed approach comparison with existing approach. It states that the accuracy results of the Decision Tree, SVM, RF and WOAANN are 83.14%, 84.68%, 90.53%, and 94.25%, respectively. In comparison to other current systems, proposed system's results reveal that it achieves higher accuracy. And also the otput accuracy graph is shown in the figure 6.

Figure 6. Accuracy Graph

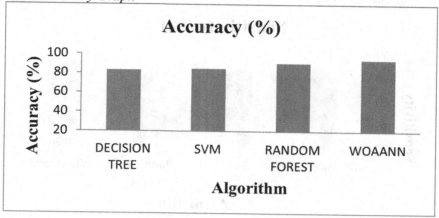

Sensitivity

To measure sensitivity, divide the total number of positives by the total number of forecasts that are precise positives (SN).

$$\text{Sensitivity} = \frac{TP}{TP + FN}$$

Table 3. Sensitivity Table

Algorithm	Sensitivity (%)
Decision Tree	81.25
SVM	85.38
Random Forest	83.91
WOAANN	93.56

The table 3 shows detailed explanation of the sensitivity of proposed approach comparison with existing approaches, which offers a superior maximum result than the existing system. The Decision Tree, SVM, RF and WOAANN sensitivity outcomes are given as 81.25%, 85.38%, 83.91%, and 93.56% respectively. The result shows that our suggested approach reaches higher sensitivity more than other existing systems. The figure 7 depicts the result of the sensitivity output for existing and proposed system.

Figure 7. Sensitivity Graph

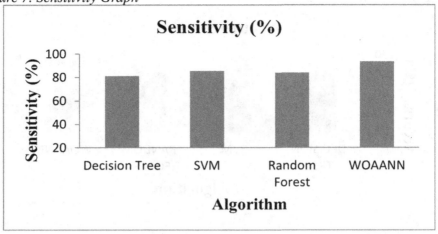

Specificity

Specificity is a number that indicates the number's value and the number's quantity of information digits.

$$\text{Specificity} = \frac{TP}{TP + FP}$$

Table 4. Specificity Table

Algorithm	Specificity (%)
Decision Tree	82.36
SVM	87.82
Random Forest	85.64
WOAANN	94.52

The table 4 shows explanation of the specificity of proposed approach comparison with existing approaches, The indicated results are 82.36%, 87.82%, 85.64%, and 94.52% for the Decision Tree, SVM, RF and WOAANN respectively. The results show that suggested approach reaches higher specificity more than other available strategies. The specificity output result graph is plotted in figure 8.

Figure 8. Specificity Graph

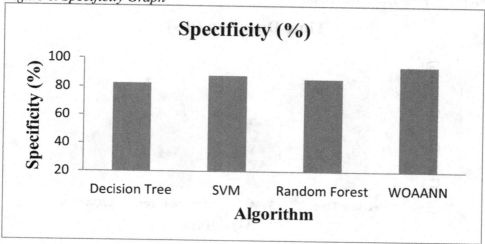

Time Duration

The total time duration is how long the something lasts, from the beginning to the end.

Table 5. Time Duration Table

Algorithm	Time Duration (ms)
Decision Tree	12.66
SVM	7.28
Random Forest	9.83
WOAANN	5.68

Figure 9. Time Duration Graph

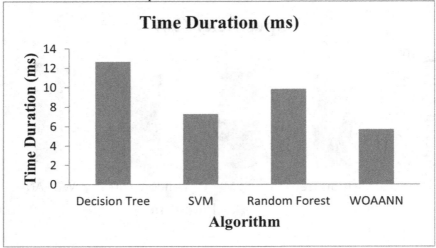

The table 5 explains the time consuming of proposed system comparison with existing systems, the indicated results are 12.66 ms, 7.28 ms, 9.83 ms, and 5.68 ms for the Decision Tree, SVM, RF and WOAANN respectively. The results show that suggested system consumes minimum time duration comparing with the other existing systems. Its output graph is plotted in the figure 9. We have learned more about the predictive models used in the application in this section. We were able to investigate several ANN algorithms with the optimization of Whale Optimization algorithm thanks to the realisation of use cases. Then, using WOAANN, we assessed each of them to determine which was the most accurate for the automated social media post monitoring for disasters utilising sentiment analysis-based artificial intelligence.

V. CONCLUSION

In order to address all of these issues with Whale Optimisation Algorithm based Artificial Neural Networks (WOAANN) and by deploying through Matlab 2013A, we devised a novel methodology in this work using sentiment from social media as an input feature. Our experimentation with the results that our suggested approach can identify a disaster monitoring with 94.25% accuracy, 93.56% sensitivity, 94.52% specificity and the computation time duration is 5.68 milliseconds. This AI base sentiment analysis for the automatic disaster monitoring method works for the better solution comparing than the other existing systems. A catastrophe strategist employed by an emergency or crisis management organisation can gain important knowledge by utilising the suggested solution, which combines AI and NLP across a variety of platforms, such as tablets and smart phones. In the future, we hope to combine historical event datasets with social media disaster data to achieve a deeper understanding of analytical intelligence using deep learning.

REFERENCES

Bouzidi, Z., Boudries, A., & Amad, M. (2020). Towards a smart interface-based automated learning environment through social media for disaster management and smart disaster education. In *Intelligent Computing: Proceedings of the 2020 Computing Conference,* Volume 1 (pp. 443-468). Springer International Publishing.

Cinnamon, J., Jones, S. K., & Adger, W. N. (2016). Evidence and future potential of mobile phone data for disease disaster management. *Geoforum*, 75, 253–264. PMID: 32287362

Dos Santos Rocha, R., Widera, A., van den Berg, R. P., de Albuquerque, J. P., & Helingrath, B. (2016). Improving the Involvement of Digital Volunteers in Disaster Management. In *Proceedings of the International Conference on Information Technology in Disaster Risk Reduction.* Springer.

Dwarakanath, L., Kamsin, A., Rasheed, R. A., Anandhan, A., & Shuib, L. (2021). Automated machine learning approaches for emergency response and coordination via social media in the aftermath of a disaster: A review. *IEEE Access : Practical Innovations, Open Solutions*, 9, 68917–68931.

Erdelj, M., & Natalizio, E. (2016). UAV-assisted disaster management: Applications and open issues. In *Proceedings of the 2016 International Conference on Computing, Networking and Communications (ICNC 2016)*. IEEE.

Fan, C., Wu, F., & Mostafavi, A. (2020). A hybrid machine learning pipeline for automated mapping of events and locations from social media in disasters. *IEEE Access : Practical Innovations, Open Solutions*, 8, 10478–10490.

Gandhi, A., Adhvaryu, K., Poria, S., Cambria, E., & Hussain, A. (2023). Multimodal sentiment analysis: A systematic review of history, datasets, multimodal fusion methods, applications, challenges and future directions. *Information Fusion*, 91, 424–444.

Guha, S., Jana, R. K., & Sanyal, M. K. (2022). Artificial neural network approaches for disaster management: A literature review (2010–2021). *International Journal of Disaster Risk Reduction*, 103276.

Jurgens, M., & Helsloot, I. (2018, March). the effect of social media on the dynamics of (self) resilience during disasters: A literature review. *Journal of Contingencies and Crisis Management*, 26(1), 79–88.

Kim, J., & Hastak, M. (2018). Social network analysis: Characteristics of online social networks after a disaster. *International Journal of Information Management*, 38(1), 86–96.

Kubat, M., & Kubat, M. (2021). Artificial neural networks. An Introduction to Machine Learning, 117-143.

Liu, D., Fan, Z., Fu, Q., Li, M., Faiz, M. A., Ali, S., & Khan, M. I. (2020). Random forest regression evaluation model of regional flood disaster resilience based on the whale optimization algorithm. *Journal of Cleaner Production*, 250, 119468.

Martinelli, E., Tagliazucchi, G., & Marchi, G. (2018). The resilient retail entrepreneur: Dynamic capabilities for facing natural disasters. *International Journal of Entrepreneurial Behaviour & Research*, 24(7), 1222–1243.

Merz, B., Kuhlicke, C., Kunz, M., Pittore, M., Babeyko, A., Bresch, D. N., ... Wurpts, A. (2020). Impact forecasting to support emergency management of natural hazards. Reviews of Geophysics, 58(4), e2020RG000704.

Nasiri, J., & Khiyabani, F. M. (2018). A whale optimization algorithm (WOA) approach for clustering. *Cogent Mathematics & Statistics*, 5(1), 1483565.

Palen, L., & Hughes, A. L. (2018). Social media in disaster communication. Handbook of disaster research, 497-518.

Park, S. B., Kim, J., Lee, Y. K., & Ok, C. M. (2020). Visualizing theme park visitors' emotions using social media analytics and geospatial analytics. *Tourism Management*, 80(104127).

Qi, W., Procter, R., Zhang, J., & Guo, W. (2019). Mapping Consumer Sentiment Toward Wireless Services Using Geospatial Twitter Data. *IEEE Access : Practical Innovations, Open Solutions*, 7, 113726–113739.

Ragini, J. R., Anand, P. R., & Bhaskar, V. (2018). Big data analytics for disaster response and recovery through sentiment analysis. *International Journal of Information Management*, 42, 13–24.

Rudra, Ganguly, Goyal, & Ghosh. (2018). Extracting and Summarizing Situational Information from the Twitter Social Media during Disasters. ACM Transactions on the Web, 12(3).

Ruz, G. A., Henríquez, P. A., & Mascareño, A. (2020). Sentiment analysis of Twitter data during critical events through Bayesian networks classifiers. *Future Generation Computer Systems*, 106, 92–104.

Schwarz, A., Binetti, J. C., Broll, W., & Mitschele-Thiel, A. (2016). New technologies and applications in international crisis communication and disaster management. The handbook of international crisis communication research, 465-477.

Sivanantham, K., Kalaiarasi, I., & Leena, B. (2022). Brain tumor classification using hybrid artificial neural network with chicken swarm optimization algorithm in digital image processing application. In *Advance Concepts of Image Processing and Pattern Recognition: Effective Solution for Global Challenges* (pp. 91–108). Springer Singapore.

Sivanantham, K., & Kumar, R. M. (2023). Different Approaches to Background Subtraction and Object Tracking in Video Streams: A Review. Object Tracking Technology: Trends, Challenges and Applications, 23-39.

Sivanantham, K., Praveen, P. B., Deepa, V., & Kumar, R. M. (2023). Cybercrime Sentimental Analysis for Child Youtube Video Dataset Using Hybrid Support Vector Machine with Ant Colony Optimization Algorithm. In *Kids Cybersecurity Using Computational Intelligence Techniques* (pp. 175–193). Springer International Publishing.

Sufi, F. K., & Alsulami, M. (2021). *Knowledge Discovery of Global Landslides Using Automated Machine Learning Algorithms* (Vol. 9). IEEE Access.

Sufi, F. K., & Khalil, I. (2022). Automated disaster monitoring from social media posts using AI-based location intelligence and sentiment analysis. *IEEE Transactions on Computational Social Systems.*

Toivonen, T., Heikinheimo, V., Fink, C., Hausmann, A., Hiippala, T., Järv, O., & Di Minin, E. (2019). Social media data for conservation science: A methodological overview. *Biological Conservation*, 233, 298–315.

Vashisht, G., & Sinha, Y. N. (2021). Sentimental study of CAA by locationbased tweets. *International Journal of Information Technology : an Official Journal of Bharati Vidyapeeth's Institute of Computer Applications and Management.* PMID: 33778365

Yu, M., Yang, C., & Li, Y. (2018). Big data in natural disaster management: A review. *Geosciences*, 8(5), 165.

Zheng, Z., Lu, X. Z., Chen, K. Y., Zhou, Y. C., & Lin, J. R. (2022). Pretrained domain-specific language model for natural language processing tasks in the AEC domain. *Computers in Industry*, 142, 103733.

Chapter 12
Optimizing Convolutional Neural Network Impact of Hyperparameter Tuning and Transfer Learning

Youssra El Idrissi El-Bouzaidi

iD https://orcid.org/0000-0003-2068-3403

Team-ISISA, Faculty of Science, Abdelmalek Essaadi University, Tetouan, Morocco

Fatima Zohra Hibbi

ISIC Research Team of ESTM, Moulay Ismail University, Meknes, Morocco

Otman Abdoun

Team-ISISA, Faculty of Science, Abdelmalek Essaadi University, Tetouan, Morocco

ABSTRACT

This chapter examines skin cancer, particularly melanoma, which has a high mortality rate, making early diagnosis essential. It explores how convolutional neural networks (CNNs) can improve melanoma detection, providing a detailed technical analysis of hyperparameters and their impact on model performance. Strategies for tuning hyperparameters, including random search and Bayesian optimization, are demonstrated. Using the HAM10000 dataset, the chapter assesses the impact of different hyperparameter settings on accuracy, sensitivity, and specificity. Issues like class imbalance are addressed with data augmentation and resampling. The optimization methods improve DenseNet121 and MobileNetV2 accuracies to 85.65% and 84.08%, respectively.

DOI: 10.4018/979-8-3693-5231-1.ch012

INTRODUCTION

Melanoma is a malignant skin cancer that has the ability to invade other tissues and become life threatening if diagnosed at an advanced stage (Maryam Naqvi et al., 2023). Among skin cancers, there are two types: skin carcinomas and skin melanomas. Carcinomas are the most prevalent type of skin cancer, which are not invasive, whereas melanomas are malignant tumors that develop from melanocytes, which are the pigment-producing cells in the skin (Dildar M et al., 2021). Melanomas are mainly located in the skin but can also occur in other organs such as the eye, mouth, vagina, anus and under the nails (Elgamal M, 2013). Melanoma is more common in the elderly, as 75% of new cases are detected in patients older than 49 years, while only 27% of cases are detected in patients aged 15-49 years (Maryam Naqvi et al., 2023). As it is well known, the diagnosis is one of the key aspects in the treatment of the disease and its outcomes. Traditional approaches of diagnosing skin cancer include biopsies, which involves the excision of a small portion of the suspicious lesion for examination (Ogundokun R. O. et al., 2023). However, this procedure has some disadvantages including pain, time consuming and high cost (Nancy V. A. et al., 2023). Artificial intelligence, specifically machine learning, is more effective and less costly than the conventional techniques of diagnosing skin cancer. Among these approaches are the machine learning and deep learning techniques especially CNNs which have been proved to be very efficient in the detection, classification and segmentation of skin cancer lesions (El Idrissi El-Bouzaidi & Abdoun, 2024), and other disease like covid-19 (El Idrissi El-Bouzaidi & Abdoun, 2023; Youssra & Otman, 2022; YOUSSRA & OTMAN, 2022) . CNNs are beneficial for learning and extracting features and therefore very valuable for image recognition. CNNs' performance depends on the selected hyperparameters including the learning rate, batch size and the number of layers in the CNN. Hyperparameters are important because they determine how well the model generalizes from the training data to the test data. Many of the hyperparameters tuning methods such as manual tuning and grid search are very time-consuming and involve a lot of iteration to arrive at the best values. To overcome these problems, better hyperparameter optimization methods have been proposed. In this study, we explore the application of random search and Bayesian optimization to refine the hyperparameters of two advanced CNN architectures: MobileNetV2 and DenseNet121 for the highest accuracy in melanoma detection. To this end, we use the HAM10000 dataset (Tschandl, 2023) containing a huge number of dermatoscopic images and study the influence of changes in hyperparameters on the values of accuracy, sensitivity, specificity, F1 score. We also deal with the problem of class imbalance in the dataset which is prevalent in medical image analysis and has an impact on learning bias. Regarding this, the methods of data augmentation and resampling are employed to enhance the stability of the model. However, this is also a consideration of how transfer learning could be employed to increase performance especially in situations where data is limited. In this work, we recommend the following ways to enhance the performance of CNN on the dataset mentioned in the paper.

The structure of this paper is as follows: In Section 2, which is the literature review section, the prior studies, which use CNNs in melanoma detection, are reviewed. In section 3, a background of CNNs, MobileNetV2, DenseNet121, parameters, and optimization. Section 4 explains the experiment that has been done and the phase which is the hyperparameters tuning phase. The section five is dealing with the results and discussion; however, the focus is on the comparison of the models. Lastly, in section 6, the conclusion of the study is given and suggestions for future research are offered.

RELATED WORK

Extensive studies have been conducted to enhance the diagnostic capabilities for early detection of skin cancer using deep learning techniques. (Ali et al., 2021) applied a deep convolutional neural network (DCNN) to distinguish between benign and malignant skin lesions using the HAM10000 dataset, achieving 93.16% accuracy in training and 91.93% in testing. In a recent study by (Gouda et al., 2022), the authors used CNN for the classification of skin tumors as benign or malignant with an accuracy of 83. 2%, while achieving a top-5 error rate of 2%, which is significantly lower than ResNet50 (83. 7%) and InceptionV3 (85. 8%). (Alwakid et al., 2022) applied ESRGAN for image enhancement and CNN for classification with a performance of 85.9%. DeepLabv3+ was used for segmentation while Vision Transformer (ViT) was used for classification and the authors of (Ahmad et al., 2024) proved it to be more effective. In their study, (Tan et al., 2024) used deep learning to detect rare non-melanoma skin cancers with high precision. (Sivakumar et al., 2024) in their study proposed a diagnostic system based on CNN and ResNet50, which yielded an accuracy of 94%. (Syed et al., 2024) suggested a method using Deep Forest algorithm where the feature extraction modules were SIFT, HoG, RIFT, LoG, and DoG and the achieved accuracy rate was 88. 5% accuracy. (Moturi et al., 2024) proposed MobileNetV2 and a custom CNN for the classification of melanoma and non-cancerous skin tumors using the HAM10000 dataset and the respective accuracies of 85% and 95%, respectively. (Munuswamy Selvaraj et al., 2024) designed a web-based AI diagnostic program using CNN-ResNet50 for malignant melanoma detection with 94% accuracy and 93. 9% F1-score. (Dai et al., 2024) developed a new model by integrating Faster R-CNN and Fuzzy K-Means for classifying and segmenting skin lesions, which was tested on ISIC-2016, ISIC-

2017, and PH2 databases with high accuracy. In (Nivedha & Shankar, 2023), AGTO and Faster R-CNN were integrated to detect melanoma, and the proposed system attained a 98. 55% success rate. The present work (El-Bouzaidi & Abdoun, 2024) intends to present a review on the application of AI in dermatology. To support the findings of the study, the authors employed the HAM10000 dataset, which reveals that preprocessing and transfer learning can improve CNN models' performance in skin cancer classification.

Despite the contribution of each of these works, hyperparameters are still a critical area of focus as far as model performance enhancement is concerned. Perhaps, by fine-tuning some of the hyperparameters in these studies, the researchers could have obtained improved performance of the model as indicated by the enhanced accuracy and other performance measures.

BACKGROUND

Convolutional Neural Networks (CNN)

Recent research has focused on the ability to employ deep learning techniques, namely CNNs, for skin cancer diagnosis (Ogundokun et al., 2023; Nancy et al., 2023; Dildar et al., 2021). Such techniques entail the utilization of large data for training and evaluating of the models. To overcome the problem of a scarcity of images, transfer learning is applied, which refines the existing networks for similar tasks, which reduces the training problem and time (Rajeshwari & Sughasiny, 2022; Sharma & Raman, 2023). This paper also assesses different CNN like DenseNet121 and MobileNetV2, known for their success in image classification tasks.

DenseNet121 Framework

DenseNet, described by (Huang et al., 2017) solves the problem of gradient loss, enhances the performance and encourages the reusing of features where each layer takes an input from all the previous layers in the dense block. The DenseNet121 architecture is made up of four dense blocks with different numbers of layers; 6, 12, 24, and 16 layers respectively. These transition layers help reduce the size of the feature maps that concatenation generates between these dense blocks. The classification layers are made up of a global average pooling layer and a fully connected layer. In DenseNet, learned filters are used to extract features from input images to obtain feature maps that indicate where features of interest are located in the images. The dense connectivity also means that each layer gets direct access to gradients of the loss function as well as the input signal which improves the network's efficiency in learning both the low-level features (in the earlier layers closer to the input) and high-level abstract features (in the deeper layers of the network). The pooling layers in DenseNet do multi-scale analysis and also helps in down sampling the input images to get feature reduction. More information of this can be found in (Huang et al., 2017).

MobileNet Framework

MobileNet is a CNN proposed by (Howard et al., 2017) from google research, which is designed to work efficiently with limited computational resources which makes it ideal for mobile and embedded systems. MobileNet is characterized by the fact that it has fewer hyperparameters than other CNN models, making it rather lightweight. MobileNetV2, the improved version, has been employed in this study as well as in other studies for the classification of skin melanoma. For instance, (Rashid et al., 2022) used transfer learning with MobileNetV2 on the ISIC 2020 dataset for melanomas classification with an average accuracy of 92. 8% by using data augmentation techniques to address the class imbalance issue. MobileNetV2's architecture consists of 19 base residual blocks, a 1x1 convolution layer, and an average pooling layer. In an attempt to fit the layers into smaller images, modifications were made on the stride, padding, and the filter size. The classification layer was also changed to work with three classes which was described by (Seidaliyeva et al., 2020).

Hyperparameters

Hyperparameters is another significant factor that describe the training procedure and functioning of machine learning models. Hyperparameters on the other hand are chosen prior to the model training process and do not change when the actual training is taking place phase (Yeh et al., 2021). Some of the parameters that can be tuned for CNN architectures include; learning rate, number of batch and the overall depth of CNN and number of units in each depth level. Hyperparameters are the only part of the model that has the capability of defining how well the model would generalize from the training data set to a data set that is new.

The learning rate is used to define the step size in terms of optimization and influences the rate of convergence as well. Batch size determines the number of training samples that are updated for each iteration affecting the training speed and gradient stability. The number of epochs, which is the total passes through the training dataset, mediates between underfitting and overfitting (Jin, 2022). Modifying these parameters during training can greatly enhance the performance of a model, even when they are set to their default values. The hyperparameters of the algorithms are adjusted using methods such as adapt learning rates, early stopping, and dropout to improve the training.

Optimization Methods

The main focus of optimization techniques is to determine whether there is an ideal set of hyperparameters that can lead to an optimal result of a model (Yang & Shami, 2020). The manual tuning and the grid search are also very inconvenient and time-consuming and it requires a lot of computational power (Liashchynskyi & Liashchynskyi, 2019). In order to surmount such limitations, some of the approaches that have been created include the random search method and the Bayesian optimization. Random search selects the hyperparameters randomly from the search space and hence is able to search a relatively larger area than the grid search, and therefore is generally better than the grid search in a given amount of computational time (Liashchynskyi & Liashchynskyi, 2019). Bayesian optimization works under the premise that there is a probability distribution model for the performance of the hyperparameters and thus assists in an efficient search (Garnett, 2023 ; Hibbi et al., 2022). The following should be noted in regard to hyperparameter optimization in the various areas of application: For example, in the study by (Antunes et al., 2023), the authors presented the hyperparameters for CNNs in pipe burst detection, which include early stopping, batch size, and learning rate. Like this study, (Aszemi & Dominic, 2019) were interested in understanding metaheuristic algorithms for enhancing CNN in the MNIST dataset. In this study, (Öztürk, 2023) aimed at enhancing the prediction capability of Echo State Networks through metaheuristic ensemble for hyperparameter initialization. (Bacanin et al., 2022) proposed the improved sine cosine algorithm for hyperparameter tuning of CNNs with remarkable performance on the CIFAR-10 dataset.

METHODOLOGY

Dataset and Preprocessing

The HAM10000 dataset (Tschandl, 2023), used in this work, comprising 10,015 dermatoscopic images of different skin lesions. For this research, we concentrated on two classes: lesions that are non-cancerous and are referred to as nevi (benign) and the cancerous lesions referred to as melanoma (malignant). First, the data set was preprocessed to include only these two classes, and their labels were converted into numerical values: 0 for nevi and 1 for melanoma. From the two classes in the HAM10000 dataset, Figure 1 below presents some of the images in each of the classes. This figure shows the variability of the pattern within the given data and presents typical examples of nevi and melanoma lesions.

Figure 1. Representative Images from Melanoma and Nevus Classes in the HAM10000 Dataset.

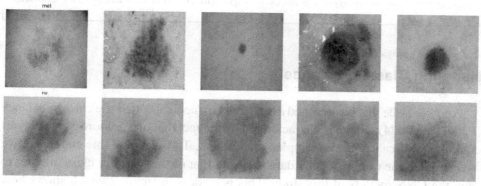

To solve the problem of class imbalance, we applied oversampling methods (SMOTE). Particularly, the number of samples in the minority class (melanoma) was increased to make the number of samples equal for both classes. The images were then scaled down to 128 x 128 pixels and normalized on the pixel values to the range of [0, 1]. It standardized the images and also normalized them in order to feed them into the CNN models. Moreover, the rotation, zoom, width and height shifts, the horizontal and vertical flips were used as the data augmentation techniques to expand the training dataset and enhance the model's generalization capability. The details of data collection and preprocessing techniques and their corresponding values are presented below in Table 1.

Table 1. Data Collection and Preprocessing Techniques

Technique	Description	Value/Parameters
Class Filtering	Selection of nevi (0) and melanoma (1) classes	Selected classes: nevi (0), melanoma (1)
Class Balancing	Oversampling of the minority class to balance the dataset	Number of samples equalized for both classes
Image Resizing	Standardizing the size of images	128x128 pixels
Image Normalization	Scaling pixel values to the range [0, 1]	Pixel values normalized between 0 and 1

continued on following page

Table 1. Continued

Technique	Description	Value/Parameters
Data Splitting	Splitting data into training, validation, and test sets	Training set: 80%, Validation set: 10%, Test set: 10%
Data Augmentation	Generating new images by transforming existing images	Rotation: 10 degrees, Zoom: 10%, Width Shift: 10%, Height Shift: 10%, Horizontal and Vertical Flip, Nearest Fill Mode

Handling Class Imbalance

Another issue that has reached a high level in medical data is the class imbalance (Park et al., 2024), which is characterized by the fact that one or more of the classes contain significantly fewer samples than others. To overcome this challenge, we oversampled the minority class data to match that of the majority class in order to train the CNN models of this study. This is evident in figure 2 which shows how the two classes initially looked like in the HAM10000 dataset which contains nevi (benign) and melanoma (malignant).

Figure 2. Initial Distribution of Nevi and Melanoma Classes in the HAM10000 Dataset.

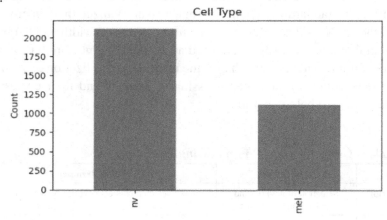

To mitigate the issue of class imbalance, we implemented a series of steps:

Class Filtering: Initially, data set was preprocessed in order to contain only two types of skin lesions, nevi (nv) and melanoma (mel). The labels for these classes were then binarized where 0 refers to nevi and 1 to melanoma.

Class Balancing: Regarding oversampling, it was used to handle the issue of class imbalance as proposed by (He & Garcia, 2009). In particular, the melanoma class was oversampled so that the size of this class in the sample would be equal to the size of the nevi class. This method is useful in addressing the problem of class imbalance since the number of synthetic instances for the minority class is produced.

Oversampling Process: First, the data was separated into two groups depending on the class labels that were incorporated into the problem. Thus, the count of the samples was taken in the minority class, namely melanoma. In order to ensure that the number of samples was the same in the two classes, the majority class, which was nevi, was down sampled while the minority class was oversampled using the resampling function. In this way, all classes receive an equal number of samples which will overcome the class imbalance issue (Daud et al., 2023).

Data Visualization: The distribution of the two classes of the remaining records after the oversampling process was also performed in order to evaluate the oversampling process as shown below. As can be observed from the distribution depicted in figure 3, oversampling has been effective because after the balancing, the classes are well distributed.

Figure 3. Balanced Distribution of Nevi and Melanoma Classes.

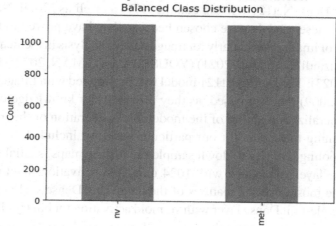

The dataset was balanced, which was composed of 1113 samples of nevi and 1113 samples of melanoma; therefore, there were 2226 samples. The data was then divided into training, validation and test data set with each set having the same class distribution as in the original data. The combined distribution of classes before and after balancing is summarized in the table 2:

Table 2. Class Distribution in HAM10000 Dataset.

Class	Initial Count	Balanced Count
Nevi (nv)	2000+	1113
Melanoma (mel)	1000+	1113

The use of the balanced dataset meant that both classes of the CNN models were trained and tested on balanced data to minimize overfitting and hence, improve on the generalization of our models in the classification of both nevi and melanoma. This strategy of dealing with class imbalance was very important in improving the stability and reliability of the models, to perform optimally and with greater flexibility in classifying skin lesion images (Daud et al., 2023). Thus, following the steps outlined above, it was possible to solve the problem of class imbalance, which will create the basis for the subsequent stages of our work, such as modeling and evaluation.

Model Architectures

In this study, we employed two advanced Convolutional Neural Network (CNN) architectures: DenseNet121 (Huang et al., 2017b) as well as MobileNetV2 (Dong et al., 2020). These models were chosen because they have proved to be useful in classification of images particularly for image pattern analysis in medical images (El Idrissi El-Bouzaidi & Abdoun, 2021) (YOUSSRA & OTMAN, 2022) (El-Bouzaidi & Abdoun, 2023). The DenseNet121 model was pre-trained with ImageNet weights (Deng et al., 2009) that were used, as they provide prior knowledge of the model and boost generalization ability of the model in consideration of the training data. When fine tuning the model for our particular task, we included the use of Glo-balAveragePooling2D layer to down sample the feature maps' spatial dimensions. Then a Dense layer was added with 1024 units and activation function ReLU in order keep the most complex features of the data. This DenseNet121 model final layer was a single-unit Dense layer with sigmoid activation for binary classification. The model was compiled using the Adam optimizer and binary cross entropy loss function to enhance the training phase of the model.

In the same manner, MobileNetV2 was pre-trained with weights of ImageNet for it to harness the training. We add a GlobalAveragePooling2D layer to convert the feature maps to a one-dimensional vector that represents the image in some global manner. This was followed by a Dense layer was added with a Total of 1024 units and ReLU to facilitate better learning of complexities. The final classification layer was a Dense layer of one unit with sigmoid activation which will be more suitable for binary classification. Like the MobileNetV2 model, the Adam optimizer and binary cross-entropy loss function were used to train this model through proper optimization which enhanced the training accuracy.

This was followed by the tuning of top hyperparameters such as the learning rate, batch size and number of epochs to optimize both models. This fine-tuning was performed with the help of Random Search and Bayesian Optimization to identify the best parameters that define the highest results for every of the models. The functions and parameters of both the model architectures are enlisted in the following table 3.

Table 3. Summary of Functions and Parameters Used in Model Architectures

Parameter/Function	Description
Pre-trained Weights	ImageNet
Additional Layers	GlobalAveragePooling2D, Dense (1024, ReLU)
Final Layer	Dense (1)
Activation Functions	ReLU, Sigmoid
Optimizer	Adam
Loss Function	Binary Cross-Entropy

Hyperparameter Tuning

In our study, we focused on optimizing three key hyperparameters: learning rate, batch, size and the number of epochs. The search spaces for these hyperparameters were defined as follows: Learning Rate: 0.0001 to 0.01 and Batch Size: From 16 to 128.

Random Search Strategy

Several crucial steps were incorporated in the random search process in order to ensure that the best hyperparameters in the given hyperplanes are found. First, we described the specific ranges within which each of the hyperparameters should be selected, which in fact defines the area of the search space. After selecting the initial search space, we then went on to use a simple random sampling technique of the hyperparameter combinations. Having obtained the lists of sampled combination, we then computed the performance of each sampled combination through k-cross validation. More pointedly, stratified formed of K-Fold cross validation was used

311

to make sure that each formed contained the class label of the initial data set in the similar proportion. This method made the evaluation very strong to a point where every group's input was representative of the cohort. After that, for every fold of the data, the results of the regulation of hyperparameters have been analyzed and the best hyperparameters for the model were used for training the model which gave better results.

Bayesian Optimization Strategy

Another approach, for Bayesian optimization, was slightly more complex and iterative in nature. At this stage, Probabilistic model, often Gaussian Process, is employed to predict the properties of various hyperparameters in question. This model gave the capacity of performing the probable outcomes of other hyperparameters that were evaluated before. This it was a process of going back to the model's predictions to select hyperparameters to further assess in the model. After each calculation, the set of hyperparameters was modified by the results obtained in the previous evaluation and used for the next round of testing. The above process of applying the cross-validation method was repeated several times till the model determined the best hyperparameters. The Gaussian Process used was probabilistic in nature, which enabled the modelling of the variance on the performance predictions; this, in turn, provided the optimal hyperparameters under uncertainty. With the help of the Bayesian guide, who constantly revised the evaluations, the search can be considered successful to optimize the hyperparameters. The following table 4 summarizes the search spaces explored during the hyperparameter tuning process:

Table 4. Hyperparameter Search Spaces

Hyperparameter	Search Space
Learning Rate	0.0001 to 0.01
Batch Size	16 to 128

Using RS and BO, we were able to exhaustively sweep the defined hyperparameters, making the models have the best performance. The systematic approach used in the hyperparameter tuning process proved to be helpful in increasing the reliability and accuracy of the convolutional neural network models.

Model Training and Evaluation

The process of training and then testing the model was done in a structured manner through experimenting with different hyperparameter values. Firstly, for each fold the original training data was split into training and validation set with cross-validation. Training was carried out based on the chosen hyperparameters and the use of early stopping to avoid overfitting, as well as the use of model checkpoint to save the best performing model. The performance on the data not used in the learning was then determined for each combination and the best hyperparameters for each fold were used to train the final model. The training process initially involved batch training, in which the data was split into batches in order to be used in the training. It let the model do forward and backward passes to compute the loss and adjust weights according to the calculated loss. To enhance generalization and determine the stop point, the model was tested at the end of each epoch for the validation set. Training was performed by training the model for up to 10 epochs or until early stopping conditions were met to avoid overfitting the model. This systematic manner of approach helped the model to be best trained and tested, and therefore it was more reliable in providing the best classification between nevi and melanoma lesions.

Training with Bayesian Optimization

During the first step of the hyperparameters tuning step using Bayesian Optimization, we started by assuming the existence of a probabilistic model, which is a Gaussian Process on the given hyperparameters in order to simulate the performance accurately. The optimization was performed again by evaluating based on prediction of the model; this process involved the selection hyperparameters to be tested. At the end of each evaluation, the result was used to train or update the model choice that would be in charge of choosing closer hyperparameters in subsequent evaluations. It entailed making adjustments to the model, testing it on the data to determine if new hyperparameters needed to be sought until the right one was found. With the best hyperparameters that resulted out of the Bayesian Hyperparameter tuning, the last part of the training of this model was then carried out. Some of the steps included in the training process include; Batching of data where the model is supposed to go forward and backward passing in order to allow updating of the weights from the computed loss. After each epoch, the accuracy for the current model on the validation set was calculated in a cross-validation manner to check generalization and for early stopping. Cro trainers were trained up to maximum of 10 epochs or until the criterion for early stopping to minimize over fitting was reached. The Termination Criteria implemented included validation loss where the model was stopped as soon as the validation loss started increasing, and optimization that considered the best model weights was selected based on the validation accuracy. At last, the trained models were tested using the test set by the metrics like accuracy, precision, recall, and F- score in order to know the efficiency of the models in differentiating the nevi and melanoma lesions.

Training with Random Search

In this study, the training process by means of Random Search included a number of steps: The primary purpose of the following steps was to have an effective search for hyperparameters. Firstly, in each hyperparameter we set its range of the values so as to set the search space where random values combination of hyperparameters were taken. For each fold the data set of training was divided into the training and the validation data sets using the cross-validation technique. The model was then trained with the sampled hyperparameters It must be noted that the process of training the model using the sampled hyperparameters may take a long time and several trials to obtain the best output. Regularization methods such as; Early stopping and Model checkpointing were used to avoid overfitting and keep check of the best model during training. half way through each of the epoch the model was tested on the validation set in order to check on the model's ability to generalize. Training was carried on for the up to 10 epochs, or until it fulfilled the early-stopping rules. In case of Random Search, a data set was divided into mini-batches and the model did forward pass and backprop to update with the loss. Every combination of the hyperparameters was then fine-tuned based on the validation accuracy. The best hyperparameters obtained in each fold of data were later on incorporated to train the final model. Cross validation was used for performance on each set of hyperparameters as to obtain solid and representative results. Depending on each of the hyperparameter combinations, all the models were trained and the best of the hyperparameters in terms of the best accuracy and generalization was chosen. The final trained models were tested on the test set by checking accuracy, precision, recall, and F1-score in order to determine the level of effectiveness in interpreting nevi and melanoma lesions. This approach enabled us to better optimize the convolutional neural network models by applying selective dereverberation and other modifications that improved the models' stability and performance.

RESULTS AND DISCUSSION

This section describes the results of the model evaluations as well as the results collected from the steps of model training and hyperparameter tuning. The accuracy, precision, recall, and F1-score of the models(DenseNet121 and MobileNetV2) optimized through Random Search and Bayesian Optimization approaches are compared.

Analysis of Randomized Search Optimization Results

DenseNet121

The obtained DenseNet121 model was optimized for hyperparameters using Randomized Search optimization allowing the model to generate three different folds. The latter unveil the level of accuracy that defines the performance of the model in question (refer to table 5).

Table 5. Summary of Functions and Parameters Used in Model Architectures

Fold	Learning Rate	Batch size	Accuracy	Precision	Recall	F1-score
1	0.002223	45	88.30%	83.71%	85.58%	84.63%
2	0.009377	93	88.02%	78.65%	86.52%	82.35%
3	0.002283	66	86.80%	78.65%	89.33%	83.66%

For Fold 1, the optimal values from the parameter search were a batch size of 45 and a learning rate of 0.002223. The best accuracy found for the model in the current investigation was 88.30%. In the first training session, the estimated accuracy was 77.91%. The first epoch achieved 88.30% and the best validation accuracy recorded in the sixth epoch. While the loss reduced its figure from 0.5628 in the first epoch to 0.2261 in the tenth epoch, accuracy was enhanced to 89.72%. The output data using measurement indices show 84.30% of accuracy, 77.69% precision, 94.39% recall, and 85.23% F1-Score. Using the confusion matrix, it displayed true negatives equal to 174, false positives equal to 58, false negatives equal to 12, and true positives equal to 202.

According to Table 5, the best parameters used in Fold 2 were a batch size of 93 and a learning rate of 0.009377. The model had the highest accuracy of 88.02%. At the start, the accuracy was 61.64% in the first epoch, while the accuracy in the seventh epoch was 88.02%. The loss reduces from 3.7847 in the initial epoch to 0.2716 within the sixth epoch while accuracy improves to 88.82% in the tenth epoch. The performance metrics show the accuracies in terms of classification as 86.52%, precision as 78.65%, recall as 86.52%, and F1-Score as 82.35%. The confusion matrix of this fold had 164 number of TN, 68 number of FP, 13 number of FN and 201 number of TP.

The best parameters for Fold 3 are batch size: 66, learning rate: 0. 002283. This interacting model could only achieve a maximum of 86.80 percent accuracy of the best kind. Firstly, the results depicted were 64.17 percent correct in the first epoch while increasing to 89.33 percent in the eighth epoch. This gives a loss reducing from 1.1957 first epoch to 0.2261 in the tenth epoch while the accuracy feature improved to 89.72%. The following performance parameters show the efficiency of the system; accuracy = 84.30%, precise= 77.69%, recall= 94.39%, F1 Score = 85.23%. From the confusion matrix, it was possible to identify that 174 subjects were classified as being negative and not prone to using social networks in different or more extensive ways, while 58 subjects were not correctly diagnosed, 12 being classified as being positive to learning different or more extensive ways to use social networks, and 202 being correctly diagnosed.

Finally, summarizing the current research, the DenseNet121 model considered relatively low standard deviations less than 3% and high validation accuracy more than 86.52% in all the folds. As it has already been seen in the training process given in the section above, it is clear that the learning rate and the batch size applied when training the model in each fold of the cross-validation method are not the same, and that makes it clear that this particular type of model is very sensitive to both the hyperparameters. The remarkable point that should be highlighted here is that all the folds have indicated very high recall value which asserts the claim that the model has retained sufficiently strong characteristics that can would enable the positive class to be categorized. Besides, the proposed F1 score which combines such measures of precision and recall is also more than 82%, which means that the proposed model is prescriptive enough and does not unbalance the two aforementioned concepts.

MobileNetV2

For the identification of the best hyperparameters for the MobileNet V2 model in the present study, the random search optimization method was performed on three different folds. The model's performance is analyzed in more detail in the following section and can be assessed from the results depicted in the table below, namely Table 6.

Table 6. Summary of Functions and Parameters Used in Model Architectures

Fold	Learning Rate	Batch size	Accuracy	Precision	Recall	F1-score
1	0.007157	99	87.73%	83.54%	85.39%	84.46%
2	0.007239	76	87.64%	83.90%	83.90%	83.89%
3	0.009798	88	86.42%	87.83%	85.96%	86.89%

By applying parameter tuning for Fold 1 the suitable parameters appeared to be; Batch size of 45 and a learning rate of 0.002223. The model was enhanced to reach 88.30% accuracy at its best performance. The training phase revealed that the accuracy of the first epoch was 77.91% and the highest validation accuracy was 88.30% in the sixth epoch of the entire training session. The loss was significantly less and came down to 0.5628 at the first epoch, but for the second epoch and onwards the figure was 0.2261 by the tenth epoch with the acceptable accuracy rates being 89.72%. It was found that the overall measure of accuracy was 84.30%, the precision was 77.69%, the recall was 94.39%, and F1-Score stands at 85.23%. When considering the confusion matrix, the following results were found; true negative: 174, false positives: 58, false negatives: 12, true positives: 202.

The best parameters in Fold 2 were a batch size of 93 and a learning rate of 0.009377. The model achieved the maximum accuracy of 88.02%, which is considered pretty high for such a task. At the beginning, accuracy was slightly high at 61.64% within the first epoch and then it increased to 88.02% in the seventh epoch. The loss dropped from 3.7847 to 0.2716 by the sixth epoch with the precision rising up to 88.82% for the tenth epoch. The results of the performance measure put accuracy at 86.52%, the precision at 78.65%, recall also at 86.52%, F1-Score at 82.35%. Cross-validation for this fold showed 164 TN, 68 FP, 13 FN, and 201 TP in the confusion matrix.

As for Fold 3, the best parameters were calculated as follows: The number of samples within a batch = 88; Learning rate = 0.009798. The final model obtained a highest accuracy of 86.42%. Initially, the accuracy estimate was at 68.67% for the first epoch while it increased to 88.47% in the tenth epoch. The validation accuracy was initially at 78.28% and it reached 85.96% at epoch value of 10. The loss, which has just gone down from 5.2848, has its value reduced to 0.2768, according to the tenth epoch. The metric outcomes of accuracy, precision, recall, and F1-Score stand at 84.07%, 83.57%, 83.18%, and 83.37% respectively. In this case, the confusion matrix for this fold is 197 TN, 35 FP, 36 FN, and 178 TP.

For folds 1 to 5, the validation accuracy of the MobileNetV2 model remain high standing at 84% and above. Due to the differences in learning rate and the size of the batch inside folds, it can be concluded that the model to some extent depends on these hyperparameters. The high recall achieved in all the folds generally indicates that the model does well in the identification of the positive class. Further, the parameter of F1-score, which measures both precision and recall together, is greater than 83% ascertain the model's stability in both aspects.

Both DenseNet121 and MobileNetV2 gave good results in the classification part, but it was slightly higher in DenseNet121 in terms of accuracy, recall, and F1-Score. Thus, it can be concluded that DenseNet121 has a higher recall and F1-Score which means it is more reliable in identifying the positive class and in terms of precision and recall. MobileNetV2 was found to have comparable levels of precision and accuracy to MobileNet for most of the folds, but the levels of variations observed were higher.

This comparative analysis thus encompasses the advantages of each of the models as well as a clear picture of their performance which can assist in proper deployment when employed practically. According to the results, DenseNet121 can be regarded as better suitable for the tasks that require high recall and balanced precision-recall rate. However, MobileNetV2 is still a pretty solid and stabilized model, especially for such tasks when precision is rather important.

Bayesian Optimization Results

MobileNetV2

The best configuration for MobileNetV2 was achieved with a batch size of 64.38 and a learning rate of 0.002983, resulting in a target accuracy of 86.52%. The performance metrics indicate strong results: accuracy of 86.52%, precision of 83.57%, recall of 83.18%, and an F1-score of 83.37%. The confusion matrix shows 197 true positives, 35 false positives, 36 false negatives, and 178 true negatives. The Bayesian optimization results for MobileNetV2 are summarized in Table 7.

Table 7. Bayesian Optimization Results for MobileNetV2

Iter	Target Accuracy	Batch Size	Learning Rate
1	84.83%	57.95	0.009512
2	83.15%	97.98	0.006027
3	83.71%	33.47	0.001644
4	79.78%	22.51	0.008675
5	82.02%	83.32	0.007110
6	81.46%	18.31	0.009702
7	82.02%	109.2	0.002202

continued on following page

Table 7. Continued

Iter	Target Accuracy	Batch Size	Learning Rate
8	81.46%	36.36	0.001916
9	83.71%	50.08	0.005295
10	86.52%	64.38	0.002983

While the model was being trained, it can be observed that it was constantly increasing in performance with MobileNetV2. In the first epoch, the specific percentages acquired include the accuracy of 73.86% and the validation accuracy of 80.90%. Huge difference in the score shows that the model was able to learn basic characteristics of the dataset in the first iteration. By the second epoch, there was an increase in validation accuracy to about 83.71% meaning that the model was able to generalize on the training data. Subsequently, the model remained at a relatively consistent performance chancing a bit to get the validation accuracy of 86.52%.

Thus, MobileNetV2 shows the feature of generalization since its validation accuracy gradually increases with each epoch. This reveals that only high precision means that every time the model comes up with a positive class it is most likely to be correct. While predicting the results, recall accuracy is slightly lower and it indicates that some positive instances are escaped. The F1-Score was calculated to be 0.538, and hence, we can believe that there is a good balance between Precision and Recall, thus proving that there is no over-look or under-look of the cases by the Algorithm. MobileNetV2, when compared to its counterpart architectures, is computationally efficient and flexible with hyperparameters making it fit for many uses, cases. However, first epochs demonstrated the ability to overfit and this problem was solved with proper selection of the learning rate.

DenseNet121

The best configuration designed for DenseNet121 indicated a batch size of 33.47 and a learning rate of 0.001644. The model achieved a target accuracy of 88.20%. Analysis of the results by means of specific parameters shows the level of accuracy to be 82.51%, the precision – 78.33%. It improves the sensitivity of the IE by 33% while the recall raises to 87.85% and the F1-score that combined between the sensitivity and the recall is 82.82%. In the confusion matrix, 180 are TP, while 52 are FP, 26 are FN, and 188 are TN. The Bayesian optimization results for DenseNet121 are summarized in Table 8.

Table 8. Bayesian Optimization Results for DenseNet121

Iter	Target Accuracy	Batch Size	Learning Rate
1	83.15%	57.95	0.009512
2	85.39%	97.98	0.006027
3	88.20%	33.47	0.001644
4	83.71%	22.51	0.008675
5	84.83%	83.32	0.007110
6	82.58%	18.31	0.009702
7	85.96%	109.2	0.002202
8	85.96%	36.36	0.001916
9	85.39%	50.08	0.005295
10	84.83%	57.95	0.009512

Based on the training accuracy, it was observed that DenseNet121 had enormous learning capacity right from the beginning. In the first epoch, the model's accuracy was 78.98% while the model's validation accuracy was 82.02%. This meant that the model used in the completion of the model's first epoch had invested 78.98% accuracy through fast learning on these complex patterns. In the second epoch, the validation accuracy stood at 83.15%, which implies the model achieved good learning and has the ability to generalize. For the rest of the epochs, the performance remained fluctuating only slightly up again and reached validation accuracy of 82.51% by the time of the last epoch.

Based on the above results, it can be noted that DenseNet121 has a generalization ability with low change in epochs and almost no sign of overfitting. From the results obtained, the work concludes that recall is higher than precision, meaning that DenseNet121 is more efficient in the detection of the positive instances than MobileNetV2, while it has relatively higher number of false positives. Presenting a shallow structure of dependency the network as described provokes it into learning deep complicated features which in turn lead to high levels of accuracy and stature in complex tasks. Thus, DenseNet121 provides very high recall that is needed for tasks, where missing a positive instance is inadmissible, though, the loss of precision has to be considered. Also, deep architecture can be more computationally expensive and may entail more RAM and CPU usage than the lightweight models like MobileNetV2.

Here, DenseNet121 reaches the target accuracy of 88.20% which is higher than that of getting 86.52% accuracy of the MobileNetV2. MobileNetV2 has very minor improvement in the precision values and therefore it is better suited for minimizing the false positives. On the other hand, DenseNet121 performs very well in the measure of recall and shows that it is very effective for the identification of instances which are positive. MobileNetV2 is suitable to be used in situations where the available resources are limited and medium accuracy is desirable. It is useful for those problems for which it is crucial to exclude false negative, like spam filtering. Therefore, DenseNet121, with its high recall, is suitable for use cases that rely on feature extraction and need high recall, as, for example, in medical image analysis. It is appropriate to use it where the nonavailability of positive examples can lead to disastrous results.

From the results obtained we can conclude that the performance of both architectures is positively affected by the process of hyperparameters tuning using Bayesian Optimization. This is because for a network to operate optimally it has to learn at uniform rates and in batches that should also be adjusted periodically. Furthermore, this detailed analysis presents a clear picture about the strength and weakness of MobileNetV2 and DenseNet121 and which architecture to use depending on the requirements of the application.

CONCLUSION

The results of this study support the detective of early melanoma as a significant aspect of improving the quality of patient care; while recognizing the CNN machine learning potential as a tool to increase accuracy of the diagnostic process. Thus, we have illustrated how multiple hyperparameter tuning approaches, including random search and Bayesian optimization, help improve the performance of CNN models. Applying the optimized hyperparameter to DenseNet121 and MobileNetV2 models on the HAM10000 dataset, our experiments showed that both of these models could get corresponding accurate rate of 85.65% and 84.08%. These findings imply that further improvement of CNN's performance for melanoma detection can be achieved if more significant work is dedicated to hyperparameters optimization. Therefore, data augmentation as well as resampling techniques realigned the classes in a way that offered adequate coverage where necessary, and also helped augment the overall model accuracy and reliability. Thus, it can be concluded that automated hyperparameter tuning is a critical feature that can improve the utility and performance of CNNs in medical imaging applications. When it comes to the identification of disease in the images, DenseNet121 has a higher recall and F1-score and therefore is useful in areas where recall is crucial. MobileNetV2 on the other hand provides reasonable accuracy and needed computation on the needed outcome making it suitable for clustered environments.

Therefore, this study contributes significantly to deeper understanding of CNN performance fields for melanoma detection and opens the direction to improve the techniques for this purpose. Further researchly studies should be conducted towards

the comparison of other forms of hyperparameter tuning and the use of more extensive samples for the models testing.

REFERENCES

Ahmad, I., & Amin, J., IkramUllah Lali, M., Abbas, F., & Imran Sharif, M. (2024). A novel Deeplabv3+ and vision-based transformer model for segmentation and classification of skin lesions. *Biomedical Signal Processing and Control*, 92, 106084. DOI: 10.1016/j.bspc.2024.106084

Ali, M. S., Miah, M. S., Haque, J., Rahman, M. M., & Islam, M. K. (2021). An enhanced technique of skin cancer classification using deep convolutional neural network with transfer learning models. *Machine Learning with Applications*, 5, 100036. DOI: 10.1016/j.mlwa.2021.100036

Alwakid, G., Gouda, W., Humayun, M., & Sama, N. U. (2022). Melanoma Detection Using Deep Learning-Based Classifications. *Health Care*, 10(12), 12. Advance online publication. DOI: 10.3390/healthcare10122481 PMID: 36554004

Antunes, A., Ferreira, B., Marques, N., & Carriço, N. (2023). Hyperparameter Optimization of a Convolutional Neural Network Model for Pipe Burst Location in Water Distribution Networks. *Journal of Imaging*, 9(3), 3. Advance online publication. DOI: 10.3390/jimaging9030068 PMID: 36976119

Bacanin, N., Zivkovic, M., Salb, M., Strumberger, I., & Chhabra, A. (2022). Convolutional Neural Networks Hyperparameters Optimization Using Sine Cosine Algorithm. In Shakya, S., Balas, V. E., Kamolphiwong, S., & Du, K.-L. (Eds.), *Sentimental Analysis and Deep Learning* (pp. 863–878). Springer. DOI: 10.1007/978-981-16-5157-1_67

Dai, W., Liu, R., Wu, T., Wang, M., Yin, J., & Liu, J. (2024). Deeply Supervised Skin Lesions Diagnosis with Stage and Branch Attention. *IEEE Journal of Biomedical and Health Informatics*, 28(2), 719-729. Advance online publication. DOI: 10.1109/JBHI.2023.3308697 PMID: 37624725

Daud, S. N. S. S., Sudirman, R., & Shing, T. W. (2023). Safe-level SMOTE method for handling the class imbalanced problem in electroencephalography dataset of adult anxious state. *Biomedical Signal Processing and Control*, 83, 104649.

Deng, J., Dong, W., Socher, R., Li, L.-J., Li, K., & Li, F.-F. (2009). ImageNet : A large-scale hierarchical image database. *2009 IEEE Conference on Computer Vision and Pattern Recognition*, 248-255. DOI: 10.1109/CVPR.2009.5206848

Dong, K., Zhou, C., Ruan, Y., & Li, Y. (2020). MobileNetV2 model for image classification. *2020 2nd International Conference on Information Technology and Computer Application (ITCA)*, 476-480. https://ieeexplore.ieee.org/abstract/document/9422058/

El-Bouzaidi, Y. E. I., & Abdoun, O. (2023). Advances in artificial intelligence for accurate and timely diagnosis of COVID-19 : A comprehensive review of medical imaging analysis. *Scientific African*, 01961.

El-Bouzaidi, Y. E. I., & Abdoun, O. (2024). Artificial Intelligence for Sustainable Dermatology in Smart Green Cities : Exploring Deep Learning Models for Accurate Skin Lesion Recognition. *Procedia Computer Science*, 236, 233–240.

El Idrissi El-Bouzaidi, Y., & Abdoun, O. (2021). DenTcov : Deep Transfer Learning-Based Automatic Detection of Coronavirus Disease (COVID-19) Using Chest X-ray Images. In Motahhir, S., & Bossoufi, B. (Eds.), *Digital Technologies and Applications* (Vol. 211, pp. 967–977). Springer International Publishing. DOI: 10.1007/978-3-030-73882-2_88

El Idrissi El-Bouzaidi, Y., & Abdoun, O. (2023). CNN-Based Deep Features with Ensemble Learning for COVID-19 Classification. In Farhaoui, Y., Rocha, A., Brahmia, Z., & Bhushab, B. (Eds.), *Artificial Intelligence and Smart Environment* (Vol. 635, pp. 325–330). Springer International Publishing. DOI: 10.1007/978-3-031-26254-8_46

El Idrissi El-Bouzaidi, Y., & Abdoun, O. (2024). Health Care Intelligent System : Deep Residual Network Powered by Data Augmentation for Automatic Melanoma Image Classification. In Bendaoud, M., El Fathi, A., Bakhsh, F. I., & Pierluigi, S. (Eds.), *Advances in Control Power Systems and Emerging Technologies* (pp. 223–230). Springer Nature Switzerland. DOI: 10.1007/978-3-031-51796-9_27

Garnett, R. (2023). *Bayesian optimization*. Cambridge University Press. https://books.google.com/books?hl=fr&lr=&id=MBCrEAAAQBAJ&oi=fnd&pg=PP1&dq=Bayesian+optimization&ots=tkKBuiYbxG&sig=Me8TEKWzwKqwa2IgvvfbsMO18Zc

Gouda, W., Sama, N. U., Al-Waakid, G., Humayun, M., & Jhanjhi, N. Z. (2022). Detection of Skin Cancer Based on Skin Lesion Images Using Deep Learning. *Health Care*, 10(7), 7. Advance online publication. DOI: 10.3390/healthcare10071183 PMID: 35885710

He, H., & Garcia, E. A. (2009). Learning from Imbalanced Data. *IEEE Transactions on Knowledge and Data Engineering*, 21(9), 1263–1284. DOI: 10.1109/TKDE.2008.239

Hibbi, F.-Z., Abdoun, O., & Haimoudi, E. K. (2022). Bayesian Network Modelling for Improved Knowledge Management of the Expert Model in the Intelligent Tutoring System. *International Journal of Advanced Computer Science and Applications*, 13(6). Advance online publication. DOI: 10.14569/IJACSA.2022.0130624

Huang, G., Liu, Z., Van Der Maaten, L., & Weinberger, K. Q. (2017a). Densely Connected Convolutional Networks. *2017 IEEE Conference on Computer Vision and Pattern Recognition (CVPR)*, 2261-2269. DOI: 10.1109/CVPR.2017.243

Huang, G., Liu, Z., Van Der Maaten, L., & Weinberger, K. Q. (2017b). Densely connected convolutional networks. *Proceedings of the IEEE Conference on Computer Vision and Pattern Recognition*, 4700-4708. https://openaccess.thecvf.com/content_cvpr_2017/html/Huang_Densely_Connected_Convolutional_CVPR_2017_paper.html

Jin, H. (2022). Hyperparameter Importance for Machine Learning Algorithms (arXiv:2201.05132).

Liashchynskyi, P., & Liashchynskyi, P. (2019). Grid Search, Random Search, Genetic Algorithm : A Big Comparison for NAS (arXiv:1912.06059). http://arxiv.org/abs/1912.06059

Moturi, D., Surapaneni, R. K., & Avanigadda, V. S. G. (2024). Developing an efficient method for melanoma detection using CNN techniques. *Journal of the Egyptian National Cancer Institute*, 36(1), 6. DOI: 10.1186/s43046-024-00210-w PMID: 38407684

Munuswamy Selvaraj, K., Gnanagurusubbiah, S., & Roby Roy, R. R., John peter, J. H., & Balu, S. (2024). Enhancing skin lesion classification with advanced deep learning ensemble models : A path towards accurate medical diagnostics. *Current Problems in Cancer*, 101077. Advance online publication. DOI: 10.1016/j.currproblcancer.2024.101077 PMID: 38480028

Nivedha, S., & Shankar, S. (2023). Melanoma Diagnosis Using Enhanced Faster Region Convolutional Neural Networks Optimized by Artificial Gorilla Troops Algorithm. *Information Technology and Control*, 52(4), 4. Advance online publication. DOI: 10.5755/j01.itc.52.4.33503

Öztürk, M. M. (2023). Initializing hyper-parameter tuning with a metaheuristic-ensemble method : A case study using time-series weather data. *Evolutionary Intelligence*, 16(3), 1019–1031. DOI: 10.1007/s12065-022-00717-y

Park, I., Kim, W. H., & Ryu, J. (2024). Style-KD : Class-imbalanced medical image classification via style knowledge distillation. *Biomedical Signal Processing and Control*, 91, 105928.

Sivakumar, M. S., Leo, L. M., Gurumekala, T., Sindhu, V., & Priyadharshini, A. S. (2024). Deep learning in skin lesion analysis for malignant melanoma cancer identification. *Multimedia Tools and Applications, 83*(6), 17833-17853. *Scopus.* Advance online publication. DOI: 10.1007/s11042-023-16273-1

Syed, S. A., Gowthami, S., Shanmukhi, M., & Mohammad, G. baig, Potluri, S., Chandragandhi, S., & Srihari, K. (2024). Registration based fully optimized melanoma detection using deep forest technique. *Biomedical Signal Processing and Control*, 93, 106116. DOI: 10.1016/j.bspc.2024.106116

Tan, E., Lim, S., Lamont, D., Epstein, R., Lim, D., & Lin, F. P. Y. (2024). Development and validation of a deep learning model for improving detection of nonmelanoma skin cancers treated with Mohs micrographic surgery. *JAAD International*, 14, 39–47. DOI: 10.1016/j.jdin.2023.10.007 PMID: 38089398

Tschandl, P. (2023). *The HAM10000 dataset, a large collection of multi-source dermatoscopic images of common pigmented skin lesions* (Version 4). Harvard Dataverse. https://doi.org/DOI: 10.7910/DVN/DBW86T

Yang, L., & Shami, A. (2020). On hyperparameter optimization of machine learning algorithms : Theory and practice. *Neurocomputing*, 415, 295–316.

Yeh, W.-C., Lin, Y.-P., Liang, Y.-C., & Lai, C.-M. (2021). *Convolution Neural Network Hyperparameter Optimization Using Simplified Swarm Optimization* (arXiv:2103.03995). arXiv. http://arxiv.org/abs/2103.03995

Youssra, E. I. E.-B., & Otman, A. (2022). Transfer Learning for Automatic Detection of COVID-19 Disease in Medical Ch*est X-ray Images. IAENG International Journal of Computer Science.*https://search.ebscohost.com/login.aspx?direct=true&profile =ehost&scope=site&authtype=crawler&jrnl=1819656X&AN=157247540&h=e EJw4oqM8bCnxIX06IKar%2Bto%2FGsNf2LDiNU3rJpHdGSl4Zk0HGMEvEYz TrGWAJCzUzrZtuNI57zq0xao3OezOQ%3D%3D&crl=c

Youssra, E. I. E.-B., & Otman, A. (2022). Application of Artificial Intelligence to X-ray Image-Based Coronavirus Diseases (COVID-19) for Automatic Detection. In M. Lazaar, C. Duvallet, A. Touhafi, & M. Al Achhab (Éds.), *Proceedings of the 5th International Conference on Big Data and Internet of Things* (Vol. 489, p. 208-220). Springer International Publishing. DOI: 10.1007/978-3-031-07969-6_16

Chapter 13
Unleashing Human Potential:
Human–AI Collaboration and Augmentation

Mehrajudin Aslam Aslam Najar

Communication University of China, China

ABSTRACT

This chapter explores how artificial intelligence (AI) augments human capabilities across sectors like healthcare, education, and business, emphasizing ethical considerations. It addresses challenges such as bias in algorithms and workforce displacement while discussing future trends like natural language interfaces and brain-computer interfaces. It advocates for ethical governance, proactive reskilling, and inclusive AI development to ensure equitable societal benefits and sustainable progress.

I. INTRODUCTION

The convergence of human intelligence and artificial intelligence (AI) is paving the way for a new era of collaboration and augmentation, as various studies have explored (Dellermann et al., 2019; Jarrahi, 2018; Shukla et al., 2021). As AI systems become increasingly sophisticated, their ability to complement and enhance human capabilities across various domains is being realized (Ravi et al., 2017; Amershi et al., 2019). This synergistic partnership between humans and AI agents, leveraging their respective strengths to achieve superior outcomes, is referred to as human-AI collaboration (Kirchkamp & Stuckenschmidt, 2020). Augmentation, on the other

DOI: 10.4018/979-8-3693-5231-1.ch013

hand, focuses on using AI as a cognitive extension to enhance human intelligence, decision-making, and performance (Shukla et al., 2021; Dellermann et al., 2019).

The potential benefits of human-AI collaboration and augmentation are vast and far-reaching. By combining the analytical prowess, speed, and scalability of AI with the creativity, emotional intelligence, and contextual understanding of humans, we can unlock new frontiers of innovation and productivity (Jarrahi, 2018; Amershi et al., 2019). However, this integration of AI into human activities also raises important social, psychological, and philosophical questions that must be addressed.

Social Impact: The widespread adoption of AI in various sectors is reshaping social structures and interactions. In the workplace, human-AI collaboration is altering team dynamics, job roles, and organizational hierarchies (Brynjolfsson & Mitchell, 2017). This shift necessitates new forms of social skills and adaptability as humans learn to work alongside AI systems. Moreover, the increasing presence of AI in public spaces and services is changing how individuals interact with technology and each other, potentially affecting social cohesion and community dynamics (Cath et al., 2018).

Psychological Considerations: The psychological impact of human-AI collaboration is multifaceted. On one hand, AI systems can reduce cognitive load and stress by handling routine tasks, potentially improving job satisfaction and mental well-being (Hancock et al., 2020). Conversely, the reliance on AI may lead to concerns about job security, feelings of inadequacy, or a sense of loss of control (Triberti et al., 2021). Understanding and addressing these psychological factors is crucial for successful implementation of human-AI collaborative systems.

Philosophical Implications: The integration of AI into human activities raises profound philosophical questions about the nature of intelligence, consciousness, and human uniqueness. As AI systems become more advanced, the boundaries between human and machine intelligence become increasingly blurred, challenging our understanding of what it means to be human (Bostrom, 2014). This convergence also prompts ethical considerations regarding decision-making responsibility, moral agency, and the potential long-term consequences of human-AI symbiosis (Floridi & Cowls, 2019).

This chapter explores the landscape of human-AI collaboration, the principles that govern effective augmentation systems, and the diverse application domains where these approaches are being employed (Shukla et al., 2021; Ravi et al., 2017). Furthermore, it addresses the ethical considerations and governance frameworks necessary to ensure responsible development and deployment of human-AI collaborative systems (Abdul et al., 2018; Yin et al., 2019).

As we delve into this complex and rapidly evolving field, we will examine not only the technological aspects but also the broader societal implications of human-AI collaboration. By understanding these multifaceted impacts, we can work towards harnessing the full potential of AI while mitigating potential risks and ensuring that the development of these technologies aligns with human values and societal goals.

BACKGROUND INFORMATION AND LITERATURE REVIEW

Background Information

This chapter provides a historical overview of AI technologies, tracing their evolution from early rule-based systems to contemporary advancements in machine learning and neural networks. Early AI systems relied on explicit programming and rule sets to perform tasks, whereas modern AI has shifted towards more flexible and data-driven approaches (Russell & Norvig, 2022). Breakthroughs in natural language processing (NLP), computer vision, and reinforcement learning have significantly enhanced AI's ability to understand and interact with human-centric activities (LeCun et al., 2015). For instance, NLP techniques such as transformers have revolutionized language understanding tasks by enabling AI systems to process and generate human-like text at unprecedented levels of accuracy (Vaswani et al., 2017).

Literature Review

In addition to technical advancements, this chapter integrates insights from social, psychological, and philosophical perspectives on AI-human interaction. AI technologies not only augment human capabilities but also influence cognition, behavior, and societal norms in profound ways (Floridi & Sanders, 2004). Studies on human perceptions of AI reveal complex dynamics where trust, acceptance, and concerns about autonomy intertwine (Waytz & Norton, 2014). Ethical dilemmas in AI ethics, such as fairness in algorithmic decision-making and privacy concerns, underscore the importance of considering broader societal impacts (Jobin et al., 2019). Philosophical debates on AI consciousness and agency further illuminate the ethical and existential implications of creating intelligent systems (Bostrom, 2014).

This holistic perspective enriches our understanding of human-AI collaboration by examining not only the technical capabilities of AI systems but also their ethical, social, and philosophical dimensions. By synthesizing insights across disciplines, this chapter aims to provide a comprehensive view of the evolving relationship between humans and AI, laying the groundwork for deeper exploration into its implications and applications in various domains.

DEFINING HUMAN-AI COLLABORATION AND AUGMENTATION

Human-AI collaboration refers to the synergistic partnership between humans and artificial intelligence (AI) systems, leveraging their respective strengths to achieve superior outcomes (Dellermann et al., 2019; Jarrahi, 2018). In this collaborative model, humans and AI agents work together, combining human cognitive abilities such as reasoning, creativity, and emotional intelligence with the computational power, data processing capabilities, and pattern recognition prowess of AI (Shukla et al., 2021; Amershi et al., 2019).

From a social perspective, this collaboration is reshaping workplace dynamics and team structures. Organizations are increasingly adopting "hybrid intelligence" models, where human teams are augmented by AI systems (Dellermann et al., 2021). For instance, in customer service, AI chatbots handle routine inquiries, allowing human agents to focus on complex issues that require empathy and nuanced understanding. This shift necessitates new social skills, as employees learn to effectively communicate and collaborate with AI systems as team members.

Psychologically, human-AI collaboration can have both positive and negative impacts. While it can reduce cognitive load and enhance decision-making capabilities, it may also lead to over-reliance on AI systems or feelings of inadequacy among workers (Triberti et al., 2021). Companies like IBM have recognized this challenge and are implementing training programs to help employees develop "AI literacy" and build confidence in working alongside AI systems (IBM, 2021).

Augmentation, on the other hand, focuses on using AI as a cognitive extension to enhance and amplify human intelligence, decision-making, and performance (Ravi et al., 2017; Dellermann et al., 2019). Rather than replacing human involvement entirely, AI augmentation aims to support and augment human capabilities by offloading specific tasks, providing decision support, and enhancing cognitive capacities (Shukla et al., 2021; Kirchkamp & Stuckenschmidt, 2020).

Corporate Strategies for Deployment: Companies are adopting various strategies to deploy human-AI collaboration systems:

1. Gradual Integration: Organizations like Accenture are taking a phased approach, introducing AI tools incrementally to allow employees to adapt and provide feedback (Accenture, 2022).
2. Customized Solutions: Microsoft's AI Builder allows businesses to create custom AI models tailored to their specific needs, facilitating smoother integration into existing workflows (Microsoft, 2023).

3. Collaborative Development: Google's "AI for everyone" initiative involves employees from various departments in the development and deployment of AI tools, fostering a culture of collaboration and reducing resistance (Google, 2022).
4. Ethical Considerations: Companies like Salesforce have established AI ethics boards to ensure responsible development and deployment of AI systems, addressing concerns about bias and fairness (Salesforce, 2021).

Case Study: Healthcare Diagnostics In the field of medical imaging, human-AI collaboration has shown remarkable results. At Stanford University Medical Center, radiologists work alongside an AI system called ChestNet to analyze chest X-rays. The AI quickly identifies potential abnormalities, allowing radiologists to focus their expertise on confirming diagnoses and developing treatment plans. This collaboration has led to a 20% increase in diagnostic accuracy and a 30% reduction in reading time (Stanford Medicine, 2023).

By understanding these nuanced aspects of human-AI collaboration and augmentation, organizations can develop more effective strategies for integrating these technologies into their operations, while also addressing the social and psychological impacts on their workforce.

IMPORTANCE AND BENEFITS OF COMBINING HUMAN AND AI CAPABILITIES

The integration of human and AI capabilities holds immense potential for driving innovation, increasing productivity, and tackling complex challenges across various domains (Dellermann et al., 2019; Jarrahi, 2018). By harnessing the complementary strengths of human intelligence and artificial intelligence, we can transcend the limitations of either working independently (Shukla et al., 2021).

Complementary Strengths

Humans possess invaluable qualities such as:

1. Creativity and innovation: The ability to generate novel ideas and think outside the box.
2. Emotional intelligence: Understanding and responding to complex emotional and social cues.
3. Contextual awareness: Grasping nuanced real-world situations and applying common sense reasoning.

4. Ethical reasoning: Making moral judgments and considering broader societal implications.
5. Adaptability: Quickly adjusting to new situations and unforeseen circumstances.

AI systems excel at:

1. Data processing: Analyzing vast amounts of data at high speeds.
2. Pattern recognition: Identifying complex patterns and correlations in data.
3. Consistency: Performing repetitive tasks without fatigue or variation in quality.
4. Scalability: Handling large-scale operations efficiently.
5. Prediction: Making accurate forecasts based on historical data and trends.

Real-World Examples

1. Financial Services: JPMorgan Chase has implemented a system called COiN (Contract Intelligence) that uses AI to analyze legal documents and extract important data points. This AI-powered system can review 12,000 annual commercial credit agreements in seconds, a task that would take lawyers 360,000 hours to complete manually. Human lawyers now focus on interpreting the results and making strategic decisions based on the AI's analysis (JPMorgan Chase, 2022).
2. Drug Discovery: Exscientia, a UK-based pharmaceutical company, has developed an AI-driven drug discovery platform that works alongside human scientists. In 2020, they announced the first AI-designed drug to enter human clinical trials. The AI system analyzed vast databases of biological and chemical data to identify potential drug candidates, while human scientists provided expertise in experimental design and interpretation of results. This collaboration reduced the typical drug discovery timeline from 4-5 years to just 12 months (Exscientia, 2021).
3. Customer Service: Zurich Insurance Group has implemented an AI-powered chatbot named Zara, which works in tandem with human customer service representatives. Zara handles routine inquiries and policy questions, freeing up human agents to deal with more complex issues that require empathy and nuanced understanding. This collaboration has resulted in a 50% reduction in query handling time and improved customer satisfaction scores (Zurich Insurance Group, 2023).

Challenges and Solutions

While the benefits are significant, implementing effective human-AI collaboration also presents challenges:

1. Trust and Transparency: Challenge: Employees may be hesitant to rely on AI recommendations if they don't understand how decisions are made. Solution: Companies like IBM are developing explainable AI tools that provide clear rationales for AI decisions, helping build trust among human collaborators (IBM Explainable AI, 2023).
2. Skill Gap: Challenge: Many employees lack the necessary skills to effectively work with AI systems. Solution: Organizations such as Google and Microsoft are investing heavily in AI literacy programs and providing extensive training to their workforce (Google AI Education, 2023; Microsoft AI School, 2023).
3. Job Displacement Concerns: Challenge: Fear of job loss due to AI automation can lead to resistance. Solution: Companies like Amazon are implementing reskilling programs, helping employees transition to new roles that focus on managing and collaborating with AI systems rather than being replaced by them (Amazon Upskilling 2025, 2023).
4. Ethical Considerations: Challenge: Ensuring AI systems make fair and unbiased decisions when collaborating with humans. Solution: Organizations such as the Partnership on AI are developing guidelines and best practices for ethical AI development and deployment, which many companies are adopting (Partnership on AI, 2023).

By combining these complementary strengths through effective human-AI collaboration and augmentation, we can achieve superior outcomes, make more informed decisions, and unlock new frontiers of problem-solving (Jarrahi, 2018; Kirchkamp & Stuckenschmidt, 2020). This symbiotic relationship has the potential to enhance human capabilities, improve efficiency, and drive innovation across various sectors, including healthcare, education, scientific research, creative industries, and business operations (Ravi et al., 2017; Amershi et al., 2019).

II. LANDSCAPE OF HUMAN-AI COLLABORATION

Current State and Examples of Human-AI Teams

The concept of human-AI collaboration has gained traction as advancements in machine learning, natural language processing, and computer vision have enabled more seamless and sophisticated interactions between humans and intelligent systems (Daugherty & Wilson, 2018). While humans have worked alongside automation and decision support systems for years, the recent progress in AI has opened up new possibilities for augmenting and enhancing human performance through collaboration (Brynjolfsson & McAfee, 2014).

Current examples of human-AI teams can be found across various sectors, leveraging the unique capabilities of AI to complement human expertise:

1. **Healthcare**: AI-assisted diagnostic tools are being used by radiologists and pathologists to improve the accuracy and efficiency of medical image analysis (Wiljer & Hakim, 2019). AI algorithms can rapidly analyze large volumes of medical data, identify patterns, and provide decision support, leading to more accurate diagnoses and personalized treatment plans (Yu et al., 2018).
2. **Finance**: In the financial industry, AI algorithms are employed to augment human traders' decision-making processes by providing real-time market insights, predictive analytics, and automated trading strategies (Bahrammirzaee, 2010). These human-AI teams can react more quickly to market fluctuations and identify investment opportunities (Dunbar & Gowree, 2020).
3. **Manufacturing**: AI-powered predictive maintenance systems work alongside human experts to monitor industrial equipment and predict potential failures, enabling proactive maintenance and minimizing downtime (Mobley, 2002). Additionally, collaborative robots (cobots) are designed to work in tandem with human workers, enhancing productivity and safety (Bauer et al., 2016).
4. **Scientific Research**: AI is increasingly being used in scientific research to accelerate discovery and analysis (Hey et al., 2009). AI algorithms can assist researchers in identifying patterns in large datasets, generating hypotheses, and designing experiments, while human researchers provide domain expertise, critical thinking, and validation (Schneiderman, 2020).

Challenges and Barriers to Effective Collaboration

Despite the promising examples and potential benefits, several challenges and barriers exist in achieving effective human-AI collaboration:

1. **Trust and Transparency**: Building trust is crucial for successful collaboration. Humans may hesitate to rely on AI recommendations or decisions if the underlying reasoning processes lack transparency or interpretability (Ribeiro et al., 2016). Explainable AI and interpretable models are essential for fostering trust and enabling humans to effectively evaluate and leverage AI capabilities (Doshi-Velez & Kim, 2017).
2. **Human Factors and Usability**: Designing intuitive and user-friendly interfaces that facilitate seamless interaction between humans and AI agents is a significant challenge (Amershi et al., 2019). Human-centered design principles must be

applied to ensure that AI systems align with human cognitive processes, work-flows, and mental models, minimizing friction and enhancing overall usability (Norman, 2013).

3. **Skill Gap and Training**: As AI systems become more prevalent, there is a growing need for individuals with the necessary skills to effectively collaborate with and leverage AI capabilities (Brynjolfsson & Mitchell, 2017). Addressing this skill gap through specialized training programs and educational initiatives is crucial for successful human-AI collaboration (Whittlestone et al., 2019).

4. **Organizational Culture and Change Management**: Integrating AI into exist-ing workflows and processes often requires cultural shifts within organizations (Davenport & Ronanki, 2018). Overcoming resistance to change, addressing potential biases or misconceptions about AI's capabilities, and fostering a culture of collaboration are critical for successful adoption of human-AI collaborative systems (Ransbotham et al., 2019).

Complementary Strengths of Humans and AI Systems

Effective human-AI collaboration relies on leveraging the complementary strengths of both humans and AI systems. While AI excels in certain areas, humans possess unique capabilities essential for optimal decision-making and problem-solving:

1. **Human Strengths**:
   a. **Creativity and Innovation**: Humans excel at generating novel ideas, think-ing outside the box, and approaching problems from unique perspectives, enabling creativity and innovation (Boden, 2004).
   b. **Emotional Intelligence**: Humans possess the ability to understand, interpret, and respond to emotions, crucial for tasks involving social interactions, communication, and empathy (Salovey & Mayer, 1990).
   c. **Context Awareness and Common Sense**: Humans have a deep under-standing of context, cultural nuances, and real-world complexities, allowing informed decisions based on situational factors and common sense reasoning (Levesque et al., 2012).
   d. **Ethical Reasoning and Judgment**: Humans have the capacity for moral reasoning, ethical decision-making, and considering broader societal im-plications, essential in high-stakes situations (Wallach & Allen, 2009).

2. AI Strengths:
   a. **Data Processing and Pattern Recognition**: AI systems excel at processing and analyzing large volumes of data, identifying patterns, and extracting insights that may be difficult for humans (Najafabadi et al., 2015).

b. **Computational Power and Speed**: AI algorithms can perform complex calculations and simulations at tremendous speeds, enabling real-time decision-making and optimization in time-critical scenarios (Ciregan et al., 2012).

c. **Consistency and Scalability**: AI systems can consistently apply decision-making rules and processes across large-scale operations, ensuring consistency and scalability (Amodei et al., 2016).

d. **Automation of Repetitive Tasks**: AI can automate repetitive and mundane tasks, freeing up human cognitive resources for more complex and creative endeavors (Brynjolfsson & McAfee, 2014).

By combining the complementary strengths of humans and AI systems, human-AI teams can achieve superior outcomes. Humans provide contextual understanding, creativity, and ethical reasoning, while AI contributes computational power, data processing capabilities, and consistent decision-making at scale.

III. CURRENT STATE OF HUMAN-AI COLLABORATION

As artificial intelligence continues to evolve, its integration into various sectors has prompted a transformation in workplace dynamics. Human-AI collaboration is not merely a theoretical concept; it is a growing reality that enhances productivity, creativity, and decision-making across multiple industries. This section delves into real-world examples of human-AI collaboration, showcasing its applications in healthcare, finance, education, and the creative industries. Additionally, it examines emerging trends that are shaping the future of work.

A. Real-World Examples by Industry

1. Healthcare

In the healthcare sector, AI is revolutionizing patient care and treatment processes. For instance, IBM's Watson Health utilizes natural language processing and machine learning algorithms to analyze vast amounts of medical literature, patient records, and clinical trial data. This system assists healthcare professionals in making evidence-based decisions for patient diagnosis and treatment plans. A notable example is Watson's collaboration with oncologists at Memorial Sloan Kettering Cancer Center, where it provided treatment recommendations based on genetic data, significantly improving patient outcomes (Abramson, 2020).

2. Finance

The finance industry is leveraging AI for enhanced risk management and fraud detection. Machine learning algorithms analyze transaction patterns to identify anomalies that may indicate fraudulent activity. For instance, Mastercard employs AI to monitor transactions in real time, allowing for rapid detection and response to potential fraud. By collaborating with AI, financial analysts can focus on strategic decision-making and complex problem-solving, while AI handles routine data processing tasks (Brynjolfsson & McAfee, 2017).

3. Education

In education, AI-driven platforms are personalizing learning experiences for students. Tools such as Coursera and Khan Academy utilize AI algorithms to assess individual learning styles and progress, tailoring educational content accordingly. AI tutors can provide instant feedback and support to students, enabling educators to concentrate on facilitating discussions and addressing broader educational needs. This collaboration enhances the learning experience and supports diverse student populations (Luckin et al., 2016).

4. Creative Industries

The creative industries are also witnessing the impact of AI in areas such as content creation and design. For example, OpenAI's GPT-3 has been used to generate written content, while AI-driven design tools like Canva allow users to create visually appealing graphics with minimal effort. These technologies augment human creativity by providing suggestions and automating repetitive tasks, enabling creators to focus on innovative and complex ideas (McCormick, 2021).

B. Emerging Trends

The integration of human-AI collaboration is not a static process; it is continuously evolving. Some key emerging trends include:

- **Interdisciplinary Collaboration**: As AI technologies permeate various fields, interdisciplinary collaboration is becoming essential. Professionals from diverse backgrounds are coming together to develop solutions that leverage AI's strengths. For example, healthcare practitioners, data scientists, and ethicists are collaborating to ensure AI applications are both effective and ethical (Dignum, 2019).

- **AI-Enhanced Decision-Making**: The use of AI tools to support decision-making processes is becoming increasingly common. Organizations are employing AI systems to analyze large datasets, providing insights that inform strategic decisions. This trend is evident in supply chain management, where AI algorithms optimize inventory levels based on predictive analytics (Bughin et al., 2018).
- **Human-Centric AI Design**: As awareness of the ethical implications of AI grows, there is a push for human-centric AI design that prioritizes user experience and inclusivity. Companies are focusing on creating AI systems that are transparent, explainable, and designed with user feedback in mind, ensuring that human-AI interactions are intuitive and beneficial (Floridi & Cowls, 2019).
- **Continuous Learning and Adaptation**: Organizations are recognizing the need for continuous learning and adaptation in the face of rapid technological advancements. By fostering a culture of innovation and adaptability, companies can better prepare their workforce for the integration of AI technologies and the evolution of job roles (Makridakis, 2017).

The current state of human-AI collaboration illustrates not only the potential benefits of integrating AI into various industries but also the challenges that organizations face in navigating this transformation. As we explore these dynamics further, it becomes crucial to understand the implications for the workforce and the necessary steps to ensure successful collaboration.

IV: CASE STUDIES OF AI-HUMAN COLLABORATION

1. IBM Watson Health in Oncology

Overview

IBM Watson Health has partnered with healthcare institutions to enhance cancer diagnosis and treatment plans through AI-driven analytics.

Collaboration

IBM collaborated with **Memorial Sloan Kettering Cancer Center** to develop Watson for Oncology, an AI system that analyzes medical literature and patient data to provide evidence-based treatment options.

Successes

- Watson can analyze vast amounts of data quickly, offering oncologists treatment recommendations based on current research, which improves the decision-making process.
- A study found that Watson's recommendations aligned with oncologists' decisions 96% of the time, demonstrating its potential to augment human expertise (Saeed et al., 2019).

Challenges

- Watson faced criticism for its initial inability to adequately analyze patient data and provide appropriate treatment plans, necessitating continuous improvement and validation of its algorithms.
- Concerns arose regarding data privacy and the ethical implications of AI in healthcare, highlighting the need for robust regulatory frameworks.

Lessons Learned

Collaboration between AI systems and human experts can lead to improved patient outcomes, but it requires ongoing monitoring, validation, and ethical considerations to ensure effective and responsible use.

2. AI-Powered Predictive Maintenance in Manufacturing

Overview

Companies like **Siemens** and **General Electric (GE)** have implemented AI systems to enhance predictive maintenance in manufacturing environments.

Collaboration

These companies utilize AI algorithms to analyze sensor data from machinery to predict when maintenance is needed, thereby reducing downtime and operational costs.

Successes

- Siemens reported a 30% reduction in maintenance costs and a 40% decrease in unplanned downtime through AI-driven predictive maintenance strategies (Siemens, 2020).
- GE's Predix platform uses AI to analyze data from jet engines, predicting failures before they occur and improving overall equipment efficiency.

Challenges

- Implementing AI in legacy systems posed integration challenges, requiring a comprehensive strategy to upgrade and adapt existing infrastructure.
- There were concerns about the skills gap among workers in understanding and leveraging AI technologies effectively.

Lessons Learned

Successful AI-human collaboration in manufacturing relies on a solid data infrastructure, employee training, and a culture of continuous improvement.

3. AI in Customer Service: Chatbots and Virtual Assistants

Overview

Many companies, such as **H&M** and **Sephora**, have employed AI chatbots to enhance customer service experiences.

Collaboration

These chatbots handle common inquiries and provide recommendations, allowing human agents to focus on more complex customer issues.

Successes

- H&M's chatbot, "Ada," helps customers find products and answer queries, improving response times and customer satisfaction ratings (H&M, 2021).
- Sephora's Virtual Artist uses AI to recommend makeup products based on user preferences, enhancing user engagement and driving sales.

Challenges

- Chatbots sometimes struggle with nuanced queries, leading to customer frustration if they cannot seamlessly hand off complex issues to human agents.
- Ensuring a smooth transition between AI and human representatives is crucial to maintaining customer satisfaction.

Lessons Learned

AI chatbots can effectively enhance customer service when used in tandem with human agents, but it's essential to establish clear protocols for escalation to ensure customer needs are met.

4. AI in Agriculture: Precision Farming

Overview

Companies like **John Deere** and **PrecisionHawk** leverage AI technologies to optimize farming practices through precision agriculture.

Collaboration

AI systems analyze data from drones, sensors, and satellite imagery to provide farmers with insights on crop health, soil conditions, and resource optimization.

Successes

- John Deere's AI-powered machinery allows farmers to apply fertilizers and pesticides more efficiently, reducing waste and environmental impact. Users have reported increased crop yields and decreased operational costs (John Deere, 2020).
- PrecisionHawk's drone technology provides farmers with actionable insights, enabling data-driven decisions that enhance productivity.

Challenges

- The adoption of AI technologies in agriculture requires significant investment and training for farmers to effectively utilize the tools.
- Data privacy and ownership issues may arise regarding the information collected from farmland and crops.

Lessons Learned

Effective collaboration between AI and farmers enhances productivity and sustainability in agriculture but necessitates investment in education and infrastructure to maximize benefits.

5. AI for Fraud Detection in Finance

Overview

Financial institutions, such as **American Express** and **PayPal**, utilize AI algorithms to detect fraudulent transactions in real-time.

Collaboration

These systems analyze transaction data to identify unusual patterns, flagging potential fraud for human review.

Successes

- American Express reported a 25% reduction in fraud losses due to its AI-powered fraud detection system, which combines machine learning with human oversight (American Express, 2021).
- PayPal's AI algorithms analyze millions of transactions per day, significantly increasing the speed and accuracy of fraud detection.

Challenges

- Balancing AI's efficiency with the need for human judgment can be challenging, particularly in distinguishing between legitimate transactions and potential fraud.
- There are concerns about false positives, where legitimate transactions are flagged as fraudulent, leading to customer dissatisfaction.

Lessons Learned

AI-human collaboration in fraud detection can enhance security and reduce losses, but it requires continuous refinement and an emphasis on maintaining customer trust.

These case studies illustrate the diverse applications of AI-human collaboration, showcasing both successes and challenges while highlighting key lessons learned from each initiative. If you need any further modifications or additional information, feel free to ask!

V. AUGMENTING HUMAN INTELLIGENCE WITH AI

AI as a Cognitive Extension and Decision Support Tool

The concept of augmenting human intelligence with AI revolves around leveraging AI systems as cognitive extensions and decision support tools (Riedl & Hennen, 2022; Kaplan & Haenlein, 2020). Rather than replacing human involvement entirely, this approach aims to enhance and amplify human cognitive abilities by offloading specific tasks and providing intelligent assistance.

One of the primary applications of AI augmentation is in decision support systems. AI algorithms can process and analyze vast amounts of data, identify patterns and trends, and generate insights or recommendations to support human decision-making processes (Akata et al., 2020). These AI-powered decision support tools can be invaluable in domains where complex decisions need to be made based on multiple factors and large datasets.

For example, in healthcare, AI-powered diagnostic tools can assist physicians in making more accurate and timely diagnoses by analyzing medical images, patient records, and clinical literature (He et al., 2019). By rapidly processing this wealth of information, AI can provide decision support to healthcare professionals, enabling them to make better-informed treatment decisions while leveraging their expertise and experience.

Similarly, in business operations, AI-driven predictive analytics and optimization algorithms can augment human decision-making by providing data-driven insights and forecasts (Duan et al., 2019). These AI systems can identify trends, simulate various scenarios, and recommend optimal strategies, empowering human decision-makers with valuable information to guide their choices.

Enhancing Human Skills and Capabilities

Beyond serving as decision support tools, AI can directly enhance and augment human skills and capabilities across various domains. By offloading specific tasks or providing cognitive assistance, AI can amplify human performance, productivity, and creativity (Jarrahi, 2018).

In education, for instance, AI-powered tutoring systems can provide personalized learning experiences by adapting to each student's learning style, pace, and knowledge gaps (Hooshyar et al., 2020). These systems can identify areas where students struggle, provide targeted feedback and exercises, and adjust the curriculum accordingly, enhancing the overall learning experience and outcomes.

In creative industries, AI can be used as a tool to augment human creativity and expression. AI algorithms can generate ideas, visualize concepts, and explore new artistic possibilities, serving as a source of inspiration and exploration for human artists, writers, and designers (Anantrazizynski et al., 2022). Additionally, AI can assist in various creative tasks, such as image editing, video processing, and music composition, amplifying human creativity and enabling new forms of artistic expression.

Furthermore, AI can enhance human cognitive abilities by offloading routine or repetitive tasks, freeing up mental resources for more complex and creative endeavors (Brynjolfsson & Mitchell, 2017). For example, AI-powered virtual assistants can handle scheduling, information retrieval, and task management, allowing humans to focus their attention on higher-level cognitive tasks that require critical thinking, problem-solving, and decision-making.

Potential Impacts on Workforce and Job Roles

As AI systems become increasingly integrated into various workflows and processes, there is a potential impact on workforce dynamics and job roles. While some routine and repetitive tasks may be automated, new roles and responsibilities will emerge that leverage human-AI collaboration and augmentation.

One potential impact is the emergence of new job roles that bridge the gap between humans and AI systems. For instance, "AI managers" or "AI translators" may be needed to facilitate effective communication and coordination between human team members and AI agents (Dellermann et al., 2019). These roles would require a deep understanding of both AI capabilities and human workflows, ensuring seamless integration and collaboration.

Additionally, existing job roles may evolve to incorporate AI-augmented skills and responsibilities. For example, healthcare professionals may need to develop expertise in interpreting AI-generated diagnostic recommendations and integrating them into their decision-making processes (Huang & Rust, 2018). Similarly, business analysts and strategists may need to become proficient in leveraging AI-driven predictive analytics and optimization tools to enhance their analytical capabilities.

While some routine tasks may be automated, the demand for human skills in areas such as critical thinking, creativity, emotional intelligence, and ethical reasoning is likely to increase (Frank et al., 2019). As AI systems take over more repetitive and data-intensive tasks, human workers will need to focus on developing skills that complement and leverage AI capabilities effectively.

To navigate these workforce transitions, proactive measures such as reskilling and upskilling initiatives will be crucial. Educational programs and professional development opportunities should be designed to equip individuals with the necessary skills to thrive in an AI-augmented workforce (Whittlestone et al., 2019). Collaboration between industry, academia, and policymakers will be vital in addressing potential job displacement and ensuring a smooth transition into new roles and responsibilities (Lee, 2018).

VI. DESIGN PRINCIPLES FOR HUMAN-AI COLLABORATION SYSTEMS

Developing successful human-AI collaboration systems requires adherence to several key design principles to ensure trust, usability, responsible implementation, and overall effectiveness. These principles should guide the development and deployment of AI systems that augment and collaborate with human intelligence.

Transparency, Explainability, and Trust

Transparency and explainability are essential for fostering trust between humans and AI systems (Arrieta et al., 2020). Humans are often hesitant to rely on AI recommendations or decisions when the underlying reasoning processes are opaque or lacking in comprehensibility (Ribeiro et al., 2016). To overcome this barrier, AI systems should be designed to provide clear and interpretable explanations for their outputs, decisions, and recommendations (Gunning & Aha, 2019).

Explainable AI (XAI) techniques, such as local interpretable model-agnostic explanations (LIME) and SHapley Additive exPlanations (SHAP), can help make complex AI models more transparent and understandable (Molnar, 2020). By providing insights into the factors and rationale that influenced the AI's decision-making process, humans can better evaluate and validate the recommendations, leading to increased trust and confidence in the system (Tomsett et al., 2018).

Furthermore, transparency should extend beyond just the AI's outputs; it should also encompass the data used for training, the algorithms employed, and the potential biases or limitations of the system (Selbst & Barocas, 2018). Clear communication and documentation of these aspects can further promote trust and enable humans to make informed decisions about when and how to leverage the AI's capabilities (Doshi-Velez & Kim, 2017).

Human-Centered Design and Usability

Effective human-AI collaboration systems must prioritize human-centered design principles and usability (Norman, 2013). These systems should be designed with a deep understanding of human cognitive processes, workflows, and mental models, ensuring that the AI augments and enhances human performance rather than hindering it (Horvitz, 1999).

User experience (UX) and human-computer interaction (HCI) best practices should be employed to create intuitive and user-friendly interfaces that facilitate seamless interactions between humans and AI agents (Amershi et al., 2019). This includes consideration of factors such as information architecture, visual design, and interaction modalities (e.g., voice, gesture, or traditional input methods) (Streitz, 2018).

Additionally, human-centered design should account for the varying levels of technical expertise and domain knowledge among users. AI systems should be accessible and usable for both domain experts and non-technical users, providing appropriate levels of guidance, training, and support to ensure effective adoption and utilization (Abdul et al., 2018).

Balancing Automation and Human Control

While AI systems can automate certain tasks or decision processes, it is crucial to maintain appropriate human oversight and the ability to intervene or override the AI when necessary (Rahwan, 2018). This balance between automation and human control is essential to ensure that AI remains a tool to augment human intelligence rather than completely replacing human decision-making (Brynjolfsson & Mitchell, 2017).

In high-stakes domains or scenarios with significant consequences, it is imperative to preserve human agency and the ability to override AI recommendations or decisions (Amodei et al., 2016). This could be achieved through mechanisms such as human approval workflows, adjustable automation levels, or manual intervention options (Parasuraman & Manzey, 2010).

Furthermore, the level of automation and human control should be tailored to the specific context and user preferences (Sauer et al., 2019). Some users may prefer a higher degree of automation for routine or low-risk tasks, while others may prefer more manual control in complex or high-risk situations (Habibovic et al., 2018). Providing configurable settings and customizable interfaces can accommodate these varying preferences and requirements (Bradshaw et al., 2004).

Data Privacy and Security Considerations

Human-AI collaboration systems often deal with sensitive or personal data, which necessitates robust data privacy and security measures (Shokri et al., 2017). Ensuring the protection of data integrity, preventing unauthorized access, and maintaining compliance with relevant regulations and ethical standards are paramount considerations (Zwetsloot et al., 2018).

Privacy-preserving techniques, such as differential privacy (Dwork & Roth, 2014), federated learning (Kairouz et al., 2021), and secure multi-party computation (Cramer et al., 2015), should be explored and implemented to protect individual privacy while enabling AI systems to learn from data without compromising sensitive information.

Furthermore, strong cybersecurity measures, including encryption, access controls, and regular security audits, should be in place to safeguard against potential data breaches or cyber threats (Cobb, 2020). Comprehensive data governance policies and procedures should be established to ensure the responsible handling, storage, and usage of data throughout the entire lifecycle of the human-AI collaboration system (Tallon et al., 2020).

Adherence to relevant data protection regulations, such as the General Data Protection Regulation (GDPR) in the European Union (Voigt & Von dem Bussche, 2017) or the California Consumer Privacy Act (CCPA) in the United States (Graff, 2020), is also crucial. Organizations should implement robust compliance frameworks and undergo regular audits to ensure they meet the necessary legal and ethical standards for data privacy and security (Bamberger, 2019).

By following these design principles, organizations can develop human-AI collaboration systems that foster trust, promote usability, maintain appropriate levels of human control, and prioritize data privacy and security. These principles are essential for responsible and effective integration of AI technologies that augment and collaborate with human intelligence.

VII. APPLICATION DOMAINS AND USE CASES

Healthcare and Medical Decision Support

The healthcare sector stands to benefit significantly from the integration of human and artificial intelligence. AI-powered systems can augment and enhance medical decision-making processes, leading to improved patient outcomes and more efficient healthcare delivery.

1. **Diagnostic Assistance**: AI algorithms can analyze medical images (e.g., X-rays, CT scans, MRIs) and patient data to assist radiologists and physicians in making accurate diagnoses (Hosny et al., 2018). These AI-assisted diagnostic tools can identify patterns and abnormalities that may be difficult for humans to detect, reducing diagnostic errors and enabling earlier intervention (Topol, 2019).

2. **Treatment Planning**: AI systems can process vast amounts of clinical data, scientific literature, and patient medical histories to provide personalized treatment recommendations (Ehteshami Bejnordi et al., 2017). By considering various factors such as genetics, comorbidities, and treatment responses, AI can support healthcare professionals in developing tailored and effective treatment plans (Jiang et al., 2017).

3. **Clinical Decision Support**: AI-powered decision support systems can assist physicians and nurses in making informed decisions at the point of care (Shameer et al., 2019). These systems can provide real-time guidance, alert healthcare professionals to potential risks or contraindications, and suggest evidence-based interventions based on the patient's specific condition and medical history (Shortliffe & Sepúlveda, 2018).

4. **Drug Discovery and Development**: AI techniques like machine learning and molecular modeling can accelerate the drug discovery and development process (Chen et al., 2018). AI can assist in identifying potential drug candidates, predicting their efficacy and safety profiles, and optimizing clinical trial designs, ultimately leading to more efficient and targeted drug development (Stephenson et al., 2019).

By leveraging the complementary strengths of human expertise and AI capabilities, the healthcare sector can achieve significant advancements in diagnosis, treatment planning, clinical decision support, and drug development, ultimately improving patient care and outcomes.

Education and Personalized Learning

AI has the potential to revolutionize education by providing personalized and adaptive learning experiences tailored to individual students' needs, abilities, and learning styles.

1. **Intelligent Tutoring Systems**: AI-driven tutoring systems can adapt to each student's pace, knowledge level, and learning preferences (Kulik & Fletcher, 2016). These systems can provide personalized feedback, customized learning materials, and targeted exercises to address specific learning gaps or reinforce strengths (Nye, 2015).
2. **Adaptive Learning Platforms**: AI-powered adaptive learning platforms can dynamically adjust the content, difficulty level, and delivery method based on a student's performance and engagement (Truong, 2016). By continuously monitoring and analyzing learner data, these platforms can optimize the learning experience for each individual student (Aleven et al., 2016).
3. **Automated Grading and Feedback**: AI algorithms can assist educators by automating the grading and feedback process for assignments, essays, and assessments (Rama & Bhasin, 2022). This can save time for teachers and provide students with faster and more consistent feedback, enabling them to identify areas for improvement and adjust their learning strategies accordingly (Jamil et al., 2022).
4. **Learning Analytics**: AI can analyze vast amounts of student data, including performance metrics, engagement levels, and learning behaviors, to provide insights and recommendations to educators (Viberg et al., 2018). These analytics can help identify at-risk students, optimize instructional methods, and inform curriculum design and resource allocation decisions (Essa & Ayad, 2012).

By leveraging AI's capabilities in personalization, adaptation, automation, and data-driven insights, the education sector can transform traditional one-size-fits-all approaches into individualized and effective learning experiences, ultimately improving student engagement, achievement, and outcomes.

Creative Industries and Artistic Collaboration

AI is increasingly being employed in creative industries as a tool to augment human creativity, explore new artistic possibilities, and collaborate with human artists, writers, and designers.

1. **Content Generation and Ideation:** AI algorithms can generate ideas, storylines, and creative content by analyzing existing works and identifying patterns. These AI-generated ideas can serve as inspiration or starting points for human creators, sparking new creative directions and facilitating the ideation process (Caselli, 2021; Zhong et al., 2022).
2. **Visual Art and Design:** AI systems can assist in various visual art and design tasks, such as image editing, style transfer, and 3D modeling. Human artists can collaborate with AI by providing initial concepts or prompts, and the AI can generate variations, visualizations, or renderings to explore different artistic directions (Elgammal et al., 2017; Gatys et al., 2016).
3. **Music and Audio Production:** AI algorithms can analyze and learn from existing music compositions, enabling them to generate new melodies, harmonies, and instrumental arrangements. Human musicians and producers can leverage these AI-generated elements as a starting point or as inspiration for their own creative processes (Bretan et al., 2019; Huang et al., 2019).
4. **Creative Writing and Storytelling:** AI language models can generate creative writing samples, storylines, and character descriptions based on provided prompts or existing works. Human writers can use these AI-generated content as a foundation, editing and refining the material to create their desired narratives or literary works (Roemmele & Gordon, 2018; Zhu et al., 2020).

While AI can augment and inspire human creativity, it is important to note that true artistic expression and emotional resonance still rely on the human touch. AI should be viewed as a powerful tool to explore new creative possibilities, but not as a replacement for human artistry and ingenuity (Colton et al., 2018; Hertzmann, 2020).

These application domains highlight the vast potential of human-AI collaboration and augmentation across various sectors. By leveraging the respective strengths of humans and AI, we can enhance decision-making processes, personalize learning experiences, and unlock new avenues for creative expression and innovation.

Scientific Research and Discovery

Human-AI collaboration holds immense potential for accelerating scientific research and driving groundbreaking discoveries across various disciplines, from physics and chemistry to biology and astronomy.

1. **Data Analysis and Pattern Recognition:** AI algorithms excel at processing and analyzing vast amounts of scientific data, identifying patterns and relationships that may be difficult or impossible for humans to discern. This capability can

lead to new insights, hypotheses generation, and the discovery of previously unrecognized phenomena (Géron, 2019; Langley, 2000).

2. **Experiment Design and Simulation:** AI can assist researchers in designing and simulating complex experiments, optimizing parameters, and exploring a vast number of scenarios. This can accelerate the research process, reduce the need for physical experiments, and enable the exploration of phenomena that may be challenging or impossible to study in real-world settings (Barde & Chaudhari, 2016; Karpatne et al., 2017).

3. **Literature Review and Knowledge Extraction:** AI-powered natural language processing (NLP) techniques can rapidly scan and extract insights from vast repositories of scientific literature, helping researchers stay up-to-date with the latest developments and discoveries in their field (Hausner et al., 2022; Lee et al., 2020).

4. **Collaborative Hypothesis Generation:** Human researchers can collaborate with AI systems to generate and evaluate hypotheses based on existing data and scientific knowledge. This synergistic approach combines the AI's ability to identify patterns and relationships with the human researcher's domain expertise, intuition, and critical thinking skills (Kanter & Veeramachaneni, 2015; Tuomi et al., 2018).

5. **Computational Modeling and Simulation:** AI algorithms can create highly accurate computational models and simulations of complex systems, phenomena, or processes, enabling researchers to study and predict their behavior under various conditions. This capability is particularly valuable in fields like climate science, materials science, and astrophysics (Bhatnagar et al., 2019; Roscher et al., 2020).

Business Intelligence and Decision-Making

In the business world, human-AI collaboration can enhance decision-making processes, drive strategic insights, and optimize operations across various functional areas, including finance, marketing, supply chain management, and risk assessment.

1. **Predictive Analytics and Forecasting:** AI algorithms can analyze historical data, market trends, and various external factors to generate accurate forecasts and predictive models. These insights can inform business decisions related to product demand, inventory management, pricing strategies, and resource allocation (Agrawal et al., 2018; Runkler, 2020).

2. **Customer Analytics and Personalization:** AI can process vast amounts of customer data, including browsing behavior, purchase histories, and demographic information, to personalize marketing campaigns, product recommendations,

and customer experiences. This level of personalization can improve customer satisfaction, loyalty, and overall business performance (Boddington, 2017; Xu et al., 2019).

3. **Fraud Detection and Risk Management:** AI systems can continuously monitor and analyze financial transactions, network activities, and other data sources to identify patterns and anomalies indicative of fraud, cybersecurity threats, or operational risks. This proactive approach can help businesses mitigate risks and comply with regulatory requirements (Chakraborty et al., 2018; Ngai et al., 2011).

4. **Supply Chain Optimization:** AI algorithms can optimize complex supply chain networks by analyzing various factors such as demand forecasts, inventory levels, transportation routes, and logistics constraints. This can lead to improved efficiency, reduced costs, and better resource utilization across the entire supply chain (Baryannis et al., 2019; Toorajipour et al., 2021).

5. **Strategic Decision Support:** AI-powered decision support systems can provide executives and strategic decision-makers with data-driven insights, scenario simulations, and recommendations to inform critical business decisions. These systems can consider multiple variables, constraints, and objectives, enabling more informed and effective strategic planning (Delen & Pratt, 2006; Shim et al., 2002).

By utalizing human-AI collaboration in these domains, businesses can gain a competitive edge, make more informed decisions, and drive innovation and growth. However, it is crucial to ensure the responsible and ethical development and deployment of AI systems, addressing concerns around data privacy, algorithmic bias, and transparency in decision-making processes (Arrieta et al., 2020; Floridi et al., 2018).

VIII. ETHICAL CONSIDERATIONS AND GOVERNANCE

As the integration of human and artificial intelligence systems becomes more prevalent, it is crucial to address the ethical implications and establish robust governance frameworks to ensure responsible development and deployment of these technologies.

Accountability and Responsibility in Human-AI Systems

One of the key challenges in human-AI collaboration is determining accountability and responsibility for the decisions and actions resulting from the interplay between humans and AI agents. Clear guidelines and mechanisms must be established to answer questions such as:

a. Who is accountable when an AI system's recommendation or decision leads to adverse outcomes or unintended consequences? (Doshi-Velez & Kortz, 2017; Rahwan, 2018)
b. How is responsibility distributed between the AI developers, the organizations deploying the system, and the human users interacting with the AI? (Bryson & Winfield, 2017; Luciano et al., 2021)
c. What processes should be in place for investigating incidents, assigning accountability, and providing recourse or compensation when necessary? (Araujo et al., 2018; Hogan, 2019)

Addressing these accountability issues requires a multifaceted approach involving technical solutions, organizational policies, and regulatory frameworks. Mechanisms such as audit trails, explainable AI techniques, and established chains of command can help attribute responsibility and enable thorough investigation of incidents (Doshi-Velez & Kortz, 2017; Wachter et al., 2017).

Additionally, ethical guidelines and codes of conduct should be developed to outline the responsibilities and expected behavior of various stakeholders involved in human-AI systems, including developers, deployers, and end-users (Arrieta et al., 2020; Floridi et al., 2018).

Bias and Fairness in Algorithmic Decision-Making

AI systems can perpetuate or amplify existing biases present in the training data or algorithms, leading to potentially discriminatory or unfair outcomes. This is particularly concerning in high-stakes domains such as lending, hiring, or criminal justice, where biased decision-making can have severe consequences.

Mitigating bias and ensuring fairness in algorithmic decision-making is a critical ethical consideration. Strategies such as bias testing, algorithmic auditing, and diverse and inclusive data practices should be employed to identify and address potential biases.

Furthermore, transparency and explainability in AI systems are crucial for understanding and mitigating bias. By making the decision-making processes of AI systems interpretable, stakeholders can scrutinize the factors influencing decisions and take corrective actions when necessary.

Interdisciplinary collaboration between AI developers, domain experts, and ethics specialists is essential to navigate the complex trade-offs between fairness, accuracy, and other desirable objectives in decision-making systems.

Workforce Displacement and Skill Transitions

The increasing adoption of AI systems and automation technologies has raised concerns about potential job displacement and the need for workforce transitions. While some routine and repetitive tasks may be automated, new roles and responsibilities will emerge that leverage human-AI collaboration and augmentation.

Proactive measures are necessary to address the impact on the workforce and ensure a smooth transition to new skill requirements. These measures may include:

1. **Reskilling and Upskilling Initiatives:** Educational programs and professional development opportunities should be designed to equip workers with the necessary skills to thrive in an AI-augmented workforce. This may involve training in areas such as data literacy, AI ethics, and collaborative problem-solving.
2. **Workforce Planning and Retraining:** Organizations should engage in strategic workforce planning to identify the roles and skills that will be in demand as AI systems are integrated into various processes. Retraining programs can then be developed to help existing employees transition to new roles or acquire the necessary skills.
3. **Social Safety Nets and Policy Reforms:** Policymakers and governments may need to consider reforms to social safety nets, such as unemployment benefits or universal basic income, to support workers affected by job displacement during the transition period.
4. **Public-Private Collaboration:** Collaboration between industry, academia, and government is essential to address the workforce challenges posed by AI and automation. This can involve joint initiatives for reskilling, curriculum development, and fostering a skilled workforce capable of leveraging AI technologies effectively.

Regulatory Frameworks and Guidelines

As human-AI collaboration systems become more prevalent, regulatory frameworks and guidelines are necessary to govern their development and deployment. These frameworks should address various aspects, including:

1. **Data Privacy and Security:** Regulations should establish clear standards for data privacy, security, and governance, ensuring the responsible handling and protection of personal or sensitive data used in AI systems (Cath et al., 2018; Mittelstadt, 2019).

2. **Algorithmic Transparency and Explainability**: Guidelines should mandate appropriate levels of transparency and explainability in AI systems, particularly in high-stakes decision-making scenarios, to enable scrutiny, auditing, and accountability (Doshi-Velez & Kortz, 2017; Guidotti et al., 2018).

3. **Ethical Principles and Standards:** Overarching ethical principles and standards should be established to guide the development and deployment of human-AI collaboration systems. These may include principles related to fairness, non-discrimination, privacy, human oversight, and responsible AI governance (Dignum, 2019; Jobin et al., 2019).

4. **Risk Assessment and Impact Evaluation:** Frameworks should require rigorous risk assessment and impact evaluation processes for AI systems, particularly in domains with potential for significant societal impact, such as healthcare, finance, or criminal justice (Amodei et al., 2016; Leslie, 2019).

5. **Compliance and Certification:** Mechanisms for compliance monitoring, auditing, and certification may be necessary to ensure that human-AI collaboration systems adhere to established regulations, ethical standards, and best practices (Brundage et al., 2020; Raji et al., 2020).

6. **Governance and Oversight:** Independent advisory boards or regulatory bodies may be established to provide ongoing governance, oversight, and guidance on the responsible development and deployment of human-AI systems (Butcher & Beridze, 2019; Whittlestone et al., 2019).

Collaboration between policymakers, industry leaders, academic experts, and civil society organizations is crucial in developing effective and widely accepted regulatory frameworks. These frameworks should strike a balance between fostering innovation and promoting the responsible adoption of human-AI collaboration technologies while safeguarding against potential risks and unintended consequences (Floridi et al., 2018; Zweig et al., 2018).

By addressing these ethical considerations and establishing robust governance frameworks, we can unlock the immense potential of human-AI collaboration and augmentation while prioritizing ethical and responsible development and deployment of these transformative technologies.

IX. FUTURE DIRECTIONS AND EMERGING TRENDS

Advancements in Natural Language Interfaces

One of the key areas of advancement that will shape the future of human-AI collaboration is the development of more advanced and intuitive natural language interfaces. Current natural language processing (NLP) technologies have made significant strides, enabling humans to communicate with AI systems using natural language input and receive contextually appropriate responses (Cambria & White, 2014; Young et al., 2018).

However, future advancements aim to create even more seamless and conversational interactions between humans and AI agents. This includes technologies such as:

1. **Multimodal Interfaces**: Combining natural language with other modalities like vision, gesture, and touch can enable more immersive and natural interactions with AI systems (Baltrušaitis et al., 2018; Ngiam et al., 2011).
2. **Contextual and Situational Awareness:** AI agents with advanced contextual and situational awareness capabilities can better understand and respond to the nuances of human communication, accounting for factors like tone, intent, and environmental context (Chai et al., 2020; Yang et al., 2019).
3. **Personalized and Adaptive Interfaces:** Natural language interfaces that can adapt to individual communication styles, preferences, and domain knowledge can provide more personalized and tailored interactions with AI systems (Haas et al., 2020; Rudovic et al., 2018).
4. **Multilingual and Cross-Cultural Support:** As AI systems become more globally integrated, natural language interfaces must be capable of supporting multiple languages and accounting for cultural differences in communication norms (Bender & Koller, 2020; Choudhury et al., 2021).

These advancements in natural language interfaces will not only enhance the efficiency and effectiveness of human-AI collaboration but also make these interactions more natural and intuitive, potentially increasing trust and adoption of AI technologies (Luger & Sellen, 2016; Wang et al., 2021).

Brain-Computer Interfaces and Neural Augmentation

While current AI systems augment human intelligence by providing external decision support and cognitive assistance, future technologies may enable more direct integration between human and artificial intelligence through brain-computer interfaces (BCIs) and neural augmentation (Rao, 2013; Wolpaw et al., 2002).

BCIs are devices that enable direct communication between the human brain and external devices or systems, potentially allowing for seamless exchange of information, control signals, and augmented cognitive capabilities. Emerging research in this field explores the possibility of enhancing human cognitive functions, such as memory, attention, and decision-making, through neural augmentation (Hampson et al., 2018; Sokoliuk & Cracco, 2021).

Potential applications of these technologies include:

1. Enhanced cognitive abilities for tasks requiring high-level processing, such as complex problem-solving, creative endeavors, or rapid decision-making in high-stakes situations (Demartini et al., 2022; Trimper et al., 2014).
2. Assistive technologies for individuals with cognitive or neurological impairments, enabling improved communication, mobility, and independence (Blabe et al., 2015; Chaudhary et al., 2016).
3. Augmented learning and knowledge acquisition by directly interfacing with external knowledge sources or AI systems (Dehghani et al., 2019; Ramakrishnan et al., 2017).
4. Collaborative problem-solving between human and AI agents, leveraging the complementary strengths of biological and artificial intelligence in a tightly coupled manner (Jiang et al., 2019; Reddy et al., 2021).

While these technologies are still in their early stages, advancements in neuroscience, brain-mapping, and neural interface engineering could pave the way for more direct and seamless integration between human and artificial intelligence, blurring the boundaries between the two (Ienca & Andorno, 2017; Nijboer et al., 2021).

Distributed and Decentralized AI Collaboration Models

Traditional AI models often rely on centralized training and deployment, with data and compute resources concentrated in a single location or organization. However, emerging trends in distributed and decentralized AI collaboration models are gaining traction, driven by concerns around data privacy, scalability, and the need for collective intelligence (Konečný et al., 2016; Shokri & Shmatikov, 2015).

One such approach is federated learning, where AI models are trained across multiple decentralized devices or servers holding local data samples, without the need to centralize the data itself. This enables collaborative training while preserving data privacy and reducing communication overhead (Kairouz et al., 2021; McMahan et al., 2017).

Another promising direction is swarm intelligence, which involves the collective behavior of decentralized, self-organized systems, inspired by the mechanisms observed in natural systems like ant colonies or flocking birds. In the context of AI, swarm intelligence could enable collaborative decision-making and problem-solving across multiple AI agents and human participants, leveraging their collective intelligence and diverse perspectives (Bayındır, 2016; Couzin et al., 2011).

These distributed and decentralized models have several potential advantages:

1. Improved data privacy and security by avoiding centralized data aggregation (Bonawitz et al., 2017; Shokri & Shmatikov, 2015).
2. Scalability and resilience through decentralized computation and decision-making (Konečný et al., 2016; Lian et al., 2017).
3. Leveraging collective intelligence and diverse perspectives from multiple stakeholders (Couzin et al., 2011; Durugkar et al., 2016).
4. Enabling collaboration across organizational boundaries and geographies (Kairouz et al., 2021; McMahan et al., 2017).

As these models continue to evolve, they could reshape the landscape of human-AI collaboration, fostering more inclusive, secure, and scalable collaborative systems that transcend traditional centralized approaches (Bonawitz et al., 2019; Lian et al., 2017).

Societal Impacts and the Future of Work

The widespread adoption of human-AI collaboration and augmentation technologies is poised to have far-reaching societal impacts, particularly on the nature of work and the future of employment. As AI systems take over certain tasks and automate specific job functions, there will be a significant shift in the types of jobs and skills required in the workforce (Autor, 2015; Frank et al., 2019).

On one hand, some routine and repetitive tasks across various industries may become increasingly automated, potentially leading to job displacement in certain sectors. However, this disruption also creates opportunities for new types of jobs and roles that leverage the unique strengths of human-AI collaboration (Brynjolfsson & McAfee, 2014; Makridakis, 2017).

Potential new job roles and responsibilities may include:

1. **AI Managers and Orchestrators:** Professionals responsible for coordinating and managing teams of human and AI agents, ensuring effective collaboration and optimal task allocation (Jarrahi, 2018; Trunk, 2019).
2. **AI Trainers and Curators:** Experts responsible for curating and annotating data, as well as training and fine-tuning AI models to ensure their accuracy, fairness, and alignment with organizational goals (Bellamy et al., 2019; Sambasivan et al., 2021).
3. **AI Ethicists and Governance Specialists:** Professionals focused on ethical AI development, monitoring for biases, and ensuring compliance with relevant regulations and governance frameworks (Arrieta et al., 2020; Dignum, 2019).
4. **AI-Human Interaction Designers:** UX/UI designers and human-computer interaction specialists focused on creating intuitive and seamless interfaces for human-AI collaboration systems (Amershi et al., 2019; Yang et al., 2018).
5. **AI-Augmented Professionals:** Existing roles across various domains, such as healthcare, education, finance, and creative industries, may evolve to incorporate AI augmentation, requiring professionals to develop skills in leveraging and collaborating with AI systems effectively (Geis et al., 2019; Miller, 2018).

As the workforce transitions, proactive measures such as reskilling initiatives, educational reforms, and policy changes will be crucial to ensure a smooth adaptation to the AI-augmented future of work. Additionally, interdisciplinary collaboration between policymakers, industry leaders, educators, and technology experts will be essential in navigating these societal shifts and preparing the workforce for the transformative impact of human-AI collaboration and augmentation (Bughin et al., 2018; Makridakis, 2017).

CONCLUSION

Throughout this chapter, we have explored the rapidly evolving landscape of human-AI collaboration and augmentation, examining the synergistic partnership between human intelligence and artificial intelligence. We have delved into the current state of human-AI teams across various sectors, the challenges and barriers to effective collaboration, and the complementary strengths that humans and AI systems bring to the table.

Furthermore, we have investigated the principles and strategies for augmenting human intelligence with AI, exploring how AI can serve as a cognitive extension and decision support tool to enhance human skills and capabilities. The chapter has showcased diverse application domains where human-AI collaboration and augmentation are being implemented, demonstrating their transformative potential across healthcare, education, creative industries, scientific research, and business operations.

Recognizing the ethical and societal implications of these technologies, we have addressed crucial considerations such as accountability, bias mitigation, workforce implications, and the need for robust governance frameworks and regulatory guidelines. Additionally, we have explored emerging trends and future directions, including advancements in natural language interfaces, brain-computer interfaces, distributed AI collaboration models, and the societal impacts on the future of work.

Opportunities and Challenges Ahead

The integration of human and artificial intelligence presents a wealth of opportunities for driving innovation, increasing productivity, and tackling complex challenges across various domains. By leveraging the complementary strengths of humans and AI, we can achieve superior outcomes, make more informed decisions, and unlock new frontiers of problem-solving and discovery (Brynjolfsson & McAfee, 2017; Jarrahi, 2018).

However, realizing the full potential of human-AI collaboration and augmentation also comes with significant challenges. Ensuring trust, transparency, and explainability in AI systems is paramount for fostering effective collaboration and responsible adoption (Arrieta et al., 2020; Guidotti et al., 2018). Additionally, addressing issues of bias, fairness, and accountability in algorithmic decision-making is crucial to mitigate potential risks and unintended consequences (Barocas & Selbst, 2016; Mehrabi et al., 2021).

The impact on the workforce and the need for proactive reskilling and upskilling initiatives is another critical challenge that must be addressed. As AI automates certain tasks and job roles evolve, it is essential to prepare the workforce for the AI-augmented future and ensure a smooth transition to new skill requirements (Frank et al., 2019; Makridakis, 2017).

Call to Action for Responsible Development

As we navigate the exciting and transformative era of human-AI collaboration and augmentation, it is imperative that we adopt a responsible and ethical approach to the development and deployment of these technologies. This requires a concerted effort from all stakeholders, including researchers, developers, policymakers, industry leaders, and civil society organizations (Floridi et al., 2018; Whittlestone et al., 2019).

We must prioritize the ethical principles of transparency, accountability, fairness, and privacy in the design and implementation of human-AI systems. Robust governance frameworks and regulatory guidelines should be established to ensure compliance with ethical standards, protect individual rights, and mitigate potential risks (Dignum, 2019; Zweig et al., 2018).

Interdisciplinary collaboration and open dialogue among experts from various domains, including AI, ethics, law, social sciences, and domain-specific fields, are essential for navigating the complex trade-offs and considerations surrounding human-AI collaboration and augmentation (Floridi & Cowls, 2019; Raisch & Krakowski, 2021).

Furthermore, we must invest in education and awareness programs to equip current and future generations with the necessary skills and knowledge to thrive in an AI-augmented world. This includes fostering data literacy, ethical reasoning, and collaborative problem-solving abilities, as well as promoting a deeper understanding of the capabilities and limitations of AI systems (Bughin et al., 2018; Miller, 2018).

REFERENCES

Amershi, S., Weld, D., Vorvoreanu, M., Fourney, A., Nushi, B., Collisson, P., & Horvitz, E. (2019). Guidelines for human-AI interaction. In *Proceedings of the 2019 CHI Conference on Human Factors in Computing Systems* (pp. 1-13).

Amodei, D., Olah, C., Steinhardt, J., Christiano, P., Schulman, J., & Mané, D. (2016). Concrete problems in AI safety. arXiv preprint arXiv:1606.06565.

Araujo, T., Helberger, N., Kruikemeier, S., & de Vreese, C. H. (2018). In AI we trust? Perceptions about automated decision-making by artificial intelligence. *AI & Society*, 33(4), 509–519.

Arrieta, A. B., Díaz-Rodríguez, N., Del Ser, J., Bennetot, A., Tabik, S., Barbado, A., & Herrera, F. (2020). Explainable Artificial Intelligence (XAI): Concepts, taxonomies, opportunities and challenges toward responsible AI. *Information Fusion*, 58, 82–115. DOI: 10.1016/j.inffus.2019.12.012

Autor, D. H. (2015). Why are there still so many jobs? The history and future of workplace automation. *The Journal of Economic Perspectives*, 29(3), 3–30. DOI: 10.1257/jep.29.3.3

Baltrušaitis, T., Ahuja, C., & Morency, L. P. (2018). Multimodal machine learning: A survey and taxonomy. *IEEE Transactions on Pattern Analysis and Machine Intelligence*, 41(2), 423–443. DOI: 10.1109/TPAMI.2018.2798607 PMID: 29994351

Bayındır, L. (2016). A review of swarm robotics tasks. *Neurocomputing*, 172, 292–321. DOI: 10.1016/j.neucom.2015.05.116

Bellamy, R. K. E., Dey, K., Hind, M., Hoffman, S. C., Houde, S., Kannan, K., & Zhang, Y. (2019). AI fairness 360: An extensible toolkit for detecting, understanding, and mitigating unwanted algorithmic bias. *IBM Journal of Research and Development*, 63(4/5), 4–1. DOI: 10.1147/JRD.2019.2942287

Bender, E. M., & Koller, A. (2020). Climbing towards NLU: On meaning, form, and understanding in the age of data. In *Proceedings of the 58th Annual Meeting of the Association for Computational Linguistics* (pp. 5185-5198). DOI: 10.18653/v1/2020.acl-main.463

Blabe, C. H., Gilja, V., Chestek, C. A., Shenoy, K. V., & Henderson, J. M. (2015). Assessment of brain-machine interfaces from the perspective of people with paralysis. *Journal of Neural Engineering*, 12(4), 043002. DOI: 10.1088/1741-2560/12/4/043002 PMID: 26169880

Bonawitz, K., Eichner, H., Grieskamp, W., Huba, D., Ingerman, A., Ivanov, V., . . . van Overveldt, T. (2019). Towards federated learning at scale: System design. arXiv preprint arXiv:1902.01046.

Bonawitz, K., Ivanov, V., Kreuter, B., Marcedone, A., McMahan, B., Patel, S., & Seth, K. (2017). Practical secure aggregation for privacy-preserving machine learning. In *Proceedings of the 2017 ACM SIGSAC Conference on Computer and Communications Security* (pp. 1175-1191). DOI: 10.1145/3133956.3133982

Brynjolfsson, E., & McAfee, A. (2014). *The Second Machine Age: Work, Progress, and Prosperity in a Time of Brilliant Technologies*. W.W. Norton & Company.

Brynjolfsson, E., & McAfee, A. (2017). What's driving the machine learning explosion? *Harvard Business Review*, 17.

Bryson, J. J., & Winfield, A. F. (2017). Standardizing ethical design for artificial intelligence and autonomous systems. *Computer*, 50(5), 116–119. DOI: 10.1109/MC.2017.154

Bughin, J., Hazan, E., Ramaswamy, S., Chui, M., Allas, T., Dahlström, P., & Trench, M. (2018). *Skill shift: Automation and the future of the workforce*. McKinsey Global Institute.

Butcher, J., & Beridze, I. (2019). What is the state of artificial intelligence governance globally? *RUSI Journal*, 164(5-6), 88–96. DOI: 10.1080/03071847.2019.1694260

Cambria, E., & White, B. (2014). Jumping NLP curves: A review of natural language processing research. *IEEE Computational Intelligence Magazine*, 9(2), 48–57. DOI: 10.1109/MCI.2014.2307227

Cath, C., Wachter, S., Mittelstadt, B., Taddeo, M., & Floridi, L. (2018). Artificial intelligence and the 'good society': The US, EU, and UK approach. *Science and Engineering Ethics*, 24(2), 505–528. PMID: 28353045

Chai, J. Y., Fang, R., Liu, C., & She, L. (2020). Collaborative language grounding toward situated human-robot dialogue. *AI Magazine*, 41(1), 20–31.

Chaudhary, U., Birbaumer, N., & Ramos-Murguialday, A. (2016). Brain-computer interfaces for communication and rehabilitation. *Nature Reviews. Neurology*, 12(9), 513–525. DOI: 10.1038/nrneurol.2016.113 PMID: 27539560

Choudhury, S., Wihardja, H., Bhardwaj, A., & Rudinac, M. (2021). Socially-aware AI for multilingual information retrieval and recommendation. *ACM Transactions on Multimedia Computing Communications and Applications*, 17(2s), 1–21.

Couzin, I. D., Ioannou, C. C., Demirel, G., Gross, T., Torney, C. J., Hartnett, A., Conradt, L., Levin, S. A., & Leonard, N. E. (2011). Uninformed individuals promote democratic consensus in animal groups. *Science*, 334(6062), 1578–1580. DOI: 10.1126/science.1210280 PMID: 22174256

Dehghani, M., Tiňo, P., & Gholipour, M. (2019). Spiking neural network learning and memory. *Neural Networks*, 111, 18–25.

Demartini, D., Pizzamiglio, S., Di Matteo, R., & Cappa, S. F. (2022). Memory enhancement: New insights from transcranial electrical stimulation. *Journal of Cognitive Enhancement: Towards the Integration of Theory and Practice*, 6(2), 187–198.

Dignum, V. (2019). *Responsible Artificial Intelligence: How to Develop and Use AI in a Responsible Way*. Springer. DOI: 10.1007/978-3-030-30371-6

Doshi-Velez, F., & Kortz, M. (2017). Accountability of AI under the law: The role of explanation. arXiv preprint arXiv:1711.01134.

Durugkar, I., Repucci, B., & Stone, P. (2016). Dynamic integration of heterogeneous swarm behaviors using mood. In *Proceedings of the 2016 International Conference on Autonomous Agents & Multiagent Systems* (pp. 1203-1204).

Floridi, L., & Cowls, J. (2019). A unified framework of five principles for AI in society. *Harvard Data Science Review*, 1(1).

Floridi, L., Cowls, J., Beltrametti, M., Chatila, R., Chazerand, P., Dignum, V., & Schafer, B. (2018). AI4People—An ethical framework for a good AI society: Opportunities, risks, principles, and recommendations. *Minds and Machines*, 28(4), 689–707. DOI: 10.1007/s11023-018-9482-5 PMID: 30930541

Frank, M. R., Sun, L., Cebrian, M., Youn, H. Y., & Rahwan, I. (2019). Small cities face greater impact from automation. *Journal of the Royal Society, Interface*, 16(151), 20180946. PMID: 29436514

Geis, J. R., Brady, A. P., Wu, C. C., Spencer, J. A., Ranschaert, E., Jaremko, J. L., Langer, S. G., Kitts, A. B., Birch, J., Shields, W. F., van den Hoven van Genderen, R., Kotter, E., Gichoya, J. W., Cook, T. S., Morgan, M. B., Tang, A., Safdar, N. M., & Kohli, M. (2019). Ethics of artificial intelligence in radiology: Summary of the joint European and North American multisociety statement. *Insights Into Imaging*, 10(1), 101. DOI: 10.1186/s13244-019-0785-8 PMID: 31571015

Guidotti, R., Monreale, A., Ruggieri, S., Turini, F., Giannotti, F., & Pedreschi, D. (2018). A survey of methods for explaining black box models. *ACM Computing Surveys*, 51(5), 1–42. DOI: 10.1145/3236009

Haas, M., Pelikan, H., & Seifert, J. (2020). Personalizing conversational agents for user engagement: Insights from a design study. In *Proceedings of the 2020 CHI Conference on Human Factors in Computing Systems* (pp. 1-14).

Hampson, R. E., Song, D., Chan, R. H., Marmarelis, V. Z., Leung, H. C., Griffin, A. L., & Deadwyler, S. A. (2018). Developing a hippocampal neural prosthetic to facilitate human memory encoding and recall. *Journal of Neural Engineering*, 15(3), 036014. DOI: 10.1088/1741-2552/aaaed7 PMID: 29589592

Hogan, P. (2019). AI accountability: Rethinking liability and blame. *Georgetown Journal of International Affairs*, 20(3), 60.

Huang, X., He, X., Gao, J., Deng, L., Acero, A., & Heck, L. (2013). Learning deep structured semantic models for web search using clickthrough data. In *Proceedings of the 22nd ACM International Conference on Information & Knowledge Management* (pp. 2333-2338). DOI: 10.1145/2505515.2505665

Hutson, M. (2018). Machine learning gets a health check. *Nature*, 555(7697), S1–S2.

Ienca, M., & Vayena, E. (2018). On the responsible use of digital data to tackle the COVID-19 pandemic. *Nature Medicine*, 26(4), 463–464. DOI: 10.1038/s41591-020-0832-5 PMID: 32284619

Jiang, F., Jiang, Y., Zhi, H., Dong, Y., Li, H., Ma, S., Wang, Y., Dong, Q., Shen, H., & Wang, Y. (2017). Artificial intelligence in healthcare: Past, present and future. *Stroke and Vascular Neurology*, 2(4), 230–243. DOI: 10.1136/svn-2017-000101 PMID: 29507784

Jobin, A., Ienca, M., & Vayena, E. (2019). The global landscape of AI ethics guidelines. *Nature Machine Intelligence*, 1(9), 389–399. DOI: 10.1038/s42256-019-0088-2

Kaplan, A., & Haenlein, M. (2019). Siri, Siri, in my hand: Who's the fairest in the land? On the interpretations, illustrations, and implications of artificial intelligence. *Business Horizons*, 62(1), 15–25. DOI: 10.1016/j.bushor.2018.08.004

Krizhevsky, A., Sutskever, I., & Hinton, G. E. (2012). ImageNet classification with deep convolutional neural networks. In Advances in Neural Information Processing Systems (pp. 1097-1105).

LeCun, Y., Bengio, Y., & Hinton, G. (2015). Deep learning. *Nature*, 521(7553), 436–444. DOI: 10.1038/nature14539 PMID: 26017442

Liang, J., Mahmood, A., & Burger, D. (2020). End-to-end relation extraction using LSTMs on sequences and tree structures. *Journal of Computational Science*, 43, 101163.

Liao, Q. V., & Cherry, E. C. (2021). Measuring and mitigating unintended bias in text classification. *Transactions of the Association for Computational Linguistics*, 9, 614–630.

Lipton, Z. C. (2016). The mythos of model interpretability. In *Proceedings of the 2016 ICML Workshop on Human Interpretability in Machine Learning (WHI 2016)* (pp. 1-8).

Mnih, V., Kavukcuoglu, K., Silver, D., Rusu, A. A., Veness, J., Bellemare, M. G., & Petersen, S. (2015). Human-level control through deep reinforcement learning. *Nature*, 518(7540), 529–533. DOI: 10.1038/nature14236 PMID: 25719670

Müller, V. C., & Bostrom, N. (2016). Future progress in artificial intelligence: A survey of expert opinion. In Müller, V. C. (Ed.), *Fundamental Issues of Artificial Intelligence* (pp. 555–572). Springer. DOI: 10.1007/978-3-319-26485-1_33

Papamichail, M., & Aritzoglou, A. (2021). Robotics and the international political economy: An inquiry into the evolving regulatory landscapes. *Regulation & Governance*, 15(3), 528–549.

Pasquale, F. (2015). *The black box society: The secret algorithms that control money and information*. Harvard University Press. DOI: 10.4159/harvard.9780674736061

Pinto, L., Gandhi, D., & Han, Y. (2016). Curious robots: Learning visual representations via physical interactions. In *Proceedings of the 2016 IEEE/RSJ International Conference on Intelligent Robots and Systems (IROS)* (pp. 2440-2447). DOI: 10.1007/978-3-319-46475-6_1

Raghavan, V., Madani, O., & Jones, R. (2006). Active learning with feedback on features and instances. *Journal of Machine Learning Research*, 7, 1655–1686.

Rudin, C. (2019). Stop explaining black box machine learning models for high stakes decisions and use interpretable models instead. *Nature Machine Intelligence*, 1(5), 206–215. DOI: 10.1038/s42256-019-0048-x PMID: 35603010

Russell, S. J., & Norvig, P. (2021). *Artificial Intelligence: A Modern Approach* (4th ed.). Pearson.

Sarathy, V., & Robertson, A. (2021). The long-term impact of artificial intelligence on the labor market. *International Journal of Forecasting*, 37(4), 1697–1707.

Schölkopf, B., & Smola, A. J. (2002). *Learning with Kernels: Support Vector Machines, Regularization, Optimization, and Beyond*. MIT Press.

Silver, D., Huang, A., Maddison, C. J., Guez, A., Sifre, L., Van Den Driessche, G., Schrittwieser, J., Antonoglou, I., Panneershelvam, V., Lanctot, M., Dieleman, S., Grewe, D., Nham, J., Kalchbrenner, N., Sutskever, I., Lillicrap, T., Leach, M., Kavukcuoglu, K., Graepel, T., & Hassabis, D. (2016). Mastering the game of Go with deep neural networks and tree search. *Nature*, 529(7587), 484–489. DOI: 10.1038/nature16961 PMID: 26819042

Singh, S. P., Wang, Z., & Xu, D. (2018). Knowledge-enhanced hybrid neural networks for recommender systems. In *Proceedings of the 24th ACM SIGKDD International Conference on Knowledge Discovery & Data Mining* (pp. 1933-1942).

Thomason, J., & Strohl, M. (2018). Artificial intelligence and the end of work. In *The Economics of Artificial Intelligence: An Agenda* (pp. 207–226). University of Chicago Press.

Vincent, J. (2020). Google claims 'quantum supremacy' with new supercomputer chip. The Verge. Retrieved from https://www.theverge.com/2020/9/23/21452256/google-quantum-supremacy-sycamore-processor-53-qubits-wsj

Chapter 14
Exploring Bias and Fairness in Machine Learning Algorithms

T. Venkat Narayana Rao
https://orcid.org/0000-0002-1996-1819
Sreenidhi Institute of Science and Technology, India

M. Stephen
Sreenidhi Institute of Science and Technology, India

E. Manoj
Sreenidhi Institute of Science and Technology, India

Bhavana Sangers
https://orcid.org/0009-0005-6134-1081
Sreenidhi Institute of Science and Technology, India

ABSTRACT

When developing and implementing machine learning algorithms, bias and fairness are essential factors to consider. Systematic mistakes or inconsistencies in the data or the algorithmic decision-making process are the root cause of bias in machine learning algorithms. In algorithmic systems, ensuring fairness is crucial to preventing harm and advancing equity and justice. In order to assess the fairness of machine learning algorithms, several measures and criteria have been put forth, such as differential impact, equal opportunity, and demographic parity. This study reviews how these algorithms work and their applications in real-world scenarios such as healthcare, hiring and recruitment, financial services, and recommender systems. In conclusion, in order to guarantee fair results and minimize potential

DOI: 10.4018/979-8-3693-5231-1.ch014

harm, machine learning algorithms must address prejudice and promote fairness. Through the chapter the authors hope the readers will be able to review the fairness on existing algorithms and become responsible AI practitioners by addressing bias and fairness.

1. INTRODUCTION

1.1 Overview of Machine Learning and Its Impact

The application of machine learning algorithms is becoming increasingly important in many aspects of our lives, such as problem decision-making in criminal justice, economics, and healthcare, as well as recommending products and services. With these applications come several problems which have to do with bias and fairness, although algorithms have great promise for added efficiency and effectiveness.

In machine learning which is a subset of artificial intelligence without known programming, computer systems are capable of learning from data and making decisions due to predicting or judgment. Machine learning algorithms would automate some tasks, strengthen business operations and pull-out information that would spark breakthroughs in different areas by deriving patterns and links from huge datasets.

1.2 Introduction to Bias and Fairness in Machine Learning Algorithms

Undoubtedly, a broad spectrum of machine learning core functions, bias, and fairness, touches people, businesses, and communities. The development of a trusted system and application of similar processes in diverse groups require knowledge of and commitment to overcome the same biases and fairness problems.

The following chapter intends to analyse the factors behind the unexpected, biased outcomes of machine learning algorithms, how they impact people's lives, and suggest some possible corrective measures and solutions. With that being said we are certain that all the aforementioned issues will undoubtedly be brought to the forefront and consequently knowledge of the ethical complications in the AI development and application as well as AI systems setup that is more inclusive and egalitarian will be improved.

2. UNDERSTANDING BIAS IN MACHINE LEARNING

In the context of machine learning, a bias is a wide-ranging mistakes or inaccuracies when the process of producing decisions which may belong to diverse sources for example: inadequate information, false assumptions, or algorithmic limitations. It is essential to comprehend the many forms of bias in order to recognize and lessen its influence on algorithmic results. (Towards Data Science, n.d) (Simplilearn, n.d)

2.1 Definition of Bias in Machine Learning

In the context of machine learning, a bias is a wide-ranging mistakes or inaccuracies when the process of producing decisions which may belong to diverse sources for example: inadequate information, false assumptions, or algorithmic limitations. It is essential to comprehend the many forms of bias in order to recognize and lessen its influence on algorithmic results.

2.2 Types of Bias

2.2.1 Data Bias

Machine learning models may not generalize to the target population when the training data used for the models is not a representative cross section of the target population. The probability of inaccurate predictions and negative results due to being overrepresented or underrepresented is higher when samples have specific groups or characteristics overrepresented or underrepresented. (Telus International, 2021) (Label Your Data, 2023)

2.2.2 Algorithmic Bias

Bias is created in the process of either the machine learning algorithm's setup or by its own design. This will express itself in a few forms where biased features are being applied, assumptions which are not granted, and bias-inclined goals during the trainings. Especially in circumstances where the algorithm on which the system is based on has high stakes decisions, algorithmic bias is able to mirror and even intensify the already existing discrimination. (IBM Data and AI Team, 2023)

2.2.3 Societal Bias

Machine learning models are trained by historical data that indexes a wider spectrum of societal prejudices and inequalities as a result of which the algorithm regurgitates the same sort of bias in a different form. Society may be biased towards one group or another and this could be manifested as discrimination, stereotypes, or historical injustices. The societal bias among the marginalized or the minority groups could be a crucial factor that aggravates inequality and keeps the social injustice very much entrenched in the society. (McKinsey & Company, 2019)

2.3 The Role of Historical Biases in Data

The variation of the accuracy of machine learning models and the performance level is highly dependent on the historical biases that exist in training data. The data employed to create algorithms may routinely be the outcome of past injustices, restrictions, and unfairness, which may then bring to light results that are biased which eventually worsen existing imbalance. The development and application of machine learning systems that provide an equal and fair environment for the decision-making process and empower the eradication of the systemic bias require uncovering and removing historical prejudice in data.

We can come with mechanisms that can mitigate prejudice and inclusiveness in machine learning algorithms by knowing the different forms of bias and the source of the bias. We will explore the methods to suppress bias and maintain fairness in algorithmic decision-making through the compensation sections that are to come.

3. THE IMPACT OF BIAS IN MACHINE LEARNING

AI algorithms that show prejudice (even unwittingly), may well result in large fallouts for the people, companies, and society as a whole. This part will look at the ethical concerns of such biases, talk about the consequences of bias and the damages caused due to bias as well as provide current cases and illustrations of real bias examples that practical systems face.

Bias in machine learning algorithms can have a variety of effects on the way they are designed, implemented, and performed. The following defines the ways in which bias impacts several aspects of machine learning algorithms:

3.1 Breakdown of Bias and its Affects

3.1.1 Model Performance and Accuracy

Bias in training data or algorithms which have been designed, may result in unjust and inferior performance of machine learning models. Whether data is used for training or to produce predictions, the issue arises when the data is biased and so does not generalize well to unseen data or even to produce biased predictions. A preferable way to illustrate the point is as such: imaging an algorithm for healthcare which is biased in regard to the training data towards some demographic groups, not accurately predict the health outcomes for the underrepresented population, and thus produce disparities in health care delivery.

3.1.2 Robustness and Reliability

Data-driven AI, instead of being a human-centred phenomenon, may turn to have biased algorithms which may be less dependable and robust because such algorithms might not be able to make correct decisions or predictions in real world scenarios. If a discrepancy between biased recognition which the algorithm recognizes during training and new data appears, the algorithm may have problems to discover decisions, and consequently it makes an error which leads to unreliable results.

3.1.3 Fairness and Equity

Bias in machine learning algorithms could aggravate or exacerbate already-existing unfair treatments thus leading to inequalities in the decision-making processes. For instance, biases supported by algorithms applied in hiring or borrowing systems may lead to systematically favoured certain demographics over others which would end up as discrimination while some will have way more chances. The issue of fairness and equity in machine learning algorithms demand to be solved, as they are the only way of social justice and of mitigation of the negative consequences which can be caused by the bias. (Zong, Z., 2018) (Kaur, A., n,d) (Arvix, n.d)

3.1.4 Interpretability and Transparency

The algorithms established in such a way may be biased in their operations without interpretability and transparency, as a result, they leave ambiguities on how and why particular decisions are made. This will erode trust in machine learning systems if they lack openness, especially in cases where they will be put to use in critical systems like health care and criminal justice systems. Knowing the root of bias and design process includes a trail of mistake observer helps build accountable and transparent AI machine learning systems(T.Venkat Narayana Rao, at el., 2020).

3.1.5 Ethical and Legal Considerations

Machine learning algorithms biasing technology issues serious ethical and legal difficulty about discrimination, privacy, and human right. Bias in algorithms might give rise to breaches of the anti-discrimination laws that are in existence or fall short of the ethical principles like transparency, accountability, and fairness. The reduction of bias demands the all-embracing method that deems both ethical and legal frameworks and guarantees the preservation and consent of human values and rights that undoubtedly should be the core essence of machine learning systems. (Ericsson, 2021) (Harvard Gazette, 2020)

3.2 Case Study 1: Biased Hiring Algorithms

3.2.1 Context

A tech company with most of its profits from IT placed an automation system that filtered the potential candidates for technical job employments by use of ML tech as shown in Figure 1.

3.2.2 Key Issues

Skill ratings of women were regularly rejected by an automatic hiring system that led to considerable disparities in employment rates by technical positions.

This analysis proved the system was biasing against women, assigning negative marks to resumes having phrases associated with females - like 'women's college' and 'women's leadership (T.Venkat Narayana Rao, at el., 2019).

3.2.3 Outcomes

A gender bias in the hiring algorithms led to the perpetuation of gender inequality in tech firms through under-representation of women in technical parts and the denial of women from managerial roles.

The company faced public criticism, and legal disputes which tainted the brand reputation and affected internal work team spirit.

3.2.4 Lessons Learned

In order to bring equal outcomes to all applicants, features selection and assessment criteria are to be carried out mindfully since addressing all other forms of prejudice in hiring algorithms is the ultimate goal.

The potential for unintended biases should be minimized to bring about the trustworthiness of automated recruitment processes therefore, transparency and accountability are critical. (Smith J., & Johnson, K, 2023).

Figure 1. Biased Hiring Scenario

3.3 Case Study 2: Biased Loan Approval Systems

3.3.1 Context

A creditworthiness assessment and a loan approval process that was quicker was made possible by the net of an artificial intelligence system used by the financial institution.

3.3.2 Key Issues

Among the several differences in approval rates noted in the loan approval data of varied economic groups of the society, minorities had a greater number of rejections.

On going investigations revealed the biases in the algorithm's decision mechanism. To be precise, the study found out that the proxies for the creditworthiness which the algorithm used was in proportion to punish the applicants of colour (T.Venkat Narayana Rao, at el., 2020).

3.3.3 Outcomes

There was detrimental effect upon socioeconomic inequalities as those people who were marginalized were rejected from loans which led to them suffering previously because of it, like in home, job, and education obtention.

The financial entity's discriminatory lending policies got noticed by regulators and were voiced in society, therefore its reputation damaged and might have affected their business future.

3.3.4 Lessons Learned

The creation of a strategy which is inclusive of the social and economic environment of lending decisions and incorporates interventions that promote fairness from the algorithmic pipeline start through to the end is required for combating bias in automated loan acceptance systems.

Balanced and all-circular lending acts that encourage banking democracy and economic equity need to be crafted together with the financial institution, the regulators, and community partners. (Smith J., & Johnson, K, 2023) as shown in figure 2.

Figure 2. Biased Loan Approval Systems

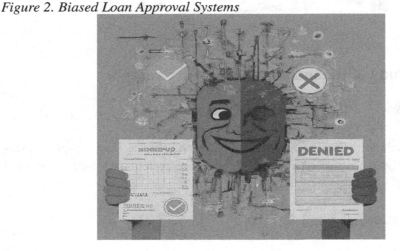

3.4 Case Study 3: Biased Predictive Policing Algorithms

3.4.1 Context

The same law enforcement organization implemented predictive policing algorithms in order to undertake the interventions and to distribute the resources in the high crime areas as shown in figure 3 .

3.4.2 Key Issues

The comparison of the work of law enforcement showed that minorities were the subject of the action of surveillance and police initiatives in crime prediction more often than others.

Hence, other studies showed the bias, which existed in the training of the algorithm and data input and also this leads to discrimination by the police against minority groups and contributed to the racial profiling (T.Venkat Narayana Rao, at el., 2011).

3.4.3 Outcomes

In minority districts, biased predictive policing algorithms across the board worsened police-community relations, causing dissent, arrests based on questionable evidence, and police brutality.

It completely destroyed the sense of justice in the mind of public at large, completely cut the bridge between the police and community and kept reaffirming the circles of anger, hatred, and discrimination over and over again.

3.4.4 Lessons Learned

Getting rid of bias from predictive policing algorithms calls for ingenious (multi-faceted) strategy that covers among others community involvement, algorithmic decision transparency and general fundamental (historical) knowledge about critical policing issues of the society.

Predictive algorithms for policing must possess of the characteristics of transparency, accountability, and being subject to control mechanisms in order to avoid the possibility of racial inequities and human rights breaches.

These studies are narrowly focused and have a uniform writing style that examines in detail the issue of biased algorithms and how people, institutions, and society as a whole have been significantly affected. (Smith J., & Johnson, K, 2023)

Figure 3. Biased Predictive Policing Algorithms

3.5 Case Study 4: Biased Health Diagnosis Algorithms

3.5.1 Context

In the past few years, healthcare providers widely utilize the machine learning algorithms in the diagnosis of the diseases and the designing of the treatment. The systems consisting of such diagnostics, are programmed to analyse the data of a patient, and thereby succeeding in predicting the probability of different health conditions including heart diseases and diabetes.

3.5.2 Key Issues

On the other hand, the usage of attention algorithms for health diagnosis has also shown prevalent biases. Experiments have observed that primarily, these programs underestimated the performance of certain demographic groups especially minority races. By way of illustration, a prediction algorithm purportedly assessing cardiovascular risk was less precise in the case of African-American individuals as compared to the Caucasian ones as illustrated by figure 4. The main reason for this difference was the absence of a big enough data set that captured African American patients. This led to a systemic underdiagnosis and misdiagnosis of patients in cases where the algorithm made predictions, which prove that there is a bias on the part of the machine.

3.5.3 Outcomes

Health diagnosis algorithms disproportionately affected ethnic minorities worsening already existing health disparities which translated to worse health outcomes for minority groups. African Americans were in the majority of cases given delayed and insufficient medical care due to which they developed complications that could have been avoided if they had been treated early. This not only led to worsening of morbidity and increased mortality rates among such patients but also reduced the popularity and trust patients had in healthcare systems. Due to the belief that discrimination and wrong judgment in the doctor is getting bigger day by day between health providers and minority communities, the whole process of public health is getting weaker.

3.6.4 Lessons Learned

The strategy of dealing with bias in health diagnosis algorithms requires complex solutions which may comprise the data diversity training, transparent decision-making in algorithms, and including the community stakeholders in the algorithm development. The primary goal is to ensure and have effective assessment and assessment mechanisms that will measure and monitor the algorithms performance in different demographic groups consistently. Addressing the problems of transparency, accountability, and inclusivity while developing diagnostic tools will mean designing the tools to be re-instilled with trust in medical systems and serve all of the patients.

These studies portray the great influence on individuals and the systems within the society of the algorithms that are biased as one can see which calls for a coordinated effort to address the issue of fairness and equity in machine learning applications.

Figure 4. Biased Health Diagnosing Algorithms

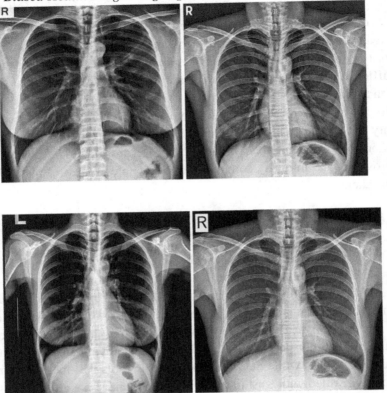

3.5 Discussion on Societal Implications

In addressing the societal consequences of bias in Machine Learning (ML) algorithms, the consequences brought to the fore abound. Innocently, algorithmic, as well as evaluation and data bias, can result in doing extremely unfair activities which respectively reasons cannot be given to certain group. For example, an algorithm that is biased against the hiring process might miss qualified candidates from marginalized communities and such a practice could continue to feed into an unequal society. An unbiased prediction model for criminal suspicious of policing, could direct its significant attention to some part of the area, resulting in more policing in that neighbourhood. On the contrary, it may enable the practice of fairness in ML in favour of equity and inclusivity. When we ensure fairness of algorithms, we can then swiftly build the systems which when interacting with people, treat all individuals in the fair manner, taking their backgrounds into consideration. On the one hand, but to say fairness in ML systemic complexity goes hand in hand with its intricate nature that demands appropriate attention to be given to the socio-cultural reality where these algorithms function. It's not only a change of algorithms technique; it's also about comprehending the social reality that embodies in the data that machine learning algorithms feed on. (Hassani, B. K., 2021) (Shah, M., & Sureja, N, 2024)

3.5.1 Reinforcement of Inequities

Attempting equity and diversity instead of biased algorithms can result in the worsening of social cleavages, and continuation of a systematic discrimination against the underprivileged groups.

3.5.2 Erosion of Trust

Bias in algorithms does not only endanger trust but also poses a great threat to consumers, institutions, and technology. When people have the perception that algorithms are biased, they may become very doubtful about the justice and correctness of the judgements which are algorithms' results. This kind of mistrust can account for the weaponization of innovations and spoil healthy equation of absorbance and adoption of new technologies. Certainly, if a hiring algorithm is screened in by discrimination against a number of groups, the credibility of the entire recruitment process might be called into question, despite being fair overall. This brigade of doubt can go worse as it can be expanded to cover the credibility of other institutions which heavily rely on algorithmic decisions. Thus, individuals may feel more resistant to take part in these technological advances, supposing technology only leads to built-in and mistrust-worthy bias. This low confidence can deter efforts to develop technologies further and consequently undermine the benefits that diverse societies could gain from technological advances. Additionally, a widespread stereotype of biased algorithms can prompt regulations to be made stronger and pertinent where responsible and well-governed development could be as well slowed down.

3.5.3 Normalization of Bias

Algorithms biased lead to a slow but steady process of mental conditioning, creating a groundwork for preconceptions and perpetuating stereotypes about selective groups and localities. When algorithms tend to exhibit bias, the biases present are commonly perpetuated as well as normalized. Such an algorithm could be applied for instance in predictive policing in a way that it would by and large target specific communities and as a consequence would continue to reproduce negative stereotypes and amplify the view that members of these groups are perhaps more involved in criminal activities. After a period, this attitude could instead normalize the discrimination as the unfair practices are accepted and become a common factor in the socio-cultural norms and behaviours. Persistent links to algorithmic discrimination impact the psyche such that they create desensitization of persons who get used to someone discrimination and ultimately start believing that discrimination is normal. This normalization can in addition closely merge the idea of the everyday injustice, therefore revealing a society in which it seems to be impossible to root out the causes of discrimination and indefinitely establish equality. However, biased algorithms can impact public narrative and form social opinion which further promote polarization and segmentation in the community. Additionally, biased AI systems can fuel a continuous cycle of unfairness and inequality where it is difficult to overcome these biased practices.

3.5.4 Legal and Ethical Concerns

To suppress within the algorithms the discrimination and keep vulnerable communities safe, the biased algorithms trigger legal and ethical dimensions about justice, duties, and individual rights. These apprehensions have been responsible for open requests for regulation and algorithmic transparency.

On this note, elimination of prejudice and the achievement of fairness in the machine learning algorithms becomes critical for the systems to avoid violation of ethical standards in algorithmic decision-making and to enable inclusivity and trust.

The next part of the section addresses the consequences associated with biased algorithms on humans and neighbourhoods. It also calls for the introduction of ethics and methods of improving fairness in machine learning activities. (Hamilton, R.H., & Davison, H.K, 2022) (Prainsack, B., & Steindl, E, 2022)

4. FAIRNESS IN MACHINE LEARNING

For fairness to be ensured, the algorithmic decision-making processes must be transparent, accountable, and impartial, hence a concern which must be addressed while designing and implementing the machine learning algorithms. The fairness of such systems can only be achieved if we take great care in considering the different dimensions that make for fairness, as well as we come up with specific approaches of fostering and measuring fairness in algorithms. (Coursera Staff, 2023) (Zong, Z., 2018)

4.1 Definition of Fairness

The idea of justice, equality, and non- discrimination during the algorithmic processes is addressed by fairness in machine learning. It involves avoiding strong positive and negative outcomes for individuals or groups due to the biased results of machine learning algorithms which are informed by sensitive attributes like race, gender, or social class.

4.2 Different Notions of Fairness

4.2.1 Statistical Parity

The algorithm distribution predictions should be constant homogeneous amongst all arranged test group demographics to achieve statistical parity, which is often referred to as demographic parity. Try describing as: It would also imply that the rejected loan applications, or unemployment, should be dispersed among different population groups.

4.2.2 Equal Opportunity

The provision of equal access promises that, for people from all the demographic groups who have same given qualifications or attributes, the chances of undesirable outcomes like not getting recruited for a job or not getting a loan, are diminish. The purpose of this universality principle is to get rid of unequal performance on the protected characteristic but to allow few variances on the reasonable grounds.

4.2.3 Predictive Parity

Equalized opportunities, also called predictive parity, which refer to the need that the algorithm's forecasts are as accurate for all demographic groups. This means that the probability of wrong classification of a person from this group into the dementia state and a healthy person in the same group into a dementia patient is the same.

4.2.4 Individual Fairness

Individual fairness foresight which is the difference of people who group in the related categories equal is the main component of equality. It means extracting the important attributes that individuals have in common and then using the similar scores for similar people when the algorithm predicts or gives a result for them. (Das Jui, T., & Rivas, P, 2024) (Makhlouf, K., et a. 2022)

4.3 The Importance of Fairness in Algorithmic Decision-Making

Creating trust, in turn, requires fairness in order to account for machine learning algorithms which might be adversely used to perpetuate or widen any prior inequalities. Algorithms based on machine learning can offer chance for fairer outcomes in case concerning many sub-groups by encouraging same treatment, which sometimes leads to removal of biases and discrimination and improvement of inclusiveness.

The upcoming few sections look at a few of the strategies and tactics like pre-treatment, in-processing and so on a fairness and bias reduction plan in the machine learning algorithms.\

5. APPROACHES TO MITIGATING BIAS AND ENSURING FAIRNESS

Effectively addressing fairness and reduction in bias in machine learning algorithms needs more than just a single tactic to be used at each stage of the machine learning pipeline. In other words, different measures and techniques should be considered and used at each stage. Fairness worries can be used to eliminate potential biases and have the result of producing outcomes related to a variety of populations by being considered at every stage from design to development, and implementation of technological systems based on machine learning. (Mehrabhi, N., et al. 2019)

5.1 Pre-Processing Techniques

The pre-processing techniques play a crucial role in the method of ridding the machine learning algorithms of bias. The approach involves routine data management - cleaning, normalization, and transformation - to make the training data representatively and impartially. Methods like oversampling, under sampling and SMOTE can be applied to handle the class imbalance (a factor of biasedness). Relevance of the input features also can be improved, using the feature selection and transformation methods, in order to address the bias interference of unrelated and repetitive features. Therefore, data upscaling becomes an indispensable aspect of the beginning processes pertaining to setting up a fair method of ML development.

5.1.1 Data Preprocessing

Data preprocessing is an inevitable component of machine learning algorithms, and it is more necessary to reduce machine learning algorithms biases. It means making raw data to be in proper form and shape before you can use its format in a machine learning model. Methods such as reassigning values, reweighting samples, and even generating artificial data could aid in rectifying the inequality of the information set. This procedure, however, helps to make sure that the data is general and fair, thereby minimizing bias in the end outputs of the model. This way, data cleaning is a keystone stage in the development of ML algorithms which promote fairness.

5.1.2 Algorithmic Adjustments

Many of the algorithmic adjustments can diminish bias through change of training approach. Techniques such as reweighting and resampling, which are inclusive methods that allow underrepresented data to make a greater contribution. Redistribution comprises of supplying more weight to raw data from underrepresented groups in comparison to more emphasis of those that are overrepresented, such an approach guarantees a fair learning process. Resampling includes an adjustment to your dataset therefore the model has instants of underrepresented, and consequently you can get rid of bias in your model. These changes are beneficial for creating equal algorithms that more accurately represent the populations of minorities, thus there is a decreased chance for a biased decision in algorithms in making.

5.2 In-Processing Techniques

Introducing fairness elements into the learning process in a direct way requires modifying the algorithm itself to include the fairness element, which is one of the processing in-processing techniques. These procedures attain high accuracy and performance scores while the algorithm computes for good biases in prediction and conclusion.

5.2.1 Fairness-Aware Algorithms

Among the main advancements in the field of machine learning with a lot of impact is fairness-aware algorithms, developed to remove bias and guarantee equality. These algorithms have considerations of fairness and equity built into all stages including design, training, and actual decision-making processes in an effort to keep bias in check and all populations at par. An alternative approach is to alter the learning process to make the model take fairness considerations into account, such as avoiding the formation of a demographic parity or ensuring the equal opportunity, into account during model training. A different approach is to create post-processing models which would serve to cut out or diminish bias in the results of the models. The 'fairness-aware' algorithms that are highly demanded in areas like the healthcare, finance, and the justice system are mainly to cater for the societal concerns out of discrimination and inequality. With the advancement of research on the fair-aware algorithm further, this design can offer a significant contribution for the achievement of fair and inclusive machine learning systems that carries principles of fairness and justice. (Pan, W., et al. 2021) (Shah, M., et al. 2024)

5.2.2 Adversarial Debiasing

There is a new trend called adversarial debiasing, that attempts to address bias issues with the ML. It is a method comprising training the model so as to anticipate the prediction while the adversary – at the same time – trains to find out possible biases in those predictions. The purpose of this is that the model predicts a fair decision, and the opponent cannot observe any kind of bias. This approach implements a dynamic and robust mechanism, which helps in equalizing the opportunities to avoid the biased algorithms. It proves to be a solid tool in the struggle for unbiased ML algorithms.

5.3 Post-processing Techniques

As the goal is to justify and level the already trained machine learning models, postprocessing methods make changes to the model outputs after the training is complete. These procedures are meant to guarantee an equal outcome for the various population groups by the specific forecast threshold adjustment and model calibration.

5.3.1 Calibration Methods

Ensuring the model's predicted probabilities or scores reflect the fairness criteria that are set, calibration methods yield that they are sampled from normal distribution. For balancing false positive or false negative rates across different demographic groups, calibration methods modify the model's output.

5.3.2 Fairness Metrics Evaluation

The assessment of fairness metrics uses metrics beneficial like discrepancy effect, equally chances, or demographic equality such that model performance may be evaluated. These measures, hence, aid in the process of determining the extent of justice and bias in algorithmic decision-making and bring about preferable alteration measures.

We can further develop machine learning systems which are not only fully functional and effective but also traceable, understandable, and fair, using pre-, in-, and post-processing methods. We will explain the moral aspect and problems with bias and fairness in machine learning as well as ways to face this issue in the follow parts of the essay. (Castlenovo, A., et al. 2021) (Barocas, S., et al. 2019)

6. ETHICAL CONSIDERATIONS AND CHALLENGES

We cannot solve the problem of prejudice and bias in data and algorithms without considering the moral issues and difficulties involved. Machine learning systems, which are designed, applied, and enforced considering ethical issues. With this, it is ensured that the tenets of integrity, equity, and justice are adhered to. (UK Statistics Authority, 2021) (Vayena, E., et al. 2018)

6.1 Ethical Considerations in Designing and Deploying Machine Learning Systems:

All steps in the machine learning process – which includes data collection and preprocessing and model building, deploying, and evaluating – are determined by ethical issues. Important moral considerations consist of:

6.1.1 Transparency and Interpretability

Makes sure that the machine learning model transparency and interpretability levels are high enough for the users and public trust and accountability in their deployment. It means to render algorithms' inner mechanisms impervious to everyone involved: developers, users, as well as regulators. Such a transparency liberates the chances of unearthing and correcting injustice and prejudice within the algorithms. Human comprehensibility, however, refers to the fact that those decisions made by such models do not defy human comprehension. It becomes vital for these cases of critical applications, including the healthcare system, financial system, and criminal justice, when knowing the justification behind the algorithm's conclusion can influence the lives of people in a big way. By setting transparency and interpretability as their priorities, companies can, therefore, have a better chance to see new technologies embraced but in an ethical way. Furthermore, it is a means to serve as watchdogs over and prospective algorithm manipulations, improving their interaction and effectiveness.

6.1.2 Accountability and Responsibility

Determining precisely what roles and responsibilities one will have in generating and applying machine learning systems is all-important for safeguarding and handling the risks carried by algorithmic decision-making. This is done by designating roles/responsibilities for each task related to ML lifecycle starting from data collection till model training, deployment, and maintenance. A clear framework which outlines who responsible for assessing the working of algorithms and correcting problems caused by algorithmic bias or inaccuracy should be established. Furthermore, it's important to have in place procedures which could help to settle defaults and errors that could occur. This involves developing policies for auditing algorithms, handling complaints from users and the processes for change and rebuild of models where necessary. The existence of clear accountability and responsibility frameworks not only improves the reliability and credibility of machine learning systems, but it also avoids the possible impediments where negative effects can be efficiently addressed. Through creating a culture of responsibility, industries can maintain a safer environment for the misappropriation of technology and so promote the implementation of machine learning technologies that are ethical, fair, and robust.

6.1.3 Privacy and Data Protection

Privacy and data anonymization in ML are very important in order to allow bias and discriminations in AI algorithms. The models trained by these algorithms commonly are based on personal data that can include sensitive info as well. This secure data will strengthen people's faith in ML systems which make them confident- using such technologies. Additionally, there are differential privacy ones that offer ways to prevent overfitting to particular data points so as to limit bias. These requirements, therefore, are not the only ways of safeguarding against bias in machine learning but are just one of the tools for fight against it.

6.2 Challenges in Achieving Fairness

Many obstacles need to be overcome in order to eliminate bias and advance fairness in machine learning algorithms:

6.2.1 Trade-offs between Fairness and Accuracy

Balancing the trade-offs between fairness and accuracy in algorithmic decision-making, as optimizing for fairness may sometimes lead to decreased accuracy or increased complexity. Addressing the dilemma of algorithmic decision-making's accuracy and justice by offering different choices, which in one case may prove to be more complex than others, while in the other case, accuracy may be sacrificed for justice.

6.2.2 Transparency and Interpretability

Transparency and interpretability are essentially in resolving fairness and bias appropriate for Machine Learning (ML) models. The transparency means to show how the machine learning works, further, the interpretability comes following the reasoning of the model's decisions. These two biases can be recognized and corrected. With the use of them, a citizen can see the process of a decision coming to be, voice their disagreement with any mismatch between the gadget's ethos and the ethical norms, and facilitate that the algorithms are in line with the society values. Therefore, they contribute significantly in establishing reliable and ethically appropriate machine learning technologies.

6.2.3 Domain-specific Challenges

The challenges of dealing with bias and impartiality in ML algorithms which are unique for field specific reason further accentuate the discriminatory nature of these algorithms. Such as in health care, when data with biases meant that the diseases were not appropriately diagnosed or was given improper treatment recommendations. In financials, algorithms with bias may cause financial activities to be not right. Every domain needs unique plan to exclude the bias and the ethical, legal, and societal community concerns in that specific field should be considered when it is being formulated. This implies that in addition to problem solving, both laws and political institutions are needed for a specific area to ensure fairness.

6.3 Ethical Guidelines and Best Practices

The practice of scripting ethical rules and remediation procedures related to creation, application, and assessment is being done by many organizations and efforts here in order the handle ethical problems and obstacles on machine learning systems. These guidelines, which intending to provide an ethical basis for AI advancement and governance, focus on values, such as justice, openness, transparency, and inclusiveness.

The application of algorithms in human decision-making can be rightfully, meticulous, and transparent by including ethical considerations in the design and use of Machine Learning Systems. The policy to be put forward will be encouraging therefore creating an equal ground for all people, individuals, and communities.

The concluding section of this chapter reflects on actions to implement some ethical principles of AI in practice along with paths of research into machine learning bias and fairness of the future.

7. EXAMPLES OF FAIRNESS-ENHANCING INTERVENTIONS

In this project, we not only try to make examples transparent and cases where bias or unfairness appeared, but we also show an initiative implemented aimed at furthering justice in machine learning algorithms. Among these instances could be:

A. Algorithmic engineering principles aiming for fairness.
B. Tackling the question of how to detect bias when data is fuelling algorithmic systems.
C. Community-based forming battling with algorithms.
D. Joint attempts for realizing justified and responsible AI systems through cooperation of academicians, industrial experts, and the legislature.

This will have the power of making us get a clear picture of the strengths and weaknesses of contemporary techniques in bias reduction and fairness in educational algorithms and show areas we must carry out more research and act.

It will wrap up the chapter during which it will examine specific suggestions for having ethics in AI, as well as other perspectives and trends in the field of machine learning aiming at studying bias and fairness.

8. FUTURE DIRECTIONS AND CONCLUSION

Quite a few new techniques and launching of novel investigations are changing the field of machine learning algorithms to be more without biases and fairness, as a future. We will sum up these different directions and outline the main thoughts in this last section with the highlight on how it is necessary to ensure fairness and reduce bias in machine learning algorithms.

8.1 Emerging Trends and Future Directions

The field of bias and fairness in machine learning settings is driven by developing new methodologies that aim to avoid and eliminate bias in the algorithms' implementation. The application of various techniques such as those used in interdisciplinary fields like ethics, law, and sociology becomes another trend, which is used during the development of machine learning systems. Added to this, we now see a trend involving the introduction of the concepts of the algorithmic fairness and reliable ways to detect and measure bias in the machine learning models. In addition, progress in things like interpretability and transparency techniques sits on the improvement of public understanding of how algorithms choose what they do, and of possible sources of bias. The joint work of researchers, policy-makers, and private-sector actors should be central to finding solutions to the multi-layer challenges of the machine learning and promote the use of the forthcoming generation of AI systems that would be ethically and socially acceptable.

8.1.1 Explainable AI (XAI)

The XAI is all about being more transparent and understandable in machine learning algorithm annotation of the algorithms process of decision-making. Through XAI, technologies that are based on algorithms explain how the automatic conclusions are obtained so as to identify and rectify the discrimination of the models. It allows actors to recognize the variables having an impact on algorithm output, resulting to a fairer allocation of the formulated punishment. Given the XAI's role in this respect in holding the ML systems accountable and their dependability, it stands out more especially in those areas where transparency and fairness dominate.

8.1.2. Algorithmic Fairness Across Domains

A multitude of future studies will explore the topic of algorithmic fairness in multiple fields including recruiting, healthcare, finance, and criminal justice, to name but a few. This holistic strategy will work to foster the creation of fairness indices specific to the domain while addressing the unique bias considerations as well as Gray areas in fairness.

8.1.3. Fairness in Reinforcement Learning

It is this concern over unjust outcomes in reinforcement learning algorithms that must be resolved, as these systems become more widespread in autonomous systems and decision-making processes. So as to ensure that equitable results are enjoyed in dynamic and uncertain contexts researchers will turn their focus to expansion of fair reinforcement learning models.

8.1.4. Ethical AI Governance and Regulation

A few voices have raised concerns about the lack of regulatory control over AI systems while a lot of discussions have been held about the ethical implications of AI technologies. Second effort will be concentrated on drafting ethical AI protocols, norms, and legal frameworks with the goals of fairness, visibility, and objectivity in the decision-making process.

8.2 Conclusion

To sum up, all the elements related building, providing, and handle the machine learning algorithms rely on fairness and bias. As well as rolling up the inequality level and no credibility of algorithmic decision-making processes, biased algorithms build up undesirable impressions on the people, groups, and overall society.

Through the cross-area proficiency of researchers, practitioners, policymakers, and other influencers, machine bias can be reduced to make the machine learning technology is fair. Fair frameworks include eliminating of biases, providing access to transparent information and equal result for all people are the basics underlining AI development process.

In other to make breakthrough in the aspect of bias and fairness e promotion of the union of ethical AI principles and interdepartmental collaborations are required. We will pay most close attention to machine learning technologies that though ensure justice, fairness, and human dignity, but do not compromise on these values in the process of AI development. In addition, we would not hesitate to involve people from diverse backgrounds and strive to develop AI that is responsive.

Thank you for taking the time to be here as we are set for some deep digging into the multifaceted and many-shaded bias and fairness aspects in machine learning algorithms. Indeed, this future world could also be artificial intelligence (AI) one, whereby system have not only intelligence but also ethics, justice, and responsibility.

9. LITERACY REVIEW

The chapter is the definition of bias and fairness in machine learning algorithm is useful in the evolving narrative of artificial intelligence to understand the interconnection between technology and ethics. It will become clear that this chapter only offers clarity, good advice, and comprehensive information on the fundamental subjects of bias and justice, which should inspire hope for anyone who finds themselves lost in the treacherous AI research.

9.1 Chapter Summary

To begin with, the first part of the chapter is devoted to building up the context – the essential roles of bias and fairness in machine learning models. It explains how, as much as they may appear impartial, when algorithms that underpin them are not built and managed well, a system continues to perpetuate past injustices and prejudices. Every person who is creating or using AI technologies in any position has to be aware of such knowledge.

The chapter makes a good attempt at illustrating the real-world implications of the use of an unfair algorithm with detailed case studies. Such illustrations clearly depict how bias impacts or affects people and the various dynamics involved, from a recruitment process that tends to offer preferences to a certain category of the population to the loan approval bias against the minority. What the story underscores, therefore, is the need to be very careful and ethically inclined when developing algorithms.

The chapter focuses on the issue of fairness and gives a detailed discussion of many definitions and approaches. This presents the reader with the policy of balances and challenges that come with the quest for justice and in so doing makes the reader understand that this is a problem. Various concepts of fairness are defined, and this is useful when applying a comprehensive approach to the development of fair AI systems.

9.2 Reader Benefits

In my opinion, readers can benefit a lot from this chapter, which helps readers obtain the information and resource to fight prejudice and work for the fairness of machine learning. It also assures that individuals reading from different sections of the globe; from the developers of AI, policymakers to the executives understand the various facets of bias and justice by breaking down complex ideas into simple parts.

Specific and achievable action-based instructions for actual steps for the reduction of bias are clearly spelled out. Some of the methodologies that are explained to the readers are fairness-aware machine learning algorithms and pre-, in-, and post-processing paradigms. The techniques involved in bias detection and reduction allow readers to reduce bias in their projects and therefore develop AI systems that are less bias.

9.3 Insights Provided

The chapter offers the following significant discoveries that broaden the reader's comprehension of bias and fairness in machine learning:

9.3.1 Comprehensive Understanding of Bias

The chapter helps the readers make the different manifestations of bias in the different types of AI systems apparent and how bias ubiquitous by characterising and categorising different types.

9.3.2 Implications for the Real World

The readers are able to be acquainted with practical examples of how biased algorithms can be used in real-life scenarios and imposed on people or society as a whole.

9.3.3 Trade-offs and Fairness Metrics

One reason for that is that the comparison of different fairness metrics enables readers to grasp the challenges and choices that should not be accomplished to increase the level of fairness because of their nature and the fact that they are still under development.

9.3.4 Useful Mitigation Ways

There is also practical information that the readers can use to achieve the fairness and equity in their own work on AI by presenting how to minimize the bias.

9.3.5 Ethical Considerations

Thus, the use of ethical concepts enables the author to make people adopt multi-faceted and ethical views of the world. This underlines the importance of the values of openness, accountability, and inclusion in AI scholarship.

9.3.6 Future Directions

Based on new trends and ideas for further studies, readers are offered a future-oriented outlook that pushes them to continue the innovations' support and contribute to the moral uplifting of artificial intelligence.

Finally, every person involved in artificial intelligence reckons "Bias and Fairness in Machine Learning Algorithms" necessary. It does this by showing the individuals how they can design fairer and more just AI systems for themselves, urging them to do something in the process. Its comprehensive roadmap towards tackling bias issues affecting this sector is developed upon a blend between theory, practical strategies, and ethical dilemmas.

REFERENCES

Albaroudi, E., Mansouri, T., & Alameer, A. (2024). A Comprehensive Review of AI Techniques for Addressing Algorithmic Bias in Job HiringAI, 5(1)1.

Algorithmic Mind. (n.d.). Understanding Bias in Machine Learning. Retrieved from https://algorithmicmind.org/bias-in-machine-learning

Arxiv. (n.d.). Bias Mitigation for Machine Learning Classifiers: A Comprehensive Survey. Retrieved from https://arxiv.org/pdf/2207.07068v2

Barocas, S., Hardt, M., & Narayanan, A. (2019). Fairness and Machine Learning.

Castelnovo, A., Crupi, R., Greco, G., & Regoli, D. (2021). The Zoo of Fairness Metrics in Machine Learning.

Coursera Staff. (2023). *What Is Machine Learning Fairness?* What You Need to Know. Coursera.

Das Jui, T., & Rivas, P. (2024). Fairness issues, current approaches, and challenges in machine learning modelsInternational Journal of Machine Learning and Cybernetics Ericsson. (2021). AI bias and human rights: Why ethical AI matters. Retrieved from https://www.ericsson.com/en/blog/2021/11/ai-bias-what-is-it

Data, I. B. M., & Team, A. I. (2023). Shedding light on AI bias with real world examples. Retrieved from https://www.ibm.com/blog/shedding-light-on-ai-bias -with-real-world-examples

DataCamp. (2023). What is Algorithmic Bias? Retrieved from https://www.datacamp .com/blog/what-is-algorithmic-bias

Hamilton, R. H., & Davison, H. K. (2022). *Legal and Ethical Challenges for HR in Machine Learning. Employee Responsibilities and Rights Journal*, 34, 19–39.

Harvard Gazette. (2020). Ethical concerns mount as AI takes bigger decision-making role. Retrieved from https://news.harvard.edu/gazette/story/2020/10/ethical-concerns -mount-as-ai-takes-bigger-decision-making-role

Hassani, B. K. (2021). Societal bias reinforcement through machine learning: A credit scoring perspective. *AI and Ethics*, 1(3), 239–247. DOI: 10.1007/s43681-020-00026-z

Kaur, A. (n.d.). Mitigating Bias in AI Algorithms: Identifying, and Ensuring Responsible AI. Retrieved from https://leena.ai/blog/mitigating-bias-in-ai

Label Your Data. (2023). Bias in Machine Learning. Retrieved from https://labelyourdata.com/articles/bias-in-machine-learning

Makhlouf, K., Zhioua, S., & Palamidessi, C. (2022). Machine learning fairness notions: Bridging the gap with real-world applications arXiv preprint arXiv:2006.16745.

McKinsey & Company. (2019). Tackling bias in artificial intelligence (and in humans). Retrieved from https://www.mckinsey.com/featured-insights/artificial-intelligence/tackling-bias-in-artificial-intelligence-and-in-humans

Mehrabi, N., Morstatter, F., Saxena, N., Lerman, K., & Galstyan, A. (2019). A Survey on Bias and Fairness in Machine Learning arXiv preprint arXiv:1908.09635.

Pan, W., Cui, S., Bian, J., Zhang, C., & Wang, F. (2021). Explaining Algorithmic Fairness Through Fairness-Aware Causal Path Decomposition.

Pickl.ai. (n.d.). Algorithmic Bias and How to Avoid It- A Complete Guide. Retrieved from https://www.pickl.ai/blog/algorithmic-bias-and-how-to-avoid-it-a-complete-guide

Prainsack, B., & Steindl, E. (2022). Legal and Ethical Aspects of Machine Learning: Who Owns the Data? In Artificial Intelligence/Machine Learning in Nuclear Medicine and Hybrid Imaging (pp. 191–201).

Shah, M., & Sureja, N. (2024). *A Comprehensive Review of Bias in Deep Learning Models: Methods*. Impacts, and Future Directions.

Simplilearn. (n.d.). Bias and Variance in Machine Learning. Retrieved from https://www.simplilearn.com/tutorials/machine-learning-tutorial/bias-and-variance

Smith, J., & Johnson, K. (2023a). Case Study 1: Biased Hiring Algorithms. In K. White & L. Brown (Eds.), Advancements in Machine Learning Applications in Hiring Processes (pp. 45-48). Publisher X.

Smith, J., & Johnson, K. (2023b). Case Study 2: Biased Loan Approval Systems. In K. White & L. Brown (Eds.), Advancements in Artificial Intelligence Applications in Financial Institutions (pp. 87-90). Publisher X.

Smith, J., & Johnson, K. (2023c). Case Study 3: Biased Predictive Policing Algorithms. In K. White & L. Brown (Eds.), Advancements in Artificial Intelligence Applications in Law Enforcement (pp. 123-126). Publisher X.

Springer. (2024). Designing Against Bias: Identifying and Mitigating Bias in Machine. Retrieved from https://link.springer.com/chapter/10.1007/978-3-031-47715-7_28

TELUS International. (2021). Seven Types Of Data Bias In Machine Learning. Retrieved from https://www.telusinternational.com/insights/ai-data/article/7-types -of-data-bias-in-machine-learning

Towards Data Science. (n.d.). Algorithm Fairness: Sources of Bias. Retrieved from https://towardsdatascience.com/algorithm-fairness-sources-of-bias

UK Statistics Authority. (2021). Ethical considerations in the use of Machine Learning for research and statistics.

Vayena, E., Blasimme, A., & Cohen, I. G. (2018). Machine learning in medicine: Addressing ethical challenges. PLOS Medicine.

Venakt Narayana Rao, Govardhan, & Jahangir Badashah. (2011). Statistical analysis for performance evaluation of image segmentation quality using edge detection algorithms. International Journal of Advanced Networking and Applications, 3(3), 1184,.

Venkat Narayana Rao & Manasa. (2019). Artificial neural networks for soil quality and crop yield prediction using machine learning. International Journal on Future Revolution in Computer Science, 14.

Venkat Narayana Rao & Reddy. (2019). Prediction Of Soil Quality Using Machine Learning Techniques. International Journal of Scientific & Technology Research, 8(11), 1309-1313.

Venkat Narayana Rao, T., & Sharma, L. (2020). Towards smart world: homes to cities using internet of things. CRC Press.

Venkat Narayana Rao, Unnisa, & Sreni. (2020). Medicine recommendation system based on patient reviews. Int J Sci Technol Res, 9, 3308-12.

Venkat Narayana Rao, T., & Yellu, K. R. (2016). Automatic Safety Home Bell System with Message Enabled Features. *International Journal of Science.Engineering and Computer Technology*, 6, 10.

Zhong, Z. (2018). A Tutorial on Fairness in Machine Learning. Towards Data Science. Retrieved from https://towardsdatascience.com/a-tutorial-on-fairness-in -machine-learning-3ff8ba1040cb

Zhong, Z. (2018). *A Tutorial on Fairness in Machine Learning*. Towards Data Science.

Chapter 15
Global Adoption of Artificial Intelligence in the Manufacturing Industries

Evariste Gatabazi
The Open University of Tanzania, Tanzania

Maad M. Mijwil
https://orcid.org/0000-0002-2884-2504
Al-Iraqia University, Iraq

Mostafa Abotaleb
https://orcid.org/0000-0002-3442-6865
South Ural State University, Russia

Saganga Kapaya
The Open University of Tanzania, Tanzania

ABSTRACT

This study reviewed a total of 3171 published articles, mainly from 1992-2024. The review was performed using scientifically cited and indexed databases, namely Dimensions, Web Science, Elsevier Scopus, and Google Scholar. This study demonstrates how AI technologies, such as computer vision and system learning, may revolutionize industrial efficiency, productivity, and satisfactory control. Superior algorithms, neural networks, and big data analytics are integrated to optimize manufacturing strategies and enable intelligent decision-making, which is where the innovation lies. Also, it was found that building workforce capacity through

DOI: 10.4018/979-8-3693-5231-1.ch015

collaborations and customized training programs can help close the skills gap, while improving cybersecurity and implementing efficient data management frameworks can help with privacy issues. However, despite the growing body of literature on AI packages, studies specializing in AI embracing on the organizational level stay restrained.

1. INTRODUCTION

A great deal of innovative ideas on how to improve the machinery and equipment used in the manufacturing industry have been proposed, including smart factories, robots, Artificial Intelligence AI, Industry 4.0, and the Internet of Things (IoT), just to name a few (Munirathinam, 2020). The term " AI" has become an umbrella term that encompasses a variety of tasks, methods, models, and learning. Specifically, in manufacturing, Lee and Yoon (2021) found that AI has a wide range of applications, which have resulted in enhancements including cost reduction, resource optimization, and process control improvement (Kim et al., 2022).

Government agencies from participating countries all acknowledge the importance of these emerging technologies in order to be competitive and to have sustainable participation in the world market. AI, including cognition, machine learning, and robotics technology in particular, is one of those key technologies identified by government agencies as the "easiest to adopt" and "most dynamic" emerging technology (Buchmeister et al., 2019). The adoption process of AI begins with the "capture phase," where derived data in production and operating processes using sensors, vision, and other types of equipment are obtained (Cascón-Morán et al., 2024). The "model" is then obtained from the captured data by machine learning with a type of neural network (Tuama et al., 2016). The resulting model is then mapped to "intent" by the implementation-related creation method, and the production process is adjusted according to this intent (Drchal et al., 2019).

The exponential growth of AI in the technology marketplace represents a current-day renaissance of manufacturers' capability building (Khan, 2025). Since the invention of the wheel, humankind has been in the business of developing tools and techniques that facilitate trade, industry, and commerce. Conservatively, the first industrial revolution was marked by the invention of the mechanized weaving loom in 1784. Others would argue that it began around 1712 with Newcomen's steam engine or later with James Watt's improvements to it in 1765 (Mijwil et al., 2024). A key characteristic of this first industrial revolution was the application of mechanical engineering principles to provide mechanical motion to utilitarian human tools. Subsequent industrial technology revolutions applied principles of electrical, chemical, and energy engineering to further enhance the end-to-end process of value creation via mining, farming, design, testing, recycling, maintenance, and all the other industrial operations embraced under the modern scope of the term "manufacturing".

Until recently, silicon-based computational technology, the fuel for today's AI revolution, had only marginal direct application to this broad cross-section of move-make-mend business enterprise (Sahai & Rath, 2021). The main thrust of everyday AI technology, as far as tool fabrication of basic machines is concerned, is the large-scale use of iterative computational procedures to converge on more effective designs for devices such as wireless handsets, vacuum cleaners, and high-performance automobiles. This is not to say that computers, computer networks, and computer-controlled robotics for manufacturing are themselves unimportant recent advances. High-speed microcomputers have been a core technology supporting the world's automated product assembly lines for the last quarter-century (McCallum, 2017). Material and component sorting systems in manufacturing plants, supply chain management via software, and systems in product engineering have made computers the very cornerstone of modern-day factory operations. Post-manufacture, there are simulation tools that deliver greatly improved capability to predict potential product or part failure at the component design stage (Turyasingura et al., 2024). Such predictive information is of great value in the ongoing refinement and enhancement of overall product functionality. The current state of AI technologies used in manufacturing industries, benefits of AI adoption, challenging issues and future research directions.

2. METHODOLOGY

2.1 Identification of Studies

This study used a literature search and synthesis of pertinent peer-reviewed papers and associated material as its methodological technique. A literature search from 1992-2024 was performed using scientifically cited and indexed databases, namely Dimensions, Web Science, Elsevier Scopus, and Google Scholar. In addition, the inclusion and exclusion criteria, peer-reviewed papers and institutional publications were used in this study in line with the study under investigation, while unpublished sources and other work that was out of the study scope were excluded from the study. As a result, over 3171 publications, government reports, AI reports, and conference proceedings were examined. E-books from the World Bank, policy papers, and published student essays were all retrieved, with 47 of them being evaluated and used in this work.

2.2 Searching Strategy

In addition, the searching strategy used included Boolean combinations like AI AND industries, SMEs AND AI, challenges AND opportunities, and AI OR machine learning AND deep learning to capture variations. Phrases such as "AI adoption in manufacturing," "AI-driven innovation in industries," and "AI for industrial growth" target specific aspects. Broader queries include AI AND entrepreneurship, AI AND business innovation, and digital transformation AND SMEs. Specific topics like AI AND customer experience in innovations, AI AND supply chain management in manufacturing industries, and AI AND marketing strategies for industries are explored.

3. LITERATURE

3.1 Artificial Intelligence Technologies in Manufacturing

3.1.1 Introduction

AI technologies, over the years, have evolved to reach a point where they can deliver faster, smarter, and cost-effective processes compared to traditional methods in the manufacturing industry. Computer vision, big data analytics, IIoT, and deep learning are some of the many AI technologies gaining traction in the manufacturing industry (Zeba et al., 2021). This chapter provides a brief insight into these technologies.

3.1.2. Computer Vision in Manufacturing

Computer vision technology, which enables machines to recognize and interpret real-world scenarios and execute appropriate actions at manufacturing centers, has gained wide acceptance in the manufacturing industry (Zhou et al., 2022). It processes digital images captured from camera-based sensors in the same fashion as the human eye and provides cost-effective solutions for demanding shop-floor modules such as part picking, process selection, vision inspection, sorting, and packaging. To execute tasks such as gauging and quality assurance, vision inspection and measurement devices are employed to assess the precision and compatibility of machined elements to machine tool parts. These devices are designed to integrate with multi-sensor metrology machines in the closed-loop process, which delivers additional data points. In extreme case scenarios, autonomous vision-guided robots are utilized for tasks that are difficult, dangerous, or impossible for plant personnel, such as painting, welding, and machine tending. Computer vision at manufacturing centers is typically regarded as AI, also reinforcing machine learning techniques, which have shown to increase efficiency and scale up performance by automating repetitive and monotonous human operator tasks (Noble, 1995).

3.1.3. Machine Learning

Machine learning (ML) refers to a class of algorithms that allow computer systems to improve their functions based on enhanced experiences and has a wide range of applicability (Sarker, 2021). At the core of these concepts is the exploration of algorithms and models that can learn from data and make data- or knowledge-based decisions over time. Manufactured products are usually of higher value than the sum of their components. Manufacturing involves complex decisions on converting materials and energy inputs into functional products or parts. Advantages of modern teaching algorithms and the exponential increase in computer power driving the growth of sophisticated computer models applied to classify complex data present in the manufacturing process have become an unprecedented opportunity for industrial productivity (Shehab et al., 2022). In the manufacturing process, large datasets with hundreds of records and many hundreds of feature parameters, with only a few remaining relevant for modeling, are often used to ensure model performance with a sufficient level of accuracy (Rokach & Maimon, 2006). Typical manufacturing data is provided by one of the following methods: human-in-the-line correction, machine-generated data, expert-based real-time correction, or evaluation of concessions from the next step of the manufacturing value chain. The last two mentioned methods represent post-mortem data, which do not help control the manufacturing process but can be used for the improvement of the next production lots. Many of the recent advances in product quality control, process optimization, new process control, or improvement of existing ones are possible due to the fast growth of two main areas in ML, smart computational approaches designed to extract relevant information from all types of industrial signals collected in the manufacturing process to serve as the base and sources of massive amounts of historical real-time data (Iqbal et al., 2020). Computer vision is a part of AI, which is a subfield that deals with how computers can gain a high-level understanding from digital images or videos (Wiley & Lucas, 2018). It is a rapidly growing field. The main vision tasks that are computationally challenging include the following: image classification. Yet, the more advanced tasks include object detection, as well as tracking in a video, tracking by following the object in the video, recognizing the activity of the object in a video, etc. Advances in the construction of artificial neural networks and through the availability of relatively large amounts of digital data that are image-labeled are responsible for the enormous progress in the field of computer vision to date (Leo et al., 2017). At this point, neural networks (and in particular convolutional neural networks), often referred to as CNNs, are being employed to perform incredibly well for various tasks in the computer vision community (Krichen, 2023). Specifically, deep CNNs are being employed to perform image recognition. Additionally, deep networks are used to make inferences about the object's location as well as the detection of the object from the given image (Bhatt et al., 2021). CNNs are attracting an enormous amount of manufacturing interest in the last year. This is demonstrated by companies acquiring startups employing such technologies. It is to a large extent that deep learning has been seen to provide groundbreaking computer vision performance over time for a variety of image-based tasks, especially as the computer vision community is willing to embrace this technology (Lindsay, 2021).

3.2. Benefits of AI Adoption in Manufacturing

The ability of AI to discover hidden patterns and correlations in data, and then make predictions based on those patterns, is of particular value in the context of manufacturing. In addition to these analytical benefits, AI can also be used to improve the ability of equipment to communicate and collaborate with each other to achieve near-operational intelligence (Shu & Ye, 2023). The main potential of AI in manufacturing environments is to support industries in the rapid discovery of untapped opportunities and new operational efficiencies. Among the analytical capabilities of AI, projection is beyond doubt one of the most valuable, and it is through this ability that many of its benefits are derived (Zhang & Zhou, 2004). Due to the real-time/near real-time processing, AI allows organizations to make decisions that potentially help the production area as well as the maintenance and repair operations (Jarrahi, 2018). The benefits of AI in manufacturing are not limited to offering new learning algorithms. AI can also provide interaction with systems in a more natural way, facilitate dealing with extremely large data sets, make more meaningful conclusions, and finally, offer the possibility of integrating information from numerous sources with unstructured multimedia. In a manufacturing context, communication is likely to be with multiple devices, images, unstructured data, sound, or other devices and is more likely to take place in a factory, plant, or similar industrial environment (Huang & Rust, 2018).

3.2.1. Increased Efficiency and Productivity

The potential to increase production efficiency via better resource scheduling is a major attraction of AI in the manufacture of electrical goods and machinery (Margono & Sharma, 2006). In view of their complex product structures and high provisions for indirect inputs, these industries are likely to face higher information and communication costs. The capital stocks of the use of AI equipment and the industry's shares of all ICT investment are low (Benson, 2022). Used for material and energy flow control, robots with their specific real-time capacities could facilitate the smart factory vision of lean production. In capital goods and transport equipment, the impact of virtual engineering (Byanyima et al., 2025), slim and printed electronics is to shorten development lead times, reduce inputs of raw materials, increase rapid prototyping, and enhance functional efficiency. By using product-like equipment in service, the machinery industries could benefit from efficiency gains similar to those visualized for the electrical and transport equipment industries. Firms would skip prototype phases and service brands. Capture-lead product development could result. Differences between AI in product and process design would remain. While in product design the proposed component or pattern would virtually fit, production scheduling and other process constraints would become more evasive for the especially shorter lead times in the final assembly process (Färe & Grosskopf, 2006). With shoppers expecting quality, low prices, plenty of options, and the ability to get what they want now, these challenges will not go away.

3.2.2. Improved Quality Control

Quality control in the production process is critical. Defective products can be costly and time-consuming to identify and could potentially cause severe harm to consumers in some cases (Björkman & Wisén, 2020). An intelligent camera system is used to inspect the 250 welds on each Camaro produced (Ke et al., 2020). A similar system is relied upon to detect gaps between doors and body panels among products. Both of these camera systems are linked to the AI network through a single data analysis function within 120 days of a company order. If a defective product comes off the line, it needs to be pulled off the production line before the defect continues. There is also a monitoring system that records trends and provides warnings if it predicts that a camera or another machine is in danger of failing. Industry data shows that camera systems and other robots are easily programmed to perform new tasks. In the automotive industry, for example, a typical production line can operate for 6 to 8 hours before it is reprogrammed by the industrial robot (Dodda et al., 2024). It is easy to reprogram the camera systems in a few hours. To do so, technicians capture an image of an authentic part with the camera system they want to program, label the part with the desired programming, and load it into the software application (Kopetz & Steiner, 2022). After doing the same with the second part, the technician releases software applications from the secure sandbox created in the AI network architecture designed for programming tools in the production robots. The second part is then visually labeled to ensure the robot continues to function, and the part is also given a letter grade. The operator traverses the network, releasing the programming directly from the main controller for the robot or the special interface created for the purpose of handling the program (Wisth et al., 2022). Then the quality control function in the robot is also programmed for the two parts.

4. CHALLENGES AND LIMITATIONS

In the race to make these advances, considerable challenges still have to be tackled. These challenges arise mainly from the diversity of manufacturing plants along with their lack of standardization in terms of structure, tools, and performance indicators (Nadella et al., 2023). Another reason for this resistance was the heavy investment in stand-alone or computer-integrated manufacturing that many companies have made before. Implementing these systems is an arduous process, and many companies are concluding it is not feasible (Wan et al., 2020). These sets of tools vary in their level of sophistication and are in use in today's plants, while others—cheaper and non-invasive—are not yet in use, waiting for companies' tests for better acceptance. Strengthening the challenge presented so far in integrating AI tools in manufacturing environments is the hierarchical vision needed in this system (Arinez et al., 2020). This means that AI is always operating in the sphere of tactical and operational issues of a production plan, which is part of a company that is integrated into various levels ranging from the strategic manufacture to the tactical organization. Even with technologies already mature and available, they are still not widely used due to existing uncertainties about starting their operation and maintenance, the company's shortage of "fast-pay" results compounded by efforts with low profitability.

4.1. Data Security and Privacy Concerns

The introduction of artificial intelligence will result in creating a wealth of data. Data is the main fuel for the successful operation of artificial intelligence applications. New knowledge can be derived only from those kinds of data. Protection measures have to be taken in order to prevent data from unauthorized access by third parties. Cybersecurity plays a key role in that. Smart factories consist of a swarm of smart devices (Murdoch, 2021). Any smart device that has an internet connection with the factory network belongs to the list of points for potential third-party access. Once an artificial intelligence-operated factory becomes a potential target for cyberattacks, its flexibility in turning both the devices and humans from resources to a source of inefficiency will put the future duty of conventional cybersecurity systems to their maximum effort to cope with that (Admass et al., 2024). They should be able to ensure real-time access governance and real-time operations. With artificial intelligence depending increasingly on data, personal data protection and privacy will also be part of the future job requirements of data hosting organizations (Rane, 2023). The challenge is how to control and manage the impacts on manufacturing industries. Artificial intelligence developers producing the applications have to be aware of this and include features in the systems they are developing so that end users will not be adversely affected. New regulations have to be laid down by governments regarding the rights of human workers controlling, overseeing, and monitoring applications, as well as the uses of such systems in the view of the collaboration paradigm of factories (Ali et al., 2023). The business and operation models have to be enhanced by manufacturers and developers as well.

5. FUTURE TRENDS AND OPPORTUNITIES

The manufacturing industries are the core of a prospering economy. Leveraging the power of AI in the manufacturing segment has immense potential and future opportunities. This sector has numerous complex systems at the level of the factory floor, accounts, inventory, learned models, etc.; AI helps to control them. Implementation stages are also significantly large, designed mainly to automatically learn and improve (Arinez et al., 2020). Diagnosis, predictive maintenance, and bi-directional supply chain logistics are some important facilities. The requirements of adaptability built into the AI models and algorithms specifically to handle the perceived challenges of manufacturing increase the intelligence awareness of these systems (Dutta et al., 2024). Deep learning and agent-based systems have been found competitive here. AI helps in the development of smart hardware. ML strategies have improved performance, simplified design, and greatly accelerated the time-to-market for a wide range of devices for manufacturing ecosystems (Mensah et al., 2024). This includes software development, architecture design, model input for hardware resources in comparison to acceleration, neuromorphic chips, and integrated photonics. Robotics has improved the design of smarter and adaptable robots and cobots by imposing minimum disruption across trading; by integrating the production of robots through deep learning without trial and error methods. Machine vision systems are tuned to handle the manufacturing sector's vigorous market dynamics due to advancements in power, size, and performance (Sabry et al., 2022). AI helps in setting high standards of traceability for both tech-based technologies and platforms to ensure the expected visible status of the final product.

6. CONCLUSION AND POLICY RECOMMENDATIONS

6.1 Conclusion

This study demonstrates how AI technologies, such as computer vision and system learning, may revolutionize industrial efficiency, productivity, and satisfactory control. Superior algorithms, neural networks, and big data analytics are integrated to optimize manufacturing strategies and enable intelligent decision-making, which is where the innovation lies. AI significantly aids in achieving the Sustainable Development Goals (SDGs), particularly Goals 9 (*Industry, Innovation, and Infrastructure*) and 12 (*Responsible Consumption and Production*), by reducing inefficiencies, reducing flaws, and automating repetitive tasks. The compatibility with the European Union's Industry 5.0 vision and Africa's Agenda 2063 highlights AI's potential to promote inclusive industrialization, commercialize technical innovation, and create sustainable economic growth, and these aligns with the current study thus its novelty. The current study is also applicable globally, benefiting sectors other than manufacturing, including power, healthcare, and logistics. However, more research is required in two important areas: (1) the ethical ramifications of AI implementation in manufacturing, and particularly with regard to data privacy and worker displacement; and (2) the advancement of AI-driven methods for SMEs to enhance accessibility and scalability.

6.2 Policy Recommendations

There is a global need to invest in AI capacity building through skills development and training for manufacturing professional in the current error, ■ Promote AI adoption incentives for SMEs to encourage inclusive growth in manufacturing industries across the world, ■ There is need for both developed and developing countries to establish data governance frameworks to ensure security and ethical AI application, ■ Also, there is need for supporting public-private partnerships to drive AI research and innovation in manufacturing supported by research think tanks.

REFERENCES

Admass, W. S., Munaye, Y. Y., & Diro, A. A. (2024). Cyber security: State of the art, challenges and future directions. *Cyber Security and Applications*, 2, 100031.

Ali, O., Abdelbaki, W., Shrestha, A., Elbasi, E., Alryalat, M. A. A., & Dwivedi, Y. K. (2023). A systematic literature review of artificial intelligence in the healthcare sector: Benefits, challenges, methodologies, and functionalities. *Journal of Innovation & Knowledge*, 8(1), 100333.

Arinez, J. F., Chang, Q., Gao, R. X., Xu, C., & Zhang, J. (2020). Artificial intelligence in advanced manufacturing: Current status and future outlook. *Journal of Manufacturing Science and Engineering*, 142(11), 110804.

Benson, T. (2022). ICT Supported, Agricultural Extension and Advisory Services in Ethiopia. *International Journal of Academic Pedagogical Research*, 6(7), 127.

Bhatt, D., Patel, C., Talsania, H., Patel, J., Vaghela, R., Pandya, S., Modi, K., & Ghayvat, H. (2021). CNN variants for computer vision: History, architecture, application, challenges and future scope. *Electronics (Basel)*, 10(20), 2470.

Björkman, J., & Wisén, S. (2020). *Investigation of defective products and how to reduce them: A case study at a Scandinavian plastic manufacturer*.

Buchmeister, B., Palcic, I., & Ojstersek, R. (2019). Artificial intelligence in manufacturing companies and broader: An overview. *DAAAM International Scientific Book*, 81–98.

Byanyima, F., Edison, M., Kadengye, D. T., Arineitwe, S., Mijwil, M. M., Gaballa, M., Veedu, R. C., & Turyasingura, B. (2025). Foreign Direct Investment and Environmental Challenges: A Case Study of Uganda With Analytical Perspective. In *Community Resilience and Climate Change Challenges: Pursuit of Sustainable Development Goals (SDGs)* (pp. 283–296). IGI Global Scientific Publishing.

Cascón-Morán, I., Gómez, M., Fernández, D., Gil Del Val, A., Alberdi, N., & González, H. (2024). Towards Zero-Defect Manufacturing Based on Artificial Intelligence through the Correlation of Forces in 5-Axis Milling Process. *Machines (Basel)*, 12(4), 226.

Dodda, S., Chintala, S., Kanungo, S., Adedoja, T., & Sharma, S. (2024). Exploring AI-driven Innovations in Image Communication Systems for Enhanced Medical Imaging Applications. *Journal of Electrical Systems*, 20(3s), 949–959.

Drchal, J., Čertický, M., & Jakob, M. (2019). Data-driven activity scheduler for agent-based mobility models. *Transportation Research Part C, Emerging Technologies*, 98, 370–390.

Dutta, P. K., Singh, B., Towfeek, A.-S. K., Adamopoulou, J. P., Bardavouras, A. N., Bamwerinde, W., Turyasingura, B., & Ayiga, N. (2024). IoT Revolutionizes Humidity Measurement and Management in Smart Cities to Enhance Health and Wellness. *Mesopotamian Journal of Artificial Intelligence in Healthcare*, 2024, 110–117.

Färe, R., & Grosskopf, S. (2006). *New directions: efficiency and productivity* (Vol. 3). Springer Science & Business Media.

Huang, M.-H., & Rust, R. T. (2018). Artificial intelligence in service. *Journal of Service Research*, 21(2), 155–172.

Iqbal, R., Doctor, F., More, B., Mahmud, S., & Yousuf, U. (2020). Big Data analytics and Computational Intelligence for Cyber–Physical Systems: Recent trends and state of the art applications. *Future Generation Computer Systems*, 105, 766–778.

Jarrahi, M. H. (2018). Artificial intelligence and the future of work: Human-AI symbiosis in organizational decision making. *Business Horizons*, 61(4), 577–586.

Ke, R., Zhuang, Y., Pu, Z., & Wang, Y. (2020). A smart, efficient, and reliable parking surveillance system with edge artificial intelligence on IoT devices. *IEEE Transactions on Intelligent Transportation Systems*, 22(8), 4962–4974.

Khan, I. (2025). *Undisrupted: Leadership Essentials on Business Transformation, Profitability and Future Readiness*. John Wiley & Sons.

Kim, S. W., Kong, J. H., Lee, S. W., & Lee, S. (2022). Recent advances of artificial intelligence in manufacturing industrial sectors: A review. *International Journal of Precision Engineering and Manufacturing*, 1–19.

Kopetz, H., & Steiner, W. (2022). *Real-time systems: design principles for distributed embedded applications*. Springer Nature.

Krichen, M. (2023). Convolutional neural networks: A survey. *Computers*, 12(8), 151.

Lee, D., & Yoon, S. N. (2021). Application of artificial intelligence-based technologies in the healthcare industry: Opportunities and challenges. *International Journal of Environmental Research and Public Health*, 18(1), 271. PMID: 33401373

Leo, M., Medioni, G., Trivedi, M., Kanade, T., & Farinella, G. M. (2017). Computer vision for assistive technologies. *Computer Vision and Image Understanding*, 154, 1–15.

Lindsay, G. W. (2021). Convolutional neural networks as a model of the visual system: Past, present, and future. *Journal of Cognitive Neuroscience*, 33(10), 2017–2031. PMID: 32027584

Margono, H., & Sharma, S. C. (2006). Efficiency and productivity analyses of Indonesian manufacturing industries. *Journal of Asian Economics*, 17(6), 979–995.

McCallum, J. C. (2017). Price-performance of computer technology. In *Digital Design and Fabrication* (pp. 1–4). CRC Press.

Mensah, G., Kayusi, F., Chavula, P., Turyasingura, B., & Amadi, O. J. (2024). *Artificial Intelligence Systems and Medical Negligence: An Overview and Perspective of a Case Study in Ghana Civil Procedure Rules, 2004 (CI 47)*.

Mijwil, M. M., Abotaleb, M., Ali, G., & Dhoska, K. (2024). Assigning Medical Professionals: ChatGPT's Contributions to Medical Education and Health Prediction. *Mesopotamian Journal of Artificial Intelligence in Healthcare*, 2024, 76–83.

Munirathinam, S. (2020). Industry 4.0: Industrial internet of things (IIOT). *Advances in Computers*, 117(1), 129–164.

Murdoch, B. (2021). Privacy and artificial intelligence: Challenges for protecting health information in a new era. *BMC Medical Ethics*, 22, 1–5. PMID: 34525993

Nadella, G. S., Satish, S., Meduri, K., & Meduri, S. S. (2023). A Systematic Literature Review of Advancements, Challenges and Future Directions of AI And ML in Healthcare. *International Journal of Machine Learning for Sustainable Development*, 5(3), 115–130.

Noble, J. A. (1995). From inspection to process understanding and monitoring: A view on computer vision in manufacturing. *Image and Vision Computing*, 13(3), 197–214.

Rane, N. (2023). Role and challenges of ChatGPT and similar generative artificial intelligence in finance and accounting. *Available at SSRN* 4603206.

Rokach, L., & Maimon, O. (2006). Data mining for improving the quality of manufacturing: A feature set decomposition approach. *Journal of Intelligent Manufacturing*, 17, 285–299.

Sabry, F., Eltaras, T., Labda, W., Alzoubi, K., & Malluhi, Q. (2022). Machine learning for healthcare wearable devices: The big picture. *Journal of Healthcare Engineering*, 2022(1), 4653923. PMID: 35480146

Sahai, A. K., & Rath, N. (2021). Artificial intelligence and the 4th industrial revolution. In *Artificial intelligence and machine learning in business management* (pp. 127–143). CRC Press.

Sarker, I. H. (2021). Machine learning: Algorithms, real-world applications and research directions. *SN Computer Science*, 2(3), 160. PMID: 33778771

Shehab, M., Abualigah, L., Shambour, Q., Abu-Hashem, M. A., Shambour, M. K. Y., Alsalibi, A. I., & Gandomi, A. H. (2022). Machine learning in medical applications: A review of state-of-the-art methods. *Computers in Biology and Medicine*, 145, 105458. PMID: 35364311

Shu, X., & Ye, Y. (2023). Knowledge Discovery: Methods from data mining and machine learning. *Social Science Research*, 110, 102817. PMID: 36796993

Tuama, A., Comby, F., & Chaumont, M. (2016). Camera model identification with the use of deep convolutional neural networks. *2016 IEEE International Workshop on Information Forensics and Security (WIFS)*, 1–6.

Turyasingura, B., Ayiga, N., Kayusi, F., & Tumuhimbise, M. (2024). Application of Artificial Intelligence (AI) in Environment and Societal Trends: Challenges and Opportunities. *Babylonian Journal of Machine Learning*, 2024, 177–182.

Wan, J., Li, X., Dai, H.-N., Kusiak, A., Martinez-Garcia, M., & Li, D. (2020). Artificial-intelligence-driven customized manufacturing factory: Key technologies, applications, and challenges. *Proceedings of the IEEE*, 109(4), 377–398.

Wiley, V., & Lucas, T. (2018). Computer vision and image processing: A paper review. *International Journal of Artificial Intelligence Research*, 2(1), 29–36.

Wisth, D., Camurri, M., & Fallon, M. (2022). VILENS: Visual, inertial, lidar, and leg odometry for all-terrain legged robots. *IEEE Transactions on Robotics*, 39(1), 309–326.

Zeba, G., Dabić, M., Čičak, M., Daim, T., & Yalcin, H. (2021). Technology mining: Artificial intelligence in manufacturing. *Technological Forecasting and Social Change*, 171, 120971.

Zhang, D., & Zhou, L. (2004). Discovering golden nuggets: Data mining in financial application. *IEEE Transactions on Systems, Man, and Cybernetics. Part C, Applications and Reviews*, 34(4), 513–522.

Zhou, L., Zhang, L., & Konz, N. (2022). Computer vision techniques in manufacturing. *IEEE Transactions on Systems, Man, and Cybernetics. Systems*, 53(1), 105–117.

Compilation of References

Abbasi, S. (2020). Advanced Regression Techniques Based Housing Price Prediction Model. *13th International Conference of Iranian Operations Research Society*, 1–10. DOI: 10.13140/RG.2.2.18572.87684

Abbas, Q. (2014, August). Semi-semantic part of speech annotation and evaluation. In *Proceedings of LAW VIII-The 8th Linguistic Annotation Workshop* (pp. 75-81). DOI: 10.3115/v1/W14-4911

Abdullah, T. A. A., Zahid, M. S. M., & Ali, W. (2021). A Review of Interpretable ML in Healthcare: Taxonomy, Applications, Challenges, and Future Directions. *Symmetry*, 13(12), 2439. DOI: 10.3390/sym13122439

Admass, W. S., Munaye, Y. Y., & Diro, A. A. (2024). Cyber security: State of the art, challenges and future directions. *Cyber Security and Applications*, 2, 100031.

Adu. (2023). Optimal Computation Resource Allocation in Energy-Efficient Edge IoT Systems With Deep Reinforcement Learning. IEEE Transactions on Green Communications and Networking. .DOI: 10.1109/TGCN.2023.3286914

Afrin, M., Jin, J., Rahman, A., Tian, Y., & Kulkarni, A. (2019). Multi-objective resource allocation for edge cloud based robotic workflow in smart factory. *Future Generation Computer Systems*, 97, 119–130.

Ağrali, Ö., & Aydin, Ö. (2021). Tweet Classification and Sentiment Analysis on Metaverse Related Messages. *Journal of Metaverse*, 1(1), 25–30.

Agrawal, P., Abutarboush, H. F., Ganesh, T., & Mohamed, A. W. (2021). Metaheuristic algorithms on feature selection: A survey of one decade of research (2009-2019). *IEEE Access : Practical Innovations, Open Solutions*, 9, 26766–26791. DOI: 10.1109/ACCESS.2021.3056407

Ahmad, M., Ali, A., & Khiyal, M. S. H. (2023). Fog Computing for Spatial Data Infrastructure: Challenges and Opportunities. In D. P. Acharjya & K. Ahmed P. (Eds.), *Multi-Disciplinary Applications of Fog Computing: Responsiveness in Real-Time* (pp. 152–178). IGI Global. DOI: 10.4018/978-1-6684-4466-5.ch008

Ahmad, F., Tarik, M., Ahmad, M., & Ansari, M. Z. (2023). Weather Forecasting Using Deep Learning Algorithms. *2023 International Conference on Recent Advances in Electrical, Electronics & Digital Healthcare Technologies (REEDCON)*, 498–502. https://doi.org/DOI: 10.1109/REEDCON57544.2023.10150439

Ahmad, I. S., Bakar, A. A., & Yaakub, M. R. (2019). A review of feature selection in sentiment analysis using information gain and domain specific ontology. *International Journal of Advanced Computer Research*, 9(44), 283–292. DOI: 10.19101/IJACR.PID90

Ahmad, I., & Amin, J., IkramUllah Lali, M., Abbas, F., & Imran Sharif, M. (2024). A novel Deeplabv3+ and vision-based transformer model for segmentation and classification of skin lesions. *Biomedical Signal Processing and Control*, 92, 106084. DOI: 10.1016/j.bspc.2024.106084

Ahmad, M., & Ali, A. (2023). Mapping the future of sustainable development through cloud-based solutions: A case study of openstreetmap. In *Promoting Sustainable Management Through Technological Innovation* (pp. 153–176). IGI Global. DOI: 10.4018/978-1-6684-9979-5.ch011

Ahmed, U., Issa, G. F., Khan, M. A., Aftab, S., Khan, M. F., Said, R. A. T., Ghazal, T. M., & Ahmad, M. (2022). Prediction of Diabetes Empowered With Fused Machine Learning. *IEEE Access : Practical Innovations, Open Solutions*, 10, 8529–8538. DOI: 10.1109/ACCESS.2022.3142097

Ahn, J. J., Byun, H. W., Oh, K. J., & Kim, T. Y. (2012). Using ridge regression with genetic algorithm to enhance real estate appraisal forecasting. *Expert Systems with Applications*, 39(9), 8369–8379. DOI: 10.1016/j.eswa.2012.01.183

Airlangga, P., & Rachman, A. A. (2022). Deployment of Location Mapping Results Based on Application Programming Interface. *NEWTON: Networking and Information Technology*, 1(3). Advance online publication. DOI: 10.32764/newton.v1i3.1922

Alam, A., & Mohanty, A. (2022). Metaverse and Posthuman animated avatars for teaching-learning process: interperception in virtual universe for educational transformation. In *International Conference on Innovations in Intelligent Computing and Communications* (pp. 47-61). Springer.

Alam, M. G. R., Hassan, M. M., Uddin, M. Z., Almogren, A., & Fortino, G. (2019). Autonomic computation offloading in mobile edge for iot applications. *Future Generation Computer Systems*, 90, 149–157.

Albaroudi, E., Mansouri, T., & Alameer, A. (2024). A Comprehensive Review of AI Techniques for Addressing Algorithmic Bias in Job HiringAI, 5(1)1.

Alelaiwi, A. (2019). An efficient method of computation offloading in an edge cloud platform. *Journal of Parallel and Distributed Computing*, 127, 58–64.

Algorithmic Mind. (n.d.). Understanding Bias in Machine Learning. Retrieved from https://algorithmicmind.org/bias-in-machine-learning

Alhaidari, F., Rahman, A., & Zagrouba, R. (2023). Cloud of Things: Architecture, applications and challenges. *Journal of Ambient Intelligence and Humanized Computing*, 14(5). Advance online publication. DOI: 10.1007/s12652-020-02448-3

Alharbi, R., Magdy, W., Darwish, K., Abdelali, A., & Mubarak, H. (2018). Part-of-Speech Tagging for Arabic Gulf Dialect Using Bi-LSTM. *Proceedings of the Eleventh International Conference on Language Resources and Evaluation(LREC 2018)*, 3925–3932.

Ali, F., Khan, P., Riaz, K., Kwak, D., Abuhmed, T., Park, D., & Kwak, K. S. (2017). A fuzzy ontology and SVM–based Web content classification system. *IEEE Access : Practical Innovations, Open Solutions*, 5, 25781–25797. DOI: 10.1109/ACCESS.2017.2768564

Ali, M. S., Miah, M. S., Haque, J., Rahman, M. M., & Islam, M. K. (2021). An enhanced technique of skin cancer classification using deep convolutional neural network with transfer learning models. *Machine Learning with Applications*, 5, 100036. DOI: 10.1016/j.mlwa.2021.100036

Ali, O., Abdelbaki, W., Shrestha, A., Elbasi, E., Alryalat, M. A. A., & Dwivedi, Y. K. (2023). A systematic literature review of artificial intelligence in the healthcare sector: Benefits, challenges, methodologies, and functionalities. *Journal of Innovation & Knowledge*, 8(1), 100333.

Aljabri, M., Altamimi, H. S., Albelali, S. A., Maimunah, A. H., Alhuraib, H. T., Alotaibi, N. K., & Salah, K. (2022). Detecting malicious URLs using machine learning techniques: Review and research directions. *IEEE Access : Practical Innovations, Open Solutions*, 10, 121395–121417. DOI: 10.1109/ACCESS.2022.3222307

Al-Jawarneh, A. S., Ismail, M. T., Awajan, A. M., & Alsayed, A. R. M. (2020). Improving accuracy models using elastic net regression approach based on empirical mode decomposition. *Communications in Statistics. Simulation and Computation*, 0(0), 1–20. DOI: 10.1080/03610918.2020.1728319

Alkhalaileh, M., Calheiros, R. N., Nguyen, Q. V., & Javadi, B. (2020). Data-intensive application scheduling on mobile edge cloud computing. *Journal of Network and Computer Applications*, 167, 102735.

Allahverdi, A., & Aydilek, H. (2015). The two stage assembly flowshop scheduling problem to minimize total tardiness. *Journal of Intelligent Manufacturing*, 26, 225–237.

Allali, K., Aqil, S., & Belabid, J. (2022). Distributed no-wait flow shop problem with sequence dependent setup time: Optimization of makespan and maximum tardiness. *Simulation Modelling Practice and Theory*, 116, 102455.

Allen, D. W., & Gerike, M. J. (2021). Focus on Geodatabases in ArcGIS Pro. *Photogrammetric Engineering and Remote Sensing*, 87(7). Advance online publication. DOI: 10.14358/pers.87.7.468

Al-Tashi, Q., Abdulkadir, S. J., Rais, H. M., Mirjalili, S., & Alhussian, H. (2020). Approaches to Multi-Objective Feature Selection: A Systematic Literature Review. *IEEE Access : Practical Innovations, Open Solutions*, 8, 125076–125096. DOI: 10.1109/ACCESS.2020.3007291

Alwakid, G., Gouda, W., Humayun, M., & Sama, N. U. (2022). Melanoma Detection Using Deep Learning-Based Classifications. *Health Care*, 10(12), 12. Advance online publication. DOI: 10.3390/healthcare10122481 PMID: 36554004

Amani, M., Ghorbanian, A., Ahmadi, S. A., Kakooei, M., Moghimi, A., Mirmazloumi, S. M., Moghaddam, S. H. A., Mahdavi, S., Ghahremanloo, M., Parsian, S., Wu, Q., & Brisco, B. (2020). Google Earth Engine Cloud Computing Platform for Remote Sensing Big Data Applications: A Comprehensive Review. *IEEE Journal of Selected Topics in Applied Earth Observations and Remote Sensing*, 13. Advance online publication. DOI: 10.1109/JSTARS.2020.3021052

Amarnath, B., & Appavu alias Balamurugan, S. (2016). Metaheuristic Approach for Efficient Feature Selection: A Data Classification Perspective. *Indian Journal of Science and Technology*, 9(4). Advance online publication. DOI: 10.17485/ijst/2016/v9i4/87039

Amershi, S., Weld, D., Vorvoreanu, M., Fourney, A., Nushi, B., Collisson, P., & Horvitz, E. (2019). Guidelines for human-AI interaction. In *Proceedings of the 2019 CHI Conference on Human Factors in Computing Systems* (pp. 1-13).

Amodei, D., Olah, C., Steinhardt, J., Christiano, P., Schulman, J., & Mané, D. (2016). Concrete problems in AI safety. arXiv preprint arXiv:1606.06565.

Amoozegar, M., & Minaei-Bidgoli, B. (2018). Optimizing multi-objective PSO based feature selection method using a feature elitism mechanism. *Expert Systems with Applications*, 113, 499–514. DOI: 10.1016/j.eswa.2018.07.013

Andersson, J. C. (2023). *Learning Microsoft Azure.* O'Reilly Media, Inc.

Antunes, A., Ferreira, B., Marques, N., & Carriço, N. (2023). Hyperparameter Optimization of a Convolutional Neural Network Model for Pipe Burst Location in Water Distribution Networks. *Journal of Imaging*, 9(3), 3. Advance online publication. DOI: 10.3390/jimaging9030068 PMID: 36976119

Apollo, M., Jakubiak, M., Nistor, S., Lewinska, P., Krawczyk, A., Borowski, L., Specht, M., Krzykowska-Piotrowska, K., Marchel, Ł., Peska-Siwik, A., Kardoš, M., & Maciuk, K. (2023). Geodata in science: A review of selected scientific fields. *Acta Scientiarum Polonorum. Formatio Circumiectus*, 22(2). Advance online publication. DOI: 10.15576/ASP.FC/2023.22.2.02

Aqil, S., & Allali, K. (2021). On a bi-criteria flow shop scheduling problem under constraints of blocking and sequence dependent setup time. *Annals of Operations Research*, 296(1), 615–637.

Araujo, T., Helberger, N., Kruikemeier, S., & de Vreese, C. H. (2018). In AI we trust? Perceptions about automated decision-making by artificial intelligence. *AI & Society*, 33(4), 509–519.

Arinez, J. F., Chang, Q., Gao, R. X., Xu, C., & Zhang, J. (2020). Artificial intelligence in advanced manufacturing: Current status and future outlook. *Journal of Manufacturing Science and Engineering*, 142(11), 110804.

Ariyadasa, S., Fernando, S., & Fernando, S. (2022). Combining long-term recurrent convolutional and graph convolutional networks to detect phishing sites using URL and HTML. *IEEE Access: Practical Innovations, Open Solutions*, 10, 82355–82375. DOI: 10.1109/ACCESS.2022.3196018

Arrieta, A. B., Díaz-Rodríguez, N., Del Ser, J., Bennetot, A., Tabik, S., Barbado, A., & Herrera, F. (2020). Explainable Artificial Intelligence (XAI): Concepts, taxonomies, opportunities and challenges toward responsible AI. *Information Fusion*, 58, 82–115. DOI: 10.1016/j.inffus.2019.12.012

Arshad, H., Khan, M. A., Sharif, M. I., Yasmin, M., Tavares, J. M. R., Zhang, Y. D., & Satapathy, S. C. (2020). A multilevel paradigm for deep convolutional neural network features selection with an application to human gait recognition. *Expert Systems: International Journal of Knowledge Engineering and Neural Networks*, 39(7), e12541. DOI: 10.1111/exsy.12541

Arshad, H., Khan, M. A., Sharif, M., Yasmin, M., & Javed, M. Y. (2019). Multi-level features fusion and selection for human gait recognition: An optimized framework of Bayesian model and binomial distribution. *International Journal of Machine Learning and Cybernetics*, 10(12), 3601–3618. DOI: 10.1007/s13042-019-00947-0

Arun, J. P., Mishra, M., & Subramaniam, S. V. (2011). Parallel implementation of MOPSO on GPU using OpenCL and CUDA. *2011 18th International Conference on High Performance Computing*, 1–10. DOI: 10.1109/HiPC.2011.6152719

Arxiv. (n.d.). Bias Mitigation for Machine Learning Classifiers: A Comprehensive Survey. Retrieved from https://arxiv.org/pdf/2207.07068v2

Asif, M., Tiwana, M.I., Khan, U.S., Ahmad, M.W., Qureshi, W.S., & Iqbal, J. (2022). Human gait recognition subject to different covariate factors in a multi-view environment. *Results in Engineering,15*, 100556.

Asif, T., Ali, A., & Malik, K. (2015). Developing a POS Tagged Resource Of Urdu. Developing a POS tagged Resource in Urdu. Punjab University College of Information Technology, University of the Punjab.

Autor, D. H. (2015). Why are there still so many jobs? The history and future of workplace automation. *The Journal of Economic Perspectives*, 29(3), 3–30. DOI: 10.1257/jep.29.3.3

Avanija, J., Sunitha, G., Reddy Madhavi, K., Korad, P., & Hitesh Sai Vittale, R. (2021). Prediction of House Price Using XGBoost Regression Algorithm. DOI: 10.17762/turcomat.v12i2.1870

Awad, M., & Khanna, R. (2015). *Efficient Learning Machines*. Editions Apress., DOI: 10.1007/978-1-4302-5990-9

Awal, M. A., Rahman, M. S., & Rabbi, J. (2018, October). Detecting abusive comments in discussion threads using Naïve Bayes. In *2018 International Conference on Innovations in Science, Engineering and Technology (ICISET)* (pp. 163-167). IEEE. DOI: 10.1109/ICISET.2018.8745565

Aws. (2023). *Amazon Redshift Cloud Data Warehouse*. https://aws.amazon.com/redshift/

Aydın, K. E., & Baday, S. (2020). Machine Learning for Web Content Classification. 2020 Innovations in Intelligent Systems and Applications Conference (ASYU), 1-7. DOI: 10.1109/ASYU50717.2020.9259833

Babaee, M., Li, L., & Rigoll, G. (2018). Gait recognition from incomplete gaitcycle. 2018 25th IEEE International Conference on Image Processing (ICIP), 768-772. DOI: 10.1109/ICIP.2018.8451785

Babaee, M., Zhu, Y., Köpüklü, O., Hörmann, S., & Rigoll, G. (2019). Gait energy image restoration using generative adversarial networks. 2019 IEEE Internationa Conference on Image Processing (ICIP), 2596-2600, DOI: 10.1109/ICIP.2019.8803236

Bacanin, N., Zivkovic, M., Salb, M., Strumberger, I., & Chhabra, A. (2022). Convolutional Neural Networks Hyperparameters Optimization Using Sine Cosine Algorithm. In Shakya, S., Balas, V. E., Kamolphiwong, S., & Du, K.-L. (Eds.), Sentimental Analysis and Deep Learning (pp. 863–878). Springer. DOI: 10.1007/978-981-16-5157-1_67

Bajeddi A. (2015). Property Valuation and Ethics in Morocco.

Bajeddi, A. (2017). Land Valuation. In Morocco. Challenges And Prospects.

Bajic, , Nikola, Slobodan, Miladin, Milos, & Aleksandar. (2023). Edge Computing Data Optimization for Smart Quality Management: Industry 5.0 Perspective. Sustainability, 15(7), 6032. DOI: 10.3390/su15076032

Bajjali, W. (2018). Geodatabase. In ArcGIS for Environmental and Water Issues (pp. 103–116). Springer International Publishing., DOI: 10.1007/978-3-319-61158-7_7

Baktir, A. C., Ozgovde, A., & Ersoy, C. (2017). How can edge computing benefit from software defined networking: A survey, use cases, and future directions. IEEE Communications Surveys and Tutorials, 19, 2359–2391.

Balacheff, N. (1994). Didactique et intelligence artificielle. Recherches En Didactique Des Mathematiques, 14(June), 9–42. https://telearn.archives-ouvertes.fr/hal-00190648/

Balazia, M., & Sojka, P. (2018). Gait recognition from motion capture data. ACM Transactions on Multimedia Computing Communications and Applications, 14(1s), 1–18. DOI: 10.1145/3152124

Baltrušaitis, T., Ahuja, C., & Morency, L. P. (2018). Multimodal machine learning: A survey and taxonomy. IEEE Transactions on Pattern Analysis and Machine Intelligence, 41(2), 423–443. DOI: 10.1109/TPAMI.2018.2798607 PMID: 29994351

Barhorst, J. B., McLean, G., Shah, E., & Mack, R. (2021). Blending the real world and the virtual world: Exploring the role of flow in augmented reality experiences. *Journal of Business Research*, 122, 423–436.

Bari, A. S. M., & Gavrilova, M. L. (2019). Artificial neural network based gait recognition using kinect sensor. *IEEE Access : Practical Innovations, Open Solutions*, 7, 162708–162722. DOI: 10.1109/ACCESS.2019.2952065

Barocas, S., Hardt, M., & Narayanan, A. (2019). Fairness and Machine Learning.

Bashir, K., Xiang, T., & Gong, S. (2010). Gait recognition without subject cooperation *Elsevier Journal of Pattern Recognition Letters,31*(13), 2052-2060.

Basiri, M. E., Nemati, S., Abdar, M., Cambria, E., & Acharya, U. R. (2021). ABCDM: An attention-based bidirectional CNN-RNN deep model for sentiment analysis. *Future Generation Computer Systems*, 115, 279–294.

Batcheller, J. K., Gittings, B. M., & Dowers, S. (2007). The performance of vector oriented data storage strategies in ESRI's ArcGIS. *Transactions in GIS*, 11(1). Advance online publication. DOI: 10.1111/j.1467-9671.2007.01032.x

Batta, M. (2020). Machine Learning Algorithms - A Review. *International Journal of Science and Research, 9*(1), 381–386. DOI: 10.21275/ART20203995

Bayındır, L. (2016). A review of swarm robotics tasks. *Neurocomputing*, 172, 292–321. DOI: 10.1016/j.neucom.2015.05.116

Bellamy, R. K. E., Dey, K., Hind, M., Hoffman, S. C., Houde, S., Kannan, K., & Zhang, Y. (2019). AI fairness 360: An extensible toolkit for detecting, understanding, and mitigating unwanted algorithmic bias. *IBM Journal of Research and Development*, 63(4/5), 4–1. DOI: 10.1147/JRD.2019.2942287

Bender, E. M., & Koller, A. (2020). Climbing towards NLU: On meaning, form, and understanding in the age of data. In *Proceedings of the 58th Annual Meeting of the Association for Computational Linguistics* (pp. 5185-5198). DOI: 10.18653/v1/2020.acl-main.463

Benson, T. (2022). ICT Supported, Agricultural Extension and Advisory Services in Ethiopia. *International Journal of Academic Pedagogical Research, 6*(7), 127.

Bertsekas, D. P. (2019). *Reinforcement Learning and Optimal Control*. Athena Scientific Belmont.

Bhargavas, W. G., Harshavardhan, K., Mohan, G. C., Sharma, A. N., & Prathap, C. (2017). Human identification using gait recognition. In 2017 International Conference on Communication and Signal Processing (ICCSP), 1510-1513, DOI: 10.1109/ICCSP.2017.8286638

Bhatt, D., Patel, C., Talsania, H., Patel, J., Vaghela, R., Pandya, S., Modi, K., & Ghayvat, H. (2021). CNN variants for computer vision: History, architecture, application, challenges and future scope. *Electronics (Basel)*, 10(20), 2470.

Birjali, M., Kasri, M., & Beni-Hssane, A. (2021). A comprehensive survey on sentiment analysis: Approaches, challenges and trends. *Knowledge-Based Systems*, 226, 107134.

Bishop, C. M. (2006). *Pattern recognition and machine learning (Information science and statistics)*. Springer-Verlag New York, Inc.

Bisong, E. (2019). Google Cloud Storage (GCS). In *Building Machine Learning and Deep Learning Models on Google Cloud Platform*. DOI: 10.1007/978-1-4842-4470-8_4

Björkman, J., & Wisén, S. (2020). *Investigation of defective products and how to reduce them: A case study at a Scandinavian plastic manufacturer.*

Blabe, C. H., Gilja, V., Chestek, C. A., Shenoy, K. V., & Henderson, J. M. (2015). Assessment of brain-machine interfaces from the perspective of people with paralysis. *Journal of Neural Engineering*, 12(4), 043002. DOI: 10.1088/1741-2560/12/4/043002 PMID: 26169880

Bolón-Canedo, V., & Alonso-Betanzos, A. (2019). Ensembles for feature selection: A review and future trends. *Information Fusion*, 52, 1–12. DOI: 10.1016/j.inffus.2018.11.008

Bolón-Canedo, V., Rego-Fernández, D., Peteiro-Barral, D., Alonso-Betanzos, A., Guijarro-Berdiñas, B., & Sánchez-Maroño, N. (2018). On the scalability of feature selection methods on high-dimensional data. *Knowledge and Information Systems*, 56(2), 395–442. DOI: 10.1007/s10115-017-1140-3

Bölücü, N., & Can, B. (2019). Unsupervised joint PoS tagging and stemming for agglutinative languages. *ACM Transactions on Asian and Low-Resource Language Information Processing*, 18(3), 1–21. DOI: 10.1145/3292398

Bonawitz, K., Eichner, H., Grieskamp, W., Huba, D., Ingerman, A., Ivanov, V., . . . van Overveldt, T. (2019). Towards federated learning at scale: System design. arXiv preprint arXiv:1902.01046.

Bonawitz, K., Ivanov, V., Kreuter, B., Marcedone, A., McMahan, B., Patel, S., & Seth, K. (2017). Practical secure aggregation for privacy-preserving machine learning. In *Proceedings of the 2017 ACM SIGSAC Conference on Computer and Communications Security* (pp. 1175-1191). DOI: 10.1145/3133956.3133982

Borde, S., Rane, A., Shende, G., & Shetty, S. (2017). Real Estate Investment Advising Using MachineLearning. *International Research Journal of Engineering and Technology (IRJET), 4*(3), 1821–1825. https://irjet.net/archives/V4/i3/IRJET-V4I3499.pdf

Bounajma, N. (2014). Cours d'expertise immobilière pour le compte de l'ONIGT / CRC, Casablanca.

Bouzidi, Z., Boudries, A., & Amad, M. (2020). Towards a smart interface-based automated learning environment through social media for disaster management and smart disaster education. In *Intelligent Computing: Proceedings of the 2020 Computing Conference,* Volume 1 (pp. 443-468). Springer International Publishing.

Brendan Brow. (2021). *Azure Blob Storage | Microsoft Azure*. Microsoft.

Brownlee, J. (2011). *Clever Algorithms: Nature-Inspired Programming Recipes* (1st ed.). Lulu.com.

Bryant, C., & Briscoe, T. (2017). *Automatic Annotation and Evaluation of Error Types for Grammatical Error Correction.* Association for Computational Linguistics. DOI: 10.18653/v1/P17-1074

Brynjolfsson, E., & McAfee, A. (2014). *The Second Machine Age: Work, Progress, and Prosperity in a Time of Brilliant Technologies.* W.W. Norton & Company.

Brynjolfsson, E., & McAfee, A. (2017). What's driving the machine learning explosion? *Harvard Business Review*, 17.

Bryson, J. J., & Winfield, A. F. (2017). Standardizing ethical design for artificial intelligence and autonomous systems. *Computer*, 50(5), 116–119. DOI: 10.1109/MC.2017.154

Buchmeister, B., Palcic, I., & Ojstersek, R. (2019). Artificial intelligence in manufacturing companies and broader: An overview. *DAAAM International Scientific Book*, 81–98.

Bughin, J., Hazan, E., Ramaswamy, S., Chui, M., Allas, T., Dahlström, P., & Trench, M. (2018). *Skill shift: Automation and the future of the workforce.* McKinsey Global Institute.

Butcher, J., & Beridze, I. (2019). What is the state of artificial intelligence governance globally? *RUSI Journal*, 164(5-6), 88–96. DOI: 10.1080/03071847.2019.1694260

Butler, H., Daly, M., Doyle, A., Gillies, S., Schaub, T., & Schmidt, C. (2016). The GeoJSON format specification. In *IRFC 7946* (Vol. 67).

Byanyima, F., Edison, M., Kadengye, D. T., Arineitwe, S., Mijwil, M. M., Gaballa, M., Veedu, R. C., & Turyasingura, B. (2025). Foreign Direct Investment and Environmental Challenges: A Case Study of Uganda With Analytical Perspective. In *Community Resilience and Climate Change Challenges: Pursuit of Sustainable Development Goals (SDGs)* (pp. 283–296). IGI Global Scientific Publishing.

Cambria, E., & White, B. (2014). Jumping NLP curves: A review of natural language processing research. *IEEE Computational Intelligence Magazine*, 9(2), 48–57. DOI: 10.1109/MCI.2014.2307227

Cao, J., Guan, Z., Yue, L., Ullah, S., & Sherwani, R. A. K. (2020). A bottleneck degreebased migrating birds optimization algorithm for the pcb production scheduling. *IEEE Access : Practical Innovations, Open Solutions*, 8, 209579–209593.

Cascón-Morán, I., Gómez, M., Fernández, D., Gil Del Val, A., Alberdi, N., & González, H. (2024). Towards Zero-Defect Manufacturing Based on Artificial Intelligence through the Correlation of Forces in 5-Axis Milling Process. *Machines (Basel)*, 12(4), 226.

Castelnovo, A., Crupi, R., Greco, G., & Regoli, D. (2021). The Zoo of Fairness Metrics in Machine Learning.

Cath, C., Wachter, S., Mittelstadt, B., Taddeo, M., & Floridi, L. (2018). Artificial intelligence and the 'good society': The US, EU, and UK approach. *Science and Engineering Ethics*, 24(2), 505–528. PMID: 28353045

Cavalieri, A. (2022). An Intelligent System for the Categorization of Question Time Official Documents of the Italian Chamber of Deputies. *Journal of Information Technology & Politics*.

Chai, J. Y., Fang, R., Liu, C., & She, L. (2020). Collaborative language grounding toward situated human-robot dialogue. *AI Magazine*, 41(1), 20–31.

Chaitanya, G. K., & Raja Sekhar, K. (2020). A human gait recognition against information theft in smartphone using residual convolutional neural network. *International Journal of Advanced Computer Science and Applications*, 11(5). Advance online publication. DOI: 10.14569/IJACSA.2020.0110544

Chalmers, D. J. (2022). *Reality+: Virtual worlds and the problems of philosophy.* Penguin UK.

Chao, H., He, Y., Zhang, J., & Feng, J. (2019). Gaitset: Regarding gait as a set for cross-view gait recognition. *Proceedings of the AAAI Conference on Artificial Intelligence*, 33(1), 8126–8133. DOI: 10.1609/aaai.v33i01.33018126

Chao, H., Wang, K., He, Y., Zhang, J., & Feng, J. (2021). GaitSet: Cross-view gait recognition through utilizing gait as a deep set. *IEEE Transactions on Pattern Analysis and Machine Intelligence*, 44, 3467–3478. DOI: 10.1109/TPAMI.2021.3057879 PMID: 33560976

Chaudhary, U., Birbaumer, N., & Ramos-Murguialday, A. (2016). Brain-computer interfaces for communication and rehabilitation. *Nature Reviews. Neurology*, 12(9), 513–525. DOI: 10.1038/nrneurol.2016.113 PMID: 27539560

Chen, J., Chen, S., Luo, S., Wang, Q., Cao, B., & Li, X. (2020). An intelligent task offloading algorithm (itoa) for uav edge computing network. *Digital Communications and Networks*, 6, 433–443.

Chen, X., Zhang, H., Wu, C., Mao, S., Ji, Y., & Bennis, M. (2019). Optimized computation offloading performance in virtual edge computing systems via deep reinforcement learning. *IEEE Internet of Things Journal*, 6, 4005–4018.

Choudhury, S., Wihardja, H., Bhardwaj, A., & Rudinac, M. (2021). Socially-aware AI for multilingual information retrieval and recommendation. *ACM Transactions on Multimedia Computing Communications and Applications*, 17(2s), 1–21.

Cinnamon, J., Jones, S. K., & Adger, W. N. (2016). Evidence and future potential of mobile phone data for disease disaster management. *Geoforum*, 75, 253–264. PMID: 32287362

Cloud, G. (2023). *Cloud Storage | Google Cloud.* Google.

Coello, C. A. C., Pulido, G. T., & Lechuga, M. S. (2004). Handling multiple objectives with particle swarm optimization. *IEEE Transactions on Evolutionary Computation*, 8(3), 256–279. DOI: 10.1109/TEVC.2004.826067

Comité d'Application de la Charte de l'Expertise en Evaluation Immobilière (CACE-EI). (2017). Charte de l'Expertise en Evaluation Immobilière. 5e édition. Editions PALaroche.Paris, 89p.

Coursera Staff. (2023). *What Is Machine Learning Fairness?* What You Need to Know. Coursera.

Couzin, I. D., Ioannou, C. C., Demirel, G., Gross, T., Torney, C. J., Hartnett, A., Conradt, L., Levin, S. A., & Leonard, N. E. (2011). Uninformed individuals promote democratic consensus in animal groups. *Science*, 334(6062), 1578–1580. DOI: 10.1126/science.1210280 PMID: 22174256

Cui, L., Xu, C., Yang, S., Huang, J. Z., Li, J., Wang, X., Ming, Z., & Lu, N. (2019). Joint optimization of energy consumption and latency in mobile edge computing for internet of things. *IEEE Internet of Things Journal*, 6, 4791–4803.

Cui, Y., Zhang, D., Zhang, T., Chen, L., Piao, M., & Zhu, H. (2020). Novel method of mobile edge computation offloading based on evolutionary game strategy for iot devices. *AEÜ. International Journal of Electronics and Communications*, 118, 153134.

Cui, Z., & Gu, X. (2015). An improved discrete artificial bee colony algorithm to minimize the makespan on hybrid flow shop problems. *Neurocomputing*, 148, 248–259.

Cutress, I. (2022). Intel's manufacturing roadmap from 2019 to 2029: back porting, 7nm, 5nm, 3nm, 2nm, and 1.4 nm. https://www.anandtech.com/show/15217/intels .manufacturing-roadmap-from-2019-to-2029

Dai, W., Liu, R., Wu, T., Wang, M., Yin, J., & Liu, J. (2024). Deeply Supervised Skin Lesions Diagnosis with Stage and Branch Attention. *IEEE Journal of Biomedical and Health Informatics, 28*(2), 719-729. Advance online publication. DOI: 10.1109/ JBHI.2023.3308697 PMID: 37624725

Danilak, R. (2022). Why energy is a big and rapidly growing problem for data centers. https://www.forbes.com/sites/forbestechcouncil/2017/12/15/why-energy -is-a-big-and-rapidly-growing-problem-for-data-centers

Darwish, K., & Abdelali, A. (2017). Arabic POS Tagging : Don't Abandon Feature Engineering Just Yet. *Proceedings of the Third Arabic Natural Language Processing Workshop*, 130–137. DOI: 10.18653/v1/W17-1316

Das Jui, T., & Rivas, P. (2024). Fairness issues, current approaches, and challenges in machine learning modelsInternational Journal of Machine Learning and Cybernetics Ericsson. (2021). AI bias and human rights: Why ethical AI matters. Retrieved from https://www.ericsson.com/en/blog/2021/11/ai-bias-what-is-it

Data, I. B. M., & Team, A. I. (2023). Shedding light on AI bias with real world examples. Retrieved from https://www.ibm.com/blog/shedding-light-on-ai-bias -with-real-world-examples

DataCamp. (2023). What is Algorithmic Bias? Retrieved from https://www.datacamp.com/blog/what-is-algorithmic-bias

Daud, A., Khan, W., & Che, D. (2017). Urdu language processing : A survey. *Artificial Intelligence Review*, 47(3), 279–311. DOI: 10.1007/s10462-016-9482-x

Daud, S. N. S. S., Sudirman, R., & Shing, T. W. (2023). Safe-level SMOTE method for handling the class imbalanced problem in electroencephalography dataset of adult anxious state. *Biomedical Signal Processing and Control*, 83, 104649.

de Lourdes Berrios Cintrón, M., Broomandi, P., Cárdenas-Escudero, J., Cáceres, J. O., & Galán-Madruga, D. (2024). Elucidating Best Geospatial Estimation Method Applied to Environmental Sciences. *Bulletin of Environmental Contamination and Toxicology*, 112(1). Advance online publication. DOI: 10.1007/s00128-023-03835-0 PMID: 38063862

De Paor, D. G., & Whitmeyer, S. J. (2011). Geological and geophysical modeling on virtual globes using KML, COLLADA, and Javascript. *Computers & Geosciences*, 37(1). Advance online publication. DOI: 10.1016/j.cageo.2010.05.003

Deberlanger, J. (2020). *Machine Learning Price Prediction on Green Building Prices*.

Deb, K., Pratap, A., Agarwal, S., & Meyarivan, T. (2002). A fast and elitist multi-objective genetic algorithm: NSGA-II. *IEEE Transactions on Evolutionary Computation*, 6(2), 182–197. DOI: 10.1109/4235.996017

Deb, K., Roy, P. C., & Hussein, R. (2021). Surrogate Modeling Approaches for Multiobjective Optimization: Methods, Taxonomy, and Results. *Mathematical & Computational Applications*, 26(1). Advance online publication. DOI: 10.3390/mca26010005

Dehghani, M., Tiňo, P., & Gholipour, M. (2019). Spiking neural network learning and memory. *Neural Networks*, 111, 18–25.

Dell'Orletta, F. (2009). Ensemble system sfor Part-of-Speech tagging. *Proceedings of EVALITA*, 1-8.

Demartini, D., Pizzamiglio, S., Di Matteo, R., & Cappa, S. F. (2022). Memory enhancement: New insights from transcranial electrical stimulation. *Journal of Cognitive Enhancement: Towards the Integration of Theory and Practice*, 6(2), 187–198.

Deng, J., Dong, W., Socher, R., Li, L.-J., Li, K., & Li, F.-F. (2009). ImageNet : A large-scale hierarchical image database. *2009 IEEE Conference on Computer Vision and Pattern Recognition*, 248-255. DOI: 10.1109/CVPR.2009.5206848

Deng, M., Wang, C., Cheng, F., & Zeng, W. (2017). Fusion of spatial-temporal and kinematic features for gait recognition with deterministic learning. *Pattern Recognition*, 67, 186–200. DOI: 10.1016/j.patcog.2017.02.014

Dhifaoui, S., Houaidia, C., & Saidane, L. A. (2024). Computing paradigms for smart farming in the era of drones: A systematic review. *Annales Des Telecommunications. Annales des Télécommunications*, 79(1–2). Advance online publication. DOI: 10.1007/s12243-023-00997-0

Dignum, V. (2019). *Responsible Artificial Intelligence: How to Develop and Use AI in a Responsible Way*. Springer. DOI: 10.1007/978-3-030-30371-6

Direction-régional-de Rabat-Sale-Kenitra. (2014). *Projections de la population de la région de Rabat-Salé-Kénitra, 2014-2030*. 1–70. https://www.hcp.ma/region - rabat/attachment/1048729/

Dodda, S., Chintala, S., Kanungo, S., Adedoja, T., & Sharma, S. (2024). Exploring AI-driven Innovations in Image Communication Systems for Enhanced Medical Imaging Applications. *Journal of Electrical Systems*, 20(3s), 949–959.

Dong, K., Zhou, C., Ruan, Y., & Li, Y. (2020). MobileNetV2 model for image classification. *2020 2nd International Conference on Information Technology and Computer Application (ITCA)*, 476-480. https://ieeexplore.ieee.org/abstract/document/9422058/

Dong, X., Yu, Z., Cao, W., Shi, Y., & Ma, Q. (2020). A survey on ensemble learning. In *Frontiers of Computer Science* (Vol. 14, Issue 2). DOI: 10.1007/s11704-019-8208-z

Dong, H., Sun, J., Sun, X., & Ding, R. (2020). A many-objective feature selection for multi-label classification. *Knowledge-Based Systems*, 208, 106456. DOI: 10.1016/j.knosys.2020.106456

Dong, X., Huang, H., & Chen, P. (2009). An iterated local search algorithm for the permutation flowshop problem with total flowtime criterion. *Computers & Operations Research*, 36(5), 1664–1669.

Dong, Z., Yang, D., Reindl, T., & Walsh, W. M. (2013). Short-term solar irradiance forecasting using exponential smoothing state space model. *Energy*, 55, 1104–1113. DOI: 10.1016/j.energy.2013.04.027

Doo, F. X., Kulkarni, P., Siegel, E. L., Toland, M., Yi, P. H., Carlos, R. C., & Parekh, V. S. (2024). Economic and Environmental Costs of Cloud Technologies for Medical Imaging and Radiology Artificial Intelligence. *Journal of the American College of Radiology*, 21(2). Advance online publication. DOI: 10.1016/j.jacr.2023.11.011 PMID: 38072221

Dorigo, M., & Stützle, T. (2019). *Ant colony optimization: overview and recent advances*. Springer International Publishing.

Dos Santos Rocha, R., Widera, A., van den Berg, R. P., de Albuquerque, J. P., & Helingrath, B. (2016). Improving the Involvement of Digital Volunteers in Disaster Management. In *Proceedings of the International Conference on Information Technology in Disaster Risk Reduction*. Springer.

Doshi-Velez, F., & Kortz, M. (2017). Accountability of AI under the law: The role of explanation. arXiv preprint arXiv:1711.01134.

Drchal, J., Čertický, M., & Jakob, M. (2019). Data-driven activity scheduler for agent-based mobility models. *Transportation Research Part C, Emerging Technologies*, 98, 370–390.

Dubey, P., Kumar Tiwari, A., & Raja, R. (2023). Amazon Web Services: the Definitive Guide for Beginners and Advanced Users. In *Amazon Web Services: the Definitive Guide for Beginners and Advanced Users*. DOI: 10.2174/97898151658211230101

Duman, E., Uysal, M., & Alkaya, A. F. (2012). Migrating birds optimization: A new metaheuristic approach and its performance on quadratic assignment problem. *Information Sciences*, 217, 65–77.

Durugkar, I., Repucci, B., & Stone, P. (2016). Dynamic integration of heterogeneous swarm behaviors using mood. In *Proceedings of the 2016 International Conference on Autonomous Agents & Multiagent Systems* (pp. 1203-1204).

Dutta, P. K., Singh, B., Towfeek, A.-S. K., Adamopoulou, J. P., Bardavouras, A. N., Bamwerinde, W., Turyasingura, B., & Ayiga, N. (2024). IoT Revolutionizes Humidity Measurement and Management in Smart Cities to Enhance Health and Wellness. *Mesopotamian Journal of Artificial Intelligence in Healthcare*, 2024, 110–117.

Dwarakanath, L., Kamsin, A., Rasheed, R. A., Anandhan, A., & Shuib, L. (2021). Automated machine learning approaches for emergency response and coordination via social media in the aftermath of a disaster: A review. *IEEE Access : Practical Innovations, Open Solutions*, 9, 68917–68931.

Ehaimir, M. E., Jarraya, I., Ouarda, W., & Alimi, A. M. (2017). Human gait identity recognition system based on gait pal and pal entropy (GPPE) and distances features fusion. In 2017 Sudan Conference on Computer Science and Information Technology (SCCSIT) 1-5. DOI: 10.1109/SCCSIT.2017.8293061

Ekbal, A., Hasanuzzaman, M., & Bandyopadhyay, S. (2009). Voted approach for part of speech tagging in bengali. Proceedings of the 23rd Pacific Asia Conference on Language, Information and Computation, 1, 120-129.

Ekbal, A., & Bandyopadhyay, S. (2008). Part of Speech Tagging in Bengali Using Support Vector Machine. *International Conference on Information Technology.* IEEE. DOI: 10.1109/ICIT.2008.12

El Idrissi Abdelwahed. (2015). Réflexions sur la politique foncière au Maroc. Travaux de la commission Foncière du Cadastre et Cartographie de l'Ordre National des Ingénieurs Géomètres Topographes (Maroc), Marrakech.

El Idrissi El-Bouzaidi, Y., & Abdoun, O. (2021). DenTcov : Deep Transfer Learning-Based Automatic Detection of Coronavirus Disease (COVID-19) Using Chest X-ray Images. In Motahhir, S., & Bossoufi, B. (Eds.), *Digital Technologies and Applications* (Vol. 211, pp. 967–977). Springer International Publishing. DOI: 10.1007/978-3-030-73882-2_88

El Idrissi El-Bouzaidi, Y., & Abdoun, O. (2023). CNN-Based Deep Features with Ensemble Learning for COVID-19 Classification. In Farhaoui, Y., Rocha, A., Brahmia, Z., & Bhushab, B. (Eds.), *Artificial Intelligence and Smart Environment* (Vol. 635, pp. 325–330). Springer International Publishing. DOI: 10.1007/978-3-031-26254-8_46

El Idrissi El-Bouzaidi, Y., & Abdoun, O. (2024). Health Care Intelligent System : Deep Residual Network Powered by Data Augmentation for Automatic Melanoma Image Classification. In Bendaoud, M., El Fathi, A., Bakhsh, F. I., & Pierluigi, S. (Eds.), *Advances in Control Power Systems and Emerging Technologies* (pp. 223–230). Springer Nature Switzerland. DOI: 10.1007/978-3-031-51796-9_27

El-Bouzaidi, Y. E. I., & Abdoun, O. (2023). Advances in artificial intelligence for accurate and timely diagnosis of COVID-19 : A comprehensive review of medical imaging analysis. *Scientific African*, 01961.

El-Bouzaidi, Y. E. I., & Abdoun, O. (2024). Artificial Intelligence for Sustainable Dermatology in Smart Green Cities : Exploring Deep Learning Models for Accurate Skin Lesion Recognition. *Procedia Computer Science*, 236, 233–240.

Elharrouss, O., Almaadeed, N., Al-Maadeed, S., & Bouridane, A. (2020). Gait recognition for person re-identification. *The Journal of Supercomputing*, 1–20. DOI: 10.1007/s11227-020-03409-5

Erdelj, M., & Natalizio, E. (2016). UAV-assisted disaster management: Applications and open issues. In *Proceedings of the 2016 International Conference on Computing, Networking and Communications (ICNC 2016)*. IEEE.

Ezugwu, A. E., Ikotun, A. M., Oyelade, O. O., Abualigah, L., Agushaka, J. O., Eke, C. I., & Akinyelu, A. A. (2022). A comprehensive survey of clustering algorithms: State-of-the-art machine learning applications, taxonomy, challenges, and future research prospects. *Engineering Applications of Artificial Intelligence*, 110, 104743.

Fan, C., Cui, Z., & Zhong, X. (2018). House prices prediction with machine learning algorithms. In *ACM International Conference Proceeding Series*. DOI: 10.1145/3195106.3195133

Fan, C., Wu, F., & Mostafavi, A. (2020). A hybrid machine learning pipeline for automated mapping of events and locations from social media in disasters. *IEEE Access : Practical Innovations, Open Solutions*, 8, 10478–10490.

Färe, R., & Grosskopf, S. (2006). *New directions: efficiency and productivity* (Vol. 3). Springer Science & Business Media.

Feng, L., Li, W., Lin, Y., Zhu, L., Guo, S., & Zhen, Z. (2020). Joint computation offloading and URLLC resource allocation for collaborative MEC assisted cellular-v2x networks. *IEEE Access : Practical Innovations, Open Solutions*, 8, 24914–24926.

Fernandez-Viagas, V., Valente, J. M., & Framinan, J. M. (2018). Iterated-greedy-based algorithms with beam search initialization for the permutation flowshop to minimise total tardiness. *Expert Systems with Applications*, 94, 58–69.

Floridi, L., & Cowls, J. (2019). A unified framework of five principles for AI in society. *Harvard Data Science Review*, 1(1).

Floridi, L., Cowls, J., Beltrametti, M., Chatila, R., Chazerand, P., Dignum, V., & Schafer, B. (2018). AI4People—An ethical framework for a good AI society: Opportunities, risks, principles, and recommendations. *Minds and Machines*, 28(4), 689–707. DOI: 10.1007/s11023-018-9482-5 PMID: 30930541

Flowers, S. (2023). *Designing and Implementing Cloud-native Applications Using Microsoft Azure Cosmos DB*.

Fois, M., Fenu, G., & Bacchetta, G. (2019). Estimating land market values from real estate offers: A replicable method in support of biodiversity conservation strategies. In *Ambio* (Vol. 48, Issue 3). Springer Netherlands. DOI: 10.1007/s13280-018-1074-3

Fonti, V., & Belitser, E. (2017). Feature selection-using lasso. *VU Amsterdam Research Paper in Business Analytics, 30*, 1–25. https://www.researchgate.net/profile/David-Booth-7/post/Regression-of-pairwise-trait-similarity-on-similarity-in-personal-attri-butes/attachment/5b18368d4cde260d15e3a4e3/AS%3A634606906785793%401528313485788/download/werkstuk-fonti_tcm235-836234.pdf

Foumani, N. M., Tan, C. W., Webb, G. I., & Salehi, M. (2024). Improving position encoding of transformers for multivariate time series classification. *Data Mining and Knowledge Discovery*, 38(1), 22–48. DOI: 10.1007/s10618-023-00948-2

Framinan, J. M., Gupta, J. N., & Leisten, R. (2004). A review and classification of heuristics for permutation flow-shop scheduling with makespan objective. *The Journal of the Operational Research Society*, 55(12), 1243–1255.

Frank, M. R., Sun, L., Cebrian, M., Youn, H. Y., & Rahwan, I. (2019). Small cities face greater impact from automation. *Journal of the Royal Society, Interface*, 16(151), 20180946. PMID: 29436514

Freitas, D., Lopes, L. G., & Morgado-Dias, F. (2020). Particle swarm optimisation: A historical review up to the current developments. *Entropy (Basel, Switzerland)*, 22(3), 362. PMID: 33286136

Freund, Y., & Schapire, R. E. (1995). A decision-theoretic generalization of on-line learning and an application to boosting. In *European Conference on Computational Learning Theory*. DOI: 10.1007/3-540-59119-2_166

Gandhi, A., Adhvaryu, K., Poria, S., Cambria, E., & Hussain, A. (2023). Multimodal sentiment analysis: A systematic review of history, datasets, multimodal fusion methods, applications, challenges and future directions. *Information Fusion*, 91, 424–444.

Gao, F., Tian, T., Yao, T., & Zhang, Q. (2021). Human gait recognition based on multiple feature combination and parameter optimization algorithms. *Computational Intelligence and Neuroscience*, 2021(1), 6693206. Advance online publication. DOI: 10.1155/2021/6693206 PMID: 33727913

Garcia, M. B., Adao, R. T., Pempina, E. B., Quejado, C. K., & Maranan, C. R. B. (2023, August). MILES Virtual World: A Three-Dimensional Avatar-Driven Metaverse-Inspired Digital School Environment for FEU Group of Schools. In *Proceedings of the 7th International Conference on Education and Multimedia Technology* (pp. 23-29).

Garnett, R. (2023). *Bayesian optimization*. Cambridge University Press. https://books.google.com/books?hl=fr&lr=&id=MBCrEAAAQBAJ&oi=fnd&pg=PP1&dq=Bayesian+optimization&ots=tkKBuiYbxG&sig=Me8TEKWzwKqwa2IgvvfbsMO18Zc

Gede Suacana, I. W., Sudana, I. W., Wiratmaja, I. N., & Rukmawati, D. (2024). Urban Land Consolidation Policy in the Context of Creating a Good Environment According to Spatial Planning in Indonesia. *Journal of Wood Science*, 3(2). Advance online publication. DOI: 10.58344/jws.v3i2.559

Geis, J. R., Brady, A. P., Wu, C. C., Spencer, J. A., Ranschaert, E., Jaremko, J. L., Langer, S. G., Kitts, A. B., Birch, J., Shields, W. F., van den Hoven van Genderen, R., Kotter, E., Gichoya, J. W., Cook, T. S., Morgan, M. B., Tang, A., Safdar, N. M., & Kohli, M. (2019). Ethics of artificial intelligence in radiology: Summary of the joint European and North American multisociety statement. *Insights Into Imaging*, 10(1), 101. DOI: 10.1186/s13244-019-0785-8 PMID: 31571015

Gelders, L. F., & Sambandam, N. (1978). Four simple heuristics for scheduling a flow-shop. *International Journal of Production Research*, 16(3), 221–231.

George, A. H., Fernando, M., George, A. S., Baskar, T., & Pandey, D. (2021). Metaverse: The next stage of human culture and the internet. *International Journal of Advanced Research Trends in Engineering and Technology*, .8(12), 1–10.

Ghaeminia, M. H., & Shokouhi, S. B. (2019). On the selection of spatiotemporal filtering with classifier ensemble method for effective gait recognition. *Signal, Image and Video Processing*, 13(1), 43–51. DOI: 10.1007/s11760-018-1326-5

Ghobaei-Arani, M., Souri, A., Safara, F., & Norouzi, M. (2020). An efficient task scheduling approach using moth-flame optimization algorithm for cyber-physical system applications in fog computing. *Transactions on Emerging Telecommunications Technologies*, 31, 2.

Ghosh, A., & Roy, S. (2023, February). An Emoticon-Based Sentiment Aggregation on Metaverse Related Tweets. In *The 3rd International Conference on Artificial Intelligence and Computer Vision (AICV2023), March 5–7, 2023* (Vol. 164, p. 358). Springer Nature.

Gmys, J., Mezmaz, M., Melab, N., & Tuyttens, D. (2020). A computationally efficient branch-and-bound algorithm for the permutation flow-shop scheduling problem. *European Journal of Operational Research*, 284(3), 814–833.

Goldberg, D. E., & Holland, J. H. (1988). Genetic Algorithms and Machine Learning. *Machine Learning*, 3(2), 95–99. DOI: 10.1023/A:1022602019183

Go, M. P. V. (2017). Using Stanford Part-of-Speech Tagger for the Morphologically-rich Filipino Language. *Proceedings of the 31st Pacific Asia Conference on Language, Information and Computation*, 81–88.

Gopalakrishnan, A., & Vadivel, V. (2023). Multi-objective metaheuristic optimization algorithms for wrapper-based feature selection: A literature survey. *Bulletin of Electrical Engineering and Informatics*, 12(5), 3061–3066. DOI: 10.11591/eei.v12i5.4757

Gos, M., Krzyszczak, J., Baranowski, P., Murat, M., & Malinowska, I. (2020). Combined TBATS and SVM model of minimum and maximum air temperatures applied to wheat yield prediction at different locations in Europe. *Agricultural and Forest Meteorology*, 281, 107827.

Gouda, W., Sama, N. U., Al-Waakid, G., Humayun, M., & Jhanjhi, N. Z. (2022). Detection of Skin Cancer Based on Skin Lesion Images Using Deep Learning. *Health Care*, 10(7), 7. Advance online publication. DOI: 10.3390/healthcare10071183 PMID: 35885710

Goyal, A., Gupta, V., & Kumar, M. (2018). Recent named entity recognition and classification techniques: A systematic review. *Computer Science Review*, 29, 21–43. DOI: 10.1016/j.cosrev.2018.06.001

Graham, R. L., Lawler, E. L., Lenstra, J. K., & Kan, A. R. (1979). Optimization and approximation in deterministic sequencing and scheduling: a survey. In *Annals of discrete mathematics* (Vol. 5, pp. 287–326). Elsevier.

Gsma. (2022). Definitive data and analysis for the mobile data industry. https://www.gsmaintelligence.com/data/

Guha, S., Jana, R. K., & Sanyal, M. K. (2022). Artificial neural network approaches for disaster management: A literature review (2010–2021). *International Journal of Disaster Risk Reduction*, 103276.

Guidotti, R., Monreale, A., Ruggieri, S., Turini, F., Giannotti, F., & Pedreschi, D. (2018). A survey of methods for explaining black box models. *ACM Computing Surveys*, 51(5), 1–42. DOI: 10.1145/3236009

Gui, R., Wang, Y., Yao, Y., & Cheng, G. (2020). Enhanced logical vibrational resonance in a two-well potential system. *Chaos, Solitons, and Fractals*, 138, 109952.

Gul, S., Malik, M. I., Khan, G. M., & Shafait, F. (2021). Multi-view gait recognition system using spatio-temporal features and deep learning. *Expert Systems with Applications*, 179, 115057. DOI: 10.1016/j.eswa.2021.115057

Gunantara, N. (2018). A review of multi-objective optimization: Methods and its applications. *Cogent Engineering*, 5(1), 1–16. DOI: 10.1080/23311916.2018.1502242

Guo, H., Li, B., Zhang, Y., Zhang, Y., Li, W., Qiao, F., Rong, X., & Zhou, S. (2020). Gait recognition based on the feature extraction of gabor filter and linear discriminant analysis and improved local coupled extreme learning machine. *Mathematical Problems in Engineering*, 2020, 1–9. Advance online publication. DOI: 10.1155/2020/5393058

433

Guo, S., Liu, J., Yang, Y., Xiao, B., & Li, Z. (2019). Energy-efficient dynamic computation offloading and cooperative task scheduling in mobile cloud computing. *IEEE Transactions on Mobile Computing*, 18, 319–333.

Gupta, S., Kaur, M., Lakra, S., & Dixit, Y. (2020). A comparative theoretical and empirical analysis of machine learning algorithms. In *Webology* (Vol. 17, Issue 1). DOI: 10.14704/WEB/V17I1/WEB17011

Gupta, V., Joshi, N., & Mathur, I. (2016). POS tagger for Urdu using Stochastic approaches. *Proceedings of the Second International Conference on Information and Communication Technology for Competitive Strategies*, 56. DOI: 10.1145/2905055.2905114

Guyon, I., & De, A. M. (2003). An Introduction to Variable and Feature Selection André Elisseeff. In *Journal of Machine Learning Research* (Vol. 3).

Haas, M., Pelikan, H., & Seifert, J. (2020). Personalizing conversational agents for user engagement: Insights from a design study. In *Proceedings of the 2020 CHI Conference on Human Factors in Computing Systems* (pp. 1-14).

Hajimani, E., Ruano, M. G., & Ruano, A. E. (2015). MOGA design for neural networks based system for automatic diagnosis of Cerebral Vascular Accidents. *2015 IEEE 9th International Symposium on Intelligent Signal Processing (WISP) Proceedings*, 1–6. DOI: 10.1109/WISP.2015.7139170

Hamdani, T. M., Won, J. M., Alimi, A. M., & Karray, F. (2007a). Multi-objective Feature Selection with NSGA II. *Lecture Notes in Computer Science (Including Subseries Lecture Notes in Artificial Intelligence and Lecture Notes in Bioinformatics), 4431 LNCS*(PART 1), 240–247. DOI: 10.1007/978-3-540-71618-1_27

Hamdani, T. M., Won, J.-M., Alimi, A. M., & Karray, F. (2007b). Multi-objective Feature Selection with NSGA II. *International Conference on Adaptive and Natural Computing Algorithms*. https://api.semanticscholar.org/CorpusID:26841901

Hamilton, R. H., & Davison, H. K. (2022). *Legal and Ethical Challenges for HR in Machine Learning. Employee Responsibilities and Rights Journal*, 34, 19–39.

Hampson, R. E., Song, D., Chan, R. H., Marmarelis, V. Z., Leung, H. C., Griffin, A. L., & Deadwyler, S. A. (2018). Developing a hippocampal neural prosthetic to facilitate human memory encoding and recall. *Journal of Neural Engineering*, 15(3), 036014. DOI: 10.1088/1741-2552/aaaed7 PMID: 29589592

Han, J., & Bhanu, B. (2005). Individual recognition using gait energy image. *IEEE Transactions on Pattern Analysis and Machine Intelligence,*28(2) 316-322. DOI: 10.1109/TPAMI.2006.38

Han, F., Li, X., Zhao, J., & Shen, F. (2022). A unified perspective of classification-based loss and distance-based loss for cross-view gait recognition. *Pattern Recognition*, 125, 108519. DOI: 10.1016/j.patcog.2021.108519

Harvard Gazette. (2020). Ethical concerns mount as AI takes bigger decision-making role. Retrieved from https://news.harvard.edu/gazette/story/2020/10/ethical-concerns -mount-as-ai-takes-bigger-decision-making-role

Hassani, B. K. (2021). Societal bias reinforcement through machine learning: A credit scoring perspective. *AI and Ethics*, 1(3), 239–247. DOI: 10.1007/s43681-020-00026-z

Hedayati, S., Maleki, N., Olsson, T., Ahlgren, F., Seyednezhad, M., & Berahmand, K. (2023). MapReduce scheduling algorithms in Hadoop: a systematic study. In *Journal of Cloud Computing* (Vol. 12, Issue 1). DOI: 10.1186/s13677-023-00520-9

He, H., & Garcia, E. A. (2009). Learning from Imbalanced Data. *IEEE Transactions on Knowledge and Data Engineering*, 21(9), 1263–1284. DOI: 10.1109/TKDE.2008.239

He, K., Zhang, X., Ren, S., & Sun, J. (2016). Deep residual learning for image recognition. *Proceedings of the 2016 IEEE Conference on Computer Vision and Pattern Recognition (CVPR)*, 27-30.

Hibbi, F.-Z., Abdoun, O., & Haimoudi, E. K. (2022). Bayesian Network Modelling for Improved Knowledge Management of the Expert Model in the Intelligent Tutoring System. *International Journal of Advanced Computer Science and Applications*, 13(6). Advance online publication. DOI: 10.14569/IJACSA.2022.0130624

Hogan, P. (2019). AI accountability: Rethinking liability and blame. *Georgetown Journal of International Affairs*, 20(3), 60.

Horbiński, T., & Lorek, D. (2022). The use of Leaflet and GeoJSON files for creating the interactive web map of the preindustrial state of the natural environment. In *Journal of Spatial Science* (Vol. 67, Issue 1). DOI: 10.1080/14498596.2020.1713237

Ho, W. K. O., Tang, B. S., & Wong, S. W. (2021). Predicting property prices with machine learning algorithms. *Journal of Property Research*, 38(1), 48–70. DOI: 10.1080/09599916.2020.1832558

Huang, G., Liu, Z., Van Der Maaten, L., & Weinberger, K. Q. (2017b). Densely connected convolutional networks. *Proceedings of the IEEE Conference on Computer Vision and Pattern Recognition*, 4700-4708. https://openaccess.thecvf.com/content_cvpr_2017/html/Huang_Densely_Connected_Convolutional_CVPR_2017_paper.html

Huang, Z., Xu, W., & Kai, Y. (2015). Bidirectional LSTM-CRF Models for Sequence Tagging. arXiv preprint arXiv: 1508.01991.

Huang, G., Liu, Z., Van Der Maaten, L., & Weinberger, K. Q. (2017). Densely connected convolutional networks. *Proceedings of the 2017IEEE Conference on Computer Vision and Pattern Recognition (CVPR)*, 21-26.

Huang, G., Liu, Z., Van Der Maaten, L., & Weinberger, K. Q. (2017a). Densely Connected Convolutional Networks. *2017 IEEE Conference on Computer Vision and Pattern Recognition (CVPR)*, 2261-2269. DOI: 10.1109/CVPR.2017.243

Huang, G., Lu, Z., Pun, C., & Cheng, L. (2020). 'Flexible gait recognition based on flow regulation of local features between key frames. *IEEE Access : Practical Innovations, Open Solutions*, 8, 75381–75392. DOI: 10.1109/ACCESS.2020.2986554

Huang, H., Zeng, X., Zhao, L., Qiu, C., Wu, H., & Fan, L. (2022). Fusion of building information modeling and blockchain for metaverse: A survey. *IEEE Open Journal of the Computer Society*, 3, 195–207.

Huang, L., Feng, X., Zhang, C., Qian, L., & Wu, Y. (2019). Deep reinforcement learning-based joint task offloading and bandwidth allocation for multi-user mobile edge computing. *Digital Communications and Networks*, 5, 10–17.

Huang, M.-H., & Rust, R. T. (2018). Artificial intelligence in service. *Journal of Service Research*, 21(2), 155–172.

Huang, X., He, X., Gao, J., Deng, L., Acero, A., & Heck, L. (2013). Learning deep structured semantic models for web search using clickthrough data. In *Proceedings of the 22nd ACM International Conference on Information & Knowledge Management* (pp. 2333-2338). DOI: 10.1145/2505515.2505665

Huang, X., Jiang, Y., & Mostafavi, A. (2024). The emergence of urban heat traps and human mobility in 20 US cities. *NPJ Urban Sustainability*, 4(1). Advance online publication. DOI: 10.1038/s42949-024-00142-3

Huang, Z., Liang, D., Xu, P., & Xiang, B. (2020). Improve transformer models with better relative position embeddings. DOI: 10.18653/v1/2020.findings-emnlp.298

Huawei. (2022). Touching an intelligent world. https://www.huawei.com/minisite/giv/Files/whitepaper_en_2019.pdf

Hu, D., Ma, S., Guo, F., Lu, G., & Liu, J. (2015). Describing data formats of geographical models. *Environmental Earth Sciences*, 74(10). Advance online publication. DOI: 10.1007/s12665-015-4737-4

Hu, J., Li, K., Liu, C., & Li, K. (2020). Game-based task offloading of multiple mobile devices with qos in mobile edge computing systems of limited computation capacity. *ACM Transactions on Embedded Computing Systems*, 19(29), 1–29.

Hu, M., Xie, Z., Wu, D., Zhou, Y., Chen, X., & Xiao, L. (2020). Heterogeneous edge offloading with incomplete information: A minority game approach. *IEEE Transactions on Parallel and Distributed Systems*, 31, 2139–2154.

Hu, S., & Xiong, C. (2023). High-dimensional population inflow time series forecasting via an interpretable hierarchical transformer. *Transportation Research Part C, Emerging Technologies*, 146, 103962. DOI: 10.1016/j.trc.2022.103962

Hutson, M. (2018). Machine learning gets a health check. *Nature*, 555(7697), S1–S2.

Ienca, M., & Vayena, E. (2018). On the responsible use of digital data to tackle the COVID-19 pandemic. *Nature Medicine*, 26(4), 463–464. DOI: 10.1038/s41591-020-0832-5 PMID: 32284619

Imani, V., Sevilla-Salcedo, C., Fortino, V., & Tohka, J. (2023). *Multi-Objective Genetic Algorithm for Multi-View Feature Selection*. http://arxiv.org/abs/2305.18352

Imran, Z. U., Waqar, M., & Zaman, A. (2021). Using Machine Learning Algorithms for Housing Price Prediction: The Case of Isalamabad Housing Data. *Soft Computing and Machine Intelligence Journal*, 1(1), 11–23.

Invernizzi, L., Thomas, K., Kapravelos, A., Comanescu, O., Picod, J. M., & Bursztein, E. (2016, May). Cloak of visibility: Detecting when machines browse a different web. In *2016 IEEE Symposium on Security and Privacy (SP)* (pp. 743-758). IEEE. DOI: 10.1109/SP.2016.50

Iqbal, R., Doctor, F., More, B., Mahmud, S., & Yousuf, U. (2020). Big Data analytics and Computational Intelligence for Cyber–Physical Systems: Recent trends and state of the art applications. *Future Generation Computer Systems*, 105, 766–778.

J. A. P & Forcada. (2001). Part-of-Speech Tagging with Recurrent Neural Networks. *International Joint Conference on Neural Networks*, IEEE.

Jahangiri, N., Kahani, M., Ahamdi, R., & Sazvar, M. (2015, January). A study on part of speech tagging. *Review - Americas Society*.

Jamil, S., Mohd,T., Masrom,S., & Ab Rahim, N.(2020). Machine Learning Price Prediction on Green Building Prices.

Janicki, A. (2004). *Application of Neural Networks for POS Tagging and Intonation Control in Speech Synthesis for Polish. Soft Computing and intelligent systems*. SCIS.

Janiesch, C., Zschech, P., & Heinrich, K. (2021). Machine learning and deep learning. *Electronic Markets*, 31(3), 685–695. DOI: 10.1007/s12525-021-00475-2

Jarrahi, M. H. (2018). Artificial intelligence and the future of work: Human-AI symbiosis in organizational decision making. *Business Horizons*, 61(4), 577–586.

Jatav, R. (2017). Improving Part-of-Speech Tagging for NLP Pipelines.

Jawaid, B., Kamran, A., & Bojar, O. (2014, May). A Tagged Corpus and a Tagger for Urdu. In *LREC* (Vol. 2, pp. 2938-2943).

Jawaid, B., & Bojar, O. (2012, December). Tagger voting for Urdu. In *Proceedings of the 3rd Workshop on South and Southeast Asian Natural Language Processing* (pp. 135-144).

Jiang, C., Cheng, X., Gao, H., Zhou, X., & Wan, J. (2019). Toward computation offloading in edge computing: A survey. *IEEE Access : Practical Innovations, Open Solutions*, 7, 131543–131558.

Jiang, F., Jiang, Y., Zhi, H., Dong, Y., Li, H., Ma, S., Wang, Y., Dong, Q., Shen, H., & Wang, Y. (2017). Artificial intelligence in healthcare: Past, present and future. *Stroke and Vascular Neurology*, 2(4), 230–243. DOI: 10.1136/svn-2017-000101 PMID: 29507784

Jin, F., Song, S., & Wu, C. (2007). An improved version of the neh algorithm and its application to large-scale flow-shop scheduling problems. *IIE Transactions*, 39(2), 229–234.

Jin, H. (2022). Hyperparameter Importance for Machine Learning Algorithms (arXiv:2201.05132).

Jobin, A., Ienca, M., & Vayena, E. (2019). The global landscape of AI ethics guidelines. *Nature Machine Intelligence*, 1(9), 389–399. DOI: 10.1038/s42256-019-0088-2

Jumelet, J., & Zuidema, W. (2023). *Feature Interactions Reveal Linguistic Structure in Language Models*. http://arxiv.org/abs/2306.12181

Jurgens, M., & Helsloot, I. (2018, March). the effect of social media on the dynamics of (self) resilience during disasters: A literature review. *Journal of Contingencies and Crisis Management*, 26(1), 79–88.

Kalpakis, K., Gada, D., & Puttagunta, V. (2001). Distance measures for effective clustering of ARIMA time-series. *Proceedings 2001 IEEE International Conference on Data Mining*, 273–280. DOI: 10.1109/ICDM.2001.989529

Kang, Y., Cai, Z., Tan, C. W., Huang, Q., & Liu, H. (2020). Natural language processing (NLP) in management research: A literature review. *Journal of Management Analytics*, 7(2), 139–172. DOI: 10.1080/23270012.2020.1756939

Kaplan, A., & Haenlein, M. (2019). Siri, Siri, in my hand: Who's the fairest in the land? On the interpretations, illustrations, and implications of artificial intelligence. *Business Horizons*, 62(1), 15–25. DOI: 10.1016/j.bushor.2018.08.004

Karaboga, D., & Basturk, B. (2007). A powerful and efficient algorithm for numerical function optimization: Artificial bee colony (abc) algorithm. *Journal of Global Optimization*, 39, 459–471.

Karacan, I., Senvar, O., & Bulkan, S. (2023). A novel parallel simulated annealing methodology to solve the no-wait flow shop scheduling problem with earliness and tardiness objectives. *Processes (Basel, Switzerland)*, 11(2), 454.

Karthikeya, T. (2019). Personalized Content Extraction and Text Classification Using Effective Web Scraping Techniques. *International Journal of Web Portals*, 11(2), 41–52. DOI: 10.4018/IJWP.2019070103

Kaur, A. (n.d.). Mitigating Bias in AI Algorithms: Identifying, and Ensuring Responsible AI. Retrieved from https://leena.ai/blog/mitigating-bias-in-ai

Kausar, S., Huahu, X. U., Ahmad, W., & Shabir, M. Y. (2019). A sentiment polarity categorization technique for online product reviews. *IEEE Access : Practical Innovations, Open Solutions*, 8, 3594–3605.

Kennedy, J., & Eberhart, R. (1995). Particle swarm optimization. *Proceedings of ICNN'95 - International Conference on Neural Networks, 4*, 1942–194. DOI: 10.1109/ICNN.1995.488968

Kennedy, M. C., Ford, E. D., Singleton, P., Finney, M., & Agee, J. K. (2007). Informed multi-objective decision-making in environmental management using Pareto optimality. *Journal of Applied Ecology*, 45(1), 181–192. DOI: 10.1111/j.1365-2664.2007.01367.x

Ke, R., Zhuang, Y., Pu, Z., & Wang, Y. (2020). A smart, efficient, and reliable parking surveillance system with edge artificial intelligence on IoT devices. *IEEE Transactions on Intelligent Transportation Systems*, 22(8), 4962–4974.

Khan, Khan, Khan, Khan, Khan, & Ullah. (2018). Urdu Word Segmentation using Machine Learning Approaches. *Inernational Journal of Advanced Computer Science and applications*, 9(6), 193–200.

Khan, A., & Baig, A. R. (2015). Multi-Objective Feature Subset Selection using Non-dominated Sorting Genetic Algorithm. *Journal of Applied Research and Technology*, 13(1), 145–159. DOI: 10.1016/S1665-6423(15)30013-4

Khanam, M. H., Madhumurthy, K. V., & Khudhus, A. (2013). Part-Of-Speech Tagging for Urdu in Scarce Resource : Mix Maximum Entropy Modelling System. *International Journal of Advanced Research in Computer and Communication Engineering*, 2(9), 3421–3425.

Khan, I. (2025). *Undisrupted: Leadership Essentials on Business Transformation, Profitability and Future Readiness*. John Wiley & Sons.

Khan, M. H., Farid, M. S., & Grzegorzek, M. (2019). Spatiotemporal features of human motion for gait recognition. *Signal, Image and Video Processing*, 13(2), 369–377. DOI: 10.1007/s11760-018-1365-y

Khan, W. Z., Ahmed, E., Hakak, S., Yaqoob, I., & Ahmed, A. (2019). Edge computing: A survey. *Future Generation Computer Systems*, 97, 219–235.

Khan, W., Daud, A., Khan, K., Nasir, J. A., Basheri, M., & Alotaibi, F. S. (2019). Part of Speech Tagging in Urdu : Comparison of Machine and Deep Learning Approaches. *IEEE Access : Practical Innovations, Open Solutions*, 7, 38918–38936. DOI: 10.1109/ACCESS.2019.2897327

Khan, W., Daud, A., Nasir, J. A., & Amjad, T. (2016). A survey on the state-of-the-art machine learning models in the context of NLP. *Kuwait Journal of Science*, 43(4), 95–113.

Khan, W., Daud, A., Nasir, J. A., Amjad, T., Arafat, S., Aljohani, N., & Alotaibi, F. S. (2019). Urdu part of speech tagging using conditional random fields. *Language Resources and Evaluation*, 53(3), 331–362. DOI: 10.1007/s10579-018-9439-6

Kilic, B., Hacar, M., & Gülgen, F. (2023). Effects of reverse geocoding on OpenStreetMap tag quality assessment. *Transactions in GIS*, 27(5). Advance online publication. DOI: 10.1111/tgis.13089

Kim, J., & Hastak, M. (2018). Social network analysis: Characteristics of online social networks after a disaster. *International Journal of Information Management*, 38(1), 86–96.

Kim, S. W., Kong, J. H., Lee, S. W., & Lee, S. (2022). Recent advances of artificial intelligence in manufacturing industrial sectors: A review. *International Journal of Precision Engineering and Manufacturing*, 1–19.

Kingsley, M. S. (2023). Cloud Platform. In *Cloud Technologies and Services: Theoretical Concepts and Practical Applications* (pp. 143–156). Springer.

Kingsley, M. S. (2024a). Amazon Web Services (AWS). In *Textbooks in Telecommunications Engineering: Vol. Part F1656*. DOI: 10.1007/978-3-031-33669-0_6

Kingsley, M. S. (2024b). Microsoft Azure. In *Cloud Technologies and Services : Theoretical Concepts and Practical Applications* (pp. 127–141). Springer International Publishing. DOI: 10.1007/978-3-031-33669-0_7

Kirisci, M., & Cagcag Yolcu, O. (2022). A new CNN-based model for financial time series: TAIEX and FTSE stocks forecasting. *Neural Processing Letters*, 54(4), 3357–3374. DOI: 10.1007/s11063-022-10767-z

Kitaev, N., Kaiser, Ł., & Levskaya, A. (2020). Reformer: The efficient transformer. *ArXiv Preprint ArXiv:2001.04451*.

Kitagawa, G., & Gersch, W. (1984). A smoothness priors–state space modeling of time series with trend and seasonality. *Journal of the American Statistical Association*, 79(386), 378–389.

Kohavi, R., & John, G. H. (n.d.). *Wrappers for feature subset selection*. http://robotics.stanford.edu/

Kohavi, R., & Sommerfield, D. (1995). Feature Subset Selection Using the Wrapper Method: Overfitting and Dynamic Search Space Topology. *Knowledge Discovery and Data Mining*. https://api.semanticscholar.org/CorpusID:5147685

Koohang, A., Nord, J. H., Ooi, K. B., Tan, G. W. H., Al-Emran, M., Aw, E. C. X., & Wong, L. W. (2023). Shaping the metaverse into reality: A holistic multidisciplinary understanding of opportunities, challenges, and avenues for future investigation. *Journal of Computer Information Systems*, 63(3), 735–765.

Koohfar, S., Woldemariam, W., & Kumar, A. (2023). Prediction of electric vehicles charging demand: A transformer-based deep learning approach. *Sustainability (Basel)*, 15(3), 2105. DOI: 10.3390/su15032105

Kopetz, H., & Steiner, W. (2022). *Real-time systems: design principles for distributed embedded applications*. Springer Nature.

Korpinen, O. J., & Aalto, M. KC, R., Tokola, T., & Ranta, T. (2023). Utilisation of Spatial Data in Energy Biomass Supply Chain Research—A Review. In *Energies* (Vol. 16, Issue 2). DOI: 10.3390/en16020893

Kotenko, I., Chechulin, A., & Komashinsky, D. (2017). Categorisation of web pages for protection against inappropriate content in the internet. *International Journal of Internet Protocol Technology*, 10(1), 61–71. DOI: 10.1504/IJIPT.2017.083038

Krichen, M. (2023). Convolutional neural networks: A survey. *Computers*, 12(8), 151.

Krietemeyer, B., Bartosh, A., & Covington, L. (2019). A shared realities workflow for interactive design using virtual reality and three-dimensional depth sensing. *International Journal of Architectural Computing*, 17(2), 220–235.

Krizhevsky, A., Sutskever, I., & Hinton, G. E. (2012). ImageNet classification with deep convolutional neural networks. In Advances in Neural Information Processing Systems (pp. 1097-1105).

Krizhevsky, A., Sutskever, I., & Hinton, G. E. (2012). *Imagenet classification with deep convolutional neural networks*. Adv. Neural Inf.Process. Syst.

Krotov, V., Johnson, L., & Silva, L. (2020). Tutorial: Legality and ethics of web scraping. *Communications of the Association for Information Systems*, 47(1), 539–563. DOI: 10.17705/1CAIS.04724

Krotov, V., & Silva, L. (2018). Legality and ethics of web scraping. *Americas Conference on Information Systems 2018: Digital Disruption, AMCIS 2018, May*.

Kubat, M., & Kubat, M. (2021). Artificial neural networks. An Introduction to Machine Learning, 117-143.

Kumar, H. & Giri, S. (2019). A flow shop scheduling algorithm based on artificial neural network.

Kumar, S., Gao, X., Welch, I., & Mansoori, M. (2016, March). A machine learning based web spam filtering approach. In 2016 IEEE 30th International Conference on Advanced Information Networking and Applications (AINA) (pp. 973-980). IEEE. DOI: 10.1109/AINA.2016.177

Kumar, H., & Giri, S. (2020). Optimisation of makespan of a flow shop problem using multi layer neural network. *International Journal of Computing Science and Mathematics*, 11(2), 107–122.

Kumar, L., & Mutanga, O. (2018). Google Earth Engine applications since inception: Usage, trends, and potential. *Remote Sensing*, 10(10). Advance online publication. DOI: 10.3390/rs10101509

Kumawat, D., & Jain, V. (2015). POS Tagging Approaches: A Comparison. *International Journal of Computer Applications*, 118(6), 32–38. DOI: 10.5120/20752-3148

Kusakunniran, W., (2014). Attribute-based learning for gait recognition using spatio-temporal interest points. *Elsevier Journal of Image and Visio Computing, 32*(12), 1117-1126.

L'Heureux, A., Grolinger, K., & Capretz, M. A. M. (2022). Transformer-based model for electrical load forecasting. *Energies*, 15(14), 4993. DOI: 10.3390/en15144993

Label Your Data. (2023). Bias in Machine Learning. Retrieved from https://labelyourdata.com/articles/bias-in-machine-learning

Lai, G., Chang, W.-C., Yang, Y., & Liu, H. (2018). Modeling long-and short-term temporal patterns with deep neural networks. *The 41st International ACM SIGIR Conference on Research & Development in Information Retrieval*, 95–104.

Lalitha, T. B., & Sreeja, P. S. (2023). Potential Web Content Identification and Classification System using NLP and Machine Learning Techniques. *International Journal of Engineering Trends and Technology*, 71(4), 403–415. DOI: 10.14445/22315381/IJETT-V71I4P235

La, Q. D., Ngo, M. V., Dinh, T. Q., Quek, T. Q., & Shin, H. (2019). Enabling intelligence in fog computing to achieve energy and latency reduction. *Digital Communications and Networks*, 5, 3–9.

Laurière, J. (1987). *Intelligence artificielle – Résolution de problèmes par l'homme et la machine Intelligence Artificielle Résolution de problème par l'Homme et la machine Jean- Louis Laurière.*

LeCun, Y., Bengio, Y., & Hinton, G. (2015). Deep learning. *Nature*, 521(7553), 436–444. DOI: 10.1038/nature14539 PMID: 26017442

Lee, J., & Toutanova, K. (2018). Pre-training of deep bidirectional transformers for language understanding. *ArXiv Preprint ArXiv:1810.04805, 3*(8).

Lee, C. P., Tan, A. W., & Tan, S. C. (2013). Gait recognition via optimally interpolated deformable contours. *Pattern Recognition Letters*, 34(6), 663–669. DOI: 10.1016/j.patrec.2013.01.013

Lee, C. P., Tan, A. W., & Tan, S. C. (2014). Gait probability image: An information-theoretic model of gait representation. *Journal of Visual Communication and Image Representation*, 25(6), 1489–1492. DOI: 10.1016/j.jvcir.2014.05.006

Lee, C. P., Tan, A. W., & Tan, S. C. (2014). Time-sliced averaged motion history image for gait recognition. *Journal of Visual Communication and Image Representation*, 25(5), 822–826. DOI: 10.1016/j.jvcir.2014.01.012

Lee, C. P., Tan, A. W., & Tan, S. C. (2015). Gait recognition with transient binary patterns. *Journal of Visual Communication and Image Representation*, 33, 69–77. DOI: 10.1016/j.jvcir.2015.09.006

Lee, C. P., Tan, A., & Lim, K. (2017). Review on vision-based gait recognition: Representations, classification schemes and datasets. *American Journal of Applied Sciences*, 14(2), 252–266. DOI: 10.3844/ajassp.2017.252.266

Lee, C. W. (2022). Application of metaverse service to healthcare industry: A strategic perspective. *International Journal of Environmental Research and Public Health*, 19(20), 13038. PMID: 36293609

Lee, D., & Yoon, S. N. (2021). Application of artificial intelligence-based technologies in the healthcare industry: Opportunities and challenges. *International Journal of Environmental Research and Public Health*, 18(1), 271. PMID: 33401373

Lee, H. J., & Gu, H. H. (2022). Empirical Research on the Metaverse User Experience of Digital Natives. *Sustainability*, 14(22), 14747.

Lemke, D., Mattauch, V., Heidinger, O., & Hense, H. W. (2015). Who Hits the Mark? A Comparative Study of the Free Geocoding Services of Google and OpenStreetMap. *Gesundheitswesen (Bundesverband der Ärzte des Öffentlichen Gesundheitsdienstes (Germany))*, 77(8–9). Advance online publication. DOI: 10.1055/s-0035-1549939 PMID: 26154258

Leo, M., Medioni, G., Trivedi, M., Kanade, T., & Farinella, G. M. (2017). Computer vision for assistive technologies. *Computer Vision and Image Understanding*, 154, 1–15.

Lezmi, E., & Xu, J. (2023). Time series forecasting with transformer models and application to asset management. *Available atSSRN* 4375798. DOI: 10.2139/ssrn.4375798

Li, L., Liu, H., Ma, Z., Mo, Y., Duan, Z., Zhou, J., & Zhao, J. (n.d.). *Multi-label Feature Selection via Information Gain.*

Liang, J., Mahmood, A., & Burger, D. (2020). End-to-end relation extraction using LSTMs on sequences and tree structures. *Journal of Computational Science*, 43, 101163.

Lian, Z., Gu, X., & Jiao, B. (2008). A novel particle swarm optimization algorithm for permutation flow-shop scheduling to minimize makespan. Chaos, Solitons &amp. *Fractals*, 35(5), 851–861.

Liao. (2020). A model-based gait recognition method with body pose and human prior knowledge. *Pattern Recognition, 98,* 107069. DOI: 10.1016/j.patcog.2019.107069

Liao, Q. V., & Cherry, E. C. (2021). Measuring and mitigating unintended bias in text classification. *Transactions of the Association for Computational Linguistics, 9,* 614–630.

Liashchynskyi, P., & Liashchynskyi, P. (2019). Grid Search, Random Search, Genetic Algorithm : A Big Comparison for NAS (arXiv:1912.06059). http://arxiv.org/abs/1912.06059

Li, C., Bai, J., Chen, Y., & Luo, Y. (2020). Resource and replica management strategy for optimizing financial cost and user experience in edge cloud computing system. *Inf. Sci., 516,* 33–55.

Li, C., Jianhang, T., & Luo, Y. (2019). Dynamic multi-user computation offloading for wireless powered mobile edge computing. *Journal of Network and Computer Applications, 131,* 1–15.

Li, C., Jianhang, T., Tang, H., & Luo, Y. (2019). Collaborative cache allocation and task scheduling for data-intensive applications in edge computing environment. *Future Generation Computer Systems, 95,* 249–264.

Li, C., Min, X., Sun, S., Lin, W., & Tang, Z. (2017). DeepGait: A learning deep convolutional representation for view-invariant gait recognition using joint bayesian. *Applied Sciences (Basel, Switzerland), 7*(3), 210. DOI: 10.3390/app7030210

Li, D., Guo, W., Chang, X., & Li, X. (2020). From earth observation to human observation: Geocomputation for social science. *Journal of Geographical Sciences, 30*(2). Advance online publication. DOI: 10.1007/s11442-020-1725-8

Li, D., & Lu, M. (2018). Integrating geometric models, site images and GIS based on Google Earth and Keyhole Markup Language. *Automation in Construction, 89.* Advance online publication. DOI: 10.1016/j.autcon.2018.02.002

Li, H., Gao, K., Duan, P.-Y., Li, J.-Q., & Zhang, L. (2022). An improved artificial bee colony algorithm with q-learning for solving permutation flow- shop scheduling problems. *IEEE Transactions on Systems, Man, and Cybernetics. Systems, 53*(5), 2684–2693.

Li, J., Gao, H., Lv, T., & Lu, Y. (2018). *Deep reinforcement learning based computation offloading and resource allocation for MEC. 2018 IEEE Wireless Communications and Networking Conference, WCNC 2018.* IEEE.

Li, J.-Z., Chen, W.-N., Zhang, J., & Zhan, Z.-H. (2015). A Parallel Implementation of Multiobjective Particle Swarm Optimization Algorithm Based on Decomposition. *2015 IEEE Symposium Series on Computational Intelligence*, 1310–1317. DOI: 10.1109/SSCI.2015.187

Li, L., Dai, S., Cao, Z., Hong, J., Jiang, S., & Yang, K. (2020). Using improved gradient-boosted decision tree algorithm based on Kalman filter (GBDT-KF) in time series prediction. *The Journal of Supercomputing*, 76(9), 6887–6900. DOI: 10.1007/s11227-019-03130-y

Lindsay, G. W. (2021). Convolutional neural networks as a model of the visual system: Past, present, and future. *Journal of Cognitive Neuroscience*, 33(10), 2017–2031. PMID: 32027584

Lin, L., Liao, X., Jin, H., & Li, P. (2019). Computation offloading toward edge computing. *Proceedings of the IEEE*, 107, 1584–1607.

Lipton, Z. C. (2016). The mythos of model interpretability. In *Proceedings of the 2016 ICML Workshop on Human Interpretability in Machine Learning (WHI 2016)* (pp. 1-8).

Li, S., Jin, X., Xuan, Y., Zhou, X., Chen, W., Wang, Y.-X., & Yan, X. (2019). Enhancing the locality and breaking the memory bottleneck of transformer on time series forecasting. *Advances in Neural Information Processing Systems*, 32.

Lishani, A. O., Boubchir, L., Khalifa, E., & Bouridane, A. (2017). Human gait recognition based on Haralick feature journal of Signal. *Signal, Image and Video Processing*, 11(6), 1123–1130. DOI: 10.1007/s11760-017-1066-y

Lishani, A. O., Boubchir, L., Khalifa, E., & Bouridane, A. (2019). Human gait recognition using GEI-based local multi-scale feature descriptors. *Multimedia Tools and Applications*, 78(5), 5715–5730. DOI: 10.1007/s11042-018-5752-8

Liu, D., Fan, Z., Fu, Q., Li, M., Faiz, M. A., Ali, S., & Khan, M. I. (2020). Random forest regression evaluation model of regional flood disaster resilience based on the whale optimization algorithm. *Journal of Cleaner Production*, 250, 119468.

Liu, M., Yu, F. R., Teng, Y., Leung, V. C. M., & Song, M. (2019). Distributed resource allocation in blockchain-based video streaming systems with mobile edge computing. *IEEE Transactions on Wireless Communications*, 18(1), 695–708.

Liu, P., Xu, G., Yang, K., Wang, K., & Meng, X. (2019). Jointly optimized energy-minimal resource allocation in cache-enhanced mobile edge computing systems. *IEEE Access : Practical Innovations, Open Solutions*, 7, 3336–3347.

Livieris, I. E., Pintelas, E., & Pintelas, P. (2020). A CNN–LSTM model for gold price time-series forecasting. *Neural Computing & Applications*, 32(23), 17351–17360. DOI: 10.1007/s00521-020-04867-x

Liwang, M., Wang, J., Gao, Z., Du, X., & Guizani, M. (2019). Game theory based opportunistic computation offloading in cloud-enabled iov. *IEEE Access : Practical Innovations, Open Solutions*, 7, 32551–32561.

Li, X., Makihara, Y., Xu, C., Yagi, Y., & Ren, M. (2019). Joint intensity transformer network for gait recognition robust against clothing and carrying status. *IEEE Transactions on Information Forensics and Security*, 14(12), 3102–3115. DOI: 10.1109/TIFS.2019.2912577

Li, Y., Ma, H., Wang, L., Mao, S., & Wang, G. (2020). Optimized content caching and user association for edge computing in densely deployed heterogeneous networks. *IEEE Transactions on Mobile Computing*. Advance online publication. DOI: 10.1109/TMC.2020.3033563

Li, Y., Xia, S., Zheng, M., Cao, B., & Liu, Q. (2019). Lyapunov optimization based trade-off policy for mobile cloud offloading in heterogeneous wireless networks. *IEEE Transactions on Cloud Computing*, 10, 491–505.

Luo, J., Zhang, J., Zi, C., Niu, Y., Tian, H., & Xiu, C. (2015). Gait recognition using GEI and AFDEI. *International Journal of Optics*, 2015, 1–5. Advance online publication. DOI: 10.1155/2015/763908

Luong, M. T., Socher, R., & Manning, C. D. (2013, August). Better word representations with recursive neural networks for morphology.

Lv, S. X., & Wang, L. (2022). Deep learning combined wind speed forecasting with hybrid time series decomposition and multi-objective parameter optimization. *Applied Energy*, 311. Advance online publication. DOI: 10.1016/j.apenergy.2022.118674

Lykousas, N. (2022). Analysis and detection of deviant and malicious behaviors in social media and beyond (Doctoral dissertation, University of Piraeus (Greece)).

Ma & Hovy. (2016). End-to-end Sequence Labeling via Bi-directional LSTM-CNNs-CRF. *Proceedings of the 54th Annual Meeting of Proceedings of the 54th Annual Meeting of the Association for Computational Linguistics*, 1, 1064–1074.

Mach, P., & Becvar, Z. (2017). Mobile edge computing: A survey on architecture and computation offloading. *IEEE Communications Surveys and Tutorials*, 19, 1628–1656.

Madan, R., & Mangipudi, P. S. (2018). Predicting computer network traffic: a time series forecasting approach using DWT, ARIMA and RNN. *2018 Eleventh International Conference on Contemporary Computing (IC3)*, 1–5. DOI: 10.1109/IC3.2018.8530608

Madhuri, C. H. R., Anuradha, G., & Pujitha, M. V. (2019). House Price Prediction Using RegressionTechniques: A Comparative Study. DOI: 10.1109/ICSSS.2019.8882834

Mahmud, M. S., Huang, J. Z., Salloum, S., Emara, T. Z., & Sadatdiyonv, K. (2020). A survey of data partitioning and sampling methods to support big data analysis. *Big Data Mining and Analytics*, 3(2), 85–101.

Ma, J., Zhang, Y., & Zhu, J. (2014). Tagging The Web: Building A Robust Web Tagger with Neural Network. *Proceedings 52nd Annual Meeting Association Computing Linguistics*, 1, 144–154. DOI: 10.3115/v1/P14-1014

Makhlouf, K., Zhioua, S., & Palamidessi, C. (2022). Machine learning fairness notions: Bridging the gap with real-world applicationsarXiv preprint arXiv:2006.16745.

Manconi, A., Gnocchi, M., Milanesi, L., Marullo, O., & Armano, G. (2023). Framing Apache Spark in life sciences. In *Heliyon* (Vol. 9, Issue 2). DOI: 10.1016/j.heliyon.2023.e13368

Margono, H., & Sharma, S. C. (2006). Efficiency and productivity analyses of Indonesian manufacturing industries. *Journal of Asian Economics*, 17(6), 979–995.

Martinelli, E., Tagliazucchi, G., & Marchi, G. (2018). The resilient retail entrepreneur: Dynamic capabilities for facing natural disasters. *International Journal of Entrepreneurial Behaviour & Research*, 24(7), 1222–1243.

Maulud, D., & Abdulazeez, A. M. (2020). A Review on Linear Regression Comprehensive in Machine Learning. *Journal of Applied Science and Technology Trends*, 1(4), 140–147. DOI: 10.38094/jastt1457

McCallum, J. C. (2017). Price-performance of computer technology. In *Digital Design and Fabrication* (pp. 1–4). CRC Press.

McClellan, M., Cervello-Pastor, C., & Sallent, S. (2020). Deep learning at the mobile edge: Opportunities for 5g networks. *Applied Sciences (Basel, Switzerland)*, 10, 4735.

McKinsey & Company. (2019). Tackling bias in artificial intelligence (and in humans). Retrieved from https://www.mckinsey.com/featured-insights/artificial-intelligence/tackling-bias-in-artificial-intelligence-and-in-humans

Mehmood, A., Tariq, U., Jeong, C., Nam, Y., Mostafa, R., & Elaeiny, A. (2022). Human Gait Recognition: A Deep Learning and Best Feature Selection Framework. *Computers, Materials & Continua*, 70, 343–360. DOI: 10.32604/cmc.2022.019250

Mehrabi, N., Morstatter, F., Saxena, N., Lerman, K., & Galstyan, A. (2019). A Survey on Bias and Fairness in Machine LearningarXiv preprint arXiv:1908.09635.

Mensah, G., Kayusi, F., Chavula, P., Turyasingura, B., & Amadi, O. J. (2024). *Artificial Intelligence Systems and Medical Negligence: An Overview and Perspective of a Case Study in Ghana Civil Procedure Rules, 2004 (CI 47).*

Merz, B., Kuhlicke, C., Kunz, M., Pittore, M., Babeyko, A., Bresch, D. N., ... Wurpts, A. (2020). Impact forecasting to support emergency management of natural hazards. Reviews of Geophysics, 58(4), e2020RG000704.

Mete, M. O., & Yomralioglu, T. (2021). Implementation of serverless cloud GIS platform for land valuation. *International Journal of Digital Earth*, 14(7). Advance online publication. DOI: 10.1080/17538947.2021.1889056

Mijwil, M. M., Abotaleb, M., Ali, G., & Dhoska, K. (2024). Assigning Medical Professionals: ChatGPT's Contributions to Medical Education and Health Prediction. *Mesopotamian Journal of Artificial Intelligence in Healthcare*, 2024, 76–83.

Mitchell, J. B. O. (2014). Machine learning methods in chemoinformatics. *Wiley Interdisciplinary Reviews. Computational Molecular Science*, 4(5), 468–481. DOI: 10.1002/wcms.1183 PMID: 25285160

Mnih, V., Kavukcuoglu, K., Silver, D., Rusu, A. A., Veness, J., Bellemare, M. G., & Petersen, S. (2015). Human-level control through deep reinforcement learning. *Nature*, 518(7540), 529–533. DOI: 10.1038/nature14236 PMID: 25719670

Mogan, J. N., Lee, C. P., & Tan, A. W. (2017). Gait recognition using temporal gradient patterns. Proceedings of the 2017 5th International Conference on Information and Communication Technology (ICoIC7), 1-4. DOI: 10.1109/ICoICT.2017.8074680

Mogan, J. N., Lee, C. P., & Lim, K. M. (2020). Gait recognition using histograms of temporal gradients. *Journal of Physics: Conference Series*, 1502(1), 012051. DOI: 10.1088/1742-6596/1502/1/012051

Mogan, J. N., Lee, C. P., Lim, K. M., & Muthu, K. S. (2022). Gait-ViT: Gait Recognition with Vision Transformer. *Sensors (Basel)*, 22(19), 7362. DOI: 10.3390/s22197362 PMID: 36236462

Mogan, J. N., Lee, C. P., Lim, K. M., & Tan, A. W. (2017). Gait recognition using binarized statistical image features and histograms of oriented gradients. *Proceedings of the 2017 International Conference on Robotics, Automation and Sciences (ICORAS)*, 1-6. DOI: 10.1109/ICORAS.2017.8308067

Moturi, D., Surapaneni, R. K., & Avanigadda, V. S. G. (2024). Developing an efficient method for melanoma detection using CNN techniques. *Journal of the Egyptian National Cancer Institute*, 36(1), 6. DOI: 10.1186/s43046-024-00210-w PMID: 38407684

Mullainathan, S., & Spiess, J. (2017). Machine learning: An applied econometric approach. In *Journal of Economic Perspectives* (Vol. 31, Issue 2). DOI: 10.1257/jep.31.2.87

Müller, V. C., & Bostrom, N. (2016). Future progress in artificial intelligence: A survey of expert opinion. In Müller, V. C. (Ed.), *Fundamental Issues of Artificial Intelligence* (pp. 555–572). Springer. DOI: 10.1007/978-3-319-26485-1_33

Munirathinam, S. (2020). Industry 4.0: Industrial internet of things (IIOT). *Advances in Computers*, 117(1), 129–164.

Munuswamy Selvaraj, K., Gnanagurusubbiah, S., & Roby Roy, R. R., John peter, J. H., & Balu, S. (2024). Enhancing skin lesion classification with advanced deep learning ensemble models : A path towards accurate medical diagnostics. *Current Problems in Cancer*, 101077. Advance online publication. DOI: 10.1016/j.currproblcancer.2024.101077 PMID: 38480028

Murdoch, B. (2021). Privacy and artificial intelligence: Challenges for protecting health information in a new era. *BMC Medical Ethics*, 22, 1–5. PMID: 34525993

Nadella, G. S., Satish, S., Meduri, K., & Meduri, S. S. (2023). A Systematic Literature Review of Advancements, Challenges and Future Directions of AI And ML in Healthcare. *International Journal of Machine Learning for Sustainable Development*, 5(3), 115–130.

Nagata, R., Mizumoto, T., Kikuchi, Y., Kawasaki, Y., & Funakoshi, K. (2018, November). A POS tagging model adapted to learner English. In *Proceedings of the 2018 EMNLP Workshop W-NUT: The 4th Workshop on Noisy User-generated Text* (pp. 39-48). DOI: 10.18653/v1/W18-6106

Nandwani, P., & Verma, R. (2021). A review on sentiment analysis and emotion detection from text. *Social Network Analysis and Mining*, 11(1), 81. PMID: 34484462

Narayanan, B. K., M, R. B., J, S. M., & M, N. (2018). Adult content filtering: Restricting minor audience from accessing inappropriate internet content. *Education and Information Technologies*, 23(6), 2719–2735. DOI: 10.1007/s10639-018-9738-y

Naseem, A., Anwar, M., Ahmed, S., Satti, Q. A., Hashmi, F. R., & Malik, T. (2017). Tagging Urdu Sentences from English POS Taggers. *International Journal of Advanced Computer Science and Applications*, 8(10), 231–238. DOI: 10.14569/IJACSA.2017.081030

Nasiri, J., & Khiyabani, F. M. (2018). A whale optimization algorithm (WOA) approach for clustering. *Cogent Mathematics & Statistics*, 5(1), 1483565.

Nawaz, M., Enscore, E.Jr, & Ham, I. (1983). A heuristic algorithm for the m-machine, n-job flow-shop sequencing problem. *Omega*, 11(1), 91–95.

Nejjarou, O., Aqil, S., & Lahby, M. (2023). Inspired nature meta-heuristics minimizing total tardiness for manufacturing flow shop scheduling under setup time constraint. In *International Conference on Digital Technologies and Applications*. Springer.

Ng, H., Tan, W. H., Abdullah, J., & Tong, H. L. (2014). Development of vision based multi-view gait recognition system with MMUGait database. *TheScientificWorldJournal*, 2014, 1–13. Advance online publication. DOI: 10.1155/2014/376569 PMID: 25143972

Nguyen, H. B., Xue, B., & Zhang, M. (n.d.). *Similarity based Multi-objective Particle Swarm Optimisation for Feature Selection in Classification.*

Nguyen, Q. H., & Dressler, F. (2020). A smartphone perspective on computation offloading—A survey. *Computer Communications*, 159, 133–154.

Nikolov, H., & Atanasova, M. (2024). Local Geodatabase as Tool for Monitoring the Landslide "Thracian Cliffs." *Advances in Science. Technology and Innovation*. Advance online publication. DOI: 10.1007/978-3-031-48715-6_27

Nivedha, S., & Shankar, S. (2023). Melanoma Diagnosis Using Enhanced Faster Region Convolutional Neural Networks Optimized by Artificial Gorilla Troops Algorithm. *Information Technology and Control*, 52(4), 4. Advance online publication. DOI: 10.5755/j01.itc.52.4.33503

Njoku, U. F., Abelló, A., Bilalli, B., & Bontempi, G. (2023). *Wrapper Methods for Multi-Objective Feature Selection*. DOI: 10.48786/edbt.2023.58

Noble, J. A. (1995). From inspection to process understanding and monitoring: A view on computer vision in manufacturing. *Image and Vision Computing*, 13(3), 197–214.

Nouri-Moghaddam, B., Ghazanfari, M., & Fathian, M. (2021). A novel multi-objective forest optimization algorithm for wrapper feature selection. *Expert Systems with Applications*, 175. Advance online publication. DOI: 10.1016/j.eswa.2021.114737

Onay, C., & Öztürk, E. (2018). A review of credit scoring research in the age of Big Data. *Journal of Financial Regulation and Compliance*, 26(3), 382–405. DOI: 10.1108/JFRC-06-2017-0054

Onwubolu, G. & Davendra, D. (2006). Scheduling flow shops using differential evolution algorithm. European Journal of Operational Research, 171(2):674–692.

Onwubolu, G. C., & Mutingi, M. (1999). Genetic algorithm for minimizing tardiness in flow-shop scheduling. Production Planning &amp. *Control*, 10(5), 462–471.

Oranç, C., & Küntay, A. C. (2019). Learning from the real and the virtual worlds: Educational use of augmented reality in early childhood. *International Journal of Child-Computer Interaction*, 21, 104–111.

Oshikawa, R., Qian, J., & Wang, W. Y. (2018). A survey on natural language processing for fake news detection. arXiv preprint arXiv:1811.00770.

Ourouadi, T. (2021). *Cours d'Expertise Immobilière au profit des étudiants du département des Sciences Géomatiques et Ingénierie Topographique*. IAV.

Öztürk, M. M. (2023). Initializing hyper-parameter tuning with a metaheuristic-ensemble method : A case study using time-series weather data. *Evolutionary Intelligence*, 16(3), 1019–1031. DOI: 10.1007/s12065-022-00717-y

Palen, L., & Hughes, A. L. (2018). Social media in disaster communication. Handbook of disaster research, 497-518.

Pan, W., Cui, S., Bian, J., Zhang, C., & Wang, F. (2021). Explaining Algorithmic Fairness Through Fairness-Aware Causal Path Decomposition.

Pan, J. C.-H., Chen, J.-S., & Chao, C.-M. (2002). Minimizing tardiness in a two-machine flow shop. *Computers & Operations Research*, 29(7), 869–885.

Papamichail, M., & Aritzoglou, A. (2021). Robotics and the international political economy: An inquiry into the evolving regulatory landscapes. *Regulation & Governance*, 15(3), 528–549.

Park, I., Kim, W. H., & Ryu, J. (2024). Style-KD : Class-imbalanced medical image classification via style knowledge distillation. *Biomedical Signal Processing and Control*, 91, 105928.

Park, S. B., Kim, J., Lee, Y. K., & Ok, C. M. (2020). Visualizing theme park visitors' emotions using social media analytics and geospatial analytics. *Tourism Management*, 80(104127).

Parsopoulos, K. E., & Vrahatis, M. N. (1 C.E.). Multi-Objective Particles Swarm Optimization Approaches. DOI: 10.4018/978-1-59904-498-9.CH002

Pasquale, F. (2015). *The black box society: The secret algorithms that control money and information*. Harvard University Press. DOI: 10.4159/harvard.9780674736061

Pászto, V., Pánek, J., & Burian, J. (2021). Geodatabase of publicly available information about czech municipalities' local administration. *Data*, 6(8). Advance online publication. DOI: 10.3390/data6080089

Paymard, P., Rezvani, S., & Mokari, N. (2019). Joint task scheduling and uplink/downlink radio resource allocation in PD-NOMA based mobile edge computing networks. *Physical Communication*, 32, 160–171.

Pérez, V., & Aybar, C. (2024). Challenges in Geocoding: An Analysis of R Packages and Web Scraping Approaches. *ISPRS International Journal of Geo-Information*, 13(6), 170.

Pfanzagl-Cardone, E. (2023). '3D'-or 'Immersive' Audio—The Basics and a Primer on Spatial Hearing. In *The Art and Science of 3D Audio Recording* (pp. 51–91). Springer International Publishing.

Phan, T. D. (2019). Housing price prediction using machine-learning algorithms: The case of Melbourne city, Australia. In *Proceedings - International Conference on Machine Learning and Data Engineering, iCMLDE 2018*. IEEE. DOI: 10.1109/iCMLDE.2018.00017

Pickl.ai. (n.d.). Algorithmic Bias and How to Avoid It- A Complete Guide. Retrieved from https://www.pickl.ai/blog/algorithmic-bias-and-how-to-avoid-it-a-complete-guide

Pinčić, D., Sušanj, D., & Lenac, K. (2022, September 21). Pinčíc, D., Sušanj, D., & Lenac, K. Gait recognition with self-supervised learning of gait features based on vision transformers. *Sensors (Basel)*, 22(19), 7140. DOI: 10.3390/s22197140

Pinto, L., Gandhi, D., & Han, Y. (2016). Curious robots: Learning visual representations via physical interactions. In *Proceedings of the 2016 IEEE/RSJ International Conference on Intelligent Robots and Systems (IROS)* (pp. 2440-2447). DOI: 10.1007/978-3-319-46475-6_1

Polignac, B., Monceau, J. P., Cussac, X., & Lesieur, P. (2019). *Expertise Immobilière, guide pratique, 7e édition*. Editions EYROLLES.

Prainsack, B., & Steindl, E. (2022). Legal and Ethical Aspects of Machine Learning: Who Owns the Data? In Artificial Intelligence/Machine Learning in Nuclear Medicine and Hybrid Imaging (pp. 191–201).

Priya, P. M, A. K., K, D. K., & Singha, N. (2021). Prediction of Property Price and Possibility Prediction Using Machine Learning. *Annals of the Romanian Society for Cell Biology, 25*(4), 3870–3882. http://annalsofrscb.ro3870

Qiu, J., & Liu, H. (2021). Gait recognition for human-exoskeleton system in locomotion based on ensemble empirical mode decomposition. *Mathematical Problems in Engineering*, 2021, 1–13. Advance online publication. DOI: 10.1155/2021/5039285

Qi, W., Procter, R., Zhang, J., & Guo, W. (2019). Mapping Consumer Sentiment Toward Wireless Services Using Geospatial Twitter Data. *IEEE Access : Practical Innovations, Open Solutions*, 7, 113726–113739.

Radha Ramanan, T., Sridharan, R., Shashikant, S. K., & Haq, A. N. (2011). An artificial neural network based heuristic for flow shop scheduling problems. *Journal of Intelligent Manufacturing*, 22, 279–288.

Raghavan, V., Madani, O., & Jones, R. (2006). Active learning with feedback on features and instances. *Journal of Machine Learning Research*, 7, 1655–1686.

Raghu, M., Balusu, B., Merghani, T., & Eisenstein, J. (2018). Stylistic Variation in Social Media Part-of-Speech Tagging. *Proceedings of the Second Workshop on Stylistic Variation*, 11-19.

Ragini, J. R., Anand, P. R., & Bhaskar, V. (2018). Big data analytics for disaster response and recovery through sentiment analysis. *International Journal of Information Management*, 42, 13–24.

Rahman, H., Janardhanan, M., Chuen, L., & Ponnambalam, S. (2021). Flowshop scheduling with sequence dependent setup times and batch delivery in supply chain. Computers &amp. *Industrial Engineering (American Institute of Industrial Engineers)*, 158, 107378.

Ramya, R., & Ramamoorthy, S. (2022). Analysis of machine learning algorithms for efficient cloud and edge computing in the loT, Challenges and Risks Involved in Deploying 6G and NextGen Networks, 72–90.

Ramya, R. (2024). *Analysis and Applications Finding of Wireless Sensors and IoT Devices With Artificial Intelligence/Machine Learning. AIoT and Smart Sensing Technologies for Smart Devices.* IGI Global. DOI: 10.4018/979-8-3693-0786-1.ch005

Ramya, R., Padmapriya, R., & Anand, M. (2024). *Applications of Machine Learning in UAV-Based Detecting and Tracking Objects: Analysis and Overview. Applications of Machine Learning in UAV Networks.* IGI Global. DOI: 10.4018/979-8-3693-0578-2.ch003

Ramya, R., & Ramamoorthy, S. (2022). Development of a framework for adaptive productivity management for edge computing based IoT applications. *AIP Conference Proceedings*, 2519, 030068.

Ramya, R., & Ramamoorthy, S. (2022)... *Survey on Edge Intelligence in IoT-Based Computing Platform, Lecture Notes in Networks and Systems, Springer*, 356, 549–556. DOI: 10.1007/978-981-16-7952-0_52

Ramya, R., & Ramamoorthy, S. (2023). Lightweight Unified Collaborated Relinquish Edge Intelligent Gateway Architecture with Joint Optimization. *IEEE Access : Practical Innovations, Open Solutions*, 11, 90396–90409. DOI: 10.1109/ACCESS.2023.3307808

Ramya, R., & Ramamoorthy, S. (2024). Hybrid Fog-Edge-IoT Architecture for Real-time Data Monitoring. *International Journal of Intelligent Engineering and Systems*, 17(1), 2024. DOI: 10.22266/ijies2024.0229.22

Ramya, R., & Ramamoorthy, S. (2024). QoS in multimedia application for IoT devices through edge intelligence. *Multimedia Tools and Applications, Springer*, 83, 9227–9250. DOI: 10.1007/s11042-023-15941-6

Rane, N. (2023). Role and challenges of ChatGPT and similar generative artificial intelligence in finance and accounting. *Available atSSRN* 4603206.

Raquel, C. R., & Naval, P. C. (2005). An effective use of crowding distance in multi-objective particle swarm optimization. *Proceedings of the 7th Annual Conference on Genetic and Evolutionary Computation*, 257–264. DOI: 10.1145/1068009.1068047

Ravikumar, A. S. (2017). Real Estate Price Prediction Using. *Machine Learning*.

Rida, I., Almaadeed, S. A., & Bouridane, A. (2015). Unsupervised feature selection method for improved human gait recognition. 23rd European Signal Processing Conference (EUSIPCO), 1128-1132.

Rida, I., Almaadeed, S.A., & Bouridane, A. (2015). Gait recognition based on modified phase-only correlation. Journal of Signal, Image and Video Processing, 463-470.

Roberts, S., Osborne, M., Ebden, M., Reece, S., Gibson, N., & Aigrain, S. (2013). Gaussian processes for time-series modelling. *Philosophical Transactions of the Royal Society A: Mathematical, Physical and Engineering Sciences, 371*(1984), 20110550.

Rodríguez, J. E., & Pimiento, J. P. O. (2017). Bayesian methods for classification inappropriate web pages. Visión electrónica, 11(2), 179-189.

Rokach, L., & Maimon, O. (2006). Data mining for improving the quality of manufacturing: A feature set decomposition approach. *Journal of Intelligent Manufacturing*, 17, 285–299.

Rokanujjaman, M., Islam, M. S., Hossain, M. A., Islam, M. R., Makihara, Y., & Yagi, Y. (2015). Effective part-based gait identification using frequency-domain gait entropy features Multimed. *Tool. Appl.*, 74(9), 3099–3120.

Roldán, J. C., Jiménez, P., & Corchuelo, R. (2020). On extracting data from tables that are encoded using HTML. *Knowledge-Based Systems*, 190, 105157. DOI: 10.1016/j.knosys.2019.105157

Rouhani, S., Fathian, M., Jafari, M., & Akhavan, P. (2010). Solving the problem of flow shop scheduling by neural network approach. *Networked Digital Technologies: Second International Conference, NDT 2010, Prague, Czech Republic, July 7-9, 2010Proceedings*, 2(Part II), 172–183.

Rowland, D. L., & Uribe, D. (2020). Pornography use: what do cross-cultural patterns tell us?. Cultural differences and the practice of sexual medicine: A guide for sexual health practitioners, 317-334.

Royal Institution of Chartered Surveyors (RICS). (2020). *RICS professional standards and guidance*.

Rudin, C. (2019). Stop explaining black box machine learning models for high stakes decisions and use interpretable models instead. *Nature Machine Intelligence*, 1(5), 206–215. DOI: 10.1038/s42256-019-0048-x PMID: 35603010

Rudra, Ganguly, Goyal, & Ghosh. (2018). Extracting and Summarizing Situational Information from the Twitter Social Media during Disasters. ACM Transactions on the Web, 12(3).

Russell, S. J., & Norvig, P. (2021). *Artificial Intelligence: A Modern Approach* (4th ed.). Pearson.

Ruz, G. A., Henríquez, P. A., & Mascareño, A. (2020). Sentiment analysis of Twitter data during critical events through Bayesian networks classifiers. *Future Generation Computer Systems*, 106, 92–104.

Rzeszewski, M. (2023). Mapbox. In *Evaluating Participatory Mapping Software*. DOI: 10.1007/978-3-031-19594-5_2

Sabry, F., Eltaras, T., Labda, W., Alzoubi, K., & Malluhi, Q. (2022). Machine learning for healthcare wearable devices: The big picture. *Journal of Healthcare Engineering*, 2022(1), 4653923. PMID: 35480146

Sadatdiynov, , Cui, Zhang, Huang, Salloum, & Mahmud. (2022). A review of optimization methods for computation offloading in edge computing networks. *Digital Communications and Networks*, 9. Advance online publication. DOI: 10.1016/j.dcan.2022.03.003

Sadki, H., Aqil, S., Belabid, J., & Allali, K. (2024). Multi-objective optimization flow shop scheduling problem solving the makespan and total flow time with sequence independent setup time. *Journal of Advanced Manufacturing Systems*, 23(01), 163–184.

Sadki, H., Belabid, J., Aqil, S., & Allali, K. (2021). On permutation flow shop scheduling problem with sequence-independent setup time and total flow time. In *International Conference on Advanced Technologies for Humanity*. Springer International Publishing.

Saeys, Y., Inza, I., & Larrañaga, P. (2007). A review of feature selection techniques in bioinformatics. In *Bioinformatics* (Vol. 23, Issue 19, pp. 2507–2517). Oxford University Press. DOI: 10.1093/bioinformatics/btm344

Safavat, S., Sapavath, N. N., & Rawat, D. B. (2020). Recent advances in mobile edge computing and content caching. *Digital Communications and Networks*, 6, 189–194.

Saha, S., & Ekbal, A. (2013). Combining multiple classifiers usin vote based classifier ensemble technique for named entity recognition. Data & Knowledge Engineering, 15-39.

Saha, S., Basu, S., Majumder, K., & Chakravarty, D. (2022). Extension of Search Facilities Provided by 'CoWIN' Using Google's Geocoding API and APIs of 'CoWIN' and 'openweathermap.org.' *Communications in Computer and Information Science, 1534 CCIS*. DOI: 10.1007/978-3-030-96040-7_14

Sahai, A. K., & Rath, N. (2021). Artificial intelligence and the 4th industrial revolution. In *Artificial intelligence and machine learning in business management* (pp. 127–143). CRC Press.

Sahingoz, O. K., Buber, E., Demir, O., & Diri, B. (2019). Machine learning based phishing detection from URLs. *Expert Systems with Applications*, 117, 345–357. DOI: 10.1016/j.eswa.2018.09.029

Sahoo, D., Liu, C., & Hoi, S. C. (2017). Malicious URL detection using machine learning: A survey. arXiv preprint arXiv:1701.07179.

Sah, S., & Panday, S. P. (2020). Model-Based Gait Recognition Using Weighted KNN. *Proceedings of the 8th IOE Graduate Conference*, 5-7.

Sajjad, H., & Schmid, H. (2009). Tagging Urdu Text with Parts of Speech: A Tagger Comparison. Proccedings 12th Conferrence Euopian, 692–700.

Saleh, A. M., & Hamoud, T. (2021). Analysis and best parameters selection for person recognition based on gait model using CNN algorithm and image augmentation. *Journal of Big Data*, 8(1), 1–20. DOI: 10.1186/s40537-020-00387-6 PMID: 33425651

Salloum, S., Dautov, R., Chen, X., Peng, P. X., & Huang, J. Z. (2016). Big data analytics on Apache Spark. In *International Journal of Data Science and Analytics* (Vol. 1, pp. 3–4). Issues. DOI: 10.1007/s41060-016-0027-9

Salmani, M., & Davidson, T. N. (2020). Uplink resource allocation for multiple access computational offloading. *Signal Processing*, 168, 107322.

Sangeetha, C., Moond, V., Rajesh, G. M., Damor, J. S., Pandey, S. K., Kumar, P., & Singh, B. (2024). Remote Sensing and Geographic Information Systems for Precision Agriculture: A Review. *International Journal of Environment and Climate Change*, 14(2). Advance online publication. DOI: 10.9734/ijecc/2024/v14i23945

Santana, L. A., & Canuto, A. M. P. (2013). Particle swarm intelligence as feature selector in ensemble systems. *Proceedings - 2013 Brazilian Conference on Intelligent Systems, BRACIS 2013*, 89–94. DOI: 10.1109/BRACIS.2013.23

Santana, L. E. A., & Canuto, A. M. P. (2012). Bi-objective Genetic Algorithm for Feature Selection in Ensemble Systems. *Lecture Notes in Computer Science (Including Subseries Lecture Notes in Artificial Intelligence and Lecture Notes in Bioinformatics), 7552 LNCS* (PART 1), 701–709. DOI: 10.1007/978-3-642-33269-2_88

Sapankevych, N. I., & Sankar, R. (2009). Time series prediction using support vector machines: A survey. *IEEE Computational Intelligence Magazine*, 4(2), 24–38. DOI: 10.1109/MCI.2009.932254

Sarangi, S., Dash, P. K., & Bisoi, R. (2023). Probabilistic prediction of wind speed using an integrated deep belief network optimized by a hybrid multi-objective particle swarm algorithm. *Engineering Applications of Artificial Intelligence*, 126. Advance online publication. DOI: 10.1016/j.engappai.2023.107034

Sarathy, V., & Robertson, A. (2021). The long-term impact of artificial intelligence on the labor market. *International Journal of Forecasting*, 37(4), 1697–1707.

Sarker, I. H. (2021). Machine learning: Algorithms, real-world applications and research directions. *SN Computer Science*, 2(3), 160. PMID: 33778771

Saroj & Jyoti. (2014). Multi-objective genetic algorithm approach to feature subset optimization. *2014 IEEE International Advance Computing Conference (IACC)*, 544–548. DOI: 10.1109/IAdCC.2014.6779383

Schölkopf, B., & Smola, A. J. (2002). *Learning with Kernels: Support Vector Machines, Regularization, Optimization, and Beyond*. MIT Press.

Schwarz, A., Binetti, J. C., Broll, W., & Mitschele-Thiel, A. (2016). New technologies and applications in international crisis communication and disaster management. The handbook of international crisis communication research, 465-477.

Sepas-Moghaddam, A., & Etemad, A. (2022). Deep gait recognition: A survey. *IEEE Transactions on Pattern Analysis and Machine Intelligence*. Advance online publication. DOI: 10.1109/TPAMI.2022.3151865 PMID: 35167443

Servotte, J. C., Goosse, M., Campbell, S. H., Dardenne, N., Pilote, B., Simoneau, I. L., & Ghuysen, A. (2020). Virtual reality experience: Immersion, sense of presence, and cybersickness. *Clinical Simulation in Nursing*, 38, 35–43.

Shah, M., & Sureja, N. (2024). *A Comprehensive Review of Bias in Deep Learning Models: Methods*. Impacts, and Future Directions.

Shakarami, A., Ghobaei-Arani, M., & Shahidinejad, A. (2020). A survey on the computation offloading approaches in mobile edge computing: A machine learning-based perspective. *Computer Networks*, 182, 107496.

Shakarami, A., Shahidinejad, A., & Ghobaei-Arani, M. (2020). A review on the computation offloading approaches in mobile edge computing: A game-theoretic perspective. *Software, Practice & Experience*, 50, 1719–1759.

Shao, Y., Hardmeier, C., & Nivre, J. (2017). Character-based Joint Segmentation and POS Tagging for Chinese using Bidirectional RNN-CRF. The 8th International Joint Conference on Natural Language Processing, 173-183.

Shao, Y., Li, C., Fu, Z., Jia, L., & Luo, Y. (2019). Cost-effective replication management and scheduling in edge computing. *Journal of Network and Computer Applications*, 129, 46–61.

Sharif, M., Attique, M., Tahir, M. Z., Yasmim, M., Saba, T., & Tanik, U. J. (2020). A machine learning method with threshold-based parallel feature fusion and feature selection for automated gait recognition. *Journal of Organizational and End User Computing*, 32(2), 67–92. DOI: 10.4018/JOEUC.2020040104

Shashi, A. (2023). Designing Applications for Google Cloud Platform. In *Designing Applications for Google Cloud Platform*. DOI: 10.1007/978-1-4842-9511-3

Shehab, M., Abualigah, L., Shambour, Q., Abu-Hashem, M. A., Shambour, M. K. Y., Alsalibi, A. I., & Gandomi, A. H. (2022). Machine learning in medical applications: A review of state-of-the-art methods. *Computers in Biology and Medicine*, 145, 105458. PMID: 35364311

Sheth, A. A., Sharath, M., Reddy, A. S. C., & Sindhu, K. (2023). *Gait Recognition Using Convolutional Neural Network*. International Journal of Online and Biomedical Engineering. DOI: 10.3991/ijoe.v19i01.33823

Shumway, R. H., Stoffer, D. S., Shumway, R. H., & Stoffer, D. S. (2017). ARIMA models. *Time Series Analysis and Its Applications: With R Examples*, 75–163.

Shu, X., & Ye, Y. (2023). Knowledge Discovery: Methods from data mining and machine learning. *Social Science Research*, 110, 102817. PMID: 36796993

Siedlecki, W., & Sklansky, J. (2011). On automatic feature selection. DOI: 10.1142/S0218001488000145

Silfverberg, M., Ruokolainen, T., Linden, K., & Kurimo, M. (2014, June). Part-of-speech tagging using conditional random fields: Exploiting sub-label dependencies for improved accuracy. In *Proceedings of the 52nd Annual Meeting of the Association for Computational Linguistics(*Volume 2*: Short Papers)* (pp. 259-264). DOI: 10.3115/v1/P14-2043

Silva, A. P., Silva, A., & Rodrigues, I. (2013). A New Approach to the POS Tagging Problem Using Evolutionary Computation. *Proceedings of the International Conference Recent Advances in Natural language Processing RANLP*, 619–625.

Silver, D., Hubert, T., Schrittwieser, J., Antonoglou, I., Lai,M., Guez, A., Lanctot, M., Sifre, L., Kumaran, D., Graepel, T., Lillicrap, T., Simonyan, K., & Hassabis, D. (2018). A general reinforcement learning algorithm that masters chess, shogi, and go through self-play. Science, 362(6419), 1140 1144. .DOI: 10.1126/science.aar6404

Silver, D., Huang, A., Maddison, C. J., Guez, A., Sifre, L., Van Den Driessche, G., Schrittwieser, J., Antonoglou, I., Panneershelvam, V., Lanctot, M., Dieleman, S., Grewe, D., Nham, J., Kalchbrenner, N., Sutskever, I., Lillicrap, T., Leach, M., Kavukcuoglu, K., Graepel, T., & Hassabis, D. (2016). Mastering the game of Go with deep neural networks and tree search. *Nature*, 529(7587), 484–489. DOI: 10.1038/nature16961 PMID: 26819042

Simonyan, K., & Zisserman, A. (2014). Very deep convolutional networks for large-scale image recognition. arXiv 2014, arXiv:1409.1556.

Simplilearn. (n.d.). Bias and Variance in Machine Learning. Retrieved from https://www.simplilearn.com/tutorials/machine-learning-tutorial/bias-and-variance

Simumba, N., Okami, S., Kodaka, A., & Kohtake, N. (2021). Comparison of Profit-Based Multi-Objective Approaches for Feature Selection in Credit Scoring. *Algorithms*, 14(9), 260. DOI: 10.3390/a14090260

Simumba, N., Okami, S., Kodaka, A., & Kohtake, N. (2022). Multiple objective metaheuristics for feature selection based on stakeholder requirements in credit scoring. *Decision Support Systems*, 155. Advance online publication. DOI: 10.1016/j.dss.2021.113714

Singh, S. P., Wang, Z., & Xu, D. (2018). Knowledge-enhanced hybrid neural networks for recommender systems. In *Proceedings of the 24th ACM SIGKDD International Conference on Knowledge Discovery & Data Mining* (pp. 1933-1942).

Sioud, A., & Gagne, C. (2018). Enhanced migrating birds optimization algorithm for the permutation flow shop problem with sequence dependent setup times. *European Journal of Operational Research*, 264(1), 66–73.

Sivakumar, M. S., Leo, L. M., Gurumekala, T., Sindhu, V., & Priyadharshini, A. S. (2024). Deep learning in skin lesion analysis for malignant melanoma cancer identification. *Multimedia Tools and Applications, 83*(6), 17833-17853. *Scopus*. Advance online publication. DOI: 10.1007/s11042-023-16273-1

Sivanantham, K., & Kumar, R. M. (2023). Different Approaches to Background Subtraction and Object Tracking in Video Streams: A Review. Object Tracking Technology: Trends, Challenges and Applications, 23-39.

Sivanantham, K., Kalaiarasi, I., & Leena, B. (2022). Brain tumor classification using hybrid artificial neural network with chicken swarm optimization algorithm in digital image processing application. In *Advance Concepts of Image Processing and Pattern Recognition: Effective Solution for Global Challenges* (pp. 91–108). Springer Singapore.

Sivanantham, K., Praveen, P. B., Deepa, V., & Kumar, R. M. (2023). Cybercrime Sentimental Analysis for Child Youtube Video Dataset Using Hybrid Support Vector Machine with Ant Colony Optimization Algorithm. In *Kids Cybersecurity Using Computational Intelligence Techniques* (pp. 175–193). Springer International Publishing.

Si, W., Zhang, J., Li, Y. D., Tan, W., Shao, Y. F., & Yang, G. L. (2020). Remote identity verification using gait analysis and face recognition. *Wireless Communications and Mobile Computing*, 2020, 1–10. Advance online publication. DOI: 10.1155/2020/8815461

Smith, J., & Johnson, K. (2023a). Case Study 1: Biased Hiring Algorithms. In K. White & L. Brown (Eds.), Advancements in Machine Learning Applications in Hiring Processes (pp. 45-48). Publisher X.

Smith, J., & Johnson, K. (2023b). Case Study 2: Biased Loan Approval Systems. In K. White & L. Brown (Eds.), Advancements in Artificial Intelligence Applications in Financial Institutions (pp. 87-90). Publisher X.

Smith, J., & Johnson, K. (2023c). Case Study 3: Biased Predictive Policing Algorithms. In K. White & L. Brown (Eds.), Advancements in Artificial Intelligence Applications in Law Enforcement (pp. 123-126). Publisher X.

Sokolova & Konushin. (2018). Pose-based deep gait recognition. *IET Biometrics,8*(2), 134-143. .DOI: 10.1049/iet-bmt.2018.5046

Spolaôr, N., Lorena, A. C., & Lee, H. D. (2011). Multi-objective Genetic Algorithm Evaluation in Feature Selection. *Lecture Notes in Computer Science (Including Subseries Lecture Notes in Artificial Intelligence and Lecture Notes in Bioinformatics), 6576 LNCS*, 462–476. DOI: 10.1007/978-3-642-19893-9_32

Spolaôr, N., Lorena, A. C., & Diana Lee, H. (2017). Feature Selection via Pareto Multi-objective Genetic Algorithms. *Applied Artificial Intelligence*, 31(9–10), 764–791. DOI: 10.1080/08839514.2018.1444334

Springer. (2024). Designing Against Bias: Identifying and Mitigating Bias in Machine. Retrieved from https://link.springer.com/chapter/10.1007/978-3-031-47715-7_28

Stankovics, P., Schillaci, C., Pump, J., Birli, B., Ferraro, G., Munafò, M., Di Leginio, M., Hermann, T., Montanarella, L., & Tóth, G. (2024). A framework for co-designing decision-support systems for policy implementation: The LANDSUPPORT experience. *Land Degradation & Development*, 35(5). Advance online publication. DOI: 10.1002/ldr.5030

Storck, C. R., & Duarte-Figueiredo, F. (2020). A survey of 5g technology evolution, standards, and infrastructure associated with vehicle-to-everything communications by internet of vehicles. *IEEE Access : Practical Innovations, Open Solutions*, 8, 117593–117614.

Straka, M., & Straková, J. (2017, August). Tokenizing, pos tagging, lemmatizing and parsing ud 2.0 with udpipe. In *Proceedings of the CoNLL 2017 shared task: Multilingual parsing from raw text to universal dependencies* (pp. 88-99). DOI: 10.18653/v1/K17-3009

Stratos, K., Collins, M., & Hsu, D. (2016). Unsupervised Part-Of-Speech Tagging with Anchor Hidden Markov Models. *Transactions of the Association for Computational Linguistics*, 4, 245–257. DOI: 10.1162/tacl_a_00096

Su & Huang. (2005). Human gait recognition based on motion analysis. *2005 International Conference on Machine Learning and Cybernetics, 7*, 4464-4468.

Sufi, F. K., & Alsulami, M. (2021). *Knowledge Discovery of Global Landslides Using Automated Machine Learning Algorithms* (Vol. 9). IEEE Access.

Sufi, F. K., & Khalil, I. (2022). Automated disaster monitoring from social media posts using AI-based location intelligence and sentiment analysis. *IEEE Transactions on Computational Social Systems*.

Sunkur, R., & Mauremootoo, J. (2024). Spatio-temporal Analysis of An Invasive Alien Species, Vachellia nilotica, on Rodrigues Island, Mauritius, Using Geographic Information Systems and Remote Sensing Techniques. *Indonesian Journal of Earth Sciences*, 4(1). Advance online publication. DOI: 10.52562/injoes.2024.835

Sun, X., He, Y., Wu, D., & Huang, J. Z. (2023). Survey of Distributed Computing Frameworks for Supporting Big Data Analysis. *Big Data Mining and Analytics*, 6(2). Advance online publication. DOI: 10.26599/BDMA.2022.9020014

Sur, F. (2021). *Introduction à l'apprentissage automatique Tronc commun scientifique FICM 2A École des Mines de Nancy.* https://members.loria.fr/FSur/

Syed, S. A., Gowthami, S., Shanmukhi, M., & Mohammad, G. baig, Potluri, S., Chandragandhi, S., & Srihari, K. (2024). Registration based fully optimized melanoma detection using deep forest technique. *Biomedical Signal Processing and Control*, 93, 106116. DOI: 10.1016/j.bspc.2024.106116

Tamenu, Y. (2021). Proptech: la Data Science appliquée à l'immobilier. Haute École de Gestion de Genève. Travail de Bachelor réalisé en vue de l'obtention du Bachelor HES.1- 77

Tan, E., Lim, S., Lamont, D., Epstein, R., Lim, D., & Lin, F. P. Y. (2024). Development and validation of a deep learning model for improving detection of nonmelanoma skin cancers treated with Mohs micrographic surgery. *JAAD International*, 14, 39–47. DOI: 10.1016/j.jdin.2023.10.007 PMID: 38089398

Tang, L., Liu, W., & Liu, J. (2005). A neural network model and algorithm for the hybrid flow shop scheduling problem in a dynamic environment. *Journal of Intelligent Manufacturing*, 16, 361–370.

Tan, Z., Yu, F. R., Li, X., Ji, H., & Leung, V. C. M. (2018). Virtual resource allocation for heterogeneous services in full duplex-enabled scns with mobile edge computing and caching. *IEEE Transactions on Vehicular Technology*, 67, 1794–1808.

Ta, Q., Billaut, J.-C., & Bouquard, J.-L. (2018). Matheuristic algorithms for minimizing total tardiness in the m-machine flow-shop scheduling problem. *Journal of Intelligent Manufacturing*, 29, 617–628.

Tchuente, D., & Nyawa, S. (2022). Real estate price estimation in French cities using geocoding and machine learning. In *Annals of Operations Research* (Vol. 308, Issues 1– 2). Springer US. DOI: 10.1007/s10479-021-03932-5

TELUS International. (2021). Seven Types Of Data Bias In Machine Learning. Retrieved from https://www.telusinternational.com/insights/ai-data/article/7-types -of-data-bias-in-machine-learning

Thomason, J., & Strohl, M. (2018). Artificial intelligence and the end of work. In *The Economics of Artificial Intelligence: An Agenda* (pp. 207–226). University of Chicago Press.

Tian, Y., & Lo, D. (2015, March). A comparative study on the effectiveness of part-of-speech tagging techniques on bug reports. In *2015 IEEE 22nd International Conference on Software Analysis, Evolution, and Reengineering (SANER)* (pp. 570-574). IEEE. DOI: 10.1109/SANER.2015.7081879

Toivonen, T., Heikinheimo, V., Fink, C., Hausmann, A., Hiippala, T., Järv, O., & Di Minin, E. (2019). Social media data for conservation science: A methodological overview. *Biological Conservation*, 233, 298–315.

Tokgöz, A., & Ünal, G. (2018). A RNN based time series approach for forecasting turkish electricity load. *2018 26th Signal Processing and Communications Applications Conference (SIU)*, 1–4.

Tong, S., Fu, Y., & Ling H. (2019). Cross-view gait recognition based on a restrictive triplet network. *Elsevier Journal of Pattern Recognition Letters, 125*, 212-219.

Tong, Z., Deng, X., Basodi, F. Ye. S., Xiao, X., & Pan, Y. (2020). Adaptive computation offloading and resource allocation strategy in a mobile edge computing environment. *Inf. Sci.*, 537, 116–131.

Toutanova, K., Klein, D., Manning, C. D., & Singer, Y. (2003). Feature-Rich Part-of-Speech Tagging with a Cyclic Dependency Network. *Association for Computational Linguistic*, (June), 173–180. DOI: 10.3115/1073445.1073478

Towards Data Science. (n.d.). Algorithm Fairness: Sources of Bias. Retrieved from https://towardsdatascience.com/algorithm-fairness-sources-of-bias

Tschandl, P. (2023). *The HAM10000 dataset, a large collection of multi-source dermatoscopic images of common pigmented skin lesions* (Version 4). Harvard Dataverse. https://doi.org/DOI: 10.7910/DVN/DBW86T

Tuama, A., Comby, F., & Chaumont, M. (2016). Camera model identification with the use of deep convolutional neural networks. *2016 IEEE International Workshop on Information Forensics and Security (WIFS)*, 1–6.

Tuli, S., Casale, G., & Jennings, N. R. (2022). Tranad: Deep transformer networks for anomaly detection in multivariate time series data. *ArXiv Preprint ArXiv:2201.07284*.

Turyasingura, B., Ayiga, N., Kayusi, F., & Tumuhimbise, M. (2024). Application of Artificial Intelligence (AI) in Environment and Societal Trends: Challenges and Opportunities. *Babylonian Journal of Machine Learning*, 2024, 177–182.

UK Statistics Authority. (2021). Ethical considerations in the use of Machine Learning for research and statistics.

Ulker, E., & Tongur, V. (2017). Migrating birds optimization (mbo) algorithm to solve knapsack problem. *Procedia Computer Science*, 111, 71–76.

Utiu, N., & Ionescu, V.-S. (2018). Learning Web Content Extraction with DOM Features. IEEE 14th International Conference on Intelligent Computer Communication and Processing (ICCP), 5-11. DOI: 10.1109/ICCP.2018.8516632

Vallada, E., & Ruiz, R. (2010). Genetic algorithms with path relinking for the minimum tardiness permutation flowshop problem. *Omega*, 38(1-2), 57–67.

Vallada, E., Ruiz, R., & Minella, G. (2008). Minimising total tardiness in the m-machine flowshop problem: A review and evaluation of heuristics and metaheuristics. *Computers & Operations Research*, 35(4), 1350–1373.

Varshney, G., Misra, M., & Atrey, P. K. (2016). A survey and classification of web phishing detection schemes. *Security and Communication Networks*, 9(18), 6266–6284. DOI: 10.1002/sec.1674

Vashisht, G., & Sinha, Y. N. (2021). Sentimental study of CAA by locationbased tweets. *International Journal of Information Technology : an Official Journal of Bharati Vidyapeeth's Institute of Computer Applications and Management*. PMID: 33778365

Vashishtha, J., Puri, V. H., & Mukesh. (2020). Feature Selection Using PSO: A Multi Objective Approach. *Communications in Computer and Information Science, 1241 CCIS*, 106–119. DOI: 10.1007/978-981-15-6318-8_10

Vaswani, A., Shazeer, N., Parmar, N., Uszkoreit, J., Jones, L., Gomez, A. N., Kaiser, Ł., & Polosukhin, I. (2017). Attention is all you need. *Advances in Neural Information Processing Systems*, 30.

Vayena, E., Blasimme, A., & Cohen, I. G. (2018). Machine learning in medicine: Addressing ethical challenges. PLOS Medicine.

Venakt Narayana Rao, Govardhan, & Jahangir Badashah. (2011). Statistical analysis for performance evaluation of image segmentation quality using edge detection algorithms. International Journal of Advanced Networking and Applications, 3(3), 1184,.

Venkat Narayana Rao & Manasa. (2019). Artificial neural networks for soil quality and crop yield prediction using machine learning. International Journal on Future Revolution in Computer Science, 14.

Venkat Narayana Rao & Reddy. (2019). Prediction Of Soil Quality Using Machine Learning Techniques. International Journal of Scientific & Technology Research, 8(11), 1309-1313.

Venkat Narayana Rao, T., & Sharma, L. (2020). Towards smart world: homes to cities using internet of things. CRC Press.

Venkat Narayana Rao, Unnisa, & Sreni. (2020). Medicine recommendation system based on patient reviews. Int J Sci Technol Res, 9, 3308-12.

Venkat Narayana Rao, T., & Yellu, K. R. (2016). Automatic Safety Home Bell System with Message Enabled Features. *International Journal of Science.Engineering and Computer Technology*, 6, 10.

Vincent, J. (2020). Google claims 'quantum supremacy' with new supercomputer chip. The Verge. Retrieved from https://www.theverge.com/2020/9/23/21452256/google-quantum-supremacy-sycamore-processor-53-qubits-wsj

Wang, D. (2022). Meta Reinforcement Learning with Hebbian Learning. *2022 IEEE 13th Annual Ubiquitous Computing, Electronics & Mobile Communication Conference (UEMCON)*, 52–58.

Wang, D. (2023c). Obstacle-aware Simultaneous Task and Energy Planning with Ordering Constraints. *2023 11th International Conference on Information and Communication Technology (ICoICT)*, 289–294.

Wang, D. (2024a). Robust Adversarial Deep Reinforcement Learning. In *Deep Learning, Reinforcement Learning, and the Rise of Intelligent Systems* (pp. 106–125). IGI Global. DOI: 10.4018/979-8-3693-1738-9.ch005

Wang, D. (2024b). Multi-agent Reinforcement Learning for Safe Driving in On-ramp Merging of Autonomous Vehicles. *2024 14th International Conference on Cloud Computing, Data Science & Engineering (Confluence)*, 644–651.

Wang, D., Hu, M., & Gao, Y. (2018). Multi-criteria mission planning for a solar-powered multi-robot system. *International Design Engineering Technical Conferences and Computers and Information in Engineering Conference*, 51753, V02AT03A026.

Wang, F. Y. (2022). The metaverse of mind: Perspectives on DeSci for DeEco and DeSoc. *IEEE/CAA Journal of AutomaticaSinica*, 9(12), 2043-2046.

Wang, P., Qian, Y., Soong, F. K., He, L., & Hai, Z. (2015). Part-of-Speech Tagging with Bidirectional Long Short-Term Memory Recurrent Neural Network. arXiv preprint arXiv: 1510.0616.

Wang, X., Ristic-Durrant, D., Spranger, M., & Gräser, A. (2017). Gait assessment system based on novel gait variability measures. 2017 International Conference on Rehabilitation Robotics (ICORR), 467-472. DOI: 10.1109/ICORR.2017.8009292

Wang, C., Wang, Y., Ding, Z., Zheng, T., Hu, J., & Zhang, K. (2022). A transformer-based method of multienergy load forecasting in integrated energy system. *IEEE Transactions on Smart Grid*, 13(4), 2703–2714. DOI: 10.1109/TSG.2022.3166600

Wang, D. (2023a). Explainable deep reinforcement learning for knowledge graph reasoning. In *Recent Developments in Machine and Human Intelligence* (pp. 168–183). IGI Global. DOI: 10.4018/978-1-6684-9189-8.ch012

Wang, D. (2023b). Reinforcement Learning for Combinatorial Optimization. In *Encyclopedia of Data Science and Machine Learning* (pp. 2857–2871). IGI Global.

Wang, D. (2023d). Out-of-Distribution Detection with Confidence Deep Reinforcement Learning. *2023 International Conference on Communications, Computing, Cybersecurity, and Informatics (CCCI)*, 1–7. DOI: 10.1109/CCCI58712.2023.10290768

Wang, D., & Hu, M. (2021). Deep Deterministic Policy Gradient With Compatible Critic Network. *IEEE Transactions on Neural Networks and Learning Systems*. PMID: 34653007

Wang, D., & Hu, M. (2023). Contrastive learning methods for deep reinforcement learning. *IEEE Access : Practical Innovations, Open Solutions*, 11, 97107–97117. DOI: 10.1109/ACCESS.2023.3312383

Wang, D., Hu, M., & Weir, J. D. (2022). Simultaneous Task and Energy Planning using Deep Reinforcement Learning. *Information Sciences*, 607, 931–946. DOI: 10.1016/j.ins.2022.06.015

Wang, D., Zhao, J., Han, M., & Li, L. (2023). 4d Printing-Enabled Circular Economy: Disassembly Sequence Planning Using Reinforcement Learning. DOI: 10.2139/ssrn.4429186

Wang, X., Ning, Z., & Guo, S. (2021). Multi-agent imitation learning for pervasive edge computing: A decentralized computation offloading algorithm. *IEEE Transactions on Parallel and Distributed Systems*, 32, 411–425.

Wang, X., & Yan, W. Q. (2021). Non-local gait feature extraction and human identification. *Multimedia Tools and Applications*, 80(4), 6065–6078. DOI: 10.1007/s11042-020-09935-x

Wang, X., Zhang, J., & Yan, W. Q. (2020). Gait recognition using multichannel convolution neural networks. *Neural Computing & Applications*, 32(18), 14275–14285. DOI: 10.1007/s00521-019-04524-y

Wan, J., Li, X., Dai, H.-N., Kusiak, A., Martinez-Garcia, M., & Li, D. (2020). Artificial-intelligence-driven customized manufacturing factory: Key technologies, applications, and challenges. *Proceedings of the IEEE*, 109(4), 377–398.

Wankhade, M., Rao, A. C. S., & Kulkarni, C. (2022). A survey on sentiment analysis methods, applications, and challenges. *Artificial Intelligence Review*, 55(7), 5731–5780.

Wen, Q., Zhou, T., Zhang, C., Chen, W., Ma, Z., Yan, J., & Sun, L. (2022). Transformers in time series: A survey. *ArXiv Preprint ArXiv:2202.07125*.

Wiley, V., & Lucas, T. (2018). Computer vision and image processing: A paper review. *International Journal of Artificial Intelligence Research*, 2(1), 29–36.

Wisth, D., Camurri, M., & Fallon, M. (2022). VILENS: Visual, inertial, lidar, and leg odometry for all-terrain legged robots. *IEEE Transactions on Robotics*, 39(1), 309–326.

Wolf, K., Dawson, R. J., Mills, J. P., Blythe, P., & Morley, J. (2022). Towards a digital twin for supporting multi-agency incident management in a smart city. *Scientific Reports*, 12(1). Advance online publication. DOI: 10.1038/s41598-022-20178-8 PMID: 36171329

Worzala, E., Lenk, M., & Silva, A. (1995). An Exploration of Neural Networks and Its Application to Real Estate Valuation. In *Journal of Real Estate Research* (Vol. 10, Issue 2). DOI: 10.1080/10835547.1995.12090782

Wu, H., & Wang, C. (2018). A new machine learning approach to house price estimation. *New Trends in Mathematical Science*, 4(6), 165–171. DOI: 10.1016/j. tins.2018.02.002

Wu, H., Weng, J., Chen, X., & Lu, W. (2018). Feedback weight convolutional neural network for gait recognition. *Journal of Visual Communication and Image Representation*, 55, 424–432. DOI: 10.1016/j.jvcir.2018.06.019

Wu, H., Xu, J., Wang, J., & Long, M. (2021). Autoformer: Decomposition transformers with auto-correlation for long-term series forecasting. *Advances in Neural Information Processing Systems*, 34, 22419–22430.

Xia, S., Yao, Z., Li, Y., & Mao, S. (2021). Online distributed offloading and computing resource management with energy harvesting for heterogeneous mec-enabled iot. *IEEE Transactions on Wireless Communications*, 20, 6743–6757.

Xu, C., Li, J., Feng, B., & Lu, B. (2023). A financial time-series prediction model based on multiplex attention and linear transformer structure. *Applied Sciences (Basel, Switzerland)*, 13(8), 5175. DOI: 10.3390/app13085175

Xu, C., Makihara, Y., Li, X., Yagi, Y., & Lu, J. (2020). Cross-view gait recognition using pairwise spatial transformer networks. *IEEE Transactions on Circuits and Systems for Video Technology*, 31(1), 260–274. DOI: 10.1109/TCSVT.2020.2975671

Xu, X., Fu, S., Yuan, Y., Luo, Y., Qi, L., Lin, W., & Dou, W. (2019). Multi objective computation offloading for workflow management in cloudlet-based mobile cloud using NSGA-II. *Computational Intelligence*, 35, 476–495.

Xu, X., Liu, X., Yin, X., Wang, S., Qi, Q., & Qi, L. (2020). Privacy-aware offloading for training tasks of generative adversarial network in edge computing. *Inf. Sci.*, 532, 1–15.

Xu, X., Li, Y., Huang, T., Xue, Y., Peng, K., Qi, L., & Dou, W. (2019). An energy-aware computation offloading method for smart edge computing in wireless metropolitan area networks. *Journal of Network and Computer Applications*, 133, 75–85.

Yadav, A., & Vishwakarma, D. K. (2020). Sentiment analysis using deep learning architectures: A review. *Artificial Intelligence Review*, 53(6), 4335–4385.

Yang, S., & Xu, Z. (2021). Intelligent scheduling for permutation flow shop with dynamic job arrival via deep reinforcement learning. In 2021 IEEE 5th Advanced Information Technology, Electronic and Automation Control Conference (IAEAC). IEEE.

Yang, L., & Shami, A. (2020). On hyperparameter optimization of machine learning algorithms : Theory and practice. *Neurocomputing*, 415, 295–316.

Yang, L., Zhong, C., Yang, Q., Zou, W., & Fathalla, A. (2020). Task offloading for directed acyclic graph applications based on edge computing in industrial internet. *Inf. Sci.*, 540, 51–68.

Yang, X., Chen, Z., Li, K., Sun, Y., Liu, N., Xie, W., & Zhao, Y. (2018). Communication-constrained mobile edge computing systems for wireless virtual reality: Scheduling and tradeoff. *IEEE Access : Practical Innovations, Open Solutions*, 6, 16665–16677.

Yang, Y., Ma, Y., Xiang, W., Gu, X., & Zhao, H. (2018). Joint optimization of energy consumption and packet scheduling for mobile edge computing in cyber-physical networks. *IEEE Access : Practical Innovations, Open Solutions*, 6, 15576–15586.

Yan, Z., & Zong, L. (2020). Spatial Prediction of Housing Prices in Beijing Using Machine Learning Algorithms. In *ACM International Conference Proceeding Series*. DOI: 10.1145/3409501.3409543

Yao, K., Peng, B., Zweig, G., Yu, D., Li, X., & Gao, F. (2014). Recurrent Conditional Random Field for Language Understanding. *2014 IEEE International Conference on Acoustics, Speech and Signal Processing (ICASSP)*, 4077–4081. DOI: 10.1109/ICASSP.2014.6854368

Yeh, W.-C., Lin, Y.-P., Liang, Y.-C., & Lai, C.-M. (2021). *Convolution Neural Network Hyperparameter Optimization Using Simplified Swarm Optimization* (arXiv:2103.03995). arXiv. http://arxiv.org/abs/2103.03995

Yenisey, M. M., & Yagmahan, B. (2014). Multi-objective permutation flow shop scheduling problem: Literature review, classification and current trends. *Omega*, 45, 119–135.

Yessenbayev, Z. (2016). Character-based Feature Extraction with LSTM Networks for POS-tagging Task. 2016 IEEE 10th International. Conference on. Application of. Information and. Communication Technologies., 1–5.

Yin, R., Wang, D., Zhao, S., Lou, Z., & Shen, G. (2021). Wearable sensors-enabled human–machine interaction systems: From design to application. *Advanced Functional Materials*, 31(11), 2008936.

You, Q., & Tang, B. (2021). Efficient task offloading using particle swarm optimization algorithm in edge computing for industrial internet of things. *J Cloud Comp*, 10, 41. DOI: 10.1186/s13677-021-00256-4

Youssra, E. I. E.-B., & Otman, A. (2022). Application of Artificial Intelligence to X-ray Image-Based Coronavirus Diseases (COVID-19) for Automatic Detection. In M. Lazaar, C. Duvallet, A. Touhafi, & M. Al Achhab (Éds.), *Proceedings of the 5th International Conference on Big Data and Internet of Things* (Vol. 489, p. 208-220). Springer International Publishing. DOI: 10.1007/978-3-031-07969-6_16

Youssra, E. I. E.-B., & Otman, A. (2022). Transfer Learning for Automatic Detection of COVID-19 Disease in Medical Chest X-ray Images. *IAENG International Journal of Computer Science.* https://search.ebscohost.com/login.aspx?direct=true&profile=ehost&scope=site&authtype=crawler&jrnl=1819656X&AN=157247540&h=eEJw4oqM8bCnxIX06IKar%2Bto%2FGsNf2LDiNU3rJpHdGSl4Zk0HGMEvEYzTrGWAJCzUzrZtuNI57zq0xao3OezOQ%3D%3D&crl=c

Yu, A. J., & Seif, J. (2016). Minimizing tardiness and maintenance costs in flow shop scheduling by a lower-bound-based ga. *Computers & Industrial Engineering*, 97, 26–40.

Yuan, W., Guan, D., Shen, L., & Pan, H. (2014). An empirical study of filter-based feature selection algorithms using noisy training data. *2014 4th IEEE International Conference on Information Science and Technology*, 209–212. DOI: 10.1109/ICIST.2014.6920367

Yue, L., Chen, W., Li, X., Zuo, W., & Yin, M. (2019). A survey of sentiment analysis in social media. *Knowledge and Information Systems*, 60, 617–663.

Yue, M., & Ma, S. (2023). LSTM-based transformer for transfer passenger flow forecasting between transportation integrated hubs in urban agglomeration. *Applied Sciences (Basel, Switzerland)*, 13(1), 637. DOI: 10.3390/app13010637

Yu, M., Yang, C., & Li, Y. (2018). Big data in natural disaster management: A review. *Geosciences*, 8(5), 165.

Yun, L., Wang, D., & Li, L. (2023). Explainable multi-agent deep reinforcement learning for real-time demand response towards sustainable manufacturing. *Applied Energy*, 347, 121324. DOI: 10.1016/j.apenergy.2023.121324

Yusuf, M. B., & Jauro, U. A. (2024). *Impact of Land Use and Land Cover Change on Deforestation in the Central Taraba State: A Geographic Information System and Remote Sensing Analysis.* Environmental Protection Research. DOI: 10.37256/epr.4120243326

Zeba, G., Dabić, M., Čičak, M., Daim, T., & Yalcin, H. (2021). Technology mining: Artificial intelligence in manufacturing. *Technological Forecasting and Social Change*, 171, 120971.

Zeng, A., Chen, M., Zhang, L., & Xu, Q. (2023). Are transformers effective for time series forecasting? *Proceedings of the AAAI Conference on Artificial Intelligence*, 37(9), 11121–11128. DOI: 10.1609/aaai.v37i9.26317

Zeng, Z., Xiao, H., Zhang, X., Koprinska, I., Wu, D., Wang, Z., Kirisci, M., & Cagcag Yolcu, O. (2018). Self CNN-based time series stream forecasting. *2018 International Joint Conference on Neural Networks (IJCNN)*, *54*(4), 1–8.

Zhang, C., Sjarif, N. N. A., & Ibrahim, R. (2024). Deep learning models for price forecasting of financial time series: A review of recent advancements: 2020–2022. *Wiley Interdisciplinary Reviews. Data Mining and Knowledge Discovery*, 14(1), e1519. DOI: 10.1002/widm.1519

Zhang, C., & Zheng, Z. (2019). Task migration for mobile edge computing using deep reinforcement learning. *Future Generation Computer Systems*, 96, 111–118.

Zhang, D., & Zhou, L. (2004). Discovering golden nuggets: Data mining in financial application. *IEEE Transactions on Systems, Man, and Cybernetics. Part C, Applications and Reviews*, 34(4), 513–522.

Zhang, G. P. (2003). Time series forecasting using a hybrid ARIMA and neural network model. *Neurocomputing*, 50, 159–175. DOI: 10.1016/S0925-2312(01)00702-0

Zhang, J., Xia, W., Yan, F., & Shen, L. (2018). Joint computation offloading and resource allocation optimization in heterogeneous networks with mobile edge computing. *IEEE Access : Practical Innovations, Open Solutions*, 6, 19324–19337.

Zhang, L., Cao, B., Li, Y., Peng, M., & Feng, G. (2021). A multi-stage stochastic programming based offloading policy for fog enabled iot-ehealth. *IEEE Journal on Selected Areas in Communications*, 39(2), 411–425.

Zhang, Q., & Li, H. (2007). MOEA/D: A Multiobjective Evolutionary Algorithm Based on Decomposition. *IEEE Transactions on Evolutionary Computation*, 11(6), 712–731. DOI: 10.1109/TEVC.2007.892759

Zhang, Q., Lin, M., Yang, L. T., Chen, Z., & Li, P. (2019). Energy-efficient scheduling for real-time systems based on deep q-learning model. *T-SUSC*, 4, 132–141.

Zhao, B. (2017). Web Scraping. DOI: 10.1007/978-3-319-32001-4_483-1

Zhao, Q., Yu, L., Li, X., Peng, D., Zhang, Y., & Gong, P. (2021). Progress and trends in the application of google earth and google earth engine. In *Remote Sensing* (Vol. 13, Issue 18). DOI: 10.3390/rs13183778

Zhao, M., Wang, W., Wang, Y., & Zhang, Z. (2019). Load scheduling for distributed edge computing: A communication-computation tradeoff. *Peer-to-Peer Networking and Applications*, 12, 1418–1432.

Zhao, P., Liu, X., Shi, W., Jia, T., Li, W., & Chen, M. (2020). An empirical study on the intra-urban goods movement patterns using logistics big data. *International Journal of Geographical Information Science*, 34(6). Advance online publication. DOI: 10.1080/13658816.2018.1520236

Zhao, S., Blaabjerg, F., & Wang, H. (2021). An overview of artificial intelligence applications for power electronics. *IEEE Transactions on Power Electronics*, 36(4), 4633–4658. DOI: 10.1109/TPEL.2020.3024914

Zhao, X., & Miao, C. (2023). Research on the Spatial Pattern of the Logistics Industry Based on POI Data: A Case Study of Zhengzhou City. *Sustainability*, 15(21). Advance online publication. DOI: 10.3390/su152115574

Zheng, T., Wan, J., Zhang, J., Jiang, C., & Jia, G. (2020). A survey of computation offloading in edge computing. 2020 International Conference on Computer, Information and Telecommunication Systems (CITS), 1–6.

Zheng, Z., Lu, X. Z., Chen, K. Y., Zhou, Y. C., & Lin, J. R. (2022). Pretrained domain-specific language model for natural language processing tasks in the AEC domain. *Computers in Industry*, 142, 103733.

Zhong, Z. (2018). A Tutorial on Fairness in Machine Learning. Towards Data Science. Retrieved from https://towardsdatascience.com/a-tutorial-on-fairness-in-machine-learning-3ff8ba1040cb

Zhong, Z. (2018). *A Tutorial on Fairness in Machine Learning*. Towards Data Science.

Zhou, H., Zhang, S., Peng, J., Zhang, S., Li, J., Xiong, H., & Informer, W. Z. (n.d.). Beyond efficient transformer for long sequence time-series forecasting. Https://Doi. Org/10.1609/Aaai

Zhou, Z., Wong, J., Yu, K., Li, G., & Chen, S. (2023). *Feature Selection on Deep Learning Models: An Interactive Visualization Approach.* https://api.semanticscholar.org/CorpusID:260140100

Zhou, J., Zhang, X., & Wang, W. (2019). Joint resource allocation and user association for heterogeneous services in multi-access edge computing networks. *IEEE Access : Practical Innovations, Open Solutions*, 7, 12272–12282.

Zhou, L., Zhang, L., & Konz, N. (2022). Computer vision techniques in manufacturing. *IEEE Transactions on Systems, Man, and Cybernetics. Systems*, 53(1), 105–117.

Zhou, Q., Shan, J., Fang, B., Zhang, S., Sun, F., Ding, W., Wang, C., & Zhang, Q. (2021). Personal-specific gait recognition based on latent orthogonal feature space. *Cognitive Computation and Systems*, 3(1), 61–69. DOI: 10.1049/ccs2.12007

Zhu, M., & Han, F. (2021). Multi-objective Particle Swarm Optimization based on Space Decomposition for Feature Selection. *Proceedings - 2021 17th International Conference on Computational Intelligence and Security, CIS 2021*, 387–391. https://doi.org/DOI: 10.1109/CIS54983.2021.00087

Zhu, J., Wang, X., Wang, P., Wu, Z., & Kim, M. J. (2019). Integration of BIM and GIS: Geometry from IFC to shapefile using open-source technology. *Automation in Construction*, 102. Advance online publication. DOI: 10.1016/j.autcon.2019.02.014

Zhu, J., Zhao, Z., Zheng, X., An, Z., Guo, Q., Li, Z., Sun, J., & Guo, Y. (2023). Time-series power forecasting for wind and solar energy based on the SL-transformer. *Energies*, 16(22), 7610. DOI: 10.3390/en16227610

Zhu, Z., Peng, J., Gu, X., Li, H., Liu, K., Zhou, Z., & Liu, W. (2018). Fair resource allocation for system throughput maximization in mobile edge computing. *IEEE Access : Practical Innovations, Open Solutions*, 6, 5332–5340.

Zobolas, G., Tarantilis, C. D., & Ioannou, G. (2009). Minimizing makespan in permutation flow shop scheduling problems using a hybrid metaheuristic algorithm. Computers &amp. *Operations Research*, 36(4), 1249–1267.

Zou, Q., Ni, L., Zhang, T., & Wang, Q. (2015). Deep Learning Based Feature Selection for Remote Sensing Scene Classification. *IEEE Geoscience and Remote Sensing Letters*, 12(11), 2321–2325. DOI: 10.1109/LGRS.2015.2475299

About the Contributors

Toufik Mzili holds the position of Assistant Professor in the Department of Computer Science at the Faculty of Science, Chouaib Doukkali University. Recognized as a distinguished researcher, he has made noteworthy contributions to the fields of metaheuristics, optimization, and scheduling problems. His scholarly impact is evident through numerous publications in esteemed Q1 journals. Additionally, Dr. Mzili Toufik has demonstrated his expertise as a peer reviewer for several prestigious journals, showcasing his commitment to advancing the academic discourse in his field.

Adarsh Kumar Arya is a distinguished Associate Professor in the Department of Chemical Engineering at Harcourt Butler Technical University (HBTU), Kanpur. With a robust career spanning over twenty years in academic institutions and industrial organizations, Dr. Arya has established himself as a leading figure in engineering education and research. He serves as the Convener for the Prime Minister- Uchhatar Siksha Abhiyan (HBTU-Kanpur), and Print & Social Media, demonstrating his commitment to advancing educational standards and outreach. Dr. Arya's previous experience includes significant roles such as Associate Dean of Incubation & Startups at HBTU and managing the Pipeline Division at Petroleum University in Dehradun, where he successfully placed numerous students in various industrial sectors. His tenure at Worley Parsons in Mumbai saw him contributing to critical projects, including the TANAP gas pipeline, further adding to his extensive knowledge in the oil and gas sector. An alumnus of prestigious institutions, Dr. Arya completed his B.Tech. at Bundelkhand Institute of Engineering & Technology, Jhansi, followed by an M.Tech. from HBTU. He also specializes in Piping Engineering from IIT Mumbai and has a Ph.D. from the University of Petroleum & Energy Studies, Dehradun. His academic rigour matches his passion for empowering students, urging them to delve into the exciting world of chemical engineering. Dr. Arya's areas of expertise span core subjects in chemical engineering, including oil and gas pipeline engineering, and he has taught more than ten subjects at both undergraduate and postgraduate levels. He has supervised over 100 graduate and 25 postgraduate students, with two earning PhDs under his guidance, while three more are currently pursuing their doctoral studies. His commitment to innovation continues as he explores projects focused on green hydrogen and hydrogen blends in natural gas pipeline networks, accompanied by the development of artificial intelligence software to tackle industrial optimization challenges. Motivated by a profound appreciation for the societal impact of chemical engineering, Dr. Arya finds fulfilment in educating the next generation of engineers. He is drawn to the field's versatility and the opportunity for impactful research, recognizing that chemical engineers are critical in addressing contemporary challenges such as climate change and sustainability. Embracing a career in academia has allowed him to continually learn, collaborate with esteemed industry experts, and contribute meaningful advancements to the engineering field. Through his innovative leadership and dedication to education, Dr. Adarsh Kumar Arya continues to inspire students and colleagues alike, ensuring a robust future for both his students and the field of chemical engineering.

* * *

Munir Ahmad is a seasoned professional in the realm of Spatial Data Infrastructure (SDI), Geo-Information Productions, Information Systems, and Information Governance, boasting over 25 years of dedicated experience in the field. With a PhD in Computer Science, Dr. Ahmad's expertise spans Spatial Data Production, Management, Processing, Analysis, Visualization, and Quality Control. Throughout his career, Dr. Ahmad has been deeply involved in the development and deployment of SDI systems specially in the context of Pakistan, leveraging his proficiency in Spatial Database Design, Web, Mobile & Desktop GIS, and Geo Web Services Architecture. His contributions to Volunteered Geographic Information (VGI) and Open Source Geoportal & Metadata Portal have significantly enriched the geospatial community. As a trainer and researcher, Dr. Ahmad has authored over 50 publications, advancing the industry's knowledge base and fostering innovation in Geo-Tech, Data Governance, and Information Infrastructure, and Emerging Technologies. His commitment to Research and Development (R&D) is evident in his role as a dedicated educator and mentor in the field.

Usama Ahmed holds an MS degree in Computer Science from Riphah International University, Lahore. He previously obtained his B.S.C.S. degree from the University of Sargodha. Currently, he is serving as a Lecturer in the Department of Artificial Intelligence in the School of Systems and Technology at the University of Management and Technology Lahore. He has research interests in applied machine learning, medical diagnosis, data mining, and image processing.

Kenza Aitelkadi is an associate Professor in the Cartography-Photogrammetry-GIS-Remote sensing department from Geomatic Sciences and surveying engineering school, Agronomic and Veterinary Hassan II Institute. Rabat Morocco. She is graduated from IAV Hassan II in 2008. She obtained her PhD in 2016. The research, publishing and teaching she provides are photogrammetry, lasergrammetry, 3D modeling and deep learning approaches. Pr. Aitelkadi is member in several national and international project related to the technical topics such as Earth observation, Data mining, GIS, Spatial data infrastructure, etc. in parallel with the thematic areas of expertise, Pr. Aitelkadi is beginning, since 2018, to operate on another potential research to IAV and the Ministry of Agriculture focused especially on the Agri-entrepreneurship the community engagement, and the knowledge management. In this sense, she coordinates three projects. The SKIM project (2018-2022) funded by IFAD with partners from Sudan, Moldova, Uzbekistan and Italy. The project facilitates and supports the growth of knowledge management and capacity development operations within the Near East and North Africa (NENA) and Central-Eastern Europe and Central Asia (CEN) regions. The second project is MunIE (2019-2022) financed by DAAD fund with Koblenz University. MUnIE is a project within the framework of the Entrepreneurial Universities in Africa (EpU) program, which involves higher education institutions working with African cooperation partners to design and implement reform measures that will increase the labor market orientation of African higher education institutions. The third project is Agriengage (2020-2023) financed by ERASMUS+ Program. This project titled "Strengthening Agri-Entrepreneurship and Community Engagement Training in East, West and North Africa (AgriENGAGE)" aims at enhancing capabilities and employability of agricultural workers in East, West and North Africa by building the skills of staff and students in community engagement, business management and entrepreneurship so, as to catalyze transformation of farming communities and industry in Africa.

Karam Allali is a Full Professor at Faculty of Sciences and Technologies, Hassan II University of Casablanca, Morocco and the head of the Mathematics Department. He received Master degree from the Faculty of Sciences at the University of Rabat, Morocco, and received a Ph.D. in Applied Mathematics from the University of Lyon, France. His research activities are mainly focused on mathematical modeling and numerical simulations. He has total academic teaching experience of more than twenty years with several publications in international journals. His research area includes numerical analysis, biomathematics, natural convection, fluid mechanics, scheduling, flow shop, manufacturing, vibration, nonlinear dynamics, dynamical systems, combustion, frontal polymerization, reaction front, chaotic systems and other areas.

Bimol Chandra Das is currently a postgraduate student at Trine University, Angola, IN, USA, pursuing a Master's degree in Business Analytics. He earned his B.Sc. degree in Statistics from the University of Dhaka, Dhaka, Bangladesh, in 2019. His research interests include Machine Learning and AI in Business, Predictive Analytics, Big Data Analytics, Data Visualization, Optimization Techniques, Consumer Behavior Analysis, Supply Chain Analytics, Financial Analytics, and Marketing Analytics. He is actively involved in various research projects aimed at ensuring sustainability in the healthcare and transportation sectors. His research findings have been published in several peer-reviewed international journals and conferences.

Hicham Hajji is an associate professor at IAV Institute, Rabat, Morocco. He received a PhD (2005) and MSc (2001) in Computer Sciences from the National Institute of Applied Sciences of Lyon – INSA-Lyon, France. In 1999 he received an Engineer degree of Surveying from IAV Institute. Since 2001, he has occupied several positions such as Lecturer, IT consultant, and Research & Development engineer. He has been involved in more than 15 projects (technical and research projects) ranging from Financial Data Warehousing, GIS to Big Data with international and national institutions such as United Nations UNIDO, USAID, Natixis Bank and European Union. His major research interests lie in Big Data management using scalable approaches and Spatial Data Management. He was recently awarded the Water Innovation Fellowship from USAID and the Azure for Research Awards for ML (Machine Learning) from Microsoft. He is leading a research group working on applications of Spatial Big Data management and Machine Learning on Urban Management, Telco, Water management and Forest management. https://orcid.org/0000-0001-9026-8980.

Ramchandra Mangrulkar is a professor in the Department of Information Technology at Dwarkadas J. Sanghvi College of Engineering in Mumbai, India. He holds various memberships in professional organizations such as IEEE, ISTE, ACM, and IACSIT. With over 22 years of combined teaching and administrative experience, Dr. Mangrulkar has established himself as a knowledgeable and skilled professional in his field. He has a strong publication record with 95 publications, including refereed/peer-reviewed international journal publications, book chapters with international publishers (including Scopus indexed ones), and international conference publications.

Maida Maqsood did MS in English from Government College Women University, Sialkot. Throughout her academic journey, she has achieved notable successes that have strengthened her foundation in literature, education and linguistics. Her Master's research reflects her dedication to exploring critical themes in literature with the use of linguistics style. Additionally, her active participation in different conferences and seminars, such as The International Conference on Modern Trends in Applied Linguistics, and 7th ASNeT International Multidisciplinary Academic Conference 2024 (AIMAC 2024) highlight her commitment to staying updated with current trends in her field.

Hetavi Mehta is a final-year student pursuing B.Tech in Computer Engineering with Honors in Intelligent Computing from the reputed institution Dwarkadas J. Sanghvi College of Engineering, Mumbai. With numerous projects, she has cultivated expertise in Python, C, and Java programming. Her strong problem-solving and analytical thinking skills complement her technical proficiency. An ardent computer scientist, Hetavi's research interests extend from deep learning and feature engineering to information security and multimedia cryptography. Along with an outstanding academic performance, she has actively participated in collegiate teams and clubs to hone her interpersonal skills.

Maad M. Mijwil is an Iraqi Academician; he is born in Baghdad, Iraq, in 1987. He received his B.Sc. degree in software engineering from Baghdad college of economic sciences university, Iraq, in 2009. He received a M.Sc. degree in 2015 from the computer science department, university of Baghdad in the field of wireless sensor networks, Iraq. Currently, he is a member of the Division of Quality Assurance and Performance, College of Administration and Economics, Al-Iraqia University and is working as a Lecturer and an academic member of staff in the Computer Techniques Engineering Department at Baghdad College of Economic Sciences University, Iraq. He has over ten years of experience in teaching, guiding projects for undergraduates, and laboratory sessions. He has authored 146 publications, including papers/ chapters (published 135 peer reviewed papers in national/international conferences and journals), preprints, presentations, and posters. He is also an editor in more than 10 international/national journals and a reviewer in more than 100 international/national journals. He has served on technical program committees for many prestigious conferences. Also, he graduated from Publons academy as a peer reviewer. His Google citations are over 2900 mark.

Mehrajudin Aslam Najar holds a Ph.D. in Communication Studies from Communication University of China and a master's degree in Convergent Journalism from Central University of Kashmir. His research interests span a wide range, from peace and conflict studies to exploring the intersections of new media and artificial intelligence. Dr. Najar's academic journey has been marked by a commitment to understanding the transformative impact of communication technologies on society, with a focus on ethical and societal implications. His work aims to bridge theoretical insights with practical applications, contributing to both academic discourse and societal development. Through his research, Dr. Mehraj seeks to uncover how media and AI can be leveraged for positive social change while navigating the complex challenges of the modern digital landscape.

Suresh Palarimath is a renowned computer science expert, prolific author, and accomplished researcher with a distinguished academic career. He has authored a staggering 25 books in computer science, covering diverse topics ranging from Database Management Systems, Computer Concepts, and C Programming to Java and Python programming. These books have been well-received by students and professionals alike and have contributed significantly to the field of computer science. In addition to his impressive writing career, Dr. Palarimath has made noteworthy contributions to computer science research. He has published 10 research articles and has 7 Indian patents and 2 United Kingdom patents. Additionally, he received a Research Grant worth $ 56,200 in 2023 for 3 research projects. Dr. Palarimath is a Senior Lecturer in Information Technology at the University of Technology and Applied Sciences, Salalah, Oman.

Ramya R. completed her B.E and M.E degree in Computer science and engineering. She had 14 years of teaching experience in various Engineering colleges. She pursuing PhD in computer science and engineering and published many articles and book chapters in her domain. She specialises in edge computing, cloud computing, Machine learning, artificial intelligence, Quality of services and resource management.

Muhammad Sarwar holds a Master's degree from COMSATS University and specializes in networking and cyber security research. With expertise in designing secure network infrastructures and identifying vulnerabilities, he remains at the forefront of technological advancements. Sarwar's commitment to excellence and innovation makes him a valuable asset in optimizing network performance and enhancing security measures.

Index

Printed in the United States
by Baker & Taylor Publisher Services

Printed in the United States
by Baker & Taylor Publisher Services